ϭⲱ ⲛ̄ⲟⲩⲓⲟⲩ ⲟⲩⲉϣⲱⲡ ⲧⲁ ⲇⲉ
ⲭⲣⲓⲁ ⲧⲉⲙⲁⲅⲉ ϭ ⲱⲛ ⲧⲁ
ϣⲱⲡⲓ ⲇⲉ ⲁⲩϣⲁⲛ ϭ ⲱ ⲅ
ⲟⲩ ⲡⲣⲟⲫⲏ ⲧ ⲏⲥ ⲛ̄ⲛⲟⲩⲁ
ⲁⲉⲉⲃ ⲁⲗ ⲛ̄ ⲁⲉⲍⲓⲁ ⲡ ⲱ
ⲙⲡⲉ ⲧⲉ ϥ ⲭⲓⲗ ⲁⲉⲓ ✝
ⲁ ⲉ ⲓⲕ ⲁ ϣⲁⲛⲧⲉϥ ⲙ ⲛ̄ⲧ ⲁⲛ
ⲧⲉ ϣⲱⲡⲓ ⲇⲉ ⲁϥ ϣⲁⲛ ⲭⲓⲁ ⲙⲛ̄ⲧ
ⲟ ⲫⲏ ⲧ ⲏⲥ ⲛ̄ⲛⲟⲩ ⲭ ⲡⲉ ⲡⲣⲟ
ⲏ ⲥ ⲛ̄ⲃⲓ ⲉⲧ ⲥⲉ ⲭⲓⲁ ⲛ̄ⲛⲟⲩ
ⲙⲡⲉⲣⲡⲓⲣⲁⲍⲉ ⲙ̄ⲙⲁ ϥ ⲟⲩ ⲁⲉ
ⲏ ⲧ ⲥ ⲛⲉ ⲟⲩ ⲉⲧ ⲃⲏⲧ ϥ ⲭ ⲉⲛ
ⲁ ⲥ ⲉ ⲛⲉ ⲕⲉ ⲟⲩ ⲏⲛ ⲧ ⲛ̄ ⲉ ⲁ
ⲁ ⲃ ⲓ ⲁ ⲉⲛ ⲧ ⲁ ϥ ⲥ ⲉ ⲛⲉ ⲕ ⲉ ⲓ
ⲧⲉ ⲉ ⲁⲗ ⲉⲛ ⲛⲟⲩ ⲁⲛ ⲙ ⲃ ⲓ ⲉⲛ
ⲭ ⲓⲁ ⲛ̄ⲛⲟⲩ ⲓ̄ⲡ ⲱ ⲛ̄ ⲉ ⲓ ⲧ ⲉ ϥ
ⲫⲏ ⲧ ⲏ ⲥ ⲛⲉ ⲁⲗ ⲗⲁ ⲉ ϣⲱⲡⲓ
ⲉ ⲛ̄ ⲁ ⲧⲙ ⲡⲉ ⲱⲁ ⲗ ⲓ ⲱ ⲁ
ⲟ ⲩ ⲛ̄ ⲓ ⲛ ⲛ̄ ⲉ ⲓ ⲥ ⲙ ⲁ ⲧ ⲧⲉ ⲉ ⲛ
ⲩ ⲉⲛ ⲡⲓ ⲡ ⲣⲟ ⲫⲏ ⲧ ⲏⲥ ⲭ ⲉ ⲟⲩ
ⲉ ⲉ ⲭ ⲟ ⲩ ⲛⲣⲟ ⲫ ⲏ ⲧ ⲏⲥ ⲛ
ⲭ ⲟ ⲛ̄ ⲛ̄ ⲟ ⲩ ⲅ ⲧⲁ ⲡ ⲉ ⲍ ⲁ ⲉ ⲩ ⲣ ⲏ
ⲩ ⲱ ⲙ ⲉ ⲇ ⲁ ⲗ ⲛ̄ ⲏ ⲧ ⲥ ⲉ ⲛ ⲡⲉ ⲓ
ⲛ ⲟ ⲩ ⲡ ⲣ ⲟ ⲫ ⲏ ⲧ ⲏ ⲥ ⲛ̄ ⲛ ⲟ ⲭ
ⲁ ⲩ ⲱ ⲡ ⲣ ⲟ ⲫ ⲏ ⲧ ⲏ ⲥ ⲛ̄ ⲃ ⲓ ⲉ ⲧ
ⲱ ⲛ ⲛ ⲟ ⲩ ⲙ ⲉ ⲧ ⲙ ⲉ ⲧ ⲉ ⲛ
ⲙⲁ ϭ ⲉ ⲛ ⲟ ⲩ ⲡ ⲣ ⲟ ⲫ ⲏ ⲧ ⲏ ⲉ ⲛ
ⲭ ⲡ ⲉ ⲡ ⲣ ⲟ ⲫ ⲏ ⲥ ⲧ ⲏ ⲥ ⲛ̄ ⲃ ⲓ ⲙ ⲉ ⲓ
ⲟ ⲉ ⲁ ⲩ ⲉ ⲣ ⲇ ⲟ ⲕ ⲓ ⲙ ⲁ ⲍ ⲉ ⲛ
ⲛ ⲉ ⲧ ✝ ⲥ ⲃ ⲱ ⲁ ⲩ ϣ ⲉ ϥ ⲉ ⲣ ⲙ ⲉ
ⲛ ⲟ ⲩ ⲡ ⲁ ⲣ ⲁ ⲇ ⲱ ⲥ ⲓ ⲥ ⲉ ϣ ⲁ ⲛ ⲱ ⲥ
ⲭ ⲟ ⲛ ⲧ ⲛ ⲧ ⲉ ⲕ ⲕ ⲗ ⲏ ⲥ ⲓ ⲁ

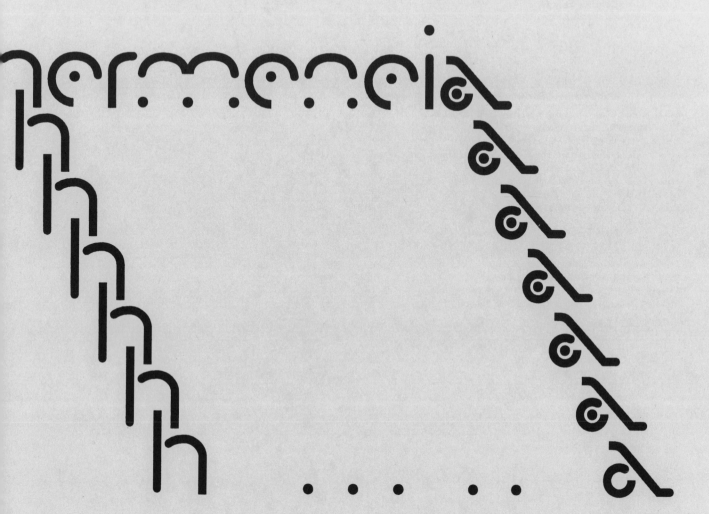

**Hermeneia
—A Critical
and Historical
Commentary
on the Bible**

The Didache
A Commentary on the Didache

Library of Congress Cataloging-in-Publication Data

Niederwimmer, Kurt.
   [Didache. English]
   The Didache : a commentary / by Kurt
Niederwimmer ; translation by Linda M. Maloney ;
edited by Harold W. Attridge.
      p.   cm. — (Hermeneia — a critical and historical
commentary on the Bible)
      Includes bibliographical references and indexes.
      ISBN 0-8006-6027-7 (alk. paper)
      1. Didache.   I. Attridge, Harold W.   II. Title.
III. Series.
BS2940.T5N54   1998
270.1—dc21   98-28758
                                        CIP

Manufactured in the U.S.A.   AF 1-6027

02 01 00 99 98 1 2 3 4 5 6 7 8 9 10

The Didache

A Commentary
by Kurt Niederwimmer

Translation by Linda M. Maloney
Edited by Harold W. Attridge

Fortress
Press   Minneapolis

Kurt Niederwimmer was born in Vienna, Austria, in 1929. He took his doctoral degree in 1956 with a dissertation on Ignatius, bishop of Antioch in the early second century, *Grundzüge der Theologie des Ignatius von Antiochien,* and completed his Habilitationsschrift in 1962. From 1973 to 1997 he held the chair in New Testament on the faculty of the Evangelisch-theologische Fakultät at the University of Vienna. His research interests have included the study of the New Testament and the early church as well as hermeneutical and philosophical issues of New Testament interpretation. In addition to his commentary on the *Didache,* his publications include *Der Begriff der Freiheit im Neuen Testament* (TBT 11; Berlin: Töpelmann, 1966); *Askese und Mysterium. Über Ehe, Ehescheidung und Eheverzicht in den Anfängen des christlichen Glaubens* (FRLANT 113; Göttingen: Vandenhoeck & Ruprecht, 1975), and his collected essays: *Quaestiones theologicae. Gesammelte Aufsätze* (ed. Wilhelm Pratscher and Markus Öhler; BZNW 90; Berlin, New York: De Gruyter, 1998).

Contents
The Didache

Commentary

The name *Hermeneia,* Greek ἑρμηνεία, has been chosen as the title of the commentary series to which this volume belongs. The word *Hermeneia* has a rich background in the history of biblical interpretation as a term used in the ancient Greek-speaking world for the detailed, systematic exposition of a scriptural work. It is hoped that the series, like its name, will carry forward this old and venerable tradition. A second, entirely practical reason for selecting the name lies in the desire to avoid a long descriptive title and its inevitable acronym, or worse, an unpronounceable abbreviation.

The series is designed to be a critical and historical commentary to the Bible without arbitrary limits in size or scope. It will utilize the full range of philological and historical tools, including textual criticism (often slighted in modern commentaries), the methods of the history of tradition (including genre and prosodic analysis), and the history of religion.

Hermeneia is designed for the serious student of the Bible. It will make full use of ancient Semitic and classical languages; at the same time, English translations of all comparative materials—Greek, Latin, Canaanite, or Akkadian—will be supplied alongside the citation of the source in its original language. Insofar as possible, the aim is to provide the student or scholar with full critical discussion of each problem of interpretation and with the primary data upon which the discussion is based.

Hermeneia is designed to be international and interconfessional in the selection of authors; its editorial boards were formed with this end in view. Occasionally the series will offer translations of distinguished commentaries which originally appeared in languages other than English. Published volumes of the series will be revised continually, and eventually, new commentaries will replace older works in order to preserve the currency of the series. Commentaries are also being assigned for important literary works in the categories of apocryphal and pseudepigraphical works relating to the Old and New Testaments, including some of Essene or Gnostic authorship.

The editors of *Hermeneia* impose no systematic-theological perspective upon the series (directly, or indirectly by selection of authors). It is expected that authors will struggle to lay bare the ancient meaning of a biblical work or pericope. In this way the text's human relevance should become transparent, as is always the case in competent historical discourse. However, the series eschews for itself homiletical translation of the Bible.

The editors are heavily indebted to Augsburg Fortress for its energy and courage in taking up an expensive, long-term project, the rewards of which will accrue chiefly to the field of biblical scholarship.

The editor responsible for this volume is Harold W. Attridge of Yale University.

June 1992

Frank Moore Cross	*Helmut Koester*
For the Old Testament	For the New Testament
Editorial Board	Editorial Board

Preface

More than one hundred years ago, in 1873, Philotheos Bryennios discovered the text of the *Didache* in an eleventh-century manuscript version. In 1883 he edited the manuscript for publication. The special fascination of this particular writing has not diminished in over a century of research.

The manuscript of the present commentary was completed in the spring of 1987. Literature on the *Didache* appearing since that time, or accessible to me only after that date, could not be considered. As far as I can see, however, I have no reason to correct my positions.

For individual references I have to thank my colleagues Georg Sauer and Alfred Raddatz in Vienna and Walter Pötscher in Graz. The clean copy of the manuscript was admirably prepared by Irene Pernet. I owe special thanks to my colleague Wilhelm Pratscher, who bore the principal burden of proofreading the manuscript, and to whom readers are also indebted for the index. Finally, I am grateful to the "Word" society for their subvention of the publication costs.

Vienna
December 1988

Kurt Niederwimmer

The text of the second edition, which became necessary rather soon after the first, remains unchanged.

In this preface I would like to discuss briefly just one improvement, one addition to the list of testimonies, namely, two citations from the *Didache* among the papyri from Tura. In the *Commentary on the Psalms* (227, 26–27) from Tura, ascribed (although not without debate) to Didymus of Alexandria, the *Didache* is mentioned, in connection with Ps 34:20, as a βίβλος τῆς κατηχήσεως ("Book of Catechesis"). The text also cites the maxim εἰρηνεύσεις μαχομένους ("you shall reconcile those who quarrel") from Did 4.3 [Michael Gronewald, ed., *Psalmenkommentar (Tura Papyrus), Teil III: Kommentar zu Psalm 29–34* (Papyrologische Texte und Abhandlungen 8; Bonn: Habelt, 1969) 398]. Something similar occurs in the *Commentary on Ecclesiastes*, which is also ascribed, without any contention, to Didymus. At 78, 22, on Eccl 3:7a, appears the reference: ἐν τῇ Διδαχῇ τῆς κ[ατη]-χ[ή]σεως τῶν ἀποσ[τ]όλων λέγεται· εἰρηνεύσεις μαχομένους [Michael Gronewald, ed., *Kommentar zum Ecclesiastes (Tura Papyrus,* Teil II: *Kommentar zu Eccl. 3–4, 12* (Papyrologische Texte und Abhandlungen 22; Bonn: Habelt, 1977) 70]. I cannot here treat the context of these passages. In general, cf. Bart D. Ehrman, "The New Testament Canon of Didymus the Blind," *VC* 37 (1983) 16–17 and 21, n 16; and Dieter Lührmann, "Das Bruchstück aus dem Hebräerevangelium bei Didymos von Alexandrien," *NovT* 29 (1987) 276.

The designation of the *Didache* as βίβλος τῆς κατηχήσεως in fact recalls, as Lührmann (p. 276) notes, the conceptuality of Athanasius, on which consult my treatment on p. 4. Ehrman comes to a different judgment. In his understanding Didymus cites the *Didache* as a canonical work, belonging to the New Testament. Only one more observation on the texts is worth making here: The second citation makes it obvious that Didymus, or Pseudo-Didymus, knew the writing under the title of διδαχὴ τῶν ἀποστόλων.

So much for the two citations in the Tura papyri. I also call attention to the bibliographical supplement. In compiling that list I must thank my assistant Markus Öhler for his help.

Vienna
October 1992

Kurt Niederwimmer

Reference Codes

1. Abbreviations

Abbeviations for ancient sources follow, with minor modifications, the *Theological Dictionary of the New Testament,* ed. Gerhard Kittel and Gerhard Friedrich, trans. Geoffrey W. Bromiley, vol. 1 (Grand Rapids: Eerdmans, 1964) xvi–xl. The following abbreviations have also been used.

AB	Anchor Bible
Act Thom.	*Acts of Thomas*
ACW	Ancient Christian Writers
AGJU	Arbeiten zur Geschichte des Judentums und Urchristentums
AKG	Arbeiten zur Kirchengeschichte
ALW	*Archiv für Liturgiewissenschaft*
ANF	Alexander Roberts and James Donaldson, eds., *The Ante-Nicene Fathers: Translations of the Fathers Down to A.D. 325* (10 vols.; New York: Scribner's, 1905–6)
ANRW	*Aufstieg und Niedergang der römischen Welt*
ANTF	Arbeiten zur neutestamentlichen Textforschung
Apoc. Elijah	*Apocalypse of Elijah*
Apoc. Pet.	*Apocalypse of Peter*
Aristides	Aristides of Athens
Apol.	*Apology*
As. Mos.	*Assumption of Moses*
(Ps.-)Athanasius	
De virg.	*De virginitate*
AThAnt	Abhandlungen zur Theologie des Alten und Neuen Testaments
ATR	*Anglican Theological Review*
AuC.E.	Antike und Christentum. Ergänzungsband
Augustine	Augustine of Hippo
Enar. in Ps.	*Enarratio in Psalmos*
b.	Babylonian Talmud
'Abod. Zar.	*'Aboda Zara*
Ber.	*Berakot*
Ḥag.	*Ḥagiga*
Men.	*Menaḥot*
Šab.	*Šabbat*
BAGD	W. Bauer, W. F. Arndt, F. W. Gingrich, and F. W. Danker, *A Greek-English Lexicon of the New Testament*
2 Bar.	*Syriac Apocalypse of Baruch*
3 Bar.	*Greek Apocalypse of Baruch*
Barn.	*Epistle of Barnabas*
BBB	Bonner biblische Beiträge
BDF	F. Blass and A. Debrunner, *A Greek Grammar of the New Testament and Other Early Christian Literature,* ed. Robert W. Funk

	(Chicago: University of Chicago Press, 1961)
BDR	F. Blass, A. Debrunner, and F. Rehkopf, *Grammatik des neutestamentlichen Griechisch* (14th ed.; Göttingen: Vandenhoeck & Ruprecht, 1975)
BenM	*Benediktinische Monatsschrift*
BETL	Bibliotheca ephemeridum theologicarum lovaniensium
BEvTh	Beiträge zur evangelischen Theologie
BFCTh	Beiträge zur Förderung christlicher Theologie
BGU	*Ägyptische Urkunden aus den Kgl. Museen zu Berlin*
BHH	B. Reicke and L. Rost, eds., *Biblisch-Historisches Handwörterbuch*
BHTh	Beiträge zur historischen Theologie
Bib	*Biblica*
BiTeu	Bibliotheca Teubneriana
BSGRT	Bibliotheca Scriptorum Graecorum et Romanorum Teubneriana
BZAW	Beihefte, *Zeitschrift für die alttestamentliche Wissenschaft*
BZNW	Beihefte, *Zeitschrift für die neutestamentliche Wissenschaft*
Can.	*Canons of the Apostles* (ed. Schermann)
CChrSL	Corpus Christianorum Series Latina
CD	Cairo (Genizah) text of the *Damascus Document*
Cicero	Cicero
Off.	*De officiis*
1 Clem.	*First Epistle of Clement*
2 Clem.	*Second Epistle of Clement*
Clement of Alexandria	
Paed.	*Paedagogos*
Protr.	*Protreptikos*
Quis dives salv.	*Quis dives salvetur*
Strom.	*Stromateis*
Const.	*Apostolic Constitutions*
Corp. Herm.	*Corpus Hermeticum*
CPS.G	Corona patrum Salesiana. Series Graeca
CQ	*Church Quarterly*
CSCO	Corpus scriptorum christianorum orientalium
CSEL	Corpus scriptorum ecclesiasticorum latinorum
CTP	Cadernos de teologia e pastoral

CUFr	Collection des universités de France	Hippolytus	Hippolytus
Cyprian	Cyprian of Carthage	*Apost. Trad.*	*Apostolic Tradition*
De aleat.	*De aleatoribus*	*De Antichr.*	*De Antichristo*
Deut. Rab.	*Deuteronomy Rabbah*	*Ref.*	*Refutatio omnium haeresium*
Did.	*Didache*	HNT	Handbuch zum Neuen Testament
Didasc.	*Didascalia apostolorum*	HNT.E	Handbuch zum Neuen Testament. Ergänzungsband
Diodorus Siculus		HThKNT	Herders theologischer Kommentar zum Neuen Testament
Bibl. Hist.	*Library of History*		
Diogn.	*Epistle to Diognetus*		
Doctr.	*Doctrina apostolorum*	*HTR*	*Harvard Theological Review*
DRev	*Downside Review*	Ignatius	Ignatius of Antioch
EdF	Erträge der Forschung	*Eph.*	*Letter to the Ephesians*
EDNT	*Exegetical Dictionary of the New Testament*	*Magn.*	*Letter to the Magnesians*
		Phld.	*Letter to the Philadelphians*
EHS.T	Europäische Hochschulschriften. Theologie	*Pol.*	*Letter to Polycarp*
EKK	Evangelisch-katholischer Kommentar	*Rom.*	*Letter to the Romans*
		Smyrn.	*Letter to the Smyrnaeans*
Ep.	Epistola(e)	*Trall.*	*Letter to the Trallians*
Ep. apost.	*Epistola apostolorum*	JAC	Jahrbuch für Antike und Christentum
Ep. Arist.	*Epistle of Aristeas*		
Epiphanius	Epiphanius of Salamis	JAC.E.	Jahrbuch für Antike und Christentum. Ergänzungsband
Pan.	*Panarion*		
Epit.	*Epitome* of the *Canons of the Apostles* (ed. Schermann)	*JBL*	*Journal of Biblical Literature*
		JLH	*Jahrbuch für Liturgie und Hymnologie*
EPRO	Études préliminaires aux religions orientales dans l'empire Romain		
		JLW	*Jahrbuch für Liturgiewissenschaft*
		Josephus	Flavius Josephus
Er.	*Eranos*	*Ant.*	*Antiquities of the Jews*
EtB	Études bibliques	*Ap.*	*Against Apion*
EThL	*Ephemerides theologicae lovanienses*	*Bell.*	*The Jewish War*
		Vita	*Autobiography*
EvTh	*Evangelische Theologie*	JSHRZ	Jüdische Schriften aus hellenistische-römischer Zeit
Exod. Rab.	*Exodus Rabbah*		
Fides patr.	(Ps.-Athanasius) *Fides CCCXVIII patrum* (ed. Batiffol)	*JTS*	*Journal of Theological Studies*
		Justin	Justin Martyr
Flor patr	Florilegium patristicum	*1 Apol.*	*First Apology*
fol.	folio	*2 Apol.*	*Second Apology*
FRLANT	Forschungen zur Religion und Literatur des Alten und Neuen Testaments	*Dial.*	*Dialogue with Trypho*
		KEK	Kritisch-exegetischer Kommentar
		KIG	Kirche in ihrer Geschichte
FThSt	Freiburger theologische Studien	KlT	Kleine Texte für Vorlesungen und Übungen
GCS	Griechischen christlichen Schriftsteller		
		Lactantius	
Gen. Rab.	*Genesis Rabbah*	*Divin. inst.*	*Divinae institutiones*
GNT	Grundrisse zum Neuen Testament	Lampe	G. W. H. Lampe, *Patristic Greek Lexicon* (Oxford: Clarendon 1961–68)
Gos. Pet.	*Gospel of Peter*		
Gos. Thom.	*Gospel According to Thomas*	LCC	Library of Christian Classics
HAT	Handbuch zum Alten Testament	LCL	Loeb Classical Library
HAW	Handbuch der Altertumswissenschaft	LD	Lectio Divina
		Lev. Rab.	*Leviticus Rabbah*
Hermas	*Shepherd of Hermas*	*Lib. grad.*	*Liber graduum*
Man.	*Mandates*	*LJ*	*Liturgisches Jahrbuch*
Sim.	*Similitudes*	LQF	Liturgiegeschichtliche Quellen und Forschungen
Vis.	*Visions*		
Hippocrates		LSJ	Liddell-Scott-Jones, *Greek-English Lexicon* (Oxford: Clarendon, 1968)
De morb. mul.	*De morbidibus mulierum*		
De nat. mul.	*De natura mulierum*		

LWQF	Liturgiewissenschaftliche Quellen und Forschungen
LXX	Septuagint
m.	Mishnah
'Abot	*'Abot*
Ber.	*Berakot*
Mik.	*Mikwa'ot*
Mart. Pol.	*Martyrdom of Polycarp*
Mek. Exod.	*Mekilta on Exodus*
MS(s).	manuscript(s)
MT	Masoretic text
NGWG	Nachrichten von der Gesellschaft der Wissenschaft zu Göttingen
NHC	Nag Hammadi Codices
NJKA	*Neue Jahrbücher für das klassische Altertum, Geschichte und deutsche Literatur*
NovT	*Novum Testamentum*
NovTSup	Supplements to *Novum Testamentum*
n.s.	new series
NTAbh	Neutestamentliche Abhandlungen
NTApoc	Wilhelm Schneemelcher, ed., *New Testament Apocrypha* (2 vols.; rev. ed., Louisville: Westminster/John Knox, 1991)
NTD	Das Neue Testament Deutsch
NTS	*New Testament Studies*
OBO	Orbis biblicus et orientalis
Odes Sol.	*Odes of Solomon*
OrChr	*Orientalia Christiana*
OrChrA	Orientalia Christiana Analecta
Origen	Origen
De orat.	*De oratione*
De princ.	*De principiis*
Hom. 6.2 in Iudic.	*Homilies on Judges 6.2*
P. Bodm.	*Bodmer Papyrus*
P. Dêr Balizeh	*Dêr Balizeh Papyrus*
P. Lond.	*Greek Papyri in the British Museum*
P. Mich.	*Michigan Papyrus*
P. Oxy.	*Oxyrhynchus Papyrus*
PFLUS	Publications de la Faculté des Lettres de l'Université de Strasbourg
PG	*Patrologia graeca* (ed. J.-P. Migne)
Philo	Philo of Alexandria
Abr.	*De Abrahamo*
Decal.	*De decalogo*
Deus imm.	*Quod Deus sit immutabilis*
Gig.	*De gigantibus*
Hyp.	*Hypothetica*
Mut. nom.	*De mutatione nominum*
Omn. prob. lib.	*Quod omnis probus liber sit*
Plant.	*De plantatione*
Poster. C.	*De posteritate Caini*
Rer. div. her.	*Quis rerum divinarum heres sit*
Sacr. AC	*De sacrificiis Abeli et Caini*
Sobr.	*De sobrietate*
Som.	*De somniis*
Spec. leg.	*De specialibus legibus*
Vit. Mos.	*De vita Mosis*
pl.	plural
PL	*Patrologia latina* (ed. J.-P. Migne)
Polycarp	Polycarp of Smyrna
Phil.	*Epistle to the Philippians*
Ps.-Clem.	*Pseudo-Clement*
Ep. ad virg.	*Epistula ad virgines*
Hom.	*Homilies*
Rec.	*Recognitions*
Ps.-Phocyl.	*Pseudo-Phocylides*
Ps. Sol.	*Psalms of Solomon*
PVTG	Pseudepigrapha Veteris Testamenti graece
QCVL	Quellen zum christlichen Verständnis der Liebe
r.	recto
RAC	*Reallexikon für Antike und Christentum*
RB	*Revue biblique*
RBén	*Revue bénédictine*
RE³	*Realencyklopädie für protestantische Theologie und Kirche*, 3d ed.
RechSR	*Recherches de science religieuse*
RHR	*Revue de l'histoire des religions*
RQ	*Römische Quartalschrift für christliche Altertumskunde und Kirchengeschichte*
RThAM	*Recherches de théologie ancienne et médiévale*
Rul. Ben.	*Rule of Benedict* (CSEL 75; SC 184)
SANT	Studien zum Alten und Neuen Testament
SBLTT	Society of Biblical Literature Texts and Translations
SBS	Stuttgarter Bibelstudien
SBT	Studies in Biblical Theology
sc.	*scilicet*, namely
SC	Sources chrétiennes
SCBO	Scriptorum classicorum bibliotheca Oxoniensis
SEÅ	*Svensk exegetisk årsbok*
Sextus Empiricus	Sextus Empiricus
Adv. math.	*Adversus mathematicos*
sg.	singular
SGKA	Studien zur Geschichte und Kultur des Altertums
SHAW.PH	Sitzungsberichte der Heidelberger Akademie der Wissenschaften. Philosophisch-historische Klasse
Shen.	*Life of Shenoute* (in Arabic)
Sib. Or.	*Sibylline Oracles*
SIG	Sylloge inscriptionum Graecarum
SNTSMS	Society for New Testament Studies Monograph Series
SO	*Symbolae Osloenses*

SPAW.PH	Sitzungsberichte der preussi-schen Akademie der Wissen-schaften. Philosophisch-historische Klasse		*ThWNT*	*Theologisches Wörterbuch zum Neuen Testament* (ed. G. Kittel and G. Friedrich; 11 vols.; Stuttgart: Kohlhammer, 1933–79)

SPAW.PH Sitzungsberichte der preussi-schen Akademie der Wissen-schaften. Philosophisch-historische Klasse

SPB Studia Post Biblica

SPLi Studia patristica et liturgica

SQS Sammlung ausgewählter kirchen- und dogmengeschichtlicher Quellenschriften

StEv *Studia Evangelica*

StLi *Studia Liturgica*

StPatr *Studia Patristica*

Str–B H. Strack and P. Billerbeck, *Kommentar zum Neuen Testament*

StrThS. S Strassburger theologische Studien. Supplement

SUC Schriften des Urchristentums

Sup Supplement

SVF *Stoicorum veterum fragmenta* (ed. J. von Arnim; 4 vols.; Stuttgart: Teubner, 1968)

SVTP Studia in Veteris Testamenti Pseudepigrapha

Synt. doctr. Ps.-Athanasius *Syntagma doctrinae* (ed. Batiffol)

TBT Theologische Bibliothek Töpel-mann

TDNT *Theological Dictionary of the New Testament* (ed. G. Kittel and G. Friedrich; trans. G. W. Bromiley; 10 vols.; Grand Rapids: Eerdmans, 1964–76)

Tertullian Tertullian of Carthage

 Adv. Marc. *Adversus Marcionem*

 Apol. *Apologia*

 De bapt. *De baptismo*

 De idol. *De idolatria*

 De ieiun. *De ieiunio adversus psychicos*

 De orat. *De oratione*

 De praescr. *De praescriptione haereticorum*

Test. 12 Patr. *Testaments of the Twelve Patriarchs*

 T. Ash. *Testament of Asher*

 T. Benj. *Testament of Benjamin*

 T. Dan *Testament of Dan*

 T. Iss. *Testament of Issachar*

 T. Jos. *Testament of Joseph*

 T. Jud. *Testament of Judah*

 T. Levi *Testament of Levi*

 T. Naph. *Testament of Naphthali*

 T. Reu. *Testament of Reuben*

 T. Sim. *Testament of Simeon*

 T. Zeb. *Testament of Zebulun*

ThBü Theologische Bücherei

ThGl *Theologie und Glaube*

ThHKNT Theologischer Handkommentar zum Neuen Testament

ThLZ *Theologische Literaturzeitung*

ThPh *Theologie und Philosophie*

ThQ *Theologische Quartalschrift*

ThR *Theologische Rundschau*

ThWNT *Theologisches Wörterbuch zum Neuen Testament* (ed. G. Kittel and G. Friedrich; 11 vols.; Stuttgart: Kohlhammer, 1933–79)

TS *Theological Studies*

TU Texte und Untersuchungen

UNT Untersuchungen zum Neuen Testament

UTB Uni-Taschenbücher

UUÅ Uppsala universitets årsskrift

v. verso

VBW Vorträge der Bibliothek Warburg

VC *Vigiliae Christianae*

VetChr *Vetera Christianorum*

VKHSM Veröffentlichungen aus dem Kirchenhistorischen Seminar, Munich

Vg Vulgate

v.l. *Varia lectio:* textual variant

VT *Vetus Testamentum*

WdF Wege der Forschung

WMANT Wissenschaftliche Monographien zum Alten und Neuen Testament

WS *Wiener Studien*

WUNT Wissenschaftliche Untersuchungen zum Neuen Testament

Xenophon Xenophon

 Mem. *Memorabilia*

ZKG *Zeitschrift für Kirchengeschichte*

ZKTh *Zeitschrift für katholische Theologie*

ZNW *Zeitschrift für die neutestamentliche Wissenschaft*

ZThK *Zeitschrift für Theologie und Kirche*

2. Short Titles

Frequently mentioned monographs or articles are cited by author and short title. For works cited only in a single note or several successive notes, the full bibli-ographical information is given in the first citation. Bibliographical information on works frequently cited throughout the commentary is given here.

Adam, "Herkunft"
    Alfred Adam, "Erwägungen zur Herkunft der Didachè," *ZKG* 68 (1957) 1–47; repr. in idem, *Sprache und Dogma: Untersuchungen zu Grundproblemen der Kirchengeschichte* (Gütersloh: Mohn, 1969) 24–70.
Altaner, "Doctrina"
    Berthold Altaner, "Zum Problem der lateinischen Doctrina Apostolorum," *VC* 6 (1952) 160–67; repr. as "Die lateinische Doctrina Apostolorum und die griechische Grundschrift der Didache," in Günter Glockmann, ed., *Kleine patristische Schriften* (TU 83; Berlin: Akademie-Verlag, 1967) 335–42.

Altaner and Stuiber, *Patrologie*
  Berthold Altaner and Alfred Stuiber, *Patrologie: Leben, Schriften und Lehre der Kirchenväter* (9th ed.; Freiburg im Breisgau, Basel, and Vienna: Herder, 1980).
Aono, *Entwicklung*
  Tashio Aono, *Die Entwicklung des paulinischen Gerichtsgedankens bei den apostolischen Vätern* (EHS.T 137; Bern, Frankfurt, and Las Vegas: Peter Lang, 1979).
Audet, "Affinités littéraires"
  Jean-Paul Audet, "Affinités littéraires et doctrinales du Manuel de Discipline," *RB* 59 (1952) 219–38.
Audet, *Didachè*
  Jean-Paul Audet, *La Didachè: Instructions des apôtres* (EtB; Paris: Gabalda, 1958).
Bammel, "Schema"
  Ernst Bammel, "Schema und Vorlage von *Didache* 16," *StPatr* 4 (1961) 253–62.
Bardenhewer, *Geschichte*
  Otto Bardenhewer, *Geschichte der altchristlichen Literatur* (2d ed.; 5 vols.; Freiburg im Breisgau: Herder, 1913–32; repr. Darmstadt: Wissenschaftliche Buchgesellschaft, 1962).
Barnard, "Later History"
  Leslie W. Barnard, "The Dead Sea Scrolls, Barnabas, the *Didache* and the Later History of the 'Two Ways,'" in idem, *Studies in the Apostolic Fathers and Their Background* (Oxford: Blackwell, 1966) 87–107.
Beck, *Literatur*
  Hans-Georg Beck, *Kirche und theologische Literatur im byzantinischen Reich* (HAW 12.2.1; Munich: Beck, 1959).
Berger, *Formgeschichte*
  Klaus Berger, *Formgeschichte des Neuen Testaments* (Heidelberg: Quelle & Meyer, 1984).
Berger, "Hellenistische Gattungen"
  Klaus Berger, "Hellenistische Gattungen im Neuen Testament," *ANRW* 2.25.2 (1984) 1031–1432.
Betz, "Eucharist"
  Johannes Betz, "The Eucharist in the *Didache*," in Draper, *Research*, 244–75; ET of "Die Eucharistie in der Didache," *ALW* 11 (1969) 10–39.
Bigg and MacLean, *Doctrine*
  Charles Bigg and Arthur J. MacLean, *The Doctrine of the Twelve Apostles* (London, New York, and Toronto: SPCK, 1922).
Bihlmeyer, *Apostolischen Väter*
  Karl Bihlmeyer, *Die apostolischen Väter: Neubearbeitung der Funkschen Ausgabe, unveränderter Nachdruck der mit einem Nachtrag von W. Schneemelcher versehen 2. Auflage* (3d ed.; Sammlung ausgewählter kirchen- und dogmengeschichtlicher Quellenschriften, 2d ser., vol. 1; Tübingen: Mohr, 1970).
Bornkamm, "Anathema"
  Günther Bornkamm, "On the Understanding of Worship. B: The Anathema in the Early Christian Lord's Supper Liturgy," in idem, *Early Christian Experience* (New York: Harper & Row, 1966) 169–79; ET of "Zum Verständnis des Gottesdienstes bei Paulus. B: Das Anathema in der urchristlichen Abendmahlsliturgie," in idem, *Das Ende des Gesetzes: Paulusstudien (Gesammelte Aufsätze I)* (5th ed.; BEvTh 16; Munich: Kaiser, 1966) 123–32.
Bosio, *Padri apostolici*
  Guido Bosio, *I Padri apostolici*, vol. 1: *Dottrina degli Apostoli–San Clemente Romano–Lettera di Barnaba. Introduzione–Traduzione–Note* (CPS.G 7; Turin: Società Editrice Internazionale, 1940; 2d ed. 1958).
Braun, *Qumran*
  Herbert Braun, *Qumran und das Neue Testament* (2 vols.; Tübingen: Mohr [Siebeck], 1966).
Bryennios, Διδαχή
  Philotheos Bryennios, Διδαχὴ τῶν δώδεκα ἀποστόλων ἐκ τοῦ ἱεροσολυμιτικοῦ χειρογράφου νῦν πρῶτον ἐκδιδομένη μετὰ προλεγομένων καὶ σημειώσεων ἐν οἷς καὶ τῆς Συνόψεως τῆς Π. Δ., τῆς ὑπὸ Ἰωάνν. τοῦ Χρυσοστόμου, σύγκρισις καὶ μέρος ἀνέκδοτον ἀπὸ τοῦ αὐτοῦ χειρογράφου (Constantinople: Voutyra, 1883). N.B. The introduction is numbered in Greek; the text and notes in Arabic.
Butler, "Relations"
  Basil C. Butler, "The Literary Relations of Didache, Ch. XVI," *JTS*, n.s. 11 (1960) 265–83.
Clerici, *Einsammlung*
  Luigi Clerici, *Einsammlung der Zerstreuten: Liturgiegeschichtliche Untersuchung zur Vor- und Nachgeschichte der Fürbitte für die Kirche in Didache 9,4 und 10,5* (LWQF 44; Münster: Aschendorff, 1966).
Connolly, "Barnabas and the Didache"
  Richard H. Connolly, "Barnabas and the Didache," *JTS* 38 (1937) 165–67.
Connolly, "Relation"
  Richard H. Connolly, "The *Didache* in Relation to the Epistle of Barnabas," *JTS* 33 (1932) 237–53.
Connolly, "Streeter on the Didache"
  Richard H. Connolly, "Canon Streeter on the Didache," *JTS* 38 (1937) 364–79.
Connolly, "Use of the *Didache*"
  Richard H. Connolly, "The Use of the *Didache* in the *Didascalia*," *JTS* 24 (1923) 147–57.
Creed, "Didache"
  John M. Creed, "The Didache," *JTS* 39 (1938) 370–87.
Cremer, *Fastenansage*
  F. G. Cremer, *Die Fastenansage Jesu: Mk 2,20 und Parallelen in der Sicht der patristischen und scholastischen Exegese* (BBB 23; Bonn: Hanstein, 1965).
Dibelius, "Mahl-Gebete"
  Martin Dibelius, "Die Mahl-Gebete der Didache," *ZNW* 37 (1938) 32–41; repr. in H. Kraft and Günther Bornkamm, eds., *Botschaft und Geschichte: Gesammelte Aufsätze*, vol. 2: *Zum Urchristentum und*

zur hellenistischen Religionsgeschichte (Tübingen:
Mohr, 1956) 117–27.

Dix, "Didache"
Gregory Dix, "Didache and Diatessaron," *JTS* 34
(1933) 242–50.

Dölger, *Taufritual*
Franz J. Dölger, *Der Exorzismus im altchristlichen
Taufritual: Eine religionsgeschichtliche Studie* (SGKA
3.1–2; Paderborn: Schöningh, 1909).

Draper, *Research*
Jonathan A. Draper, ed., *The Didache in Modern
Research* (AGJU 37; Leiden: Brill, 1996).

Drews, "Apostellehre"
Paul Drews, "Apostellehre (Didache)," in Edgar
Hennecke, ed., *Handbuch zu den neutestamentlichen
Apokryphen* (Tübingen: Mohr, 1904) 256–83.

Drews, "Untersuchungen"
Paul Drews, "Untersuchungen zur Didache," *ZNW*
5 (1904) 53–79.

Duensing, "Briefe"
Hugo Duensing, "Die dem Klemens von Rom
zugeschriebenen Briefe über die Jungfräulichkeit,"
ZKG 63 (1950/51) 166–88.

Ehrhard, *Altchristliche Litteratur*
Albert Ehrhard, *Die altchristliche Litteratur und ihre
Erforschung von 1884–1900*, vol. 1: *Die vornicänische
Litteratur* (StrThS.S 1; Freiburg: Herder, 1900).

Finkelstein, "Birkat Ha-Mazon"
Louis Finkelstein, "The Birkat Ha-Mazon," *JQR*,
n.s. 19 (1928/29) 211–62.

Frank, "Maleachi 1,10ff."
K. S. Frank, "Maleachi 1,10ff. in der frühen
Väterdeutung: Ein Beitrag zu Opferterminologie
und Opferverständnis in der alten Kirche," *ThPh*
53 (1978) 70–78.

Funk (or Funk and Diekamp), *Patres apostolici*
Franz Xaver Funk, ed., *Patres apostolici* (2d ed.; 2
vols.; Tübingen: Laupp, 1901); vol. 2, ed. Franz
Diekamp (3d ed.; Tübingen: Laupp, 1913).

Funk, *Abhandlungen*
Franz Xaver Funk, *Kirchengeschichtliche
Abhandlungen und Untersuchungen* (3 vols.;
Paderborn: Schöningh, 1899).

Funk, "Didache"
Franz Xaver Funk, "Die Didache in der afrikanischen Kirche," *ThQ* 76 (1894) 601–4.

Funk, *Didascalia*
Franz Xaver Funk, ed., *Didascalia et Constitutiones
apostolorum* (2 vols.; Paderborn: Schöningh, 1905;
repr. Turin: Bottega d'Erasmo, 1962).

Gero, "Ointment Prayer"
Stephen Gero, "The So-called Ointment Prayer in
the Coptic Version of the Didache: A Re-evaluation," *HTR* 70 (1977) 67–84.

Giet, *L'Énigme*
Stanislas Giet, *L'Énigme de la Didachè* (PFLUS 149;
Paris: Ophrys, 1970).

Glover, "Quotations"
Richard Glover, "The *Didache*'s Quotations and the
Synoptic Gospels," *NTS* 5 (1958/59) 12–29.

Goodspeed, *Apologeten*
Edgar J. Goodspeed, ed., *Die ältesten Apologeten:
Texte mit kurzen Einleitungen* (Göttingen:
Vandenhoeck & Ruprecht, 1914; repr. 1984).

Goodspeed, "Doctrina"
Edgar Goodspeed, "The Didache, Barnabas and
the Doctrina," *ATR* 27 (1945) 228–47.

Greiff, *Pascharituale*
Anton Greiff, *Das älteste Pascharituale der Kirche,
Did 1–10, und das Johannesevangelium* (Johan-
neische Studien 1; Paderborn: Schöningh, 1929).

Grenfell and Hunt, *Papyri*
Bernard P. Grenfell and Arthur S. Hunt, *The
Oxyrhynchus Papyri*, vol. 15 (London: Egypt
Exploration Fund, 1922).

Hagner, *Use*
Donald A. Hagner, *The Use of the Old and New
Testaments in Clement of Rome* (NovTSup 34;
Leiden: Brill, 1973).

de Halleux, "Ministers"
André de Halleux, "Ministers in the *Didache*," in
Draper, *Research*, 300–320; ET of "Les Ministères
dans le Didachè," *Irénikon* 53 (1980) 5–29.

Harnack, *Apostellehre*
Adolf von Harnack, *Die Apostellehre und die jüdischen beiden Wege* (2d ed.; Leipzig: Hinrichs,
1896).

Harnack, "Bezeichnung"
"Die Bezeichnung Jesu als 'Knecht Gottes' und
ihre Geschichte in der alten Kirche," SPAW.PH
(1926) 212–38.

Harnack, *Geschichte*
Adolf von Harnack, *Geschichte der altchristlichen
Litteratur bis Eusebius* (2 vols.; Leipzig: Hinrichs,
1893–97).

Harnack, *Lehre*
Adolf von Harnack, *Die Lehre der zwölf Apostel nebst
Untersuchungen zur ältesten Geschichte der
Kirchenverfassung und des Kirchenrechts* (TU 2.1, 2;
1884; repr. Berlin: Akademie-Verlag, 1991).

Harnack, "Prolegomena"
Adolf von Harnack, "Prolegomena," in idem, *Die
Lehre der zwölf Apostel nebst Untersuchungen zur
ältesten Geschichte der Kirchenverfassung und des
Kirchenrechts* (TU 2.1, 2; 1884; repr. Berlin:
Akademie-Verlag, 1991) 1–286.

Harris, *Teaching*
James Rendel Harris, *The Teaching of the Apostles
(Διδαχὴ τῶν ἀποστόλων)* (London: Clay;
Baltimore: Johns Hopkins University Press, 1887).

Hemmer, *Doctrine*
Hippolyte M. Hemmer, Gabriel Oger, and A.
Laurent, *Doctrine des apôtres: Épître de Barnabé* (2d
ed.; Textes et documents 5, Les Pères apostoliques
1–2; Paris: Picard, 1926).

Hennecke, "Grundschrift"
Edgar Hennecke, "Die Grundschrift der Didache und ihre Recensionen," *ZNW* 2 (1901) 58–72.

Holtzmann, *Berakot*
Oscar Holtzmann, *Die Mischna: Text, Übersetzung und ausführliche Erklärung*, I.1: *Berakot* (Giessen: Töpelmann, 1912; repr. Berlin and New York: de Gruyter, 1970).

Horner, "New Papyrus Fragment"
George W. Horner, "A New Papyrus Fragment of the *Didaché* in Coptic," *JTS* 25 (1924) 225–31.

Hruby, "Birkat Ha-Mazon"
Kurt Hruby, "La 'Birkat Ha-Mazon,'" in *Mélanges liturgiques offerts au R. P. Dom Bernard Botte à l'occasion du cinquantième anniversaire de son ordination sacerdotale (4 juin 1972)* (Louvain: Abbaye du Mont César, 1972) 205–22.

Jacquier, *Doctrine*
Eugene Jacquier, Διδαχὴ τῶν δώδεκα ἀποστόλων: *La Doctrine des douze Apôtres et ses Enseignements* (Lyons: Vitte; Paris: Lethielleux, 1891).

Jefford, *Context*
Clayton N. Jefford, ed., *The Didache in Context: Essays on Its Text, History and Transmission* (NovTSup 77; Leiden: Brill, 1995).

Jeremias, *Abba*
Joachim Jeremias, *Abba: Studien zur neutestamentlichen Theologie und Zeitgeschichte* (Göttingen: Vandenhoeck & Ruprecht, 1966); partial ET: *The Prayers of Jesus* (SBT 2.6; London: SCM, 1967).

Jeremias, *Eucharistic Words*
Joachim Jeremias, *The Eucharistic Words of Jesus* (trans. Norman Perrin; 3d ed.; London: SCM, 1966); ET of *Die Abendmahlsworte Jesu* (4th ed.; Göttingen: Vandenhoeck & Ruprecht, 1967).

Jeremias, *Theologie*
Joachim Jeremias, *Neutestamentliche Theologie* (3d ed.; Gütersloh: Mohn, 1979); ET of 1st ed.: *New Testament Theology: The Proclamation of Jesus* (trans. John Bowden; New York: Scribner's, 1971).

Johnson, "Motive"
Sherman E. Johnson, "A Subsidiary Motive for the Writing of the Didache," in Massey H. Shepherd and Sherman E. Johnson, eds., *Munera Studiosa: Studies Presented to W. H. P. Hatch on the Occasion of His Seventieth Birthday* (Cambridge, Mass.: Episcopal Theological School, 1946) 107–22.

Kahle, *Bala'izah*
Paul E. Kahle Jr., *Bala'izah: Coptic Texts from Deir El-Bala'izah in Upper Egypt* (2 vols.; Oxford and London: Oxford University Press, 1954).

Kamlah, *Paränese*
Ehrhard Kamlah, *Die Form der katalogischen Paränese im Neuen Testament* (WUNT 7; Tübingen: Mohr, 1964).

Klauck, *Herrenmahl*
Hans-Josef Klauck, *Herrenmahl und hellenistischer Kult: Eine religionsgeschichtliche Untersuchung zum ersten Korintherbrief* (NTAbh 15; Münster: Aschendorff, 1982).

Klauser, *Doctrina*
Theodor Klauser, *Doctrina duodecim apostolorum, Barnabae epistula* (Flor Patr 1; Bonn: Hanstein, 1940).

Klauser, "Taufet"
Theodor Klauser, "Taufet in lebendigem Wasser! Zum religions- und kulturgeschichtlichen Verständnis von Didache 7,1–3," in Theodor Klauser and A. Rükker, eds., *Pisciculi: Studien zur Religion und Kultur des Altertums, F. J. Dölger zum 60. Geburtstage dargeboten* (AuC.E. 1; Münster: Aschendorff, 1939) 157–64; repr. Klauser, ed., *Gesammelte Arbeiten zur Liturgiegeschichte, Kirchengeschichte und christlichen Archäologie* (ed. Ernst Dassmann; JAC.E 3; Münster: Aschendorff, 1974) 177–83.

Klein, "Gebete,"
Gottlieb Klein, "Die Gebete in der Didache," *ZNW* 9 (1908) 132–46.

Kleist, *Didache*
James A. Kleist, *The Didache, The Epistle of Barnabas, The Epistles and the Martyrdom of St. Polycarp, The Fragments of Papias, The Epistle to Diognetus* (ACW 6; Westminster, Md.: Newman, 1948).

Kloppenborg, "Matthaean Tradition"
John S. Kloppenborg, "Didache 16.6–8 and Special Matthaean Tradition," *ZNW* 70 (1979) 54–67.

Kmosko, *Liber graduum*
Mihaly Kmosko, ed., *Liber graduum* (Patrologia Syriaca 1.3; Paris: Didot, 1926).

Kneller, "Zum 'schwitzenden Almosen'"
C. A. Kneller, "Zum 'schwitzenden Almosen,'" *ZKTh* 26 (1902) 779–80.

Knopf, *Lehre*
Rudolf Knopf, *Die Lehre der zwölf Apostel. Die zwei Clemensbriefe* (HNT.E. Die apostolischen Väter 1; Tübingen: Mohr [Siebeck], 1920).

Koester, *Synoptische Überlieferung*
Helmut Koester, *Synoptische Überlieferung bei den apostolischen Vätern* (TU 65; Berlin: Akademie-Verlag, 1957).

Kraft, *Didache*
Robert A. Kraft, *Barnabas and the Didache* (The Apostolic Fathers; A New Translation and Commentary 3; New York: Nelson, 1965).

Kretschmar, "Askese"
Georg Kretschmar, "Ein Beitrag zur Frage nach dem Ursprung frühchristlicher Askese," *ZThK* 61 (1964) 27–67; repr. in K. S. Frank, ed., *Askese und Mönchtum in der Alten Kirche* (WdF 409; Darmstadt: Wissenschaftliche Buchgesellschaft, 1975) 129–79, with an addendum, 179–80.

Lake, "Didache"
Kirsopp Lake, "The Didache," in J. Vernon Bartlet, Kirsopp Lake, et al., *The New Testament in the Apostolic Fathers* (Oxford: Clarendon, 1905) 24–56.

Layton, "Sources"

Bentley Layton, "The Sources, Date and Transmission of *Didache* 1.3b–2.1," *HTR* 61 (1968) 343–83.

Lefort, *Pères apostoliques*

L. Theophile Lefort, *Les Pères apostoliques en Copte* (2 vols.; Scriptores Coptici 17–18; CSCO 135–36; Louvain: Durbecq, 1952).

Leipoldt, "Schenute"

Johannes Leipoldt, "Schenute von Atripe und die Entstehung des national ägyptischen Christentums" (TU 25.1; Leipzig: Hinrichs, 1903).

Lietzmann, *Didache*

Hans Lietzmann, *Die Didache* (Kleine Texte für Vorlesungen und Übungen 6; Bonn: Marcus and Weber, 1903).

Lietzmann, *Mass*

Hans Lietzmann, *Mass and Lord's Supper: A Study in the History of the Liturgy* (trans. and with appendices by Dorothea H. G. Reeve, with introduction and further inquiry by Robert Douglas Richardson; Leiden: Brill, 1979); ET of *Messe und Herrenmahl: Eine Studie zur Geschichte der Liturgie* (AKG 8; Bonn: Marcus and Weber, 1926).

MacLean, "Introduction"

Arthur J. MacLean, "Introduction," in Charles Bigg and Arthur J. MacLean, *The Doctrine of the Twelve Apostles* (London, New York, and Toronto: SPCK, 1922).

Massaux, *Influence*

Edouard Massaux, *The Influence of the Gospel of Saint Matthew on Christian Literature before Saint Irenaeus* (3 vols.; New Gospel Studies 5.1–3; Louvain: Peeters; Macon, Ga.: Mercer University Press, 1990–93); ET of *Influence de l'Évangile de Saint Matthieu sur la littérature chrétienne avant Saint Irénée. Réimpression anastatique présentée par F. Neirynck. Supplément: Bibliographie 1950–1985 par B. Dehandschutter* (BETL 75; Leuven: Leuven University Press and Peeters, 1986).

Mattioli, *Didache*

Umberto Mattioli, *La Didache, dottrina dei dodici apostoli: Introduzione, traduzione e note* (Rome: Edizione Paoline, 1969; 3d ed., 1980).

Michaelis, "ὁδός"

Wilhelm Michaelis, "ὁδός," *TDNT* 5 (1967) 42–114.

Middleton, "Eucharistic Prayers"

R. D. Middleton, "The Eucharistic Prayers of the Didache," *JTS* 36 (1935) 259–67.

Moll, *Opfer*

Helmut Moll, *Die Lehre von der Eucharistie als Opfer: Eine dogmengeschichtliche Untersuchung vom Neuen Testament bis Irenäus von Lyon* (Theophaneia 26; Cologne and Bonn: Hanstein, 1975).

Moule, "Note"

Charles F. D. Moule, "A Note on *Didache* IX.4," *JTS*, n.s. 6 (1955) 240–43.

Muilenburg, *Literary Relations*

James Muilenburg, *The Literary Relations of the Epistle of Barnabas and the Teaching of the Twelve Apostles* (diss. Yale; printed, Marburg, 1929).

Nautin, "Composition"

Pierre Nautin, "La composition de la 'Didachê' et son titre," *RHR* 78 (1959) 191–214.

Nestle-Aland

Novum Testamentum Graece (ed. Eberhard Nestle, Erwin Nestle, Kurt Aland, et al.; 26th ed.; 4th rev. printing; Stuttgart: Deutsche Bibelstiftung, 1981).

Niederwimmer, *Askese*

Kurt Niederwimmer, *Askese und Mysterium: Über Ehe, Ehescheidung und Eheverzicht in den Anfängen des christlichen Glaubens* (FRLANT 113; Göttingen: Vandenhoeck & Ruprecht, 1975).

Niederwimmer, "Itinerant Radicalism"

Kurt Niederwimmer, "An Examination of the Development of Itinerant Radicalism in the Environment and Tradition of the *Didache*," in Draper, *Research*, 321–39; ET of "Zur Entwicklungsgeschichte des Wanderradikalismus im Traditionsbereich der Didache," *WS*, n.s. 11 (1977) 145–67.

Niederwimmer, "Textprobleme"

Kurt Niederwimmer, "Textprobleme der Didache," *WS*, n.s. 16 (1982) 114–30.

Nissen, *Gott und der Nächste*

Andreas Nissen, *Gott und der Nächste im antiken Judentum: Untersuchungen zum Doppelgebot der Liebe* (WUNT 15; Tübingen: Mohr, 1974).

Peradse, "Lehre"

G. Peradse, "Die 'Lehre der zwölf Apostel' in der georgischen Überlieferung," *ZNW* 31 (1932) 111–16.

Peterson, *Εἷς θεός*

Erik Peterson, *Εἷς θεός: Epigraphische, formgeschichtliche und religionsgeschichtliche Untersuchungen* (FRLANT 41; Göttingen: Vandenhoeck & Ruprecht, 1926).

Peterson, *Frühkirche*

Erik Peterson, *Frühkirche, Judentum und Gnosis: Studien und Untersuchungen* (Rome, Freiburg, and Vienna: Herder, 1959).

Peterson, "Probleme"

"Über einige Probleme der Didache-Überlieferung," in idem, *Frühkirche*, 146–82.

Pillinger, "Taufe"

Renate Pillinger, "Die Taufe nach der Didache: Philologisch-archäologische Untersuchung der Kapitel 7, 9, 10 und 14," *WS*, n.s. 9 (1975) 152–62.

Poschmann, *Paenitentia secunda*

Bernhard Poschmann, *Paenitentia secunda: Die kirchliche Buße im ältesten Christentum bis Cyprian und Origenes: Eine dogmengeschichtliche Untersuchung* (Theophaneia 1; Bonn: Hanstein 1940, repr. 1964).

Preuschen, *Analecta*

Erwin Preuschen, ed., *Analecta: Kürzere Texte zur Geschichte der Alten Kirche und des Kanons*, vol. 2: *Zur Kanonsgeschichte* (SQS 1.8.2; 2d ed.; Tübingen: Mohr, 1910)

Quasten, *Patrology*
Johannes Quasten, *Patrology* (3 vols.; 1950–60; repr. Utrecht and Antwerp: Spectrum; West-minster, Md.: Newman, 1975).

Reitzenstein, "Frühchristliche Schrift"
Richard Reitzenstein, "Ps.-Cyprian, *De centesima, de sexagesima, de tricesima*: Eine frühchristliche Schrift von den dreierlei Früchten des Lebens," *ZNW* 15 (1914) 60–90.

Rengstorf, "σημεῖον,"
Karl Rengstorf, "σημεῖον κτλ.," *TDNT* 7 (1971) 200–269.

Resch, *Agrapha*
Alfred Resch, *Agrapha* (2d ed.; Leipzig: Hinrichs, 1906; repr. Darmstadt: Wissenschaftliche Buch-gesellschaft, 1967).

Richardson, "Teaching"
Cyril Charles Richardson, "The Teaching of the Twelve Apostles, Commonly Called the Didache," in idem, *The Early Christian Fathers* (LCC 1; Philadelphia: Westminster, 1953; repr. New York: Macmillan, 1970) 161–79.

Riesenfeld, "Brot von den Bergen"
Harald Riesenfeld, "Das Brot von den Bergen. Zu Did. 9,4," *Eranos* 54 (1956) 142–50.

Roberts and Capelle, *Euchologium*
Colin H. Roberts and Bernard Capelle, eds., *An Early Euchologium: The Dêr-Balizeh Papyrus Enlarged and Reedited* (Bibliothèque du Muséon 23; Louvain: Bureau du Muséon, 1949).

Robinson, "Barnabas and the Didache"
Joseph Armitage Robinson, "The Epistle of Barnabas and the Didache" (ed. R. H. Connolly), *JTS* 35 (1934) 113–46, 225–48.

Robinson, *Didache*
Joseph Armitage Robinson, *Barnabas, Hermas, and the Didache: Being the Donnelan Lectures Delivered before the University of Dublin in 1920* (London: SPCK; New York: Macmillan, 1920).

Robinson, "Problem"
Joseph Armitage Robinson, "The Problem of the Didache," *JTS* 13 (1912) 339–56.

Rordorf, "Baptism"
Willy Rordorf, "Baptism according to the Didache," in Draper, *Research,* 212–22; ET of "Le baptême selon la *Didachè*," in *Mélanges liturgiques offerts au R. P. Dom Bernard Botte O.S.B. de l'Abbaye du Mont César à l'occasion du cinquantième anniver-saire de son ordination sacerdotale (4 Juin 1972)* (Louvain: Abbaye du Mont César, 1972) 499–509.

Rordorf, "Didachè"
Willy Rordorf, "La Didachè," in *L'Eucharistie des premiers chrétiens* (Le Point théologique 17; Paris: Beauchesne, 1976) 7–28.

Rordorf, "Gebrauch des Dekalogs"
Willy Rordorf, "Beobachtungen zur Gebrauch des Dekalogs in der vorkonstantinischen Kirche," in William C. Weinrich, ed., *The New Testament Age: Essays in Honor of Bo Reicke* (2 vols.; Macon, Ga.: Mercer, 1984) 2.431–42.

Rordorf, "Rémission des péchés"
Willy Rordorf, "La rémission des péchés selon la Didachè," *Irénikon* 46 (1973) 283–97.

Rordorf, "Tradition apostolique"
Willy Rordorf, "La tradition apostolique dans la Didachè," *L'Année canonique* 23 (1979) 105–14.

Rordorf, "Transmission textuelle"
Willy Rordorf, "Le problème de la transmission textuelle de *Didachè* 1.3b–2.1," in F. Paschke, ed., *Überlieferungsgeschichtliche Untersuchungen* (TU 125; Berlin: Akademie-Verlag, 1981) 499–513.

Rordorf, "Two Ways"
Willy Rordorf, "An Aspect of the Judeo-Christian Ethic: The Two Ways," in Draper, *Research*, 148–64; ET of "Un chapitre d'éthique judéo-chré-tienne: les deux voies," *RechSR* 60 (1972) 109–28.

Rordorf and Tuilier, *Doctrine*
Willy Rordorf and André Tuilier, *La Doctrine des douze apôtres (Didachè): Introduction, Texte, Traduction, Notes, Appendice et Index* (SC 248; Paris: Cerf, 1978).

Sandvik, *Kommen des Herrn*
Bjørn Sandvik, *Das Kommen des Herrn beim Abendmahl im Neuen Testament* (AThANT 58; Zurich: Zwingli, 1970).

Schaff, *Church Manual*
Philip Schaff, *The Oldest Church Manual, Called the Teaching of the Twelve Apostles* (2d ed.; New York: Funk & Wagnalls, 1886).

Schermann, *Elfapostelmoral*
Theodor Schermann, *Eine Elfapostelmoral oder die X-Rezension der "beiden Wege"* (VKHSM 2.2; Munich: Lentner, 1903).

Schille, "Recht"
Gottfried Schille, "Das Recht der Propheten und Apostel — gemeinderechtliche Beobachtungen zu Didache Kapitel 11–13," in Paul Wätzel and Gott-fried Schille, eds., *Theologische Versuche* (Berlin: Evangelische Verlags-Anstalt, 1966) 84–103.

Schlecht, *Doctrina XII Apostolorum*
J. Schlecht, *Doctrina XII Apostolorum: Die Apostel-lehre in der Liturgie der katholischen Kirche* (Freiburg im Breisgau: Herder, 1901).

Schmidt, "Koptische Didache-Fragment"
Carl Schmidt, "Das koptische Didache-Fragment des British Museum," *ZNW* 24 (1925) 81–99.

Schöllgen, "Church Order"
Georg Schöllgen, "The *Didache* as a Church Order: An Examination of the Purpose for the Composition of the *Didache* and Its Consequences for Its Interpretation," in Draper, *Research*, 43–71; ET of "Die Didache als Kirchenordnung: Zur Frage des Abfassungszweckes und seinen Konsequenzen für die Interpretation," JAC 29 (1986) 5–26.

Schümmer, *Altchristliche Fastenpraxis*
Johannes Schümmer, *Altchristliche Fastenpraxis: Mit besonderer Berücksichtigung der Schriften Tertullians* (LQF 27; Münster: Aschendorff, 1933).

Seeberg, *Wege*
Alfred Seeberg, *Die beiden Wege und das Apostel-dekret* (Leipzig: Deichert, 1906).

Staerk, *Gebete*
Willy Staerk, ed., *Altjüdische liturgische Gebete aus-gewählt und mit Einleitungen* (KIT 58; Bonn: Marcus and Weger, 1910).

Stempel, "Lehrer"
H.-A. Stempel, "Der Lehrer in der 'Lehre der zwölf Apostel,'" *VC* 34 (1980) 209–17.

Stenzel, "Bibelkanon"
M. Stenzel, "Der Bibelkanon des Rufin von Aqui-leja," *Bib* 23 (1942) 43–61.

Stommel, "Σημεῖον"
E. Stommel, "Σημεῖον ἐκπετάσεως (Didache 16,6)," *RQ* 48 (1953) 21–42.

Streeter, "Much-Belaboured *Didache*"
B. H. Streeter, "The Much-Belaboured *Didache*," *JTS* 37 (1936) 369–74.

Stuiber, "Drei σημεῖα"
Alfred Stuiber, "Die drei σημεῖα von Didache XVI," JAC 24 (1981) 42–44.

Stuiber, "Eulogia"
Alfred Stuiber, "Eulogia," *RAC* 6 (1966) 900–929.

Stuiber, "Ganze Joch"
Alfred Stuiber, "'Das ganze Joch des Herrn' (Didache 6,2–3)," *StPatr* 4.2 (TU 79; Berlin: Akademie-Verlag, 1961) 323–29.

Suggs, "Two Ways Tradition"
M. Jack Suggs, "The Christian Two Ways Tradition: Its Antiquity, Form, and Function," in David E. Aune, ed., *Studies in New Testament and Early Christian Literature: Essays in Honor of Allen P. Wikgren* (NovTSup 33; Leiden: Brill, 1972) 60–74.

Taylor, *Teaching*
Charles Taylor, *The Teaching of the Twelve Apostles with Illustrations from the Talmud* (Cambridge and London: Deighton Bell, 1886).

Theissen, "Nonviolence"
Gerd Theissen, "Nonviolence and Love of Our Enemies (Matthew 5:38–48; Luke 6:27–38): The Social Background," in idem, *Social Reality*, 115–56.

Theissen, *Social Reality*
Gerd Theissen, *Social Reality and the Early Christians: Theology, Ethics and the World of the New Testament* (trans. Margaret Kohl; Minneapolis: Fortress, 1992).

Theißen, *Studien*
Gerd Theißen, *Studien zur Soziologie des Urchristen-tums* (WUNT 19; 2d ed.; Tübingen: Mohr, 1983).

van der Horst, *Sentences*
Pieter van der Horst, *The Sentences of Pseudo-Phocylides with Introduction and Commentary* (SVTP 4; Leiden: Brill, 1978).

van Haelst, "Nouvelle reconstitution"
J. van Haelst, "Une nouvelle reconstitution du Papyrus liturgique de Dêr Balizeh," *EThL* 45 (1969) 444–55.

Vielhauer, *Geschichte*
Philipp Vielhauer, *Geschichte der urchristlichen Lite-ratur: Einleitung in das Neue Testament, die Apo-kryphen und die apostolischen Väter* (Berlin and New York: de Gruyter, 1975).

Vokes, *Riddle*
Frederick E. Vokes, *The Riddle of the Didache: Fact or Fiction, Heresy or Catholicism?* (London: SPCK; New York: Macmillan, 1938).

Vööbus, *Didascalia*
Arthur Vööbus, ed., *The Didascalia Apostolorum in Syriac* (CSCO 401–2, 407–8; Louvain: Secrétariat du Corpus SCO, 1979).

Vööbus, *Liturgical Traditions*
Arthur Vööbus, *Liturgical Traditions in the Didache* (Papers of the Estonian Theological Society in Exile 16; Stockholm: Estonian Theological Society in Exile, 1968).

Weinreich, *Privatheiligtums in Philadelphia*
Otto Weinreich, ed., *Stiftung und Kultsatzungen eines Privatheiligtums in Philadelphia in Lydien* (SHAW.PH 16; Heidelberg: Winter, 1919).

Wengst, *Barnabasbrief*
Klaus Wengst, *Tradition und Theologie des Barnabasbrief* (AKG 42; Berlin and New York: de Gruyter, 1971).

Wengst, *Didache*
Klaus Wengst, *Didache (Apostellehre), Barnabasbrief, Zweiter Klemensbrief, Schrift an Diognet: Eingeleitet, herausgegeben, übertragen und erläutert* (SUC 2; Munich: Kösel, 1984).

Wibbing, *Tugend- und Lasterkataloge*
Siegfried Wibbing, *Die Tugend- und Lasterkataloge im Neuen Testament und ihre Traditionsgeschichte unter besonderer Berücksichtigung der Qumran-Texte* (BZNW 25; Berlin: Töpelmann, 1959).

Wrege, *Bergpredigt*
Hans Theo Wrege, *Die Überlieferungsgeschichte der Bergpredigt* (WUNT 9; Tübingen: Mohr, 1968).

Zahn, *Geschichte*
Theodor Zahn, *Geschichte des Neutestamentlichen Kanons* (2 vols.; Erlangen and Leipzig: Deichert, 1890–92).

Zahn, *Kanon*
Theodor Zahn, *Forschungen zur Geschichte des neu-testamentlichen Kanons und der altkirchlichen Litera-tur* (3 vols.; Erlangen: Deichert, 1881–84).

Zimmermann, *Lehrer*
Alfred F. Zimmermann, *Die urchristlichen Lehrer: Studien zum Tradentenkreis der διδάσκαλοι im frühen Urchristentum* (WUNT 2.12; Tübingen: Mohr, 1984).

3. Sigla in the Translation

< >   Textual addition or deletion
[ ]   Translation supplement
*   Textual emendation

The English translation of the *Didache* is based on the translation by Aelred Cody in Jefford, *Context,* 5–14, modified to reflect Professor Niederwimmer's exegetical decisions. Other biblical texts are usually from the New Revised Standard Version. Translations of Jewish pseudepigrapha are from James H. Charlesworth, ed., *The Old Testament Pseudepigrapha* (2 vols.; Garden City, N.Y.: Doubleday, 1983–85). Translations from Latin and Greek authors, except where noted, are from the Loeb Classical Library.

The endpapers display the Coptic fragment of the *Didache,* discovered in 1923 and now in the British Library (Or. 9271).

1. Structure and Genre

a. Structure

This document, which is approximately the length of Paul's letter to the Galatians,[1] consists of four clearly separate sections. It begins (I) with a fairly long tractate that can be called the "Tractate on the Two Ways," from its opening words (1.1–5.2). It concludes with an epilogue (6.1) and a short addition (6.2–3). In 7.1 the reader learns after the fact that the *Sitz im Leben* of this tractate is baptismal instruction. This part (which may accordingly be designated baptismal catechesis) is followed (II) by a lengthy section that announces itself as a ritual or set of instructions for action (liturgy) by its rubrical notes, περὶ δὲ τοῦ βαπτίσματος ("on baptism," 7.1), and περὶ δὲ τῆς εὐχαριστίας ("on the Eucharist," 9.1). Then follows (III) a section whose content shows it to be a church order (11.1–15.4). The whole document concludes (IV) with an eschatological epilogue, consisting of a short eschatological parenesis (16.1–2) and a brief apocalypse (16.3–8).[2]

The detailed outline of the writing is as follows:

The Title
I. Baptismal catechesis: The Tractate on the Two Ways (1.1–6.3)
  1. Statement of the theme (1.1)
  2. The way of life (1.2–4.14)
    a. The fundamental commandment and introduction to its performance (1.2–3a)
    b. The *sectio evangelica* (1.3b–2.1)
    c. A list of prohibitions (2.2–7)
    d. The "*teknon*" sayings (3.1–6)
    e. The "*anawim*" sayings (3.7–10)
    f. Rules for life in society (4.1–11)
    g. Epilogue on the "way of life" (4.12–14)
  3. The way of death (5.1–2)
    a. Introduction (5.1a)
    b. Catalog of vices (5.1b–2)
    c. Final admonition (5.2c)
  4. Epilogue (6.1) and appendix (6.2–3)
II. The liturgy (7.1–10.7)
  1. On baptism (7.1–4)
  1a. Addition: On fasting and prayer (8.1–3)
    a. How to fast (8.1)
    b. How to pray (8.2–3)
  2. On the Eucharist (9.1–10.7)
    a. Prayers for the full meal (9.1–5)
    b. Prayer of thanksgiving (Eucharist) (10.1–7)
III. The church order (11.1–15.4)
  1. Transition (11.1–2)
  2. On the reception of itinerant apostles and prophets (11.3–12)
    a. Introduction (11.3)
    b. On itinerant apostles (11.4–6)
    c. On itinerant prophets (11.7–12)
  3. First appendix: On the reception of other traveling brothers and sisters (12.1–5)
    a. Reception and testing of new arrivals (12.1)
    b. Travelers passing through (12.2)
    c. Persons newly arrived who desire to remain (12.3–5)
  4. Second appendix: On the duty to support prophets who desire to remain in the community, and duties toward teachers (13.1–7)
    a. Fundamental principles (13.1–2)
    b. Directions for action (13.3–7)
  5. On confession and reconciliation (14.1–3)
  6. On the election of bishops and deacons (15.1–2)
  7. On church discipline (15.3–4)
IV. Eschatological conclusion (16.1–8)
  1. Eschatological parenesis (16.1–2)
  2. The apocalypse (16.3–8)
    a. The appearance of false prophets and the collapse of the Christian community (16.3–4a)
    b. The appearance of the Antichrist (16.4b–d)
    c. The great apostasy and the preservation of the faithful (16.5)
    d. The revelation of the three signs of the truth (16.6–7)
    e. The arrival of the *Kyrios* (16.8)

b. Genre

It is immediately apparent that the document is a generically mixed composition. Each individual part (tractate on the "ways," liturgy, church order in the narrower sense, apocalypse) belongs to a different literary genre

---

1   Schaff, *Church Manual*, 23.
2   The conclusion of the book in the Bryennios manuscript has unfortunately been lost. More will be said about this below. After 16.8 (the arrival of the *Kyrios*), another short passage on the judgment of the world must have followed. On this, also, see below.

1

and could stand alone.[3] Indeed, this writing was composed by a compiler or redactor using very diverse extant materials. (We must inquire later about the particular parts possibly attributable to the redactor himself.) The resultant whole cannot be easily classified. Ordinarily, scholars refer to it as a "church order,"[4] "community order," "church manual," or something similar.[5] Karl Bihlmeyer, for instance, speaks of a "handbook of religion"; Alfred Adam of a "church book."[6] In this book, the compiler (a church leader of the early 2d century) has produced an instruction, a rule, a kind of *regula vitae christianae* for his own sphere of influence; it is entirely aimed at practical needs and lacks any theoretical or even speculative exposition of Christian belief. The compiler is no "theologian."[7] It would be foolish to attempt to derive the complete teaching or views of the Didachist from the *Didache*.[8] The *Didache* is not a "theological" work but a rule for ecclesiastical praxis, a handbook of church morals, ritual, and discipline.

The Didachist possessed no direct literary model from which to construct this work.[9] The elements of church order in the Pastoral Epistles (1 and 2 Timothy and Titus) are certainly not sufficient to constitute a model, to say nothing of the fact that the Didachist could scarcely have been acquainted with the Pastorals.[10] Nonetheless, we should not overestimate our author's originality. The construction of a rule for a church community of limited size is predetermined by the nature of the task itself,[11] and the literary form of such a document was also prescribed by presuppositions governing

---

3   Cf. the brief analysis in Rordorf and Tuilier, *Doctrine,* 17–18.

4   Most recently, again, Wengst, *Didache,* 18.

5   Audet (*Didachè,* 248, 436–41) differs, preferring (on the basis of an assumption of the apostolicity of the document) to distinguish the *Didache* quite sharply from the genre of later canonical literature. In this matter, however, Audet (pp. 249–53) permits his statements about the literary genre of the writing to be determined by the original title, as he himself has deduced it; this approach is questionable. Some reservations about the assumption that the writing is to be interpreted as a church order are also voiced by Rordorf and Tuilier, *Doctrine,* 21 n. 2.

6   Bihlmeyer, *Apostolischen Väter,* xiii; Adam, "Herkunft," 60–63. Stempel ("Lehrer," 214–15) regards the *Didache* as a "religious pedagogical document." This judgment corresponds to his thesis about the special role of the διδάσκαλος in the community of the *Didache* (see below). The Didachist is regarded as one of these teachers.

7   Cf. Wengst, *Didache,* 17. This is also emphasized by Kraft, *Didache,* 65; however, he makes the "author-editor" of the *Didache* a mere copyist (pp. 1–2). Proceeding on this basis, Schöllgen now asserts that "theological problems play no role explicitly" ("Church Order," 63).

8   There are passing and sometimes implicit details that make clear what the teaching and views of the Didachist (or the Didachist's sources) were; but it would be wrong to try to construct a "theology" of the Didachist from those details. The teaching and views of the Didachist cannot be reduced to what emerges, en passant and implicitly, from this writing. The same is a fundamental objection to all attempts to determine the "theology" of the *Didache* and to distinguish it from others (e.g., Matthew's or

Paul's); on this, see, e.g., Aono, *Entwicklung,* 163–210, esp. 190–96 and 208–10. Such attempts violate the principle that forbids direct comparison of texts that indicate different levels of reflection.

9   Günther Bornkamm differs ("Eschatology and Ecclesiology in the Gospel of Matthew," in Günther Bornkamm, Gerhard Barth, and Heinz Joachim Held, *Tradition and Interpretation in Matthew* [trans. Percy Scott; Philadelphia: Westminster, 1963] 17). Bornkamm establishes a parallel structure for Matthew's Sermon on the Mount and the *Didache* (parenesis as Torah for admission, individual questions regarding the life of worship and behavior in the church, eschatological outlook). "One may draw the conclusion that a settled 'catechism pattern' provided the basis for their composition and in the *Didache* this actually acquires the character of an ecclesiastical discipline" (ibid.). In a later essay ("Der Aufbau der Bergpredigt," *NTS* 24 [1978/79] 432) Bornkamm again refers to this question. Once more he discovers points of contact, but this time he gives stronger emphasis to the peculiarities of the *Didache:* "The Sermon on the Mount differs from the *Didache,* however, in that it lacks all those elements that give the latter its character as a church order" (ibid.). In my opinion, the points of structural contact are scarcely adequate to justify the assumption of a common catechetical schema, and in any case, the *Didache* cannot be understood on the basis of such a schema alone (as Bornkamm himself emphasizes).

10 See below.

11 One may think of 1QS and 1QSa. In the pagan sphere, reference can be made to the stele from Philadelphia: SIG 3.985 (pp. 113–18). On this, see Weinreich, *Privatheiligtums in Philadelphia,* 1–68. The rules can be divided "into four sections: I.

such an enterprise. The "basic document" that the Didachist used as a source afforded a foundation of sorts for the construction of the *Didache*. Once the plan of producing a book of rules had been conceived, the very nature of the enterprise suggested that instructions for baptism and the Eucharist, as well as questions regarding order within the community, should be added. The eschatological conclusion, as a further additional element, may have been suggested by the model of the basic document.[12] The whole composition is unpretentious as literature, nourished by praxis and intended for immediate application. There may have been a particular occasion or cause that impelled the influential but unknown author to produce this compilation. We do not, however, know what that occasion may have been,[13]

and we cannot reconstruct it from what we can learn of the author's tendencies — except to say, in general terms, that the *Didache* was written in a time of transition and its author is clearly making an effort to harmonize ancient and revered traditions of the church with new ecclesial necessities. The book does not claim to regulate the behavior of the entire church;[14] it appears to have only local situations in view. Still, from the very fact that it preserves the archaic traditions of a particular locality, this document is of great importance.[15]

Reasons for the dedication, listing of the group of gods (lines 2–11); II. Prescriptions of a religious and moral nature (lines 12–50); III. Agdistis, guardian of the sanctuary, who also watches over the disposition of the members of the cult (lines 51–60); IV. Concluding prayer to Zeus for a blessing (lines 60–64)" (p. 4).

12 I do not believe that chap. 16 of the *Didache* goes back to the "basic document," but I think that this chapter may have replaced the epilogue of that document. On this, see below.

13 See now the speculations of Wengst, *Didache,* 18. Of course, one may produce specific suggestions if one adopts the fictional hypothesis and a late dating of the document. Johnson ("Motive," 107–22) distinguishes three motives that are supposed to have led to the composition of the *Didache*: (1) the intention to write "a catechetical manual" (p. 108); (2) the intention to create a handbook "for a matured church" (ibid.); and (3) (this is Johnson's special thesis) to solve some problems left open by the evangelists. The *Didache* thus becomes a commentary on the Gospels. It is, among other things, "a commentary on the gospels and other Christian books"

(p. 110). The authority of the document is supported by a recourse to the twelve apostles. In sum: the *Didache* appears "as an expansion of Matthew 28:19–20. . . . It purports to be the Lord's teaching through the Twelve to the Gentiles. It tells how disciples are to be made (catechetical section, chapters 1–6), how they are to be baptized (chapter 7), and what the Lord has commanded them to observe (chapters 8–15), and finally it encourages them to wait for the end of the age (chapter 16)" (p. 122).

14 One may not attempt to interpret the *Didache* on the basis of the two titles of the document as found in H. See below.

15 Schöllgen ("Church Order," 43–64, and passim) now emphasizes the merely selective character of the *Didache*. According to Schöllgen, the document "has a limited purpose in its composition and is, as a selective church order, a polemical text on particular problems of community life" (p. 63). Behind this judgment lies an accurate insight, but one that should not be overdrawn. For example, I would not call the *Didache* a "polemical text."

2. Attestation of the *Didache*
a. References in Ancient Canonical Lists

Before the discovery of the Bryennios manuscript, the existence of the *Didache* was known only from other witnesses. Among these, the attestations in the canonical lists play a special but not entirely unproblematic role.

Eusebius's canonical list (*Hist. eccl.* 3.25) first mentions the generally acknowledged writings of the New Testament, the *homologoumena* ("recognized books"), followed by the group of *antilegomena* ("disputed books"), the latter divided into two subgroups, the "*antilegomena*, yet familiar to most" (3.25.3) and the *νόθα* ("spurious," 3.25.4), including the *Acts of Paul*, the *Shepherd (of Hermas)*, the *Apocalypse of Peter*, καὶ πρὸς τούτοις ἡ φερομένη Βαρναβᾶ ἐπιστολὴ καὶ τῶν ἀποστόλων αἱ λεγόμεναι Διδαχαί ("also the alleged Epistle of Barnabas and the so-called Teachings of the Apostles") — and finally the Johannine Apocalypse (which, however, Eusebius also lists among the *homologoumena*), as well as (with some reservations) the *Gospel to the Hebrews*, used primarily by Jewish Christians. As Eusebius notes, these are writings that are not included in the canon but are among the disputed books; nevertheless, they are acknowledged by a great many ἐκκλησιαστικοί (i.e., ἄνδρες): οὐκ ἐνδιαθήκους μὲν ἀλλὰ καὶ ἀντιλεγομένας, ὅμως δὲ παρὰ πλείστοις τῶν ἐκκλησιαστικῶν γινωσκομένας ("not canonical but disputed, yet familiar to most churchmen," *Hist. eccl.* 3.25.6). A clear distinction is drawn between both groups of the *antilegomena* and the absolutely rejected heretical writings (3.25.6–7). Thus as far as our question is concerned we learn two

things. Eusebius knows of a writing entitled τῶν ἀποστόλων Διδαχαί ("Teachings of the Apostles").[1] The insertion of the phrase αἱ λεγόμεναι ("so-called") expresses his doubt either about the apostolicity of the writing or about the title of the document itself.[2] At the same time we learn that, although this writing does not enjoy canonical recognition, it belongs to a group that follows the canonical writings, and as part of that group the document enjoys the respect of the ἐκκλησιαστικοὶ ἄνδρες.[3] Of course, this welcome news is rendered somewhat problematic. Is Eusebius really referring to our *Didache* (which I consider likely), or to the Greek tractate on the Two Ways whose Latin translation is retained for us in the *Doctrina apostolorum* (which I consider less likely)? The question remains open.[4]

It is probable that the same document (i.e., our *Didache*) appears in the Thirty-ninth Easter Letter of Athanasius of Alexandria from the year 367, a document of great importance for the history of the biblical canon of the Greek church.[5] After listing the canonical writings of the Old and New Testaments, Athanasius mentions ἕτερα βιβλία τούτων ἔξωθεν, οὐ κανονιζόμενα μέν, τετυπωμένα δὲ παρὰ τῶν πατέρων ἀναγινώσκεσθαι τοῖς ἄρτι προσερχομένοις καὶ βουλομένοις κατηχεῖσθαι τὸν τῆς εὐσεβείας λόγον ("other books not recognized as canonical, but recommended by our ancestors for reading by those who have recently entered and wish to learn the word of faith") — that is, books that, although not included in the canon, nevertheless enjoy a certain regard as (we might say) books approved by the church and, accordingly, appropriate reading for

---

1   Rufinus's translation has the singular: *Doctrina quae dicitur apostolorum* (GCS 2.1.253), as does the Syriac version. The Armenian translation (from Syriac) reads: "those that are called Teachings" (cf. GCS 2.1.252).

2   Cf. the remarks of Audet, *Didachè*, 83.

3   Bihlmeyer (*Apostolischen Väter*, xvi) infers regarding the *Didache* that "it was thus counted by some as part of the New Testament canon." Adolf von Harnack ("Prolegomena," 6–7) had already said something similar. This judgment, however, is very questionable. It is a matter of dispute whether Clement of Alexandria cites our *Didache* as γραφή; see below.

4   It should be noted that Eusebius mentions the Διδαχαί immediately after the letter of Barnabas. We will have to deal later with the tractate on the "Two Ways" (sometimes called the "basic docu-

ment" underlying the *Didache*). In the following discussion of the witnesses, we will presume this "basic document" hypothesis.

5   *Festal Letter* 39 §11 (Preuschen, *Analecta*, 45). According to Barnard ("Later History," 101) this reference is to the Two Ways tractate. Kraft is skeptical: "Probably *our* document or something very similar to it is meant" (*Didache*, 73).

6   The ἀπόκρυφα are then clearly distinguished from these.

7   The Coptic text can now be found in Athanasius, *Lettres festales et pastorales en Copte* (trans. and ed. L.-Theophile Lefort; CSCO 150–51; Louvain: Durbecq, 1955) 150.19–20. The Paris fragment (B. N. 151) of Codex B contains (p. 177), at the crucial point for our question, a text that Lefort (*Lettres festales*, CSCO 151.37) renders as follows: "la DI <DA> SCALIKÈ DES APÔTRES, — je ne parle pas de celle

baptismal candidates.[6] In this group are Wisdom of Solomon, Sirach, Esther, Judith, Tobit, καὶ Διδαχὴ καλουμένη τῶν ἀποστόλων ("and the 'Teachings' said to be 'of the Apostles'"), and *Hermas*.[7] This time our writing is called Διδαχὴ τῶν ἀποστόλων. It is not clear what Athanasius means by the added καλουμένη; cf. the parallel ἐπιστολαὶ καθολικαὶ καλούμεναι τῶν ἀποστόλων ("catholic epistles said to be 'of the apostles,'" §8).[8]

There are additional references in later canonical lists. First is Ps.-Athanasius *Synops. script. sacr.* 76 (*PG* 28.432),[9] where our document appears as Διδαχὴ ἀποστόλων.[10] Then there is *Indicium scriptorum canonicorum sexaginta*,[11] where, among the apocryphal writings, in seventeenth place, we find Περίοδοι καὶ διδαχαὶ τῶν ἀποστόλων,[12] followed by *Barnabas, Acts of Paul, Apocalypse of Paul,* and

so on. Finally, our writing appears under the title Διδαχὴ ἀποστόλων in the stichometry attributed to Patriarch Nicephoros of Constantinople[13] in sixth place in the list of the New Testament apocrypha,[14] with the stich number 200.[15] These numbers are "for the most part round, sometimes very much rounded figures."[16] According to Zahn,[17] the figure given for the *Didache* by the stichometry of Nicephoros is much too low.[18] Rordorf and Tuilier, who give the number of stichoi in *Codex Hierosolymitanus* 54 as 204,[19] see the information in the stichometry of Nicephoros as evidence that the text of *Cod. Hier.* 54 goes back to a "prototype from Christian antiquity."[20]

One may doubt that the information given by Eusebius and Athanasius really refers to our *Didache,* and

---

qui passe pour corriger le Deutéronome (the DIDASCALIA OF THE APOSTLES — I am not referring to the one that serves to correct Deuteronomy)." According to the Coptic version the writing was called ἡ διδασκαλικὴ τῶν ἀποστόλων, but that is certainly corrupt (perhaps a conflation of διδαχή and διδασκαλία). Nothing at all sensible can be made of the strange addition ("je ne parle pas de celle . . ."). It seems to me very questionable that the scribe (the codex probably comes from the 9th–10th century: cf. Lefort, *Lettres festales,* CSCO 150.viii) knew the *Didache* at all. Thus for our purposes the Coptic text is of no value.

8 Cf. Audet's remarks, *Didachè,* 85.

9 For the synopsis, see Quasten, *Patrology,* 3.39; and esp. Zahn, *Geschichte,* 2.302–18, according to which the synopsis is a compilation, and the passage that describes the *antilegomena* and apocrypha is older and was incorporated by the compiler; in fact, the text depends on a list that is closely related to that of Nicephoros (see below). "The compilation certainly did not originate before the sixth century; it may have been later" (Zahn, *Geschichte,* 2.315).

10 Τῆς νέας πάλιν Διαθήκης ἀντιλεγόμενα ταῦτα. Περίοδοι Πέτρου, Περίοδοι Ἰωάννου, Περίοδοι Θωμᾶ, Εὐαγγέλιον κατὰ Θωμᾶ, Διδαχὴ ἀποστόλων, Κλημέντια, ἐξ ὧν μετεφράσθησαν ἐκλεγέντα τὰ ἀληθέστερα καὶ θεόπνευστα. Ταῦτα τὰ ἀναγινωσκόμενα ("These are the disputed books of the new covenant: The *periodoi* [travels] of Peter, the *periodoi* of John, the *periodoi* of Thomas, the Gospel according to Thomas, the Teachings of the Apostles, the Clementines, parts of which may be considered more faithful and inspired by God. These are the books that are read").

11 See Preuschen, *Analecta,* 2.69; Zahn, *Geschichte,* 2.289–93. This is a list transmitted by a number of

manuscripts. The idea of sixty canonical books Zahn finds attested (pp. 292–93) as early as the 7th century by Antiochus, a monk of Sabas (*PG* 89.1428).

12 It is doubtful what one should understand by this title. The expression περίοδος is reminiscent of the apostolic "Acts."

13 In Preuschen, *Analecta,* 2.64. On this, see Zahn, *Geschichte,* 2.295–301: the stichometry (which, in the more extensive recension, constitutes the conclusion to the chronography) is not part of the original text of Nicephoros, but is (according to Zahn, *Geschichte,* 2.297) "a redaction of it undertaken in about 850."

14 It is preceded by the *periodoi* of Paul, Peter, John, and Thomas, and the Gospel of Thomas, and is followed by the thirty-two (books?) of Clement, etc.

15 Διδαχὴ ἀποστόλων στίχ. σ΄.

16 Zahn, *Geschichte,* 2.403.

17 Cf. Zahn's overall assessment of the numbers in the stichometry of "Nicephoros," *Geschichte,* 2.403.

18 *Geschichte,* 2.403. Cf. Ehrhard, *Altchristliche Litteratur,* 44. Audet (*Didachè,* 111) attempted (with some provisos) to make use of the information in the stichometry to promote his hypothesis that the *Didache* was formed in stages (see below). Accordingly, the number of stichoi would refer only to the first edition.

19 Rordorf and Tuilier, *Doctrine,* 109 n. 3. The numbers of stichoi in the stichometry of Nicephoros probably refer (according to Rordorf and Tuilier, *Doctrine,* 110) to an uncial text.

20 Rordorf and Tuilier, *Doctrine,* 109.

one could posit that ultimately they are speaking of the tractate on the Two Ways (which was also transmitted separately in antiquity) in one of its recensions.[21] Similarly, the information in Rufinus cannot be applied with certainty to particular writings. In the translation in Eusebius's church history (*Hist. eccl.* 3.25.4), the Greek source is represented by *Doctrina quae dicitur apostolorum* ("The Teaching called 'of the Apostles,'" GCS 2.1.253). In the canonical list in *Expositio symboli* 36 (CChrSL 20.171)[22] Rufinus mentions among the *alii libri . . . qui non canonici, sed ecclesiastici a maioribus appellati sunt* ("other books . . . which by most are called not canonical, but ecclesiastical")[23] in the New Testament series *libellus qui dicitur Pastoris sive Hermae, et his qui appellatur Duae viae, vel Iudicium secundum Petrum* ("little book called 'The Pastor' or 'of Hermas,' and the one called 'Two Ways,' or 'Sentences according to Peter'").[24] Whether by *Duae viae* and *Iudicium secundum Petrum* Rufinus is referring to two different writings[25] or only

one[26] is uncertain.[27] I consider it very improbable that he identifies all three writings (referring thereby to our *Didache*).[28] Instead, the more likely conclusion is that with *Doctrina apostolorum* Rufinus refers to our *Didache*, and with *Duae viae* to the independent tractate on the Two Ways.[29] The reference of the title *Iudicium secundum Petrum* is a question that can remain open.

b. Quotations in Early Church Literature

Of the instances of quotations from the *Didache* in the literature of the early church that have been pointed out in the course of time, only a few are conclusive. Moreover, some of them are rendered questionable by the fact that they belong to the "two ways" section of the book, so that it is uncertain whether the citation in question can really be traced to our *Didache*, rather than to the independent tractate on the "ways" that is one of the sources of our document.

(1) This ambiguity is true of the very first citation

---

21 This doubt could also apply to Ps.-Athanasius. The *Indiculus* probably indicates no knowledge at all of the writing he mentions. By contrast, the information in the stichometry of Nicephoros very probably refers to our *Didache*.

22 On this, see Stenzel, "Bibelkanon," 43–61.

23 On the *libri ecclesiastici* of the NT in Rufinus, cf. Stenzel, "Bibelkanon," 57–60. This refers to the "books that are read in the churches" (p. 57).

24 Variae lectiones: *Iudicium petri: Iudicium petrum* (cf. the text-critical information, CChrSL 2.171). Rufinus continues: *Quae omnia legi quidem in ecclesiis voluerunt, non tamen proferri ad auctoritatem ex his fidei confirmandam. Ceteras vero scripturas apocryphas nominarunt, quas in ecclesia legi noluerunt* ("All of which they wished to be read in the churches, not, however, in order to thereby support the faith. But they mention other, apocryphal writings which they did not want read in the church").

25 Jerome mentions a writing called *Iudicium* (*Liber de viris inlustribus* 1, ed. Ernest C. Richardson [TU 14.1a; Leipzig: Hinrichs, 1896] 7). Stenzel ("Bibelkanon," 58–60) attempts to show that *Duae viae* and *Iudicium secundum Petrum* are two different writings. He interprets *vel* as the equivalent of *et* (with Zahn). Stenzel ("Bibelkanon," 58) wishes to think of the *Duae viae* as referring to the first six chapters of the *Didache*, "disseminated as a special edition." For the *Iudicium*, Stenzel refers to the information in Jerome and regards the writing mentioned there as having been lost.

26 This would then be a reference to the *Apostolic Church Order* (= *Canons of the Apostles*); cf. Ehrhard, *Altchristliche Litteratur*, 44–45; Bardenhewer, *Geschichte*, 2.260 (as probable). Barnard ("Later History," 101) suggests that the reference is to the Two Ways tractate.

27 Skeptical are Rordorf and Tuilier, *Doctrine*, 108 n. 5. Audet (*Didachè*, 85–86, n. 2) thinks of reading the *vel* as well as the preceding *sive* as indications of an alternative title, which would lead to an identification of the *Duae viae* with the *Iudicium*. But Audet refuses to decide whether this writing is also identical with the *Didache*.

28 Thus already Bryennios, Διδαχή, κδ´ and κε´. Cf. also the suggestions of Harnack, "Prolegomena," 21–24; and Schaff, *Church Manual*, 137.

29 Cf. Rordorf and Tuilier, *Doctrine*, 108–9.

30 There are no examples from the time *before* Clement. The parallel between *Did.* 1.2 and Justin *1 Apol.* 16.6 (Goodspeed, *Apologeten*, 37) – τὸν ποιήσαντά σε ("the one who made you") – proves nothing about Justin's knowledge of the *Didache*, as Franz Xaver Funk thought ("Zur Apostellehre und apostolischen Kirchenordnung," *ThQ* 69 [1887] 357–59). Justin's knowledge of the *Didache* was asserted particularly by Taylor (*Teaching*, 98, 113, 116); he even (116) wanted to see some relationship in their theologies. On *Did.* 1.3 and Justin *1 Apol.* 15.9 (Goodspeed, *Apologeten*, 35), see below. According to M. A. Smith ("Did Justin Know the Didache?" *StPatr* 7.1 [TU 92; Berlin: Akademie-Verlag, 1966] 287–90), Justin's account in *1 Apol.* 61–65 appears to depend on *Did.* 7–14. But the par-

worth serious consideration,[30] which has played a certain role in research on the *Didache* as well, Clement of Alexandria *Strom.* 1.20, 100.4 (GCS 2³.64). The context is Clement's polemic against the claims of Greek philosophy, which arrogated to itself the teachings of the Old Testament. We would call it intellectual plagiarism. Clement writes: ἔμπαλιν οὖν ἀδικεῖ ὁ σφετερισάμενος τὰ βαρβάρων καὶ ὡς ἴδια αὐχῶν, τὴν ἑαυτοῦ δόξαν αὔξων καὶ ψευδόμενος τὴν ἀλήθειαν. οὗτος "κλέπτης" ὑπὸ τῆς γραφῆς εἴρηται. φησὶ γοῦν· "υἱέ, μὴ γίνου ψεύστης· ὁδηγεῖ γὰρ τὸ ψεῦσμα πρὸς τὴν κλοπήν" ("On the other hand, therefore, whoever appropriates what belongs to the barbarians, and boasts it is his own, does wrong by increasing his own glory and falsifying the truth. It is this kind of person scripture calls a 'thief.' Therefore it is said, 'Son, be not a liar, for falsehood leads to theft'"). The text Clement cites corresponds, with slight variations,[31] to the text of *Did.* 3.5. Or is this a quotation from the independent "ways" tractate?[32] Clement does not name the document he is quoting. There is also disagreement about the value Clement assigns to the work. As a rule, ὑπὸ τῆς γραφῆς is interpreted to mean that the quoted text has the status of (sacred) Scripture.[33] Thus Clement would be calling the *Didache* γραφή — on the assumption that it is the *Didache*, and not, for example, the independent tractate on the "ways" in one of its versions, that is being quoted. As early as 1913, Otto Stählin raised some doubts about this opinion.[34] He thought that γραφή referred to John 10:8, πάντες ὅσοι ἦλθον (πρὸ ἐμοῦ) κλέπται εἰσὶν καὶ λῃσταί ("all who came [before me] are thieves and ban-

dits"), and that the following φησὶ simply means "so it says, so it has been handed down,"[35] but that there is no intention to qualify the subsequent quotation as "Scripture."[36]

It has repeatedly been suggested that Clement of Alexandria quotes the *Didache* in other places besides *Strom.* 1.20, 100.4, or at least indicates that he is familiar with it.[37]

(a) Some passages in which Clement quotes a series of prohibitions recall *Did.* 2.2: οὐ φονεύσεις, οὐ μοιχεύσεις, οὐ παιδοφθορήσεις, οὐ κλέψεις, οὐ ψευδομαρτυρήσεις ("thou shalt not kill, thou shalt not commit adultery, thou shalt not corrupt boys, thou shalt not steal, thou shalt not bear false witness," *Protr.* 10.108.5 [GCS 1³.77]); οὐ πορνεύσεις, οὐ μοιχεύσεις, οὐ παιδοφθορήσεις ("thou shalt not engage in harlotry, thou shalt not commit adultery, thou shalt not corrupt boys," *Paed.* 2.10, 89.1 [GCS 1³.211]); οὐ μοιχεύσεις, οὐκ εἰδωλολατρήσεις, οὐ παιδοφθορήσεις, οὐ κλέψεις, οὐ ψευδομαρτυρήσεις ("thou shalt not commit adultery, thou shalt not worship idols, thou shalt not corrupt boys, thou shalt not steal, thou shalt not bear false witness," 3.12, 89.1 [GCS 1³.285]); τὸ μὲν "οὐ μοιχεύσεις" καὶ "οὐ παιδοφθορήσεις" καὶ ὅσα εἰς ἐγκράτειαν συμβάλλεται ("the commands 'thou shalt not commit adultery,' and 'thou shalt not corrupt boys,' and all the commandments enjoining purity," *Strom.* 3.4, 36.5 [GCS 2³.212]). Striking here is παιδοφθορεῖν, which is absent from

---

allels are not so extensive as to cause us to think of a genuine literary dependence. [Ed. For the suggestion that Ignatius of Antioch was familiar at least with the traditions underlying the *Didache*, and perhaps with an early form of the text itself, cf. Clayton N. Jefford, "Did Ignatius of Antioch Know the *Didache*?" in Jefford, *Context*, 330–51.]

31 | *Didache* | Clement of Alexandria |
|---|---|
| τέκνον μου, | υἱέ |
| μὴ γίνου ψεύστης | μὴ γίνου ψεύστης |
| ἐπειδὴ ὁδηγεῖ τὸ ψεῦσμα | ὁδηγεῖ γὰρ τὸ ψεῦσμα |
| εἰς τὴν κλοπήν . . . | πρὸς τὴν κλοπήν . . . |

32 According to Muilenburg, *Literary Relations*, 33–34, Clement is citing a Jewish apocryphon that underlies *Did.* 3.1–6. Cf. Robinson, *Didache*, 62; idem, "Barnabas and the Didache," 242; Vokes, *Riddle*, 76.

33 Thus first of all Bryennios, Διδαχή, πγ΄; then Harnack, "Prolegomena," 15; idem, *Apostellehre*, 22;

Jacquier, *Doctrine*, 110 n. 4; Schaff, *Church Manual*, 114 ("an inspired book in a wider sense"); cf. 121; Hemmer, *Doctrine*, xviii; Knopf, *Lehre*, 15; Rordorf and Tuilier, *Doctrine*, 97 n. 6.

34 Otto Stählin, "Zu dem Didachezitat bei Clemens Alexandrinus," *ZNW* 14 (1913) 271–72.

35 Stählin, 272.

36 This in turn was disputed by John E. L. Oulton, "Clement of Alexandria and the Didache," *JTS* 41 (1940) 177–79, but not cogently.

37 For an expansive treatment, see Francis R. M. Hitchcock, "Did Clement of Alexandria Know the *Didache*?" *JTS* 24 (1923) 397–401. The only material that can really be considered is that cited by Giet, *L'Énigme*, 36 n. 96; and Rordorf and Tuilier, *Doctrine*, 125 n. 1.

the biblical Decalogues but is found in the series in *Did.* 2.2. Cf. also *Barn.* 19.4 (a "ways" tractate).

(b) In *Strom.* 5.5, 31.1 (GCS 2³.346) we read: Πάλιν αὖ δύο ὁδοὺς ὑποτιθεμένου τοῦ εὐαγγελίου καὶ τῶν ἀποστόλων ὁμοίως τοῖς προφήταις ἄπασι καὶ τὴν μὲν καλούντων "στενὴν καὶ τεθλιμμένην" τὴν κατὰ τὰς ἐντολὰς καὶ ἀπαγορεύσεις περιεσταλμένην, τὴν δὲ ἐναντίαν τὴν εἰς ἀπώλειαν φέρουσαν "πλατεῖαν καὶ εὐρύχωρον" κτλ. ("But again, the gospel supposes two ways, as do the apostles, and similarly all the prophets; and they call that one 'narrow and confined' that is circumscribed according to the commandments and prohibitions, and the opposite one, which leads to perdition, [they call] 'broad and roomy' . . ." [with a subsequent reference to the fable of Prodicus: 31.2]). Rordorf and Tuilier (*Doctrine*, 125 n. 1) conclude from the expression καὶ τῶν ἀποστόλων ὁμοίως τοῖς προφήταις ἄπασι that Clement is probably thinking of our *Didache*. This is not very persuasive.

(c) Finally, there is the liturgical expression οὗτος (ὁ) τὸν οἶνον, τὸ αἷμα τῆς ἀμπέλου τῆς Δαβίδ, ἐκχέας ("you pour out this wine, the blood of the vine of David," *Quis dives salv.* 29.4 [GCS 3².179]; cf. *Did.* 9.2). The *Didache* and Clement, however, may be independently quoting the same liturgical tradition. For the fragment from the Nicetas catena in *Mon. Gr.*

36, fol. 107v., cf. the remarks in GCS 3².xxvii–xxviii.

Problematic as a witness is Origen *De princ.* 3.2.7 (GCS 5.255): *Propterea docet nos scriptura divina omnia quae accidunt nobis tamquam a deo illata suscipere, scientes quod sine deo nihil fit* ("that is why divine Scripture teaches us to receive everything that happens to us as coming from God, knowing that without God nothing comes to be"). The text recalls *Did.* 3.10 (especially in the final phrase).[38] But in light of the sententious character of the expression, this cannot be a quotation, and Origen must simply intend to introduce appropriate biblical passages such as Job 1:13–22 (to which he has referred just before) or Matt 10:29 (which he cites afterward). Moreover, the text of *Did.* 3.10 is almost identical to that of *Barn.* 19.6c, and both come from the "ways" tractate.[39] Similarly, one can scarcely claim the equally sententious expressions in Dorotheus Archimandrita *Doctr.* 13.1 (*PG* 88.1761B) and *Ep.* 3 (*PG* 88.1840C) as witnesses for the *Didache*.[40] Finally (with an extreme stretch), there could be a play on *Did.* 1.4 in Johannes Climacus *Scala paradisi gradus* 26 (*PG* 88.1029A): εὐσεβῶν μέν, τὸ παντὶ αἰτοῦντι διδόναι, εὐσεβεστέρων δὲ καὶ τῷ μὴ αἰτοῦντι. Τὸ δὲ ἀπὸ τοῦ αἴροντος μὴ ἀπαιτεῖν δυναμένους μάλιστα, τάχα τῶν ἀπαθῶν καὶ μόνων ἴδιον καθέστηκεν[41] ("It is characteristic of the pious to 'give to everyone who asks,' but of the more pious still to 'give to one who does not ask.' Not to

---

38 Hemmer (*Doctrine*, xviii) and Schaff (*Church Manual*, 116) take this to be a quotation.

39 Of course, we cannot exclude the possibility that Origen is quoting unconsciously.

40 Still more remote is Dionysius of Alexandria (?) in John of Damascus *Sacra parallela* 33 (*PG* 96.320A).

41 The contacts between Origen *Hom. 6.2 in Iudic.* (Origenis, *Opera Omnia*, vol. 11: *In Libros Josuae Judicum et I Samuelis Homiliae* [ed. C. H. E. Lommatzsch; Berlin: Haude and Spener, 1841] 258) and *Did.* 9.2 do not rest on literary dependence (thus Hemmer, *Doctrine*, xviii; Schaff, *Church Manual*, 116) but on the common language of the liturgy. According to Adam ("Herkunft," 48) the Ps.-Clementine *Epistula ad Virgines* is dependent on the *Didache*. Adam thinks that Ps.-Clement *Ep. ad virg.* 1.11.8 (Hugo Duensing, "Die dem Klemens von Rom zugeschriebenen Briefe über die Jungfräulichkeit," *ZKG* 63 [1950/51] 176) is a "deliberate challenge to *Did.* 11.11." This can scarcely be correct. On the question of the key word χριστέμπορος (making a business of Christ) and the suggestions about quotations of the *Didache* connected with it,

see below at *Did.* 12.5. Franz Xaver Funk, in turn (in an untitled note on the *Didache*, *ThQ* 74 [1892] 522) indicated a passage in the Latin *Passio beati Phileae episcopi de civitate Thmui* (3 end): *dicit enim sacra et divina scriptura: Diliges Dominum Deum tuum qui te fecit* ["for the sacred and divine scripture says: You shall love the Lord your God who made you"] (Herbert Musurillo, ed., *The Acts of the Christian Martyrs* [Oxford: Clarendon, 1972; repr. 1979] 346). Meanwhile, a Greek version of the Acts has been found in *P. Bodm.* XX (Musurillo, *Acts*, xlvi–xlvii), which unfortunately has a gap just at the parallel passage. But lines 14 (end) and 15 (beginning) could have read (in Martin's conjecture): ἀγαπή-σεις κ̄ν̄ τὸν θ̄ν̄ ὅς σε | ἐποίησεν ("you shall love the Lord your God who made you"). Cf. Musurillo, *Acts*, 338. The Greek text stems from the beginning of the 4th century (Musurillo, *Acts*, xlvii). The quotation is from Deut 6:5, but with an expansion (*qui te fecit* ["who made you"]), the sense of which also appears in *Did.* 1.2. The same addition is also found in Justin *1 Apol.* 16.6 (cf. n. 30 above). Here, as there, we cannot conclude that it is derived from

refuse one who takes something away, when one is able to do so, is perhaps characteristic of those who have no emotion, and them alone.")

Almost certainly the liturgical texts can be eliminated from the list of witnesses: (Ps.-)Athanasius *De virg.* 13 recalls motifs from *Did.* 9.3–4;[42] Serapion of Thmuis *Euchologion* 13.13 recalls *Did.* 9.4;[43] *P. Dêr Balizeh,* fol. IIv., lines 3–11, is reminiscent of *Did.* 9.2, 4, and perhaps also 10.5.[44] It is true that they illustrate individual expressions from the Didachistic prayers in a most fortunate way, but it is difficult to suppose that they are dependent on the *Didache.* The agreements must, rather, rest on common liturgical tradition.

(2) The Latin witnesses begin with an interesting example, Ps.-Cyprian *De aleat.* 4 (CSEL 3.3.96): *et in doctrinis apostolorum: si quis frater delinquit in ecclesia et non paret [v.l. apparet] legi, hic nec colligatur [v.l. colligitur], donec paenitentiam agat, et non recipiatur, ne inquinetur et inpediatur oratio vestra* ("and in the teachings of the apostles: if a brother offends in the church and disobeys the law, let him not be considered until he does penance, nor received, lest he defile and obstruct your prayer").[45] The text recalls *Did.* 14.2 or 15.3.[46] That the unknown

author of the writings of Ps.-Cyprian[47] really quotes the *Didache* is suggested by the specific naming of the writing.[48] The passage involves a free quotation that mixes 14.2 with 15.3.[49] This quotation is a welcome proof of the existence of a Latin translation of the *Didache* (and not merely of the tractate on the "ways") around 300 (in Africa?), as well as of the title it bore: "*doctrinae apostolorum.*"[50]

Table 1

Did. 14.2	*Did.* 15.3	*De aleat.*
πᾶς δὲ ἔχων τὴν ἀμφιβολίαν	καὶ παντὶ ἀστοχοῦντι	*si quis frater*
μετὰ τοῦ ἑταίρου αὐτοῦ	κατὰ τοῦ ἑτέρου	*delinquit*
—	—	*in ecclesia*
—	—	*et non paret legi,*
μὴ συνελθέτω ὑμῖν	μηδεὶς λαλείτω μηδὲ παρ᾽ ὑμῶν ἀκουέτω,	*hic nec colligatur*
ἕως οὗ διαλλαγῶσιν	ἕως οὗ μετανοήσῃ.	*donec paenitentiam agat,*
—	—	*et non recipiatur,*
—	—	*ne inquinetur et inpediatur*
ἵνα μὴ κοινωθῇ	—	*oratio vestra.*
ἡ θυσία ὑμῶν.		

---

the *Didache.* See Altaner, "Doctrina," 337–38.

42 Eduard von der Goltz, ed., *Ps.Athanasius, De virginitate: λόγος σωτηρίας πρὸς τὴν παρθένον (de virginitate): Eine echte Schrift des Athanasius* (TU, n.s. 14.2a; Leipzig: Hinrichs, 1905) 47. According to MacLean, "Introduction," xxvi; Hemmer, *Doctrine,* xix; Muilenburg, *Literary Relations,* 39; and Vokes, *Riddle,* 73–74, and frequently elsewhere, this set of parallels indicates familiarity with the *Didache.* Adam ("Herkunft," 34) believes that *Did.* 9.3–4 was used as a table prayer.

43 Serapion, *Euchologion,* in Funk, *Didascalia,* 2.174. Dependence on the *Didache* is postulated by MacLean, "Introduction," xxvi; Creed, "Didache," 374; Vokes, *Riddle,* 73–74 and frequently elsewhere; van Haelst, "Nouvelle reconstitution," 451.

44 Roberts and Capelle, *Euchologium,* 26. Also in van Haelst, "Nouvelle reconstitution," 449, who also (pp. 449, 451) thinks there are citations from the *Didache.* Cf. also Cyprian *Ep.* 63.13 (CSEL 3.2.712) and 69.5 (CSEL 3.2.754).

45 The quotation is marked in the editions.

46 Cf. the synopsis in table 1. I do not think that the text also recalls *Did.* 4.14 (so Harnack, "Prolegomena," 20–21; Rordorf and Tuilier, *Doctrine,* 80).

47 On this document, earlier much disputed, cf. Bardenhewer, *Geschichte,* 2.49–99; Hugo Koch, "Zur

Schrift *adversus aleatores,*" in *Festgabe von Fachgenossen und Freunden Karl Müller zum siebzigsten Geburtstag dargebracht* (Tübingen: Mohr, 1922) 58–67; Altaner and Stuiber, *Patrologie,* 177: "a vulgar Latin sermon against dice-players. . . . The author may have been a Catholic bishop in Africa writing around 300."

48 The text extract is contained within a series of quotations. Chap. 4 first cites texts from the Pastorals, then introduces a quotation from 1 Cor 5:11 with *et iterum* ("and again"); there follows, *alio loco* ("elsewhere"), a quotation of unknown origin; then, after the introductory words *in doctrinis apostolorum* ("in the teachings of the apostles"), comes our quotation from the *Didache.* Then follows *et apostolus iterum dicit* ("and again the apostle says"), with a quotation from 1 Cor 5:13. The conclusion is a corollary referring to the *multorum testium unitas et consonans monitio* ("single and harmonious admonition of a multitude of witnesses"). The conclusion: *doctrina apostolorum* ("teachings of the apostles") was regarded by the author (probably without much reflection) as an apostolic writing having apostolic authority.

49 This free and mixed quotation has no consequences for the text of the *Didache* itself.

50 Altaner ("Doctrina," 340) also supports the position

In 1914 Richard Reitzenstein edited Ps.-Cyprian's *De centesima, sexagesima, tricesima*,[51] which may go back to an anonymous North African of the fourth century.[52] Chapter 14 (p. 79, lines 132–35) reads: *et alio in loco scriptura haec testatur et admonet dicens: 'Si potes quidem, fili, omnia praecepta domini facere, eris consummatus; sin autem, vel duo praecepta, amare*[53] *dominum ex totis praecordiis et similem tibi quasi (te ipsum)'* ("and at another place this scripture bears witness and admonishes, with the words, 'If you are able, son, to do all the commandments of the Lord, you will be perfect; but if only one or two commandments, love the Lord with all your heart and those like you as [yourself]'"). This could be a citation of *Did.* 6.2[54] (as Reitzenstein already indicated).[55] Interesting in that case (but not to be overvalued) would be the qualification of the source as "*scriptura.*"[56]

The *Gesta apud Zenophilum*[57] is problematic: *quosdam diligo super animam meam* ("certain ones I love more than my soul," CSEL 26.192)[58] is supposed to be a reflection of *Did.* 2.7, οὓς δὲ ἀγαπήσεις ὑπὲρ τὴν ψυχήν σου ("others you shall love more than your soul"). But it is equally possible that the text of the Two Ways tractate is being quoted — if this is a quotation at all.[59] When

Optatus of Mileve *Contra Parmen.* 1.21 (CSEL 26.23) writes *denique inter cetera praecepta etiam haec tria iussio divina prohibuit: non occides, non ibis post deos alienos, et in capitibus mandatorum: non facies scisma* ("finally, among other commandments, these three also the divine order prohibits: you shall not kill, you shall not run after other gods, and in the chapters of commandments: you shall not cause schism"), the last expression, taken by itself, suggests a play on 1 Cor 1:10; however, there is a greater similarity to *Did.* 4.3, οὐ ποιήσεις σχίσμα ("you shall not cause division") — a text that comes from the Two Ways tractate; cf. *Barn.* 19.12 (where the text is the same), and *Doctrina apostolorum*: *non facies dissensiones* ("you shall not cause dissensions").[60] It is thus quite possible here that the Latin text of the independent tractate on the Two Ways is being quoted.[61] In that case, would *capita mandatorum* ("chapters of commandments")[62] be one of its names? It should be noted that the quotation reappears in 3.7 (CSEL 26.88–89): *non sacrificabis idolis idem deus locutus est et: non facies scisma et . . .* ("you shall not sacrifice to idols, as God has said, and: you shall not cause schism, and . . ."), and it is striking that the quotation that recalls the "ways" tractate is introduced by *deus locu-*

---

that a Latin translation of the *Didache* (14.2 certainly, 15.3 possibly) is being quoted.

51 Richard Reitzenstein, ed., "Ps.-Cyprian, *De centesima, de sexagesima, de tricesima*: Eine frühchristliche Schrift von den dreierlei Früchten des Lebens," *ZNW* 15 (1914) 60–90 (the edition at 74–90). Cf. *PL* Sup 1.53–67 (with text-critical notes by Donatien de Bruyne).

52 Reitzenstein thought of a gnosticizing author, who may just as well have belonged to the great church ("Frühchristliche Schrift," 68). Donatien de Bruyne ("Un traité gnostique sur les trois récompenses," *ZNW* 15 [1914] 280–84) considered the 3d century a possibility (dependence on Cyprian). Hugo Koch ("Die ps.-cyprianische Schrift De centesima, sexagesima, tricesima in ihrer Abhängigkeit von Cyprian," *ZNW* 31 [1932] 248–72) attempted to demonstrate literary dependence on Cyprian (North Africa, 4th century). Jean Daniélou ("Le traité de centesima, sexagesima, tricesima et le Judéo-Christianisme Latin avant Tertullien," *VC* 25 [1971] 171–81) posited an African tractate of Jewish-Christian encratite provenance from the end of the 2d century. To the contrary, cf. the arguments of A. P. Orbán ("Die Frage der ersten Zeugnisse des Christenlateins," *VC* 30 [1976] 214–38), who dates the writing between 251/257 and 383. Altaner and Stuiber (*Patrologie,*

178) opt for North Africa, probably 4th century; see also Quasten, *Patrology*, 2.372.

53 "Ama *or* amabis?" Reitzenstein, "Frühchristliche Schrift," 79.

54 *Did.* 6.2   *De centesima*:
εἰ μὲν γὰρ δύνασαι   *Si potes quidem, fili,*
βαστάσαι
ὅλον τὸν ζυγὸν τοῦ   *omnia praecepta domini facere,*
κυρίου,
τέλειος ἔσῃ·   *eris consummatus;*
εἰ δ᾽ οὐ δύνασαι   *sin autem,*
ὃ δύνῃ, τοῦτο ποίει.   *vel duo praecepta . . . [etc.]*

55 Reitzenstein, "Frühchristliche Schrift," 79.

56 The quotation of the Golden Rule in its negative form at 42 (ibid., 86, lines 340–41) does not go back to the *Didache* (nor to the Two Ways tractate). See below, at *Did.* 1.2.

57 Bardenhewer, *Geschichte*, 3.494. According to Altaner, "Doctrina," 338, it should be dated ca. 320.

58 *Item alia recitata:* "*Fratri Forti Sabinus in domino aeternam salutem! quae sit caritas, iuxta omnes collegas certus sum peculiariter; tamen secundum dei voluntatem, qui dixit: quosdam diligo super animam meam, Silvanum te coluisse certus sum.*"

59 Funk held for dependence on the *Didache* ("Didache," 603; cf. the same passage in the revision of this article in idem, *Abhandlungen*, 2.109).

tus est ("God said"). Nevertheless, one must avoid any overhasty conclusions about the tractate — or the *Didache*.[63]

The extent to which Lactantius can be adduced for knowledge of the Two Ways tractate (or even the *Didache*?) is not clear to me. In *Divin. inst.* 6.3.1 (CSEL 19.485) we read: *Duae sunt viae per quas humanam vitam progredi necesse est, una quae in caelum ferat, altera quae ad inferos deprimat: quas et poetae in carminibus et philosophi in disputationibus suis induxerunt* ("There are two ways by which it is necessary for human life to go, one that leads to heaven, another which leads down to hell: as also the poets have shown in their songs, and the philosophers in their disputations"). The "ways" motif controls the entire section that follows (6.3–4 = 19.485–94). It should be compared especially with *Inst. epitome* 54 (59)–62 (67) (CSEL 19.734–50).[64] One cannot deny a certain relationship with the tractate in the motifs (partly also in the structure). Is literary dependence present? I note one striking detail: *non sit asper in filium neque in servum: meminerit quod et ipse patrem habeat ac dominum* ("be not harsh to your son nor to your slave: remem-

ber that you also have a father and Lord," *Inst. epit.* 59[64].3 = CSEL 19.744). Compare *Did./Doctr.* 4.10 and *Barn.* 19.7. From a literary point of view, however, the passages in Commodian *Instructiones* 1.22.15 (CSEL 15.28) and *Carmen apologeticum* 699 (CSEL 15.160) can scarcely be traced to the Two Ways tractate.[65]

Epistula Titi is a problematic witness:[66] *praeconante prudentia gesta futura hoc est quod mandat semper dicens: Fuge filiole, omnem malum et ab omne simile illi* ("while wisdom announces the future, this is what it always orders: Avoid, my child, every evil and everything that resembles it"). One is reminded of *Did.* 3.1 or *Doctr.* 3.1,[67] so that here again, if there really is a quotation from one of the two documents (the *Didache* or the independent tractate on the Two Ways),[68] it is entirely possible that the Latin text of the Two Ways tractate is being quoted.[69]

At the same time, we find apparent instances (not of references to the Two Ways tractate, but only to our *Didache*) in Augustine. In his commentary on the Psalms, he quotes four times the striking sentence about "sweating alms" that appears in *Did.* 1.6: *De alio enim dictum est: Omni petenti te da; et de alio dictum est: Desudet eleemosyna*

Altaner ("Doctrina," 338) opted for the Latin translation of the "ways" tractate and regarded "dependence on *Doctr.* 2.7" as "very probable." "It is not essential for our question that in the *Acta Zenophili* a superabundant love of neighbor is acclaimed of God, while in the *Doctrina* the same command is given to human beings by the apostles, and so by God" (ibid.). The Latin *Doctrina* reads: *quosdam amabis super animam tuam* ("certain ones you will love more than your own soul"). The version in *Barnabas* (19.5) is more remote in this instance.

60 The *Canons of the Apostles* and *Apostolic Constitutions* have the plural σχίσματα.

61 Funk considered a *Didache* citation possible ("Didache," 602; cf. idem, *Abhandlungen*, 2.109). Altaner ("Doctrina," 338) differs: he chose the Latin translation of the tractate on the "ways." Altaner explained the shift from *dissensiones* to *scisma* in terms of the occasion for the writing (Optatus was polemicizing against the Donatist schism).

62 Such a title would not be ill suited to the Two Ways tractate.

63 For the contrary position, see Funk, "Didache," 602; idem, *Abhandlungen*, 2.109.

64 On this see Willy Rordorf, "An Aspect of the Judeo-Christian Ethic: The Two Ways," in Draper,

Research, 148–64 (ET of "Un chapitre d'éthique judéo-chrétienne: les deux voies," *RechSR* 60 [1972] 109–28).

65 Altaner ("Doctrina," 337) sees no dependence of Lactantius or Commodian on the tractate.

66 Donatien de Bruyne, ed., "*Epistula Titi, discipuli Pauli, de dispositione sanctimonii*," *RBén* 37 (1925) 47–72, lines 261–315. This writing probably comes from the 5th century and may have been written in Spain, under the influence of the Priscillianist movement. It is transmitted in several isolated MSS. (University of Würzburg, 8th century), which de Bruyne published. Cf. Adolf von Harnack, "Der apokryphe Brief des Paulusschülers Titus 'De dispositione sanctimonii,'" SPAW.PH (1925) 180–213; Aurelio de Santos Otero, "The Pseudo-Titus Epistle," in *NTApoc*, 2.53–74. Harnack ("Der apokryphe Brief," 195) pointed out the possibility of a quotation from the *Didache*.

67 There is no parallel in *Barnabas*.

68 Of course, there could also be reference to a text of related content from Sirach; the mention of *prudentia* may in itself indicate something of the sort: de Santos Otero, "The Pseudo-Titus Epistle," *NTApoc*, 2.53 n. 1.

69 The text of *Doctrina apostolorum* creates some difficulties in this passage. The Munich MS. has: *Fili, fuge*

in manu tua, donec invenias iustum, cui eam tradas ("For in another [place] it is said: Give to all who ask of you; and in another it is said: Let your charitable gift sweat in your hands until you know to whom you are giving it," *Enar. in Ps.* on Ps 102:12 [CChrSL 40.1462]); *Sicut enim de illo qui te quaerit dictum est: Omni petenti te, da, sic de illo quem tu debes quaerere dictum est: Sudet eleemosyna in manu tua, donec invenias iustum cui eam tradas* ("For as it is said of the one who asks you: Give to all who ask you, and of the one of whom you should inquire it is said: Let your charitable gift sweat in your hands until you know to whom you are giving it," *Enar. in Ps.* on Ps 103:3, 10 [CChrSL 40.1509]); *utrumque dictum est, fratres mei, et: Omni petenti te da, modo lectum est; et alio loco scriptura dicit: Sudet eleemosyna in manu tua, quousque invenias iustum cui eam tradas. . . . Omni enim petenti te da: sed alius est quem tu debes quaerere; Sudet eleemosyna in manu tua quousque invenias iustum cui des* ("and again it is said, my brothers, also: Give to all who ask you, as we just read; and another place in Scripture says: Let your charitable gift sweat in your hands until you find a just person to whom to give it. . . . give to all who ask you, but there is another whom you should seek; Let your charitable gift sweat in your hand until you find a just person to whom to give it," *Enar. in Ps.* on Ps 146:17 [CChrSL 40.2135]).[70] The quotation then appears in post-Augustinian authors (Cassiodorus *Expositio in Psalterium* 40 [*PL* 70.295D]; 103 [*PL* 70.733 B]; Gregory the Great *Regula Pastoralis* 3.20 [*PL* 77.84D]) and relatively often in the medieval Christian literature of the West (see further on this in the commentary, at *Did.* 1.6). It is interest-ing that Augustine once explicitly refers to the sentence as "*scriptura*."[71] We are confronted with the following alternative:[72] either we really have here the Latin transla-tion of a Greek alternate translation of Sir 12:1 (thus Audet, *Didachè*, 275–80) — which would eliminate Augustine (and his followers with him) as witness(es) to knowledge of the *Didache*; or the saying comes from the *Didache*, as Altaner maintained.[73] In that case, Altaner (in light of the Augustinian view of Scripture) must sup-pose that the bishop of Hippo "did not derive [his words] from a Latin *Didache* available to him," but "the sentence, perhaps circulating as a familiar quotation, would have reached Augustine by a route unknown to us."[74] Nevertheless, in this way Augustine would become a witness (although indirectly) for the existence of a Latin translation of the *Didache* in the fourth/fifth cen-tury.[75] The quotations from the subsequent period would then be dependent, directly or indirectly, on Augustine.[76]

(3) Finally, there are the Syrian witnesses. Among those in question[77] are the Messalianic *Liber graduum*,[78] which may attest to knowledge and use of the *Didache*.[79] The insertions of the Golden Rule at 7.1 (l. 146); 15.16 (l. 375); 30.26 (ll. 922–23) are not significant. Similarly, 13.1 (l. 307), *iustitia autem nullos habet inimicos* ("for jus-tice has no enemies") need not be traced to *Did.* 1.3. More important is 7.20 (l. 183), *Quare non ieiunamus bis in hebdomade, sicut iustis scriptum est? . . . Et cur* (l. 186) *non oramus ter in die et mane et vespere, sicut iustis scriptum est* ("Why should we not fast twice a week, as it is written for the just? . . . And why should we not pray three times

---

ab homine malo, et homine simulatore ("Child, flee from the evil person, and what resembles a human being"). This not only represents a false interpreta-tion of the Greek παν πονηρόν ("every evil") as *homo malus* ("evil person"), but the last word of the Munich ms. is problematic: *sim* is clear, but the rest is *in rasura* (f3); f1 read either *simili illi* (thus Schlecht, *Doctrina XII Apostolorum,* 50) or *simili illius* (thus Leo Wohleb, *Die lateinische Übersetzung der Didache kritisch und sprachlich untersucht* [SGKA 7.1; Paderborn: Schöningh, 1913; repr. New York: Johnson, 1967] 26). Altaner ("Doctrina," 339) sup-poses that the *Epistle of Ps.-Titus* had a better Latin text at its disposal than f, and therefore he emends — following the *Epistle* — *simile illi.* Altaner sees the reference to *prudentia* as an indication that the source of the *Epistle of Ps.-Titus* was probably the

Two Ways tractate. To the contrary, however, cf. de Santos Otero (n. 68 above).

70	*Didache*	Augustine
	Ἱδρωσάτω	*(De-)sudet*
	ἡ ἐλεημοσύνη σου	*eleemosyna*
	εἰς τὰς χεῖράς σου,	*in manu tua*
	μέχρις ἂν γνῷς,	*donec (quousque) invenias*
	—	*iustum*
	τίνι δῷς	*cui eam tradas (cui des).*

71 Cassiodorus and Gregory the Great also write *scrip-tum est* and *de quo* [or *quod*] *scriptum est.*

72 See the remarks below on *Did.* 1.6.

73 This is the older opinion represented by Altaner, "Doctrina," 340–41.

74 Altaner, "Doctrina," 341. He does not wish to exclude the possibility that Augustine, according to this, did in fact know the *Didache* or the *Doctrina.*

a day, both morning and evening, as it is written for the just"). The *Liber graduum* seems here to be making a play on *Did.* 8.1 and/or 8.3, and to cite the *Didache* as "Scripture."[80] Also striking is 2.2 (l. 27), *Qui te percusserit in maxilla tua, admove ei alteram et ora pro ipso et esto perfectus* ("If anyone strikes you on the cheek, turn the other to him and pray for him and be perfect"), as well as 22.15 (l. 671), *qui te percusserit in maxilla tua, admove ei aliam et eris perfectus* ("If anyone strikes you on the cheek, turn the other to him and you will be perfect"). The *Liber graduum* quotes the Synoptic logion with an addition similar to that in the *Didache* (καὶ ἔσῃ τέλειος). We must regard this either as a peculiarity of the Syriac text tradition (while taking note of the fact that the *Liber graduum* customarily quotes the *Diatesseron*), or — and this I consider more probable — as representing dependence on the *Didache*.[81] In addition, there is 16.4 (l. 395), *Dixit autem tibi: Dilige fratrem tuum plus quam teipsum* ("He also says to you: Love your brother more than yourself"); cf. *Did.* 2.7, and note that the *Liber graduum* introduces the saying as *dictum domini* ("a saying of the Lord"). Finally, 13.2 (l. 307), *sacerdotes honorat eorumque verbis obedit, eos adit* ("give honor to priests and obey their words that they speak to you"); cf. *Did.* 4.1(?); and *sacerdotibus suis primitias omnium proventuum suorum et primitias alveorum praestat et primogenita omnium, quae possidet* ("let him give to his priests the firstfruits of all his produce

and the firstfruits of the vats and the firstborn of all that he possesses"); cf. *Did.* 13.3–7. Adam maintained, "The accumulation of quotations from the *Didache* in this context can only be understood as the use of a written source, and it must have been a Syriac version."[82] I do not share Adam's certainty, but I do not consider it impossible that the author of the *Liber graduum* knew and used a Syriac version of the *Didache*. Thus in this case we would have to say that there was a (lost) Syriac translation of the *Didache*, the origins of which would have to lie at least as far back as the fifth century.[83]

c. Use of the *Didache* in Later Church Orders

In the previous discussion I have not referred to specific texts in canonist and monastic literature to which a literary association with the *Didache* has been attributed (sometimes on the basis of evidence, sometimes problematically, and sometimes unjustly). In this section I will consider those texts.

The so-called *Apostolic Church Order* or *Canons of the Holy Apostles* (= *Can.*)[84] chaps. 4–13 parallels *Did.* 1.1–4.8[85] (i.e., the "way of life" in the "two ways" section, but without its conclusion).[86] Something similar is true of the *Epitome*, which is related to the *Canons* (and in which the conclusion of the "way of life" is retained).[87] It is rather certain, however, that these two writings are not dependent on the *Didache* (as is

---

75 Cf. what was said above regarding Ps.-Cyprian *De aleat*.

76 Cf. Altaner's suggestions in "Doctrina," 342.

77 The Syriac version of the *Didascalia apostolorum* rests on a Greek original. Something analogous is true of Ps.-Clement *Epistula ad virgines*, but in this case it is rather improbable that the writer knows and cites the *Didache*. See n. 41 above.

78 Mihaly Kmosko, ed., *Liber graduum* (Patrologia Syriaca 1.3; Paris: Didot, 1926). The writing probably comes from Messalianic circles.

79 On what follows, cf. Kmosko, *Liber graduum*, clxvii, and at the individual passages mentioned. In addition, see Adam, "Herkunft," 49–50 (examples and discussion).

80 That the prescriptions of the *Didache* are here adapted to Messalianic doctrine is a topic for another day.

81 Or is this an accidental parallel arising out of the

He was then thinking of the reversal of the fifth and sixth commandments in Augustine, and tried to establish a connection with *Doctr.* 2.2.

teaching of the *Liber graduum* about the "*perfecti*"?

82 Adam, "Herkunft," 49.

83 For Adam's hypothesis of a Syriac original, see below. We should also note in passing that there are supposed parallels to the *Didache*, or material from the "ways" tractate, in Chinese Nestorian texts: Joan H. Walker, "An Argument from the Chinese for the Antiochene Origin of the *Didache*," *StPatr* 8.2 (TU 93; Berlin: Akademie-Verlag, 1966) 44–50.

84 The text is found in Theodor Schermann, *Die allgemeine Kirchenordnung, frühchristliche Liturgien und kirchliche Überlieferung*, vol. 1: *Die allgemeine Kirchenordnung des zweiten Jahrhunderts* (SGKA Sup 3.1; Paderborn: Schöningh, 1914; repr. New York: Johnson, 1968) 12ff. Cf. Bardenhewer, *Geschichte*, 2.256–62; Altaner and Stuiber, *Patrologie*, 254–55; Quasten, *Patrology*, 2.119–20. This document probably stems from Egypt at the beginning of the 4th century.

85 *Canons* lacks the *sectio evangelica*: *Did.* 1.3b–2.1.

86 But there is a parallel to *Did.* 4.13b in *Can.* 14.3.

87 Schermann, *Elfapostelmoral*, text at pp. 16–18. An

already evident from the absence of the *sectio evangelica, Did.* 1.3b–2.1). Instead, the two documents go back to a particular recension of the Two Ways tractate, which was also available to the author of the *Didache* (but in a different recension). In the same way, it is probable that other parallel texts rest not on the *Didache* but on recensions of the Two Ways tractate. These include passages from Ps.-Athanasius *Syntagma doctrinae*,[88] from *Fides CCCXVIII patrum*,[89] and (parallel to the "two ways" section) from the Arabic *Life of Shenoute*.[90] The generically similar *Fragmenta*

Anastasiana and *Sentences* derive from other sources.[91] We should probably include in the group of texts dependent on the Two Ways tractate (with some reservation) the *Rule of Benedict* 4 (CSEL 75².31–32), where Benedict draws on the *Rule of the Master*. Whether the latter (and with it, then, the *Rule of Benedict*) is dependent in a literary sense, or only through oral tradition, on the beginning of the Two Ways tractate, I cannot

---

88 analogy to the *sectio* is also lacking in the *Epitome*.

88 Cf. *PG* 28.836A–845B. Pierre Batiffol later edited this text: "Le Syntagma Doctrinae dit de Saint Athanase," in idem, ed., *Studia Patristica* (Études d'ancienne littérature chrétienne, fasc. 2; Paris: Leroux, 1890) 119–60.

89 Cf. *PG* 28.1637A–1644B. There is another edition by Pierre Batiffol, "Canones Nicaeni pseudepigraphi," *Revue archéologique* 3d ser. 6 (1885) 134–41. The variants are often considerable. I quote the text from Batiffol, but include the parallels in *PG*. There is a Coptic version: Eugène Revillout, *Le concile de Nicée d'après les textes coptes et les diverses collections canoniques* (2 vols.; Paris: Maisonneuve, 1881–98) 1.33–50 (text) and 2.475–92 (French translation). I was unfortunately unable to obtain Pierre Batiffol, *Didascalia CCCXVIII patrum pseudepigrapha e graecis codicibus rec. Petrus Batiffol, coptico contulit Henricus Hyvernat* (Paris, 1887).

90 On Shenoute, cf. Johannes Leipoldt, *Schenute von Atripe und die Entstehung des nationalägyptischen Christentums* (TU 25.1; Leipzig: Hinrichs, 1903); Bardenhewer, *Geschichte,* 4.98–100; Altaner and Stuiber, *Patrologie,* 268–69; Quasten, *Patrology,* 3.185–87. The originally Coptic *Vita,* now retained in Arabic, is in Émile Amélineau, *Mémoires publiés par les membres de la Mission archéologique française au Caire, 1885–1886,* vol. 4: *Monuments pour servir à l'histoire de l'Égypte chrétienne aux IVᵉ et Vᵉ siècles* (Paris: Leroux, 1888); chap. 6: *Vie de Schnoudi* (Arabic and French) 289–478. In the first part of the text there is a version of the Two Ways tractate (pp. 291–93 in Amélineau's edition). Cf. also H. Benigni, "Didachê coptica: 'Duarum viarum' recensio coptica monastica, Shenudii homiliis attributa, per arabicam versionem superstes," *Bessarione* 3 (1898) 311–29, and Leipoldt, *Schenute von Atripe,* 14–15 ("naturally not original at this point," p. 15). For a German translation, see Ludwig E. Iselin, *Eine bisher unbekannte Version des ersten Teiles der "Apostellehre," gefunden und besprochen von L. E. Iselin,*

übersetzt von A. Heusler (TU 13.1b; Leipzig: Hinrichs, 1895) 6ff. [Ed. An English translation is now available in Cyprian Davis, O.S.B., "The *Didache* and Early Monasticism in the East and West," in Jefford, *Context,* 352–67.]

91 The so-called *Fragmenta Anastasiana* (Funk, *Didascalia,* 2.51–71), by contrast, derive from the *Apostolic Constitutions* (see below). For the "Sentences" of Isaac Syrus (M. Besson, "Un recueil de sentences attribué à Isaac le Syrien," *Oriens Christianus* 1 [1901] 46–60, 288–98), see below.

92 The question of the relationship between the *Rule of Benedict* and the *Didache* has often been discussed: Schlecht, *Doctrina,* 86–91; Edward C. Butler, "The Rule of St. Benedict," *JTS* 11 (1910) 279–88; *JTS* 12 (1911) 261–68; Heinrich Boehmer, "Hat Benedikt von Nursia die Didache gekannt?" *ZNW* 12 (1911) 287. Adalbert de Vogüé (*La Règle de Saint Benoît* IV [SC 184; Paris: Cerf, 1971] 131–33) surmises, probably correctly, that there is a connection between *Rule of Benedict* 4 by way of the *Rule of the Master* to the tradition of the Two Ways tractate. Rordorf ("Two Ways," 163) sees dependence not only in chap. 4 but also in the prologue.

93 Adam ("Herkunft," 47) suggests Berea-Aleppo.

94 For fragments of the Greek text, see J. Vernon Bartlet, "Fragments of the *Didascalia Apostolorum* in Greek," *JTS* 18 (1917) 301–9. The Syriac version is now found in Vööbus, *Didascalia,* 1, chaps. 1–10, edited text (Scriptores Syri 175; CSCO 401; Louvain: Secrétariat du Corpus SCO, 1979), and English translation (Scriptores Syri 176; CSCO 402; Louvain: Secrétariat du Corpus SCO, 1979) 2, chaps. 11–26, edited text (Scriptores Syri 179; CSCO 407; Louvain: Secrétariat du Corpus SCO, 1979), and English translation (Scriptores Syri 180; CSCO 408; Louvain: Secrétariat du Corpus SCO, 1979). The Syriac version exists in two recensions, which Vööbus has studied: *Didascalia,* CSCO 402.33*–34*. The remnants of the Latin version have been newly edited by Erik Tidner: *Didascalia*

say.[92] At any rate, the Latin translation of the Two Ways tractate was known in the West as late as the eleventh century. (On this, see below.)

The case of the *Didascalia apostolorum* is different. It may have been written in Syria[93] in the third century, perhaps even before 250.[94] I consider it possible that the unknown author of the *Didascalia apostolorum* knew our *Didache* and occasionally made use of it (without citing it as a source),[95] although this is not certain.[96] The following passages are those that deserve primary consideration:[97]

Did. 1.3d	*Didasc.* (Syriac) 1 (402.12)	*Didasc.* (Latin) 2.28–31 (75.4)
—	And again, he says in the Gospel: "Love those who hate you, and pray over those who curse you, and you shall have no enemy."	*Nam iterum in evangelio dicit: Diligite odientes vos et orate pro maledicentibus vos et inimicum nullum habebitis.*
ὑμεῖς δὲ φιλεῖτε τοὺς μισοῦντας ὑμᾶς καὶ οὐχ ἕξετε ἐχθρόν		

The connection with the *Didache* occurs through the agreement in the first line (against the Gospel text) and primarily through the unusual last line of the quoted passage.[98] One is strongly tempted to think that this is a quotation from the *Didache*; otherwise one would have to suppose that the two documents are both dependent on an apocryphal gospel tradition.

Did. 1.5c	*Didasc.* (Syriac) 17 (408.161)	*Didasc.* (Latin) 37.25–29 (75.63)
οὐαὶ τῷ λαμβάνοντι	Indeed, woe from God to those who have, and receive in falsehood.[100]	*Vae autem his, qui habent et cum dolo accipiunt*[99]
εἰ μὲν γὰρ χρείαν ἔχων λαμβάνει τις, ἀθῷος ἔσται·		*aut qui possunt sibi iuvare et [accipiunt].*[101]
ὁ δὲ μὴ χρείαν ἔχων δώσει δίκην,	Indeed, everyone of those who receive shall give an account to the Lord God [in the day of judgment],	*Unusquisque vero de accipientibus dabit rationem domino deo in die [iudicii],*
ἱνατί ἔλαβε καὶ εἰς τί.	how he (used what he) received.	*quare acceperit.*

The assumption that this is a quotation from the *Didache* is again possible, even though not absolutely certain (it could be a free quotation). In addition, one may not suppress the fact that the wording of the *Didascalia apostolorum* in two passages is closer to *Hermas Man.* 2.5 than to the *Didache*: *cum dolo accipiunt* ("receive deceitfully")[102] recalls the passage in *Hermas*, οἱ δὲ ἐν ὑποκρίσει λαμβάνοντες, and the expression *unusquisque . . . dabit rationem domino deo* is reminiscent of *Hermas Man.* 2.5: ἀποδώσουσιν λόγον τῷ θεῷ ("they will render an account to God"). At the same time, there can be no stringent proof of dependency on *Hermas*.[103]

Apostolorum, Canonum Ecclesiasticorum, Traditionis Apostolicae versiones latinae (TU 75; Berlin: Akademie-Verlag, 1963). The Latin text of *Didascalia* is on pp. 2–102. As indirect witness we may mention (with major reservations) *Constitutions* 1–6, where the Greek text of the *Didascalia* is written out with alterations. Cf. Funk, *Didascalia*, 1. For the Ethiopic and Arabic tradition, cf. Altaner and Stuiber, *Patrologie*, 85. See also Bardenhewer, *Geschichte*, 2.304–12; Altaner and Stuiber, *Patrologie*, 84–85; Quasten, *Patrology*, 2.147–52; Vööbus, *Didascalia*, CSCO 402.23*–33*.

95 Funk, *Abhandlungen*, 2.125–27, 136–37; Connolly, "Use of the *Didache*," 147–57; Muilenburg, *Literary Relations*, 36–38; Vokes, *Riddle*, 67–71; Adam, "Herkunft," 47 (*Didascalia* is here said to be a deliberate rewriting of the *Didache*); Barnard, "Later History," 101–2, etc. Giet (*L'Énigme*, 143–45) takes a different position.

96 In the following remarks, the text from *Canons of the Apostles* that was inserted in later recensions of the Syriac *Didascalia* at the end of chap. 3 will be left out of account. On this text, see Vööbus, *Didascalia*, CSCO 402.40*–41*.

97 In what follows, I will cite the English translation of the Syriac *Didascalia* by Vööbus, and the Latin *Didascalia* from Tidner.

98 See below, commentary on 1.3.

99 Cf. n. 100 below.

100 The same expression is also found in 17 (408.162); cf. the Latin version at 38.18 (75.64): *Qui autem habet (et accipit) in hypocrisim.*

101 There is nothing corresponding to this line in the Syriac text, but see *Const.* 4.3.2 (Funk, *Didascalia*, 1.221).

102 *Const.* 4.3.2 has Οὐαὶ τοῖς ἔχουσιν καὶ ἐν ὑποκρίσει λαμβάνουσιν.

103 Connolly ("Use of the *Didache*," 149) rightly refers especially to the fact that what we find in the *Didache* and the *Didascalia* (but not in *Hermas*) is a "woe."

Did. 1.5c	Didasc. (Syriac) 17 (408,162)	Didasc. (Latin) 38.23–25 (75.64)
μακάριος ὁ διδοὺς κατὰ τὴν ἐντολήν· ἀθῷος γάρ ἐστιν.	But the one who gives simply to everyone, does well to give, and is justified.	Qui ergo dat simpliciter omnibus, bene dat, sicut est illi, et est innocens.[104]

Again, one is not compelled to conclude that this is an instance of dependence on the *Didache*. Cf. also *Hermas Man.* 2.6a, ὁ οὖν διδοὺς ἀθῷός ἐστιν ("the one, therefore, who gives is innocent").

From among other parallels that have been suggested (cf. especially Connolly's work), the following should be mentioned.

- The quotation of the Golden Rule in *Didasc.* (Syriac) 1 (402.11); (Latin) 2.12–13 (75.4) need not (and does not) come from *Did.* 1.2.
- *Did.* 2.4 (= *Barn.* 19.7), οὐκ ἔσῃ διγνώμων οὐδὲ δίγλωσσος ("thou shalt not be double-minded or double-tongued"), may be compared to *Didasc.* (Syriac) 4 (402.48), where it is said (of the bishop): "And let him not be double-minded or double-tongued" (*Const.* 2.6.1 μὴ δίγνωμος, μὴ δίγλωσσος ["neither double-minded nor double-tongued"]). The expression in *Didache* and *Barnabas* comes from the Two Ways tractate. If one presumes that the *Didascalia apostolorum* knows and uses the *Didache*, this expression could, of course, be taken from the *Didache* as well.
- Further, *Did.* 3.8: Connolly ("Use of the *Didache*," 150–51) points especially to the addition of διὰ παντός ("at all times") to the quotation from Isa 66:2. (Other references he proposes are rather incidental.) This should be compared with *Didasc.* (Latin) 10.7–8 (75.17): *et trementem verba mea semper* ("and tremble ever at my words?"). The Syriac version, in contrast, reads (at 4 = 402.44–45) "that tremble at my sayings?" and thus lacks the διὰ παντός. In *Const.* 2.1.5, διαπαντός is probably the primitive text, even though it is absent from part of the manuscript tradition.[105] Connolly assumes (probably correctly) that it was also in the original Greek text of the *Didascalia*, and concludes from this (questionably, in my opinion) that the passage

comes from the *Didache*. This addition, however, is also found in *Syntagma doctrinae* and *Fides patrum*, which can scarcely be dependent on the *Didache*. In addition, διὰ παντός is absent from the compilation of passages from the *Didache* in *Const.* 7.8.3. The quotation from Isaiah must have circulated in two versions (with and without διὰ παντός). (It is true, however, that Josef Ziegler's edition of the LXX, *Isaias* [Vetus Testamentum graecum 14; Göttingen: Vandenhoeck & Ruprecht, 1983³] indicates no variants in this connection.)

- *Didasc.* (Syriac) 21 (408.191–92) prescribes fasting on Wednesdays and Fridays. I consider it improbable that it is dependent on *Did.* 8.1 for this.
- *Didasc.* (Syriac) 9 (402.100) speaks of the sacrifices of the old covenant, now replaced by the offerings of the bishops, "for they are your high priests." Cf. the Latin version, 25.20–21 (75.41): *Isti enim primi sacerdotes vestri*; cf. *Did.* 13.3. The echo is surprising, but the meaning is different. In the *Didache*, the prophets are understood to be the Christian high priests, while in the *Didascalia apostolorum* (as in Tertullian *De bapt.* 17.1 [CChrSL 1.291]) these are the bishops. The idea that the bishops have taken the place of the high priests of the Old Testament must certainly have seemed reasonable, even without literary models.
- Finally, there is also σημεῖον ἐκπετάσεως ("sign of extension") in *Did.* 16.6, which is recalled by *Didasc.* (Latin) 49.8 (75.80): *apex vero signum est extensionis ligni* ("the crowning sign indeed is the extension of the wood"). (The Syriac version, 26 [408.225] does not have "sign," which Connolly attempts to explain ["Use of the *Didache*," 153].) I am not persuaded that there is a literary connection here.

In conclusion, the widespread conviction that the author of the *Didascalia apostolorum* silently used our *Didache* as a source has some points in its favor, but it is not secure. If one grants that the author of the *Didascalia apostolorum* did know our *Didache*, one may (apart from the acceptance of some occasional quotations) go one step farther and suppose that this author garnered

---

104 Earlier there is a macarism: "And truly blessed is everyone who is able to help himself" (17; [408.161]); *Nam vere beatus est, qui potest invare se* (37.22–23; [75.63]).

105 See Funk, *Patres apostolici*, 1.33.

106 In Funk's edition, *Didascalia*, 1.386–423.

107 Bryennios pointed this out already in the editio princeps (Διδαχή, λε′–λζ′).

from the *Didache* the idea and inspiration for creating a new "church order" of his own.

Although in the case of the *Didascalia apostolorum* one can only suspect, but not prove with certainty, that the *Didache* was used, the case is completely different with the so-called *Apostolic Constitutions*. Here, for the first time, we arrive at a matter that is of eminent importance for the textual and tradition history of the *Didache*, and that has been respected accordingly from the beginning of research on the *Didache*, namely, the author of the seventh book of the *Constitutions,* in 7.1.2–32.4[106] — thus at the beginning of this particular book — silently copied out the entire text of the *Didache*.[107] In doing so, the author continually commented on the text of the source, while also paraphrasing and altering it. In this way, *Constitutions* 7 became not only a witness to knowledge of the *Didache* around 300 (although, unfortunately, we cannot determine with certainty where the *Constitutions* were written:[108] Constantinople or Syria are possibilities).[109] Beyond this, *Constitutions* 7 (which in chaps. 1–32 are nothing but an expanded and reorganized edition of the *Didache*)[110] thus becomes a valuable textual witness to the indirect tradition — of which I will have more to say below.[111]

Finally, we should make reference to the *Ethiopic Church Order,*[112] in which is embedded a fragment of the *Didache* (namely, 11.3–13.7, and afterward 8.1–2). I will have to speak later of the importance of this text for the *constitutio textus* of the *Didache*. This text may have entered the *Ethiopic Church Order* in the fourth century, but it is difficult to determine what reasons may have occasioned its introduction.[113]

Let us attempt to summarize the results. The *Didache* was used as a source by later authors or compilers of canonistic works; this is true first of all of the compiler

we find at work in the seventh book of the *Apostolic Constitutions*; it is true to a much lesser degree of the unknown redactor of the *Ethiopic Church Order*, who introduced a small portion of the *Didache* into that work. Both documents point to the fourth century. Whether the *Didache* was used even earlier in a similar way cannot be determined with certainty. It is possible that this is true for the unknown author of the *Didascalia apostolorum*, which comes from the third century. In contrast, the apparent connections between the *Didache* and *Canons of the Apostles*, the *Epitome*, *Syntagma doctrinae*, *Fides patrum*, and *Life of Shenoute* (and in some ways also to the *Rule of the Master* and the *Rule of Benedict*) can be otherwise explained; they all go back to a common source, the tractate that researchers refer to as the "Two Ways."

d. The *Didache* in Byzantine Authors of the Twelfth–Fourteenth Centuries

John Zonaras (first half of the 12th century)[114] mentions the *Didache* in his commentary on Athanasius, "Festal Letter" 39 (*PG* 138.564C),[115] but in a way that forces us to conclude that he no longer had the document itself before him: Μετὰ δέ γε τὴν ἀπαρίθμησιν, φησὶν [i.e., Athanasius], ὅτι ἔστιν ἕτερα βιβλία τούτων ἔξωθεν, οὐ κανονιζόμενα μὲν, ἀναγινωσκόμενα δὲ, ἅτινα λέγει εἶναι τὴν σοφίαν Σιράχ, Ἐσθήρ, Ἰουδήθ, καὶ Τωβήτ, καὶ διδαχὴν καλουμένην τῶν ἀποστόλων λέγουσιν εἶναι τὰς διὰ τοῦ Κλήμεντος συγγραφείσας τῶν ἀποστόλων διατάξεις, ἃς ἡ λεγομένη ἕκτη σύνοδος ἀναγινώσκεσθαι οὐ συγχωρεῖ, ὡς νοθευθείσας καὶ φθαρείσας ὑπὸ αἱρετικῶν ("After the enumeration, he [i.e., Athanasius] says that there are other books apart from these which are not canonized, but are read, and he says that they are the Wisdom of Sirach, Esther,

---

108 This is quite apart from the question whether the whole work can be attributed to a single author. This could scarcely be true of 8.47.

109 For the *Apostolic Constitutions* in general, cf. Funk, *Didascalia*, 1.xv–lii; Bardenhewer, *Geschichte*, 4.262–75; Altaner and Stuiber, *Patrologie*, 255–56. Eunomian origins are asserted by Günter Wagner, "Zur Herkunft der Apostolischen Konstitutionen," in *Mélanges liturgiques offerts au R. P. Dom Bernard Botte O.S.B. de l'Abbaye du Mont César à l'occasion du cinquantième anniversaire de son ordination sacerdotale (4 Juin 1972)* (Louvain: Abbaye du Mont César, 1972) 525–37.

110 In books 1–6 (as mentioned above), the *Didascalia apostolorum* is copied. For the sources of book 8, see Bardenhewer, *Geschichte*, 4.266.

111 For the *Fragmenta Anastasiana* and Isaac of Syria, see below.

112 Bardenhewer, *Geschichte*, 4.274–75.

113 See below.

114 Cf. Beck, *Literatur*, 655–56. J. Pitra (in Beck, 656): *Facile omnium juris byzantini magistrorum princeps* ("Easily the prince of all the masters of Byzantine law").

115 The commentary on the canons "could scarcely

Judith, and Tobit, and they say that the so-called Teaching of the Apostles consists of the ordinances of the apostles collected in writing by Clement. The so-called sixth council did not permit these to be read, on the grounds that they had been adulterated and corrupted by heretics"). The expression διδαχὴ καλουμένη τῶν ἀποστόλων comes entirely from Athanasius. It appears, however, that Zonaras is not acquainted with the writing itself.[116] Instead, he knows and cites the opinion according to which what Athanasius calls the *Didache* is identical to the apostolic "*Constitutions.*"[117] Matthew Blastares[118] also refers, in his *Syntagma alphabeticum*[119] at B, chap. 11 (*PG* 144.1141B), to Athanasius's canonical list and mentions the *Didache* among other extracanonical writings including Wisdom, Sirach, Esther, Judith, Tobit, τὸν Ποιμένα, καὶ τὴν Διδαχὴν

τῶν ἁγίων ἀποστόλων· ταύτην δὲ καὶ ἡ ϛ´ σύνοδος ἠθέτησεν, ὡς δεδήλωται ("The Shepherd, and the Teaching of the Holy Apostles, which the sixth council set aside, as already indicated"). Blastares also confuses the *Didache* with the *Apostolic Constitutions*,[120] and therefore had no direct knowledge of the *Didache*. Nicephoros Callistos Xanthopolous (died ca. 1335 or 1312),[121] in his *Ecclesiastica historia* 2.46 (*PG* 145.888B), counts the *Didache* among the νόθα ("illegtimate books"): Ἐν νόθοις καὶ ἡ Βαρνάβα φερομένη ἐπιστολὴ, καὶ αἱ λεγόμεναι τῶν ἀποστόλων διδαχαί ("Among the illegitimate books are the Epistle attributed to Barnabas and the so-called Teachings of the Apostles"), followed then by the *Gospel to the Hebrews*. It is very questionable that he still knew the *Didache* from having actually seen it.

---

have been completed before 1159" (Beck, *Literatur*, 656).

116 Harnack, "Prolegomena,"10; Schaff, *Church Manual*, 118 n. §; Hemmer, *Doctrine*, xxii; Audet, *Didachè*, 90.

117 It would be difficult to infer from this that this confusion is based on knowledge that one document is the source of the other.

118 Beck, *Literatur*, 786–87.

119 Written in 1335, this is "an alphabetical handbook of canon law" (Beck, *Literatur*, 786).

120 What Zonaras supposed, Blastares promulgates "as established truth" (Harnack, "Prolegomena," 10).

121 Beck, *Literatur*, 705–6.

3. The Direct Tradition

a. The Bryennios Manuscript (H)

Sometimes in antiquity the *Didache* (as we have seen in the preceding sections) was altogether forgotten (as in the West), and sometimes (as in the East) only a rather indirect knowledge of it was retained; its confusion with the *Apostolic Constitutions* shows that the writing itself was no longer familiar.[1] Therefore it was a first-class sensation when, at the end of the nineteenth century, an (almost) complete text of the *Didache* surfaced in a Byzantine manuscript – a text that attracted the interest of researchers at its first publication and introduced a new era in the history of the *Didache*'s influence. The discoverer of the manuscript was the Byzantine metropolitan Philotheos Bryennios.

Bryennios,[2] born in Constantinople in 1833, studied theology in East and West, and then became a teacher in the theological schools of the Byzantine Church. In 1875 he became metropolitan of Serrae in Macedonia, and in 1877 transferred to Nicomedia. In 1873 he found, in the library of the Monastery of the Holy Sepulchre ("Jerusalem Monastery") in Constantinople, a parchment manuscript of 120 leaves, bound in leather. It turned out to be a manuscript collection dated by the scribe, who calls himself Λέων νοτάριος καὶ ἀλείτης ("Leon the notary and sinner"),[3] in colophon folio 120a. He completed the manuscript on Tuesday, 11 June 1056 (of our reckoning). The manuscript is written in a careful and handsome minuscule script.[4] Only one hand is discernible, and obvious mistakes in orthography are relatively few.

This manuscript contains:

1. Ps.-Chrysostom *Synopsis Veteris et Novi Testamenti* (cf. *PG* 56.313–86): fol. 1a–38b[5]
2. *Epistle of Barnabas*: fol. 39a–51b

3. *1 Clement*: fol. 51b–70a
4. *2 Clement*: fol. 70a–76a
5. A list of the ὀνόματα τῶν βιβλίων παρ' ἑβραίοις ("names of the books of the Hebrews"), with the Hebrew and Aramaic titles in Greek transcription, followed by the Greek title of the respective book: fol. 76a[6]
6. *Didache*: fol. 76a–80b
7. The letter of Maria of Cassoboloi to Ignatius of Antioch: fol. 81a–82a
8. Twelve letters of Ignatius (*recensio longior*): fol. 82a–120a; the text of the letters of Ignatius is followed by the colophon (see above)

Finally, there is:

9. a discussion of the genealogy of Jesus: fol. 120a–120b.

The text of the *Didache* is thus found in folios 76a–80b. Bryennios published the *Didache* text in 1883, ten years after the discovery of the manuscript.[7] The whole manuscript was transferred in 1887 to the Greek patriarchate of Jerusalem, where it remains today (under the signature Κῶδ. πατρ. 54).[8]

The *Didache* text begins at folio 67a, line 20, with the superscription: διδαχὴ τῶν δώδεκα ἀποστόλων ("teaching of the twelve apostles"). A "second" superscription begins at line 21 (preceded by an initial Δ): Διδαχὴ κυρίου διὰ τῶν δώδεκα ἀποστόλων τοῖς ἔθνεσιν ("the Lord's teaching through the twelve apostles to the nations"). The text then continues on the same line with ὁδοὶ δύο ("two ways").

The end of the *Didache* text is not contained in H. The situation[9] is this. The scribe filled each page with 23 lines of text, but folio 80b breaks off in the middle of

---

1. The reason for this is probably that this once highly respected writing was not included within the canon. On this, cf. the remarks of Rordorf and Tuilier, *Doctrine*, 11–12.
2. See the autobiographical note in Schaff, *Church Manual*, 289–96.
3. The name "Leon," however, is uncertain. Cf. the photograph of the colophon in Schaff, *Church Manual*, 6.
4. Details in Bryennios, Διδαχή, ϛε´–ϛϛ´.
5. For this synopsis, cf. Bardenhewer, *Geschichte*, 3.352; Altaner and Stuiber, *Patrologie*, 328; Quasten, *Patrology*, 3.472.

6. On this, cf. Jean-Paul Audet, "A Hebrew-Aramaic List of Books of the Old Testament in Greek Transcription," *JTS*, n.s. 1 (1950) 135–54; Charles C. Torrey, "Ein griechisch transkribiertes und interpretiertes hebräisch-aramäisches Verzeichnis der Bücher des Alten Testaments aus dem 1. Jahrhundert n. Chr. (aus dem Englischen übersetzt und mit Anmerkungen versehen von Otto Eißfeldt)," *ThLZ* 77 (1952) 249–54.
7. Editio princeps: Bryennios, Διδαχή.
8. There is a photocopy in the appendix to Harris, *Teaching*.
9. On this whole subject, see Audet, *Didachè*, 73–74.

line 16, with the words ἐπάνω τῶν νεφελῶν τοῦ οὐρανοῦ ("coming upon the clouds of heaven"), after which the scribe sets a period; the remaining half line and the following seven lines are left blank. (The next document, the letter of Maria of Cassoboloi, begins on the next page.)[10] There is no notation after the words quoted to indicate that the copyist considered the text complete at τοῦ οὐρανοῦ.[11] One must conclude that the copyist by no means thought that the text of the *Didache* ended with the words τοῦ οὐρανοῦ, but apparently the source only went as far as these words. Therefore, seeing correctly that the conclusion of the *Didache* was no longer available, the scribe left the remaining lines on the page empty — hoping, perhaps, that the end of the writing could at some point be added on the basis of a different source. That the document does not end with the words ἐπάνω τῶν νεφελῶν τοῦ οὐρανοῦ is obvious from the structure of the *Didache* apocalypse (16.3–8), as well as from the paraphrasing conclusions to this section in the *Apostolic Constitutions* and the Georgian version.[12] Moreover, in my opinion one should not draw any conclusions about the format and type of writing in the source on the basis of the seven and a half empty lines left by the copyist,[13] as Audet has done.[14] The scribe simply left the rest of the page empty, based on the correct supposition that the conclusion of the document he was copying was missing, but without knowing for certain how much text had been lost. The entire procedure also shows that the copyist was a thoughtful worker who did not simply make a mechanical copy of the source.

The Bryennios manuscript offers us the only complete text of the *Didache* (except for the final lines) that we have thus far. That alone gives it special value. But what about the quality of the text in H?[15] Here judgments diverge widely. Erik Peterson considers the Bryennios text to be a late recension of the *Didache*, and thinks that the high regard in which it is traditionally held is a fundamental fault in scholarship.[16] If Peterson were right, we could neither make an edition of the *Didache* nor write a serious commentary on it. To give expression, by way of example, to the counterposition, we note the completely different judgment of Rordorf and Tuilier.[17] They consider the *Didache* text of H to be one that rests on a source from the fourth or fifth century.[18] That is possible, but it still would say nothing decisive about the quality of the H text. A real decision about that would be possible only if we possessed a greater wealth of alternative manuscript material for the *Didache* than we have in our hands at this time. The few lines in *P. Oxy.* 1782, the versions, and the indirect tradition give us a picture of the rather severe instability of the textual tradition of the *Didache* (understandable for a writing whose transmission was not protected by canonical validity), but they do not permit us to make a definitive judgment about the value of the form of text found in H.

If we examine that text without permitting ourselves to be overcome by pessimism or optimism, the results are ambivalent. On the one hand, it appears that H has been distorted by some later glosses and interpolations (although these are only brief expressions or passages: cf. at 1.4a; 2.5b; 10.5; 13.4), but that its text can also be corrected in some places with a greater or lesser degree

---

10 This long blank space is contrary to the scribe's practice elsewhere: cf. Audet, *Didachè*, 73–74.

11 For the usage in this regard, see Audet, *Didachè*, 74.

12 On this, see below.

13 Audet concludes (*Didachè*, 75) to a separate *Didache* codex that was available to the copyist.

14 Audet, *Didachè*, 75–78. He believes it was a miniature codex with uncial script.

15 The text of *1* and *2 Clement*, the letters of Ignatius, and *Barnabas* appear to be the result of revision. Of course, that in itself says nothing about the text of the *Didache*; see Audet, *Didachè*, 25–26.

16 Peterson, "Probleme," passim. Peterson thought that the H text went back to a late recension (perhaps stemming from ascetic circles [150, 181, and passim], and more precisely from Novatianist circles [162–63]). What we find in H is not the text of the *Didache* but a subsequent revision of the text. "Our

editions of the *Didache*, and our *Didache* exegesis, prevent us from recognizing the total insecurity of the manuscript tradition. It is still customary to explain the text as if we had, in the manuscript discovered by Bryennios, something like the authentic version of the *Didache*. In reality, it appears to me that the Bryennios text represents a late recension of the *Didache*" (181). "We can only describe the aporiae, but cannot communicate the original text" (182).

17 Rordorf and Tuilier, *Doctrine*, 102–10.

18 Rordorf and Tuilier, *Doctrine*, 104–7. Audet (*Didachè*, 32) had made a similar estimation beforehand.

19 For this whole question, see Niederwimmer, "Textprobleme," 114–30. Wengst, in his edition, offers a text that deviates rather sharply from H.

20 See below, at 9.3–4; and Niederwimmer, "Textprobleme," 125.

of assurance (cf. at 1.3d; 2.7b; 3.4c; 5.1 end; 9.3a and 4a; 10.3 end; 10.4a; 12.1a). On the other hand, the absence of the interpolation after 10.7 (*myron* [oil] prayer) shows that H goes back to a text that, at least in this passage, is better than the textual tradition of the Coptic or the source for the *Apostolic Constitutions*.[19] All this suggests that the H tradition should neither be damned nor simply passed on as the authentic text of the *Didache*. The Bryennios manuscript seems to me to present a *Didache* text that must remain subject at every point to inquiries of a text-critical nature, but one should not feel compelled to the desperate conclusion that what we have before us is a late and tendentiously falsified recension of the original writing. There are demonstrable changes in individual passages, and they may be suspected elsewhere; but that the H text is the result of a thorough, tendentious recension is not demonstrable. A final judgment would be possible only if the textual basis of the *Didache* could be expanded. Everything we can say about the original home of the archetype of H can be reduced to the inference that, at *Did.* 9.3–4, it inserted the expression κλάσμα (fragment), which was characteristic of the liturgical language of Egypt; from this in turn one can infer that the archetype of H originated in Egypt.[20]

b. Papyrus Oxyrhynchus 1782 (P)

In 1922 B. P. Grenfell and A. S. Hunt edited[21] two fragmentary parchment leaves of a miniature codex[22] from the end of the fourth century.[23] These leaves (hereafter "P") are now to be found in the Ashmolean Museum in Oxford. The pages, which are worn and badly discolored in places, especially at the edges, are 5.5 cm. by 4.5 cm. (fol. 1) and 5.7 cm. by 4.8 cm. (fol. 2), and are written on both sides. Folio 1 recto has seven short lines, while folios 1 verso and 2 recto and verso have eight short

lines each.[24] Folio 1 contains the Greek text of *Did.* 1.3c, οὐχὶ καὶ τὰ ἔθνη τοῦτο ποιοῦσιν . . . ("do not even the nations do that . . .") to 1.4a, ἀπόσχου τῶν σαρκε[ι]κῶν ἐπιθυμειῶν ("avoid the fleshly and bodily passions"). Folio 2 contains *Did.* 2.7b, ἐλέγξεις περὶ ὧν δὲ προσεύξῃ . . . ("some . . . for whom you shall pray . . ."), to 3.2a, ἡ ὀργὴ πρὸς τὸν φόνον ("anger [leads to] murder"). These two leaves must come from the same book, which originally contained the whole text of the *Didache* (and perhaps more besides). The leaves are covered with irregular uncials written in brownish ink.[25] "That the writer was a person of no great culture is clear also from his spelling and division of words (e.g., επιθυμειων, υμ|εις)."[26] In folio 2 recto, line 20, after the word σου, the copyist has completed the line with wedge-shaped symbols written alternately in red ink and in the usual brown (nine of these are still visible, but the symbols must have extended to the end of the line). In the following line (21) there are three repeatedly interrupted horizontal lines (the first and third in red ink); in the middle, and extending beyond the lines, one can discern the symbol ⚡ written in the ordinary brown ink.[27] It is natural to assume that the copyist wished to designate the beginning of a new section in line 21 (probably on the basis of the source) by means of the horizontal lines there,[28] while the symbols in line 20 serve to show that no text is missing at this point.[29]

---

21   *Papyri*, no. 1782, pp. 12–15.

22   For miniature codices of this type, see Grenfell and Hunt, *Papyri*, 12; Audet, *Didachè*, 26 n. 2; Leiv Amundsen, "Christian Papyri from the Oslo Collection," *SO* 24 (1945) 126–28; Eric G. Turner, *The Typology of the Early Codex* (Haney Foundation Series 18; Philadelphia: University of Pennsylvania Press, 1977) 22, 29–30.

23   "It may perhaps date from the fourth century rather than the fifth" (Grenfell and Hunt, *Papyri*, 12–13).

24   See immediately below for the *signum dispositionis* in fol. 2 recto.

25   The letters in fol. 1 recto are somewhat larger than those on the other pages.

26   Grenfell and Hunt, *Papyri*, 13.

27   It is also possible to discern a brownish horizontal line and (above and below it) two red horizontal lines between lines 19 and 20. One gets the impression that these horizontal lines were inserted by the copyist at a later time.

28   Audet differs (*Didachè*, 55). He does not presume a *signum dispositionis* here: "It is much more natural to suppose a projected addition, omitted after the fact for one reason or another."

29   The new section would begin just where we also place the beginning of a new chapter. I find it ques-

We need not mince words regarding the significance of these two leaves for the manuscript tradition of the *Didache*. They are some 650 years older than the Bryennios manuscript and represent the oldest manuscript witness to date for the *Didache* text. One should also keep in mind that these two leaves come from approximately the time when the compiler of the *Apostolic Constitutions* was copying the *Didache* into book 7.

The text presented by P is important, in the first instance, as evidence for the so-called *interpolatio christiana* ("Christian interpolation") or *sectio evangelica* ("gospel section"). In folio 1, P gives us, of all things, a bit of text from the very passage that is sometimes regarded (wrongly, I believe) as a later gloss.[30] Otherwise, the deviations from the H text (in the brief passage contained in P) are numerous enough to strengthen the thesis stated above concerning the instability of the text of the *Didache*. In table 2, I illustrate this situation by setting the P text alongside the H text (whereby the order of lines is retained only in the presentation of the P text).[31]

Table 2

	H		P
(1.3c)	οὐχὶ καὶ τὰ ἔθνη		(fol. 1r.) ουχι και τα ε
	τὸ αὐτὸ		θνη τουτο
(3d)	ποιοῦσιν; ὑμεῖς		ποιουσιν υμ
	δὲ ἀγαπᾶτε		εις δε φιλειτ
	τοὺς μισοῦντας	5	ε τους μισοῡ
	ὑμᾶς καὶ		τας υμας και
	οὐχ ἕξετε		ουχ εξετε εχ
	ἐχθρόν·	(fol. 1v.)	θρον ακου
			ε τι σε δει ποι
		10	ουντα σωσαι
			σου το πνᾱ π[ρ]ω
			τον παντω̄
(1.4)	ἀπέχου τῶν		αποσχου των
	σαρκικῶν καὶ σωματικῶν		σαρκε[ι]κων ε
	ἐπιθυμιῶν·	15	πιθυμειων
(2.7b)	...ἐλέγξεις· περὶ δὲ	(fol. 2r.)	ἐλεγξεις περι ω̄

	H/P		
	ὧν προσεύξῃ· οὓς		δε προσευξει ους
	δὲ ἀγαπήσεις		δε αγαπησεις
	ὑπὲρ τὴν ψυχήν		υπερ την ψυχη̄
	σου·	20	σου > > > > >

═══ 𝓵 ═══

(3.1)	τέκνον μου		τεκνον μου
	φεῦγε ἀπὸ		φευγε απο
	παντὸς	(fol. 2v.)	[[απο]] παντος
	—	25	πραγματος
	πονηροῦ καὶ		πονηρου και
	ἀπὸ παντὸς ὁμοίου αὐτοῦ·		ομοιου αυτου
(3.2)	μὴ γίνου ὀργίλος·		μη γεινου οργει
	ὁδηγεῖ γὰρ		λος επειδη οδη
	ἡ ὀργὴ πρὸς		γει η οργη προς
	τὸν φόνον·...		τον φονον

I will discuss only the most important textual variants.[32] At some points, P appears to have the better text: in line 2, P reads τοῦτο (as does *Apostolic Constitutions*) against τὸ αὐτό in H. The reading in P and *Apostolic Constitutions* is preferable; H apparently assimilates to Matt 5:46 or Luke 6:33. In lines 4–5, P reads φιλεῖτε (again with the *Apostolic Constitutions*), which is preferable to H's ἀγαπᾶτε. One may ask whether H again reveals an influence from the Synoptic Gospels (Matt 5:44/Luke 6:27). In lines 13–15, P has an older variant of the interpolation that has entered the text of the *Didache* at this point.[33] H shows what is already a later form (apart from ἀπέχου, which is preferable). In lines 16–17, P reads περὶ ὧν δέ (as do the *Canons of the Apostles* and the *Epitome*), probably rightly (against H's περὶ δὲ ὧν).[34] The P text also reveals a series of secondary elements, however: lines 8–12 are certainly a later addition to the interpolation in *Did.* 1.4. I will have more to say below about the successive expansions the *Didache* text underwent at this point. In lines 24–26, P has (as a clarification) ἀπὸ παντὸς πράγματος πονηροῦ instead of H's ἀπὸ παντὸς πονηροῦ (which is also secured by *Canons of the Apostles*; *Apostolic Constitutions* reads ἀπὸ παντὸς κακοῦ, as does the *Epitome*). The

---

tionable whether one can read the symbol in the middle of line 21 as a numeral (as Hans Lietzmann supposes: "Notizen," *ZNW* 21 [1922] 238).

30 On this, see below.
31 For P I cite the text of the editio princeps, but with an altered numbering of the lines at the end.
32 See also Audet, *Didachè*, 28; Niederwimmer, "Textprobleme," 122–23.
33 See at *Did.* 1.4 below.
34 *Barnabas*, *Doctrina apostolorum*, and *Apostolic Constitutions* do not offer a witness here.

trend toward clarification appears also in *Doctrina apostolorum*: *ab homine malo*. Both these clarifications are textually secondary, but that in P is at least correct in its tendency. In lines 26–27, P omits ἀπὸ παντός. In lines 29–30, P's ἐπειδὴ ὁδηγεῖ (against H, *Canons*, *Epitome* ὁδηγεῖ γάρ) is probably a later assimilation to *Did*. 3.4, 5, 6.

P apparently rests on an archetype different from that of H. Neither of the two forms of the text is always superior to the other. It is interesting that P (perhaps on the basis of its source) appears to indicate the first signs of a division of the *Didache* into chapters, as is suggested by the *signum dispositionis* in line 21.

4. The Versions

a. The Coptic Fragment: Br. Mus. Or. 9271 (Copt.)

In the spring of 1923 there appeared in Cairo a papyrus sheet of unusual size and style of writing, written on both sides in Coptic (with a lavish waste of space). L.-Theophile Lefort examined it but chose not to acquire it. The sheet ultimately came into the possession of the British Museum, where it remains, designated Or. 9271. The editio princeps was by G. Horner.[1] Carl Schmidt was able to prepare a better edition based on a photograph, followed by an inspection of the original.[2] Finally, Lefort offered a new edition of the Coptic text with an extensive introduction and notes, as well as a French translation in separate volume.[3]

This papyrus leaf, which when Lefort first inspected it was still in good condition, apparently suffered by being transported to Europe.[4] It appears to come from a papyrus scroll, and could have been the last part of it. The sheet has a remarkably large format: 44 cm. long, 28.5 cm. high. It is written on both sides but with a strange arrangement. The recto (horizontal strands) contains two columns. Column 1 has 29 lines measuring 21.5 cm. by 17 cm. Column 2 has 32 lines[5] measuring 23 cm. by 12 cm. Between the two columns is a space of 2–4 cm.; the left margin (where it is best preserved) is 2.5 cm., and between the right edge of column 2 and the edge of the sheet there is a space of 11 cm. The verso (vertical strands) contains only one column; this (col. 3) has only 18 lines measuring 12.5 cm. by 11 cm. The text breaks off about halfway down the page,[6] and in the middle of a sentence. The whole right side is blank (leaving about 29 cm. to the right edge).[7]

It seems that the scribe changed his calamus (and ink?) at line 14 of column 1. Beginning with line 14, he writes in somewhat larger letters.[8] Nevertheless, the whole text is certainly from the same hand. The scribe frequently uses the apostrophe as a *signum dispositionis*.[9] At the end of column 1, the scribe has filled out the line with five symbols. The manuscript probably comes from the fifth century. Horner adds: "the Greek authorities at the British Museum would put it even as early as A.D. 400."[10] Schmidt did not want to go that far.[11]

We find here the Coptic text of *Did.* 10.3b–12.2a. From what has been said, it is clear that this cannot be a section of a complete manuscript of the *Didache*, but only a more or less casual excerpt.[12] How should we

---

1 "New Papyrus Fragment," 225–31. On p. 225, Horner gives a brief description of the sheet, and, on pp. 226–29, the Coptic text with notes; at pp. 230–31 there is an English translation.

2 "Koptische Didache-Fragment," 81–99. Schmidt presents a description of the papyrus with notes (81–83), an edition of the Coptic text with German translation and notes (84–89), and additional discussion (90–99).

3 *Pères apostoliques*, introduction on pp. ix–xv; Coptic text with notes on pp. 32–34 (though it should be noted that Lefort has normalized the orthography of the original); on pp. 25–28 Lefort presented a French translation with notes. [Ed. Most recently see F. Stanley Jones and Paul A. Mirecki, "Considerations on the Coptic Papyrus of the *Didache* (British Library Oriental Manuscript 9271)," in Jefford, *Context*, 47–87.]

4 On this, and on the whole history of its discovery as outlined above, cf. Lefort, *Pères apostoliques*, ix–x.

5 Column 2 begins one line above col. 1 and ends one line lower.

6 There remain about 13–14 cm. between the end of the text and the bottom of the sheet.

7 Audet (*Didachè*, 31) gives some strong arguments for thinking that text has been lost from what is now col. 1. Schmidt ("Koptische Didache-Fragment," 81) differs. In lines 25 and 26 it is possible that one can really discern fragments of letters on the outer edge, which would mean that there was a column before col. 1.

8 Most of the letters are now about 3–4 mm. tall. ⲫ clearly reaches above and below the line, † slightly above. ⲩ extends slightly above and below the line, as does ⲉ in some cases.

9 For the supposed initial letters in col. 1, line 27 (Horner), see the correction by Audet, *Didachè*, 30–31 n. 4. The ⲉ in ⲉⲧⲃⲉ is really not an initial, but only (like other ⲉs) somewhat enlarged.

10 "New Papyrus Fragment," 225. Rordorf and Tuilier, *Doctrine*, 112: end of the 4th or beginning of the 5th century. Cf. also Wengst, *Didache*, 11.

11 "Koptische Didache-Fragment," 82.

12 "Mr. Bell of the British Museum suggests that the papyrus may be a casual extract" (Horner, "New Papyrus Fragment," 225).

13 "Koptische Didache-Fragment," 82.

14 *Pères apostoliques*, xii.

15 Adam ("Herkunft," 26) has proposed the hypothesis that this is the project for a translation (from Syriac, he thinks): "the pages with the completed translation were, in turn, to serve as a source for copyists, and could then be thrown away; therefore they could be written on waste scraps." This is highly

interpret this? Schmidt thought it was a "scribal exercise" written on a "scrap of waste papyrus."[13] Lefort presents the matter thus: "it is clear, as I. Bell remarked at the outset, that we have to do with an *excerptum*; probably someone, for a reason unknown to us, transcribed this passage from the *Didache* on the end of a roll that was otherwise free of writing."[14] Why the scribe begins in the middle of the text (10.3b) and stops with equal abruptness (12.2a) is completely unclear. The manuscript presents more puzzles than the editors admit.[15]

The location of this fragment within the linguistic history of the text is also problematic.[16] Schmidt supposed that there was a Greek source.[17] Lefort proposes the hypothesis that the orthographic oddities of the text may be explained if it was a Fayyumic version of a

Sahidic source.[18] Quite different is the opinion of Paul E. Kahle Jr., who writes, concerning the dialect of the text: "It was merely a later development of Middle Egyptian proper under Fayyumic or Bohairic influence, and was superseded by Fayyumic in the second half of the fifth century."[19] "The manuscript of the *Didache* is probably the latest text in this dialect, being written about the beginning of the fifth century."[20] In my view, it remains an open question whether, in Or. 9271, we have a section from a Coptic source or an ad hoc translation from a Greek text.[21]

The text form presented by the Coptic is remarkable in many places.[22] On the whole, it does not offer a better text than H. I consider the famous prayer for the *stinŏufi* (col. 1, ll. 15–20) to be a later addition to the *Didache*

---

improbable. I tend to think rather (with Schmidt) that this is a writing exercise.

16 The page was presumably discovered in the neighborhood of Oxyrhynchus, in the nome of Cynopolis. See Horner, "New Papyrus Fragment," 225.

17 "Koptische Didache-Fragment," 93.

18 Lefort, *Pères apostoliques,* xiii–xiv. That a relatively early Sahidic translation of the *Didache* existed is an acceptable hypothesis, but the demonstration Lefort proposes is fragile. The text from the Pachomiana that he adduces at p. xiii n. 5 (Ernest A. W. Budge, *Coptic Apocrypha in the Dialect of Upper Egypt* [London: British Museum, 1913] no. VI: "The Instructions of Apa Pachomius, the Archimandrite," Br. Mus. Or. 7024, fol. 18a [p. 146, with English translation at p. 352]: "My son, listen. Make thyself wise, and receive the instruction of truth[?]. There are two ways [which thou canst follow]") is not a witness for the *Didache*, and is not even decisive for a literary dependence on the Two Ways tractate. The Arabic "Vita of Apa Shenute" (see above) next adduced by Lefort (*Pères apostoliques,* xiii n. 6) simply presumes the existence of a Coptic (Sahidic?) version of the Two Ways tractate, but not a Sahidic version of the *Didache*, as Lefort thinks. On the whole question, cf. also the cautious opinion of Audet, *Didachè,* 29 n. 1, and 32.

19 Kahle, *Bala'izah,* 1.225. For Kahle, also, the question of purpose in writing remains open, as long as *P. Mich.* 3520 and 3521 have not been published (Kahle, *Bala'izah,* 224–25). Kahle offers an analysis of the dialect used in the Coptic *Didache* fragment at 225–26.

20 Kahle, *Bala'izah,* 226. He continues, "If the dialect existed originally as a separate dialect, we should expect it to have been current outside the Fayyum

in the Nile valley north of Oxyrhynchus. It certainly must have been the spoken language in that neighbourhood during the early Coptic period before it was superseded by Fayyumic" (*Bala'izah*, 226–27). Of course, one should compare what Kahle has said, self-critically, in the addenda (Kahle, *Bala'izah,* 2.888–89) on the topic of dialects and their influence.

21 Adam differs ("Herkunft," 26–38). He attempts to give foundation to the idea that this is a translation not from the Greek but from a Syriac source. I would like to set aside the question whether the individual arguments Adam presents are compelling. This deserves a separate investigation. In at least two cases I am very skeptical about the attempt to trace this text to a Syriac original: in *Did.* 11.11 (the supposed *crux interpretum*), the Coptic has its own text (col. 2, ll. 30–32; on this, see below). Adam supposes that the striking παράδοσις goes back to Syriac ܐܠܡ ("Herkunft," 30). But it is a much more probable assumption that the Coptic text is corrupt at this point (due to misunderstanding of the Greek source?). Adam understands the disputed term cϯⲛⲟⲩϥⲓ (col. 1, ll. 16 and 18) as a translation of Syriac ܚܒ or ܐܚܒ, which at this point would mean "*agape* celebration" ("Herkunft," 31–32). In contrast, see my explanation at 11.11

22 On what follows, see Niederwimmer, "Textprobleme," passim, and the individual passages in the commentary. Audet (*Didachè,* 33–34) offers a complete collation of the Coptic with H. I will restrict myself to a few characteristics. [Ed. See now also Boudewijn Dehandschutter, "The Text of the *Didache*: Some Comments on the Edition of Klaus Wengst," in Jefford, *Context,* 37–46.]

text.[23] Since we also find a similar passage in *Const.* 7.27, both go back to a recension of the Greek text of the *Didache* that already had an interpolation at this point (even though the Greek source of the Coptic makes, on the whole, a very different impression).[24] I believe the repeated "Amens" (after 10.4, 5, 6a) to be liturgical additions.[25] The omission of δεχθήτω ὡς κύριος in 11.4 (also in Ethiopic) is a corruption of the text; the famous crux at 11.11 was already misunderstood by the Coptic (or its source), perhaps deliberately; what we find here in the Coptic is a corrupted text. Characteristic of this textual corruption is also 10.6: the Coptic presupposes ἐλθέτω ὁ κύριος [instead of H's χάρις] καὶ παρελθέτω ὁ κόσμος οὗτος. ἀμήν [H lacks "Amen"]. ὡσαννὰ τῷ οἴκῳ Δαυίδ [instead of τῷ θεῷ Δαυίδ in H] . . . ὁ κύριος ἦλθεν [instead of μαραναθά· ἀμήν as in H]. But there are some passages in which the Coptic appears to be in the right when differing from H.[26] In particular: in 10.4 we should probably read περὶ πάντων with the Coptic (against πρὸ πάντων in H). The role of the Coptic text of the *Didache* can be compared with that of the so-called D text of the New Testament: in the Coptic, we must distinguish a few ancient readings from numerous later additions and alterations.[27]

b. The Ethiopic Version (Eth.)

From the existence of part of the *Didache* tradition in the Ethiopian language (of which I will speak presently), we may conclude that there was a complete translation of the *Didache* into Ethiopic, drawing on either Greek or Coptic; the date of this translation cannot be given with certainty. The translation as a whole has been lost, but parts of it (namely, *Did.* 8.1–2 and 11.3–13.7) have been preserved — not, however, as an independent writing, but (without designation of the source) as an insertion in the Ethiopian church order.[28] In canons 49–52 there is an insertion, within which, in canon 52, a piece of the *Didache* appears, namely, *Did.* 11.3–13.7 (Horner, 54,20–55,24). This is followed immediately by *Did.* 8.1–2 (Horner, 55,25ff.).[29] We need not introduce a discussion here of how these portions of the *Didache* (and in reverse order) came to be included in the text of the Ethiopian church order.[30] What is interesting is that the insertion of the *Didache* text occurs only in the Ethiopian version of the church order, not in the Arabic of the *Canones ecclesiastici*, and not in the Sahidic version of the Egyptian collection of laws. According to Audet's exhaustive investigations, the insertion (from the *Didascalia* and) from the *Didache* (both said to have been inserted by the same interpolator) must have happened soon after 350.[31] "The fragment of the version of the *Didache* that Horner made known by his publication, in 1904, of the Ethiopic recension of the *Apostolic Canons* is an independent witness, detached from the rest of the tradition at a date that cannot be much later than the middle of the fourth century."[32]

The significance of the Ethiopic version for the establishment of the text of the *Didache* is small.[33] This version reveals a slight attraction to paraphrase, and the textual variants "are of unequal weight."[34] For example, in 11.4 δεχθήτω ὡς κύριος is omitted in Ethiopic and in Coptic; 11.6 is entirely omitted; in 11.10 τὴν ἀλήθειαν

---

23 On this, see below, pp. 165–67.

24 On this, see below.

25 Schmidt ("Koptische Didache-Fragment," 93–96) concluded that the *Didache* text underwent redaction in Egypt.

26 In this connection, we should note 10.3 only in passing, because Ἰησοῦ, which the Coptic correctly offers, has been omitted from H only by a scribal error. The same is true of 10.4, where H reads δυνατὸς εἶ σὺ [sic] ἡ δόξα, which Bryennios had already improved to δυνατὸς εἶ· σοὶ ἡ δόξα, and this is confirmed by the Coptic. Also, the πρὸς ὑμᾶς in 12.1, which is wrongly omitted by H in 12.1 (the correct text is in Coptic, Ethiopic, Georgian, and *Apostolic Constitutions*), is absent only because of a copyist's mistake.

27 Audet (*Didachè*, 32) assesses the text of the Coptic fragment thus: it represents an individual form of

the text that probably goes back to a Sahidic source, the text of which Audet wishes to place in the first half of the 4th century, and perhaps even in the 3d century.

28 Cf. George W. Horner, *The Statutes of the Apostles or Canones Ecclesiastici* (London: Williams and Norgate, 1904) 54–55 and 193–94.

29 For the English translation of *Did.* 11.3–13.7, see his pp. 193,7–194,23; of *Did.* 8.1–2: pp. 194,24–28. Hugo Duensing gives a German translation in Adam, "Herkunft," 36–37.

30 The complicated process of tradition is discussed at length by Audet, *Didachè*, 34–45; he also presents hypotheses about the origins of canons (49–52).

31 Audet, *Didachè*, 41–42. Audet attempted to explain (*Didachè*, 42) how, in particular, the interpolation of the *Didache* was supposed to have occurred.

32 Audet, *Didachè*, 43. Horner ("New Papyrus

is missing; in 12.3 καὶ φαγέτω is omitted, as is χριστιανός in 12.4; 13.2 is also entirely missing; 8.2 lacks
αὐτοῦ after εὐαγγελίῳ and the conclusion of the verse
as well. There are major additions in 11.8 and 12.3,
lesser in 12.4 (after τέχνην add καὶ οὐκ ἐργάζεται), in
13.6 (after ἐλαίου add καὶ μέλιτος), and in 13.7 (after
ἐντολὴν add τοῦ κυρίου). There are characteristic alterations in 11.5 (where the stay of the traveling apostles
may be extended to *three* days, if necessary), in 11.7, and
in 11.11 (where the Ethiopic shows that the author no
longer understood the Greek source). In 11.12 ἀργύρια
is replaced by χρυσόν (cf. 13.7), and in 13.6 the prophets
are replaced by the poor. The Ethiopic text is important
in three passages: it secures εἰ μή in 11.5 and πρὸς ὑμᾶς
in 12.1 (together with the Coptic and *Apostolic
Constitutions*), and it shows that the gloss in 13.4 must be
old (although the Ethiopic presupposes τῷ πτωχῷ).

c. Appendix: The Georgian Version (Georg.)

We thus come to a somewhat dubious chapter in the
Didache text tradition. In 1923, in Constantinople, a
young Georgian named Simon Pheikrishvili copied the
Georgian text of the *Didache* from a manuscript that
contained, besides the *Didache* in Georgian, a number of
other texts in Georgian and Armenian. The manuscript
from which he copied was, unfortunately, destroyed, but
we are told that it was supposed to have come from the
first half of the nineteenth century. G. Peradse saw
Pheikrishvili's copy in Paris, copied it, and collated it
with the Greek text of the *Didache* as found in Harnack's
large (German) edition.[35] This collation is all that we

possess of the Georgian version of the *Didache*.[36] Peradse
("Lehre," 112–14) made some daring suggestions about
the age of the Georgian version,[37] but there is little reason to rely on them.[38] In reality, we are faced here with a
very late, modern translation; nothing more in detail
can be said about it. Nevertheless, Rordorf and Tuilier
(*Doctrine*, 115 n. 2) wish to suppose that the vanished
Constantinople manuscript goes directly back to H. I do
not think that is probable. Against it are the readings of
the Georgian in 3.4 (beginning with αὐτὰ βλέπειν ἢ
ἀκούειν, against H, which contains only the first two
words) and in 12.1 (πᾶς δὲ ἐρχόμενος πρὸς ὑμᾶς, with
Coptic, Ethiopic, *Apostolic Constitutions*, against πᾶς δὲ
ἐρχόμενος in H).[39] Instead, the Georgian version probably goes back to a recension of the Greek text that is
closely related to that of H.

From Peradse's collation, we can observe the following. The Georgian presents a complete text of the
Didache (lacking only 1.5–6 and 13.5–7); the text is
inclined to paraphrasing additions (beginning even with
the title); after 16.8 there is a brief and partly quite plausible conclusion of the whole book (whereas the conclusion is lacking in H: see above). I consider it excessive to
omit the Georgian altogether from consideration in
determining the reconstruction of the text, as Rordorf
and Tuilier do. Nevertheless, in light of its late and dubious tradition, the Georgian version is not to be regarded
as an equal witness. One may adduce it only in individual cases, and then with reservations.

Fragment," xxxvi–xxxvii) gives a description of the
MSS. of the Ethiopian church order. The variants in
the Ethiopic MSS. for this portion of the text are listed by Horner, "New Papyrus Fragment," 401–2, and
reproduced by Audet, *Didachè*, 44–45, who gives a
collation of the deviations from H; cf. also Vokes,
Riddle, 15–16. In the following remarks I will discuss
only those variants that are especially characteristic.

33 There is a characterization of the *versio ethiopica*
     also in Audet, *Didachè*, 71–72.

34 Rordorf and Tuilier, *Doctrine*, 115.

35 Peradse, "Lehre," 111–16 (with the collation on pp.
     115–16).

36 In 1932 Peradse was convinced that there were still
     a number of MSS. of the *Didache* in Tbilisi ("Lehre,"
     112).

37 In the colophon there is mention of "a certain
     Jeremias from Orhai," who is supposed to have

translated the *Didache* from a Greek source. Cf.
Peradse, "Lehre," 113. Peradse considers the
colophon an interpolation, but wishes to retain the
core of the information contained in it (p. 113 n. 5).
He identifies the translator with Bishop Jeremias
the Iberian, who was a contemporary of the
Council of Ephesus (p. 114).

38 Cf. Audet, *Didachè*, 46–47.

39 It is possible that one could also adduce the conclu-
     sion of the Georgian version. On the whole, it does
     not look like an ad hoc invention of the copyist (or
     his source), even though the talk about "holy right-
     eousness" sounds strange in the framework of the
     Didache. The translator of the Georgian may, in any
     case, have possessed a complete copy of the *Didache*.

5. The Indirect Tradition: *Apostolic Constitutions* 7.1.2–32.4

I already noted (in §2c) that the unknown compiler of the *Apostolic Constitutions* copied the whole of the *Didache* in the first, major part of book 7, making some changes in the text of the source and sometimes paraphrasing. The extent of this dependency is visible in the edition by Funk.[1] In 7.1.1–2 the compiler placed before the "Two Ways" tractate of the *Didache* a proemium of scriptural citations, in order then to begin quoting the source in 7.1.2. This quotation extends to 32.4.[2]

The "Constitutor's" way of working can be illustrated by the following selected examples:[3] (1) The Constitutor interpreted the text continuously, by giving examples from the Old and New Testament, very frequently by citations from both testaments, and finally by interpretations from his own pen as well. The whole document, at times, reads like a commentary on the text of the *Didache*. The glossing interpretation of the text is, however, uneven. Thus the compiler has included the quotation from the "way of death" almost without addition (7.18). (2) Passages of the source are occasionally omitted, for example, *Did.* 1.5b–6 or 6.2 (the latter probably because the compiler no longer understood the source, or better, because he did not accept the motive expressed there).[4] In the same way, it is no accident that ἐλθέτω χάρις καὶ παρελθέτω ὁ κόσμος οὗτος is absent (whereas "maranatha" and "hosanna," both sanctified by biblical texts, have been retained): 7.26.5. (3) There are characteristic additions to the text, for example, in 7.16, where the compiler adds to the household code in his source a section about the βασιλεύς and the ἄρχοντες; also typical is the Christianizing addition at the end of the "way of life" (7.17.2) or the augmentation of the baptismal fast (7.22.4–5) and the weekly fast (7.23.2–3). The meal prayers are liturgically expanded (7.25–26), and the compiler interprets the prohibition in *Did.* 9.5 in a casuistical manner (7.25.5-6). (4) Above all, however, the compiler repeatedly adapts the text, without comment, to his own situation. Thus the admonition περὶ τοῦ βαπτίσματος is, for him, directed to bishops and presbyters (7.22.1); the permission to improvise the prayers of thanksgiving freely is given not, as in *Did.* 10.7, to the prophets, but to the presbyters (7.26.6); so also with regard to the firstfruits, the priests take the place of the prophets (7.29.1 and 3). While *Didache* 15 speaks of the choice of bishops and deacons, the *Apostolic Constitutions* has an *ordo triplex* in 7.31, and the discussion in *Didache* 11 and 12, which was long since anachronistic for the *Apostolic Constitutions*, is sharply curtailed (7.28).[5] There is an important addition at 7.22.2: baptism is preceded by the anointing with ἔλαιον and followed by the anointing with *myron*. In my opinion, the *Apostolic Constitutions* found the famous *myron* prayer (7.27) in the source;[6] that it is not the Constitutor's own work (except for possible stylization) is evident from the parallel in Coptic.[7]

In reconstructing the text, the *Apostolic Constitutions* should be adduced as an indirect but constant witness. That the recension behind the source of the *Apostolic Constitutions* is different from the H recension is seen from the myrrh prayer. We should warn against an overvaluation of the *Apostolic Constitutions* (as happens, e.g., with Peterson).[8] On the one hand, we should note that the *Apostolic Constitutions* was already dependent on a text containing the interpolated myrrh prayer; on the other hand, we should continually be aware that the compiler of the *Constitutions* alters the source without misgivings whenever he thinks it necessary (e.g., in the sense of the motives sketched above).

---

1 *Didascalia*, 1.386–423. Previously in Bryennios, Διδαχή, λζ′–ν′; then in Harnack, "Prolegomena," 178–92; and Harris, *Teaching*, 25ff. I am following the text of Funk's edition.

2 It is very improbable that 32.5 belongs with it; it probably comes directly from the pen of the "Constitutor," who repeatedly compiles scriptural citations. It is at least possible that some elements of the *Didache* are concealed in 32.4b; that conclusion is missing from H. At any rate, the Constitutor still possessed a complete copy of the *Didache*.

3 For more detail, see Harnack, "Prolegomena," 173–78. There is some information also in Giet, *L'Énigme*, 136–39.

4 Harnack, "Prolegomena," 176: The Constitutor rejects a Christianity of the *perfecti*. In fact, he also removed the corresponding passage in 7.2.4.

5 In *Const.* 7.28.5 the Constitutor suffered a lapse. While he otherwise omits what the source says about the prophets, we find here προφήτης ἀληθινός. See Harnack, "Prolegomena," 174, 177.

6 See below the excursus on the addition in the Coptic version, pp. 165–67.

7 See below.

8 "Probleme," 158–66, and passim.

The so-called *Fragmenta Anastasiana*[9] go back not to the *Didache* but to the *Apostolic Constitutions*. Interesting for us are the following passages: 9 (p. 61,10 in Funk: *Anastasius Quaestiones* 64), where *Const.* 7.23 (depending on *Didache* 8) is quoted with alterations and omissions; also 12 (pp. 63–67, more precisely, in Funk 64,5–67,19; *Anastasius Quaestiones* 15), where the Two Ways section appears; the section comes from *Const.* 7.1.2–18 (dependent on *Didache* 1–6), but Anastasius has radically shortened the source.[10] The *Fragmenta Anastasiana* do not enter into consideration for the critical reconstruction of the text of the *Didache*.

The same is true of the *Sentences* edited by M. Besson and attributed (in one of the two MSS.) to one "Isaac the Syrian."[11] These *Sentences*[12] are preserved in two manuscripts: *Vaticanus graecus* 375, 14th century, fol. 157r. ff., which attributes the text to a Syrian anchorite named Isaac,[13] and *Palatinus graecus* 146,

15th century, fol. 44r. ff. Besson thought of the Nestorian bishop and ascetic Mar Isaac (Isaac of Nineveh), who died about the end of the seventh century.[14] The text begins with Δύο ὁδοί εἰσιν, ἀγαπητοί, πρὸ προσώπου ἡμῶν [ποῖαι αὗται] τοῦ θανάτου καὶ τῆς ζωῆς ("There are before us, beloved, two ways. [What are they?] Of death and of life," Besson, p. 49, 4–5), but then does not continue with any allusions to the Two Ways tractate. These appear only at pp. 51, 10–54,1, where (with extensive additions, omissions, and some rearrangements) elements from the "way of life" are found. Moreover, analysis shows that the *Sentences* are dependent either on the *Apostolic Constitutions* 7[15] or (more probably) on an extract from the *Apostolic Constitutions* similar to that used by the *Fragmenta Anastasiana*.[16] Thus, like the latter, they may be eliminated from consideration for the reconstruction of the text of the *Didache*.

---

9   Edited by Funk, *Didascalia,* 2.51–71; there is an introduction to the text in Funk, *Didascalia,* 2.viii–xi.

10   Cf. the remarks in Funk, *Didascalia,* 2.67.

11   Cf. M. Besson, "Un recueil des sentences attribué à Isaac le Syrien," *OrChr* 1 (1901) 46–60, 288–98.

12   Besson ("Recueil," 46) characterizes this work as "a compilation of moral maxims apparently for religious."

13   The text, found only in *Vatic.*, reads: Κεφάλαια διάφορα τοῦ σοφοῦ πατρὸς ἡμῶν Ἰσαὰκ τοῦ Σύρου καὶ ἀναχωρητοῦ ἐκλελεγμένα τοῦ ἁγίου Ἰωάννου τοῦ Χρυσοστόμου διάφορα καὶ πάνυ ὠφέλιμα ("Altogether various and useful chapters of our wise father and anchorite Isaac the Syrian, selected by Saint John Chrysostom").

14   For Isaac of Nineveh, cf. Altaner and Stuiber, *Patrologie,* 350. "His literary legacy, which was very extensive, must be severely limited . . . because of confusion with other authors of the same name" (ibid.). In the information on the literary works of Isaac of Nineveh the title of the present work does not appear; see Besson, "Recueil," 46. Altaner and Stuiber (*Patrologie,* 350) do not discuss the *Sentences* edited by Besson.

15   Besson's proposal ("Recueil," 47) that there are also occasional contacts with *Barnabas* (19.1) and *Doctrina* (6.5) is without foundation. Dix ("Didache," 242–50) thought that the author of the *Sentences* was dependent on the *Didache*. "The author of the 'Maxims' may well have known A. C. VII itself, but he clearly had independent knowledge of its *Didache* also" (p. 245 n. 1). In saying this, Dix is thinking of an old recension of the *Didache*. To the contrary, see Richard H. Connolly, "Didache and Diatessaron," *JTS* 34 (1933) 346: Isaac is dependent on the *Apostolic Constitutions*. See Audet, *Didachè,* 51 n. 2; Rordorf and Tuilier, *Doctrine,* 123–24 n. 3.

16   Giet (*L'Énigme,* 141) supports (with good reason) the opinion that the *Sentences* do not go back directly to the *Apostolic Constitutions*, but to an extract from it similar to that used by the *Fragmenta Anastasiana*. See *L'Énigme,* 141 n. 16.

6. The Relationship of the *Didache* to the "Two Ways" Tractate

a. The Findings

The *Didache* begins, in chaps. 1–6 (more precisely, in 1.1–6.1), with a tractate on the two ways the human being can go: the way to (eternal) life, or the way to (eternal) death. There are numerous parallels to this motif of the two ways in the literature of popular philosophy and religion.[1] But there are also (and this is what interests us here) striking parallels to the *Didache* tractate itself in the literature of earliest Christianity that must stand in a close literary relationship to the *Didache*. The only question is, What is that relationship? The writings in question are (1) the *Epistle of Barnabas* 18–20,[2] (2) the *Doctrina apostolorum*, (3) the first part of the so-called *Apostolic Church Order* or *Canons of the Apostles* (more precisely, chaps. 4–13),[3] and the related *Epitome*, (4) part of the Arabic *Life of Shenoute*, and finally (5) sections in Ps.-Athanasius *Syntagma doctrinae* (ed. Batiffol),

or the related *Fides patrum* (*PG* 28.1637–1643C, more precisely 1639C-1643C). If (3) and (5) are each counted as two, and the *Didache* added, we have altogether eight different but somehow related recensions of the Two Ways tractate before us.[4]

1. While the *Didache* begins with a version of the Two Ways tractate, the analogous tractate in the *Epistle of Barnabas* is near the end of the document (chaps. 18–21). Almost the whole of the material included in these chapters of the *Epistle of Barnabas* recurs in the *Didache*, with the exception that in *Barnabas* 18 and 19.1–2 the material is only about half equivalent; at 20.1 *Barnabas* has a somewhat different introduction, but beginning with the catalog of vices, the sections are again equivalent, with but few exceptions, and from 20.2 onward even their order is the same.[5] There is a strong likelihood of literary relationship. But how should we think of it? Is the *Didache* dependent on *Barnabas*,[6] or *Barnabas* on the *Didache*?[7] If the *Didache* were dependent

---

1 On this, see below.

2 I will later express the opinion that parts of the Two Ways tractate are also concealed in chap. 21.

3 On the traces of the tractate in chap. 14, see below.

4 The number increases if we include *Const.* 7.1.2–19 or the parallels in the *Fragmenta Anastasiana* and in Isaac of Syria (see above). To count them would, however, distort the picture, because the *Apostolic Constitutions* is dependent on the *Didache*, and the *Fragmenta Anastasiana* and Isaac of Syria are directly or indirectly dependent on the *Apostolic Constitutions*.

5 The absence of the "*teknon* sayings" (*Did.* 3.1–6) in *Barnabas* is striking. The omission of the *sectio evangelica* (*Did.* 1.3b–2.1) should in my opinion be considered in another context.

6 Thus Bryennios, Διδαχή, πδ′-ϛ′. Other early advocates of this position are listed in Ehrhard, *Altchristliche Litteratur*, 49–50. Later advocates were Robinson (*Didache,* esp. 69–70), supposing that the Two Ways tractate stems from *Barnabas,* and that the *Didache* is dependent on *Barnabas;* also, in detail, Muilenburg (*Literary Relations*, 130), who considers *Barnabas* to be the originator of the Two Ways tractate, and attempts to show (pp. 140–58) that the *Didache* is dependent on *Barnabas.* Thus the compiler of the *Didache* may be using a Jewish apocryphon in 3.1–6 (p. 149; there was a similar suggestion earlier by Robinson, *Didache*, 62). Arguments along the same line appear in Francis C. Burkitt, "Barnabas and the Didache," *JTS* 33 (1932) 25–27; cf. also Connolly, "Relation," 237–53; idem, "Bar-

nabas and the Didache," 166–67; idem, "Streeter on the Didache," 374, 376–77. Cf. then the new version of Robinson's work in idem, "Barnabas and the Didache," 119–20, 146, 238–40; Vokes, *Riddle*, 27–51 (p. 44: "There seems no legitimate reason for denying that the 'Two Ways' is the original composition of Barnabas, used by the *Didache*"). John Lawson (*A Theological and Historical Introduction to the Apostolic Fathers* [New York: Macmillan, 1961] 75) "inclines to the view that *Barnabas* adopted 'The Two Ways' from a Jewish source, and that the writer of *Didache* took it over from him."

7 E.g., Zahn, *Geschichte*, 3.310–12; Schaff, *Church Manual*, 20, 121 (but Schaff also suggests the possibility of a common source); etc. Other early advocates of this hypothesis are listed in Ehrhard, *Altchristliche Litteratur*, 49–50. Funk, in turn, wrote frequently in favor of this hypothesis; cf. Funk, *Abhandlungen*, 2.109–11, 117–24, 131–34; idem, "Didache und Barnabasbrief," *ThQ* 87 (1905) 161–79; later Bosio, *Padri apostolici*, 1.3.

8 Also striking is the agreement of *Barn.* 18.1c with *Doctr.* 1.1b against *Did.* 1.1, quite apart from the mutual absence of the *sectio evangelica* in *Barnabas* and *Doctrina apostolorum*.

9 Muilenburg (*Literary Relation*, 161–64) differs, seeing further contacts between *Didache* and *Barnabas* outside the Two Ways tractate. But the parallels he adduces are quite far-fetched. Cf. also the list in Vokes, *Riddle*, 27–28. (Of course, the strength of proof in the individual passages is very differently evaluated by Vokes himself.) In my opinion, how-

on *Barnabas* (or vice versa), one would expect that literary relationships would be evident elsewhere, not merely within the limited field of the tractate *de duabus viis*. But the literary relationship between the two documents is strikingly restricted to that tractate.[8] Outside the Two Ways tractate there is no demonstrable contact between *Barnabas* and the *Didache* (because the only parallel worth considering,[9] *Barn.* 4.9/*Did.* 16.2, can rest on common oral tradition: see below, in the commentary at 16.2). This in itself makes the model of a common dependence of *Barnabas* and the *Didache* on a third entity the most plausible solution. Further indications of the existence of such a source will appear in the course of the following presentation.

2. Much closer to the *Didache* text of the tractate on the Two Ways than *Barnabas* is the text of the *Doctrina apostolorum*. There are two manuscripts of this writing (thus far found only in Latin): one is complete (Cod. lat. Monac. 6264,[10] 11th century, in the Bavarian

Staatsbibliothek in Munich, fol. 102b–103b) and was edited by Joseph Schlecht.[11] The other is incomplete, containing the text only as far as 2.6[12] (Cod. Mellic. 597,[13] 9th century [?], Melk, Stiftsbibliothek, fol. 115b). It was most recently edited by Kurt Niederwimmer.[14] The two manuscripts appear to go back to a common archetype. *Doctrina apostolorum* follows the Two Ways tractate of the *Didache* very differently from the way *Barnabas* does. It is sometimes so close that, at first, it was thought that *Doctrina apostolorum* was the (or a) Latin translation of the *Didache*, or at least of its first section.[15] This opinion is very improbable, however, not only because of the deviations of *Doctrina apostolorum* from the *Didache* parallels, which remain striking,[16] but primarily because *Doctrina apostolorum* contains only the Two Ways tractate (and omits from it the *sectio evangelica*). Again, it is the more probable supposition that *Doctrina apostolorum* and *Didache* 1–6 are dependent on a

---

ever, the only passage that can be seriously considered is *Barn.* 4.9/*Did.* 16.2.

10 Formerly labeled frising 64.

11 Schlecht, *Doctrina,* 101–4. In an appendix, Schlecht included photographic plates of the ms. which he discovered in 1900.

12 The ms. ends with *Nec conten* . . . on the last page of the codex. The rest of the codex has been lost. (Vokes is incorrect in writing, "Von Gebhardt's fragment is merely a short extract" [*Riddle*, 17].) Naturally, there is no parallel text to *Did.* 1.3b–2.1 in Codex Mellicensis, any more than in Codex Monacensis. That is, however, not a gap in the tradition; it appears that the *sectio evangelica* was never part of the *Doctrina apostolorum*.

13 Formerly labeled Q 52 or 914.

14 Kurt Niederwimmer, "Doctrina apostolorum (Cod. Mellic. 597)," in Hans Christoph Schmidt-Lauber, ed., *Theologia scientia eminens practica; F. Zerbst zum 70. Geburtstag* (Vienna, Freiburg, and Basel: Herder, 1979) 266–72. For the history of the discovery of the Melk fragment of the *Doctrina apostolorum* (B. Pez or O. von Gebhardt and F. X. Funk) and a description of the ms., see pp. 266–67. In research on the *Didache*, Codex Monacensis bears the symbol f (f[1] for corrections by a first hand, f[2] for corrections by a second hand, f[3] for corrections by a third hand); Codex Mellicensis bears the symbol g (g[1] for corrections by a first hand). Important for the language and text of the two mss. is Leo Wohleb, *Die lateinische Übersetzung der Didache kritisch und sprachlich untersucht* (SGKA 7.1; Paderborn: Schöningh,

1913; repr. New York: Johnson, 1967).

15 Thus, e.g., Funk; cf. his *Abhandlungen,* 2.109; Streeter, "Much-Belaboured *Didache,*" 360–74, in which he writes that *Doctrina apostolorum* is nothing but the Latin version of the *Didache,* although the translator simply omitted chaps. 7–16 because of the changed state of canon law (p. 374). This may be the writing to which Rufinus refers as "*Duae viae.*" For Muilenburg and Vokes, see below.

16 Examples: at 1.1 after *viae duae sunt* add *in saeculo*; and after *mortis* add *lucis et tenebrarum, in his constituti sunt angeli duo, unus aequitatis, alter iniquitatis* (for this, cf. *Barn.* 18.1c). At the end of 1.3: *interpretatio autem horum verborum haec est* fits well before 2.2: *Non moechaberis* . . . , while the Didachist's δευτέρα δὲ ἐντολὴ τῆς διδαχῆς (*Did.* 2.1) is obviously secondary. At 4.8c *omnibus enim* . . . is probably in the right place, and was removed by the Didachist to avoid a repetition (1.5). Especially striking are the differences between the *Didache* and *Doctrina apostolorum* in the catalog of vices in the "way of death" (5.1). The hypothesis of multiple versions is badly hampered by the absence of the *sectio evangelica* in *Doctrina apostolorum*. These indications speak clearly against the idea that *Doctrina apostolorum* is only the Latin translation of the *Didache*. On the double conclusion of *Doctrina apostolorum*, see below.

common tradition. In that case, *Doctrina apostolorum* appears to be an independent writing, or better, the Latin translation (made in antiquity) of a Greek original containing nothing but the Two Ways tractate.[17] The Greek original has been lost.[18] Whether the Greek original was already entitled διδαχὴ τῶν ἀποστόλων, or whether that title was first given to the Latin translation (as [*de*] *doctrina apostolorum*)[19] is a point deserving further consideration.[20]

3. The Two Ways tractate in the so-called *Apostolic Church Order* or *Canons of the Apostles* (*Can.* 4.1—13.4 or 14)[21] would be related to the text of the *Didache* in somewhat similar fashion, if it were not that the tractate is here attributed to the words of individual apostles (certainly a later stylization of the material).[22] Remarkably

enough, however, the quotation from the Two Ways tractate extends at first only as far as 13.4 (cf. *Did.* 4.8), πόσῳ μᾶλλον ἐν τοῖς θνητοῖς. The rest of the "way of life" (with the exception of *Did.* 4.13b, for which see immediately below), and the whole "way of death" have not been incorporated into the canon. (Something from the epilogue to the tractate, which is absent in the *Didache*, could be concealed in 14.3a: see below. The expression in 14.3b, φυλάξεις ἃ παρέλαβες μήτε προσθεὶς μήτε ὑφαιρῶν ["You shall keep what you have received, without adding or subtracting anything"] is reminiscent of *Did.* 4.13.) It is tempting to see the text as dependent on the *Didache*,[23] the more so as *Can.* 12.3 includes the expression ἠξίωσέν σοι δοθῆναι πνευματικὴν τροφὴν καὶ ποτὸν καὶ ζωὴν αἰώνιον ("He graced you with spiri-

---

17 Those (e.g., Muilenburg) who derive the Two Ways tractate from *Barnabas,* and consider *Doctrina apostolorum* the Latin translation of the *Didache,* typically get into serious difficulties. They must explain not only the (in this case) "epitomatic" character of *Doctrina apostolorum,* but also its occasional resemblance to *Barnabas* (against the *Didache*). But how? "The Latin version of the *Teaching of the Twelve Apostles* shows clear traces of familiarity with the Epistle of Barnabas" (Muilenburg, *Literary Relations,* 27; cf. 45). This, and the homiletic context of the tradition, "supports the belief that the Latin version is in actuality a homiletical extract and not a true copy or translation of an original Two Ways Teaching" (ibid., 42). Cf. 45: "The homiletic character of the Latin version. . . ." Cf. earlier Robinson, *Didache,* 73–83; and thereafter Vokes, *Riddle,* 17–21, and passim (the Latin version is simply a homiletic extract and corrected the *Didache* by using *Barnabas*).

18 For the type of Latin translation, see the general opinion of Giet, *L'Énigme,* 118. But his supposition that there were two stages of translation remains arbitrary.

19 *Doctrina apostolorum* g: *de doctrina apostolorum* f. The title in g may be the more original.

20 For more on this, see below.

21 On this writing, see above.

22 *Can.* 4 (John) = *Did.* 1.1–1.2b.
Can. 5 (Matthew) = *Did.* 1.2c; 3a.
Can. 6 (Peter) = *Did.* 2.2-7.
Can. 7 (Andrew) = *Did.* 3.1–2.
Can. 8 (Philip) = *Did.* 3.3a. (This canon inserts a rather long excursus on the key word ἐπιθυμία.)
Can. 9 (Simon) = *Did.* 3.3b.
Can. 10 (James) = *Did.* 3.4.
Can. 11 (Nathanael) = *Did.* 3.5–10.

Can. 12 (Thomas) = *Did.* 4.1–2. (This canon again inserts a short excursus.)
Can. 13 (Cephas [!]) = *Did.* 4.3–8.
On *Can.* 14 (Bartholomew), see below.
The rest of the text is also attributed to apostles, but the material is no longer taken from the Two Ways tractate. On the list of apostles, see below.

23 Thus Bryennios, Διδαχή, ξθ′ and ο′ (dependent on *Barnabas, Didache, Apostolic Constitutions,* and others); Schaff, *Church Manual,* 19, 127–32 (dependent on *Didache*); Vokes, *Riddle,* 72, and passim (dependent on *Didache* and *Barnabas*); Barnard, "Later History," 103–4 (*Duae viae, Barnabas,* and *Didache*); for Harnack and Wengst, see below.

24 ἡμῖν δὲ ἐχαρίσω πνευματικὴν τροφὴν καὶ ποτὸν καὶ ζωὴν αἰώνιον διὰ τοῦ παιδός σου, *Did.* 10.3c and *Canons,* would show that its author also knows the second part of the *Didache,* and this would support the idea of literary dependence in the *first* part. Cf. Harnack, "Prolegomena," 210–11 n. 34. (Harnack supported, on pp. 210–11, the opinion that the *Canons of the Apostles* was dependent on the *Didache* and *Barnabas.*) Of course, Harnack wished to establish dependence not only on *Did.* 10.3 but also on 13.1–2. In *Apostellehre,* 31–32, he attempted to understand the whole complex in light of his hypothesis of a basic document (see below), and this led him to a singular variant on this hypothesis. Against the thesis that *Can.* 12.3 rests on *Did.* 10.3 + 13.1–2, see Ehrhard, *Altchristliche Litteratur,* 57.

25 Kraft (*Didache,* 10) complicates the matter: "Most witnesses also include brief verbal parallels to *Didache* 10.3b and 13.1/2 (?) in the expansion which follows the admonitions of *Didache* 4.2, but this material is not extensive enough to encourage the belief that our full *Didache* was used for the Two Ways of *CO* [= Apostolic Church Order]. Rather, *CO*

tual food and drink and eternal life"), which is reminiscent of *Did.* 10.3.[24] One must admit that this is a relatively strong argument. Still, while noting that this is a liturgical expression that the *Canons* did not necessarily derive from the *Didache*, I wish to maintain the hypothesis that the text also received the tractate not directly from the *Didache* but from a tradition common to it and to the author of the *Didache*.[25] The same will apply, consequently, to the *Epitome*, which stands in a literary relationship to the *Canons*.[26] Here again, the material of the tractate is attributed to apostles (eleven in number),[27] and this time the whole "way of life" is written out (but the "way of death" is again absent).[28] In making a decision about dependence on an independent Two Ways tractate, one should not be led astray by the expression ἠξίωσέ σε δι᾿ αὐτοῦ δοθῆναι πνευματικὴν τροφὴν καὶ ζωὴν αἰώνιον (*Epit.* 9), which appears again here, somewhat shortened.[29]

In his investigation of the relations existing here, Wengst reached a different result.[30] He discusses (*Didache*, 10) the deviations between *Epitome* 9 and *Canons* 12, referring first to the passage ἐκζητ. δὲ . . . κτλ. (I add the *Didache* parallels):

Epit. 9	*Can.* 12.2	*Did.* 4.2
Ἐκζητήσεις δὲ αὐτὸν	Ἐκζητήσεις δὲ τὸ πρόσωπον αὐτοῦ καθ᾽ ἡμέραν	Ἐκζητήσεις δὲ καθ᾽ ἡμέραν τὰ πρόσωπα τῶν ἁγίων
—		
καὶ τοὺς λοιποὺς ἁγίους	καὶ τοὺς λοιποὺς ἁγίους	—

Wengst thinks that the deviations between *Epitome* and the *Canons* derive from an additional use of the *Didache* or its Two Ways tractate. The text of the *Canons* is said to be a combination of the "Moral Teaching of the Twelve Apostles" and the *Didache*. But *Barn.* 19.10 offers something similar:

Καὶ ἐκζητήσεις
καθ᾽ ἑκάστην ἡμέραν
τὰ πρόσωπα τῶν ἁγίων

In my opinion, it is not the text of the *Canons* but that of *Epitome* that requires explanation. It rests simply on an abbreviation of the source of its version of the Two Ways tractate. Wengst supposes that there is a similar phenomenon a little later:

---

seems to have added excerpts from at least Barnabas and possibly the *Didache* to the *Dctr*-like form of the Two Ways on which it is based."

26 On this document, see below.

27 *Epit.* 1 (John) = *Did.* 1.1–2b.
Epit. 2 (Matthew) = *Did.* 1.2c.
Epit. 3 (Peter) = *Did.* 2.2–7.
Epit. 4 (Andrew) = *Did.* 3.1–2.
Epit. 5 (Philip) = *Did.* 3.3a (without the excursus found at this point in the *Canons*).
Epit. 6 (Simon) = *Did.* 3.3b.
Epit. 7 (James) = *Did.* 3.4.
Epit. 8 (Nathanael) = *Did.* 3.5–10.
Epit. 9 (Thomas) = *Did.* 4.1–2.
Epit. 10 (Cephas [!]) = *Did.* 4.3–4, 6, 8.
Epit. 11 (Bartholomew) = *Did.* 4.9, 14a, 13a, 14b, 12, 13b, 14c [*sic*].
For this list of eleven apostles, cf. Giet, *L'Énigme*, 122–23; and idem, "La Didachè: Enseignement des douze Apôtres?" *Melto* 3 (1967) 223–36. It is clear (1) that the distribution of the material among the apostles is a subsequent stylization; it is also clear (2) that this stylization must go back to a revision of the Two Ways tractate, on which both *Canons* and *Epitome* are dependent; the origins of the list of eleven apostles (despite Giet's investigation) requires a new analysis; (3) that the text attributed to Bartholomew is different, because *Epitome* con-

tains the whole "way of life" (without the piece found in *Did.* 4.5, 7, 10–11), while *Canons* breaks off at *Did.* 4.8 and then follows immediately with the epilogue of the tractate (as I suspect; see above); (4) that the two writings (*Canons* and *Epitome*) present only the way of life from the Two Ways tractate (and in *Canons* it is already abbreviated) is connected with this naive stylization in terms of utterances of the eleven: the text breaks off when the list has been exhausted (cf. Giet, "Enseignement," 235). Wengst's opinion is somewhat different (*Didache*, 10): "The way of death is also omitted, probably as a result of the division of the material among the eleven apostles, who preach the way of life, not the way of death." There is still another proposal in Rordorf and Tuilier, *Doctrine*, 119 n. 1.

28 That in *Epitome* the stylization of the material of *Did.* 3.1–6 in "*teknon* sayings" is lacking is not something that I consider a sign of greater originality with respect to the *Canons* (where it is present). I think that it was available to the author of the *Epitome*, but that it was removed in the course of the development of the fiction.

29 Schermann attributed excessive significance to what he called the "X recension" of the two ways, and turned the genealogy of the tradition on its head (*Elfapostelmoral*, 18–23, 80–88).

30 Wengst, *Didache*, 7–14, esp. 10–11.

Epit. 9 (end)	*Can.* 12.3	*Did.* 10.3 (end)
Ὁ γὰρ κύριος	Εἰ γὰρ ὁ κύριος	
ἠξίωσέ σε	δι᾽ αὐτοῦ	
δι᾽ αὐτοῦ	ἠξίωσέν σοι	ἡμῖν δὲ
δοθῆναι	δοθῆναι	ἐχαρίσω
πνευματικὴν	πνευματικὴν	πνευματικὴν
τροφὴν	τροφὴν	τροφὴν
	καὶ ποτόν	καὶ ποτὸν
καὶ ζωὴν αἰώνιον	καὶ ζωὴν αἰώνιον	καὶ ζωὴν αἰώνιον

This is the passage already mentioned above. According to Wengst, the added καὶ ποτόν in *Canon* 12 should suggest that the *Canons* is additionally dependent on the *Didache* (*Didache*, 11). But if the *Didache* is already supposed to be in use (which I, nota bene, do not believe), it is much more inviting to suppose that *both* versions (*Canons* and *Epitome*) used the *Didache*, or (better) that their common source used the *Didache*,[31] and that καὶ ποτόν in the *Epitome* has (for unknown reasons) been omitted. The two conditions for supposing independence of the *Canons* from the *Didache*, as proposed by Wengst (*Didache*, 11) are that the Didachist "reproduced his source word for word" and the *Canons* used "exactly the same source as the Didachist." In my opinion, these should be distinguished. The Didachist was fairly faithful in copying his source, but I do not believe that he used exactly the same source as did the *Canons*. What he had as a source was *similar* to that used by the *Canons*, because the relationship between the *Didache* and the *Canons* is not so exclusive as Wengst's reasoning implies.[32] This is evident especially in the passages where the *Canons* (and *Epitome*)

agree with *Barnabas against* the *Didache*. (These will be discussed below.)[33] In my opinion, this phenomenon suggests a different genealogical relationship among these writings. In sum, despite Wengst's objections, I wish to maintain the hypothesis that the *Canons* was not influenced by the *Didache*.

(4) In the Arabic *Life of Shenoute of Atripe*[34] the introduction to the speech of Visa (in Amélineau, 291, ll. 6ff.) is followed by a didactic section having the character of a set of rules: in content, it is nothing but a (fairly late) version of the Two Ways tractate. We are no longer surprised to discover that the *sectio evangelica* is missing. Otherwise, the tractate reappears with numerous alterations, including the ὁδὸς τοῦ θανάτου (which, however, is treated very cursorily).[35] It is interesting that the shaping of the material into *teknon* sayings does not begin with the section corresponding to *Did.* 3.1–6, but already in that corresponding to *Did.* 2.6 (and extends past *Did.* 3.6). There can probably be no question of the author's knowing the whole *Didache*.[36]

(5) Finally, I should mention two texts with a mutual literary relationship: Ps.-Athanasius *Syntagma doctrinae* (ed. Batiffol), and *Fides patrum* (ed. Batiffol; also *PG* 28.1637–43).[37] As regards the *Fides patrum*, the quotations or allusions to the Two Ways tractate begin only in the second part of the writing, from chap. 3 (Batiffol), equivalent to *PG* 28.1639C. The literary relationship of the two writings to one another seems to be best understood if we suppose that the *Fides patrum* (in its second part) draws either on the *Syntagma doctrinae*[38] or on a source common to both.[39] This whole question (includ-

---

31 It is true that Wengst himself (*Didache*, 11) raises the objection that this could also be a tradition "from which the compiler acquired knowledge by other means as well." But for him this objection is not conclusive in light of the considerations that follow.

32 Wengst himself (*Didache*, 10 n. 24) mentions "four exceptions," where the *Canons* and *Epitome* agree against the *Didache*.

33 Wengst supposes (*Didache*, 10 n. 23) that the *Canons* used *Barnabas*, but does not wish to explain *Can.* 12.1 (ἀγαπήσεις ὡς κόρην ὀφθαλμοῦ σου; cf. *Epit.* 9 and *Barn.* 19.9) by dependence on *Barnabas*. Instead, he explains it as showing dependence on the Two Ways tractate, because according to Wengst the *Canons* is dependent on *Barnabas*, but *Epitome* is not.

34 See above.

35 Striking here is the absence of the material contained in *Did.* 4.9–14.

36 H. Benigni attempted to derive the material from the *Didache*, but from a recension of the writing that would have been available to the *Canons* as well ("Didachê coptica: 'Duarum viarum' recensio coptica monastica, Shenudii homiliis attributa, per arabicam versionem superstes," *Bessarione* 3 [1898] 326). According to Vokes (*Riddle*, 72) the use of the Two Ways tractate stems from the *Didache*, with the author assimilating *Did.* 1.2 to *Barnabas* and the Gospels. Barnard ("Later History," 104–5) writes that *Didache* and the *Canons* may have been used in addition to the Two Ways tractate. "The 'Two Ways' known to Schnudi was probably the Greek Original of the *Doctrina*" (p. 105).

37 On these two writings, see above.

38 Cf. Connolly, "Use of the *Didache*," 156; Vokes, *Riddle*, 72; Barnard, "Later History," 105.

39 Thus Harnack, *Apostellehre*, 28. Pierre Batiffol writes

ing the relationship of the Coptic version of the *Fides patrum* to the other documents) requires a new investigation. Quotations from the Two Ways tractate are distributed throughout both documents:

Synt. doctr. 1.4 = *Fides patr.* 3 (1639C): cf. *Did.* 1.2.
Synt. doctr. 1.5 = *Fides patr.* 3 (1639C): cf. *Did.* 2.2.
Synt. doctr. 1.9 = *Fides patr.* 4 (1639D): cf. *Did.* 2.4; 3.5, 6.
Synt. doctr. 2.4 = *Fides patr.* 5 (1640A): cf. *Did.* 2.2.
Synt. doctr. 2.5 = *Fides patr.* 5 (1640A): cf. *Did.* 3.4.
Synt. doctr. 3.1 = *Fides patr.* 7 (1641B): cf. *Did.* 3.5.
Synt. doctr. 4.1 = *Fides patr.* 8 (1641D):[40] cf. *Did.* 3.8.

Add to these *Fides patr.* 3 (1639C): cf. *Did.* 6.1 (lacking a parallel in *Syntagma doctrinae*). All these passages have their parallels only in the Two Ways tractate of the *Didache*,[41] and quotations from the *sectio evangelica* are (of course) absent.[42] All other parallels, which would indicate knowledge of later passages in the *Didache* (and thus knowledge of the *Didache* itself) are questionable: *Synt. doctr.* 2.10 (cf. *Fides patr.* 6 [1640B]) knows of fasting on Wednesdays and Fridays, but it cannot be proved that the passage is borrowed from *Did.* 8.1. *Synt. doctr.* 3.2, ἐὰν τέχνας μὴ ἔχωσιν ἀναγκάζονται πραγματεύεσθαι (cf. *Fides patr.* 7 [1641B]), can, but need not, stem from *Did.* 12.4. *Synt. doctr.* 3.10 (cf. *Fides patr.* 7 [1641C]) can scarcely come from *Did.* 13.3, no more than *Synt. doctr* 6.4 (cf. *Fides patr.* 10 [1642D]) can come from *Did.*

12.4. For *Synt. doctr.* 6.6 (cf. *Fides patr.* 10 [1642D]) as well, dependence on *Did.* 13.3 cannot be demonstrated with certainty.[43] The result is that these two writings have a secure relationship only to the Two Ways section.[44] The corresponding items probably do not go back to the *Didache*,[45] but to the independent Two Ways tractate in one of its forms.[46]

b. Further Details on the Hypothesis of an Independent "Ways" Tractate

In the preceding section, we have discussed the relationship between the Two Ways portion of the *Didache* and similar passages in *Barnabas*, *Doctrina apostolorum*, the *Canons of the Apostles*, *Epitome*, the *Life of Shenoute*, *Syntagma doctrinae*, and *Fides patrum*. We could not emerge from this without positing the idea of an independent tractate *de duabus viis*, a tractate handed on in different versions and used as a source in various ways. This model of interpretation (sometimes called the "basic document hypothesis") appeared early in the history of *Didache* research, was presented in the widest variety of versions, and dominates research today (although the more precise genealogical relationships are differently described).[47] I cannot enter into detail on these kinds of differences and nuances here. I will restrict myself to a description of what, in light of the history of research, appears to me most probable.

---

that the two versions of the *Fides patrum* (Greek and Coptic) go back, independently of one another, to the same source, from which the *Syntagma doctrinae* also derives ("Le Syntagma Doctrinae dit de Saint Athanase," in idem, ed., *Studia Patristica* [Études d'ancienne littérature chrétienne, fasc. 2; Paris: Leroux, 1890] 135).

40 *Synt. doctr.* 4.1 and *Fides patr.* 8 (1641D) read (with *Didache* and against *Barnabas*, *Canons*, *Epitome*; *Doctrina apostolorum*: omnia verba) διὰ παντός. One would strike this expression in *Didache* if it were not found in *Syntagma doctrinae* and *Fides patrum*. Const. 2.1.5 probably reads thus (it is uncertain whether the source, the *Didascalia apostolorum*, also had this reading); in 7.8.3 (from the *Didache*), διὰ παντός is absent.

41 In fact, in *Syntagma doctrinae* only from the beginning of the Two Ways tractate (analogous to *Didache* 1–3).

42 Differently Dix ("Didache," 247), who sees *Did.* 1.5a quoted in *Synt. doctr.* 3.8–9.

43 Dependence of *Syntagma doctrinae* and *Fides patrum* on the *Didache* is advocated by Edgar Hennecke,

"Die Grundschrift der Didache und ihre Recensionen," *ZNW* 2 (1901) 59 n. 3, and passim; Muilenburg, *Literary Relations*, 39; Vokes, *Riddle*, 72–73 (with complicated demonstrations); Dix, "Didache," 246–47; Barnard, "Later History," 105, suggested both dependence on the *Duae viae* and on the *Didache* and *Canons*.

44 Goodspeed, "Doctrina," 233.

45 Giet (*L'Énigme*, 146–47, 150) differs, and gives a complicated and quite arbitrary hypothesis.

46 Interesting is *Synt. doctr.* 1.6, a reminiscence of the James clauses; cf. *Fides patr.* 3 (1639C).

47 This model of interpretation stems from the very earliest period of research. Ehrhard (*Altchristliche Litteratur*, 53) formulated it this way: "The first part, the description of the two ways, is Jewish in origin and may have been formulated even before Christ as a catechism for proselytes." (The description of the source as a catechism for proselytes is not, however, shared by all defenders of this hypothesis.) On p. 54, Ehrhard also names the earliest representatives of this opinion. Its principal founder (after some precursors) was Taylor, "Early Jewish Manual

1. The different versions of the tractate go back to an originally Jewish basic model, which began as a pre-Christian, Jewish tractate on the Two Ways[48] and whose original wording can no longer be restored in detail on the basis of the related material.[49] One of these versions also served the Didachist as a source. In any case, this hypothesis enables us to place the temporal origins of the Jewish tractate in the first century; the preliminary literary forms are still older and go back to pre-Christian times.[50]

2. The Jewish character of the original Two Ways trac-tate was noted very early[51] and in recent times has been given additional support as a result of the discovery of the Qumran texts, especially the analogy to 1QS 3.18–4.26. It is characteristic of the special form in which the motif of the "ways" appears in the tractate that the nearest parallels are to be found in Jewish and Jewish-Christian texts: 1QS 3.18–4.26; *T. Ash*. 1:3–5; *Ps.-Clem. Hom*. 7.3.3–5 (GCS 1.117–18); 7.1–2 (GCS 1.119). I will say more in detail about this below. In explicating the details of the tractate as a whole, one encounters an Old Testament-Jewish milieu at every turn; in the earlier pas-

---

of Two Ways," in *Teaching*, 18–23. The model was then developed primarily by Harnack (*Apostellehre*, 14, 25–34), although he originally had a different opinion. While other scholars were critical, the model received a particularly sustained attack in the early period from Franz Xaver Funk ("Zur Apostel-lehre und apostolischen Kirchenordnung," *ThQ* 69 [1887] 281–89; idem, *Abhandlungen*, 2.137–41). For the deliberations on this question until 1900, see Ehrhard, *Altchristliche Litteratur*, 53–58. Important opponents of the hypothesis of a basic document at a later period were Robinson (*Didache*, 70–83, 120, 146), Muilenburg (*Literary Relations*, 41–44, and passim), and Vokes (*Riddle*, 31–51, and frequently). Later adherents of the basic document hypothesis included, e.g., Drews, "Untersuchungen," 54, and passim; J. Vernon Bartlet, "The Didache Recon-sidered," *JTS* 22 [1921] 243–46; MacLean, "Intro-duction," viii ff.; Creed, "Didache," 377–79. In recent research there are Goodspeed, "Doctrina," 230–47; Altaner, "Doctrina," 335–42; Richardson, "Teaching," 161–79, esp. 162; Audet, *Didachè*, 122–63; Basil C. Butler, "The 'Two Ways' in the Didache," *JTS*, n.s. 12 (1961) 27–38; Kraft, *Didache*, 4–16; Barnard, "Later History," 97–99; Adam, "Herkunft," 53–54; Giet, *L'Énigme*, 39–55, and pas-sim; Suggs, "Two Ways Tradition," 62–63; Rordorf and Tuilier, *Doctrine*, 22–34, esp. 28; Wengst, *Didache*, 20–23.

48 Nevertheless, the interpretative model also has some variants that accept the Two Ways tractate as very probably an independent source for the *Didache*, but regard the hypothesis of the originally *Jewish* character of the source document as not com-pelling, or reject it outright: Hennecke, "Grund-schrift," 61; Goodspeed, "Doctrina," 236–37. These objections have been eliminated by 1QS 3.18–4.26, because there we find a preliminary Jewish form constituting a literary analogy to the Two Ways tractate.

49 I consider Harnack's attempt to restore the source (*Apostellehre*, 57–65) a failure. The attempts by Klaus

Wengst (*Tradition und Theologie des Barnabasbrief* [AKG 42; Berlin and New York: de Gruyter, 1971] 65–66) are also problematic.

50 We may also suppose an oral tradition of the Two Ways teaching before and alongside the literary tradition, but it cannot be reconstructed. What we have to trace here is the reconstruction of the liter-ary tradition. In this connection it is appropriate to recall the attempts of Alfred Seeberg (cf. *Der Kate-chismus der Urchristenheit* [TB 26; 1903, repr. Munich: Kaiser, 1966]; *Die beiden Wege und das Aposteldekret* [Leipzig: Deichert, 1906]; *Die Didache des Judentums und der Urchristenheit* [Leipzig: Deichert, 1908]. Seeberg made a number of attempts to reconstruct an orally transmitted, origi-nally Jewish catechism schema (sometimes called "proselyte catechism": *Wege*, 47 n. 3) with a more or less fixed body of teaching. He posited that this was, in turn, taken over by the Christian tradition (with appropriate modifications). He also asso-ciated the Two Ways teaching with this schema in various ways: it was to be understood as part of this catechetical schema. For an evaluation and critique of Seeberg's overall conception, see Ferdinand Hahn's introduction to the reprinting of *Der Katechismus* (esp. xxi–xxii and xxiv–v). As far as our subject is concerned, we may say that it is very doubtful whether there ever was such a generally circulating and more or less fixed catechism schema in Judaism, containing various teachings including the Two Ways doctrine, and the attempt to bring this into a relationship with the Two Ways teaching (or ultimately the whole *Didache*) remains corre-spondingly dubious (quite apart from the question-able character of many details in the whole description). In a broader sense, the proposals of Gottlieb Klein in *Der älteste christliche Katechismus und die jüdische Propaganda-Literatur* (Berlin: Reimer, 1909) belong here. Klein constructed a separate, orally transmitted tradition, part of which was the "Ur-*Didache*."

51 Harris (*Teaching*, 91) and Muilenburg (*Literary*

sages especially, parallels to *Ps.-Phocylides* play a certain role.[52] In the *teknon* sayings (which, however, I consider an outgrowth of the original tractate) we encounter Jewish sapiential thought. At no point does the original tractate speak of Jesus[53] (the *sectio evangelica* of the *Didache* is excluded). Nowhere do we encounter the christological or soteriological kerygma of passion, resurrection, and return.[54] Finally, it is characteristic that the typically Christian text of *Did.* 1.3b–2.1 is absent from the Two Ways tractate in *Barnabas, Doctrina apostolorum,* the *Canons of the Apostles, Epitome, Life of*

Shenoute, Syntagma doctrinae, and *Fides patrum.*[55] That is, as far as the source, the Two Ways tractate, is concerned, we are dealing in the first instance with a purely Jewish text. It probably belonged within the broader context of the community rules of Jewish religious communities (as did 1QS, 1QSa in Qumran).[56] The often expressed idea that the document was a "proselyte catechism"[57] is

---

52 *Relations,* 107–8) objected that chaps. 7–16 also have a strongly Jewish coloration. But such a judgment overlooks a characteristic difference: the Two Ways tractate is *Jewish* in substance, and was later superficially Christianized; chaps. 7–16 are not a unit, but are shaped on the whole by Jewish-Christian tradition that was then redacted by the author.

52 The text of *Sib. Or.* 2.56–148, parallel to *Ps.-Phocyl.* 5–79, in the ms. group ψ, entered the *Sibylline Oracles* only at a late period (when there were additions and expansions during the Christian era): see van der Horst, *Sentences,* 84–85; Nikolaus Walter, "Pseudo Phokylides," in Ernst Vogt and Nikolaus Walter, *Poetische Schriften* (JSHRZ 4, 3; Gütersloh: Mohn, 1983) 186–87. I will therefore cite the parallels in parentheses. The discovery of the *Didache* "constituted a turning-point in the research on Ps-Phoc." (van der Horst, *Sentences,* 14). It should be noted marginally that the parallels in the moral instructions of the Philadelphia stele (ll. 12–50; cf. SIG 3.985, pp. 116–18; and the table in Weinreich, *Privatheiligtum in Philadelphia,* 59) should not confuse the assessment of the Jewish character of the Two Ways tractate. In addition, it appears to me that Jewish influence on the section of the stele in question cannot be excluded.

53 *Kyrios* (*Did.* 4.1) probably refers to Jesus, but that is not the oldest text of the tractate. See below at 4.1c, and the following footnote.

54 The double love commandment (*Doctr.* 1.2; *Did.* 1.2; *Can.* 4.2–3; *Epit.* 1), typically lacking in *Barnabas,* probably goes back to the later Christianizing of the Jewish source. On this, see below. Does the passage about the Spirit in *Doctr.* 4.10 and *Did.* 4.10 (cf. *Barn.* 19.7c) presuppose Christian editing? I think it does. *Doctr.* 4.1c; *Did.* 4.1c; *Can.* 12.1 is uncertain. (The corresponding parallel in *Epit.* 9 is Christianized, but it is a subsequent clarification.) Uncertain also is *Did.* 4.1b par. In both cases, I suppose that there has been some Christianizing. Ἐν ἐκκλησίᾳ in *Did.* 4.14 is probably an addition by the

Didachist (and is absent in *Barnabas, Doctrina apostolorum,* and *Epitome*). We see that the Jewish source has been revised (hesitantly at first, and then more extensively).

55 In the *Apostolic Constitutions* it is traceable to the *Didache.* The three principal arguments for supposing an originally altogether Jewish source (the numerous parallels in the Jewish milieu, the absence of anything specifically Christian, and the absence of the *sectio evangelica* in the parallel texts) were listed already by Ehrhard, *Altchristliche Litteratur,* 54.

56 Suggs ("Two Ways Tradition," 68) says that 1QS 3.18–4.26 is "a kind of homiletic exhortation concerned with group identity," and that *T. Ash.* 2 is a "school discourse in the interest of ethical instruction." The *Sitz im Leben* of the Two Ways teaching in *Barnabas* seems identical with that of the analogous teaching in 1QS, "an instrument of group identity. . . . an initiatory setting." The same is said to be true also of the *Doctrina apostolorum* (p. 71). The Two Ways tractate in the *Didache* is also said to be initiatory (p. 72). "In early Christianity the Two Spirits/Ways form had its primary (but not exclusive) Sitz in relation to initiation" (p. 72). Klaus Berger wishes to assign *Didache* 1–6 (i.e., the Two Ways tractate) to the genre of προτρεπτικὸς λόγος. Typical of this genre, according to Berger ("Hellenistische Gattungen," 1139), is also chap. 6. "The frame corresponds to that of a *protreptikos,* and its filling out with a 'way of life' is parenesis (*hypothetikos*)."

57 Cf. n. 47 above. In addition: Harnack, *Apostellehre,* 14, 29–30; Drews, "Untersuchungen," 54 (there is "a Jewish proselyte catechism at the basis" of the "Ur-Didache," and Paul knew it in a similarly "Christianized form"). The proposals in Adam, "Herkunft," again go especially far: "The Two Ways teaching could have originated in the Judaism of Adiabene as a handbook for the instruction of catechumens" (pp. 53–54). At p. 53 n. 97, Adam suggests that the Ananias known from Josephus *Ant.*

Table 3

Can. 12.1 (cf. Epit. 9)	Barn. 19.9, 10	Did. 4.1 (cf. Doctr. 4.1)
τὸν λαλοῦντά σοι τὸν λόγον τοῦ θεοῦ καὶ παραίτιόν σοι γινόμενον τῆς ζωῆς καὶ δόντα σοι τὴν ἐν κυρίῳ σφραγίδα ἀγαπήσεις[1] ὡς κόρην ὀφθαλμοῦ σου,	ἀγαπήσεις ὡς κόρην τοῦ ὀφθαλμοῦ σου πάντα τὸν λαλοῦντά σοι τὸν λόγον κυρίου.	τοῦ λαλοῦντός σοι τὸν λόγον τοῦ θεοῦ[6]
μνησθήσῃ δὲ[2] αὐτοῦ νύκτα καὶ ἡμέραν,[3] τιμήσεις[4] αὐτὸν ὡς τὸν[5] κύριον.	μνησθήσῃ ἡμέραν κρίσεως νυκτὸς καὶ ἡμέρας ...	μνησθήσῃ νυκτὸς καὶ ἡμέρας, τιμήσεις δὲ αὐτὸν ὡς κύριον.

[1] Epitome adds αὐτόν.
[2] Epitome omits δέ.
[3] Epitome: νυκτὸς κ. ἡμέρας.
[4] Epitome adds δέ.
[5] Epitome omits τόν.
[6] Doctrina: domini dei.

Table 3a

Can. 14	Barn. 21.2c–4, 6a
...	...
(1) ὡς ἔτι καιρός ἐστι καὶ οὐκ ἔχετε εἰς οὓς ἐργάζεσθε μεθ᾽ ἑαυτῶν, μὴ ἐκλίπητε ἐν μηδενί, ἐξουσίαν ἐὰν ἔχητε.	(2c) ἔχετε μεθ᾽ ἑαυτῶν, εἰς οὓς ἐργάζεσθε τὸ καλόν· μὴ ἐλλείπητε.
(2) Ἐγγὺς γὰρ ἡ ἡμέρα κυρίου ἐν ᾗ συναπολεῖται πάντα σὺν τῷ πονηρῷ· ἥξει γὰρ ὁ κύριος. καὶ ὁ μισθὸς αὐτοῦ.	(3) ἐγγὺς ἡ ἡμέρα, ἐν ᾗ συναπολεῖται πάντα τῷ πονηρῷ· ἐγγὺς ὁ κύριος καὶ ὁ μισθὸς αὐτοῦ.
(3) Ἑαυτῶν γίνεσθε νομοθέται, ἑαυτῶν γίνεσθε σύμβουλοι ἀγαθοί· θεοδίδακτοι· [φυλάξεις ἃ παρέλαβες μήτε προσθεὶς μήτε ὑφαιρῶν Cf. Epit. 11 (end)]	(4) ἔτι καὶ ἔτι ἐρωτῶ ὑμᾶς· ἑαυτῶν γίνεσθε νομοθέται ἀγαθοί, ἑαυτῶν μένετε σύμβουλοι πιστοί ... (6a) γίνεσθε δὲ θεοδίδακτοι ... Cf. Barn. 19.11b; Did. 4.13b; Doctr. 4.13b.

dubious.[58] In its original form the tractate may have had the function of a community rule for Jewish enthusiasts who gathered in the house of study[59] and who encouraged each other to mutual social support.[60] Nevertheless, some things point to a mission among the Gentiles.[61] The complete absence of any ritual prescriptions is very striking. They were either erased by the Christian revisers, or (and this may be more probable) they had no place in the group's moral catechism.[62]

3. The original form of the Jewish tractate of which we have been speaking has disappeared, but it lived on (in a variety of modifications) in ancient Christian literature. The first Christians (probably Jewish Christians at the outset) adopted this text and arrogated it to

20.34–96 was its author. For Adam, the basic document of chaps. 1–6 of the *Didache* was, in any case, a Jewish proselyte catechism from Adiabene (p. 54, and frequently).

58 The cautions in Rordorf and Tuilier (*Doctrine*, 31 n. 5) are correct. Cf. earlier Wilhelm Michaelis, "ὁδός," *TDNT* 5 (1967) 92, 99, and frequently; Wibbing, *Tugend- und Lasterkataloge*, 5–7.

59 Wengst (*Barnabasbrief*, 67) supposed that "the Two Ways teaching, like the traditions used in *Barnabas* in chaps. 2–16, may have had its *Sitz im Leben* in a school setting."

60 Cf. at 4.8 below.

61 Cf. 2.2.

62 P. Savi introduced the idea that the substance of the final part of the *Didache* (chap. 16) also came from the source, i.e., from the Jewish Two Ways text (*La dottrina degli apostoli: Ricerche critiche sull' origine del testo con una nota intorno all' eucaristia* [1893] 55–56 [not available to me; I quote from Ehrhard]; cf. Ehrhard, *Altchristliche Litteratur*, 51 and n. 1, as well as 55). This idea was frequently accepted later (sometimes with variations). I consider it, too, to be false. For this question, see the remarks below at 16.1. I also believe that, in the course of its Christianizing, the tractate acquired an (originally brief) eschatological epilogue. But this epilogue had its own history, and in any case *Didache* 16 does not come from it, but has replaced it.

63 Goodspeed ("Doctrina," 234) says, with reference to the tractate, "The evidence for its literary influence is much greater than is that for the influence of *Didache*."

64 *Barnabas* often has the corresponding parallels in a different sequence. In Barnabas, the *teknon* sayings found in the *Canons* and known also to the *Epitome*

themselves, and from then on it has had a historical impact within Christian literature.[63] Whether that history can still be clarified in all its details is a difficult question.

One of the fundamental problems that emerges in this connection is as follows: the *Canons of the Apostles/Epitome* to a large extent parallel *Didache/ Doctrina apostolorum* against *Barnabas*.[64] Nonetheless, the proemium to the *Canons*[65] (χαίρετε υἱοί κτλ.) recalls *Barn.* 1.1 (omitted in *Didache/Doctrina*);[66] *Can.* 4.2, καὶ δοξάσεις τὸν λυτρωσάμενόν σε ἐκ θανάτου ("You will glorify the one who has redeemed you from death"),[67] recalls *Barn.* 19.2 (against *Didache/ Doctrina*, where the expression is missing);[68] *Can.* 12.1 (*Epit.* 9) contains a text that deviates from *Didache/ Doctrina*, wherein the characteristic expression ὡς κόρην ὀφθαλμοῦ σου ("as the pupil of your eye") again recalls *Barnabas* (19.9): cf. table 3. Finally, *Can.* 14 (omitted in *Epitome*) matches *Barn.* 21.2c–4, 6a against *Didache* and *Doctrina* (cf. table 3a).

It would be difficult to persuade oneself that *Can.* 14 stems directly from *Barnabas*. The text in the *Canons* has a more immediate application;[69] it seems more likely that the epilogues in *Canon* 14 and *Barnabas* 21 are traceable to a common source. The text of the *Canons* is probably based on the end of one of the recensions of the Two Ways tractate, and a

similar recension was read by *Barnabas* (without φυλάξεις κτλ., which was not at the end of this author's source, or in that used by the *Canons*);[70] but *Barnabas* made changes and expansions. Similarly, the agreements between the *Canons* (and once *Epitome* as well) and *Barnabas* against *Didache/Doctrina* mentioned above can scarcely be traced to a use of *Barnabas* as an additional source by the *Canons*, or by it and *Epitome*, or by their common source. In view of *Can.* 12.1 (*Epit.* 9) it is impossible to understand why *Barnabas*, of all documents, should have been used at this point.[71] The problem, rather, is evidently that the *Canons* (and the *Epitome*) move largely in tandem with *Didache/Doctrina*, in both matter and structure, but in the rare cases mentioned above the *Canons* (and, in one instance, *Epitome* as well) corresponds to *Barnabas* against *Didache* and *Doctrina*. In my opinion, that suggests the idea that the text of the tractate for all four (or five) witnesses (*Barnabas*, *Didache*, *Doctrina*, the *Canons*, and the *Epitome*, or the common source of the last two) should ultimately be traced to a common primitive form (B), which was copied

---

are missing (although it is true that the *teknon* apostrophe is also lacking in the *Epitome*). That the "way of death" is absent from the *Canons* and *Epitome* (and the *Canons* also lacks the conclusion of the "way of life") does not disprove the hypothesis of a close relationship between *Didache/Doctrina apostolorum* and the *Canons/Epitome*. The reasons for these omissions have been discussed above. In addition, the fact that in *Epit.* 10–11 the material found in *Didache* 4 is in a different order does not destroy the above hypothesis.

65 It was especially Hennecke ("Grundschrift," 62–69) who pointed out the combination *Barnabas/Canons* against *Didache/Doctrina*, although he arrives at a different *stemma* by this process than I do.

66 The corresponding material is also lacking in the *Epitome*. In addition, cf. the suggestions by Goodspeed, "Doctrina," 232–33. According to Goodspeed, the opening greeting in the *Canons* goes back to *Barnabas*. That is not true, however, of the remainder of the document.

67 This expression is missing from the *Epitome*.

68 That *Canons*, after τὸν ποιήσαντά σε, also adds ἐξ ὅλης σου καρδίας (as does *Epitome*), something that is paralleled neither in *Didache* and *Doctrina apostolorum* nor in *Barnabas,* says nothing about the dependency relationships. It is a biblical reminiscence (very similar to *Synt. doctr.* 1.4 or *Fides patr.* 3: cf. *PG* 28.1639C).

69 Hennecke, "Grundschrift," 65.

70 *Didache* and *Doctrina apostolorum* have the text in 4.13, which I believe to be its original location. The redactor of the *Epitome* followed his source up to the text corresponding to *Did.* 4.13, and accordingly had φυλάξῃ δέ κτλ. as a sensible conclusion. The *Canons* at first did not have this passage, because the quotation from the Two Ways tractate broke off for the present, at the text corresponding to *Did.* 4.8. Therefore, *Canons* transferred an appropriate text to the conclusion of the epilogue.

71 Wengst (*Didache*, 10 n. 23) supposes that the *Canons* knew *Barnabas*, while *Epitome* was independent of *Barnabas*. Hence the parallels in *Can.* 12.1/*Epit.* 9 (cf. *Barn.* 19.9) would come not from *Barnabas* but

directly by *Barnabas*,[72] whereas the rest are dependent on an archetype (C) derived from (B), and, more precisely, *Didache* and *Doctrina* are taken from a sub-archetype (C^1), and the *Canons* and *Epitome* from another sub-archetype (C^2). Using this model (for which, see the hypothetical *stemma* in table 4) as a working hypothesis, one can incorporate the observations already made above.

If these observations are accurate, we should picture the genealogy of the Two Ways tractate more or less as follows:

(a) In the beginning was a Jewish "primitive form" (A) that has been lost.[73] Even this "primitive form" was not a unified composition, however, but rather a compilation.[74]

(b) Dependent on (A) was the first Christian recension (B). The Christianizing of the material in this first recension was probably very superficial; still, the redactor probably added an eschatological epilogue with Christian character (to replace the original, Jewish eschatological epilogue). Materially, this epilogue still forms the basis of *Canon* 14 and *Barnabas* 21.

(c) Dependent on this first recension is *Barnabas* 18–21. The author of *Barnabas* sometimes copied his source very freely and (with some exceptions) represented the order of the source less perfectly than did some later derivations.[75] In addition, *Barnabas* has incorporated the Two Ways tractate at the end of his text. The introductory χαίρετε υἱοί κτλ. was probably also something he took from his source, and he

Table 4

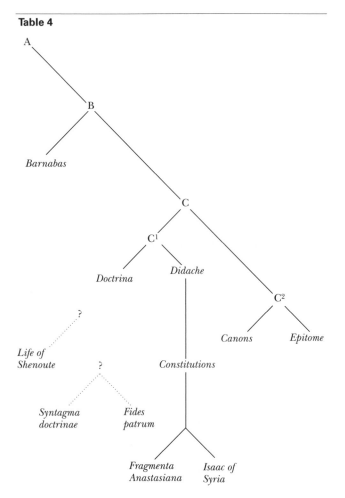

---

from a recension of the Two Ways tractate. But is it not more plausible to explain the parallels between *Canons/Epitome/Barnabas* against *Didache* and *Canons/Barnabas* against *Didache* in the same way?

72 While, at the same time (with some exceptions), he altered and rearranged the sequence.

73 The reference is to the "primitive form" of the Two Ways tractate whose existence we have deduced, and to which can be traced, either directly or indirectly, all the filiated documents to be named. One can also go behind "A" to a "pattern" that would include 1QS 3.18–4.26 and *T. Ash.* 1–5. Cf. Barnard, "Later History," 107; Suggs, "Two Ways Tradition," 62–63.

74 It would have consisted of (1) an introduction with fundamental rule, (2) a list of prohibitions, (3) the *anawim* sayings, and (4) sayings regarding social relationships, including a household code; all these

sections would have been redacted to form a "way of life," and to them was added (5) a vice list that was formed into the "way of death." The whole was concluded (6) with an eschatological epilogue. The *teknon* sayings were added in Christian times, even though materially (apart from a few additions) they would have been Jewish in origin. In a clever analysis, Audet (*Didachè*, 308–20) has attempted to sketch a different primitive form.

75 The alternative supposition that it was only the redactor of C who put the text in the order we find in *Didache*, etc., is not as good. The sections of the Two Ways tractate as they are sequenced in the *Didache* belong to different genres; that kind of order would scarcely be created at a subsequent time. On this, cf. the suggestions of Audet, *Didachè*, 320. Differing is, e.g., Kraft (*Didache*, 12), who is inclined to think "that the Doctrina-Didache form

has displaced this sentence to the beginning of his entire work.

(d) More important for the subsequent history was a second Christian recension of the tractate (C). It intervened much more strongly in the tradition. This redactor (1) transformed the traditional basic commandment into a double love commandment;[76] (2) added the *teknon* sayings; (3) made an additional, minor expansion of the text. Dependent on (C) is a sub-archetype (C[1]), characterized by the alteration of the eschatological epilogue. Dependent in turn on (C[1]) are the *Doctrina apostolorum*[77] and the *Didache*. The author of the *Doctrina* appears to have reproduced his source with overall fidelity. *Doctr.* 6.6 was first added in the Latin text tradition. The redactor of the *Didache* dealt quite differently with the source; this will be discussed more fully below.[78]

(e) A later recension (C[2]) proceeded to put the material of the Two Ways tractate in the mouths of the (eleven) apostles: that is, it stylized the whole document as apostolic teaching. In the process, the text of the "way of death" was eliminated. Dependent on this recension (but independent of one another) are the *Canons of the Apostles* and the *Epitome*; *Epit.* 11 contains the conclusion of the "way of life," which is missing from the *Canons*, while — in contrary fashion — the *Canons* has substantially preserved the old eschatological material in chap. 14, which is missing from the *Epitome*. (We need not discuss the further differences between the *Canons* and the *Epitome* here.)

(f) Finally, the material of the Two Ways tractate (meanwhile long since part of Christian tradition) migrated, not accidentally, into particular segments of monastic literature (*Life of Shenoute, Syntagma doctrinae*) and the *Fides patrum*. I do not presume to give information on the more precise genealogical context of these texts (apart from the fact that I judge them to be late filiations from recension C).

Of course, the presentation attempted here remains purely hypothetical.[79] It serves merely as a working hypothesis. What seems to me fundamentally important is only that we should posit an independent, originally Jewish source document that existed in a variety of recensions. In one of those recensions, it was available as a source for the Didachist.

The fate suffered by the Two Ways tractate in its Latin translation in the West is striking. A version of the tractate in Latin survived in the West into the eleventh century (under the title *[De] doctrina apostolorum*). We cannot deal here with the influence of this version on Latin church literature.[80] It is probable that the tractate was even used by Boniface in connection with prebaptismal catechesis. A new investigation of the history of our tractate in the Latin church might be desirable.[81]

---

of especially the Way of Life has been extensively reworked with respect to sequence." Cf. also Wengst, *Didache*, 21 n. 77, and further at 92 n. 2; idem, *Barnabasbrief*, 59ff.

76 This probably already reveals Christian motivation; see below, on *Did.* 1.2.

77 More precisely the Greek original, the Latin translation of which we have in *Doctrina apostolorum*.

78 Literarily dependent on the *Didache* is the *Apostolic Constitutions*, on which depend *Fragmenta Anastasiana* and Isaac of Syria, directly or indirectly.

79 Cf. the agreements and disagreements with this presentation in Giet, *L'Énigme*, passim (see merely the *stemma*, p. 152); and Wengst, *Didache*, 7–14,

20–23; cf. the *stemma* on p. 22.

80 Schlecht, *Doctrina*, 43, 75–91 (but under the false assumption that the two Latin mss. f and g are Latin versions of the *Didache*); further Rordorf and Tuilier, *Doctrine*, 206.

81 The more precise relationship between our tractate and the *Rule of the Master* and the *Rule of Benedict* would need to be investigated again in this connection. On this, see above, p. 14 n. 92.

7. Reconstruction of the Origin of the *Didache*

a. The Sources and Their Redaction by the Didachist

The following reflections presume that the *Didache* represents an original writing in Greek. Adam, who thought it possible to detect a Syrian text stage, was unwilling to decide whether the *Didache* was originally written in Greek or Syriac, or whether the document had existed from the beginning in two versions (Greek and Syriac).[1] These proposals have (I think rightly) met with no assent. We may reckon with an early Syriac version of the *Didache* (although it has disappeared),[2] but the original text of the *Didache* could scarcely have been anything but Greek, and any Syriac version could only have been a subsequent translation. These considerations are the starting point for the question of the *Didache*'s origins, which remains to be discussed below.[3] How should we picture this more precisely?

I do not share Audet's opinion[4] that we should imagine three stages or levels in the composition of the work:[5] one and the same (apostolic) author (Audet, *Didachè*, 119–20)[6] would first have completed 1.1–11.2,[7] and then added 11.3–16.8[8] in a second phase.[9] Finally, a contemporary (apostolic? cf. Audet, *Didachè*, 120) interpolator altered the work. To this interpolator we owe the passages 1.3b–2.1 (except for 1.4a), as well as 6.2–3; 7.2–4; and 13.3, 5–7.[10] In my opinion, not only the early point of origin (in apostolic times) is false in this conception, but also (and this is of special interest to us in this section) the model of the evolution of the work in stages at the hand of one and the same author (to whom is added the interpolator).[11] In contrast, the initiative of Richardson, Mattioli, Giet, Rordorf and Tuilier, and Wengst appears to me correct in principle. These scholars draw a fundamental distinction (although differing in details) between a predidachistic tradition and didachistic redaction, and they make an attempt to deduce the history of the writing's origins.[12] It appears to me only that the notion of a *double* redaction shared

---

1 "Herkunft," 35.

2 See above, §2.

3 I am not persuaded by Adam's historical location of the *Didache*. Adam points (I think correctly) to the region of Syria, but wishes to locate the addressees of the writing more precisely in eastern Syria, in Adiabene. He adduces a series of varied arguments to support this position. For him, the history of the *Didache*'s origins is connected to the primitive history of the church in eastern Syria. The *Didache* thus appears as "the church book for the recently missionized communities in eastern Syria" ("Herkunft," 60). "We may suggest that the *Didache*, in its original form, was written in Pella between 90 and 100, for the purpose of serving the young east Syrian communities as a guideline for structuring their congregations. In this conclusion, the limitation of the purpose is a thesis with a high degree of probability; the temporal location ranks as a well-grounded hypothesis; but the determination of the place of writing remains in the realm of hypothetical suggestion" (p. 70). In reality, however, the precise location of the addressees in Adiabene is entirely arbitrary. The same is true of the hypothesis that the document was written in Pella.

4 Audet, *Didachè*, 104–20.

5 The idea that the *Didache* was composed in a series of stages is quite old. J. Vernon Bartlet ("The Didache Reconsidered," *JTS* 22 [1921] 246–49) suggested that the *Didache* had progressed through two editions, an *editio princeps* and an *editio altera, emendata et glossata*. In his *Church-Life and Church-Order*

during the First Four Centuries with Special Reference to the Early Eastern Church-Orders (ed. Cecil J. Cadoux; Oxford: Blackwell, 1943) 35–36, 53–54, Bartlet further developed this suggestion. A survey of the assignment of passages to three stages of development (according to Bartlet's picture of the growth of the *Didache*) was given by C. J. Cadoux in Bartlet, *Church-Order*, 55. With a great deal of fantasy, Greiff (*Pascharituale*, 139, and frequently elsewhere) supports three versions of this writing, one of them a church order (chaps. 1–16), another a ritual book (chaps. 1–10).

6 "Apostle" is used in the broader sense, not as one of the Twelve.

7 Apart from the interpolations that Audet attributes to a later hand. More on this immediately below. To be more precise, the first level would have contained 1.1–3a; 2.2–5.2; 7.1; 8.1–11.2.

8 Again without the later interpolations, thus more precisely 11.3–13.2 and 14.1–16.8.

9 The gospel to which the *Didache* refers in the second part would have been written between the first and second phases.

10 Audet thus distinguishes between D 1 and D 2 (the same author), and the interpolator. He counts 1.4a; 7.1b; and 13.4 as subsequent glosses.

11 Against Audet's presentation are Nautin, "Composition," 193–95 (with argumentation that is sometimes questionable, but on the whole persuasive); and Rordorf and Tuilier, *Doctrine*, 19. Kraft's proposal is immeasurably more complicated. He investigates the "stages of development" behind the

by Giet and Rordorf and Tuilier is unnecessary;[13] I see no reason for positing it.[14] In my opinion, the positing of a single redaction is sufficient to solve the existing problems.[15] The resulting picture is as follows: At the beginning of the second century (more will be said below about the temporal location), a Christian author living in an originally Jewish-Christian milieu created, by

compilation, a kind of book of rules that is our *Didache*. Thus we should make a basic distinction between the sources (literary sources and oral traditions) and the redactor or compiler of the book.[16] (Of course, the later glosses are not part of the history of the book's origins, but belong to the story of its textual transmission.) The sources available to the Didachist were as follows:

Didache. The result is that the book becomes a complicated literary conglomerate (Kraft, *Didache*, 63–65), and the author appears merely as an editor, that is, simply an arranger at a particular stage of development. Kraft speaks (*Didache*, 1–2) very instructively of the genre of "evolved literature" to which the *Didache* is said to belong, and rightly describes the author of the *Didache* as an "author-editor." Nevertheless, it seems to me that Kraft underestimates the literary contribution of the Didachist to the writing.

12 Richardson ("Teaching," 164–66) develops a kind of two-source theory: the compiler had two older literary sources, the Two Ways tractate and a church order. Richardson does not attempt to make a more precise assignment of chaps. 7–15 to the source or the redaction, but he considers chap. 16 probably redactional (as well as the *sectio evangelica*). Mattioli distinguishes between the work of the Didachist and his sources, namely: the Two Ways tractate with an apocalyptic appendix, NT material, and the eucharistic prayers (Richardson, "Teaching," 33, and passim). For Wengst and Schöllgen, see immediately below.

13 Rordorf and Tuilier, *Doctrine*, 49, 63, 92–94: an unknown author (= the first redactor) took over the Two Ways tractate and altered it through additions (1.3b–2.1 and 6.2–3), forming chaps. 1–6. The same redactor also took over chaps. 7–10, archaic liturgical traditions from the Syrian church (7.2–3, 4b are from the hand of the redactor). It was probably the same author (= the first redactor) who also created chaps. 11–13, for which he also had old tradition at his disposal. Chaps. 14–15 could not be from the same author, however, because they presume a different set of canonical preconditions. These chapters should be traced to a second redactor, and this may also be true of chap. 16 (where again old tradition has been reworked). Chaps. 14–16 consequently come from a later period. The Didachist also appears in Giet's work (*L'Énigme*, passim) as a redactor in possession of a variety of old source materials. But Giet recognizes postdidachist materials in addition. Chap. 15 is a later addition (p. 243), and chap. 16 may also stem from the same postdidachist author (Giet, *L'Énigme*, 256).

14 I have arrived at a different position from that of Rordorf and Tuilier because I (unlike them) do not regard chaps. 11–13 as a literary unit. As indicated in the discussion below, I consider 11.4–12 to be a predidachistic tradition, and chaps. 11–13 not to be a literary unit; instead, I believe that chaps. 12–15 constitute both a tradition-historical and literary unit. The consequence of this is that I can avoid the awkward positing of a second redaction.

15 A single redaction is also posited by Richardson and Mattioli (see n. 12 above). That these two authors differ somewhat in their estimation of the state of the sources, and so differ also from my opinion, is a separate issue. The positing of a double redaction is now rejected also by Wengst (*Didache*, 17 n. 57; cf. 20–23). Still, Wengst differs from my opinion in that he regards chaps. 11–15 as a literary unit (p. 23). Against Rordorf and Tuilier's hypothesis, see now also Schöllgen, "Church Order," 67–69.

16 Cf. Wengst, *Didache*, 20–23. Schöllgen ("Church Order," 64–67) now offers a separate opinion. He opposes "arbitrariness" in "division of sources" (p. 65) and prefers to recognize only old pieces of tradition that were worked together by the author.

Of course, one comes to a completely different conclusion if one regards the *Didache* as a deliberate *literary fiction*. This is the opinion of some English-speaking scholars. The forerunner was Robinson, who, in "Problem," 339–56, undertook a first foray in this direction. The thesis was further developed in his Donnellan Lectures in 1920 (*Didache*, esp. 43–68). Part of the subsequent edition of this book appeared as "Barnabas and the Didache," 113–46, 225–48. For Robinson, the *Didache* is the camouflage of a later author who artificially placed himself in the apostolic period and imitated (using copious amounts of NT material) and faked apostolicity. (The material in the Two Ways part is said to come from the *Epistle of Barnabas*.) The liturgical formulae and the canonical situation that is presupposed are, correspondingly, the products of fantasy. Cf. further Richard H. Connolly, "The *Didache* and Montanism," *DRev* 55 (1937) 339–47 (the *Didache* as a proto-Montanist work); Middleton, "Eucharistic Prayers," 259, 267; William Telfer, "The 'Plot' of the *Didache*," *JTS* 45 (1944) 141–42 (the author

- a superficially Christianized, originally Jewish document *de duabus viis*;
- a (written or oral) archaic liturgical tradition concerning baptism and Eucharist;[17]
- a (probably written) also archaic tradition concerning the reception of itinerant charismatics;[18] and finally:
- a brief apocalyptic description of the events of the end time.[19]

This material the Didachist compiled to form a whole (the Didachist is the compiler), expanded it by means of insertions, and interpreted it (the Didachist is the redactor). Particularly in the final section (before the apocalypse, i.e., in chaps. 12–15) the Didachist expanded the work with text from his own pen (the Didachist is, to a modest degree, also an independent author). He had two principal tendencies: on the one hand, he wished to create a book of rules for his communities; on the other hand, at the same time he did not wish to create something of his own but to hand on the traditions of his church (which amounted primarily to Jewish-Christian traditions).[20] That it was necessary, in the process, to augment the tradition to accommodate the changes that

had taken place in the situation of the churches, or, as far as the Two Ways section is concerned, expressly to bring the tradition to the level of specifically Christian eschatological awareness, is another issue.[21]

In what follows, I will show (1) how the Didachist dealt with his sources in detail, and (2) what can be said about the possible New Testament sources of the *Didache*.

1. The Didachist placed the *Two Ways tractate* at the beginning of his book, commencing the citation at 1.1 without any introduction or preparation. The quotation of this source extends from 1.1 to 6.1;[22] nevertheless, the Didachist (as redactor) made additions to the tractate that gave it a new meaning:

- He reinterpreted the older tractate as a baptismal catechesis ($\tau\alpha\hat{\upsilon}\tau\alpha$ $\pi\acute{\alpha}\nu\tau\alpha$ $\pi\rho\sigma\epsilon\iota\pi\acute{\sigma}\nu\tau\epsilon\varsigma$, $\beta\alpha\pi\tau\acute{\iota}\sigma\alpha\tau\epsilon$ in 7.1 is redactional).
- He more strongly Christianized the tractate, which had already been superficially Christianized, by inserting in 1.3b–6 (in the so-called *sectio evangelica*) typically Christian passages from the Jesus tradition as well as other traditions available to him (the quotation in 1.6 is also an addition by the Didachist to an existing tradition);[23] all of which places the Two

---

fabricated his writing "to be the work of the apostolic council of Jerusalem," 142). The thesis is systematically developed by Vokes, *Riddle*, passim: the author of the *Didache* is said to be a moderate Montanist, and his work "is an attempt to express Montanism in apostolic terms" (p. 144). "The *Didache* is Montanism dressed up in an ill-fitting New Testament garb" (p. 172). (Vokes, however, later lost faith in his Montanism thesis: Rordorf, "Two Ways," 150 n. 18.) In the tradition of the fiction hypothesis is also Layton, in his study of the *sectio evangelica* ("Sources," 343–83). The following objections may be raised against the fiction hypothesis: (1) It is usually combined with the supposition that *Didache* 1–6 depends on *Barnabas* 18–20; this supposition is false, however, as shown above. (2) The liturgical parts of the *Didache* are ancient and are not fictional; they differ even in their language from the diction of the Didachist. (3) In chaps. 11–16 there are two different layers, one predidachist and one redactional; this alone destroys the fiction hypothesis.

17   This is the common opinion today, e.g.: Vööbus, *Liturgical Traditions*, passim, esp. 169–70; Rordorf and Tuilier, *Doctrine*, 92–93; Wengst, *Didache*, 23.

18   I believe I have shown ("Itinerant Radicalism," 323–27) that there is predidachistic tradition in 11.4–12, which was partly modified by the Didachist

in chaps. 12–13. See below. Now to the contrary: Wengst, *Didache*, 23 n. 83.

19   I am inclined to trace 16.3–8 also to a written source. Wengst, *Didache*, 23: "Chapter 16 contains a little apocalypse that, at least in its individual components, is altogether traditional. Whether it was found by the Didachist as a complete whole or whether he himself put it together is a question that must remain open."

20   Stempel ("Lehrer," 214–15) sees the Didachist as $\delta\iota\delta\acute{\alpha}\sigma\kappa\alpha\lambda\sigma\varsigma$. De Halleux ("Ministers," 319) desires to see in the Didachist a noncharismatic $\delta\iota\delta\acute{\alpha}\sigma\kappa\alpha$-$\lambda\sigma\varsigma$, and emphasizes (certainly correctly) his attitude of fidelity to tradition.

21   Unlike the representatives of the fiction hypothesis, I do indeed believe that both the sources and the redaction of the *Didache* reflect real situations.

22   It is possible that at 5.1 the redactor altered the source by rearranging part of it.

23   Also redactional is $\kappa\alpha\tau\grave{\alpha}$ $\tau\grave{\eta}\nu$ $\dot{\epsilon}\nu\tau\sigma\lambda\acute{\eta}\nu$ in 1.5, and $\dot{\epsilon}\nu$ $\dot{\epsilon}\kappa\kappa\lambda\eta\sigma\acute{\iota}\alpha$ in 4.14 is probably didachistic redaction as well.

24   This problem did not exist for the Two Ways tractate. The underlying tradition considers the demands of the Jewish catechism as obviously capable of being fulfilled. They have no eschatological character.

Ways tractate in an entirely different light: it is now clear to the readers that they are confronted not only with a rigorous Jewish or Jewish-Christian moral catechism, but beyond that with what could be called (in our terms) the eschatological demands of Jesus — although, certainly, the problem of the possibility of fulfilling such demands immediately arises here as well.[24] The Didachist solves the problem with the aid of the concept of τέλειος (καὶ ἔσῃ τέλειος in 1.4 is his addition to the sayings tradition), which recurs in 6.2 (again from the pen of the Didachist):[25] the fulfillment of Jesus' paradoxical demands is a matter for the τέλειος ("perfect").[26]

- The insertion of the *sectio evangelica*, however, caused the Didachist to make another alteration. Now the introduction in 1.2 and the additions in 1.3b–6 are seen to be (or we must understand them to be) πρώτη ἐντολή, and he causes the further text of the tractate to follow from 2.2, calling it explicitly δευτέρα ἐντολὴ τῆς διδαχῆς (2.1 is redactional). With this, the significance of the *sectio evangelica* for the understanding of the whole is once again underscored. One cannot call this division into πρώτη and δευτέρα ἐντολή an especially skillful arrangement, but it should be sufficiently clear what the Didachist intended to achieve by it.

- At the end of the text available to him, the Didachist made another redactional intervention: the tractate ended (as we can now see from *Doctrina apostolorum*) with a parenetic epilogue, including an eschatological prospect; the Didachist retained only the beginning (5.2 [end], and 6.1), eliminating the rest, or that part that he could not use, and replacing it with an appendix from his own pen (6.2–3). As a result, 6.2 (as I have already shown) acquires a function with respect to the interpretation that the Didachist gives to the demands of the *sectio*; 6.3, in contrast, touches a special problem that was not in the source but that the Didachist wanted to cover.

So much for the redactional interventions in the reproduction of the tractate. It is difficult to decide whether the Didachist made other interventions. The double love commandment in 1.2, as well as 4.1b, 4.1c, and the conclusion of 4.10 probably belong to the predidachistic recension of the tractate.

In 7.1 the Didachist begins to reproduce the *liturgical tradition* of his church (7.1–10.7). It is possible that he already had a fixed, written "agenda" as a source. What is clear is that he expanded his tradition by commenting on it. The detailed assignment of the text to tradition or redaction, however, is not always easy. The baptismal formula and the rule for baptismal fasting (7.4a) are taken from the tradition; I am inclined also to regard the rubric (περὶ δὲ τοῦ βαπτίσματος, οὕτω βαπτίσατε in 7.1a) as a quotation from the source (if we really can suppose that a written source was in use). I have already noted that 7.1b (ταῦτα πάντα προειπόντες, βαπτίσατε, "Having said all of these things, baptize") is redactional. I consider vv. 2–3 redactional as well. The Didachist here interprets and corrects the Jewish-Christian demand of his tradition, according to which baptism should be done ἐν ὕδατι ζῶντι ("in living water"). Probably redactional also is 7.4b.[27] What the Didachist writes in 8.1 about fasting in general certainly stems from tradition. The same is true of 8.2–3, where only the reference to the gospel in 8.2 (ὡς ἐκέλευσεν ὁ κύριος ἐν τῷ εὐαγγελίῳ αὐτοῦ, "As the Lord commanded in his gospel") is the work of the Didachist. We will encounter other, similar references to the "gospel" later. The table prayers (9.2–4) certainly come from tradition; and if one may suppose a written source, the rubrics (9.1, 2a, 3a) must stem from it. In contrast, I consider 9.5 redactional. In καὶ γὰρ περὶ τούτου εἴρηκεν ὁ κύριος ("For also concerning this the Lord has said"), the Didachist betrays his presence (cf. 1.6); v. 5a can also be traced to him. The prayers after the meal (10.1–7) are certainly another old liturgical tradition, but it is difficult to determine where the end point comes. Probably

---

25   See the respective passages in the commentary.
26   Willy Rordorf, in particular, has instructively shown that the Didachist desires to establish a connection between the *sectio evangelica* and his remarks in 6.2: cf. "Tradition apostolique," 108–9, and Rordorf and Tuilier, *Doctrine*, 32–33.
27   Rordorf, "Baptism," 212–22: 6.3 (except for the concession) and 7.1 belong to the *Didache*'s liturgical source (in 7.1, ταῦτα πάντα προειπόντες is redactional). Redactional also are 7.2–3 and 7.4b. Cf. Rordorf and Tuilier, *Doctrine*, 92–93.

the tradition extends to 10.6 (inclusive), and only 10.7 again belongs to the Didachistic redaction. But we will have to treat this difficult question below.

The analysis is easier in the "*canon law*" part of the *Didache*. I believe that this part is based on an old tradition (which I now think was written) that forms the core of it (11.4–12) and in which the Didachist may have intervened redactionally in v. 11. Everything else is from his pen (11.1–2, 3; 12.1–15.4),[28] with only 13.4 to be bracketed as a later gloss. Here the Didachist seeks throughout to apply the motifs of his old tradition to the new situation in which he finds himself; here, and here alone, does the Didachist emerge in lengthy passages as a genuine "author."[29]

Finally, the Didachist desired to close his writing with an *eschatological conclusion*. I infer that the special impulse to do this grew out of the conclusion of the "basic document," the Two Ways tractate. There is such an eschatological conclusion now in chap. 16, but it is immediately obvious that 16.3–8, which represent a little apocalypse, are a separate unit. I believe that here, too, the Didachist is quoting an older tradition (probably written). Thus I consider 16.3–6, 8 the quotation of an old, predidachistic apocalypse, and 16.7 an addition by the didachistic redaction.[30] An assessment of 16.1–2 is more difficult. In any case, the Didachist is not formulating with entire freedom here either: the logion in 16.1 derives ultimately from the Jesus tradition, and the admonition in 16.2 has parallels elsewhere, although one need not suppose that there was a written source.

To sum up: (1) Traceable to the Didachist are: the additions to the *sectio evangelica* (καὶ ἔσῃ τέλειος 1.4; κατὰ τὴν ἐντολήν 1.5; and the quotation without introduction in 1.6); also the transition in 2.1; perhaps ἐν ἐκκλησίᾳ in 4.14, but in any case 6.2–3 (as

didachistic conclusion to the Two Ways tractate). Also from the Didachist are ταῦτα πάντα προειπόντες, βαπτίσατε in 7.1b; 7.2–3; 7.4b; the reference to the gospel in 8.2b; 9.5 and 10.7; the transition in 11.1–2; the superscription in 11.3 (with reference to the gospel); from the subsequent piece of tradition, possibly δεδοκιμασμένος ἀληθινός in 11.11 (or the entire verse?). Didachistic are also 12.1–15.4 (without 13.4) and 16.7. In addition, there are passages formulated by the Didachist, even though based on tradition. (2) Characteristic of the Didachist's *language*[31] are expressions like προσέχειν ἀπό (6.3; 12.5); διδόναι κατὰ τὴν ἐντολήν (1.5; 13.5, 7); τέλειος εἶναι (1.4; 6.2); δύνασθαι (6.2, 3; 7.2); also typical of him are the expressions he uses to introduce quotations (including those from Scripture): ἀλλὰ καὶ περὶ τούτου δὲ εἴρηται (1.6); καὶ γὰρ περὶ τούτου εἴρηκεν ὁ κύριος (9.5); ἀλλ' ὡς ἐρρέθη (16.7). (3) The redactor is a *traditionalist*. He makes an effort to recur to traditions, but is equally anxious to apply the traditions (here I am referring to liturgy and law) to the circumstances of his own time; the Jewish-Christian moral catechism in chaps. 1–6 is "eschatologized" (*sit venia verbo*) by additions. (4) The constant effort to secure what is said by recourse to the γραφή or to the κύριος (who speaks in the "gospel") is striking: 1.6; 8.2; 9.5; 11.3; 14.3; 15.3, 4; 16.7.[32]

In all this, the redactional activity of the Didachist is evident. It is clear what he has in mind, and what he intends to accomplish. There is, however, still a question to be discussed in this connection, one we previously set aside: that of the possible use of New Testament texts in the *Didache*. We now turn to this issue.

2. The question of the possible *use of New Testament texts in the Didache* is especially complicated.[33] Are any

28 To the contrary now Wengst, *Didache*, 23.
29 Characteristic for him is the reference to the "gospel" in 15.3 and 4.
30 The scriptural proof (cf. also 1.6 and 14.3, both didachistic) is redactional.
31 In Muilenburg, *Literary Relations*, 137–39, some correct information is combined with a great deal that is misleading.
32 The OT is cited explicitly, in the form of a reflective quotation, only twice in the *Didache* (cf. Hagner, *Use*, 25). Both quotations are attributable to the redactor: 14.3 = Mal 1:11, 14; 16.7 = Zech 14.5. A

possible third citation is 1.6, although it is uncertain what text is cited. See below, ad loc.
33 Ehrhard, *Altchristliche Litteratur*, 58–60; Harnack, "Prolegomena," 69–81; Schaff, *Church Manual*, 78–94; Lake, "Didache," 24–36; Robinson, "Problem," 340–42; idem, *Didache,* 48–68; idem, "Barnabas and the Didache," 227–38; MacLean, "Introduction," xx–xxii; Greiff, *Paschariuale*, 163–94; Muilenburg, *Literary Relations*, 73–75; Middleton, "Eucharistic Prayers," 249, 266; Vokes, *Riddle*, 93–119; Goodspeed, "Doctrina," 231, and frequently; Erwin R. Goodenough, "John a

New Testament texts used, and if so, which? At an early stage attention was drawn primarily to quotations from the Gospel of Matthew, or mixed texts from Matthew and Luke.[34] In addition, dependence on the Gospel of John has occasionally been suggested.[35] There have also been suspicions of literary dependence on individual

Primitive Gospel," *JBL* 64 (1945) 174–75; Johnson, *Motive*, 112, and passim; Massaux, *Influence*, 3.144–82; Moule, "Note," 240–43; Richardson, "Teaching," 163–66; Koester, *Synoptische Überlieferung*, 159–60, and passim; Audet, *Didachè*, 166–86; Glover, "Quotations," 12–29; Bosio, *Padri apostolici*, 10–11; Lucien Cerfaux, "La multiplication des pains dans la liturgie de la Didachè," *Bib* 40 (1959) 943–58; Barnard, "Later History," 99 n. 2; Layton, "Sources," 343–72; Hagner, *Use*, 280; Eduard Schweizer, *Matthäus und seine Gemeinde* (SBS 71; Stuttgart: KBW, 1974) 140–41, 164–65; Aono, *Entwicklung*, 174–89; Rordorf and Tuilier, *Doctrine*, 83–91; Rordorf, "Transmission textuelle," 499–513; Kloppenborg, "Matthaean Tradition," 54–67; Wengst, *Didache*, 24–31.

34   For early scholarship: Ehrhard, *Altchristliche Litteratur*, 58–60. I mention only selected works from more recent scholarship. The question is treated at length by Massaux, *Influence*, 3.145: in all four passages where the key word εὐαγγέλιον occurs (8.2; 11.3; 15.3, 4), it reveals "a definite literary contact" with the Gospel of Matthew (3.145). "Gospel" in the *Didache* means the Gospel of Matthew (which does not exclude the possibility that the author also knows and makes use of Lukan and other NT materials); but "the gospel" as such for this author is Matthew. Cf. also 3.176, 179. Massaux (*Influence*, 3.144–76) attempts to demonstrate in detail that the *Didache* is, in fact, literarily dependent on Matthew in a great many places. According to Massaux (*Influence*, 3.180), the way in which the *Didache* quotes the First Gospel recalls Justin's manner of citation. For Massaux, the *Didache* as a whole seems "like a catechetical summary of the First Gospel" (*Influence*, 3.179, 180). See further Bosio, *Padri apostolici*, 11; Johnson, "Motive," 112, and passim: the *Didache* is dependent on Matthew and Luke (and Acts as well). "Matthew was his favorite" (p. 112); the mixtures of Matthew and Luke are explained by quotation from memory (p. 112 n. 14). Richardson ("Teaching," 163, 165–66) distinguishes between sources and redaction; in the *sectio evangelica* and chap. 16 (redactional) the Didachist reveals "a wide knowledge of New Testament Scripture" (p. 165). "He conflates Matthew with Luke and cites, among other things, *Barnabas* and *Hermas*" (ibid.). "The rest of the work reveals only a knowledge of Matthew's Gospel" (ibid.). Barnard, "Later History," 99 n. 2: the *Didache* "depends on the Matthaean stream of the Gospel tradition." Eduard Schweizer

considers "that . . . the Gospel of Matthew or an extract from it was available to the author of the *Didache*, although changes brought about by oral use in the *Didache* community are to be reckoned with. These changes could have been affected also by the Old Testament, Jewish apocalyptic ideas, or other Jesus logia" (*Matthäus und seine Gemeinde*, 141 n. 12); cf. 164–65: "The dependence on Matthew or his tradition is unmistakable." Inspired by Schweizer (but not completely identical with the opinions discussed above) is the hypothesis of Aono, *Entwicklung*, 164–89: the *Didache* is not directly (literarily) but indirectly dependent on Matthew. Aono (*Entwicklung*, 186) supposes "that the author of the *Didache* probably did not even have a written copy of the Gospel of Matthew before him, but he knew the quoted phrases by heart because they were repeated again and again in the community, literally or with variations; it is not impossible that the wording of Ps 36:11 or the recollection of Jewish sayings or of an older form of a dominical saying may have influenced the reformulation of the words as found in Matthew, and that the baptismal formula and Our Father are written in the form in which they were used in the community's liturgy, which is to say in a liturgy with a Matthean stamp." Aono himself (*Entwicklung*, 186–87) sees the difficulty created for this hypothesis by the unique character of *Did.* 1.3–5 (where there are echoes not only of Matthew but clearly of Luke as well), but he thinks he can resolve it by a hypothesis of addition: *Did.* 1.3–5 may reflect a "collection of dominical sayings," formed "primarily from Matthew" but enriched by Lukan elements (p. 187). Wengst (*Didache*, 19) now thinks of the Gospel of Matthew, and it alone ("the compiler of the *Didache* knew only one written gospel, probably that of Matthew"); see further pp. 24–31, but note also that Wengst regards the *sectio evangelica* as an interpolation.

35   The older discussion is in Greiff, *Pascharituale*, 163–94. From more recent research, cf. Erwin R. Goodenough, "John a Primitive Gospel," *JBL* 64 (1945) 174–75; Moule, "Note," 240–43. It is one of the curiosities of *Didache* scholarship that the contrary has also been posited, namely, dependence of the Gospel of John on the *Didache*. See Greiff, *Pascharituale*, 184–94.

Pauline letters and other New Testament writings.[36] The advocates of the fictional hypothesis have obviously been most prominent in positing dependence on New Testament writings. According to them, the author of the *Didache* — with the intention of faking a location within apostolic times — used a generous quantity of New Testament material and also imitated New Testament expressions.[37]

Two initial observations are in order, and they are fundamental to the whole discussion: (1) If there are any New Testament allusions or quotations in the *Didache* at all, they are found without exception in the last stage of the document, in the work of the redactor.[38] In the *Didache*'s sources (Two Ways tractate, agenda, church order, but with all probability in the apocalypse as well) there is no literary dependence on New Testament texts.[39] This circumstance is adequately explained by the age of the sources in question. (2) It is uncertain whether the redactor made a literary use of New Testament texts. This question will be discussed below. Still, it is characteristic that the only texts that deserve serious consideration are from the Synoptic tradition, more specifically the Gospels of Matthew and Luke. There are no genuinely demonstrable allusions in the *Didache* to the Gospel of John, and one may well question whether the author of the *Didache* knew that Gospel at all. The *Didache* lives in an entirely different linguistic universe, and that is true not only of its sources[40] but of its redactor as well. In this context we should add immediately that there is no echo of the corpus Paulinum in the *Didache* either.[41] One may not assume that the Christians of the *Didache* communities knew nothing at all of the apostle to the Gentiles, but it would be difficult to suppose that they had access to the corpus Paulinum (even though their Antiochene contemporary, Ignatius, did). Just as there is no specific reference in the *Didache* to the Gospel of John, so also there is none to the Pauline tradition, and obviously, therefore, no

---

36 For example, MacLean, ("Introduction," xx–xxii) mentions Matthew, Luke, Acts, and perhaps 1 Corinthians, the Thessalonian correspondence, 1 Peter, and 1 John. Muilenburg (*Literary Relations*, 73–75) lists the sources that he thinks have been compiled in the *Didache*; cf. the later remarks at pp. 91–96. The compiler certainly used Matthew and Luke. "Other N. T. traces in the Teaching are numerous, but . . . they are more obscure and vague than those just referred to" (p. 94). Cf. p. 96: "the abundant use made of the N. T." Goodspeed ("Doctrina," 231, and frequently) posits, for the *sectio evangelica*, dependence on Matthew, Luke, 1 Peter, and *Hermas*. For Massaux and Richardson, see n. 34 above.

37 Robinson, "Problem," 340–56; idem, *Didache*, 48–68; idem, "Barnabas and the Didache," 227–38; Middleton, "Eucharistic Prayers," 259, 266; Vokes, *Riddle*, 95–115, and passim. Vokes found reflections of the "language" and "subject-matter" of the New Testament writings everywhere (cf. p. 95). "The *Didache* knew nearly all of our New Testament, not as 'oral tradition,' but as written documents" (p. 115). In a later essay ("The *Didache* and the Canon of the New Testament," *StEv* 3.2 [TU 88; Berlin: Akademie-Verlag, 1964] 427–36) Vokes attempted to found his late dating of the writing (with the supposition that the *Didache* quotes the Gospels) in terms of canonical criticism. Cf. from recent research also Layton, "Sources," 343–72 (according to whom the *sectio evangelica* depends on Matthew, Luke, and *Hermas*).

38 Something analogous is true, strikingly enough, of the two or three quotations from the OT. All explicit quotations are from the Didachist, i.e., they belong to the last stage of the writing.

39 I must admit that this assessment is insecure with regard to the concluding apocalypse (16.3–8); however, I wish to maintain it for this section as well. On this issue, see the commentary.

40 From time to time connections have been posited between the table prayers (*Didache* 9–10) and Johannine expressions (esp. from John 17): on this, see below at 9.1. Of these parallels, the only ones that deserve serious consideration are γνωρίζειν in *Did.* 9.2, 3; 10.2 (John 17:26; cf. 15:15); the motif of ἐν γενέσθαι in *Did.* 9.4 (cf. John 17:11, 21–22; and perhaps also 11:52); the address πάτερ ἅγιε in *Did.* 10.2 (cf. John 17:11); the saving of the church ἀπὸ παντὸς πονηροῦ in *Did.* 10.5 (cf. John 17:15); the motif of τελείωσις in *Did.* 10.5 (cf. John 17:23). One should note in all this that these contacts all rest only on individual expressions that are found here and there in different contexts. That there are contacts at all is probably explained by the fact that John 17 (and the other parallels mentioned as well) has been penetrated by motifs from eucharistic language (cf. Vööbus, *Liturgical Traditions*, 128 n. 98). That is all. By contrast, precisely those things that are specifically Johannine are absent from the *Didache*.

41 Audet (*Didachè*, 340–43) expressed the suggestion that Paul (the reference is actually to the deutero-Pauline letters) was dependent in some way on the

polemic engagement.[42] The only New Testament contact the *Didache* shows is with the Synoptic tradition.[43] This is a remarkable circumstance. Together with the Jewish-Christian character of its sources, this gives the *Didache* its unique aspect.

If we attempt to make this latter relationship more precise, we may also begin with the judgment that the *sources* of the *Didache* reveal no literary dependence on the Synoptic Gospels (and it is only the Synoptic Gospels, more precisely Matthew and Luke, that can be considered at all, in light of what has already been said). Dependence could, at most, be present in the insertions and expansions produced by *redaction*. But is that the case?

We begin the discussion with an analysis of the four instances of εὐαγγέλιον in the *Didache*.[44] Like Koester,[45] I will first list the passages:

8.2: ὡς ἐκέλευσεν ὁ κύριος ἐν τῷ εὐαγγελίῳ αὐτοῦ, οὕτω προσεύχεσθε . . . (the Lord's Prayer follows);

11.3: περὶ δὲ τῶν ἀποστόλων καὶ προφητῶν κατὰ τὸ δόγμα τοῦ εὐαγγελίου οὕτω ποιήσατε (followed by rules for behavior toward itinerant teachers);

15.3: ἐλέγχετε δὲ ἀλλήλους μὴ ἐν ὀργῇ, ἀλλ' ἐν εἰρήνῃ, ὡς ἔχετε ἐν τῷ εὐαγγελίῳ.

15.4: τὰς δὲ εὐχὰς ὑμῶν καὶ τὰς ἐλεημοσύνας καὶ πάσας τὰς πράξεις οὕτω ποιήσατε, ὡς ἔχετε ἐν τῷ εὐαγγελίῳ τοῦ κυρίου ἡμῶν.[46]

What is immediately obvious is the symmetry of the diction:

ἐν τῷ εὐαγγελίῳ αὐτοῦ (8.2)
ἐν τῷ εὐαγγελίῳ (15.3)
ἐν τῷ εὐαγγελίῳ τοῦ κυρίου ἡμῶν (15.4)
ὡς ἐκέλευσεν ὁ κύριος (8.2)
κατὰ τὸ δόγμα τοῦ εὐαγγελίου (11.3)
οὕτω προσεύχεσθε (8.2)
οὕτω ποιήσατε (11.3)
οὕτω ποιήσατε (15.4).

All these formulations express the same concept, and it should be obvious that all of the texts can be traced to one and the same author, namely, the redactor.

Thus we must maintain, first of all, that all the examples of the key word "gospel" belong to the *redactional layer* of the *Didache*, as Koester had already noted.[47] It

---

"instruction for the poor." On this claim, see my remarks below at 4.1.

42 Johnson ("Motive," 114) writes somewhat differently: "The Twelve are the *Didache*'s heroes, not Paul. The *Didache* is not necessarily anti-Pauline, but it is certainly non-Pauline." Still, Johnson sees a possibility that one could find an anti-Pauline polemic in *Did.* 6.3 (pp. 114–15). In these suggestions, only one thing is correct: the *Didache* has no recognizable relationship to Paul, or in any case no polemical relationship. See also Andreas Lindemann, *Paulus im ältesten Christentum* (BHTh 58; Tübingen: Mohr, 1979) 174–77, esp. the summary on p. 177. Lindemann considers it probable that the Didachist "knows nothing of Paul" and founds this on the supposition "that the Pauline tradition appears to have been completely unknown in Syria toward the end of the first century." That is no more than a supposition. Lindemann concludes correctly with the observation, "it [would be] wrong to reproach the *Didache* for its neglect of Pauline elements, or to see it as representative of an anti-Pauline church establishment" (p. 177). Cf. also Aono, *Entwicklung*, 163–64. Aono posits the location of the *Didache* "outside the sphere of Pauline influence" (p. 209). Of course, he attempts to understand the "theology" of the Didachist and to perceive its omissions.

43 This approach is highly problematic; see above, §1b. It would be wrong to see here an analogy to the *Gospel of Thomas*, for we must immediately add that, of all things, Gnosticism plays no part at all in the *Didache*. The communities addressed were neither threatened by Gnosticism nor are there latent gnostic or even gnosticizing motifs in its sources or redactor. Gnosticism is not a problem for the *Didache*.

44 For the whole, see Koester, *Synoptische Überlieferung*, 6–12, esp. 10–11.

45 *Synoptische Überlieferung*, 10.

46 A fifth passage is clearly to be understood as the quotation of a dominical saying, even though the key word "gospel" is not used: 9.5: καὶ γὰρ περὶ τούτου εἴρηκεν ὁ κύριος· Μὴ δῶτε τὸ ἅγιον τοῖς κυσί·

47 Koester, *Synoptische Überlieferung*, 10. In accordance with his own conception, Audet (*Didachè*, 112) wanted to establish a difference between the use of "gospel" in D¹ and D². To the contrary, and correctly, Nautin, "Composition," 195–96. For Audet, *Did.* 11.2 does not quote a written gospel, but this is the case in the additions by D² from 11.3 onward; here, according to Audet, a gospel similar to Matthew is being quoted. Cf. pp. 178–79, 442.

was the redactor who first introduced the key word "gospel" into his sources, or, to put it another way, this key word appears only in redactional passages.[48]

Next, it is striking that (setting aside the question still to be discussed, whether "gospel" in the *Didache* refers to oral tradition or to a literary text) at no point does the *content* of "gospel" refer to the christological kerygma. In the *Didache*, "gospel" refers not to the missionary message of the epiphany, death, and resurrection of Jesus for our sake. The word always and exclusively refers to the *words of the Lord* as handed down,[49] the Jesus tradition in the Synoptic sense, or more precisely, the reference is always solely to the words of Jesus.[50] This, obviously, does not mean that the Didachist did not know the christological kerygma or did not accept it, but simply that the word "gospel" is connected, whether consciously or unconsciously, with the logia of the Lord as transmitted. *They* are the gospel of which the *Didache* speaks, and in this sense it is called τὸ εὐαγγέλιον τοῦ κυρίου ἡμῶν ("the gospel of our Lord," 15.4; cf. 8.2).

Moreover, because the words of the Lord are obligatory norms (something that was a matter of course for all of primitive Christianity and for every period there-after), the didachistic concept of "gospel" has the character of a new (eschatological) commandment; one might almost say that it is a "new law of Christ."[51] The word of Jesus is a word that brings salvation — that is why it is "good news" — but it is also, and at the same time, the binding norm for Christian behavior, and to that extent the Lord "commands" in his gospel (ὡς ἐκέλευσεν ὁ κύριος ἐν τῷ εὐαγγελίῳ αὐτοῦ, 8.2), or the gospel reveals the binding commands that Christians must obey (hence: τὸ δόγμα τοῦ εὐαγγελίου, 11.3).[52] Characteristic of him are also the occasions that cause the redactor to reflect on the gospel, the moments when it is time to establish clear and binding rules. From the gospel, one may derive the correct rules for daily prayer (8.2), for dealing with apostles and prophets (11.3), for conduct within the community (15.3), and in general for prayer, almsgiving, and the whole of life (15.4).[53] The gospel grounds the parenetical imperatives οὕτω προσ-εύχεσθε (8.2), οὕτω ποιήσατε (11.3; 15.4), ἐλέγχετε (15.3). Overall, "gospel" for the Didachist is, so to speak, the "*regula Christi*,"[54] and indeed he writes: ἐν τῷ εὐαγγελίῳ τοῦ κυρίου ἡμῶν (15.4) and ἐν τῷ εὐαγγελίῳ αὐτοῦ (8.2). Jesus' words (= his gospel) regulate the life

---

48   In my opinion, *Did.* 9.5 (see n. 46 above), which quotes a dominical saying without using the key word "gospel," is also to be traced to the didachistic redaction.

49   Koester, *Synoptische Überlieferung*, 11: "gospel" refers to the "rules and admonitions" of Jesus.

50   Glover, "Quotations," 28: there are no biographical details; the words "all refer to teaching." Glover concludes from this that a sayings collection existed. On this, see below.

51   That the Didachist understands the words of Jesus as *eschatological* admonitions is clear from the way in which he fixes and concretizes the Two Ways tractate by means of the *sectio evangelica*, but also from his tentative efforts to accommodate Jesus' demands for perfection to the moral possibilities of the majority.

52   One should not accuse the Didachist, in this connection, of confusing law and gospel. That would be a misunderstanding of the *Didache*. Paul himself never applies the dialectical relationship between law and gospel to the words and commands of Jesus. When he speaks of the law that kills, he means the law of the old covenant as it was misused by human beings. It would be meaningless — at least for Paul — to understand Jesus' commands as "law" in this sense. Instead, for Paul, Jesus' commands are

the "law of Christ," thus not "a law consisting of works," but "a law of faith," a "law of the Spirit," the "law without legalism," the law of the new eon that is no longer misused by the flesh, and that therefore no longer alienates. The Didachist did not indulge in reflections on the question of law, commandments, and instruction comparable to those of Paul. But in equating "Jesus' commands" as "absolutely binding" with "gospel" he cannot be criticized from the point of view of Pauline theology, unless it is falsely understood in modernist fashion.

53   The question of admission to the meal is regulated in 9.5 by application of a dominical saying.

54   Cf. Koester, *Synoptische Überlieferung*, 11; Rordorf, "Tradition apostolique," 108–10. This "rule" consists of the sum total of the traditional words of Jesus. The question then arises: What is the relationship of the *Didache* as rule to the gospel as rule (even if the author of the *Didache* may not have posed this question to himself)?

55   In this connection, one must attend (cf. Rordorf, "Tradition apostolique," 110) to the multitude of things definitively regulated by words of Jesus: the life of the τέλειοι (1.3b–5.2), prayer (8.2), the exclusion of the unbaptized from the meal celebration (9.5), the way to treat apostles and prophets (11.3–12), discipline within the community (14.3),

and behavior of his followers.[55] *That* is what "gospel" means in the *Didache*.[56]

While the language of the *Didache* (in this case we should say the Didachist, or the redactor) is clear and consistent in itself, there remains the difficult problem of saying whether the Didachist simply understands the *regula Domini* that he calls εὐαγγέλιον (and the readers' knowledge of which he presumes) as *oral tradition*, or whether it already exists in a literary work — that is, whether the word "gospel" in this case already refers to an *evangelium scriptum* (a written gospel, or more than one). Unfortunately, this question cannot be answered with certainty. Three solutions deserve serious consideration.

(a) All four passages refer to oral tradition (but can 15.3–4 be understood in this way?). (b) Εὐαγγέλιον refers to different things in the four passages: in 8.2, and perhaps in 11.3 as well, we are still dealing with the older usage (meaning the "living voice of the good news" [*viva vox evangelii*]); in contrast, εὐαγγέλιον in 15.3 and 4 (but also in 11.3?) already refers to a gospel in written form (*evangelium scriptum*): thus Koester.[57] Audet adopted a similar opinion, seeing in 8.2 and 9.5 reference to an oral gospel, and in 11.3 and 15.3–4 to a written gospel.[58] Rordorf and Tuilier employed this notion to distinguish a hypothetical second layer of redaction: only the second redactor could have under-

stood εὐαγγέλιον in 15.3–4 as *evangelium scriptum*.[59] But not only is this hypothesis of a double redaction questionable, in my opinion; the conceptual consistency of the clauses in which the key word "gospel" appears does not suggest such an idea. Finally, we cannot completely exclude (c), the possibility that the redactor means the same thing in all four passages, namely, a written gospel,[60] known to him and his readers and, because it preserves the words of Jesus, serving as a norm of faith and life. Koester also accepted this construal for 15.3–4, and considered it possible for 11.3; even for 8.2 he did not wish to exclude it absolutely.[61] (Nota bene: This understanding does not mean that the author also *quotes* this gospel.) If this position is accurate, we might have in *Did.* 8.2; 11.3; 15.3–4 the oldest instances of εὐαγγέλιον meaning a written gospel or gospel book. But to which gospel would they refer? Could it be canonical Matthew?[62] Or should we suppose that it means an apocryphal gospel[63] to which the Didachist refers and which he may quote in various places? In that case, one might think of an apocryphal collection of sayings of the same type as the Synoptic Sayings Source.[64] That, however, is only a hypothesis. The jury is still out.

3. By way of note, we should at least mention the question of the dependence of the *Didache* on *Hermas*. In research on the *Didache*, this question is usually discussed together with that of dependence

---

and the expectation of the end (16.1–2).

56   I should add that the term εὐαγγέλιον appears regularly only in the singular. This fact need not mean that the term intends — presuming a *written* gospel — to refer only to one individual gospel, but it does suggest the possibility of such an intention.

57   *Synoptische Überlieferung*, 10–11. Cf. Koester's very cautious judgment at pp. 203 and 240.

58   At the time of D[1] there was not yet a written gospel in the milieu for which the author wrote (Audet, *Didachè*, 173). The case is different with D[2]. In the meantime, such a written gospel was prepared and circulated in the milieu of the *Didache* (Audet, *Didachè*, 176; cf. earlier at p. 114). D[2] refers to this writing. This gospel was known to the *Didache* communities and accepted by them. This text was not, however, our Gospel of Matthew (pp. 178–83) but merely the written version of a tradition related to Matthew (p. 182).

59   Rordorf and Tuilier, *Doctrine*, 88. Cf. earlier, Rordorf, "Rémission des péchés," 293.

60   Thus now also Wengst (*Didache*, 26), who thinks that the reference is probably to the Gospel of Matthew.

"In the community of the Didachist the Gospel of Matthew was probably known as 'the gospel' or 'the gospel of our Lord,' and he used it for his own writing" (p. 30).

61   Cf. esp. *Synoptische Überlieferung*, 203.

62   The *sectio evangelica*, with its "Lukan" elements alongside the "Matthean," need not refute this hypothesis, not even if (differently from Wengst) one considers the *sectio* to be authentic, because the author need not quote the written gospel that he knows. The elements of the Jesus tradition in the *Didache* (in the *sectio* and elsewhere) could stem from the *oral* tradition that still circulated *alongside* the written gospel that the communities now possessed. Cf. the suggestions in Koester, *Synoptische Überlieferung*, 240.

63   Audet's reflections tend in this direction (although only for D[2]), when he presupposes for this stage of the writing the knowledge of a gospel book that was related to Matthew but was not quoted word for word. Cf. n. 58 above. Cf. also the suggestions of Rordorf, "Rémission des péchés," 293 and n. 4.

64   Ultimately, the remarks of Glover ("Quotations")

on *Barnabas*; we have already discussed the latter above. Regarding *Hermas*, the only passage worth serious consideration[65] is *Did.* 1.5c (cf. *Hermas Man.* 2.4–6).[66] On this parallel, see the discussion below at 1.15c, where I will show that dependence on *Hermas* is improbable.[67] The agreements are more probably attributable to a common tradition.

b. Time and Place of Writing

We should begin[68] with a distinction between tradition and redaction. The predidachistic traditions, that is, in the narrower sense the *sources* of the *Didache,* have an altogether archaic character. This is true of the Two Ways tractate, the liturgical formulae, and with special clarity of the piece of tradition about the reception of itinerant charismatics; the only thing one might possibly doubt is whether the predidachistic apocalypse can be called "archaic" tradition. In general, one can say that the sources, that is, the predidachistic traditions, should probably be located in the first century C.E., most likely toward the end of the century. It is impossible to make any more precise determination. One should also consider that the predidachistic traditions are varied in

character and stem from different strands of tradition.

Characteristic of the Didachist is a mentality that holds fast to tradition while, at the same time, having a tendency to reconcile traditions with the changed circumstances of a church undergoing a process of stabilization. This observation alone provides little information, however, with regard to a temporal location of the writing.[69] In order to proceed farther, one could argue that the archaic elements that apparently speak in favor of an early origin of the *Didache* all belong to the work's sources; thus the redactor cannot be located very early. On the contrary, the redactional sections do not reveal any great degree of church development; there are still itinerant prophets in the *Didache*'s field of tradition, although some of them seem to be in the process of becoming resident (13.1). There is still no monarchical episcopate or *ordo triplex* (cf. the ἐπίσκοποι and διάκονοι in 15.1), and the relationship between the local clergy and the charismatics is not without conflict (15.1–2).[70] Thus one cannot move too far into the second century, even if one keeps in mind that the development of canon law within the tradition of different regions of the church as a whole proceeded at widely

tend in this direction (variants of Q?): "Out of my examination grew the convictions, first, that the *Didache* does not bear witness to our gospels, but quotes directly from sources used by Luke and Matthew; secondly, that Justin possessed the same sources, at least in part; thirdly, that the *Didache* may sometimes preserve our Lord's sayings in a more authentic, or, at least, more primitive, form than that formed in either Luke or Matthew" (p. 12). Glover posits as source "a collection of sayings" (p. 28). "At the least, then, it seems sound to say that Justin and the *Didache* are witnesses who should be examined alongside Luke and Matthew when the text of Q is discussed" (p. 29). Rordorf ("Rémission des péchés," 293) also considers the possibility that (although only in 15.3–4) "gospel" may mean an apocryphal gospel of the Q type (and that it may also be quoted in other places?). For possible quotations, cf. the cautious questions on p. 293 n. 4.

65 Harnack (*Lehre,* 18; and "Prolegomena," 87) still referred to *Didache* 5/*Hermas Man.* 8.3–5. This is not obvious. Harnack originally ("Prolegomena," 66, 87) supposed dependence, but later he found it doubtful (*Apostellehre*, 13). The references in Connolly, "Streeter on the Didache," 377–78, are very far-fetched.

66 Dependence of the *Didache* on *Hermas* was posited

by Bryennios, Διδαχή, πδ´; Zahn, *Geschichte,* 3.315–18; Hennecke, "Grundschrift," 71; Muilenburg, *Literary Relations,* 33, 46, 167, and passim; Dix, "Didache," 243–44; Robinson, "Barnabas and the Didache," 233–38; Connolly, "Streeter on the Didache," 372, 377–79; Vokes, *Riddle,* 48, 51–61, and passim; Richardson, "Teaching," 163, 165: the Didachist (not his sources) is dependent on *Barnabas* and *Hermas;* Layton, "Sources," 361–72.

67 On the contrary, positing dependence of *Hermas* on the *Didache* are Harris, *Teaching,* 38; MacLean, "Introduction," xxiii (probable).

68 Early scholarship is reviewed by Ehrhard, *Altchristliche Litteratur,* 62–65. Origins ca. 50 C.E. constitute the earlier limit, and origins in the 4th and 5th century are the late limit. (With regard to the latter, Ehrhard remarks that such opinions "can in any case only arouse a pathological interest" [p. 62].)

69 Recourse to the witnesses does not bring us any farther: on the one hand, because the oldest testimonies are not clear, as we have seen above, and on the other hand because we do not know how far behind the testimonies we may go.

70 No certain argument can be derived from what is said about the εὐαγγέλιον or the elements of Synoptic tradition found in the *Didache,* because these instances themselves are not absolutely clear

differing rates. In sum, the date of the *Didache* is a matter of judgment. An origin around 110 or 120 C.E. remains hypothetical,[71] but there are as yet no compelling reasons to dismiss this hypothesis.

Regarding provenance, we are completely in the dark.[72] The strongly Jewish-Christian character of the *Didache* does not function as an argument. From that character — whether of the sources or of the redactor — one cannot deduce anything about location. On the one hand, it has occasionally been said that the *Didache* comes from Egypt,[73] with support derived from the writ-

ing's early circulation in Egypt.[74] A number of details also suggest an Egyptian origin.[75] In any case, the liturgical expression about bread on the mountains (9.4) can scarcely be used as a counterargument, because 9.4 is part of the sources of the *Didache*. Moreover, this expression is also found in Egyptian liturgical sources.[76] On the other hand, 7.2 does not favor Egypt but rather Syria or Palestine, and in fact that region is frequently claimed as the locus of the *Didache*. For Syria, or the borderland between Syria and Palestine,[77] one can adduce primarily

---

(is the "gospel" oral or written? canonical or apocryphal? Are the Synoptic elements from oral tradition?). I have spoken of this above. Nevertheless, these findings in themselves give some support to the hypothesis that the *Didache* should be located at the beginning of the 2d century.

71 Examples of attempts at dating from the history of research include: Audet, *Didachè*, 187–210: "contemporary with the first gospel writings" (197); Hemmer, *Doctrine*, xxxv: 80–100; Funk, *Abhandlungen*, 2.112: perhaps 80–90; Kleist, *Didache*, 6: "before the end of the first century"; Ehrhard, *Altchristliche Litteratur*, 65: probably "80–100, or possibly 90–110 or 120"; Schaff, *Church Manual*, 122: between 90 and 100; Adam ("Herkunft," 70) suggested that the primitive form of the *Didache* originated between 90 and 100; Aono, *Entwicklung*, 207: "toward the end of the first century"; Vielhauer, *Geschichte*, 737: "beginning of the second century"; also MacLean, "Introduction," xxxvi; and Wengst, *Didache*, 63; Barnard, "Later History," 99 n. 2: 100–130; Altaner and Stuiber, *Patrologie*, 81; and Quasten, *Patrology*, 1.37: 100–150; Bryennios, Διδαχή, κ´: between 120 and 160; Richardson, "Teaching," 165: ca. 150; Kraft, *Didache*, 76: after 150; Johnson, "Motive," 108: between 150 and 175; Vokes, *Riddle*, 86 (cf. 87, 216): between 155 and 250; Robinson, *Didache*, 82: 3d century ("very probable").

72 From the early research: Ehrhard, *Altchristliche Litteratur*, 65–66. He observed correctly (p. 66): "But only Egypt or Syria-Palestine can be considered." Ehrhard himself decided for the latter.

73 To begin with, Harnack ("Prolegomena," 159–60, 167–70) was the primary proponent of Egypt; later (*Apostellehre*, 25) he was less sure ("probably, but by no means . . . certain"); idem, *Geschichte*, 2.1.431 n. 1: "No certain decision between Egypt and Syria-Palestine can be given." Possibly Egypt: Middleton, "Eucharistic Prayers," 267; probably Egypt: Richardson, "Teaching," 165; cf. Glover, "Quotations," 27; Kraft, *Didache*, 77: rather Egypt than Syria.

74 Athanasius; *P. Oxy.* See above, §§2a, 3b.

75 Κλάσμα in 9.4 does indeed point to Egypt, but is this the original reading? Cf. the commentary at 9.4. The correspondence of the doxology of the Lord's Prayer in *Did.* 8.2 (end) and Matt 6:13 in parts of the Coptic translation is striking (see the commentary at 8.2). Is that, however, sufficient to allow us to argue for an Egyptian origin of the *Didache*?

76 The expression is found in Serapion *Euchologion* 13.13 (Funk, *Didascalia*, 2.174) and *P. Dêr Balizeh* IIv., l. 4 (Roberts and Capelle, *Euchologium*, 26; and van Haelst, "Nouvelle reconstitution," 449 — although there partly expanded, but the expansion is fairly certain). See below at *Did.* 9.4. No argument for or against a particular place of origin for the *Didache* can be made from this datum.

77 Examples: Taylor, *Teaching*, 116: northern Palestine; Jacquier, *Doctrine*, 81: Palestine, particularly Jerusalem; Ehrhard, *Altchristliche Litteratur*, 66: Syria-Palestine; Dix, "Didache," 249: Syria; Muilenburg, *Literary Relations*, 41: more likely Syria; Knopf, *Lehre*, 3: "rather Syria and Palestine . . . than Egypt"; Bardenhewer, *Geschichte*, 1.96: "Syria or Palestine" (more probable than Egypt); Altaner and Stuiber, *Patrologie*; Quasten, *Patrology*, 1.37: most probably Syria; Bosio, *Padri apostolici*, 14: probably Syria or Palestine; Vielhauer, *Geschichte*, 737: with great caution: Syria; Adam, "Herkunft," 37–42, and passim: the book stems from Palestine, perhaps from Jewish Christians from Pella, but is directed to the newly missionized communities in eastern Syria, in Adiabene; Robert M. Grant, *The Apostolic Fathers: A New Translation and Commentary*, vol. 1: *An Introduction* (New York: Nelson, 1964) 75–76: Syria, probably not Antioch; Barnard, "Later History," 99–100: Syria; Aono, *Entwicklung*, 208: probably Syria; Rordorf and Tuilier, *Doctrine*, 97–98: western Syria, rural regions; Wengst, *Didache*, 62: "a rural region in Syria."

the fact that the redactor still knows the movement of Jesus' disciples or its later offshoots (otherwise he would not have had to cite 11.4–12 and interpret it with chaps. 12–13). It appears that in the communities of the *Didache* the offshoots of the Jesus-discipleship movement are still alive; such a thing is most naturally to be sought in Palestine or Syria. Such argumentation, placing the *Didache* in Syria-Palestine, is not very strong but has some things in its favor. In the question of a more precise location, *Did.* 13.3–7 has sometimes played a role. Most recently, Georg Schöllgen[78] has attempted to show that an origin of the *Didache* in a rural area cannot be deduced from this passage. The *Didache* could certainly have come from an urban setting. I do not think, however, that the major city of Antioch should be considered as its location.

---

78   "Die Didache – ein frühes Zeugnis für Landgemeinden?" *ZNW* 76 (1985) 140–43. Schöllgen discusses the theme of the gift of firstfruits in the early period and gives instances from Rome and Caesarea. "Christians from town and even urban milieus without an agriculture of their own were apparently also in a position to produce the gift of firstfruits required for the support of the prophets and the clergy; these were probably acquired by purchase" (p. 142). He then continues, "Yet even if the gifts of firstfruits in v. 3 come from one's own produce, this would say nothing against the origins of the *Didache* in an urban milieu" (ibid.). Note the following remarks about agriculture as the basis of the economy in the majority of the small cities of the empire (pp. 142–43).

The Didache

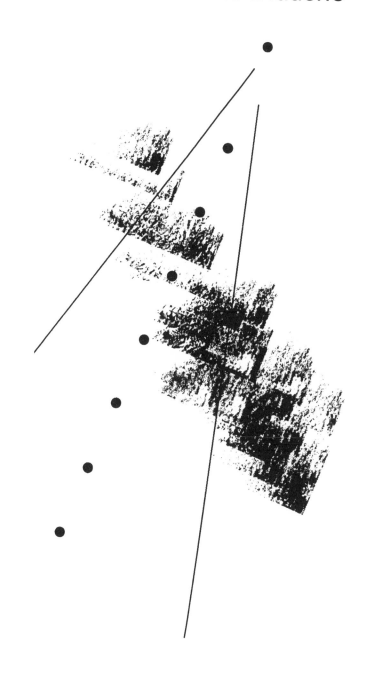

The twofold title borne by this document in H has confused scholars from the beginning. The *short title* (which stands in a separate line above the text in H) is διδαχὴ τῶν δώδεκα ἀποστόλων ("teaching [or doctrine] of the twelve apostles").[1] The *long title* is not placed in an individual line in H, but forms the beginning of the text:[2] Διδαχὴ κυρίου διὰ τῶν δώδεκα ἀποστόλων τοῖς ἔθνεσιν ("teaching of the Lord through the twelve apostles to the nations"). The text continues in the same line with ὁδοὶ δύο ("two ways").[3] Much has been written about the originality of these two titles (is the long title the older and the short title only an abbreviation of it?)[4] and their significance (especially as regards the interpretation and unique character of the book as a whole). It is probable, however, that neither title is original.

On the basis of the witnesses that testify to the document[5] it is much more likely that the original title was διδαχὴ (or διδαχαὶ) τῶν ἀποστόλων ("teaching of the apostles").[6] (The reference to the "Twelve," as found also in the short title, would have been incorporated later.) Two difficulties then arise. First, the document itself nowhere lays explicit claim to apostolic authority;[7] second, the witnesses are, in part, subject to the suspicion that they do not refer to the *Didache* at all but to versions of the Two Ways tractate. In fact, according to the witness of *Doctrina*, the Two Ways tractate (at least in *one* version) bore the title *(de) doctrina apostolorum* ("[of the] teaching of the apostles").[8] There is very good reason to suppose that, at a relatively early period, this was the title of the Christianized Two Ways tractate,[9] and that

---

1 It is written in minuscules (like the rest of the text), but framed by the symbol ·∴·.

2 The first letter (Δ) is a large initial extending into the margin.

3 The way in which the copyist presents the two titles may perhaps indicate that he regarded the short title as the title of the document itself.

4 Cf. Harnack, "Prolegomena," 24–37.

5

τῶν ἀποστόλων (. . .) διδαχαί	Eusebius *Hist. eccl.* 3.25.4 (GCS 2.1.252)
Doctrina (. . .) *apostolorum*	Rufinus ibid. (253)
Διδαχὴ (. . .) τῶν ἀποστόλων	Athanasius *Festal Letter* 39 §11 (Preuschen, *Analecta*, 2.45)
Διδαχὴ ἀποστόλων	Ps.-Athanasius *Synopsis scripturae sacrae* 76 (*PG* 28.432)
περίοδοι καὶ διδαχαὶ τῶν ἀποστόλων	*Indicium scriptorum canonicorum sexagesima* (Preuschen, *Analecta*, 2.69)
Διδαχὴ ἀποστόλων	Ps.-Nicephorus *Stichometry* (Preuschen, *Analecta*, 2.64)
doctrin(ae) apostolorum	Ps.-Cyprian *De aleat.* 4 (CSEL 3.3.96).

6 For the interpretation of the word διδαχή in this context, Adam ("Herkunft," 60 n. 116) has referred to Friederich Preisigke, ed., *Wörterbuch der griechischen Papyrusurkunden* (4 vols.; Berlin: Selbstverlag, 1924–71) 1.371, where (at B 140, 16, p. ii) ἡ στρατιωτικὴ διδαχή is attested in the sense of "military order." On this, see the discussion above (Introduction, § 1b) on the genre of the document as

regula vitae christianae ("rule for the Christian life").

7 Vielhauer, *Geschichte*, 723–24.

8 For the similar title of the *Canons of the Apostles* in some mss., see Audet, *Didachè*, 94–95.

9 MacLean, "Introduction," xxxii n. 1 (probable); Goodspeed, "Doctrina," 231; Koester, *Synoptische Überlieferung*, 218 (he suggests the possibility that the Christian Two Ways tractate bore the title "apostolic teaching" before it was incorporated into the *Didache*); Nautin, "Composition," 213: the *Duae viae* in their Christian form bore the title διδαχὴ τῶν ἀποστόλων (*doctrina apostolorum*), and this title was transferred to the *Didache*; the long title would have been an addition by the copyist. The original Jewish *Duae viae* would simply have been called διδαχή. Barnard, "Later History," 99–100: the Egyptian version of the tractate bore the title διδαχὴ τῶν ἀποστόλων; the Syriac version was entitled διδαχὴ τῶν δώδεκα ἀποστόλων, and from that the Didachist composed the long title.

10 Did *Barnabas* know the Two Ways tractate under the title διδαχή? Cf. *Barn.* 18.1: μεταβῶμεν δὲ καὶ ἐπὶ ἑτέραν γνῶσιν καὶ διδαχήν ("Let us proceed to another insight and teaching").

11 Vielhauer (*Geschichte*, 725 n. 9) has disputed the idea that the title stems originally from the Two Ways tractate and was transferred from it to the *Didache*. For him, the short title (without δώδεκα) is older, but was applied to the *Didache* only at a later time (pp. 723–24). According to Wengst (*Didache*, 15) the title was added later. Audet's thesis (*Didachè*, 91–103, 247–54) combines some correct and some bizarre ideas. According to him, the Two Ways tractate (even before it was in Christian usage) had the title διδαχὴ κυρίου (= YHWH) τοῖς ἔθνεσιν. The author of D[1] entitled his instructions: διδαχαὶ τῶν ἀποστόλων (but not referring to the Twelve). That

this title was then transferred to the *Didache*,[10] either by the author of the document itself or in a subsequent process.[11] No matter how one answers this last question, however, one should by no means understand the title διδαχὴ (or διδαχαὶ) τῶν ἀποστόλων as an indication of how the document is to be read. Even if it was imposed by the Didachist, it is a label after the fact, and its refer-ence to the ἀπόστολοι has no significance for the docu-ment itself.[12] It would be utterly aberrant to derive an instruction for reading from the long title in H, and to see that title as an expression of the document's own self understanding.[13] The two titles in H both come from a later time[14] and are irrelevant for the interpretation of the document.[15]

---

was the original and proper title of the document. In the later tradition, this became διδαχὴ τῶν δώδε-κα ἀποστόλων. A copyist inserted the phrase διὰ τῶν δώδεκα ἀποστόλων into the original title of the *Duae viae*. Thus the long title came into being. The title διδαχὴ τῶν ἀποστόλων was transferred from the *Didache* to the *Duae viae* (as the Latin *Doctrina* shows). Nautin ("Composition," 211–12) previously offered a critique of these ideas; see further Rordorf and Tuilier, *Doctrine*, 14–15.

12 This is true, mutatis mutandis, for the title of the tractate, *if* it is supposed to have read διδαχὴ τῶν ἀποστόλων.

13 False, therefore, are the judgments, respectively, of Harnack, "Prolegomena," 24–27, 30; and Knopf, *Lehre*, 3. Correct is that of Rordorf and Tuilier, *Doctrine*, 16–17: one should not be guided by either title in interpreting this work.

14 The Georgian has a still longer title: "Teaching of the Twelve Apostles, Written in the Year 90 or 100 after the Lord Christ: Teaching of the Lord, Con-veyed to Humanity through the Twelve Apostles."

15 By way of example, I list a number of positions on the question of the title. Schaff, *Church Manual*, 162 (cf. as early as p. 14): the long title rests on Acts 2:42 and Matt 28:19 and is probably original; Vokes, *Riddle*, 208: the title combines Matt 28:19–20 with Acts 2:41–42: "It seems evident that the two pas-sages at the end of Matthew and beginning of Acts explain the title and form of the Didache." According to Bartlet (*Church-Order*, 53) the long title may possibly come from the *editio altera et emendata*, with possible influence from Matt 28:19. Johnson, "Motive," 113–15: the author does not presume to write a gospel, but composes (among other things) a commentary, and supports his authority by pre-tending composition by the Twelve. Kleist, *Didache*, 153 n. 1: the short title was written on the outside of the scroll. Rordorf, "Tradition apostolique," 106: the short title refers to Acts 2:42, and the long title to Matt 28:19; cf. also Rordorf and Tuilier, *Doctrine*, 15–16.

1

1   **There are two ways, one to life and one to death, but the difference between the two ways is great.**

The document begins abruptly, without any particular introduction.[1] The Didachist commences with a quotation from the original Jewish didactic document, "On the Two Ways," which has already been superficially Christianized. In the macrocontext, however, he gives this writing a new overall meaning; for him, the tractate now serves (as 7.1 shows) as a model for instruction of baptismal candidates. In what follows (chaps. 1–6) is found what catechumens should be taught.[2]

■ **1** The initial clause (Ὁδοὶ δύο εἰσίν, μία τῆς ζωῆς καὶ μία τοῦ θανάτου, v. 1a) is a formulation of the *theme* of the tractate that follows. Human beings should know that they are faced with the alternative of two "ways," one of which leads to life, the other to death.[3] The following clause, about the difference between the two

ways (διαφορὰ δὲ πολλὴ μεταξὺ τῶν δύο ὁδῶν, v. 1b), underscores the character of the decision. Human beings stand before a parting of the ways: each individual can choose only one of the two paths. There is no compromise.

Excursus: The "Two Ways"

The topos of the "two ways"[4] was a widespread commonplace of ancient (and not only ancient) moral philosophy. For popular Greek moral thought, cf. Hesiod *Works and Days* 287–92 (Rzach, 70);[5] then the fable of Prodicus of Cheos retold by Xenophon *Mem.* 2.1.21–34 (Marchant);[6] in addition, see Theognis 911–14 (Diehl and Young, 56); Plutarch *Vita*

---

1   William Telfer ("The 'Plot' of the *Didache*," *JTS* 45 [1944] 149–50) thought that this document could not begin so abruptly; as it is now received, its beginning must be mutilated. Telfer (p. 150) reconstructs the supposed introductory text in very imaginative fashion.

2   It remains obvious that the instruction provided in chaps. 1–6 is incomplete (in spite of the additions by the Didachist). Still, it appears that the Didachist, to whom systematic theological reflection is something foreign, did not give any particular thought to this limitation. In any case, it would be wrong to try to restrict his confession of faith to the teachings in chaps. 1–6.

3   (Ὁδὸς) τῆς ζωῆς and τοῦ θανάτου involve objective genitives.

4   Knopf, *Lehre*, 4–5; Anton Vögtle, *Die Tugend- und Lasterkataloge im Neuen Testament: Exegetisch, religions- und formgeschichtlich untersucht* (NTAbh 16.4–5; Münster: Aschendorff, 1936) 113–20, 196–98; Wibbing, *Tugend- und Lasterkataloge*, 33–42, 61–64; Kamlah, *Paränese*, 149–50, 171–75; Suggs, "Two Ways Tradition," passim; Wilhelm Michaelis, "ὁδός," *TDNT* 5 (1967) 42–114; J. Bergman, "Zum Zwei-Wege Motiv," *SEÅ* 41/42 (1976–77) 27–56; Norbert Brox, *Der Glaube als Weg: Nach biblischen und altchristlichen Texten* (Munich and Salzburg:

Pustet, 1968); Bruno Snell, "Das Symbol des Weges," in idem, *Die Entdeckung des Geistes: Studien zur Entstehung des europäischen Denkens bei den Griechen* (4th ed.; Göttingen: Vandenhoeck & Ruprecht, 1975) 219–30.

5   *Τὴν μέν τοι κακότητα καὶ ἰλαδὸν ἔστιν ἐλέσθαι ῥηιδίως· λείη μὲν ὁδός, μάλα δ᾽ ἐγγύθι ναίει· τῆς δ᾽ ἀρετῆς ἱδρῶτα θεοὶ προπάροιθεν ἔθηκαν ἀθάνατοι· μακρὸς δὲ καὶ ὄρθιος οἶμος ἐς αὐτὴν καὶ τρηχὺς τὸ πρῶτον· ἐπὴν δ᾽ εἰς ἄκρον ἵκηται, ῥηιδίη δὴ ἔπειτα πέλει, χαλεπή περ ἐοῦσα.* ("Badness can be got easily and in shoals: the road to her is smooth, and she lives very near us. But between us and Goodness the gods have placed the sweat of our brows: long and steep is the path that leads to her, and it is rough at the first; but when a man has reached the top, then is she easy to reach, though before that she was hard"). The text is found within a longer admonition to exercise *dike*.

6   To show that the καλά τε κἀγαθὰ ἔργα ("noble deeds") can only be gained through effort, Xenophon's Socrates (*Mem.* 2.1.20) cites the passage from Hesiod, adding a quotation from Epicharmus and then referring (1.21–34) in his own words to the fable of Prodicus. Heracles is faced with the characteristic decision for νέοι· εἴτε τὴν δι᾽ ἀρετῆς ὁδὸν τρέψονται ἐπὶ τὸν βίον εἴτε τὴν διὰ

59

Demosthenis 26.7 (Ziegler, 306); and so on.[7] The parallels extend to Islamic[8] and even Buddhist tradition.[9]

This topos is also found in the Old Testament, explicitly in Ps 1:1-6 (1:6: ὁδὸς δικαίων/ὁδὸς ἀσεβῶν, "the way of the righteous"/"the way of the impious"); Ps 139 (138):24; Prov 2:13; 4:18-19 (combined with the pairing of light and darkness); 11:20; 12:28 LXX (combined with ζωή/θάνατος, "life/death"). But it may also lie behind expressions such as those in Deut 11:26-28; 30:15-20; Jer 21:8 (ὁδὸς τῆς ζωῆς/ὁδὸς τοῦ θανάτου, "way of life"/"way of death"); Ps 119 (118):29-30, and others. In texts from early Judaism[10] see, e.g., 1 Enoch 94:1-5; 2 Enoch, long recension 30:15 (Bonwetsch, 29): "And I showed him two ways, light and darkness";[11] shorter recension 42:10 (Bonwetsch, 89).[12] See the rabbinic material in Str-B 1.461-62; 4.1080; Wilhelm Michaelis, "ὁδός," TDNT 5 (1967) 58-60; cf. especially m. 'Abot 2.9; then b. Ber.

28b; b. Ḥag. 3b (with parallels in each case): Str-B 1.461; b. Men. 99b (Str-B 4.1080); Siphre Deut. 11.26 §53 on 11:26 (cf. Str-B 1.461-62); Exod. Rab. 30.20 on 21:1 (cf. Str-B 1.462); Deut. Rab. 4.4 on 11:22 (cf. Str-B 1.462).[13] It is important to note that in some areas of tradition in early Judaism the topos of the two ways was combined with a teaching about two spirits (or two angels).[14] Both are found most clearly in T. Ash. 1:3-5. Cf. especially: Δύο ὁδοὺς ἔδωκεν ὁ θεὸς τοῖς υἱοῖς τῶν ἀνθρώπων καὶ δύο διαβούλια καὶ δύο πράξεις καὶ δύο τρόπους (v.l. τόπους or πόνους) καὶ δύο τέλη (1:3, "God has granted two ways to the sons of men, two intentions and two behaviors and two manners"); Ὁδοὶ δύο, καλοῦ καὶ κακοῦ (1:5, "Two ways, of good and evil"), with an eschatological conclusion and the teaching about the two spirits that is associated with it:[15] ὅτι τὰ τέλη τῶν ἀνθρώπων δείκνυσι τὴν δικαιοσύνην αὐτῶν, γνωρίζοντες τοὺς

κακίας, ἐξελθόντα εἰς ἡσυχίαν καθῆσθαι ἀποροῦντα ποτέραν τῶν ὁδῶν τράπηται ("whether in life they will take the road through virtue or that through vice, going out to a quiet spot, he sat down perplexed as to which of the roads he should take," 1.21 [trans. Amy L. Bonnette, Xenophon, Memorabilia [Ithaca, N.Y.: Cornell University Press, 1994] 39). In his aporia, the arete and kakia appear to him in female forms, each recommending her own way (22-25). For the literature, see Berger, "Hellenistische Gattungen," 1089. Michaelis points out problems in the received interpretation of the fable ("ὁδός," 43-46), even though he went too far in some details. For the later impact of the fable, cf. Berger, "Hellenistische Gattungen," 1090; for Christian reception, Michaelis, "ὁδός," 46 n. 12; cf. Justin 2 Apol. 11.3-8 (Goodspeed, 86-87); Cf. Clement of Alexandria Strom. 2.20, 107.4-5 (GCS³ 2.171-72); in 5.5.31.1-2 (GCS³ 2.346), the Prodicus fable is associated with Matt 7:13-14 par. Lactantius writes of the two ways: quas et poetae in carminibus et philosophi in disputationibus suis induxerunt ("Which poets have introduced into their poems and philosophers into their disputations," Divin. Inst. 6.3.1; CSEL 19.485). Basil mentions the fable in his Sermo de Leg. Libr. Gent. 4 (PG 31.573); in Hom. in Ps. I 5 (PG 29.221) he may be alluding to it. Berger ("Hellenistische Gattungen," 1090 with citations) refers to the "series of allegorical agones, disputations between two women appearing in a vision" that follow the Prodicus fable.

7 Probably to be included in a broader sense are those passages that speak of the two ways that the soul has before it after death; cf. Plato Gorgias 524A (Burnet); Rep. 10.614C (Burnet); Diphilos the comic poet in Clement of Alexandria Strom. 5.14, 121.1 (GCS³

2.407); cf. Eusebius Praeparatio Evangelica 13.13.47 (GCS 8/2.219); Vergil Aeneid 6.540-43 (Hirtzel).
    hic locus est partis ubi se via findit in ambas:
    destera quae Ditis magni sub moenia tendit,
    hac iter Elysium nobis; at laeva malorum
    exercet poenas et ad impia Tartara mittit.
("Here is the place where the road parts in twain; there to the right, as it runs under the walls of great Dis, is our way to Elysium, but the left wreaks punishment of the wicked and sends them on to pitiless Tartarus.") The ideas in the "Book of the Two Ways" of the Egyptians are quite different. On that see J. Bergman, "Zum Zwei-Wege Motif," SEA 41/42 (1976-77) 51-52.

8 The conclusion of the opening sura of the Koran reads:
    "Guide us in the straight path,
        the path of those whom thou hast blessed,
    not of those against whom thou art wrathful,
        nor of those who are astray."
(Translation by Charles Arberry, The Koran Interpreted [London: Allen & Unwin; New York: Macmillan, 1955] 1.)

9 See the examples in Knopf, Lehre, 5.

10 Sir. 33(36):7-15? On this, see Paul Winter, "Ben Sira and the Teaching of 'Two Ways,'" VT 5 (1955) 315-18 (problematic).

11 For this, cf. also the similar statements in Mek. Exod. on 14:29 (Lauterbach, 1.248) and Gen. Rab. 21.5 on 3:22 (Str-B 1.461).

12 The examples in Philo are a chapter in themselves: see, e.g., Deus imm. 180; Plant. 37; Abr. 269; Vit. Mos. 2.138; Spec. leg. 4.108, διττὴ ὁδός, ἡ μὲν ἐπὶ κακίαν, ἡ δ᾽ ἐπ᾽ ἀρετὴν ἄγουσα ("the road is divided, one leads to vice and the other to virtue"), etc. The examples from Philo deserve a new study. To

ἀγγέλους κυρίου καὶ τοῦ σατανᾶ. Ἐὰν γὰρ τεταραγ-
μένη ἡ ψυχὴ ἀπέρχεται, βασανίζεται ὑπὸ τοῦ
πονηροῦ πνεύματος, οὗ καὶ ἐδούλευσεν ἐν ἐπιθυμί-
αις καὶ ἔργοις πονηροῖς· ἐὰν δὲ ἡσύχως ἐν χαρᾷ,
ἐγνώρισε τὸν ἄγγελον τῆς εἰρήνης, (ὃς) παρακαλέ-
σει αὐτὸν ἐν ζωῇ (6:4–6, "For the ultimate end of
human beings displays their righteousness, since they
are made known to the angels of the Lord and of
Beliar. For when the evil soul departs, it is harassed
by the evil spirit that it served through its desires and
evil works. But if one departs peacefully with joy, he
comes to know the angel of peace and enters eternal
life").[16]

In 1QS 3.18–4.26 the two-ways schema (the way of

light and the way of darkness: 3.20–21) is similarly
combined with the teaching about the two spirits
(two spirits are found in 3.18–19: "the spirits of truth
and of wickedness," and this is expanded in the subsequent passage).[17] The Qumran doctrine presents a
certain parallel to the combination of the teaching
about the two spirits or two angels with the two-ways
schema in the *Testament of Asher* and in the Jewish
source for the Two Ways tractate that interests us
here. This combination still appears in the Christian
recension in *Barnabas* and *Doctrina apostolorum*,[18]
while the teaching about the two spirits is absent
from the recension of the Two Ways tractate in the
Didache[19] (and in later recensions).[20] In fact, the com-

what extent was the fable of Prodicus here combined with OT tradition? How is the motif of the
ways more closely connected with the motif of the
βασιλικὴ ὁδός (the "royal road" to virtue)?

13 The use of the image in the sense of a middle way
between two extremes is something different. See
examples in Str-B 1.462–63.

14 Judaism may have received the impulse to the development of the teaching about the two spirits from
Iranian tradition, but the religio-historical connections cannot be traced here. Kamlah, in particular,
has given an instructive treatment of this; cf. esp.
Paränese, 163–68. There is a different version in
Berger, *Formgeschichte*, 150–51. According to him, it
is more likely that the conception of the two spirits
or angels is derived from *Greek* tradition, and in particular from the concept of the two women that
appears as early as the Prodicus fable and experienced many further developments (cf. idem, "Hellenistische Gattungen," 1090–91). "I find the two
women in Greek tradition transformed, in the
Jewish and Christian field, into two angels, two pow-
ers infused at birth, two types of spirits, or—as in
Galatians 5—related to spirit . . . and flesh as two
'spheres.' The occasion for me to make this suggestion is the fact that there is always a series of virtues
and vices associated with each of the two figures. A
connecting link between pagan and Jewish-Christian
forms of the tradition is the analogy in Silius Italicus
Punica 15.20–21: It is said of *virtus* and *voluptas* that
they are '*per auras allapsae.*' It is also understandable
from this tradition why this kind of catalog was combined, in *Barnabas* 18 and *Didache* 1, with the two
ways, because the (divided) way motif is proper to
this tradition. It is true that there are also two ways
in the Old Testament, but without any connection
with catalogs" (*Formgeschichte*, 150–51). The combination of the two-ways schema with the conception
of the two spirits would thus be—transformed—
Greek or Hellenistic tradition; then the conjunction
of both conceptions with parenetic catalogs would
also be traceable to Greco-Hellenistic tradition. For

convenience, I include here the passage from Silius
Italicus *Pun.* 15.18–22 (Bauer, 108) that is important
for Berger's argumentation:

> Has, lauri residens iuvenis viridante sub umbra,
> Aedibus extremis volvebat pectore curas,
> Cum subito assistunt, dextra laevaque per auras
> Allapsae, haud paulum mortali maior imago,
> Hinc Virtus, illinc virtuti inimica Voluptas.

("These anxious thoughts filled the young man's
mind, as he sat beneath the green shadow of a
baytree that grew behind the dwelling; and suddenly two figures, far exceeding mortal stature,
flew down from the sky and stood to right and left
of him: Virtue was on the one side, and Pleasure,
the enemy of Virtue, on the other.") The verbal battle between the two then follows, in vv. 32–120.

15 For the two-spirits teaching in *Testaments of the 12
Patriarchs*, and for the combination of that teaching
with parenetic material (outside the context of the
two-ways teaching), cf. Wibbing, *Tugend- und
Lasterkataloge*, 35–39.

16 When Philo (*Sacr. AC* 20–44, allegorizing Deut
21:15–17) speaks of the two women he calls ἡδονή
("pleasure") and ἀρετή ("virtue"; the parallel in
Sobr. 22–25 is less instructive), he has in mind of
course the material of the Prodicus fable.

17 In 1QS 3–4 as well, parenetic catalogs are combined
with the two-spirits doctrine and the two-ways
schema (4.2–14). Between the virtue and vice catalogs stands (in 4.6–8) an eschatological prospect. Cf.
also the eschatological conclusion after the vice catalog (4.11–14).

18 *Barn.* 18.1 and *Doctr.* 1.1.

19 For the whole, cf. Audet, "Affinités littéraires,"
219–38; Braun, *Qumran*, 2.185–89. We cannot discuss *Hermas Man.* 5.1.2, 4; 6.1. 1; 1.3–4; 2.1 here.
Does 1 John 1:6–7 belong here also? Cf. Wolfgang
Nauck, *Die Tradition und der Charakter des ersten
Johannesbriefes* (WUNT 3; Tübingen, Mohr, 1957)
59–62.

20 Audet ("Affinités littéraires," 234–35) associates the
Two Ways tractate and the exposition in 1QS too

bination of the two-ways schema and the two-spirit teaching reflects distant contacts between the Jewish source of the Two Ways tractate and the Qumran doctrine. Note that these are *distant* contacts, and of course represent no material identity. Nevertheless, the literature that interests us here also, naturally, contains other examples of the two-ways schema that are *not* combined with the teaching on the two spirits or angels: cf. Matt 7:13–14 par.; 2 Pet 2:15.[21] The two-ways motif also appears, not combined with the doctrine of two spirits, in *Sib. Or.* 8.399–401: αὐτὸς ὁδοὺς προέθηκα δύο, ζωῆς θανάτου τε, καὶ γνώμη προέθηκ᾿ ἀγαθὴν ζωὴν προελέσθαι· αὐτοὶ δ᾿ ἐς θάνατον καὶ πῦρ αἰώνιον ἦξαν ("I myself proposed two ways, of life and death, and proposed to the judgment to choose good life. But they turned eagerly to death and eternal fire").[22] But *Ps.-Clem. Hom.* 7.3.3–5 (GCS[2] 1.117–18) again reveals a distant analogy to the Qumran teaching on the two spirits, to the extent that there is reference to two ἄρχοντες or ἡγεμόνες, to the right and to the left, who apparently are placed as rulers over the respective ways. Still, the two-ways motif is only hinted at here. In contrast, the motif appears explicitly in 7.7.1–3 (GCS[2] 1.119)—although it is true that the two-spirits doctrine is again absent: ταύτας τοίνυν τάς τε ἀγαθὰς καὶ κακὰς πράξεις εἰδὼς προμηνύω ὑμῖν ὡς ὁδοὺς δύο. . . . (2) ἡ μὲν οὖν

τῶν ἀπολλυμένων ὁδὸς πλατεῖα μὲν καὶ ὁμαλωτάτη, ἀπολλύουσα δὲ ἄνευ τοῦ πόνου, ἡ δὲ τῶν σῳζομένων στενὴ μὲν καὶ τραχεῖα, σῴζουσα δὲ πρὸς τῷ τέλει τοὺς διαπορευθέντας ἐπιπόνως· (3) τούτων δὲ τῶν δύο ὁδῶν προκαθέζεται ἀπιστία καὶ πίστις ("Knowing, then, these good and evil deeds, I make known unto you as it were two paths. . . . The path of the lost, then, is broad and very smooth — it ruins them without troubling them; but the path of the saved is narrow, rugged, and in the end it saves, not without much toil, those who have journeyed through it. And these two paths are presided over by unbelief and faith" [ANF 8.269]).[23]

If we attempt to understand the concrete form in which the two-ways motif more specifically appears in the tradition that particularly interests us here, the result is a picture somewhat like this: the topos of the two ways (known already in the OT) was combined (and from the point of view of the material itself this is understandable and even conclusive) in certain traditions of early Judaism and thus of Christianity with the doctrine of the two spirits or angels. We may set aside the question whether impulses from Iranian tradition or models from Greek or Hellenistic traditions were determinative. In any case, we must suppose that in certain streams of tradition within Judaism and early Christianity the two-ways doctrine was

closely, despite the difference he also describes. Braun also (*Qumran,* 2.188) sees the differences (the contrasting pair ζωή–θάνατος is the very one that is absent in 1QS; the fact that the *Didache* does not speak of a light/darkness contrast, nor present the motif of the two angels, is another subject altogether). Nevertheless, Braun concludes that "1QS as direct or indirect source for the texts of the Fathers is not unthinkable" (ibid.). Instead of calling it a "source," I would prefer to speak of a common tradition. That is more adequate to the idea of a variable editing and variable meaning acquired by insertion into different contexts. Incidentally, Wengst (*Barnabasbrief,* 63) wished to attribute the tradition that recalls 1QS 3–4 not to the original tractate but to a redactor of the archetype of *Barnabas* and *Didache.* This is improbable.

21 1 Cor 4:17 ὁδοί = teaching (cf. Hans Conzelmann, *1 Corinthians* [Hermeneia; Philadelphia: Fortress Press, 1975] 92–93).

22 It is true that *Ps.-Phocylides* offers numerous parallels to individual sayings in the tractate, but what is lacking is any explicit example of the two-ways motif. Hence there is no direct tradition-historical relationship to the tractate. For the history of research, see van der Horst, *Sentences,* 14–16, 23–24, 42, 45.

23 Note the framework: baptismal catechesis. In addition, is there an influence from Matt 7:13–14 par.?

24 According to Berger ("Hellenistische Gattungen," 1091) it is true in general that parenetic catalogs arose "through *ekphrasis* . . . and *prosopopoeia* . . . from the two fundamental ways." Cf. pp. 1202–3. The catalogs of virtues and vices, in any case, originate in the Hellenistic realm.

25 Cf. Kamlah, *Paränese,* 210; Suggs, "Two Ways Tradition," 63–67, and the alternative proposals by Berger, "Hellenistische Gattungen," 1090–91; idem, *Formgeschichte,* 150–51.

26 Nota bene: 1QS 3.18–4.26 naturally does not constitute the literary source of our Two Ways tractate, but represents a distant analogy. 1QS 3.18–4.26 and *T. Ash.* 1.3–5 point to a particular literary type, a literary "pattern" from which the Jewish-Christian Two Ways tractate with which we are dealing here also originated.

27 Cf. above, Introduction, 6.b, esp. n. 47.

28 For Rordorf ("Two Ways," 153) the answer to the question of the origin of the tractate is posed hypothetically as follows: "the Old Testament ethical tradition attached to the *Bundesformular* [covenant formulary] has undergone, in certain circles of late Judaism (not in all), a clearly dualistic modification under Persian influence. . . . Christianity has inher-

oriented to that of the two spirits; we should further suppose that both were given additional and concrete form within different types of parenesis.[24] A concluding eschatological warning was then added. From the combination of these elements (two ways, doctrine of the two spirits, forms of parenesis, eschatological epilogue)[25] arose, among other things, the tractate that was the earliest ancestor of *Didache* 1–6.[26] Thus what appeared in this instance was only a particular development, a special type of the two-ways motif that, in a variety of other forms, continued to be influential alongside it and independent of it, both in Judaism and in early Christianity. It may be doubted whether one can fix the *Sitz im Leben* of the Jewish tradition underlying the tractate in contemporary instruction for proselytes.[27] I would prefer to think of Jewish religious societies of the "awakened," for whom the tractate served as a community rule. The Christians then received the whole thing from Jewish tradition, altered it, and gave the tradition a new *Sitz im Leben*.[28]

Hence the quotation of the *Didache*'s source begins immediately at *Did.* 1.1. It is a citation from one version of the Two Ways tractate. It can no longer be said with certainty whether this source spoke not only of the two ways but also of the two angels or spirits who are placed over those ways (as we now find it, mutatis mutandis, in the version in *Barnabas* and *Doctrina*).[29] It is probable, though. If that is the case, the Didachist would have

omitted the motif of the *angeli duo*, perhaps because it plays no part in the exposition that follows.[30] In the wake of this omission, then, anything about the "way of light and darkness" would also have dropped out.[31] What remains has the character of a sententious formulation: ὁδοὶ δύο εἰσί, μία τῆς ζωῆς καὶ μία τοῦ θανάτου, διαφορὰ δὲ πολλὴ μεταξὺ τῶν δύο ὁδῶν ("There are two ways, one of life and one of death, but there is a great difference between the two"). In the overall context of the *Didache*, the two-ways schema acquires an additional and concrete specification. The educational lecture is directed (as the structure of the book shows, and as one discovers after the fact in 7.1) to the catechumens, and the decision before which they are placed by the two-ways schema is now whether to become Christians. Accepting baptism is connected with the acceptance of a certain way of life, at the end of which is eschatological life (ζωή). The concept of ζωή now includes the salvation of the end time, mediated by Christ, and that of θάνατος includes the final judgment. In this sense, the Didachist adopted the tradition and adapted it.

---

ited both these currents, dualistic and non-dualistic." Here I find dubious not only the concept of "dualism" but also the reference to the so-called covenant formulary. The attempt by Klaus Baltzer to find a "covenant formulary" also behind *Barnabas* and the *Didache* (*Das Bundesformular* [2d ed.; WMANT 4; Neukirchen-Vluyn: Neukirchener Verlag, 1964] 128–37, ET of 1st ed.: *The Covenant Formulary; in Old Testament, Jewish, and Early Christian Writings* [trans. David E. Green; Philadelphia: Fortress, 1975] 123–32) I consider unsuccessful. A critique of the derivation of the two-spirits teaching from 1QS 3 from the covenant formulary was found as early as Kamlah, *Paränese*, 163 n. 1. Incidentally, Rordorf later (in *Doctrine*, 26, n. 3) issued a more critical judgment on Baltzer's relevant observations. For the *Sitz im Leben* of the tractate tradition in the Christian realm, and for later changes in the *Sitz im Leben*, cf. Rordorf, "Two Ways," 153–59. [Ed. On the development of the Two Ways tradition, see now John Kloppenborg, "The Transformation of

Moral Exhortation in *Didache* 1–5," in Jefford, *Context*, 88–109.]

29 Ὁδοὶ δύο εἰσὶν διδαχῆς καὶ ἐξουσίας, ἥ τε τοῦ φωτὸς καὶ ἡ τοῦ σκότους . . . ἐφ᾿ ἧς μὲν γάρ εἰσιν τεταγμένοι φωταγωγοὶ ἄγγελοι τοῦ θεοῦ, ἐφ᾿ ἧς δὲ ἄγγελοι τοῦ σατανᾶ ("There are two ways of teaching and power, one of light and one of darkness . . . on one of which angels of God are stationed as light-bearers; on the other are angels of Satan," *Barn.* 18.1). *Viae duae sunt in saeculo, uitae et mortis, lucis et tenebrarum, in his constituti sunt angeli duo, unus aequitatis, alter iniquitatis* ("There are two ways in the world, one of light and one of darkness, and in these are stationed two angels, one of justice and one of iniquity," *Doctr.* 1.1). Cf. 1QS 3.18–19, and *T. Ash.* 6.4.

30 The motif is also lacking in *Canons* and *Epitome*.

31 Again in agreement with *Canons* and *Epitome*. Drews had already inferred ("Apostellehre," 257) that the light/darkness motif and the expressions about the two angels were not absent from the source.

**a. The Fundamental Commandment (1.2) and
Introduction to Its Performance (3a)**

2. The Way of Life (1.2–4.14)

2 The way to life is this: "First, you shall love
God, who has created you; second, your
neighbor as yourself. Whatever you do not
want to happen to you, do not do to another."

3a This is the teaching [that comes] from these
words:

■ **2** The superscription, ἡ μὲν οὖν ὁδὸς τῆς ζωῆς ἐστιν αὕτη (2a, "The way of life is this"), is followed by a kind of basic demand or summary of all commandments that, if kept, will lead to the attainment of life. The double love commandment appears as this kind of basic demand. It is constructed from Deut 6:5 and Lev 19:18b,[1] in the form πρῶτον ἀγαπήσεις τὸν θεὸν τὸν ποιήσαντά σε, δεύτερον τὸν πλησίον σου ὡς σεαυτόν[2] (2b, "You shall love first the God who created you, then your neighbor as yourself"). One should compare the double commandment in the *Didache* text with Mark 12:30–31/Matt 22:37–39, where it is found on the lips of Jesus, and Luke 10:27, where it appears in the mouth of a νομικός τις. The series πρῶτον–δεύτερον is the same as in Matthew and Mark (but is absent in Luke).[3] As found in *Did.* 1.2b, however, the form of the double commandment can scarcely come from one of the Synoptic Gospels (e.g., Matthew).[4] The differences are too great.[5] First, the text of the *Didache* form is, in contrast to

Deuteronomy and the Synoptics, significantly shortened. It is even shorter than Justin *Dial.* 93.2 (Goodspeed, 208). In the quotation from Deut 6:5 the reference to "heart," "soul," and "power," "mind," or "strength" (καρδία, ψυχή, and δύναμις [or διάνοια and ἰσχύς]) is absent. Instead of "the Lord your God" (κύριον τὸν θεόν σου) we find, against Deuteronomy, but also against the Synoptic tradition, "God who made you" (τὸν θεὸν τὸν ποιήσαντά σε).[6] As the parallel in *Barn.* 19.2 shows (ἀγαπήσεις τὸν ποιήσαντά σε), these characteristic expressions were already part of the text of the older version of the Two Ways tractate.[7] Finally, the double commandment also stands alone in the *Didache*—unlike in the Synoptic tradition—without being inserted into a narrative framework.[8] There is thus no dependence on Matthew (or any other Synoptic Gospel), but an independent tradition.[9] It is obvious that the double commandment appears only in the (later) recension of the Two Ways tractate that was used for the *Didache* and the

1 This is different from the recension of the tractate available for *Barn.* 19.1–12, where love of God and neighbor are commanded, but these are not joined to form a double commandment. Cf. *Barn.* 19.2 and 5, and see further below.

2 *Canons, Epitome, Constitutions* read ἑαυτόν, which Wengst (*Didache*, 66) also adopts for the *Didache*. The σεαυτόν in H could be an unconscious adaptation to the Gospel text.

3 Matthew: αὕτη ἐστὶν ἡ μεγάλη καὶ πρώτη ἐντολή (22:38); δευτέρα δὲ ὁμοία αὐτῇ . . . (22:39); Mark: ἐντολὴ πρώτη πάντων (12:28); and δευτέρα αὕτη (12:31).

4 Thus, e.g., Connolly, "Relation," 245; Massaux, *Influence,* 3.147.

5 See the synopsis in table 5.

6 Cf. also Ps.-Menander, 65 (Rießler, 1055): "Do not despise God who created you."

7 Koester, *Synoptische Überlieferung*, 172. The same expression (τὸν ποιήσαντα αὐτούς) is also in *Barn.* 20.2/*Did.* 5.2, but see the commentary on that passage. It is striking that Justin also (*2 Apol.* 16.6

[Goodspeed, 37]) uses a similar expression in his quotation from Deut 6:5. In turn, Franz Xaver Funk ("Zur Apostellehre und apostolischen Kirchenordnung," *ThQ* 69 [1887] 357–59) concluded from this that Justin knew the *Didache* (see above, Introduction, §2b). Something analogous is true of the *Passio beati Phileae* 3 (end) (see above, Introduction, §2b).

8 Koester, *Synoptische Überlieferung*, 172.

9 Koester, *Synoptische Überlieferung*, 172.

10 Koester, *Synoptische Überlieferung*, 172. The result was that in *Did.* 2.7 and in the parallel versions (cf. *Barn.* 19.5) the commandment of love of neighbor appears a second time (p. 171).

11 On this, cf. Günther Bornkamm, "Das Doppelgebot der Liebe," in Walther Eltester, ed., *Neutestamentliche Studien für R. Bultmann* (2d ed.; BZNW 21; Berlin: Töpelmann, 1954) 85–93, repr. in idem, *Geschichte und Glaube* (*Gesammelte Aufsätze* 3–4) (2 vols.; BevTh 48; Munich: Kaiser, 1968–71) 1.37–45; Christoph Burchard, "Das doppelte Liebesgebot in der frühen christlichen Überliefe-

Table 5

Deut 6:5	Matt 22:37–39	Mark 12:29–31	Luke 10:27	*Did.* 1.2
—	—	(29) πρώτη ἐστίν . . .	—	πρῶτον
καὶ ἀγαπήσεις	(37) ἀγαπήσεις	(30) καὶ ἀγαπήσεις	ἀγαπήσεις	ἀγαπήσεις
κύριον τὸν θεόν σου	κύριον τὸν θεόν σου	κύριον τὸν θεόν σου	κύριον τὸν θεόν σου	τὸν θεὸν τὸν
ἐξ ὅλης τῆς καρδίας σου	ἐν ὅλῃ τῇ καρδίᾳ σου	ἐξ ὅλης τῆς καρδίας σου	ἐξ ὅλης [τῆς] καρδίας σου	ποιήσαντά σε
καὶ ἐξ ὅλης τῆς ψυχῆς σου	καὶ ἐν ὅλῃ τῇ ψυχῇ σου	καὶ ἐξ ὅλης τῆς ψυχῆς σου	καὶ ἐν ὅλῃ τῇ ψυχῇ σου	
—	καὶ ἐν ὅλῃ τῇ διανοίᾳ σου.	καὶ ἐξ ὅλης τῆς διανοίας σου	καὶ ἐν ὅλῃ τῇ ἰσχύϊ σου	
καὶ ἐξ ὅλης τῆς δυνάμεώς σου	—	καὶ ἐξ ὅλης τῆς ἰσχύος σου.	καὶ ἐν ὅλῃ τῇ διανοίᾳ σου,	
	(38) αὕτη ἐστὶν ἡ μεγάλη καὶ πρώτη ἐντολή.			
Lev 19:18b:	(39) δευτέρα ὁμοία αὐτῇ·	(31) δευτέρα αὕτη·		δεύτερον
καὶ ἀγαπήσεις	ἀγαπήσεις	ἀγαπήσεις	καὶ	—
τὸν πλησίον σου	τὸν πλησίον σου	τὸν πλησίον σου	τὸν πλησίον σου	τὸν πλησίον σου
ὡς σεαυτόν·	ὡς σεαυτόν.	ὡς σεαυτόν.	ὡς σεαυτόν	ὡς σεαυτόν.

Justin *1 Apol.* 16.6 (Goodspeed, 37): Μεγίστη ἐντολή ἐστι· Κύριον τὸν θεόν σου προσκυνήσεις καὶ αὐτῷ μόνῳ λατρεύσεις ἐξ ὅλης τῆς καρδίας σου καὶ ἐξ ὅλης τῆς ἰσχύος σου, κύριον τὸν θεὸν τὸν ποιήσαντά σε.

Dial. 93.2 (Goodspeed, 208): ἐν δυσὶν ἐντολαῖς πᾶσαν δικαιοσύνην καὶ εὐσέβειαν πληροῦσθαι· εἰσὶ δὲ αὗται· Ἀγαπήσεις κύριον τὸν θεόν σου ἐξ ὅλης τῆς καρδίας σου καὶ ἐξ ὅλης τῆς ἰσχύος σου, καὶ τὸν πλησίον σου ὡς σεαυτόν.

Canons of the Apostles and *Epitome*, and that is behind the Latin *Doctrina* (but not in the older recension on which *Barnabas* 18–20 builds). We must apparently imagine that the Two Ways tractate, in its introduction, originally spoke only of the commandment to love God (*Barn.* 19.2). At some point a redactor expanded the command to love God by adding the commandment to love one's neighbor, and so constructed the double commandment. In doing so, he made the doubling explicit by inserting "first" and "second" (πρῶτον and δεύτερον).[10] *Doctrina*, *Didache*, *Canons*, and *Epitome* (each in its own way) rest on this recension. The sense in which even contemporary Judaism recognized something like a "double commandment" of love need not be discussed here.[11] For

rung," in Eduard Lohse, Christoph Burchard, and B. Schaller, eds., *Der Ruf Jesu und die Antwort der Gemeinde: Exegetische Untersuchungen Joachim Jeremias zum 70. Geburtstag gewidmet* (Göttingen: Vandenhoeck & Ruprecht, 1970) 39–62; Klaus Berger, *Die Gesetzesauslegung Jesu*, vol. 1: *Markus und Parallelen* (WMANT 40; Neukirchen-Vluyn: Neukirchener Verlag, 1972) 136–65; Andreas Nissen, *Gott und der Nächste im antiken Judentum: Untersuchungen zum Doppelgebot der Liebe* (WUNT 15; Tübingen: Mohr, 1974) 230–44; Wolfgang Schrage, *Ethik des Neuen Testaments* (NTD Ergänzungsreihe 4; Göttingen: Vandenhoeck & Ruprecht, 1982) 69–72; Karl Kertelge, "Das Doppelgebot der Liebe im Markusevangelium," in *À Cause de l'Évangile: Études sur les Synoptiques et les Actes offertes à P. Jacques Dupont, O.S.B., à l'occasion de son 70ᵉ anniversaire* (LD 123; Paris: Cerf, 1985) 303–22. The closest examples are the *Testaments of the 12 Patriarchs*, esp. *T. Sim.* 5.2; *T. Iss.* 5.1–2; 7.6; *T. Dan* 5.1, 3; *T. Zeb.* 5.1; *T. Jos.* 11.1; *T. Benj.* 3.1, 3; 10.3. But for the characteristic restrictions in the *Testaments* see Nissen, *Gott und der Nächste*, 232–44. Approaching a double love commandment, at least, are the demands of the Essenes transmitted by Josephus in *Bell.* 2.139 (with πρῶτον and ἔπειτα) and *Ant.* 15.375. Philo knows a threefold love commandment: ὅροις καὶ κανόσι τριττοῖς χρώμενοι, τῷ δὲ φιλοθέῳ καὶ φιλαρέτῳ καὶ φιλανθρώπῳ ("taking for their defining standards these three, love of God, love of virtue, love of men," *Omn. prob. lib.* 83; this is expanded in 84). Cf. also *Spec. leg.* 2.63, where he speaks of two principal commandments (toward God and human beings), although not of *agape*: ἔστι δ᾽ ὡς ἔπος

our passage I would like to posit that the characteristic formulation in *Did.* 1.2b (or its source) already points to Christian tradition.[12] Probably favoring this understanding is also the combined quotation of Deut 6:5 and Lev 19:18b that is lacking also in the Jewish "parallels," although this quotation is not explicit in the *Didache*.

■ **2c** The insertion of the so-called Golden Rule, "whatever you do not want to happen to you, do not do to another" (πάντα δὲ ὅσα ἐὰν θελήσῃς μὴ γίνεσθαί σοι,[13] καὶ σὺ ἄλλῳ μὴ ποίει), goes back to the same (later) recension of the Two Ways tractate. Here, as in most cases, it is formulated in the negative,[14] whereas in Matt 7:12/Luke 6:31 it appears in a positive form.[15] A literary quotation (from Matthew, for example)[16] cannot be demonstrated,[17] nor is it probable, given the widespread popularity of the rule.[18] In context, it is quite unlikely that the Golden Rule here represents the "third part of the principal commandment."[19] Instead, it is simply an interpretation of the commandment to love the neighbor, and more precisely an interpretation of that characteristic "as yourself" (ὡς σεαυτόν) with which love of self is made the model and measure of love of neigh-

---

εἰπεῖν τῶν κατὰ μέρος ἀμυθήτων λόγων καὶ δογμάτων δύο τὰ ἀνωτάτω κεφάλαια, τό τε πρὸς θεὸν δι' εὐσεβείας καὶ ὁσιότητος καὶ τὸ πρὸς ἀνθρώπους διὰ φιλανθρωπίας καὶ δικαιοσύνης· ὧν ἑκάτερον εἰς πολυσχιδεῖς ἰδέας καὶ πάσας ἐπαινετὰς τέμνεται ("But among the vast number of particular truths and principles there studied, there stand out practically high above the others two main heads: one of duty to God as shewn by piety and holiness, one of duty to men as shewn by humanity and justice, each of them splitting up into multiform branches all highly laudable"). Cf. also *Decal.* 110, and for the whole, Nissen, *Gott und der Nächste*, 498–502.

12 Of course, I presume that the older version available to *Barnabas* (in which the double commandment is still lacking) stemmed from a Christian as well.

13 Wengst (*Didache*, 66) reads (with *Constitutions*): καὶ πᾶν ὃ μὴ θέλεις γενέσθαι σοι.

14 Cf. *Ep. Arist.* 207 (SC 89, 196); Tob 4:15 BA; Philo *Hyp.* 1 in Eusebius *Praep. ev.* 8.7.6 (GCS 8/1.430); *b. Šab.* 31a; *T. Naph.* (Hebrew) 1.6 (Str–B 1.460); Christian examples: Acts 15:20, 29 D et al.; *Ep. apost.* 18 (29) (*NTApoc*, 1.259); Theophilus *Ad Autolycum* 2.34 (*PG* 6.1108); Aristides *Apol.* 15.5 (Goodspeed, 20); *Gos. Thom.* (Coptic) 6 (Leipoldt, 27); cf. Greek *P. Oxy.* 654.5 (Fitzmyer, 528); Irenaeus *Adv. haer.* 3.12.14 (SC 211, 242, and 244, adopting the D text of Acts 15:20, 29); Clement of Alexandria *Strom.* 2.23, 139.2 (GCS³ 2.190); *Ps.-Clem. Rec.* 8.56.7 (GCS 2.253); *Didasc.* (Syriac) 1 (CSC 401.13; 402.11), (Latin) 2.12–13 (TU 75.4); Ps.-Cyprian *De Centes.* 42 (Reitzenstein, 86.340–41); *Lib. grad.* 7.1 (Kmosko, 146); 30.26 (922–23), etc.

15 Cf. (*1 Clem.* 13.2); Clement of Alexandria *Paed.* 3.12.88.1 (GCS³ 1.284); *Ps.-Clem. Hom.* 7.4.3 (GCS 1.118); 11.4.4 (1.155); *Lib. grad.* 15.16 (Kmosko, 375).

16 Matt 7:12: πάντα οὖν ὅσα ἐὰν θέλητε ἵνα ποιῶσιν ὑμῖν οἱ ἄνθρωποι ("Whatever you wish that people would do to you"); *Did.* 1.2: πάντα δὲ ὅσα ἐὰν θελήσῃς ("everything that you wish").

17 Massaux (*Influence*, 3.147) differs, pointing out, among other things, that the *regula aurea* is found both in Matthew and in the *Didache* in connection with the motif of the two ways (cf. Matt 7:12 + 7:13–14). Robinson ("Barnabas and the Didache," 229–30) went still farther, seeing in *Did.* 1.2 a combination of the "Western" text of Acts 15:20, 29 with Matt 7:12.

18 Koester, *Synoptische Überlieferung*, 168–70. On the *regula aurea* in general, see Leonidas J. Philippidis, *Die "Goldene Regel" religionsgeschichtlich untersucht* (Inaugural Dissertation Leipzig; Eisleben: Klöppel, 1929); idem, *Religionswissenschaftliche Forschungsberichte über die "goldene Regel"* (Athens, n.p., 1933); Albrecht Dihle, *Die goldene Regel* (Studienhefte zur Altertumswissenschaft 7; Göttingen: Vandenhoeck & Ruprecht, 1962); Hans Werner Bartsch, "Traditionsgeschichtliches zur 'goldenen Regel' und zum Aposteldekret," *ZNW* 75 (1984) 128–32; Hans-Peter Mathys, "Goldene Regel I: Judentum," *TRE* 13 (1984) 570–73; and Roman Heiligenthal, "Goldene Regel II: Neues Testament und frühen Christentum," *TRE* 13 (1984) 573–75. For the relationship between negative and positive forms, see Dihle, *Die goldene Regel*, 10–11.

19 Knopf, *Lehre*, 5.

20 Audet (*Didachè*, 262) compares this expression (unnecessarily) with 1QpHab. 5.3: פשר הדבר.

21 *Doctrina* reads *interpretatio* for διδαχή.

22 *Doctrina* reverses these: *non moechaberis* (*mechaberis* f), *non homicidium facies*.

23 This was a subsequent construction by the redactor of the source, for originally the list of prohibitions in 2.2–7 had nothing to do with the idea of an all-encompassing twofold basic commandment. In the explication, moreover, the double focus of the basic commandment (love of God and love of neighbor) does not appear. In the recension available to *Barnabas*, then, the construction with a double

66

bor. That means, however, that the fundamental commandment whose fulfillment leads "to life" is:

1. Love God (demand) who created you (reason).
2. Love your neighbor as yourself (demand), because your relationship to your neighbor rests on mutual avoidance of evil (reason).

The summary may be secondary, but it is, in any case, well thought out. It clearly bears a didactic, catechetical character.

■ **3a** The quotation of the "basic commandment" was followed, in the source, by a kind of explication of this demand. It is indicated and introduced by the expression "This is the teaching[20] [that comes] from these words" (τούτων δὲ τῶν λόγων ἡ διδαχή[21] ἐστιν αὕτη). In the source, this was followed immediately by the text of

2.2–7 (οὐ φονεύσεις, οὐ μοιχεύσεις κτλ.),[22] that is, by a list of prohibitions that, in the context of the source, had the function of expanding and concretizing the basic commandment through special commands.[23] The text attested in H, Georgian (without 1.5–6), and indirectly in *Constitutions* (up to 5a) offers, before this, a rather long insertion (1.3b–2.1) that appears to be specifically Christian.[24] Its great antiquity is demonstrated also by P (for 1.3c–4a).[25] There would be further evidence if 1.3d and 5c were really attested by quotations in the Syrian *Didascalia apostolorum* 1.[26] The insertion at *Did.* 1.3b–2.1 can be described as a "Christian interpolation" or "*sectio evangelica.*" The paired questions of the originality of the *sectio* and the source of its material are among the crucial problems of the *Didache*.

---

commandment and an explication through a series of prohibitions is lacking. Rordorf ("Gebrauch des Dekalogs," 432–34) has pointed out that in early Christian times there was a tradition of combining the Golden Rule with the second table of the Decalogue. The *Didache* is the oldest example of this, but we should also note that here the *Didache* is quoting an originally Jewish source.

24 More precisely: the text fragment (fol. 1) begins with οὐχὶ καὶ . . . and ends with σαρκεικῶν ἐπιθυμειῶν. See above, Introduction, §3b.

25 By contrast, 1.3b–2.1 is lacking in *Barnabas*, *Doctrina apostolorum, Canons of the Apostles, Epitome,*

and there is nothing corresponding to it in the *Life of Shenoute, Syntagma doctrinae,* and *Fides patrum.*

26 (CSCO 401.41 and 402.12), Latin 2.28–31 (TU 75.4); also Syriac 17 (407.177 and 408.161), Latin 37.25–26 (75.63) and Syriac 17 (407.179 and 408.162), Latin 38.23–25 (75.64): see above, Introduction, §5.

b. The *sectio evangelica* (1.3b–2.1)

General

Without any doubt, 1.3b–2.1 represents a subsequent interpolation in the text of the "basic document." The text of the *sectio* is lacking, as we have just observed, in all the recensions of the Two Ways tractate except for that in the *Apostolic Constitutions* and its derivatives.[1] The *sectio* is thus found only in the *Didache* and in writings that directly or indirectly derive from the *Didache*. From the point of view of content also, it is quite clear that the *sectio* can never have belonged to the original Jewish Two Ways tractate; here, in the *sectio*, we find characteristic motifs from Jesus' preaching, elements of the Synoptic tradition that are otherwise completely absent from the Two Ways tractate. Add to this, finally, that 2.2 follows seamlessly after 1.3a. In 2.1 the redactor had to create a more or less successful transition, a subsequent connection designed to restore the direct link in the source that had been destroyed. From this point of view it is sensible to describe 1.3b–2.1 as a Christian interpolation.

The only question remaining is: Who functioned as interpolator? A whole group of interpreters assumes that this section represents a *post*didachistic interpolation, that is, an insertion that belongs not to the original history of the document but to the history of its transmission.[2] The contrary opinion holds that the *sectio* comes from the Didachist.[3] In that case, what we have before us would not be an interpolation in the strict sense but a piece of redaction that was of special significance for the Didachist and his writing. A series of good arguments can be advanced for this second opinion. First, the *sectio* is well attested in the *Didache* tradition; it appears already in P (P witnesses to 1.3c–4a), which is the oldest text fragment of the *Didache* we possess; the *Apostolic Constitutions* also presumes a *Didache* text that already contained the *sectio*. There would be further evidence of this if 1.3d and 5c were really attested by quotations in the *Didascalia apostolorum*. It is true that these arguments are not sufficient by themselves, but an observation regarding the content may be brought forward in addition: κατὰ τὴν ἐντολήν (1.5) is a typical redactional expression of the Didachist; ἀλλὰ καὶ περὶ τούτου δὲ εἴρηται, with a quotation following (1.6) points to his hand; and finally, the significant expression καὶ ἔσῃ τέλειος (1.4) is taken up, as τέλειος ἔσῃ, in 6.2, which is certainly redactional. Indeed, it is only at 6.2 that a decisive light is shed on what the text of the *sectio* is meant to convey in the context of the whole document.[4] In conclusion, 1.3b–2.1 goes back to the Didachist, who interrupts his source at this point and enriches it with a series of reminiscences drawn from the Synoptic tradition. It is therefore better to speak of the *sectio evangelica*.[5] That does not mean that the material of the *sectio* must have been an ad hoc invention of the Didachist. It may have existed, in whole or in part,

---

1 *Fragmenta Anastasiana* (Funk, *Didascalia*, 2.64); something analogous is true of Isaac the Syrian (ed. Besson, 51–52). For these two documents, see above, Introduction, §5.

2 Harnack, *Apostellehre*, 32–33; Streeter, "Much-Belaboured *Didache*," 369–70; Creed, "Didache," 374–79; Audet, *Didachè*, 261–80. (For Audet the argument that the text of the *sectio* differs from its context by being couched in the second person singular also plays a role. Against the attempt to draw literary-critical consequences from this, see Nautin, "Composition," 199–200, and passim.) In addition, Vielhauer (*Geschichte*, 733) considers the *sectio* probably a subsequent interpolation. Wengst (*Didache*, 20, and passim) now also speaks in favor of interpolation.

3 For example, Drews, "Apostellehre," 258; MacLean, "Introduction," ix (probably); Nautin, "Composition," 200–201; Glover, "Quotations," 12; Koester, *Synoptische Überlieferung*, 220–26, 238–41 (the interpolation stems from the compiler of the *Didache*, who is to be distinguished from the redactor of the material in the *sectio*). See Umberto

Mattioli, *La Didache dottrina dei dodici apostoli: Introduzione, traduzione e note* (Rome: Edizione Paoline, 1969; 3d ed., 1980) 42–43, 130; Rordorf and Tuilier, *Doctrine*, 100, and frequently; Rordorf, "Transmission textuelle," 513. The advocates of the fiction hypothesis have also argued for an origin with the Didachist (but with both correct insights and, in part, false presumptions, and sometimes with questionable argumentation): Muilenburg, *Literary Relations*, 44–47, 144; Dix, "Didache," 243–45 (at least for 1.3b, 4, and 5a); Robinson, *Didache*, 56–58; idem, "Barnabas and the Didache," 230–38; Connolly, "Streeter on the Didache," 364–79; Vokes, *Riddle*, 32–33, and passim. The authenticity of the section 1.3b–2.1 was important for the advocates of the fiction hypothesis, because here in particular it appeared possible to demonstrate that the *Didache* is dependent on the NT and *Hermas*. But the question of the origins of the *sectio* is to be kept separate from the question of its possible sources.

4 See below.

5 The principal difficulty in accepting the authentic-

68

Table 6

Did. 1.3b–d	Matt 5:44, 46–47	Luke 6:27–28, 32–33
	(44) . . .	(27) . . .
	ἀγαπᾶτε	ἀγαπᾶτε
	τοὺς ἐχϑροὺς ὑμῶν	τοὺς ἐχϑροὺς ὑμῶν,
		καλῶς ποιεῖτε
		τοῖς μισοῦσιν ὑμᾶς,
(3b) εὐλογεῖτε		(28) εὐλογεῖτε
τοὺς καταρωμένους		τοὺς καταρωμένους
ὑμῖν		ὑμᾶς,
καὶ προσεύχεσϑε	καὶ προσεύχεσϑε	–προσεύχεσϑε
ὑπὲρ		
τῶν ἐχϑρῶν ὑμῶν,		
νηστεύετε δὲ		
ὑπὲρ τῶν διωκόντων ὑμᾶς.	ὑπὲρ τῶν διωκόντων ὑμᾶς (. . .)	περὶ τῶν ἐπηρεαζόντων ὑμᾶς.
(3c) ποία γὰρ χάρις ἐὰν ἀγαπᾶτε	(46) ἐὰν γὰρ ἀγαπήσητε	(32) καὶ εἰ ἀγαπᾶτε
τοὺς ἀγαπῶντας ὑμας;	τοὺς ἀγαπῶντας ὑμᾶς,	τοὺς ἀγαπῶντας ὑμᾶς,
	τίνα μισϑὸν ἔχετε;	ποία ὑμῖν χάρις ἐστίν
	οὐχὶ καὶ οἱ τελῶναι	καὶ γὰρ οἱ ἁμαρτωλοὶ
	τὸ αὐτὸ ποιοῦσιν;	τοὺς ἀγαπῶντας αὐτοὺς ἀγαπῶσιν.
	(47) καὶ ἐὰν ἀσπάσησϑε	(33) καὶ γὰρ ἐὰν ἀγαϑοποιῆτε
	τοὺς ἀδελφοὺς ὑμῶν μόνον,	τοὺς ἀγαϑοποιοῦντας ὑμᾶς,
	τί περισσὸν ποιεῖτε;	ποία ὑμῖν χάρις ἐστίν;
οὐχὶ καὶ τὰ ἔϑνη	οὐχὶ καὶ οἱ ἐϑνικοὶ	καὶ οἱ ἁμαρτωλοὶ
τοῦτο ποιοῦσιν;	τὸ αὐτὸ ποιοῦσιν;	τὸ αὐτὸ ποιοῦσιν.
(3d) ὑμεῖς δὲ φιλεῖτε	[(44) ἀγαπᾶτε	[(27) ἀγαπᾶτε
τοὺς μισοῦντας ὑμᾶς,	τοὺς ἐχϑροὺς ὑμῶν . . .]	τοὺς ἐχϑροὺς ὑμῶν,
καὶ οὐχ ἕξετε ἐχϑρόν.		καλῶς ποιεῖτε τοῖς μισοῦσιν ὑμᾶς . . .]

P. Oxy. 1224, fol. 2r., col. 1 (Grenfell and Hunt, x) = κ]αὶ π[ρ]οσ-
εύχεσϑε ὑπὲρ [τῶν ἐχϑ]ρῶν ὑμῶν.

as fixed oral tradition or written source.[6] The apparent occasion for the Didachist's interpretation was the key phrase "love of neighbor," which he—as a Christian—saw as being made concrete and fulfilled in terms of Jesus' commandment of love of *enemies*. In this way the baptismal candidates are made acquainted at the very beginning with a unique characteristic of their new condition.[7]

The sequence of the interpolation does not adhere to the dominical saying about love of enemies. The Didachist includes (on his own initiative, or because these things were already combined in his tradition?) the prohibition against resistance (v. 4b–d). This is followed in vv. 4e–5a, by way of transition, by the admonition to permit oneself to be robbed, and this in turn is followed, in v. 5b–d, by a parenetical statement about right giving. (There is a parallel in *Hermas Man.* 2.4–6.) All this concludes with a scriptural quotation (v. 6). The material of

---

ity of the section was always its omission in the parallel versions. But this is easily explained if one supposes that this section was not in the Two Ways tractate and was first introduced by the Didachist in his own text. That explains the literary evidence as a whole.

6 The expressions of Koester (*Synoptische Überlieferung*, 217–19) tend in the latter direction.

Koester thus distinguishes between the compiler of the *Didache* and the redactor of the *sectio* (p. 218).

7 "The motive for the insertion is clear . . . it has Christianized this Jewish morality. This addition to the *Duae viae* is thus inspired by a desire to adapt it to Christians" (Nautin, "Composition," 201). Similarly Rordorf, "Tradition apostolique," 108.

Table 7

Did. 1.4b–5a	Matt 5:39–42	Luke 6:29–30
(4b) ἐάν τίς σοι δῷ ῥάπισμα εἰς τὴν δεξιὰν σιαγόνα στρέψον αὐτῷ καὶ τὴν ἄλλην, καὶ ἔσῃ τέλειος.	(39b) ἀλλ᾽ ὅστις σε ῥαπίζει εἰς τὴν δεξιὰν σιαγόνα σου, στρέψον αὐτῷ καὶ τὴν ἄλλην …	(29a) τῷ τύπτοντί σε ἐπὶ τὴν σιαγόνα πάρεχε καὶ τὴν ἄλλην,
(4c) ἐὰν ἀγγαρεύσῃ σέ τις μίλιον ἕν, ὕπαγε μετ᾽ αὐτοῦ δύο.	(41) καὶ ὅστις σε ἀγγαρεύσει μίλιον ἕν, ὕπαγε μετ᾽ αὐτοῦ δύο.	
(4d) ἐὰν ἄρῃ τις τὸ ἱμάτιόν σου, δὸς αὐτῷ καὶ τὸν χιτῶνα· (4e) ἐὰν λάβῃ τις ἀπὸ σοῦ τὸ σόν, μὴ ἀπαίτει· οὐδὲ γὰρ δύνασαι.	(40) καὶ τῷ θέλοντί σοι κριθῆναι καὶ τὸν χιτῶνά σου λαβεῖν, ἄφες αὐτῷ καὶ τὸ ἱμάτιον.	(29b) καὶ ἀπὸ τοῦ αἴροντός σου τὸ ἱμάτιον καὶ τὸν χιτῶνα μὴ κωλύσῃς.
(5a) παντὶ τῷ αἰτοῦντί σε δίδου καὶ μὴ ἀπαίτει.	(42) τῷ αἰτοῦντί σε δός καὶ τὸν θέλοντα ἀπὸ σοῦ δανίσασθαι μὴ ἀποστραφῇς	(30) παντὶ αἰτοῦντί σε δίδου, καὶ ἀπὸ τοῦ αἴροντος τὰ σὰ μὴ ἀπαίτει.

the *sectio* is thus not homogeneous. Where does it come from?[28]

The literary data have not been clearly analyzed to date. (1) The simplest assumption is that the *Didache* is dependent on our Synoptic Gospels, in this case Matthew and Luke. This position was advocated especially (in the wake of some precursors)[9] by Massaux.[10] It is consistent with this position to suppose that *Did.* 1.5 shows additional literary dependence on *Hermas*. This is supported, for example, by Muilenburg,[11] Goodspeed,[12] and Richardson.[13] The same position is upheld, of course, by representatives of the fiction hypothesis, Robinson,[14] Connolly,[15] and Vokes.[16] Within this tradition is also the attempt of Layton,[17] but he investigated only the *sectio evangelica*. For him, the "compositor" of 1.3b–2.1 was a very deliberate writer who took material from Matthew, Luke, and *Hermas*, and in v. 6 from the Old Testament as well,[18] while making stylistic changes in his sources.[19] In this the author of the interpolation was guided by an intention to make his text give an archaic, "apostolic" impression, corresponding to the fictionalized title with its claim to apostolic authority.[20]

8 Cf. tables 6–8. These tables are adapted from Koester, *Synoptische Überlieferung*, 220, 227, and 231.

9 E.g., Funk, *Patres apostolici*, 1.4–59; Bigg and MacLean, *Doctrine*, 2.

10 *Influence*, 3.144–82. This section is primarily dependent on Matthew, but there are additional influences from the Gospel of Luke. Hagner (*Use*, 280) also held that the *Didache* had used the Gospel of Matthew.

11 *Literary Relations*, 46, 167.

12 "Doctrina," 231. Goodspeed sees material from Matthew 5, Luke 6, 1 Peter (!), and *Hermas Man.* 2.4–6 redacted here.

13 "Teaching," 163, 165.

14 *Didache*, 47–50; "Barnabas and the Didache," 230–38. The modifications and additions by the Didachist are supposed to serve to cloak this dependency (p. 230). Beyond this Robinson even considered (p. 232) the possibility of influences from 1 Pet 2:11; John 18:22; 19:3, and—with reservations— even 1 Cor 7:7 (p. 236).

15 "Streeter on the Didache," 367–70.

16 *Riddle*, 51–61.

17 "Sources," 343–72.

18 This, in turn, has consequences for one's decision about what the "compositor" thought of *Hermas*: he

Table 8

Did. 1.5		*Hermas Man.* 2.4–6		Luke 6:30
(5a)	παντὶ τῷ αἰτοῦντί σε <u>δίδου</u> καὶ μὴ ἀπαίτει·	(4c)	πᾶσιν <u>δίδου</u>·	(30)	παντὶ αἰτοῦντί σε δίδου, καὶ ἀπὸ τοῦ αἴροντος τὰ σὰ μὴ ἀπαίτει.

| (5b) | <u>πᾶσι γὰρ</u> <u>θέλει δίδοσθαι</u> <u>ὁ πατὴρ</u> <u>ἐκ τῶν ἰδίων</u> χαρισμάτων. | | <u>πᾶσιν γὰρ</u> <u>ὁ θεὸς</u> <u>δίδοσθαι θέλει</u> <u>ἐκ τῶν ἰδίων</u> δωρημάτων. | *Doctr.* 4.8 omnibus enim dominus dare vult de donis suis. |

| (5c) | μακάριος ὁ <u>δίδους</u> κατὰ τὴν ἐντολήν· <u>ἀθῷος γάρ ἐστιν.</u> οὐαὶ τῷ λαμβάνοντι· εἰ μὲν γὰρ χρείαν ἔχων λαμβάνει τις, ἀθῷος ἔσται· ὁ δὲ μὴ χρείαν ἔχων δώσει <u>δίκην,</u> ἱνατί ἔλαβε <u>καὶ εἰς τί·</u> | (6a)

 (5a) | <u>ὁ οὖν διδοὺς</u>

 <u>ἀθῷός ἐστιν</u> . . .

 οἱ οὖν λαμβάνοντες

 ἀποδώσουσιν λόγον τῷ θεῷ διατὶ ἔλαβον <u>καὶ εἰς τί·</u> | *Hermas*
 (5c) οἱ δὲ ἐν ὑποκρίσει λαμβάνοντες

 τίσουσιν <u>δίκην.</u> |

| (5d) | ἐν συνοχῇ δὲ γενόμενος ἐξετασθήσεται περὶ ὧν ἔπραξε, καὶ οὐκ <u>ἐξελεύσεται</u> <u>ἐκεῖθεν,</u> μέχρις οὗ <u>ἀποδῷ</u> <u>τὸν ἔσχατον κοδράντην.</u> | Matt 5:25c–26
 (25c)

 (26) | . . . καὶ εἰς φυλακὴν βληθήσῃ.

 ἀμὴν λέγω σοι, οὐ μὴ <u>ἐξέλθῃς</u> <u>ἐκεῖθεν,</u> <u>ἕως ἂν ἀποδῷς</u> <u>τὸν ἔσχατον κοδράντην.</u> | Luke 12:58c–59
 (58c) . . . καὶ . . . σε βαλεῖ εἰς φυλακήν.

 (59) λέγω σοι, οὐ μὴ <u>ἐξέλθῇς</u> <u>ἐκεῖθεν,</u> ἕως καὶ τὸ ἔσχατον λεπτὸν <u>ἀποδῷς.</u> |

Layton's stylistic judgments are interesting, but whether they are sufficient to demonstrate literary dependence on Matthew, Luke, and *Hermas*[21] is debatable.[22]

(2) Among the older opinions that, in my view, have by no means been overcome by Layton is Glover's hypothesis,[23] assigning the passages in the *Didache* that

---

may have regarded it as a canonical work (Layton, "Sources," 362).

19 "Rhetorical climax, chiasmus, Blessing-and-woe, refrain" ("Sources," 370 n. 51; cf. the analyses on pp. 352–61). Layton explains the differences from the source texts as the consequence of stylistic metamorphosis.

20 "Sources," 371–72.

21 Wengst (*Didache*, 19) expresses cautious agreement.

22 Out of the question is the idea (previously advanced from time to time: cf. Dix, "Didache," 242–50) that the Didachist was quoting the *Diatessaron*. To the contrary, see Connolly, "Didache and Diatessaron,"

JTS 34 (1933) 347; Audet, *Didachè*, 269–70; Koester, *Synoptische Überlieferung*, 229–30; Layton, "Sources," 351.

23 "Quotations," 12–29.

recall the Synoptic material to a tradition parallel to Q. As regards the material in 1.3b–5a, this is interesting to the extent that virtually all the parallels[24] point to the Q tradition.[25]

(3) The already venerable hypothesis that posits an otherwise unknown apocryphal sayings collection as the basis for the interpolation goes a step farther: thus, first of all, Drews,[26] who thought that this was a written source of dominical sayings bearing the title ἐντολή; the material in vv. 1, 3, 4, 5a, and the core of v. 5b–d, as well as v. 6 would have been derived from that source. Koester's reflections tend, to some degree, in a similar direction.[27] He gave this text an extensive analysis and came to the very complicated conclusion that the interpolator's basic source was a "finished collection of sayings"[28] produced by an unknown redactor who used texts from Matthew and Luke (expanding and altering them) and inserted a piece of Jewish traditional material and a scriptural quotation, the derivation of which is problematic.[29] This source was copied by the compiler (i.e., the Didachist).[30]

(4) It is also possible, however, to set aside the idea of any written source and to consider the possibility of a purely oral tradition[31] that would then—as far as the dominical sayings are concerned—constitute a parallel tradition to the canonical description. This is Audet's position.[32] It would then be possible in individual cases to find formulations that, under certain circumstances, might be older than the corresponding expressions in the Matthean and Lukan tradition. That represents more or less the opposite of Layton's position.

(5) The most recent attempt at an extended literary analysis is that of Rordorf.[33] His results lie somewhere between those of Koester and Audet. Rordorf assesses[34] 1.3b–4 and 1.5–6 as two passages that were brought together even before they were introduced into the Two Ways tractate. The core of 1.3b–4 is said to go back to old tradition, contemporary with our Synoptic Gospels but independent of them. The independence of the traditions is said to be shown by expressions like ἔθνη in 1.3 and διδόναι ῥάπισμα in 1.4.[35] In addition, according to Rordorf, 1.4 (apart from the expression καὶ σωματικῶν) could go back to this old tradition. The original text of 1.3b–4 has, however, been amplified. Did. 1.5 is an old tradition that recalls Luke without quoting him, but 1.5 has grown in stages and was also amplified at a later time. Thus one must distinguish between the old (and partly augmented) tradition behind 1.3b–4 and 1.5 and the later didachistic redaction. The old tradition was redacted by the Didachist, from whom come the commandment about fasting (1.3; see later at 8.1), the expressions καὶ ἔσῃ τέλειος and οὐδὲ γὰρ δύνασαι (1.4; cf. 6.2), as well as the end of v. 5 (ἐν συνοχῇ κτλ.) and v. 6. Important in Rordorf's exposition are above all the references to archaic elements in the *sectio* and to later, didachistic redaction, by means of which the text as given was integrated into the macrocontext. In the nature of things, some details must remain debatable.

---

24 It is true that the only parallel to *Did.* 1.4c is Matt 5:41. One may at least ask whether the Matthean text also goes back to Q.

25 The parallels to 1.5b–d are a subject in themselves. [Ed. For dependence on traditions related to Q, see now also Clayton N. Jefford, *The Sayings of Jesus in the Teaching of the Twelve Apostles* (VCSup 11; Leiden: Brill, 1989) 38–53; and André Tuilier, "La *Didachè* et le problème synoptique," in Jefford, *Context*, 110–30.]

26 "Untersuchungen," 64–67.

27 *Synoptische Überlieferung*, 217–19.

28 *Synoptische Überlieferung*, 239.

29 Cf. esp. the summary in *Synoptische Überlieferung*, 238–39.

30 Aono (*Entwicklung*, 186–87) supposed for the *sectio* (differently from the rest of the *Didache*, in which the author was indirectly dependent on Matthew)

dependence on a collection of dominical sayings substantially derived from Matthew but expanded from memory (and thus including some Lukan reminiscences).

31 Wrege (*Bergpredigt*, 77 n. 1) points to the repetitions (δῷ ῥάπισμα in 1.4b; δὸς αὐτῷ in 1.4d, and several instances of διδόναι in 1.5). "This constant repetition of one verb is part of the technique of oral tradition."

32 Audet, *Didachè*, 166–69, 183–86, 264–65. Cf. "oral style" (p. 264). Still, the interpolator made some additions. Audet counts among these νηστεύετε δὲ ὑπὲρ τῶν διωκόντων ὑμᾶς / καὶ οὐχ ἕξετε ἐχθρόν/καὶ ἔσῃ τέλειος /οὐδὲ γὰρ δύνασαι (p. 271, and passim). Regarding 1.5, Audet is uncertain about the extent of the interpolator's intervention. Michael Mees ("Die Bedeutung der Sentenzen und ihrer *auxesis* für die Formung der Jesusworte nach

1

(1) The Commandment of Love of Enemies (1.3b–4a)

3b–d   **Bless those who curse you, and pray for your
        enemies, and fast for those who persecute you.
        For what grace do you expect if you (only) love
        those who love you? Do not even the nations do
        that? As for you, love those who hate you, and
        you will not have any enemy.**

[4a   **Avoid the fleshly and bodily passions.]**

■ **3b** The commandment that introduces and, in a sense, dominates the *sectio*,[36] to love one's enemies (3b–d),[37] appears (without being expressly designated a saying of the Lord) in a form that is structurally independent, while its content recalls the Synoptic tradition (particularly the logia in Q):

(3b) εὐλογεῖτε τοὺς καταρωμένους ὑμῖν,[38]

καὶ προσεύχεσθε ὑπὲρ τῶν ἐχθρῶν ὑμῶν,[39]
νηστεύετε δὲ ὑπὲρ τῶν διωκόντων ὑμᾶς.

(3c) ποία γὰρ χάρις, ἐὰν ἀγαπᾶτε τοὺς ἀγαπῶντας
       ὑμᾶς;[40]
οὐχὶ καὶ τὰ ἔθνη τοῦτο[41] ποιοῦσιν·

Didache 1,3b–2,1," *VetChr* 8 [1971] 55–76) comes in his own way to what is in principle a similar conclusion: the text as handed down does not stem from Matthew and Luke, but is a new version of motifs from the Jesus tradition composed according to the rhetorical laws of *auxesis*.

33   "Transmission textuelle," 499–500.

34   "Transmission textuelle," 509–10.

35   The problem of the two variants was seen by Glover ("Quotations," 14), as Rordorf notes ("Transmission textuelle," 502). Glover drew his own conclusions from them. Regarding διδόναι ῥάπισμα, Rordorf refers to Wrege, *Bergpredigt*, 76 n. 2: "*Did.* 1.4, with its διδόναι ῥάπισμα, recalls Isa 50:6, and in any case is independent of Matthew."

36   Theissen ("Nonviolence," 118 n. 5) draws attention to the special place of the commandment of love of enemies in the Matthean and Lukan compositions. "Something similar is true of the Didache (*Did.* 1.3ff.). Love of enemies always has a prominent compositional placement."

37   Koester (*Synoptische Überlieferung*, 223–24) has correctly pointed out that the logion first appears as a command to *pray* for enemies; this, then, represents a characteristic reformulation of the kind experienced by the tradition in the postapostolic period. Cf. Koester's examples, p. 221. The *Didache*'s logion is, however, constructed in such a way that, while at first it commands *prayer* for enemies (εὐλογεῖτε, προσεύχεσθε), this is done in order to formulate the commandment to *love* (φιλεῖτε) them. Thus (at least as far as the *Didache* is concerned) it cannot be said that Jesus' original command was softened (Koester, *Synoptische Überlieferung*, 224). On the commandment of love of enemies in the Synoptic tradition, cf. John Piper, *"Love Your Enemies": Jesus' Love Command in the Synoptic Gospels and in the Early*

Christian Paraenesis: A History of the Tradition and Interpretation of Its Uses (SNTSMS 38; Cambridge: Cambridge University Press, 1979); Luise Schottroff, "Gewaltverzicht und Feindesliebe in der urchristlichen Jesustradition," in Georg Strecker, ed. *Jesus Christus in Historie und Theologie: Neutestamentliche Festschrift für Hans Conzelmann zum 60. Geburtstag* (Tübingen: Mohr, 1975) 197–221; Theissen, "Nonviolence," 115–56; Fritz Neugebauer, "Die dargebotene Wange," *ThLZ* 110 (1985) 865–76.

38   Καταρᾶσθαί τινι is Attic (in place of τινά, as in Luke 6:28; cf. Mark 11:21; Jas 3:9): BDF §152(1); BDR, §152(1).

39   Cf. Justin *1 Apol.* 15.9 (Goodspeed, 35): Εὔχεσθε ὑπὲρ τῶν ἐχθρῶν ὑμῶν . . . , where the *Didache* text agrees with Justin *against* the Synoptics. Glover ("Quotations," 14) referred to the connection as an indication of the possible use of Q material. The *Didache* text is, however, even more literally in agreement with *P. Oxy.* 1224. Georg Strecker ("Eine Evangelienharmonie bei Justin und Pseudo-klemens?" *NTS* 24 [1978] 310) explained the agreement between Justin and the *Didache* on the basis of a statement going back to the written gospel tradition in Matthew and Luke, but freely quoted.

40   Audet reads, with the *Apostolic Constitutions*, φιλῆτε τοὺς φιλοῦντας ὑμᾶς.

41   H has τὸ αὐτό, probably an assimilation to Matt 5:46 (where a variant reading also offers τοῦτο) and Luke 6:33. The correct text is in P (and *Constitutions*).

(3d) ὑμεῖς δὲ φιλεῖτε[42] τοὺς μισοῦντας ὑμᾶς
καὶ οὐχ ἕξετε ἐχθρόν.

Structurally, v. 3b is presented in three lines with *parallelismus membrorum*, but one may suppose (see below) that, in the history of the tradition, the third line was added at a later time, and that the whole pericope is marked throughout by a system of paired lines in *parallelismus membrorum*. The introduction (v. 3b) offers an apparently paradoxical commandment—deliberately formulated, in fact, as a paradox—for which the reasons will be given in the lines to follow. The structure and content point to wisdom (*ḥokmah*) tradition.

A saying similar to v. 3b was found in Q, from which it entered Matt 5:44/Luke 6:27–28. Jesus' saying very quickly became proverbial among Christians, however; cf. Rom 12:14; *P. Oxy.* 1224, fol. 2r., col. 1 (Grenfell and Hunt, x);[43] *2 Clem.* 13.4; Polycarp *Phil.* 12.3; and so on.[44] The paradox of Jesus' eschatological proclamation is clearly evident. Ἐχθρός is the enemy who acts aggressively against me by cursing me; the "normal" reaction would be to return the curse. But no! For Jesus' followers in such a situation, the commandment was: a blessing for the one who curses, and a prayer for the enemy![45]

The third line, "fast for those who persecute you," νηστεύετε δὲ ὑπὲρ τῶν διωκόντων ὑμᾶς, has no parallel in the Synoptic tradition of this logion. From the point of view of tradition history it may be, and probably is, a later addition.[46] It is parallel to the two preceding clauses (εὐλογεῖτε, . . . καὶ προσεύχεσθε). Fasting supports and strengthens prayer: Polycarp *Phil.* 7.2; *Act. Thom.* 20, p.131; 145, p.253. What is intended in this passage is probably a special, private fast,[47] which has the same petitionary character as prayer (cf. νηστεύετε ὑπέρ . . .). Comparable for this subject could be such texts as 2 Sam 12:15–23; Esth 4:16; *Didasc.* (Syriac) 21 (CSCO 407.209–10; 408.193–94). The point of this logion, however, is that the deed of love is to be done for the *persecutor*.[48] This is the spirituality of the "Sermon on the Mount."[49]

The paradoxical commandment calls for foundation and explanation (v. 3c–d). These are offered in two forms:

(a) "To love only one's friends would be nothing special: the pagans do that, too![50] It is only the love of *enemies* that obtains special favor and a special reward,[51] that is, before God!" The content of the logion in v. 3c

---

42 H has ἀγαπᾶτε. The correct text is in P and the *Apostolic Constitutions*. Was H influenced by Matt 5:44 and Luke 6:27?

43 For this, see *NTApoc*, 1.100.

44 The variant προσεύχεσθε ὑπὲρ τῶν ἐχθρῶν ὑμῶν (against Q) is also found in *P. Oxy.* 1224; Justin *1 Apol.* 15.9 (Goodspeed, 35); cf. also *1 Apol.* 14.3 (Goodspeed, 34); 96.3 (Goodspeed, 211); 133.6 (Goodspeed, 256); *Didasc.* Syriac) 21 (CSCO 407.209; 408.192): *Pray for your enemies.* Arthur Vööbus considered "pray for your enemies" an archaic reading of Matt 5:44 (*Studies in the History of the Gospel Text in Syriac* [CSCO 128; Louvain: Secrétariat du Corpus SCO, 1951] 137–38). He pointed not only to the passage in Justin but also to *Passio Ignatii* 8.5 (Funk and Diekamp, *Patres apostolici*, 2.374; Vööbus's citation is incorrect): *et orare pro inimicis et persequentibus nos* ("and to pray for enemies and those who persecute us"); also Gregory *Magna moralia* 34.19 (*PL* 76.739A): *Pro inimicis vestris orate* ("pray for your enemies"); idem, *Dial.* 4.44 (*PL* 77.404C); *Missale Mozarabicum* (*PL* 85.939): *cuius* (sc. Leocadiae) *fiducialis oratio superbum conterruit inimicum* ("whose trusting prayer terrified the haughty foe"). He also offers examples from the Syriac textual tradition (pp. 137–38). I suggest that in the beginning this was not a unique reading but

a variant of the free oral tradition or something drawn from free citation.

45 Karlmann Beyschlag describes Jesus' command of love of enemies as the "most radical demand of Jesus for Christians in the first centuries" ("Zur Geschichte der Bergpredigt in der Alten Kirche," *ZThK* 74 [1977] 314).

46 Koester (*Synoptische Überlieferung*, 224) finds here "influence of church custom. . . . Undoubtedly, this reduction to a practical moral admonition is also a sign of a later time." Does the description of this as a "reduction" really fit? Layton ("Sources," 353) calls it "an extra-Synoptic addition by the compositor of the *Didache* passage." Thus also Rordorf, "Transmission textuelle," 501–2, 510 (the redactor). In fact, one cannot exclude the possibility that the passage is redactional.

47 Audet, *Didachè*, 265: the reference is to fasting from one evening to the next.

48 Rordorf ("Transmission textuelle," 502) sees the addition in light of 8.1 and the Syrian *Didascalia* and concludes that the reference is to *Jewish* persecutors, and that the fasting refers to the two fast days in 8.1. Cf. also Rordorf and Tuilier, *Doctrine*, 144–45 n. 2. Cremer, *Fastenansage*, 77: "primarily the Jews"; 78: "By καταρώμενοι, ἐχθροί, and διώκοντες the *Didache* means the Jews."

corresponds to the Synoptics: Matt 5:46–47/Luke 6:32–33 Q.[52]

(b) "Those who love the ones who hate them will ultimately have no enemies!" (v. 3d). The beginning of the logion recalls Matt 5:44/Luke 6:27 Q, but there is nothing corresponding to καὶ οὐχ ἕξετε ἐχθρόν in the Synoptic tradition.[53] Parallel is *Didasc.* (Syriac) 1 (CSCO 401.14; 402.12): "*And again, He says in the Gospel: 'Love those who hate you, and pray over those who curse you, and you shall have no enemy.'*"[54] This passage in the *Didascalia apostolorum* may be dependent on the *Didache*.[55] The exact meaning of the *Didache* passage is not clear.[56] We may probably interpret it as: "Those who persist in loving their enemies will ultimately paralyze their aggression. Love destroys enmity."[57]

Excursus: Relationship to the Synoptics

Concerning relationships to the Synoptic tradition: v. 3b recalls Luke 6:28; καὶ προσεύχεσθε are common

to *Didache* and Matt 5:44b against Luke 6:28 (προσεύχεσθε); the concluding ὑπὲρ τῶν διωκόντων ὑμᾶς is found in Matt 5:44, but Matthew refers this expression to προσεύχεσθε, and *Didache* to νηστεύετε, which is unique to *Didache* and absent from the Synoptic tradition. The expression προσεύχεσθε ὑπὲρ τῶν ἐχθρῶν ὑμῶν is not in Matthew or Luke, but apparently in the fragment, already cited, from a sayings collection as found in *P. Oxy.* 1224, fol. 2r., col. 1 (Grenfell and Hunt, x).[58] Verse 3c recalls Matt 5:46–47/Luke 6:32–33, but the introductory ποία γὰρ χάρις is reminiscent only of the latter. Nevertheless, the *Didache* version is markedly shorter when measured against Matt 5:46–47/Luke 6:32–33. Finally, v. 3d recalls the beginning of the Synoptic logion (Matt 5:44/Luke 6:27). The Synoptic logion begins with the commandment of love of enemies, and the logion in the *Didache* ends with it. The last line, καὶ οὐχ ἕξετε ἐχθρόν, is again entirely without a Synoptic parallel. For the *Didache* we may entertain the hypothesis of a parallel oral tradition (without any literary connection), or (perhaps better) the

49 In contrast, the reference to fasting for the sake of charity (suggested as an alternative by Knopf, *Lehre*, 7; cf. *Hermas Sim.* 5.3.7–8; Aristides *Apol.* 15.9 [Goodspeed, 21]; Origen *Hom. 10.2 In Lev.* [Lommatzsch, 9.372]; *Didasc.* [Syriac] 21 [end] [CSCO 407.217–18; 408.201]) is a misreading of this passage.

50 The *Didache* has τὰ ἔθνη; Matt 5:46 οἱ τελῶναι, v. 47 οἱ ἐθνικοί; Luke 6:32–33 οἱ ἁμαρτωλοί. Glover ("Quotations," 14) places high value on τὰ ἔθνη in the *Didache* version and suggests that here the *Didache* may have retained what is (from a tradition-historical point of view) the more original word.

51 Χάρις, as in the parallels in Luke 6:32–35; *2 Clem.* 13.4; Ignatius *Polycarp* 2.1; cf. 1 Cor 9:16 ℵ* D* F G; more remotely 1 Pet 2:19.

52 In its form, the *Didache* version is notably shorter than the one in Matthew and Luke.

53 Hemmer (*Doctrine*, xc) thought of a quotation from a lost gospel. According to Koester, *Synoptische Überlieferung*, 221, it is probably "a concluding construction added by the redactor to the logia in *Did.* 1.3." Layton ("Sources," 355) differs: "καὶ οὐχ ἕξετε ἐχθρόν seems to be the work of the compositor" (cf. already at p. 354).

54 The Latin version: *Nam iterum in evangelio dicit: Diligite odientes vos et orate pro maledicentibus vos et inimicum nullum habebitis* (2.28–31; TU 75.4). For the agreements between the *Didache* and *Didascalia apostolorum*, see above, Introduction, §2c. In addition, cf. also *Lib. grad.* 13.1 (Kmosko, 307); and above, Introduction, §2b.

55 See above, Introduction, §2c. Something analogous is true of *Liber grad.* 13.1. Cf. above, Introduction, §2b.

56 Audet (*Didachè*, 265) wishes to understand it as future imperative. Worth considering as possible distant parallels are Prov 25:21–22; *T. Benj.* 5.1: Ἐὰν ἔχητε ἀγαθὴν διάνοιαν, τέκνα, καὶ οἱ πονηροὶ ἄνθρωποι εἰρηνεύουσιν ὑμῖν ("If you have a good attitude, children, even wicked men deal peacefully with you"). Also Aristides *Apol.* 15.5 (Goodspeed, 20): τοὺς ἀδικοῦντας αὐτοὺς παρακαλοῦσι καὶ προσφιλεῖς αὐτοὺς ἑαυτοῖς ποιοῦσι ("They exhort those who do them wrong and make them friendly to themselves"); Justin *1 Apol.* 14.3 (Goodspeed, 34); Clement of Alexandria *Strom.* 2.19, 102.4 (GCS³, 2.169): ἐχθρῷ δὲ ἐπικουρητέον, ἵνα μὴ μείνῃ ἐχθρός· ἐπικουρίᾳ γὰρ εὔνοια μὲν συνδεῖται, λύεται δὲ ἔχθρα ("One must take care of an enemy, so that he might not remain an enemy. For good will is linked to concern and enmity is thereby dissolved"). Cf. also 7.12.69.4 (GCS², 3.50).

57 This saying has nothing to do with the Stoic maxim that the wise person has no enemy.

58 See n. 44 above.

suggestion of dependence on an apocryphal sayings collection.[59]

At this point there have been *a number of interpolations* in the original text of the *Didache* (v. 4a). The text traditions are:

P: ἄκουε τί σε δεῖ ποιοῦντα σῶσαι σου τὸ πνεῦμα· π[ρ]ῶτον πάντων ἀπόσχου τῶν σαρκε[ι]κῶν ἐπιθυμειῶν.

Η: ἀπέχου τῶν σαρκικῶν καὶ σωματικῶν ἐπιθυμιῶν.[60]

Constitutions: ἀπέχου τῶν σαρκικῶν καὶ κοσμικῶν ἐπιθυμιῶν.[61]

In my opinion, the history of the interpolation can be reconstructed as follows:[62] (1) At an early time a glossator intervened in the traditional text, because he missed the motif of resistance to fleshly desires in the previous lines, and this was one of the fundamental motifs of early Christian catechesis. Compare, for example, ἀγαπητοί, παρακαλῶ . . . ἀπέχεσθαι τῶν σαρκικῶν ἐπιθυμιῶν αἵτινες στρατεύονται κατὰ τῆς ψυχῆς ("Beloved, I urge you . . . to abstain from the desires of the flesh that wage war against the soul," 1 Pet 2:11); ἀρνησάμενοι τὴν ἀσέβειαν καὶ τὰς κοσμικὰς ἐπιθυμίας ("renounce impiety and worldly passions," Titus 2:12). I think, then, that this motif was introduced by means of a gloss (in some such form as *ἀπέχου τῶν σαρκικῶν ἐπιθυμιῶν, "avoid fleshly passions").[63]

(2) The archetype of P (or the scribe of P itself?) inserted a further gloss. For this glossator, the admonition ἀπέχου τῶν σαρκικῶν ἐπιθυμιῶν (which is rather casual) was not sufficient. He introduced it with a phrase intended to point out the significance of the subsequent clause. The result was: ἄκουε τί σε δεῖ ποιοῦντα σῶσαι σου τὸ πνεῦμα· πρῶτον πάντων ἀπόσχου τῶν σαρκεικῶν ἐπιθυμειῶν ("hear what you

---

59   For Drews, see above. Koester (*Synoptische Überlieferung*, 226) distinguishes among borrowings from Matthew and from Luke, "influence of free tradition," and (predidachistic) redaction. Layton ("Sources," 352–53) makes v. 3b literarily dependent on Luke 6:28 and Matt 5:44, although the author has made deliberate stylistic alterations in the literary source. According to Layton, the literary source for v. 3c–d is Luke 6:32 + Matt 5:46 + Matt 5:47b + Luke 6:27 + (Matt 5:48). For Layton's conjecture about the conclusion of the logion, see below. For Rordorf's analysis, see above and "Transmission textuelle," 501–2, 509–10.

60   Likewise Georgian. Bryennios (Διδαχή, 6) conjectures καὶ κοσμικῶν (instead of καὶ σωματικῶν).

61   Instructive for the compilers' ways of dealing with their source in this area is Isaac the Syrian, 51.21ff. M. Besson, "Un recueil de sentences attribué à Isaac le Syrien," *OrChr* 1 (1901) 46–60, 288–98: Ἀπέχου τῶν σαρκικῶν καὶ βιωτικῶν ἐπιθυμιῶν καὶ τῶν ἡδονῶν τοῦ κόσμου ("Abstain from desires of the flesh and of earthly life and from the pleasures of the world"). The text is derived, mediately, from *Const.* 7.2.4. See above, Introduction, §5.

62   Cf. Niederwimmer, "Textprobleme," 116–18. For the following explication, cf. also Audet, *Didachè*, 55–56, 265–66. He arrives at a conclusion that is effectively similar. Differing is, e.g., Rordorf, "Transmission textuelle," 503–4, who sees v. 4a as by no means a subsequent interpolation, but instead counts it among the predidachistic material. Ἐπιθυμίαι σαρκικαί ("fleshly passions"), as ἐπιθυμίαι τῆς σαρκός ("passions arising from the flesh"), is to be understood in light of 1 Pet 2:11– 3:17 or Gal 5:13–26. *Did.* 1.4a is said to be, in this sense, the introduction to 1.4b–e. This can scarcely be correct. Moreover, Rordorf ("Transmission

textuelle," 504, 510) also regards καὶ σωματικῶν as a subsequent clarification. Cf. also Rordorf and Tuilier, *Doctrine*, 145 n. 6.

63   The singular is an accommodation to the clauses that follow. It is difficult to understand the content of the text from its context: cf. the previous note. Theissen ("Nonviolence," 129) differs: "Renunciation of self-defense presupposes control of inward aggressive impulses." Aono (*Entwicklung*, 167) connects this clause with the expression ἔση τέλειος.

64   The expression ἐπιθυμίαι σωματικαί is striking. In 4 Macc 1:31–32 there is reference to ἐπιθυμίαι ψυχικαί, distinguished from ἐπιθυμίαι σωματικαί: σωφροσύνη δὴ τοίνυν ἐστὶν ἐπικράτεια τῶν ἐπιθυμιῶν, τῶν δὲ ἐπιθυμιῶν αἱ μέν εἰσιν ψυχικαί, αἱ δὲ σωματικαί, καὶ τούτων ἀμφοτέρων ἐπικρατεῖν ὁ λογισμὸς φαίνεται ("Temperance, as I understand it, is control over desires, and of desires some relate to the soul and others to the body, over both of which reason obviously holds sway").

65   Σαρκικαί and κοσμικαί are synonymous.

66   Layton ("Sources," 375–78) makes a much more complicated (but hypothetical) reconstruction of the textual history of the gloss in v. 4a. I am simplifying here: the oldest text form had no gloss, and the interpolation may at first have been only marginal, with its most extensive form *ἄκουε . . . πρῶτον . . . ἀπέχου τῶν σαρκικῶν καὶ κοσμικῶν ἐπιθυμιῶν. Layton then pictures the further development as follows: the marginal gloss was inserted into the text, with the ἔσεσθε . . . τέλειοι postulated by Layton at the end of 1.3 (see below) changed to singular and adapted to the grammatical structure of the gloss. The form ἀπόσχου in P, instead of ἀπέχου, is a corruption of the text. The absence of καὶ

must do to save your spirit: first of all avoid fleshly passions"). This formulation is a distant echo of 1 Cor 5:5.

(3) At the same time, however, the text of the shorter gloss was handed on and clarified by additions. We find a form like this in H: ἀπέχου τῶν σαρκικῶν καὶ σωματικῶν ἐπιθυμιῶν ("avoid fleshly and bodily passions"),[64] or in *Constitutions*: ἀπέχου τῶν σαρκικῶν καὶ κοσμικῶν ἐπιθυμιῶν ("avoid fleshly and worldly

passions").[65] Compare Titus 2:12; *2 Clem.* 17.3. This passage is instructive for the question of the reliability of the text of H.[66] For this, see above, Introduction, §3a.

κοσμικῶν in P is explained by homoioteleuton. In the archetype of H, it became a metathesis, καικ-σομικων [*sic*], which explains the H reading καὶ σωματικῶν. At the same time, ἄκουε τί σε . . . πάν-

των was excised and the phrase καὶ ἔση τέλειος was transferred to the position now given by H. Cf. the *stemma* on p. 377.

(2) The Renunciation of Violence (1.4b–5a)

4b–e   **If anyone strikes you on your right cheek, turn your other one to him too, and you will be perfect. If someone presses you into one mile of service, go along with him two. If someone takes your cloak, give him your tunic as well. If someone takes away from you what is yours, do not demand it back—(since you cannot do so anyway).**

5a   **Give to everyone what he asks of you and do not ask for it back . . .**

The logion about love of enemies is continued in v. 4b–e and v. 5a with a sequence of four or five logia that also have contiguous parallels in the Synoptic tradition, where they are combined, as here, with the commandment of love of enemies:

(4b)   ἐάν τις σοι δῷ ῥάπισμα εἰς τὴν δεξιὰν[67] σιαγόνα,
       στρέψον αὐτῷ καὶ τὴν ἄλλην,
       καὶ ἔσῃ τέλειος.

(4c)   ἐὰν ἀγγαρεύσῃ σέ τις μίλιον ἕν,
       ὕπαγε μετʼ αὐτοῦ δύο.

(4d)   ἐὰν ἄρῃ τις τὸ ἱμάτιόν σου,
       δὸς αὐτῷ καὶ τὸν χιτῶνα.

(4e)   ἐὰν λάβῃ τις ἀπὸ σοῦ τὸ σόν,
       μὴ ἀπαίτει· οὐδὲ γὰρ δύνασαι.

(5a)   παντὶ τῷ αἰτοῦντί σε δίδου
       καὶ μὴ ἀπαίτει.

The first four logia belong together, both formally and in content (cf. the fourfold ἐάν . . . , στρέψον, ὕπαγε, δός, μὴ ἀπαίτει). The fifth logion is obviously a doublet

of the fourth (or vice versa). Common to the logia of this pericope is the hyperbolic admonition to unrestricted submission: If someone strikes you[68] on the face—namely, on the right cheek[69]—do not strike back, but instead present the other cheek as well (v. 4b; cf. Matt 5:39b/Luke 6:29a Q).[70] If someone forces you to do a menial task, namely, to accompany him or her for a mile,[71] do not refuse; instead, go two miles (v. 4c; cf. Matt 5:41 [Q?]). If someone takes your cloak, do not resist; give your shirt, too (v. 4d; cf. Matt 5:40/Luke 6:29b Q).[72] If someone robs you of what is yours, let it be; do not ask for it back (vv. 4e–5a; cf., for v. 5a, Matt 5:42/Luke 6:30 Q).[73] The total abandonment of violence and of one's right is documented in v. 4b by the fact that the person who has been insulted freely offers the aggressor another opportunity to mete out disgraceful treatment; in v. 4c and 4d the one oppressed or robbed gives the aggressor even more than was asked. In v. 4e and 5a, he or she refrains from making any demand for

---

67   According to Dix ("Didache," 242–43) δεξιάν was lacking in the original *Didache* text. Cf., to the contrary, Connolly, "Didache and Diatessaron," *JTS* 34 (1933) 346–47; Koester, *Synoptische Überlieferung*, 227 n. 1, 229–30; Rordorf, "Transmission textuelle," 504 n. 10.

68   Διδόναι ῥάπισμά τινι as in John 18:22; 19:3.

69   It is the *right* cheek in *Didache* and Matthew (against Luke), perhaps as a special challenge: "a blow on the right cheek is given with the back of the hand and is regarded as especially insulting" (Wrege, *Bergpredigt*, 75–76).

70   For the third line, καὶ ἔσῃ τέλειος, see below.

71   For ἀγγαρεύειν, see BAGD, *s.v.*; Gerhard Schneider, "ἀγγαρεύω," *EDNT* 1 (1990) 12.

72   Wrege, *Bergpredigt*, 76–77, and 77 n. 1: Luke and the *Didache* think of this as robbery (Matthew differs: this version contemplates a court proceeding

designed to collect a pledge).

73   For the peculiar expression οὐδὲ γὰρ δύνασαι in v. 4e, see below. Did Johannes Climacus quote *Did.* 1.4? For this, see above, Introduction, §2b.

74   This is true even though the key phrase "reign of God" is not found in the logia themselves.

75   The Didachist (as we will see) calls attention in his own way to these connections by means of his own inserted καὶ ἔσῃ τέλειος. See below.

76   It is true that the same addition is found in *Lib. grad.* 2.2 (Kmosko, 27) and 22.15 (671)—dependent on the *Didache*? See above, Introduction, §2b(1).

77   This addition is thus an interpretation. Καὶ ἔσῃ τέλειος in 1.4 recalls τέλειος ἔσῃ in 6.2, where the Didachist is also speaking (see below); cf. Rordorf and Tuilier, *Doctrine*, 32–33; and Rordorf, "Transmission textuelle," 504–5, 510. It will become clearer in the context of 6.2 what the Didachist's

restitution. The *Didache* version of the dominical sayings expresses no fundamental motive different from that in the Q version: in the renunciation of a violent enforcement of one's own right the law of a higher, although paradoxical, order becomes visible: the law of the reign of God.[74] At the same time the attitude of those who are insulted, oppressed, and robbed (which is grotesque according to ordinary and customary standards) reveals the peculiar powerlessness of aggression. Those who live according to these precepts have removed themselves from the ordinary norms and rules of society and set themselves on a road that (as far as *this* world is concerned) leads to the discipleship of the cross and (in light of what is *to come*) to the reign of God.[75]

Essentially (except for the possibly important variant διδόναι ῥάπισμα), v. 4b agrees with Matt 5:39b. The last line (καὶ ἔσῃ τέλειος) falls outside the *parallelismus membrorum* and is, in my view, a redactional addition, namely, a gloss by the Didachist,[76] who thus

attempts to interpret the existing tradition in a particular direction.[77] Verse 4c is almost identical to Matt 5:41 (for which there is no Lukan parallel); however, the succession of the logia (4c/4d) is the reverse of that in Matthew (5:41/40). Verse 4d is again close to Luke (6:29b); the Matthean κριθῆναι is lacking and the succession of garments is the reverse of that in Matthew: ἱμάτιον–χιτών, which causes us to think of a robbery (differently from Matthew).[78] Verses 4e and 5a are doublets,[79] and yet v. 5a is more strongly reminiscent of the Synoptic tradition (and particularly Luke 6:30), while v. 4e only distantly resembles the Synoptic parallels. In v. 4e the expression οὐδὲ γὰρ δύνασαι (which has no parallel in the Synoptic tradition) stands out. This little clause has confused interpreters from the beginning.[80] The most obvious interpretation is: "Let yourself be robbed, because you cannot really defend yourself, no matter what!" The clause, thus understood, would make obvious the

---

more precise intention in the use of this phrase is. Koester (*Synoptische Überlieferung*, 222) finds no motive that could have impelled the compiler to make such an insertion. "But even if the compiler is identical with the redactor, what interest could he have had in introducing such a clause just here, in the middle of *Did.* 1.4, if not to replace, as quickly as possible, something in the source that had been overlooked, because it may have appeared important to him?" (ibid.). Koester thus comes to a complicated hypothesis: the passage belongs to the source but is now in the wrong place; originally (in the form ἔσεσθε οὖν ὑμεῖς τέλειοι according to Matt 5:48) it would have constituted the end of the logia series in 1.3. The redactor of the logion collection (who is not the Didachist) would have omitted it there (replacing it with καὶ οὐχ ἕξετε ἐχθρόν) and now inserted it, in the wrong place and with grammatical alterations. Layton has allowed himself to be persuaded by Koester's inferences to go even farther: cf. "Sources," 348–49, 354–55, 374–75. He emends v. 4e to ὧδε γὰρ δύνασαι (τέλειος εἶναι), attributes the expression καὶ οὐχ ἕξετε ἐχθρόν in v. 3d to the compositor, and conjectures immediately after that phrase (following Matt 5:48) ἔσεσθε οὖν ὑμεῖς τέλειοι ὡς ὁ πατὴρ ἡμῶν ὁ οὐράνιος τέλειός ἐστιν ("you will be perfect as your heavenly Father is perfect") *vel simile*. Layton ("Sources," 375–76) associates the origin and placement of the present text, καὶ ἔσῃ τέλειος, with the textual history of the gloss in v. 4a (see above).

78 Koester's analysis is in *Synoptische Überlieferung*,

226–38; Layton ("Sources," 355–61) sees Matt 5:39b + 4:41 + Luke 6:29 + Matt 5:40 + Matt 5:42 + Luke 6:30 as having been used, from a literary point of view, and makes an effort to explain the differences from the sources as deliberate stylistic alterations. See Rordorf, "Transmission textuelle," 504–5, 509–10.

79 Koester (*Synoptische Überlieferung*, 228) argues that the redactor of the source has "separated [Luke 6:30] into two commandments . . . presumably in order to introduce the admonitions about giving, which follow in *Did.* 1.5, with a dominical saying." The clumsy repetition of μὴ ἀπαίτει is said (pp. 228–29) to show that the author is not formulating freely (according to Koester, he is here dependent on the Synoptic tradition). There is a protest from Wrege, *Bergpredigt*, 78 n. 2: "But what Koester considers literary reworking is really a mnemonic technique for simplifying the clauses in community parenesis." The expression in v. 4e is, instead, assimilated to the preceding logion in v. 4d. In both cases, it is robbery that is contemplated.

80 Cf. Harnack, *Lehre*, 6, who suspected a corruption of the text but later retracted his emendation (καίπερ δυνάμενος) in "Prolegomena," 51 n. 6. Even the Georgian text sought to correct the text through a paraphrase. For οὐδὲ γὰρ δύνασαι, the Georgian reads: "and you cannot do this even for the sake of the faith."

social milieu of those who handed on this text: they are exploited and helpless people who cannot and will not defend themselves.[81] Other attempts to understand the text[82] remain artificial; it seemed necessary to suppose a corruption of the text (and this has happened) and to emend it.[83] I consider this unnecessary. For the whole pericope it is again easy to suppose that we have before us an oral tradition parallel to that of the Synoptics, or (better) the use of the same apocryphal sayings collection that was already suggested for 1.3b–5a. The Didachist expanded and commented on his tradition with the clause $\kappa\alpha\grave{\iota}\ \check{\epsilon}\sigma\eta\ \tau\acute{\epsilon}\lambda\epsilon\iota o\varsigma$.

---

81 It is true that Schaff (*Church Manual*, 165) considers this interpretation trivial.

82 Knopf (*Lehre*, 9) considers not social pressure but ethical mind-set: "it is impossible for him, in spirit, to take back what is his with counterforce or by legal means." Cf. also Koester (*Synoptische Überlieferung*, 229), who regards this clause as part of the redaction of the source; cf. in addition the interpretation in Rordorf ("Transmission textuelle," 505, 510), who connects this text with 6.2 and attributes it to the didachistic redaction.

83 For Harnack's original suggestions, see n. 80 above. Layton ("Sources," 348–49) emends to $\hat{\omega}\delta\epsilon\ \gamma\grave{\alpha}\rho\ \delta\acute{\upsilon}\nu\alpha\sigma\alpha\iota\ (\tau\acute{\epsilon}\lambda\epsilon\iota o\varsigma\ \epsilon\hat{\iota}\nu\alpha\iota)$. The phrase $\tau\acute{\epsilon}\lambda\epsilon\iota o\varsigma\ \epsilon\hat{\iota}\nu\alpha\iota$ is said to have fallen out because of homoioteleuton $(\epsilon\hat{\iota}\nu\alpha\iota/\delta\acute{\upsilon}\nu\alpha\sigma\alpha\iota)$, and then $\hat{\omega}\delta\epsilon$ was wrongly written as $o\grave{\upsilon}\delta\acute{\epsilon}$.

1

(3) Almsgiving (1.5b–6) and Transition (2.1)

5b–d   **For the Father wants people to give to everyone from the gifts that have been freely granted to them. Blessed is the person who gives according to the commandment, for he is guiltless. Woe to the person who takes. If someone takes something because he is in need, he is guiltless, but if he is not in need he shall have to give an account of why he took and for what purpose; if he is imprisoned he shall be interrogated about what he has done, and shall not go free until he has paid back the last penny.**

6   **But then about this sort of thing it has also been said, "Let your charitable gift sweat into your hands until you know to whom you are giving it."**

2.1   **The second commandment of the teaching:**

Analysis

On the saying παντὶ τῷ αἰτοῦντί σε δίδου (v. 5a "to everyone who asks of you, give") follows now a little reflection on right giving (of alms) in v. 5b–d. The material in v. 5b and 5c is no longer taken from the Jesus tradition but from a Jewish or Jewish-Christian parenesis that appears also in *Hermas Man.* 2.4–6.[84] The transition from one tradition to the other is not marked in the *Didache* in any way.

Excursus: Hermas and the Didache

Verse 5a is the connecting phrase between the Jesus tradition quoted in what went before and the parenetic section that follows. The tie between v. 5a and 5b is purely associative (παντὶ τῷ αἰτοῦντί σε δίδου–πᾶσι . . . θέλει δίδοσθαι). Verse 5b agrees essentially with *Hermas Man.* 2.4c (ὁ πατήρ/ὁ θεός and χαρισμάτων/δωρημάτων are unimportant variants).[85] In v. 5c the agreement with *Hermas* is looser. What *Hermas* presents as an aphorism appears in the *Didache* version in the form of a macarism (or woe).[86] *Hermas Man.* 2.6a and *Did.* 1.5a/5c are reversed, while *Man.* 2.5b is completely missing. The *Didache* version avoids the doublet in *Hermas Man.* 2.5a and 5c. In *Did.* 1.5c the added κατὰ τὴν ἐντολήν is certainly redactional

(namely, a gloss by the Didachist).[87] The saying in v. 5c ends with an eschatological warning. With this (additionally in the *Didache*, but no longer in *Hermas*) is associated another saying that is also known from the Synoptic tradition: Verse 5c corresponds to Matt 5:25–26 (cf. Luke 12:58–59), but the contexts of the Q saying (judicial process) and the *Didache* version (unjustified acceptance of alms) are different.[88] In summary, the aphorism about almsgiving, also found in *Hermas*, has in its *Didache* version been framed at beginning and end with reminiscences from the Jesus tradition (and thus Christianized). The form of the aphorism in *Hermas* may well be the older from the point of view of the history of the tradition.[89] It still shows a purely Jewish aspect.

---

84   *Didasc.* (Syriac) 17 (CSCO 407.177–79; 408.161–62)/Latin 37.25–27 (TU 75.63) and 38.23–25 (75.64) may come from the *Didache*. See above, Introduction, §2c. *Const.* 4.3.1–2 is dependent on the *Didascalia apostolorum.*

85   For the parallel in *Doctr.* 4.8, see below.

86   Layton ("Sources," 363) considers it possible that the author of the interpolation is formally orienting

87   the text to Luke 6:20–26.
Layton's reference ("Sources," 360) to *Hermas Man.* 2.7a is misleading.

88   Rordorf and Tuilier, *Doctrine*, 147 n. 4.

89   Koester, *Synoptische Überlieferung*, 230, 232.

Literary dependence on *Hermas*[90] is improbable.[91] It is more likely that the aphorism about right alms-giving attested in both *Hermas* and the *Didache* goes back to a common tradition. It is uncertain whether the combination of the Jesus tradition with the Jewish parenetical material was the work of the Didachist or whether it already existed beforehand. In the former case (which I regard as more probable) the Didachist would have proceeded in a similar manner to that adopted later at 16.1-2, where he also joined Jesus tradition with parenetical material.[92]

Comment

■ **5b–d** The reflection begins with the aphorism πᾶσι γὰρ θέλει δίδοσθαι ὁ πατὴρ ἐκ τῶν ἰδίων χαρισμάτων (5b).[93] Πατήρ = God, and the ἴδια χαρίσματα (*Hermas Man.* 2.4c: δωρήματα)[94] are the gifts of God's creation.[95]

This is a very Jewish idea: God's creative gifts are given for all;[96] therefore poor people have a right to alms, and the wealthy are obligated in turn to give them. Moreover, it should be noted that the gifts given by the rich to the poor are really *God's* gifts.[97] Thus the one who gives alms is only a manager, one who distributes the divine gifts.[98] This fundamental idea is then (v. 5c) clarified in the form of a macarism (to be followed by a woe): μακάριος ὁ διδοὺς[99] κατὰ τὴν ἐντολήν· ἀθῷος γάρ ἐστιν ("blessed is the person who gives according to the commandment, for he is guiltless").[100] The expression κατὰ τὴν ἐντολήν ("according to the commandment"), typically, has no parallel in *Hermas Man.* 2.6;[101] I consider this phrase an addition by the Didachist (cf. *Did.* 13.5, 7). It probably refers to a command of the

---

90   See above, Introduction, §7a(3). According to Layton ("Sources," 361–72) the *Didache* is dependent on *Hermas* from v. 5a onward, and in v. 5d on Matt 5:25–26.

91   Cf. also Glover, "Quotations," 15–16; Koester, *Synoptische Überlieferung*, 230–31; Audet, *Didachè*, 163–66, 271–75; Kraft, *Didache*, 140–41; Rordorf, "Transmission textuelle," 507.

92   Is it possible that he also intervened redactionally in the stylization of the given material in v. 5bc (beyond κατὰ τὴν ἐντολήν)?

93   Irritatingly, this single sentence from the *sectio christiana* (1.3b–2.1) has a parallel in *Doctrina*, but in a very different place—in 4.8: *omnibus enim dominus dare vult de donis suis* ("The Lord wishes to give to all from his gifts"). One may suppose that this sentence was also in the *Didache*'s source, at the same place (i.e., after 4.8). The Didachist omitted it there (at 4.8), understandably enough, in order to avoid having a doublet. Cf. Koester, *Synoptische Überlieferung*, 233 n. 2. On the one hand, if this consideration is correct, it would also be an argument for assigning the *sectio* to the Didachist. On the other hand, if we interpret the *sectio* as a postdidachistic interpolation, the omission of the text corresponding to *Doctr.* 4.8 (end) remains inexplicable. (It is true that the hypothesis is slightly hampered by the absence of the text in question also in the *Canons of the Apostles* and the *Epitome*. *Canons* completely breaks off its quotation from the tractate at this point, however, and *Epitome* has other omissions in its version of the text corresponding to *Did.* 4.3–11.)

94   *Hermas Sim.* 2.7: δωρήματα τοῦ κυρίου.

95   This (unusual) sense of χαρίσματα is secured by the parallels in *Hermas*. There is special reference to

the ψυχή in *Sib. Or.* 2.54: Πᾶσά τε γὰρ ψυχὴ μερόπων θεοῦ ἐστι χάρισμα ("For every soul of mortals is a gracious gift of God"). But Philo *Leg. all.* 3.78 (to which Audet refers, *Didachè*, 274) can scarcely be a parallel, because there χάρισμα = χάρις (besides which, χάρισμα in both places in §78 is text-critically problematic: cf. Ludwig Cohn, "Philo von Alexandria," *NJKA* 1 [1898] 539 n. 1). Other non-Christian instances of χάρισμα are late: see BAGD, *s.v.*; Hans Conzelmann, "χαίρω κτλ.," *TDNT* 9 (1974) 402–3.

96   Cf. *Ps.-Phocyl.* 29–30 (*Sib. Or.* 2.89–90ψ); also *T. Zeb.* 6.7; 7.2.

97   Deut 15:14b; *m. ʾAbot* 3.7a: Rabbi Eleazer b. Yehuda from Bartota said: "Give to [God] from what is God's; for you and what are yours belong to God." (See the translation and commentary by Marti and Beer, 71.)

98   Cf. *Lev. Rab.* 34.2, on Lev 25:25 (see Str–B 4.540).

99   Acts 20:35 appears to me only a Christian variant on the Jewish aphorism. *Const.* 4.3.1–2 has combined the saying about giving (copied from *Didascalia apostolorum*) with Acts 20:35, and also declares the woe saying to be a word of the Lord. For the parallel with the woe in the Nicetas catena, cf. Clement of Alexandria GCS², 3.xxvii–xxviii; and see above, Introduction, §2b.

100 For a possible quotation in *Didascalia apostolorum*, see above, Introduction, §2c.

101 Moreover, in *Hermas* the text is not a macarism.

102 Glover ("Quotations," 15–16) and Drews ("Untersuchungen," 64–65) believes that it means μακάριος ὁ διδούς, and that ἐντολή is the title of the collection of commandments being quoted here. *1 Clem.* 2.1, ἥδιον διδόντες ἢ λαμβάνοντες ("giving more gladly than

Lord, but it is not clear which concrete commandment the Didachist has in mind.[102] Is there a reference here to the word of the Lord quoted just before (in v. 5a)?[103] Or does it simply mean "in the right way, as the Lord has commanded us," without any thought of a specific saying? Ἀθῷος ("guiltless") describes the giver as a person righteous and blameless before God.[104] As the rich are enjoined to give, however, so the poor are warned not to exploit the obligation of the devout to give alms (cf. again *Hermas Man.* 2.5): οὐαὶ τῷ λαμβάνοντι ("woe to the person who takes")—and this is immediately clarified: those who are in want[105] may, of course, accept alms. But woe to those who are not in need and nevertheless take alms! They must expect to be called on to explain[106] why and for what reason (ἱνατί . . . καὶ εἰς τί)[107] they have accepted alms.[108] The accounting will be unavoidable—and here the text again slips into the tone of the Synoptic tradition (v. 5d):[109] the one who accepts alms will be thrown into prison (συνοχή)[110] like a thief,

and there will be grilled about this behavior.[111] Such a one will not be released from prison until the last penny is paid. These last words recall Matt 5:25c–26 (cf. Luke 12:58c–59).[112] The underlying tradition in *Did.* 1.5d can scarcely be understood except as eschatological; συνοχή probably refers to an eschatological place of punishment or purification.[113]

■ **6** At this point, I believe, the Didachist introduces a quotation from Sacred Scripture (which of course meant the "Old" Testament),[114] to serve as a warning against too-hasty giving and also as a scriptural foundation for such a warning (v. 6).[115] The introduction to the quotation, ἀλλὰ καὶ περὶ τούτου δὲ[116] εἴρηται (cf. the similar introduction to quotations in 9.5 and 16.7), betrays the hand of the Didachist.[117] The subsequent quotation is a *crux interpretum*, because to date it has not been possible

---

103 This is the interpretation of Knopf, *Lehre*, 9; and Layton, "Sources," 365–66; Rordorf ("Transmission textuelle," 507) also considers it probable.

104 Ἀθῷος (ϑωή) does not have the usual meaning of "guiltless" here, but rather means "not blameworthy." The one in question has acted rightly, as the commandment asks. *Hermas Man.* 2.6 has the same sense.

105 Χρείαν ἔχειν, as in Mark 2:25; Acts 2:45; 4:35; Eph 4:28; 1 John 3:17.

106 Δίκην διδόναι is identical with δίκην τίνειν (*Hermas Man.* 2.5). According to Layton ("Sources," 366) the expression in the *Didache* is compounded from *Hermas Man.* 2.5a, ἀποδώσουσιν λόγον . . . διατί, and 5c, τίσουσιν δίκην.

107 Ἱνατί is made up of ἵνα τί (sc. γένηται): BDF, §299(4); BDR §299(3).

108 For a possible quotation in *Didascalia apostolorum* (including certain contacts with *Hermas*), see above, Introduction, §2c.

109 There is no parallel to v. 5d in *Hermas*.

110 *P. Lond.* II, 354.24. Here συνοχή does not mean "danger, fear" but "prison," as the parallel in Matt 5:26 shows. See Helmut Koester, "συνοχή," *TDNT* 7 (1971) 887.

111 Ἐξετάζειν is the technical term for examination under torture. See BAGD, *s.v.*

112 According to Koester (*Synoptische Überlieferung*, 237) the author may have used Matt 5:26, but *Did.* 1.5d

receiving"), seems to be an idea related to Acts 20:35, but the saying in *1 Clement* is not declared a word of the Lord.

appears "no longer to be part of the piece of tradition . . . used by the redactor of *Did.* 1.3ff. at 1.5" (p. 237). Accordingly, for Koester v. 5b (part of the Jewish tradition) and the subsequent quotation in v. 6 belong to the predidachistic source (p. 238). According to Layton ("Sources," 366–67) *Did.* 1.5c is dependent on Matthew.

113 Cf. Rordorf ("Transmission textuelle," 508 and n. 9), pointing out the eschatological interpretation of the corresponding tradition in Tertullian *De anima* 35.2–3 (CChrSL 2.836–37); 58.8 (869); cf. idem, *De orat.* 7 (CChrSL 1.261–62); and Sextus *Sentences* 39 (Chadwick, 16).

114 This is not a word of the Lord, as Drews supposed ("Untersuchungen," 65); cf. also Alfred Resch, *Agrapha* (2d ed.; Leipzig: Hinrichs, 1906; repr. Darmstadt: Wissenschaftliche Buchgesellschaft, 1967) 91–92. The sense of the quotation is intended to be identical with Eph 4:28. "But both the linguistic relationship with Eph 4:28 and the Synoptic character of the logion are—apart from ἱδρωσάτω—undeniable" (p. 92). Glover ("Quotations," 16–17) calls it a Jesus logion.

115 If the Didachist really had a scripturally formulated source before him for vv. 3–4 or for v. 5, in any case v. 6 was not part of it. Drews ("Untersuchungen," 65) differs, as does Koester (*Synoptische Überlieferung*, 238). For the connection between the ideas in 1.4–5 and 1.6, cf. below.

116 Bryennios (Διδαχή, 8) conjectured δή.

117 Thus v. 6 is not a gloss (as Peterson supposed, "Probleme," 147–49).

to give a secure demonstration of its source: ἱδρωσάτω[118] ἡ ἐλεημοσύνη σου εἰς τὰς χεῖράς σου, μέχρις ἂν γνῷς, τίνι δῷς.

Among the texts suggested are Sir 12:1: Ἐὰν εὖ ποιῇς, γνῶθι τίνι ποιεῖς, καὶ ἔσται χάρις τοῖς ἀγαθοῖς σου (Vg: *Si benefeceris, scito cui feceris, et erit gratia in bonis tuis multa;* "if you do a favor, know the person to whom you are doing it, and there will be favor for your good deeds"). But a derivation from the LXX version as we have it is not really possible. *Ps.-Phocyl.* 23, πληρώσει[119] σέο χεῖρ'. ἔλεον χρήιζοντι παράσχου ("you must fill your hand. Give alms to the needy"), is not a genuine parallel; however, it seems that *Sib. Or.* 2.79 ψ (from *Ps.-Phocylides*) is a distant echo of this saying, ἱδρώσῃ σταχύων χειρὶ χρήζοντι παράσχου ("with perspiring hand give a portion of corn to one who is in need"). Strikingly enough, Latin writers from Augustine onward know the saying in a form closely related to the *Didache* version; moreover, they frequently quote it as "Scripture."[120] Augustine *Enar. in Ps.* 102:12 (CCSL 40.1462): *De alio enim dictum est: Omni petenti te da; et de alio dictum est: Desudet eleemosyna in manu tua, donec invenias iustum, cui eam tradas* ("About one it is said, 'Give to everyone who asks of you'; about another it is said, 'Let alms sweat in your hand until you find a righteous person to whom to give'"); *Enar. in Ps.* 103; *Sermo* 3.10 (CCSL 40.1509): *Sicut enim de illo qui te quaeret dictum est: Omni petenti te, da, sic de illo quem tu debes quaerere dictum est: Sudet eleemosyna in manu tua, donec invenias iustum cui eam tradas* ("For so it is said about him who asks of you, 'To everyone who asks of you, give.' So about the one whom you ought to ask, 'Let alms sweat in your hand until you find a righteous person to whom to give'"); *Enar. in Ps.* 146:17 (CCSL 40.2135): *Utrumque dictum est, fratres mei, et: Omni petenti te da, modo lectum est; et alio loco scriptura*

dicit: Sudet eleemosyna in manu tua, quousque invenias iustum cui eam tradas. Alius est qui te quaerit, alium tu debes quaerere. Nec eum qui te quaerit relinquas inanem; Omni enim petenti te da: sed alius est quem tu debes quaerere; Sudet eleemosyna in manu tua quousque invenias iustum cui des ("My brethren, it is both said and read, 'To everyone who asks give,' and in another place Scripture says, 'Let alms sweat in your hand until you find a righteous person to whom to give.' One person begs of you, another you ought to seek out. But do not leave empty the person who begs of you. 'To everyone who begs of you, give,' but there is another whom you ought to seek out. 'Let alms sweat in your hand until you find the just person to whom to give'"). Cassiodorus *Expositiones in Psalterium* 40 (*PL* 70.295D): *Legitur enim: Omni petenti te tribue. Scriptum est etiam: Desudet eleemosyna in manu tua, donec invenias justum, cui eam tradas* ("The text is read, 'Provide to everyone who asks of you.' It is written, 'Let alms sweat in your hand until you find a just person to whom to give'"); *Expositio in Psalterium* 103 (*PL* 70.733B): *Herbam vero servituti hominum, hoc est, ut illi necessaria tribuantur, de quo scriptum est: Desudet eleemosyna in manu tua, donec invenias justum cui eam tradas* ("Grass is for the service of people, that is, so that what is necessary might be provided to him of whom it is written, 'Let alms sweat in your hand, until you find a just person to whom to give them'"). Gregory the Great *Regula Pastoralis* 3.20 (*PL* 77.84CD): *Ne sub obtentu largitatis ea quae possident inutiliter spargant, audiant quod scriptum est: Sudet eleemosyna in manu tua* ("Lest they squander uselessly what they possess under the guise of generosity, let them listen to what is written, 'Let alms sweat in your hand'").[121] *Vita Chrodegangi episcopi Mettensium* 11.27 (*Monumenta Germaniae historica* 10.568, 28ff., ed. Pertz): *Memoratus est scriptum: Sudet elemosina in manu tua, donec*

---

118 H reads ἱδρωτάτω. Bryennios (Διδαχή, 8–9) had already conjectured ἱδρωσάτω.

119 On this difficult πληρώσει, cf. Nikolaus Walter, "Pseudo-Phokylides," in Ernst Vogt and Nikolaus Walter, *Poetische Schriften* (JSHRZ 4.3; Gütersloh: Mohn, 1983) 199, n. 23a.

120 For the following list of attestations, cf. Ehrhard, *Altchristliche Litteratur*, 48 n. 5; Resch, *Agrapha*, 91–92 (history of the findings); Kneller, "Zum 'schwitzenden Almosen,'" 779–80; Cuthbert H. Turner, "Adversaria patristica," *JTS* 7 (1906) 593–95; Charles Taylor, "Traces of a Saying of the Didache," *JTS* 8 (1907) 115–17 (history of the find-

ings); Anselm Manser, "Zur Didache I,6 aus der Vita Chrodegangi," *ThR* 8 (1909) 459–60; Altaner, "Doctrina," 340–41; Audet, *Didachè*, 276–80.

121 This passage was copied in Taio Caesaraugustomus Sententiae 3.34 (*PL* 80.892B).

122 Charles Taylor, "Traces of a Saying of the Didache," *JTS* 8 (1907) 115: the text of Piers Plowman may be corrupt. The correct text might be *Sudet elemosina tua in manus tuas, donec scias cui des* ("Let your alms sweat in your hands until you know to whom to give it").

The instances cited in Kneller ("Zum 'schwitzenden Almosen,'" 779–80) and elsewhere from a fast-

invenias iustum cui eam tradas ("Recall the Scripture, 'Let alms sweat in your hand until you find a just person to whom to give them'"). Abelard *De Eleemosyna Sermo* (*Opera*, ed. Cousin, 1.552): *Sed sudet, sicut scriptum est, eleemosyna in manu tua, donec invenias qui dignus sit* ("As is written, 'Let alms sweat in your hand until you find one who is worthy'"). Bernard of Clairvaux *Ep.* 95 (*PL* 182.228C): *Ideo ait: Desudet eleemosyna in manu tua, donec invenias (v.l. videas) justum cui des* ("Therefore it says, 'Let alms sweat in your hand until you find [*v.l.* see] a just man to whom to give them'"). Peter Comestor *Historia Scholastica;* Liber Deuteronomii 5 (*PL* 198.1251C): *Desudet eleemosyna in manu tua, donec invenias justum, cui des, id est illum cui debes* ("Let alms sweat in your hand until you find a just person to whom to give, that is, one to whom you owe something'"). Piers Plowman, B, Passus 7.75 (in Resch, *Agrapha*, 92): *Sit elemosina tua in manu tua, donec studes cui des* ("Let your alms remain in your hand while you ponder to whom to give them'").[122] Peter Cantor *Verbum abbreviatum* 47 (*PL* 205.150B): *Cui etiam des, considerandum, juxta illud poetae: Videto cui des. Et iterum: Desudet eleemosyna in manu tua etc.* ("You must give thought to the person to whom you would give, as the poet says, 'Look to the one to whom you give,' and again, 'Let alms sweat in your hand, etc.'"). Guntherus Cisterciensis *De Oratione, Ieiunio et Eleemosyna* 13.1 (*PL* 212.211BC): *Ne dederis indigno, si dignus aeque indigens valeat reperiri, quemadmodum scriptum est: Sudet eleemosyna in manu tua, donec invenias justum cui des* ("Do not give to one who is not worthy, if it might be possible to find someone who is both worthy and poor, as is written, 'Let alms sweat in your hand until you find a just person to whom to give'"). Innocent III *De Eleemos.* 5 (*PL* 217.756B): *Non dicit indiffinite, qui recipit hominem, sed determinate, "qui recipit justum" quemadmodum alibi legitur:*

"Desudet eleemosyna in manu tua, donec invenias justum cui des." Hinc alibi dicit Scriptura: "si benefeceris, scito cui feceris, et erit gratia in bonis tuis multa" ("It does not say, in a general way, 'who receives a person,' but specifically, 'who receives a just person.' Likewise it is said elsewhere, 'Let alms sweat in your hand until you find a just person to whom to give them.' Elsewhere Scripture says, 'If you give a benefaction, know the one to whom you do so and there will be much grace in your good deeds'").[123]

Finally, the following example from the "Postille" of Hugh of St. Cher (Venetian ed. [1600], 3.194) is especially important: *Scito cui feceris, idest antequam des, attende cui des. Unde infra eodem secundum aliam translationem. Desudet eleemosyna in manu tua, donec invenias cui des, vel cui dare debes* ("Know the person to whom you would do something, that is, before you give, pay attention to the one to whom you give. The same point is made according to another translation, 'Let alms sweat in your hand until you find one to whom to give, or one to whom you ought to give'").[124] Kneller had already pointed emphatically to this instance[125] because it could provide an indication of the supposed scriptural citation: Hugh of St. Cher quotes the aphorism in connection with his explication of Sir 12:1. Audet discussed this question in depth.[126] He took up this suggestion and, emphasizing the note that this saying represents an *alia translatio*, he proposed the hypothesis that the aphorism is the Latin translation (deviating from the ordinary Vg text) of a different version of the Greek text of Sirach than the one attested in the great uncials.[127] "*Did.* 1.6 uses, with a certain freedom, a Greek *Ecclesiasticus* related to, if not identical with, the one that served as the basis for at least one of the ancient Latin versions or revisions of the

ing poem from Ivrea (p. xi), and from B. Jonas of Orléans, are not quotations but only reminscences of this aphorism.

123 This passage is especially interesting because it combines our aphorism with the familiar Vg text of Sir 12:1. Note also: "*Hinc alibi dicit Scriptura. . . .*"

124 Audet (*Didachè*, 277) quotes the Venetian ed. 2.194. For the transmission of the exegetical work of Hugh of St. Cher (S. Caro), cf. Friedrich Stegmüller, *Repertorium Biblicum Medii Aevi* (11 vols.; Madrid, 1940–58) 3.114–73. The *editio princeps* of Venice (1487) was unfortunately inaccessible to me. I am quoting above from *Ugonis de S. Scharo S. Romanae*

Ecclesiae tit. S. Sabinae Cardinalis primi ordinis praedicatorum (Venice, 1600) vol. 3.

125 Kneller, "Zum 'schwitzenden Almosen,'" 780.

126 Audet, *Didachè*, 276–80.

127 Audet, *Didachè*, 277. The existence of a second Greek translation of the book of Sirach is undisputed. On this question, cf. simply J. Ziegler, ed., *Sapientia Jesu Filii Sirach* (Septuaginta 12.1; 2d ed.; Göttingen: Vandenhoeck & Ruprecht, 198) 73–74. According to Ziegler, Sirach was translated into Greek several times (p. 74). For the alternative translations, of special importance are the variant readings of the Vetus Latina.

same writing."[128] He posits[129] that this Greek form of the text must have been known in Syria-Palestine from the first half of the first century; the Greek text is said to go back to a Hebrew text form that had already distanced itself from the original. Patrick W. Skehan[130] (taking up Audet's suggestions) has pointed to the textual form of Sir 12:1 in a manuscript from the Cairo Geniza (arising out of a scribal error in the Hebrew text tradition). This form is said, in turn, to be a precondition for the form of the text proposed by Audet in the Greek tradition.

Audet's (and Skehan's) suggestions are impressive but not compelling. Altaner[131] has asserted with assurance that the Latin authors after Augustine who quote this aphorism "have acquired their knowledge of the *Didache* quotation directly or indirectly from Augustine."[132] Here Altaner refers to the broad circulation of Augustine's *Enarrationes in Psalmos*. Indeed, Augustine alone could have been both the direct and indirect source of the Latin quotations. In that case, the following is possible: With the authority of the African church father, people quoted the saying received from him as Scripture and ultimately sought a source for it in the Bible; Innocent III is demonstrably the first to have connected the aphorism with Sir 12:1 (although only dubiously), and Hugh of St. Cher's "Postille"[133] then fabricated the idea that our aphorism stems from the *alia translatio* of Sir 12:1. The result is that the origin of the quotation in *Did.* 1.6 seems to me uncertain, despite the extensive proofs presented by Audet.

The aphorism (wherever it comes from) uses a witty image to warn against too hastily squandering alms on the unworthy. One receives the impression that the Didachist wanted, by quoting this aphorism, to restrict the appeal to unconditional almsgiving that existed in his tradition. He affirms the tradition. Indeed, blessed is the one who gives! But at the same time he warns against giving too quickly, and therefore challenges the hearer not to forget the scriptural saying he quotes in v. 6.[134]

■ **2.1** With the quotation in 1.6 the *sectio* in the narrower sense is complete. There follows, in 2.1, a brief remark that bears the marks of tradition: δευτέρα δὲ ἐντολὴ τῆς διδαχῆς ("the second commandment of the teaching"). We recall that the compiler of the *Didache* interrupted the text of his source (the "basic document") at 1.3a in order to introduce the *sectio evangelica*, as we call it. Now, having completed the interpolation, he saw himself faced with the task of creating a transition to the source. This is accomplished by 2.1. The Didachist was apparently inspired by the final clause of the source (τούτων δὲ τῶν λόγων ἡ διδαχή ἐστιν αὕτη: 1.3a). In the source this refers to the series of prohibitions that follows (2.2–7). It now occurred to the compiler that he could describe the commandments in the *sectio* and the series of prohibitions in the basic document as two successive concretions of the fundamental commandment (1.2). Therefore he writes δευτέρα δὲ ἐντολὴ τῆς διδαχῆς (2.1) and thus implicitly makes the commandments in the *sectio* the πρώτη ἐντολή, and the following commandments the δευτέρα ἐντολή (but without any thought of such a thing as the double love commandment).[135] One cannot call this arrangement particularly

---

128 Audet, *Didachè*, 279–80, with agreement from Layton, "Sources," 368; Rordorf, "Transmission textuelle," 508–9.
129 Audet, *Didachè*, 280.
130 "*Didache* 1,6 and Sirach 12,1," *Bib* 44 (1963) 533–36, with agreement from Layton, "Sources," 368 n. 49; Rordorf, "Transmission textuelle," 508–9.
131 "Doctrina," 342.
132 Augustine himself (according to Altaner, "Doctrina," 340–41) could scarcely have derived the quotation from a Latin *Didache*. Rather, the aphorism would have "come to him perhaps as a familiar saying . . . by an avenue unknown to us" (p. 341). Similarly Adam, "Herkunft," 42–43, who, however (in accord with his interest in combinations), suggests with an "uncertain perhaps" (p. 43) the Abelonii as vehicles of the tradition, and accordingly makes both *Doctr.* 4.8 and *Did.* 1.6 dependent on Sir 12:1 (pp. 56–57).

133 Or a tradition to which Hugh of St. Cher refers?
134 In the tradition as given, only the one who unjustly receives was threatened. Now, through the scriptural saying, the one who gives is also warned. There is a certain tension between 1.5 and 1.6. It is explained by the situation of the Didachist, who wanted to preserve the old tradition but at the same time to protect it from misuse.
135 Correctly Drews, "Apostellehre," 259; Rordorf, "Transmission textuelle," 509. It would be mistaken to interpret (with Harnack, "Prolegomena," 45–47) 1.3–6 as interpretation of the πρώτη ἐντολή (love of God), and 2.2–4.14 as interpretation of the δευτέρα ἐντολή (love of neighbor). Ulricus Hüntemann divides as follows: 1.3–6 is an exposition of the πρῶτον ἀγαπήσεις, chap. 2 an exposition of the δεύτερον . . . μὴ ποίει ("Ad cap. 1 Doctrinae XII apostolorum," *Antonianum* 6 [1931] 195–96).

skillful. The division thus created remains an emergency construction behind which there is not a deeply reflective theological conception but simply a literary principle of order. The construct is not significant except as a reconnection to the quotation of the source. The (emergency) transition in 2.1 is then followed immediately by the continuation of the text of the source (2.2ff.).

But let us pause for a moment before leaving the *sectio*, and attempt to review and summarize the results of our observations. (1) The text section 1.3b–2.1 was inserted by the hand of the Didachist. This section is redactional, not a postdidachistic interpolation. (2) The Didachist is not formulating freely here, but is making use of a variety of materials whose origins are uncertain. In vv. 3, 4b–5a, and 5d there is reliance on logia from the Jesus tradition, but we cannot point with certainty to the source from which the Didachist derived them; in v. 5b and 5c he makes use of a parenetic aphorism from Jewish or Jewish-Christian tradition that is also to be found in an earlier form in *Hermas Man.* 2.4–6. Probably this represents mutual dependence on some other source; it is unlikely that the Didachist is borrowing from *Hermas*. (3) The Didachist redacted the tradition, however; the phrase καὶ ἔσῃ τέλειος ("and you will be perfect," v. 4b) is his, as are the references to the ἐντολή (v. 5c) and to the scriptural saying whose origin is unclear (v. 6). If the coupling of traditional logia and parenesis also comes from his hand, one may also surmise redactional interventions in v. 5b–c (even though their precise extent cannot be demonstrated). (4) If this analysis is correct we can also determine the Didachist's

bias: (a) He wished to give a stronger Christian character to the existing Two Ways tractate; this he accomplished through quotation of dominical sayings that adjure the Christian to pray for his or her enemies and demand submission to opponents. In this way candidates for baptism are presented with some of the special characteristics of Christian life and teaching. (b) With the addition of καὶ ἔσῃ τέλειος, the Didachist gives a special interpretation to the sayings of the Lord that have been quoted: fulfilling these commands is a matter of the one who is τέλειος ("perfect"). In this way the Didachist expresses, in his own fashion, the eschatological character of the *lex Christi*, and raises the instruction of neophytes to the level of eschatological motivation.[136] (c) The additional logion about almsgiving recalls a further unique feature of the new community into which the neophyte is entering. It was characteristic of early Christians that they accepted the Old Testament and Jewish obligation to care for the poor, and when possible even intensified it. (In later chapters, we will learn of Christian hospitality and charity.) At the same time, the Didachist is already aware of some bad experiences: the Christian obligation to give support can also be misused and exploited. Through the addition of v. 6 the Didachist seeks to protect the Christian willingness to give alms (which he affirms, and to which the neophytes are invited) against exploitative misuse. (5) Only after the completion of the work was the text in v. 4a interpolated, in a series of stages, by means of a subsequent gloss.

---

136 Vokes (*Riddle*, 143) wished to see in the emphasis on the τελειότης (here and in 6.2) an indication of the Montanist character of the *Didache*. But in the *Didache* it is a question of the problem of fulfilling the "Sermon on the Mount," a problem that existed from the beginning. It is not an issue of heretical *perfecti*.

2

c. A List of Prohibitions (2.2–7)

2   **You shall not murder. You shall not commit adultery. You shall not corrupt children. You shall not fornicate. You shall not steal. You shall not practice magic. You shall not mix poison. You shall not murder a child, whether by abortion or by killing it once it is born. You shall not covet what belongs to your neighbor.**

3   **You shall not swear falsely. You shall not bear false witness. You shall not speak evil of anyone. You shall not harbor resentment.**

4   **You shall not equivocate, either in what you think or in what you say, for equivocation is a mortal snare.**

5   **Your word shall not be false or empty [but shall be fulfilled by deed].**

6   **You shall not be given to greed, or robbery, or wickedness, or malice, or pride. You shall not plot evil against your neighbor.**

7   **You shall not hate anyone. Some people, though, you shall call to task; for others you shall pray. Others you shall love more than yourself.**

Analysis

At 2.2–7 the Didachist returns to quoting the basic document. Originally this section followed immediately after 1.3a, and thus was the διδαχή of the fundamental commandment. Now (after the wooden transitional verse 2.1) it forms the beginning of the δευτέρα ἐντολή. De facto, we are dealing with a piece of parenesis in the form of a catalog, namely, a list of prohibitions arranged as follows:

οὐ φονεύσεις,

οὐ μοιχεύσεις,

    οὐ παιδοφθορήσεις, οὐ πορνεύσεις,

οὐ κλέψεις,

οὐ μαγεύσεις,

    οὐ φαρμακεύσεις, οὐ φονεύσεις τέκνον ἐν φθορᾷ,

    οὐδὲ γεννηθὲν ἀποκτενεῖς,

οὐκ ἐπιθυμήσεις τὰ τοῦ πλησίον,

οὐκ ἐπιορκήσεις,

    οὐ ψευδομαρτυρήσεις, οὐ κακολογήσεις,

οὐ μνησικακήσεις,

οὐκ ἔση διγνώμων οὐδὲ δίγλωσσος (παγὶς γὰρ θανάτου ἡ διγλωσσία),

οὐκ ἔσται ὁ λόγος σου κενός, οὐ ψευδής.

οὐκ ἔση πλεονέκτης

    οὐδὲ ἅρπαξ οὐδὲ ὑποκριτὴς οὐδὲ κακοήθης οὐδὲ ὑπερήφανος·

    οὐ λήψῃ βουλὴν πονηρὰν κατὰ τοῦ πλησίον σου.

οὐ μισήσεις πάντα ἄνθρωπον (general conclusion)

    ἀλλὰ οὓς μὲν . . . ὑπὲρ τὴν ψυχήν σου.

If necessary, one may further acknowledge the second table of the Decalogue as funishing the basic structure for the whole.[1] The author of the tractate used this structure with a great deal of freedom.[2] As a rule, the prohibitions are expanded by additional prohibitions of related content. *Οὐ μισήσεις κτλ.* constitutes the summary conclusion. The catalog of vices in 5.1–2 is (not in

---

1   Cf. Audet, *Didachè*, 283.

2   The independent οὐ μαγεύσεις and its entire series is striking. *Οὐκ ἐπιθυμήσεις κτλ.* is misplaced. See below.

3   Koester (*Synoptische Überlieferung*, 162) judged "that *Barnabas* abbreviates and rearranges, whereas the *Didache* has preserved this series in its more original form" (with reference to Windisch, *Barnabasbrief,*

404–5). On this, see above, Introduction §6b. Still, we may count on finding some exceptions. Thus οὐκ ἐπιθυμήσεις in *Didache* may not be in the right place. Audet (*Didachè*, 283) surmised that 5.1 originally followed immediately after 2.2–7, and thus regarded 3.1–4.14 as a later addition (within the predidachistic history of the Two Ways tractate). According to him, the additional growth consisted

form but certainly in content) a doublet of this one. It is difficult to form a judgment about the tradition-historical relationship between *Did.* 2.2–7 and *Barn.* 19.4–7. It seems to me, however, that here the *Didache* generally (although not in every detail) presents a form of the tractate tradition that is closer to the original than that of *Barnabas.*[3]

Comment

■ **2** The sequence begins with a quotation of the fifth and sixth commandments of the Old Testament Decalogue. Οὐ φονεύσεις, οὐ μοιχεύσεις ("You shall not murder . . . commit adultery"):[4] cf. Exod 20:13–14 (MT); Deut 5:17–18[5] Mark 10:19 par.[6] The final prohibition is expanded by οὐ παιδοφθορήσεις ("you shall not corrupt children")[7] and οὐ πορνεύσεις. Πορνεύειν, μοιχεύειν,

and παιδοφθορεῖν can only refer to unnatural sexual acts of all kinds.[8] Οὐ κλέψεις ("You shall not steal") again follows the Decalogue (Exod 20:15, MT; Deut 5:19, MT).[9]

A new series of prohibitions begins with οὐ μαγεύσεις. Forbidding the use of magic is as characteristic of Old Testament Jewish religion[10] as is the prohibition of sexual offenses. Both vices, taken together, are especially abhorrent[11] when practiced by Gentiles.[12] Οὐ φαρμακεύσεις specifically prohibits compounding poisons.[13] Οὐ φονεύσεις τέκνον ἐν φθορᾷ[14] forbids abortion: "you shall not kill a child by [procuring] miscarriage."[15] This passage, derived from the Jewish tractate, offers the oldest explicit Christian instance of the prohibition of

---

of two parts: 3.1–6 and 3.7–4.14. Thus Audet arrived at three parts (in addition to the introduction) in the *Via vitae,* namely: "the instruction for the Gentiles" (2.2–7), "the instruction of the wise" (3.1–6), and "the instruction for the poor" (3.7–4.14). The second and third instruction are said to have been added subsequently (*Didachè,* 308–22, esp. 311). In my opinion, all that is definitely established in this analysis is that 3.1–6 is a later addition. The other conjectures remain uncertain. Also, a clearer division should be made between 3.7–10 and 4.1–14.

4 In *Doctrina* this pair is reversed and a third member is inserted: *non falsum testimonium dices.*

5 The rearrangement of the commandments in LXX with respect to the MT (with influence on Luke 18:20 and some ms. variants of Mark 10:19) cannot be discussed here. Nevertheless, cf. *Doctrina: Non mechaberis (moechaberis* g), *non homicidium facies* ("You shall not commit adultery, you shall not commit murder").

6 Cf. the prohibitions for participants in the private cult in Philadelphia: μὴ φόνον, "not to [commit] murder" (SIG 3.985, l.21, p. 117) and to avoid sexual sins (ll. 25–46, pp. 117–18); also the commentary by Weinreich, *Privatheiligtums in Philadelphia,* 60.

7 Παιδοφθορεῖν appears to be a constructed word that first appears in the Jewish-Christian tradition, replacing παιδεραστεῖν; so Audet, *Didachè,* 286; and Rordorf and Tuilier, *Doctrine,* 149 n. 4. In Justin *Dial.* 95.1 (Goodspeed, 210) it appears with εἰδωλολατρεῖν; cf. also Tatian *Apology* 8.1 (Goodspeed, 274); Clement of Alexandria *Protr.* 10.108.5 (GCS[3] 1.77); *Paed.* 3.12.89.1 (GCS[3] 1.285). The verb is probably derived from παιδοφθόρος, *T.Lev.* 17.11 (in a vice list); *Barn.* 10.6. On this subject, cf. also Lev 18:22; 20:13; Rom 1:27; 1 Cor 6:9; 1 Tim 1:10.

Compare also the prohibition on the Philadelphia stele (SIG 3.985, ll.27–28, p. 117): μὴ φθερε[ῖν μηδὲ παῖδα μηδὲ] παρθένον ("corrupt neither boy nor virgin").

8 On the whole subject, cf. *Ps.-Phocyl.* μήτε γαμοκλοπέειν μήτ᾽ ἄρσενα Κύπριν ὀρίνειν ("neither commit adultery nor rouse homosexual passion"); and van der Horst, *Sentences,* 110–11.

9 Οὐ κλέψει, οὐ μαγεύσεις, οὐ φαρμακεύσεις has no parallel in Barnabas. Οὐ κλέψεις has no parallel in *Doctrina.* Have they been omitted through homoioteleuton? (Schlecht, *Doctrina,* 47).

10 Cf. Exod 22:17 LXX; Lev 19:26, 31; Deut 18:9–14; 1 Sam 15:23; 2 Kgs 9:22; *Sib. Or.* 3.224–30.

11 The association of οὐ μαγεύσεις with the preceding prohibitions is to be understood in this way.

12 That there was also a rich fund of Jewish magical lore is quite a different subject. Cf. van der Horst, *Sentences,* 213.

13 Cf. Exod 22:17 LXX; Deut 18:10 LXX; Wis 12:4; *Ps.-Phocyl.* 149: Φάρμακα μὴ τεύχειν, μαγικῶν βίβλων ἀπέχεσθαι ("Make no potions, keep away from magical books"). For Christian polemic against the vice of φαρμακεία, see Gal 5:20; Rev 9:21; 18:23; 21:8; 22:15; *Hermas Vis.* 3.9.7. The warning against μαγεία and φαρμακ(ε)ία returns once more in the vice list in *Did.* 5.1; cf. *Barn.* 20.1. The association of μαγεύειν and φαρμακεύειν is obvious; cf. the parallels in van der Horst, *Sentences,* 212–13. In the prohibitions on the Philadelphia stele, the magical material is called φάρμακον πονηρόν, which is made concrete in what follows: ἐπωιδαὶ πονηραί and φίλτρον (SIG 3.985, ll. 18–20, p. 117). Cf. Weinreich, *Privatheiligtums in Philadelphia,* 55.

14 Cf. *Barn.* 19.5.

15 Φθορά (or ἀποφθορά) = *abortus*: SIG 3.1042, l. 7, p. 196; Clement of Alexandria *Paed.* 2.10.96.1 (GCS[3]

abortion.[16] But it is certain that from the beginning, Christians, following Old Testament and Jewish custom, rejected abortion. That there is no specific prohibition of it in the New Testament is accidental. As in *Did.* 5.2 (and as we find frequently in Jewish and Christian texts)[17] the prohibitions on abortion and exposing of infants are connected. Thus the next command is οὐδὲ γεννηθὲν[18] ἀποκτενεῖς,[19] prohibiting the killing of newborn children and thus implicitly forbidding that they be exposed.[20] The following command, οὐκ ἐπιθυμήσεις τὰ τοῦ πλησίον ("You shall not covet what belongs to your neighbor"),[21] following Exod 20:17; Deut 5:21 (MT), really belongs with the series οὐκ ἔσῃ πλεονέκτης κτλ., and has been wrongly placed here.[22] In contrast, *Barn.* 19.6 preserves the correct order, although only in the case of the two phrases οὐ μὴ γένῃ ἐπιθυμῶν and οὐ μὴ γένῃ πλεονέκτης.

■ **3–5** Now follows a series of prohibitions[23] related to "sins of the tongue."[24] Οὐκ ἐπιορκήσεις ("You shall not swear falsely") forbids either false oaths or the breaking of an oath or vow.[25] One should note that here (differently from Matt 5:33–37; Jas 5:12) it is perjury or the

1.215); cf. Plutarch *De tuenda sanitate praecepta* (*Moralia* 134F; Babbitt, 278), where it is said of the ἀκόλασται γυναῖκες ἐκβολίοις χρώμεναι καὶ φθορίοις ("licentious women who employ drugs and instruments to produce abortion"). A prohibition for fellow members of a pagan cult to make use of φθορεῖον ἀτοκεῖον is found in the Philadelphia stele (SIG 3.985, l. 20, p. 117), although here this may be, as Weinreich (*Privatheiligtums in Philadelphia*, 5) surmises, a reference to magical practices. The stele does not refer to the ritual impurity caused by abortion but "places all the emphasis on the ethical question as such" (ibid.). For abortion in antiquity generally, see Jan Hendrik Waszink, "Abtreibung," *RAC* 1 (1950) 55–59. The broad use of abortion in the imperial period is well known (ibid., 57). It was especially common among the more well-to-do classes in that society (p. 59). "Medicine was strictly opposed to abortion, from the hippocratic oath . . . until the end of antiquity" (p. 57). It is equally well known that Jewish piety rejected abortion: cf., e.g., Philo *Spec. leg.* 3.108–9, 117; Josephus *Ap.* 2.202; *Ps.-Phocyl.* 184: μηδὲ γυνὴ φθείρῃ βρέφος ἔμβρυον ἔνδοθι γαστρός ("Do not let a woman destroy the unborn babe in her belly"). See *Sib. Or.* 2.281; Waszink, "Abtreibung," 58; van der Horst, *Sentences*, 233–34.

16   This prohibition, and the entire context, derives from the Jewish Two Ways tractate.

17   Van der Horst, *Sentences*, 233–34.

18   Read γεννηθέν with *Canons, Constitutions, Barnabas*, against γεννηθέντα in H.

19   Cf. *Barn.* 19.5.

20   See the Jewish and Christian examples in van der Horst, *Sentences*, 233–34.

21   Ἐπιθυμεῖν with accusative rather than the classical usage with the genitive: BDF, §171(1); BDR, §171(2).

22   We find the same wrong order in the version in *Doctrina, Canons,* and *Epitome.* In v. 6, however, *Doctrina* has *non eris cupidus* ("you shall not covet"), and thus offers a version that stands genetically

between *Barnabas* and the *Didache.*

23   There is no parallel to the first three members in *Barnabas,* and *Doctrina* lacks the parallel to οὐ ψευδομαρτυρήσεις.

24   Strictly speaking, οὐ μνησικακήσεις (v. 3) is an exception.

25   Cf. BAGD, *s.v.*; Lev 19:12; Zech 8:17 (*Barn.* 2.8); Sir 23:11; Wis 14:28–29; *3 Bar.* 4.17; 13.4; *Ps.-Phocyl.* 16–17: μὴ δ᾽ ἐπιορκήσῃς μήτ᾽ ἀγνῶς μήτε ἑκοντί· ψεύδορκον στυγέει θεὸς ἄμβροτος ὅστις ὀμόσσῃ ("And do not commit perjury, neither ignorantly nor willingly. The immortal God hates a perjurer, whosoever it is who has sworn"; cf. *Sib. Or.* 2.68–69 Ψ); 1 Tim 1:10; and further examples in van der Horst, *Sentences*, 123–24.

26   Knopf, *Lehre*, 11. The material in the prohibition series (stemming from the tractate) is pre-Christian Jewish. It lacks Jesus' eschatological motivation. Cf., in contrast, 1.3b–2.1.

27   Mark 10:9 par.; Rom 13:9 *v.l.* Further: Lev 19:16; Deut 19:16–19; Prov 21:28; 25:18; *Ps.-Phocyl.* 12: μαρτυρίην ψευδῆ φεύγειν ("Flee false witness," cf. *Sib. Or.* 2.64 Ψ); *Apoc. Pet.* 29 (Akhmim) (*NTApoc*, 2.631). The parallel in the vice list of the way of death has ψευδομαρτυρίαι (*Did.* 5.1; cf. Matt 15:19; 26:59; Polycarp *Phil.* 2.2; 4.3; *Hermas Man.* 8.5).

28   Contrast κακολογεῖν τινα: Exod 21:16 (cf. Prov 20:9a; Ezek 22:7; Mark 7:10/Matt 15:4); Mark 9:39; Acts 19:9.

29   As in *Hermas Man.* 9.3; *Diogn.* 9.2.

30   *Barn.* 19.4: οὐ μνησικακήσεις τῷ ἀδελφῷ σου ("Do not bear malice against your brother").

31   Zech 7:10: καὶ κακίαν ἕκαστος τοῦ ἀδελφοῦ αὐτοῦ μὴ μνησικακείτω ἐν ταῖς καρδίαις ὑμῶν ("and do not devise evil in your hearts against one another"; cf. *Barn.* 2.8); 1 Clem. 2.5: εἰλικρινεῖς καὶ ἀκέραιοι ἦτε καὶ ἀμνησίκακοι εἰς ἀλλήλους ("you were sincere and innocent and bore no malice to one another"); 1 Clem. 62.2: ὁμονοοῦντας ἀμνησικάκως ἐν ἀγάπῃ καὶ εἰρήνῃ ("to live in concord, bearing no malice, in love and peace").

32   Cf. *Barn.* 19.7.

breaking of oaths that is forbidden, not swearing itself.[26] Ψευδομαρτυρεῖν means to make a false statement (before a judge), to tell a lie when giving testimony (cf. Exod 20:16; Deut 5:20, MT).[27] Κακολογεῖν ("to speak evil") is used here absolutely.[28] Τὸ μνησικακεῖν ("to harbor resentment" in the absolute)[29] should be added τινί τι κακόν:[30] to be unable to forget the evil one has undergone; to be irreconcilable.[31]

■ **4** This verse continues the prohibitions against sins of the tongue:[32] οὐκ ἔση διγνώμων[33] οὐδὲ δίγλωσσος. Διγνώμων (or δίγνωμος)[34] is the false person who says one thing and thinks another. In fact, δίγλωσσος has the same meaning here: "double-tongued."[35] The warning against false, double-tongued speech is supported by an aphorism (breaking the schema of the context): παγὶς γὰρ θανάτου ἡ διγλωσσία ("for equivocation is a mortal snare").[36] The style[37] and content[38] resemble the Old Testament.

■ **5** Finally, there comes a warning against empty and deceptive chatter:[39] οὐκ ἔσται ὁ λόγος σου κενός, οὐ ψευδής.[40]

Excursus: The Text of 2.5

The text is uncertain at this point (and has been expanded by a later gloss).[41] The witnesses are:

H: ψευδής, οὐ κενός, ἀλλὰ μεμεστωμένος πράξει.
Canons: κενὸς οὐδὲ ψευδής.
Doctrina: vacuum nec mendax
Epitome: κενός,
Constitutions: κενός . . . οὐ ψεύσῃ.

The result is that (1) the clause ἀλλὰ μεμεστωμένος πράξει ("but fulfilled by deed")[42] represents a later gloss,[43] which does not speak for the quality of the H text, and suggests the possibility of glosses in other

---

33 *Doctrina* interprets with *duplex in consilium dandum.*

34 Text uncertain. Wengst decides for δίγνωμος. H and *Barnabas* read διγνώμων. In the parallel passages, *Contitutions, Canons,* and *Epitome* read δίγνωμος (and the word is also in *Const.* 2.6.1). *Synt. doctr.* 1.9: μὴ εἶναι δίλογον, μὴ δίνωμον. *Fides patr.* 4 (cf. *PG* 28.1639D): μὴ εἶναι δίγλωσσον μὴ (*PG* has the variant reading ἢ) δίγνωμον. Διγνώμων is found in a Greek scholion on Euripides 633 (Dindorf, 1.172); δίγνωμος in Simplicius on Epictetus (Dübner, 134.53); Hippolytus *Ref.* 5.26.1 (GCS 3.127); 10.15.2 (276); Maximus Confessor *Opuscula* (*PG* 91.56B); *Etymol. magn.* (ed. Gaisford) on ἀλλο-πρόσαλλος.

35 BAGD, *s.v.* Δίγλωσσος does not mean "bilingual" here but instead "false, dishonest." Cf. esp. Prov 11:13; Sir 5:9, 14–15; 28:13; Philo *Sacr.* 32 (vice list); *Sib. Or.* 3.37 (vice list); *Constitutions* also, at 2.6.1 (vice list).

36 The word διγλωσσία occurs only here and in the parallels in *Barn.* 19.7 and *Canons.* In *Constitutions* we read παγὶς γὰρ ἰσχυρὰ ἀνδρὶ τὰ ἴδια χείλη ("a man's own lips are a strong snare" = Prov 6:2). Διγλωσσία was probably constructed from δίγλωσσος and represents a characteristic expression of the Two Ways tractate, perhaps an ad hoc construction by the author.

37 Παγὶς θανάτου: Prov (13:14); 14:27; 21:6; Tob 14:10; Ps 17:6. Cf. the similar expression in 1QH 2.21; CD 14.2.

38 The fool is caught by his or her own speech: Prov 6:2; the mouth or tongue as παγίς: Prov (12:13); 18:7; Sir 51:2. The danger of the tongue: Sir

28:13–26; cf. Jas 3:1–12. Closer to the OT tradition is the version in *Barn.* 19.8: παγὶς γὰρ τὸ στόμα θανάτου ("the mouth is a snare of death"). That is probably more original than the version in the *Didache.* Cf. also *Doctrina: tendiculum enim mortis est lingua.*

39 This is lacking in *Barnabas.*

40 Cf. *T.Naph.* 3.1.

41 For what follows, see Niederwimmer, "Text-probleme," 118–19.

42 Cf. Jas 1:22; 1 John 3:18; *1 Clem.* 38.2; *2 Clem.* 4.1–5; Justin *1 Apol.* 14.5 (Goodspeed, 35); 16.8 (37). Knopf (*Lehre,* 12), however, also points to *Corp. Herm.* 16.2 (Nock and Festugière, 2.232): Ἕλληνες γάρ . . . λόγους ἔχουσι κενοὺς ἀποδείξεων ἐνεργητικούς, καὶ αὕτη ἐστὶν Ἑλλήνων φιλοσοφία λόγων ψόφος. ἡμεῖς δὲ οὐ λόγοις χρώμεθα, ἀλλὰ φωναῖς μεσταῖς τῶν ἔργων ("For the Greeks have empty speeches, O king, that are energetic only in what they demonstrate, and this is the philosophy of the Greeks, an inane foolosophy of speeches. We, by contrast, use not speeches but sounds that are full of action"; trans. Brian Copenhaver, *Hermetica* [Cambridge: Cambridge University Press, 1992] 58); and see Theognis 979 (Young, 60): Μή μοι ἀνὴρ εἴη γλώσσηι φίλος, ἀλλὰ καὶ ἔργωι ("I would have no man my friend with lips only, but also in deed").

43 This was already suggested by Schlecht, *Doctrina,* 48; Knopf, *Lehre,* 12: "probably to be regarded as an addition." Drews ("Apostellehre," 260) considers it probable that this is "an addition by our redactor," as does Giet, *L'Énigme,* 94. This can scarcely be the case.

passages as well. (2) Following the indirect witnesses, I conjecture the original text as κενός, οὐ ψευδής.[44]

■ **6–7** The next verses begin with prohibitions recalling the ninth and tenth commandments of the Decalogue, but then move to phraseology opposing offenses against love of neighbor. At the beginning is the πλεονέκτης ("one given to greed").[45] The content probably reflects Exod 20:17; Deut 5:21 (MT), but this is no longer clear because of the rearrangements that have occurred in the text.[46] The πλεονέκτης is then followed by the ἅρπαξ ("robber").[47] The sequence of the following parts is suggested merely by association: Οὐδὲ ὑποκριτής (here not "hypocrite," but "wicked, far from God godless"),[48] οὐδὲ κακοήθης,[49] οὐδὲ ὑπερήφανος,[50] οὐ λήψη βουλὴν πονηρὰν κατὰ τοῦ πλησίον σου[51] forbid evil and hostile intentions toward one's neighbor.[52]

■ **7** The series concludes with a general warning: οὐ μισήσεις πάντα[53] ἄνθρωπον, ἀλλὰ οὓς μὲν ἐλέγξεις, περὶ ὧν δὲ[54] προσεύξῃ, οὕς δὲ ἀγαπήσεις ὑπὲρ τὴν ψυχήν σου.[55] The meaning of this overloaded expression (alluding to Lev 19:17?),[56] which also gives an impres-

---

44 Wengst, *Didache,* 68: κενὸς οὐδὲ ψευδής.

45 This was originally introduced by a prohibition against coveting the neighbor's goods, as still evident in *Barn.* 19.6 and *Doctrina* (*non eris cupidus*). *Barnabas* lacks the parts of the sentence beginning with πλεονέκτης.

46 The warning against greed recurs in the vice list at 5.1 (= *Barn.* 20.1). For πλεονεξία and πλεονέκτης in lists, cf. Mark 7:22; Rom 1:29; 1 Cor 5:10–11; 6:10; Eph 5:3; Col 3:5; *1 Clem.* 35.5; Polycarp *Phil.* 2.2; *Hermas Man.* 8.5; *Sim.* 6.5.5. See also Luke 12:15; 2 Cor 7:2; 9:5 (12:17–18); Eph 4:19; 5:5; 1 Thess 2:5 (4:6); 2 Pet 2:3, 14; *Hermas Man.* 6.2.5; *Barn.* 10.4.

47 For ἅρπαξ, cf. also 1 Cor 5:10–11; 6:10; Luke 18:11 (in vice lists); also on this theme: Matt 12:29; 23:35 par.; *Barn.* 10.4. The sin of theft appears again in the vice list of the way of death: *Did.* 5.1 (= *Barn.* 20.1).

48 Behind the meaning "wicked" for ὑποκριτής is חָנֵף, which Audet (*Didachè,* 293–94) has pointed out, correctly in my opinion. This meaning (remarkable in relation to classical and other Hellenistic usage) begins with the translation of חָנֵף as ὑποκριτής ("godless") in LXX (Job 34:30; 36:13), and was continued in later translations (Audet, *Didachè,* 293; Ulrich Wilckens "ὑποκρίνομαι κτλ.," *TDNT* 8 [1972] 564). For general information on this linguistic usage by diaspora Judaism, see Wilckens, "ὑποκρίνομαι," 563–66, with reflections on how the usage may have arisen. Of course, the equation of ὑποκριτής with חָנֵף is still not a sure indication of the origins of the tractate in diaspora Judaism. Nota bene: NT usage of ὑποκριτής also largely derives from that of diaspora Judaism: cf. Wilckens, "ὑποκρίνομαι," 566–69; Ὑπόκρισις in *Did.* 4.12 should probably be interpreted similarly; while the ὑποκρίσεις in 5.1 are probably "hypocrisies." That Wilckens himself (p. 570) interprets the word differently in *Did.* 2.6 is a separate issue.

49 *Sib. Or.* 3.37: ψευδῶν διγλώσσων ἀνθρώπων καὶ κακοηθῶν ("false, double-tongued men and immoral").

50 In vice lists: Rom 1:30; 2 Tim 3:2; cf. also the quotation of Prov 3:34 in Jas 4:6; 1 Pet 5:5; *1 Clem.* 30.2; also Luke 1:51; *1 Clem.* 49.5; 57.2; 59.3 (= Isa 13:11); Ignatius *Eph.* 5.3. Ὑπερηφανεῖν: Ignatius *Eph.* 5.3; *Smyrn.* 10.2; *Pol.* 4.3; ὑπερηφανία in the list in Mark 7:22 and *Hermas Man.* 8.3; cf. also *Man.* 6.2.5; *Sim.* 8.9.1; *1 Clem.* 16.2; 30.1; 35.5. The word family plays a special role in *1 Clement.* For the sequence, cf. esp. *1 Clem.* 35.5: πλεονεξίαν … κακοηθείας … ὑπερηφανίαν. The vice list of the way of death in *Did.* 5.1 (= *Barn.* 20.1) has ὑπερηφανία.

51 Cf. *Barn.* 19.3.

52 Cf. BAGD, *s.v.* βουλή.

53 Οὐ—πάντα is a Hebraism (cf. Schaff, *Church Manual,* 170).

54 Περὶ ὧν δέ in P, *Canons, Epitome;* Wengst, *Didache,* 68; against περὶ δὲ ὧν in H. For the text of *Doctrina* and *Constitutions,* see below.

55 Only the last clause has a parallel in *Barnabas* (19.5): ἀγαπήσεις τὸν πλησίον σου ὑπὲρ τὴν ψυχήν σου ("You shall love your neighbor beyond yourself"; cf. ἀγαπᾶν ὑμᾶς ὑπὲρ τὴν ψυχήν μου, 1.4; πάντας ἀγαπῶν ὑπὲρ τὴν ψυχήν μου, 4.6). *Barn.* 19.5 has certainly preserved the older version of the tractate. The version we now read in the *Didache* is secondary from a tradition-historical standpoint. *Doctrina* has a shorter text (without a climax): *neminem hominum oderis, quosdam amabis super animam tuam* ("you shall hate no human beings, some you will love more than your own soul"). This leads to the suspicion that the source of the *Didache* may have been similar (i.e., without a climax), so that the climax found here (clumsy as it is) may be a clarification by the Didachist. But the climax is also found in the *Canons* and *Epitome.* It must therefore have been in the same source, and there is simply an omission in *Doctrina.* "*Quosdam* indicates that L is not original" (Drews, "Apostellehre," 260). The formally related climax in Jude 22–23 is striking, see Sakae Kubo, "Jude 22–23," in Eldon J. Epp and Gordon D. Fee, eds., *New Testament Textual Criticism: Its Significance for Exegesis: Essays in Honour of*

92

sion of being secondary,[57] is uncertain. There appear to be two or three[58] classes of people:[59] a first class who have committed faults—they are to be reproved and set straight (οὒς μὲν ἐλέγξεις);[60] a second class, perhaps those who show themselves resistant to correction—one should pray for them (περὶ ὧν δὲ προσεύξῃ); finally, a third class: we should probably assume that these are members of one's own group. For them the commandment is: ἀγαπήσεις ὑπὲρ τὴν ψυχήν σου ("You shall love more than yourself").[61] Ψυχή here probably means one's own "life," or one's own "person": one is one's own

ψυχή.[62] To love someone more than one's own life means to love that one more than oneself.[63] Thus what is probably being said is that the demand for love, the "love commandment," applies to everyone, but the concrete realization of the love commandment is different as regards the different groups of human beings. The commandment of love is most stringent toward the members of one's own group. Here it is not merely "love your neighbor as yourself," but even "love your neighbor *more* than yourself."

Bruce M. Metzger (New York: Oxford University Press, 1981) 239–53; Knopf, *Lehre*, 13: "There appears to be some kind of relationship between [*Did.* 3].7 and Jude 22–23." True, but what kind? In addition, our *Didache* passage may be quoted in *Lib. grad.* 16.4 (Kmosko, 395): see above Introduction, §2b.

56 Lev 19:17: οὐ μισήσεις τὸν ἀδελφόν σου τῇ διανοίᾳ σου, ἐλεγμῷ ἐλέγξεις τὸν πλησίον σου καὶ οὐ λήμψῃ δι᾽αὐτὸν ἁμαρτίαν ("You shall not hate in your heart any one of your kin; you shall reprove your neighbor, or you will incur guilt yourself"). Cf. A. de Vogüé, "'Ne haïr personne,'" *RThAM* 44 (1968) 3–9. The biblical τὸν ἀδελφόν σου (or τὸν πλησίον σου) has been replaced by the universal πάντα ἄνθρωπον (de Vogüé, 4). *Apostolic Constitutions* has the maxim οὐ μισήσεις πάντα ἄνθρωπον three times (in 7.5.3 from *Didache,* with the Constitutor having expanded the text by using Lev 19:17b; then in 7.2.3 in the middle of a review of the *sectio,* and finally in 2.53.6 as a gloss in a review of the *Didascalia,* where the Constitutor this time includes the whole of Lev 19:17). Later instances can be found in de Vogüé, 7–9. The *Nullum odire* in *Regula Magistri* 3.71 (SC 105.370) and *Rul. Ben.* 4.65 (CSEL² 75.36) is important. There are possible distant relationships to some version of the Two Ways tractate. See de Vogüé, 8. See above, Introduction, §2c.

57 *Canons* apparently read the version offered by the *Didache.* The compiler of the *Canons* inserted, after ἐλέγξεις: οὒς δὲ ἐλεήσεις (Funk, *Patres apostolici,* 1.8 considered this version original; it is also regard-

ed as probable by Drews, "Apostellehre," 260). Knopf (*Lehre,* 13) explained the addition in light of Jude 23. *Epitome,* however, lacks οὒς δὲ ἐλεήσεις.

58 Harnack, *Lehre,* 10; Knopf, *Lehre,* 13; Kleist, *Didache,* 155; Wengst, *Didache,* 93.

59 The following interpretation follows Harnack. Is it correct? Knopf (*Lehre,* 13) differs very little: "The first [group] contains those people who can still be saved, even though they have been affected by sin; they can be found inside or outside the community. . . . The second type of people encompasses those who, according to human opinion, are lost, the unapproachable. . . . Finally, the third type are the full-fledged members of the community." Cf. also Wengst, *Didache,* 93.

60 *Did.* 4.3; 15.3: ἐλέγχειν.

61 *Gesta ap. Zenophilum* (CSEL 26.192) quotes this passage, either from the *Didache* or from the tractate: see above, Introduction, §2b.

62 Audet, *Didachè,* 294: "more than one's self." Wengst, *Didache,* 94 n. 13 (with reference to BAGD, *s.v.* ψυχή).

63 For this whole subject, cf. also *Rul. Ben.* 2.25 (CSEL² 75.25), where, of course, the reference is to members of one's own group, the monastic community.

d. The "*Teknon*" Sayings (3.1–6)

1	My child, flee from all evil and from everything like it.
2	Do not be an angry person, for anger leads to murder; nor should you be a zealot or a quarrelsome or hot-tempered person, for from all of these [traits of character] flow murderous acts.
3	My child, do not be a person given to passion, because passion leads to fornication; nor should you be given to obscene speech or to bold gazes, for from all of these [actions] flow acts of adultery.
4	My child, do not practice augury, because this leads to idolatry; nor should you be an enchanter, or an astrologer, or a person who performs purificatory rituals; you should not even want to see <or hear> such things, for from all of these [activities] idolatry is spawned.
5	My child, do not be a liar, because lying leads to theft; nor should you be given to avarice or to vainglory, for from all of these [traits of character] theft is spawned.
6	My child, do not be a grumbler (against God), because this leads to blasphemy; nor should you be presumptuous or disposed to invent evil, for from all these [attitudes] blasphemies are spawned.

Analysis

The next group of sayings is characterized by a constant address from the fatherly teacher to his student, who is called τέκνον ("child") (3.1, 3, 4, 5, 6). We can call this group the "*teknon* sayings." They also come from the source, the tractate. Noteworthy is that there are no parallels to the *teknon* sayings as such (3.1–6) in *Barnabas*. They therefore must not have been present, as yet, in that (probably older) recension of the Two Ways tractate that served as a source for *Barnabas*.[1] Parallels in *Barnabas* then reappear at (3.7 and) 3.8c–10.[2] *Doctrina* offers a parallel text to 3.1–6 (and for 3.7–10), but 3.1–6 is not characterized by the constant address "my child," which instead is found only at the beginning, in 3.1: "*Fili, fuge. . . .*" In addition, there is no parallel to 3.3 and 4a. (This can be interpreted either as an omission,[3] or—though this is less likely—3.3, 4a were missing from *Doctrina* from the beginning.) The *teknon* sayings also return in *Canons*, including the material corresponding to *Did.* 3.3, 4a (*Canons* also has a parallel to *Did.* 3.7–10); however, the apostrophe in the second saying is doubled (something that is certainly secondary and explained by

---

1 Muilenburg (*Literary Relations*, 34, 149) has expressed the opinion that *Did.* 3.1–6 was derived from a Jewish apocryphon. This notion had been expressed earlier by Robinson, *Didache*, 62; idem, "Barnabas and the Didache," 242 (a Jewish or early Christian apocryphon as the source); Vokes, *Riddle*, 76: "a fragment of an earlier writing incorporated bodily into the Didache"; Connolly, "Relation," 242: "To my mind there can be no doubt in the world that this piece was found by the Didachist in some earlier writing—possibly some 'Testament,' or parting admonitions of a father to his son—and inserted by him in his version of the Two Ways." The correct

version is in Audet, *Didachè*, 311, who recognizes 3.1–6 as a later addition to the original Two Ways tractate. The other hypotheses associated with this can be set aside here.

2 The parallels to 3.7 are only rudimentary.

3 Drews ("Apostellehre," 261) explained the absence of vv. 3 and 4a in *Doctrina* as "probably only the result of a mistake."

4 The respective sources of the *Life of Shenoute* and of *Syntagma doctrinae* and *Fides patrum* also contained the *teknon* sayings. In the *Life*, the whole text of *Did.* 2.6–4.8 has been revised into *teknon* sayings. (This is certainly secondary.) By contrast, in *Syntagma doctri-*

the rather long insertion found in *Canons* at this point). Finally, *Epitome* also contains the material of the *teknon* sayings, although it is not stylized in the same way (the apostrophe is lacking in *Epitome*).[4] These observations can be explained if we adopt the following model: On the one hand, *Barnabas* rests on a recension of the Two Ways tractate in which the *teknon* sayings were yet absent (B recension of the tractate). On the other hand, *Doctrina, Didache, Canons,* and *Epitome* go back to a (later) recension that already contained the *teknon* sayings (C recension).[5] More precisely: *Didache* and *Doctrina* rest on sub-archetype C[1], in which the *teknon* sayings were retained in the form found in C. (*Doctrina* reveals some omissions that are secondary and may have arisen only in the Latin textual tradition.) *Canons* and *Epitome* rest on sub-archetype C[2], which is characterized by a stylization of the entirety of the material, and thus also of the *teknon* sayings, into apostolic sayings (the omission of the apostrophe in the material of the *teknon* sayings in *Epitome* is secondary). For the whole, see above, pp. 35–41, where the corresponding hypotheses are discussed.

The disposition in the *Didache* is now as follows:
First saying: general introduction; wrath leads to murder (3.1–2).
Second saying: lust leads to fornication and adultery (3.3).

Third saying: reading omens, magic, and the like lead to idolatry (3.4).
Fourth saying: lying leads to theft (3.5).
Fifth saying: grumbling leads to blasphemy (3.6).

This is sapiential material[6] in a psychologized form. The primary intention of the series is to reveal apparently minor vices as, in fact, dangerous temptations, which (if one surrenders to them) lead to serious sins. The warning appeals—in the style of *ḥokmah* (divine Wisdom)—to the understanding and assent of reason.[7] The student (the τέκνον instructed by the experienced teacher) is to recognize and learn the danger in time: *principiis obsta!* In the nature of things, this section belongs within the context of early Jewish rigoristic morality. The same motif of sharpening the moral sense through understanding is inherent in the psychological contexts that we recognize in other contemporary Jewish sources, and that (although with eschatological intensification) also shape some elements of the Jesus tradition (Matt 5:21–26). Still, the tractate lacks the eschatological inexorability that characterizes the Jesus tradition.[8] Closest to this mentality are certain passages in the *Testaments of the Twelve Patriarchs*.[9] Formally the *teknon* sayings are relatively well organized. We find five sayings, each of them (except for the first) introduced by an address, followed by a first warning, a first reason, a second warning, and a second reason. The third saying is

---

nae and *Fides patrum* (where only rudiments of the material of the *teknon* sayings are present) the apostrophe has disappeared completely. In addition, the apostrophe is lacking (naturally enough) in the *Apostolic Constitutions*, which derived this section directly from the *Didache*.

5 The sources of the *Life of Shenoute* and of *Syntagma doctrinae* and *Fides patrum* must also, ultimately, go back in some fashion to this recension (C). Because they are unacquainted with the stylization of the material into apostolic sayings, we can think more precisely of a C[1], but nothing more certain can be said about it.

6 Audet, *Didachè*, 301: "a sapiential adaptation of the Decalogue," may go too far.

7 Audet speaks (*Didachè*, 305) very accurately of a "didactic imperative, rather than juridical or legal."

8 For the motif of radicalizing in general, see Rordorf, "Gebrauch des Dekalogs," 437–38. The Jesus tradition is more radical than the *Didache*: in it, wrath already *is* murder. In the tractate, by contrast, wrath *leads* to murder. Cf. Knopf, *Lehre*, 14. Moreover, the tractate lacks the eschatological con-

text within which Jesus' interpretation of the law stands.

9 Cf., e.g., *T. Jud.* 14.1: Καὶ νῦν, τέκνα μου, μὴ μεθύσκεσθε οἴνῳ· ὅτι ὁ οἶνος διαστρέφει τὸν νοῦν ἀπὸ τῆς ἀληθείας, καὶ ἐμβάλλει ὀργὴν ἐπιθυμίας, καὶ ὁδηγεῖ εἰς πλάνην τοὺς ὀφθαλμούς ("And now, my children, I tell you, Do not be drunk with wine, because wine perverts the mind from the truth, arouses the impulses of desire, and leads the eyes into the path of error"); 19.1: Τέκνα μου, ἡ φιλαργυρία πρὸς εἴδωλα ὁδηγεῖ (!), ὅτι ἐν πλάνῃ δι᾽ ἀργυρίου τοὺς μὴ ὄντας θεοὺς ὀνομάζουσιν, καὶ ποιεῖ τὸν ἔχοντα αὐτὴν εἰς ἔκστασιν ἐμπεσεῖν ("My children, love of money leads to idolatry, because once they are led astray by money they designate as gods those who are not gods. It makes anyone who has it go out of his mind"); *T. Reub.* 2.8–9 (in the context of the teaching on the seven vices): ἕβδομον πνεῦμα σπορᾶς καὶ συνουσίας, μεθ᾽ ἧς συνεισέρχεται διὰ τῆς φιληδονίας ἡ ἁμαρτία· (9) διὰ τοῦτο ἔσχατόν ἐστι τῆς κτίσεως καὶ πρῶτον τῆς νεότητος, ὅτι ἀγνοίας πεπλήρωται καὶ αὕτη τὸν νεώτερον ὁδηγεῖ ὡς τυφλὸν ἐπὶ βόθρον καὶ ὡς

overloaded. The following system of organization[10] asserts itself:

3.2

(τέκνον μου)	address
μὴ γίνου ὀργίλος,	first warning
ὁδηγεῖ γὰρ ἡ ὀργὴ πρὸς τὸν φόνον,	first reason
μηδὲ ζηλωτὴς μηδὲ ἐριστικὸς μηδὲ θυμικός·	second warning
ἐκ γὰρ τούτων ἁπάντων φόνοι γεννῶνται.	second reason

3.3

τέκνον μου,
μὴ γίνου ἐπιθυμητής,
ὁδηγεῖ γὰρ ἡ ἐπιθυμία πρὸς τὴν πορνείαν,
μηδὲ αἰσχρολόγος μηδὲ ὑψηλόφθαλμος·
ἐκ γὰρ τούτων ἁπάντων μοιχεῖαι γεννῶνται.

3.4

τέκνον μου,
μὴ γίνου οἰωνοσκόπος,
ἐπειδὴ ὁδηγεῖ εἰς τὴν εἰδωλολατρίαν,
μηδὲ ἐπαοιδὸς μηδὲ μαθηματικὸς μηδὲ περικαθαίρων,
μηδὲ θέλε αὐτὰ βλέπειν μηδὲ ἀκούειν·
ἐκ γὰρ τούτων ἁπάντων εἰδωλολατρία γεννᾶται.

3.5

τέκνον μου,
μὴ γίνου ψεύστης,

ἐπειδὴ ὁδηγεῖ τὸ ψεῦσμα εἰς τὴν κλοπήν,
μηδὲ φιλάργυρος μηδὲ κενόδοξος·
ἐκ γὰρ τούτων ἁπάντων κλοπαὶ γεννῶνται.

3.6

τέκνον μου,
μὴ γίνου γόγγυσος,
ἐπειδὴ ὁδηγεῖ εἰς τὴν βλασφημίαν,
μηδὲ αὐθάδης μηδὲ πονηρόφρων·
ἐκ γὰρ τούτων ἁπάντων βλασφημίαι γεννῶνται.

As the original *Sitz im Leben* of the *teknon* sayings we may posit the Jewish house of study.[11]

Comment

■ **1** This verse constitutes the introduction to the sayings that follow. The teacher speaks to the student. This teacher-student relationship is conceived in a thoroughly patriarchal fashion: the teacher takes the role of the father, and the student is his child. Hence the address, τέκνον μου ("my child"), which is constantly repeated in the sayings that follow. The model is the style of address in Jewish sapiential traditions.[12] The comprehensive warning to "flee from all evil," φεῦγε ἀπὸ παντὸς πονηροῦ[13] καὶ ἀπὸ παντὸς ὁμοίου αὐτοῦ,[14] precedes the following examples. Πονηροῦ should probably be taken as neuter, and thus impersonal, here.[15] P paraphrases correctly: ἀπὸ[16] παντὸς πράγματος πονηροῦ ("from every evil thing").[17] The expression ἀπὸ παντὸς ὁμοίου αὐτοῦ ("from everything like it") clarifies the universality

---

κτῆνος ἐπὶ κρημνόν ("The seventh is the spirit of procreation and intercourse, with which come sins through fondness for pleasure. For this reason, it was the last in the creation and the first in youth, because it is filled with ignorance; it leads the young person like a blind man into a ditch and like an animal over a cliff"); *T. Sim.* 4.8, on the πνεῦμα τοῦ φθόνου ("spirit of envy"); and so on.

10 Cf. esp. the divisions in Schermann, *Elfapostelmoral*, 52.

11 Audet's suggestion (*Didachè*, 300) that the original tradition was oral cannot be proved, of course. The same is true of the idea (p. 312) that the section's original *Sitz im Leben* was domestic instruction. But Audet himself continues: "However, we should not be too precise about things that can never be verified" (ibid.).

12 The student is here (as in Proverbs and Sirach) the υἱός or τέκνον. Cf. Rainer Riesner, *Jesus als Lehrer: Eine Untersuchung zum Ursprung der Evangelien-Überlieferung* (Tübingen: Mohr [Siebeck], 1981) 109. The constant address "τέκνα (μου)" in *Testaments of the*

Twelve Patriarchs is somewhat different; it there arises from the fictional situation (or at any rate, that is one occasion for it). For the whole, see Riesner, *Jesus als Lehrer*, 102–10. For early Christian usage, cf. 1 Cor 4:14–15, 17; 2 Cor 6:13; Gal 4:19; Phil 2:22; 1 Tim 1:2, 18; 2 Tim 1:2; 2:1; Titus 1:4; Phlm 10; 1 John 2:1, 12, 28; 3:7, 18; 4:4; 5:21; 3 John 4. For the patristic period see Bardenhewer, *Geschichte*, 1.38–46. It is important in this context that the metaphor of the teacher as father and his student as his spiritual son played a role in later times especially in the monastic sphere. Cf. only Hilarius Emonds, "Abt," *RAC* 1 (1950) 51–55.

13 For φεύγειν ἀπό τινος (in part "already possible in classical usage . . . , but favored by the Semitic") see BDF, §149; BDR, §149.1. Cf. 1 Cor 10:14.

14 For ὁμοίου αὐτοῦ cf. BDF, §182(4); BDR, §182(6).

15 Cf. *Did.* 5.2, as well as 10.5. Is 8.2 different? For the interpretation as neuter in this passage see Harnack, *Lehre* 11, and elsewhere.

16 In the text ἀπὸ recurs twice more, by mistake.

17 *Doctrina* differs: *ab homine malo et homine simulatore*

of the warning. This much is introduction.

■ **2** The first example begins only with v. 2.[18] This is an admonition against wrath: μὴ γίνου ὀργίλος,[19] ὁδηγεῖ γὰρ[20] ἡ ὀργὴ πρὸς τὸν φόνον (first warning and reason). Ὀδηγεῖ insinuates the "psychological" considerations: a supposedly harmless passion, quickly passing, in fact "leads" one in a direction whose end is murder and death dealing.[21] The problem of "righteous anger" is not discussed. Matt 5:21–22 is not the source for this text but rather a (certainly more radical) parallel to the idea expressed here. In the (stylistically compatible) second warning, ὀργίλος ("angry person") is varied with ζηλωτής ("zealot," here *sensu malo*),[22] ἐριστικός ("quarrelsome"), and θυμικός ("hot tempered").[23] In accordance with the style, the warning appears with a reason: ἐκ γὰρ τούτων ἀπάντων φόνοι[24] γεννῶνται ("For from all of these flow murderous acts"). Γεννᾶσθαι insinuates the same psychological considerations as ὁδηγεῖν in the first warning.

■ **3** The next verse contains the second *teknon* saying.[25] It warns against lust, meaning, as the continuation shows, sexual libido. The psychological warning (including the reason for it) corresponds to the preceding example: sexual desire leads (leads astray, one would say) to πορνεία ("fornication"). The background of this warning is found in contemporary Jewish traditions observed particularly by pious, enlightened circles.[26] The second warning replaces ἐπιθυμητής[27] with αἰσχρολόγος and ὑψηλόφθαλμος. Αἰσχρολόγος is someone who likes to tell dirty jokes.[28] Ὑψηλόφθαλμος[29] is one who lifts up the eyes; as the context indicates, this does not refer to pride but to lechery.[30] The word is explained by *T. Iss.* 7.2: οὐκ ἐπόρνευσα ἐν μετεωρισμῷ ὀφθαλμῶν μου ("I did not commit lewdness in the lifting of my eyes").[31]

("from an evil man and a lying man"; the last word *in rasura*). For the original text see above, p. 11 n. 69. For the question of a possible quotation in *Epistula Ps. Titi*, see ibid. For the expression ἀπὸ παντὸς (πράγματος) πονηροῦ, cf. Job 1:1 LXX; 1 Thess 5:22, and (more distantly) αἰσχρῶν δ᾽ ἔργων ἀπέχεσθαι in *Ps.-Phocyl.* 76 ("abstain from shameful deeds"; cf. *Sib. Or.* 2.145Ψ).

18 The absence of the apostrophe here is explained by the fact that the introduction and first saying were apparently felt to be a unit.

19 P has οργειλος. For ὀργίλος, cf. Ps 17:49; Prov 21:19, and elsewhere; Titus 1:7; see also *Hermas Man.* 12.4.1.

20 P has ἐπειδὴ ὁδηγεῖ (probably incorrectly) rather than ὁδηγεῖ γάρ (H, *Canons, Epitome*). The text of *Doctrina* reads: *quia . . . ducit. . . .*

21 On this subject (admonitions about the destructive consequences of bitter wrath, with some psychologizing considerations), cf. *T. Dan* 1–6 (although the word here is θυμός). Wis 10:3 recalls the example of Cain. For the whole, see Erik Sjöberg and Gustav Stählin, "ὀργή κτλ.," *TDNT* 5 (1967) 413.

22 The pejorative sense appears only here in our literature. Ζῆλος in the negative sense is found in Acts 5:17; 13:45; Rom 13:13; 1 Cor 3:3; 2 Cor 12:20; Gal 5:20; Jas 3:14, 16; *Hermas Sim.* 8.7.4; and very frequently, indeed as a key concept, in *1 Clem.* (3.2, 4; 4.7–8; etc.).

23 Both these last appear only here in our literature. Cf. *Apostolic Constitutions*; BAGD, *s.v.* Wengst (*Didache*, 68) decides, with *Canons*, for θυμώδης.

24 *Doctrina* reads *irae nascuntur* ("angers are born"), which is certainly bad. One would expect something like *homicidia nascuntur*.

25 There is no parallel in *Doctrina*.

26 Niederwimmer, *Askese*, 27–28.

27 Here *sensu malo*; cf. Prov 1:22, τῆς ὕβρεως ὄντες ἐπιθυμηταί ("Being desirers of violence"). Close to the meaning of ἐπιθυμητής in *Did.* 1.3 are Num 11:34 (ὁ λαὸς ὁ ἐπιθυμητής) and 1 Cor 10:6 (ἐπιθυμητὰι κακῶν). *Constitutions* has, perhaps as allusion to the latter passage, ἐπιθυμητὴς κακῶν.

28 Αἰσχρολόγος is a rare word: cf. the parallels in *Canons, Epitome*, and *Apostolic Constitutions*. Lampe does not have the word. LSJ and BAGD, *s.v.,* refer to Pollux *Onomasticon* 6.123 (Bethe, 34) and 8.80–81 (Bethe, 126–27). More common is αἰσχρολογία, e.g., in Col 3:8; *Did.* 5.1.

29 The word is found only here and in the parallels in *Canons* and *Epitome*. Cf. BAGD, *s.v.,* referring to *Script. Physiogn.* 1.327.2 (ed. Foerster) (εἰ δὲ ὑψηλοὶ ὄντες ὀφθαλμοί). *Constitutions* has ῥιψόφθαλμος. The word ὑψηλόφθαλμος is characteristic of the language of the tractate. Knopf (*Lehre*, 14) unnecessarily suggested a corruption of the text.

30 Cf. BAGD, *s.v.*

31 Cf. also οὐ πλανᾶται μετεωρισμοῖς ὀφθαλμῶν ("nor is he led astray by visual excitement"), *T. Benj.* 6.3; Gen 39:7; μετεωρισμὸν ὀφθαλμῶν μὴ δῷς μοι καὶ ἐπιθυμίαν ἀπόστρεψον ἀπ᾽ ἐμοῦ ("do not give me haughty eyes, and remove evil desire from me"), Sir 23:4b–5a; πορνεία γυναικὸς ἐν μετεωρισμοῖς ὀφθαλμῶν ("The haughty stare betrays an unchaste

The second reason replaces πορνεία with μοιχεῖαι ("acts of adultery").

■ **4** The third saying[32] warns against various forms of pagan superstition. They are definitely not harmless; instead, they lead directly to idolatry. An οἰωνοσκόπος[33] is someone who understands the "art" of making predictions from a bird's flight or call. Εἰδωλολατρία here has the general sense of "service to idols, superstition." The reference is to the religious practice that is contrary to Old Testament and Jewish faith in God. In the second warning, three other forms of pagan superstition are condemned: μηδὲ (sc. γίνου) ἐπαοιδὸς (the "enchanter"),[34] μηδὲ μαθηματικὸς[35] (the astrologer, the "reader of stars"),[36] μηδὲ περικαθαίρων (referring to someone who performs a magical work of expiation).[37] After this,

one should read μηδὲ θέλε αὐτὰ βλέπειν, μηδὲ ἀκούειν.[38] With the sharpened emphasis that one should not only not do such things but not even pay attention or listen to others who engage in such practices, the text does abandon its set literary schema; but by that very fact it emphasizes the special importance of this warning. Ἐκ γὰρ τούτων ἁπάντων εἰδωλολατρία γεννᾶται ("from all of these idolatry is spawned") gives the concluding, second reason, in harmony with the style adopted throughout.[39]

■ **5** The fourth saying warns against lying.[40] The idea that lying leads to theft[41] establishes a surprising connection. It is possible that ψεῦσμα[42] here refers not so much to lying in the narrow sense as to dishonesty in the broader sense: deception, betrayal, treachery,[43] just as

---

wife"), Sir 26:9; *Ps. Sol.* 4.4a; CD 2.16; 2 Pet 2:14. In connection with idolatry: Num 15:39; Ezek 6:9; 1QS 1.6. The opposite is described in *T. Benj.* 8.2: ὁ ἔχων διάνοιαν καθαρὰν ἐν ἀγάπῃ οὐχ ὁρᾷ γυναῖκα εἰς πορνείαν· οὐ γὰρ ἔχει μιασμὸν ἐν καρδίᾳ, ὅτι ἀναπαύεται ἐν αὐτῷ τὸ πνεῦμα τοῦ θεοῦ ("For a person with a mind that is pure with love does not look on a woman for the purpose of having sexual relations. He has no pollution in his heart, because upon him is resting the spirit of God").

32 The beginning of this verse has no parallel in *Doctrina apostolorum*. See above.

33 BAGD and LSJ, *s.v.* See esp. Philo *Mut. nom.* 202 (of Balaam); *Spec. leg.* 1.60; 4.48 (mantic arts, among others); LXX has οἰωνισμός (Gen 44:5, 15; Num 23:23; Sir 34:5), οἰώνισμα (1 Sam 15:23; Jer 14:14; 34:9); οἰωνός (Num 24:1), and οἰωνίζεσθαι (Gen 30:27; 44:5, 15; Lev 19:26; Deut 18:10; 1 Kgs 21(20):33; 2 Kgs 17:17B; 21:6; 2 Chr 33:6); cf. οἰωνοσκοπεῖν, Josephus *Ant.* 18.125.

34 BAGD, *s.v.* Ἐπαοιδός in place of ἐπῳδός is frequent in LXX; Philo *Migr. Abr.* 83 (with φαρμακευταί); *Sib. Or.* 3.225, οὐ μάντεις, οὐ φαρμακούς, οὐ μὴν ἐπαοιδούς ("nor seers, nor sorcerers, nor soothsayers"); Irenaeus *Adv. haer.* 2.32.5 (SC 294.342): *incantationes.* Cf. Epictetus *Dissertationes* 3.24.10 (metaphorically, of philosophers). The Philadelphia stele knows the prohibition [μὴ ἐπωι]δὰς πονηρὰς . . . [μὴ] φίλτρον (SIG 3.985, ll. 18–20, p. 117).

35 *Doctrina* recommences here: *Noli esse mathematicus neque delustrator.* . . .

36 BAGD, *s.v.* Μαθηματικός in this passage does not refer to the scholarly mathematicians of the time but to astrologers. For this meaning, cf. BAGD, *s.v.;* and LSJ, *s.v.*, 2b. For special usage: Philo *Mut. nom.* 71; Marcus Aurelius *Meditations* 4.48.1 (Haines, 92), πόσοι δὲ μαθηματικοὶ ἄλλων θανάτους ὥς τι μέγα

προειπόντες ("how many astrologers [are dead] after making a great parade of predicting the deaths of others"); Sextus Empiricus *Adv. Math.* 4.34 (Mutschmann and Mau, 3.140); 5.2 (141), ἀλλὰ πρὸς γενεθλιαλογίαν, ἣν σεμνοτέροις κοσμοῦντες ὀνόμασιν οἱ Χαλδαῖοι μαθηματικοὺς καὶ ἀστρολόγους σφᾶς αὐτοὺς ἀναγορεύουσιν ("the casting of nativities, which the Chaldeans adorn with more high-sounding titles describing themselves as 'mathematicians' and 'astrologers'"); *mathematicus* in this sense is found, e.g., in Tertullian *Apol.* 43.1 (CChrSL 1.158); *Adv. Marc.* 1.18.1 (1.459); *Idol.* 9.2–3, 8 (2.1108).

37 Περικαθαίρειν is metaphorical here, namely, in the ritual sense. Perhaps the author of the tractate is dependent, at this point, on Deut 18:10 (suggested by W. L. Knox, "περικαθαίρων (*Didache* iii, 4)," *JTS* 40 [1939] 148): οὐχ εὑρεθήσεται ἐν σοὶ περικαθαίρων τὸν υἱὸν αὐτοῦ ἢ τὴν θυγατέρα αὐτοῦ ἐν πυρί ("No one shall be found among you who makes a son or daughter pass through fire"). In that case our text (as shown by the omission of τὸν υἱὸν αὐτοῦ) would have changed the sense into "a prohibition of a superstitious rite of purification" (ibid.). The Constitutor reinserted τὸν υἱόν σου, recalling Deut 18:10; but it seems to me unclear exactly what concrete action he wishes to forbid. Knox (ibid.) thinks of a prohibition of circumcision.

38 H has only αὐτὰ βλέπειν. A μηδὲ ἀκούειν has been omitted, as the Georgian shows; so do the parallel versions: αὐτὰ ἰδεῖν (*Epitome* εἰδέναι) μηδὲ ἀκούειν, *Canons, Epitome,* and *ea videre nec audire, Doctrina.* See Niederwimmer, "Textprobleme," 123.

39 This appears to have been omitted from *Doctrina*. One should add something like: *de his enim omnibus vana superstitio nascitur* ("From such things as these does empty superstition arise").

κλοπή can have similar meanings.[44] From this point of view the terms ψεύστης/ψεῦσμα and κλοπή approximate one another. In the second warning, ψεύστης is replaced by φιλάργυρος and κενόδοξος. The vice of φιλάργυρος[45] can lead to theft; but what the κενόδοξος[46] (the ambitious, the vainglorious, the boaster) has to do with κλοπαί is hard to guess. Ἐκ γὰρ τούτων ἁπάντων κλοπαὶ γεννῶνται ("from all of these theft is spawned") makes up the conclusion, in accordance with the style.

■ 6 The fifth and last of the *teknon* sayings warns against muttering or "grumbling" about the way in which we are led. Γόγγυσος[47] = the γογγυστής.[48] Γογγύζειν is the word in the LXX for לון.[49] In this passage, however, there is no allusion to the central Old Testament examples in Exodus 15–17 and Numbers 14–17. Instead, there is a general warning against grumbling, because it leads[50] to βλασφημίαι ("acts of blasphemy").[51] In the second warning, γόγγυσος is varied by αὐθάδης, "self-satisfied,"[52] here probably in the special sense of "arrogant," and πονηρόφρων, a hapax legomenon[53] whose meaning is nevertheless clear: to be intent on evil, to give voice to a wicked intent. The stylistically regular conclusion is found in the expression: Ἐκ γὰρ τούτων ἁπάντων βλασφημίαι γεννῶνται ("from all these blasphemies are spawned").

---

40 This passage is cited (either directly from a version of the tractate, or from the *Dìdache*) by Clement of Alexandria *Strom.* 1.20, 100.4 (GCS³ 2.64). See above, Introduction, §2b.

41 Wengst (*Didache*, 70) gives ἐπὶ τὴν κλοπήν (with *Canons*).

42 Rom 3:7; *Hermas Man.* 3.5; 8.3 (here in a vice list). For κλοπαί, see Matt 15:19/Mark 7:21; later *Did.* 5.1 (all in vice lists). Κλοπαί also appears at the end of 3.5.

43 There is a similar connection in Sir 5:14, although there the idea seems to be that the calumniator steals someone's good name. *Hermas Man.* 3.2 (where the liar in some sense robs the *Kyrios*) contributes nothing to the understanding of our passage.

44 LSJ, *s.v.*, II.

45 See 4 Macc 2:8; Philo *Poster. C.* 116; *Gig.* 37; *T. Levi* 17.11 (vice list); Luke 16:14; 2 Tim 3:2 (vice list).

46 *Ep. Arist.* 8 (SC 89.104); Philo *Som.* 2.105; Gal 5:26.

47 Γόγγυσος is also found in the parallels in *Canons, Epitome,* and *Constitutions:* cf. Prov 16:28 Theodotion; Herodianus Technicus, ed. Lentz, 1.213.19; Arcadius Περὶ τόνων (ed. Barkerus) 78 (γόγγυσσος).

48 Γόγγυσος = γογγυστής, Jude 16.

49 Karl H. Rengstorf, "γογγύζω," *TDNT* 1 (1964) 730.

50 Wengst, *Didache*, 70: ἄγει πρός (with *Canons*). This is very improbable.

51 Hermann Wolfgang Beyer, "βλασφημέω," *TDNT* 1 (1964) 621–25; Otfried Hofius, "βλασφημία," *EDNT* 1 (1990) 219–21; βλασφημία in the Apostolic Fathers: *1 Clem.* 47.7; *2 Clem.* 13.3; Ignatius *Eph.* 10.2; *Hermas Man.* 8.3; *Sim.* 6.2.3; βλασφημεῖν: *1 Clem.* 1.1; *2 Clem.* 13.1, 2 (ter), 4; Ignatius *Trall.* 8.2 (bis); *Smyrn.* 5.2; *Hermas Vis.* 2.2.2; *Sim.* 6.2.4; 8.6.2, 4; 8.8.2; 19.3; βλάσφημος: *Sim.* 9.18.3; 9.19.1, 3.

52 BAGD, *s.v.* Cf. Gen 49:3, 7; Prov 21:24 (with θρασύς); Josephus *Ant.* 1.189; 4.263; Titus 1:7; *1 Clem.* 1.1, πρόσωπα προπετῆ καὶ αὐθάδη ("rash and self-willed persons"); *Hermas Sim.* 5.4.2; 5.1; 9.22.1, πιστοὶ μέν, δυσμαθεῖς δὲ καὶ αὐθάδεις καὶ ἑαυτοῖς ἀρέσκοντες, θέλοντες πάντα γινώσκειν ("believers, but slow to learn and presumptuous and pleasing themselves wishing to know everything"); 2 Pet 2:10b combines αὐθάδεις with βλασφημεῖν, but the meaning is somewhat different from that in our text (namely, an attitude of the gnosticizing false teachers): τολμηταὶ αὐθάδεις, δόξας οὐ τρέμουσιν βλασφημοῦντες ("bold and willful, they are not afraid to slander"). Cf. also αὐθάδεια in the vice list of the way of death in *Did.* 5.1.

53 The word occurs otherwise only in *Canons, Epitome,* and *Apostolic Constitutions.* This, once again, represents a word characteristic of the Two Ways tractate. *Doctrina* has *male sapiens.*

e. The *"Anawim"* Sayings (3.7–10)

7	On the contrary, be mild tempered, since those who are mild tempered will inherit the land.
8	Be patient and merciful, without guile, tranquil and good, holding constantly in awe the words you have heard.
9	You shall not exalt yourself or let yourself be arrogant. You shall not attach yourself to those who are highly placed but shall associate with those who are just and humble.
10	Accept as good the experiences that come your way knowing that nothing happens without God.

Analysis

The *teknon* sayings end with 3.6. The section that follows in 3.7–10 is no longer structured like the aphorisms in 3.1–6; instead, it presents an independent profile[1] whose content is marked by the motif of quiet, gentle humility as a way of life. These next lines (3.7–10) express an attitude that recalls the Old Testament and Jewish piety of the *anawim*.[2] Therefore the following section may be entitled "the *anawim* sayings."[3] While the *teknon* sayings contained no parallel to *Barnabas*, *Did.* 3.7 recalls *Barn.* 19.4, at least in rudimentary fashion: ἔση πραΰς. The full parallelism then begins at *Did.* 3.8c.

Comment

■ **7** The section begins with the characteristic ἴσθι δὲ πραΰς κτλ. The use of πραΰς represents the adoption of a key word from the Old Testament and Jewish tradition (*anawim* piety).[4] The πραεῖς are the oppressed who hope in the Lord in quiet patience, without grumbling.[5] Socioeconomic oppression becomes a challenge to a type of devotion that lends meaning to it: suffering is accepted with resignation, and help is awaited all the more from God.[6] This attitude toward life is apparently regarded also as the ideal of the group behind the tractate, and it is characteristic that the Didachist can make the text of the source his own without any comment. Also part of the *anawim* piety is the quotation, οἱ πραεῖς κληρονομήσουσι τὴν γῆν (= Ps 36:11a, οἱ δὲ πραεῖς κληρονομήσουσιν γῆν), which is from the Old Testament, not from Matt 5:5.[7] The quotation from the psalm promises compensation: those who are now oppressed and without possessions, who in their silent humility hope in the Lord, will eventually (an eschatological hope, but not for the near future) be the possessors of the (holy) land.[8]

■ **8** Beginning with an imperative,[9] this verse mentions (in a purely associative sequence) a series of goals of *anawim* piety: long-suffering, mercy, guile-

1 Audet clearly recognized the tradition-historical break between 3.6 and 3.7 (*Didachè*, 308; cf. his subsequent suggestions). He ignored the further break between 3.10 and 4.1, however, and consequently subsumed 3.7–4.14 within the same tradition-historical context.

2 Audet speaks (*Didachè*, 311, and passim) of "instruction for the poor," but also considers 4.1–11 part of it. For the background of this passage in *anawim* piety, see Audet, *Didachè*, 316, and frequently elsewhere. The key word πραΰς in the LXX frequently represents ענו: Friedrich Hauck and Siegfried Schulz, "πραΰς," *TDNT* 6 (1968) 647–48.

3 The connection with what precedes it is associative, but *e contrario* (cf. Knopf, *Lehre*, 16): the last *teknon* saying (v. 6) forbade grumbling. The opposite attitude is πραΰτης, which leads its life in quiet humility before God (Hauck and Schulz, "πραΰς," 647).

4 The use of πραεῖς in *Did.* 15.1 (didachistic) is characteristically different.

5 Cf. Hauck and Schulz, "πραΰς," 647. *Barn.* 19.4d: ἔση πραΰς, ἔση ἡσύχιος ("you shall be meek, you shall be peaceful").

6 "Above all when one has begun to make this humble condition a humility of the heart" (Audet, *Didachè*, 316).

7 Muilenburg (*Literary Relations*, 97) suggests the contrary.

8 *Doctrina: possidebunt sanctam terram* ("they will possess the holy land"). This may be original. *Canons* reads τὴν βασιλείαν τῶν οὐρανῶν (*Epitome*: τοῦ θεοῦ) ("the kingdom of heaven [of God]"). This is certainly secondary.

9 Γίνου = ἴσθι (as in 3.7): BDF, §98; BDR, §98 (3). Cf. ἔση in *Barn.* 19.4. For the shift between adjective (μακρόθυμος κτλ.) and participle (τρέμων) after γί-

lessness, quiet, goodness.[10] Nothing is surprising here except the subsequent warning: καὶ τρέμων τοὺς λόγους διὰ παντὸς[11] οὓς ἤκουσας.[12] This resolution reminds us that the text of the tractate is here influenced by Isa 66:2b: καὶ ἐπὶ τίνα ἐπιβλέψω ἀλλ᾽ ἢ ἐπὶ τὸν ταπεινὸν καὶ ἡσύχιον καὶ τρέμοντα τοὺς λόγους μου ("To whom will I look but to the humble and contrite in spirit, who trembles at my words").[13] The reference here is to the λόγοι τοῦ θεοῦ, which the pious hear with fear and trembling.[14]

■ **9** In this verse[15] are grouped some admonitions marked by the ideal of ταπεινοφροσύνη ("humility").[16] Cf. Rom 12:16 (although the text is not at all dependent on the Letter to the Romans). Οὐχ ὑψώσεις[17] σεαυτόν warns against arrogance and conceit.[18] The next expression is striking: οὐδὲ δώσεις τῇ ψυχῇ σου θράσος[19]—something like "do not give your soul (mind, feelings) [the opportunity for] impudence, superciliousness, boldness; do not be self-important!"[20] Verse 9b, with οὐ κολληθήσεται κτλ., warns the pious against toadying to the powerful and influential. A pious person does not belong in such company. Instead, such a one should seek the society of the *anawim* (it is probably they who are considered the δίκαιοι and ταπεινοί). Piety is also evident in one's choice of companions.

■ **10** The next verse[21] takes up a special problem: the humble and pious person not only accepts everything that befalls him or her[22] without grumbling (*Dominus dedit, Dominus abstulit . . . sit nomen Domini benedictum:* "The Lord gave, and the Lord has taken away . . . blessed be the name of the Lord"), but regards the adversity that comes his or her way as something good, even if (as we may reasonably expand the thought) he or she does not understand the meaning of this fate. In any case, it is true that

---

νου, cf. again *Barn.* 19.4 (ἔσῃ πραΰς, ἔσῃ ἡσύχιος, ἔσῃ τρέμων . . .): BDF, §353 (7); BDR, §353 (10). For γίνου with the participle, cf. BDF, §354; BDR, §354 (1).

10 *Doctrina* has a short text that is certainly defective: *Esto patiens et tui negotii, bonus et tremens omnia verba quae audis.* Wengst (*Didache*, 70) offers: γίνου μακρόθυμος καὶ ἐλεήμων, ἄκακος καὶ ἡσύχιος, ἀγαθὸς καὶ τρέμων τοὺς λόγους οὓς ἤκουσας.

11 H, after τοὺς λόγους, reads διὰ παντός. This phrase is absent from *Barnabas, Canons, Epitome,* and *Doctrina apostolorum* (which does have omnia verba). It is also absent from *Const.* 7.8.3 (although it was probably part of the original text in 2.1.5). Cf. Funk, *Didascalia,* 1.33. It is uncertain whether the source of 2.1.5 (the *Didascalia*) also read διαπαντός; see above, Introduction, §2c. In *Synt. doctr.* 4.1 and in *Fides patr.* 8 (*PG* 28.1641D) it reappears, although these texts can scarcely be directly dependent on the *Didache.* See above, Introduction, §6a.

12 *Barn.* 19.4: ἔσῃ τρέμων τοὺς λόγους, οὓς ἤκουσας ("you shall tremble at the words that you have heard").

13 The Isaiah quotation is also in *1 Clem.* 13.4.

14 Cf. *Acts of Paul and Thecla* 6 (Lipsius and Bonnet, 1.239). Knopf (*Lehre,* 16) incorrectly asserts that this concluding warning "again clearly [shows] that the writing is intended for neophytes."

15 Verse 9a/*Barn.* 19.3a; οὐδὲ δώσεις κτλ./*Barn.* 19.3 (end); οὐ κολληθήσεται κτλ./*Barn.* 19.6b; *Doctrina* has, after *non altabis te,* the additional clause *nec honorabis te apud homines.* This is probably a later gloss. See Giet, *L'Énigme,* 96, 139.

16 It is possible that these are two couplets in *parallelismus membrorum* (cf. Schaff, *Church Manual,* 96):
οὐχ ὑψώσεις σεαυτὸν
   οὐδὲ δώσεις τῇ ψυχῇ σου θράσος.
οὐ κολληθήσεται ἡ ψυχή σου μετὰ ὑψηλῶν,
   ἀλλὰ μετὰ δικαίων καὶ ταπεινῶν ἀναστραφήσῃ.

17 H reads ὑψώσει [*sic*], which must be emended to ὑψώσεις.

18 *T. Jos.* 17.8; Matt 23:12; Luke 14:11; 18:14; *Hermas Man.* 11.12; *Sim.* 9.22.3.

19 Θράσος (and θάρσος) are found in classical literature both *sensu bono* and *sensu malo:* cf. LSJ, *s.v.* In this passage it is *sensu malo.* Cf. *1 Clem.* 30.8 (with αὐθάδεια and τόλμα); cf. also θρασύτης in *Did.* 5.1.

20 BAGD, *s.v.,* compares this to Diodorus Siculus *Bibl. Hist.* 5.29.3, although Oldfather's edition (3.172) reads τὸ θάρσος [*sic*] τῆς ψυχῆς.

21 Verse 10/*Barn.* 19.6c.

22 Τὰ συμβαίνοντά σοι ἐνεργήματα: *Doctrina* correctly explains this as *Quae tibi contraria contingunt.* The use of the word ἐνέργημα in this sense is unusual. Cf. also in *Barnabas, Canons,* and *Epitome.* The Constitutor replaced it with πάθη ("sufferings") and περιστάσεις ("afflictions").

ἄτερ θεοῦ οὐδὲν γίνεται ("nothing happens without God").

In these admonitions the ideal of the group is sketched in a few strokes: it is not the condition of the wealthy and influential but that of the poor and exploited, if, and to the extent that, their condition is associated with an attitude of humble submission to God. Then is given to these, and especially to these, the great promise: the inheritance of the land. Submission and hope are founded on the unimpeachable certainty that fate is governed by God, and therefore it can only serve to benefit the pious.

Excursus: The Ideal "Accept Whatever Comes"

The last aphorism (v. 10) is so general that it finds numerous parallels[23] in the Stoic, biblical, Jewish, and Christian traditions. I restrict myself to a few examples, but in each case one should note the overall mentality that gives the idea its concrete meaning in context. From the Stoa, cf. Cleanthes *Hymn to Zeus,* οὐδέ τι γίγνεται ἔργον ἐπὶ χθονὶ σοῦ δίχα, δαῖμον ("no work on earth takes place without you, O deity," *SVF* 1.122.11); *Optimum est pati, quod emendare non possis, et deum, quo auctore cuncta proveniunt, sine murmuratione comitari* ("It is best to suffer what you cannot change, and commit yourself to god, who is the author of all things, without complaint," Seneca *Epistulae Morales* 107.9 [Gummere, 3.226, 228]). Jewish parallels include: πᾶν, ὃ ἐὰν ἐπαχθῇ σοι, δέξ-αι (Sir 2:4a);[24] "All that is, he governs according to his plan, and without him nothing occurs" (1QS 11.11); *b. Ber.* 60b (Str–B 3.256). For Christian parallels, see Matt 10:29 par. Q; Acts 27:34b; τοῖς ἀγαπῶσιν τὸν θεὸν πάντα συνεργεῖ εἰς ἀγαθόν, τοῖς κατὰ πρόθεσιν κλητοῖς οὖσιν ("all things work together for good for those who love God, who are called according to his purpose," Rom 8:28); *Ps.-Clem. Hom.* 2.36.2 (GCS[2] 1.50); *Rec.* 1.21.4 (GCS 2.19); *Propterea docet nos scriptura divina omnia quae accidunt nobis tamquam a deo illata suscipere, scientes quod sine deo nihil fit* ("the divine Scripture teaches us to accept all things that happen to us as if they were brought about by God," Origen *De princ.* 3.2.7 [GCS 5.255]);[25] Μηδὲν τῶν συμβαινόντων χωρὶς ἂν γενέσθαι θεοῦ πεπεῖσθαι χρή· εἶναι δὲ ἀγαθὰ παρ᾽ αὐτοῦ πάντα κἂν ἀλγεινὰ ᾖ ("it is necessary to believe that none of the things that happen takes place without God; and that all that comes from him is good, even if it be painful," Dionysius of Alexandria [?] in John of Damascus *Sacra parallela* 33 [*PG* 96.320A]);[26] πιστεύων ὅτι οὐδὲν ἄνευ τῆς προνοίας τοῦ θεοῦ γίνεται ("believing that nothing takes place apart from the providence of God," Dorotheus *Doctrina* 13.1 [*PG* 88.1761B]); Πάντα τὰ ἐπερχόμενά σοι ὡς ἀγαθὰ προσδέχου, ἵνα ὁ σκοπὸς τῆς Προνοίας εἰς εὐάρεστον αὐτῇ πληρωθῇ ἐπὶ σοί, τέκνον μου ("Accept everything that comes upon you as good, so that, my child, the aim of providence might be fulfilled in you in a way pleasing to her," *Ep.* 3 [1840C]).[27]

---

23   Cf. Windisch, *Barnabasbrief,* 399–400.

24   Windisch (*Barnabasbrief,* 400) wished to derive the expression in *Barnabas* from Sir 2:4.

25   It has occasionally been suggested that Origen is here quoting the *Didache.* See above, p. 8 n. 39.

26   This is not a quotation from the *Didache.* See above, p. 8 n. 41.

27   This is introduced by κατὰ τὸν λέγοντα ("according to the one who says"). For the question of a possible *Didache* quotation, see above, Introduction, §2b.

4

f. Rules for Life in Society (4.1–11)

1   My child, you shall be mindful day and night of the one who speaks to you the word of God. You shall honor him as the Lord, for at the source of proclamation of the lordship [of the Lord], the Lord is there.

2   You shall seek out the countenances of the holy persons every day to find support in their words.

3   You shall not cause division; instead, you shall reconcile those who quarrel. You shall judge justly. You shall not show partiality in calling people to task for their faults.

4   You shall not show doubt whether [something] will be or not.

5   Do not be the sort of person who holds out his hands to receive but draws them back when it comes to giving.

6   If you have [something] through the work of your hands, you shall give [it as] redemption of your sins.

7   You shall not hesitate to give, and when you give you shall not grumble, for you will know who the paymaster is who gives good wages.

8   You shall not turn away anyone who is in need; on the contrary, you shall hold everything in common with your brother, and you shall not say that anything belongs [only] to you, for if you [pl.] are partners in what is immortal, [should you not be so] all the more in things that perish?

9   You shall not withhold your hand from your son or your daughter, but shall teach them reverence for God from their youth.

10   You shall not give a command in bitterness to your slave or your maid, those who hope in the same God [as you], lest they stop revering the God who is over both [you and them]. For he comes not to call [people] according to their personal status but [he comes] upon those whom the Spirit has prepared.

11   As for you [pl.] who are slaves, with respect and reverence you shall be subject to your masters as replicas of God.

Analysis

Although only partially structured, *Did.* 4.1–11 constitutes a kind of unit. The arrangement agrees with that of *Doctrina*.[1] In contrast, the passages from *Didache/Doctrina* are also found, as a rule, in *Barnabas* 19, but in a completely different arrangement. The version of the Two Ways tractate that underlies the *Didache* and *Doctrina* has a fairly discernible structure[2] whereby the obligations of the addressees are formulated according to certain social relationships (as we would now say):

1   Behavior toward teachers (4.1–2)
2   Behavior within the community (?) (4.3–4)
3   Behavior toward the poor (4.5–8)
4   Behavior toward one's own children (4.9)

---

1   This is true also of the *Canons of the Apostles* (apart from a few additions), but the text breaks with the text corresponding to that of the *Didache* at 4.8 (in order then in chap. 14—as I believe—to quote from the epilogue of the source). *Epitome* has the material that appears in *Didache* 4, with minor variations. There is no parallel to *Did.* 4.5, 7, 10–11.

2   This would have been the more original, while *Barnabas* has destroyed the structure.

5 Behavior toward slaves, and their behavior toward their masters (4.10–11).

Only the last part (4.9–11) recalls the literary form of the so-called household codes[3] (the origins and function of which are disputed in recent research),[4] and only in 4.10–11 does the mutuality of admonition that is characteristic of the "household codes" appear (although even there it is not always consistent): in v. 10 it is the κύριοι, and in v. 11 the δοῦλοι who are addressed.[5] In contrast, the section 4.1–8 contains nothing that could recall the literary form of the "household code." The whole is structurally disparate.

Comment

■ **1–2** The opening verses[6] regulate the relationship to one's teachers. The original situation (before the Christianization of the tractate) may have been that of a Jewish synagogue or house of study. In that case, the λαλῶν σοι τὸν λόγον τοῦ θεοῦ ("the one who speaks the word of God")[7] may have been the scribe, the one learned in the Law, and the τέκνον[8] his pupil. The Christian redactors of the Jewish source can only have meant the Christian διδάσκαλος when they wrote λαλῶν σοι τὸν λόγον τοῦ θεοῦ. Finally, the Didachist was probably already thinking (if he gave any thought to it at all) of the Christian teachers of *his own* time, who, together with the prophets, form the charismatic orders in the communities.[9] He will speak of them in more detail in later parts of his writing (namely, in 13.1–7). At this point he does not go into this subject, but in this passage he appears to have adopted the text of his

---

3 Cf. *Ps.-Phocyl.* 175–227; Philo *Decal.* 165–67; Josephus *Ap.* 2.198–210; Col 3:18–4:1; Eph 5:22–6:9; 1 Pet 2:18–3:7; 1 Tim 2:8–15, 6:1–2; Titus 2:1–10; *1 Clem.* 1.3; 21.6–9; Polycarp *Phil.* 4.2–6.3; more remotely: Ignatius *Poly.* 5.1–2. The text in *Barn.* 19.5–7, which is frequently cited in this connection, does not belong here, in my opinion. Note that Leonhard Goppelt (*A Commentary on I Peter* [ed. F. Hahn; trans. John E. Alsup; Grand Rapids: Eerdmans, 1993] 162–63) wanted to differentiate among the household code in the narrower sense (Colossians, Ephesians, 1 Peter), the sets of admonitions for "members of stations and groups within the congregation" (among which he counts the corresponding texts from 1 Timothy, Titus, *1 Clement*, Ignatius, and Polycarp), and a third group, in which he listed *Did.* 4.9–11 (and *Barn.* 19.5–7). The last group "according to form and content . . . belong to the classification of proverbial wisdom" (Goppelt, *I Peter*, 163); "only *Did.* 4:11 takes over a 'household code tradition'" (p. 163). Cf. also p. 167, where this assignment to the proverbial literature is repeated, and *Ps.-Phocylides,* Tob 4:3–4, Josephus *Ap.* 2.198–208, and Philo *Decal.* 165–67 are seen as the closest parallels to *Did.* 4.9–11. For a critique of Goppelt's attempt at a new categorization, cf. Klaus Thraede, "Zum historischen Hintergrund der 'Haustafeln' des NT," *Pietas* (1980) 359 n. 1.

4 Cf. Karl Weidinger, *Die Haustafeln: Ein Stück urchristlicher Paränese* (UNT 14; Leipzig: Hinrichs, 1928); Martin Dibelius and Heinrich Greeven, *An die Kolosser. Epheser. An Philemon* (HNT 12; 3d ed.; Tübingen; Mohr [Siebeck], 1953) 48–50; James E. Crouch, *The Origin and Intention of the Colossian Haustafel* (FRLANT 109; Göttingen: Vandenhoeck & Ruprecht, 1972); Wolfgang Schrage, "Zur Ethik der neutestamentlichen Haustafeln," *NTS* 21 (1975)

1–22; Goppelt, *I Peter*, 162–63. Among those who have recently proposed an origin of the "household codes" in ancient economics are Dieter Lührmann, "Neutestamentliche Haustafeln und antike Ökonomie," *NTS* 27 (1981) 83–97; Klaus Thraede, "Zum historischen Hintergrund der 'Haustafeln' des NT," *Pietas* (1980) 359–68. Berger goes his own way in "Hellenistische Gattungen," 1078–86; and in his *Formgeschichte*, 135–41 (in which he presents some propositions that are, in part, contrary to those in the essay, as well as being highly complicated). Despite the efforts of the last few years, the whole question of the origins and development of this literary "genre" requires more clarification.

5 There is a remote similarity between *Did.* 4.9–11 and Col 3:21–4:1, Eph 6:4–9. This similarity can be explained, however, from their use of the same tradition; it does not require us to suppose any literary connection, either with *Did.* 4.9–11 depending on Colossians/Ephesians, or with both (*Didache* on the one hand, Colossians and Ephesians on the other) going back to a common literary source. Audet (*Didachè*, 340–43) sees the relationship as closer: "In one way or another, the instruction to the poor [referring to 3.7–4.14; see above], if not the *Duae viae* itself, was found at some point within Paul's environment, either in the written form that we possess or in the form it may have had in the local διδαχή" (p. 343).

6 Verses 1–2/*Barn.* 19.9b, 10a.

7 *Didache, Canons, Epitome, Constitutions*: (τὸν λόγον) τοῦ θεοῦ; *Barnabas*: κυρίου; *Doctrina*: domini dei.

8 *Canons*: τέκνον (Wengst, *Didache*, 72); H: τέκνον μου; omitted in *Doctrina, Epitome, Constitutions*.

9 Harnack, *Lehre*, 14; idem, "Prolegomena," 54–55:

source unchanged, without sensing any incompatibility with what follows in 13.1–7.

How is the relationship of the pupil to the teacher determined? It is shaped by the fundamental commandment of piety, which in turn is concretized in two ways: the pupil shall continually keep the teacher in mind,[10] and shall honor him[11] like the *Kyrios* himself.[12] The additional ὡς κύριον refers apparently to the Lord Jesus.[13] The command τιμήσεις δὲ αὐτόν (i.e., τὸν λαλοῦντά σοι τὸν λόγον τοῦ θεοῦ) ὡς κύριον ("You shall honor him as Lord") is given its foundation in v. 1c:[14] ὅθεν[15] γὰρ ἡ κυριότης λαλεῖται,[16] ἐκεῖ κύριός ἐστιν. This language of the phrase is unusual, but it is easily understood in context. Κυριότης ("lordship")[17] here probably refers to the characteristic of *Jesus* as κύριος.[18] Thus the

Didache text means that the place from which the proclamation about the κυριότης of Jesus goes forth is at the same time the place of his presence. There, in the mouth of the teacher and in his teaching, the *Kyrios* himself is present. Thus the teacher himself should be honored as if the *Kyrios* himself were standing before you. In the word of the teacher, the *Kyrios* is present.[19]

the reference is first of all to the apostles, prophets, and teachers, secondarily to bishops and deacons. So also Drews, "Apostellehre," 262; more cautiously Knopf, *Lehre*, 16 (who does not think that the apostles are included). But in 1.1ff. the Didachist simply quoted the source without expressly adapting it to his own "canonical" circumstances. In the source it was probably Jewish sages who were originally intended. See Audet, *Didachè*, 327.

10 He is to think of the teacher night and day (Jewish sequence), i.e., at all times (hyperbole). The formulation μιμνήσκεσθαί τινος resembles that in Heb 13:7; cf. also 12:25. But we should not suppose (as Connolly, "Relation," 246, insinuates) that the *Didache* quotes Heb 13:7.

11 For τιμᾶν αὐτόν cf. *1 Clem.* 21.6 (presbyter) and Ignatius *Smyrn.* 9.1 (bishop).

12 The didachistic passage is (despite the contrary opinion of Drews, "Apostellehre," 262; Wengst, *Barnabasbrief*, 65, including n. 131; and Giet, *L'Énigme*, 77–78) a later form (in my opinion) of the advice of the tractate on this subject. The original version can still be found in *Barn.* 19.9b: ἀγαπήσεις ὡς κόρην τοῦ ὀφθαλμοῦ [cf. Deut 32:10; Ps 16:8; Prov 7:2] σου πάντα τὸν λαλοῦντά σοι τὸν λόγον κυρίου ("you shall love as the apple of your eye everyone who speaks to you the word of the Lord"), with the continuation in v. 10α: μνησθήσῃ ἡμέραν κρίσεως νυκτὸς καὶ ἡμέρας ("you shall remember the day of judgment night and day"). *Can.* 12.1 has a mixed form: τέκνον, τὸν λαλοῦντά σοι τὸν λόγον τοῦ θεοῦ καὶ . . . ἀγαπήσεις ὡς κόρην ὀφθαλμοῦ σου μνησθήσῃ δὲ αὐτοῦ νύκτα καὶ ἡμέραν, τιμήσεις αὐτὸν ὡς τὸν κύριον ("My child, you shall love as the apple of your eye the one who speaks to you the word of God and you shall remember him night and day; you shall honor him as the Lord"). Cf.

Epit. 9. In the version behind *Doctrina* and *Didache*, ἀγαπήσεις ὡς κόρην τοῦ ὀφθαλμοῦ σου has been omitted. The change in the object of μιμνήσκεσθαι (in *Barnabas* it is the ἡμέρα κρίσεως, and in the other versions it is the teacher) is still older than the filiation that led to *Doctrina* and *Didache* (and thus goes back to C and not to C[1]). It is too much to say (as does Peterson, "Probleme," 153) that something nonsensical has entered the text thereby. This passage is very instructive as regards the genealogy of the Two Ways tractate. See above.

13 Both C and C[1] are Christian revisions. See above.

14 Verse 1c has no parallel in *Barnabas*. The passage comes from a later version of the tractate.

15 This ὅθεν is not to be understood as οὗ. Literally: "Whence, that is, lordship is proclaimed" or "For whence the proclamation of the lordship comes."

16 *Doctrina*: Unde enim dominica procedunt.

17 Cf. *Hermas Sim.* 5.6.1.

18 If we suppose that the tractate version on which the *Didache* rests was still Jewish (and not yet subjected to Christian redaction) in this passage, too, the original meaning must have been: *Kyrios* = YHWH; the *Kyriotes* = the Shekinah. According to Taylor (*Teaching*, 36–37) the meaning is "the Name of the Lord" (37). But does 4.1c really go back to a *Jewish* version of the tractate? In my opinion, 4.1b and 4.1c are part of the (superficial) Christianization of the original Jewish tractate (for v. 1c, this is also suspected by Knopf, *Lehre*, 17).

19 On this subject, cf. *m. ʼAbot* 4.12: וּמוֹרָא רַבְּךָ כְּמוֹרָא שָׁמָיִם (Marti and Beer, 102: "Let the fear of your teacher be as the fear of heaven"); Luke 10:1b, afterward *Did.* 11.2, 4 (q.v.).

■ 2 The next verse[20] also refers to the teacher: ἐκζητήσεις δὲ καθ᾿ ἡμέραν[21] τὰ πρόσωπα τῶν ἁγίων, ἵνα ἐπαναπαῇς[22] τοῖς λόγοις αὐτῶν calls for daily contact with teachers[23] in order to be enriched by their words, that is, to find in their words peace of heart.[24] The expression οἱ ἅγιοι ("the holy persons") can only refer (as the final reference to their λόγοι shows) to the teachers: this is a striking appellation of honor for the λαλοῦντες τὸν λόγον τοῦ θεοῦ.[25]

■ 3–4 The next verses speak of right behavior within the religious community or group—originally, perhaps, of right behavior in the Jewish house of study but now (we would like to say) ἐν ἐκκλησίᾳ. Verse 3a[26] still recalls the Jewish house of learning (as the original situation): the pupil is sternly instructed not to cause divisions[27] but rather to reconcile those who are at odds.[28] Verse 3b may possibly be understood in the same sense:[29] the future wise person, when called on to judge, shall not make bad use of the office,[30] and when required to set

someone straight shall proceed impartially.[31] In any event, the Didachist drew this admonition from the situation within the Christian communities: every Christian is required to be impartial when he or she feels it necessary to call a brother or sister to account.[32] (In *Did.* 15.3 the Didachist will address this question again in his own words.)

Verse 4 is a famous *crux interpretum*: οὐ διψυχήσεις, πότερον ἔσται ἢ οὔ.[33] The text forbids indecision or doubt about "whether it will be or not." What that means concretely[34] can no longer be determined with precision.[35] The compiler of *Canons* offers an interpretation (13.2): Ἐν προσευχῇ σου μὴ διψυχήσεις ("do not be double-minded in your prayer");[36] so also *Const.* 7.11: Μὴ γίνου δίψυχος ἐν προσευχῇ σου, εἰ ἔσται ἢ οὔ ("Do not be double-minded in your prayer, doubting whether it will happen or not"), for which the example of Peter sinking in Matt 14:28–31 is adduced as a warning.[37] The Georgian version interprets differently: "in this also you

---

20   Verse 2/*Barn.* 19.10b.

21   Καθ᾿ ἡμέραν is omitted from *Doctrina*, and is also absent from *Epitome*.

22   For this form of the aorist, cf. BDF, §76.1; BDR, §76.1 and (1).

23   Ἐκζητεῖν τὰ πρόσωπα means to make personal contact with them, to appear before them (BAGD, *s.v.* ἐκζητεῖν).

24   Τοῖς λόγοις αὐτῶν ἐπαναπαύεσθαι means to find rest in their words. The teacher appears as the sage whose words lead the pupil to clarity and inner peace. The motif is drawn from the sapiential tradition; cf. Sir 6:28; Matt 11:28; it is gnosticized in *Gospel to the Hebrews* (in Clement of Alexandria *Strom.* 5.14, 96.3 [GCS³ 2.389]; and 2.9, 45.5 [GCS³ 2.137]), and still more strongly in *Gos. Thom.* Greek 2 (*P. Oxy.* 654.1; Fitzmyer, 516–17) and Coptic 2 (Leipoldt, 27); cf. also *Corp. Herm.* 9.10 (Nock, 1.100).

25   The idea that ἅγιοι refers to the Christians as a whole (so Harnack, *Lehre*, 14; idem, "Prolegomena," 54; Drews, "Apostellehre," 263) corresponds to the normal usage. It is charming to note how *Can.* 12.2 escapes from this dilemma: ἐκζητήσεις δὲ τὸ πρόσωπον αὐτοῦ καθ᾿ ἡμέραν καὶ τοὺς λοιποὺς ἁγίους ("you shall seek his face by day as well as the rest of the saints"). *Epit.* 9 is similar.

26   Verse 3a/*Barn.* 19.12a. The text of *Did.* 4.3a may reveal a *parallelismus membrorum* (Schaff, *Church Manual*, 96):
οὐ ποιήσεις σχίσμα,
    εἰρηνεύσεις δὲ μαχομένους.

27   H has mistakenly written ποθήσεις. The correct version is ποιήσεις, as the parallels show. For Optatus of Mileve *Contra Parmenianum* 1.21 (CSEL 26.23), see above, Introduction, §2b.

28   Εἰρηνεύειν, factitive: BDF, 309 (1); BDR, §309 (2).

29   Verse 3b/*Barn.* 19.11e, 4c. In this vein, cf. Lev 19:5; *Ps.-Phocyl.* 9 (cf. *Sib. Or.* 2.61Ψ); Polycarp *Phil.* 6.1.

30   Κρίνειν δικαίως: Deut 1:16; Prov 31:9.

31   Οὐ λήψῃ πρόσωπον ἐλέγξαι ἐπὶ παραπτώμασιν (the parallels read παραπτώματι, as does Wengst, *Didache*, 72, for the *Didache*): the infinitive follows without ὥστε. See BDF, §391.4; BDR, §391 (8). After *iudica iuste*, *Doctrina* reads: *sciens quod tu iudicaberis. Non deprimes quemquam in casu suo* ("Knowing that you will be judged. You shall not oppress anyone in his suit").

32   We read something similar as an admonition to presbyters in Polycarp *Phil.* 6.1.

33   *Doctrina: nec dubitabis verum erit an non erit* ("you shall not doubt whether it will be true or not"). *Barn.* 19.5a: οὐ μὴ διψυχήσῃς, πότερον ἔσται ἢ οὔ. *Can.* 13.2: Ἐν προσευχῇ σου μὴ διψυχήσεις, πότερον ἔσται ἢ οὔ. *Epit.* 10: ἐν προσευχῇ σου μὴ διψυχήσῃς. For *Constitutions*, see above.

34   The warning against διψυχία is common Jewish-Christian tradition: (Sir 1:28; *T. Ash.* 3.1–2); 1QH 4.14; Jas 1:8; 4:8; etc. But what is *concretely* intended in *Did.* 4.4?

35   Equally uncertain is the parallel in *Hermas Vis.* 3.4.3: διὰ τοὺς διψύχους, τοὺς διαλογιζομένους ἐν ταῖς καρδίαις αὐτῶν εἰ ἄρα ἔστιν ταῦτα ἢ οὐκ

shall not doubt: whether the judgment of God will come upon all human beings according to their works."[38] In light of the enigmatic expression in the *Didache,* one could think more precisely of the problem of the delay of the parousia. In that case the statement would be a warning not to give up hope in the coming of the *Kyrios.*[39] But apart from the fact that such a warning would appear completely without preparation in the context of the *Didache,* it would have no meaning in the *pre-*Christian source we are positing. In context, only one interpretation seems probable:[40] this sentence could refer to the scruples of a judge who does not dare to decide or regrets the decision that has been reached.[41] Perhaps we can straighten the matter out as follows: in the sapiential tradition there existed a general warning against the temptation to doubt and to scrupulosity. This general warning could be made concrete in different ways. Here in *Did.* 4.4 (and in the original tractate), the warning is applied to the situation of a timid judge. (How the Didachist may have understood the text, if he thought about it at all, remains an open question.)

■ **5–8** We continue within the accustomed milieu. In these verses the subject is the behavior of members of the group within the limits of their own group, and in particular the typically Jewish demand for the greatest possible degree of charity (and thus concerning attitudes toward the poor).[42] Verse 5:[43] μὴ γίνου πρὸς μὲν τὸ λαβεῖν ἐκτείνων τὰς χεῖρας,[44] πρὸς δὲ τὸ δοῦναι συσπῶν is, in form and content, a typical sapiential maxim; in particular it recalls Sir 4:31: μὴ ἔστω ἡ χείρ σου ἐκτεταμένη εἰς τὸ λαβεῖν καὶ ἐν τῷ ἀποδιδόναι συνεσταλμένη ("Do not let your hand be stretched out to receive and closed when it is time to give").[45] The image in the final clause of the *Didache* formulation is not entirely clear: (τὰς χεῖρας) συσπῶν probably means "to withdraw (the hands)."[46] The sense of the maxim—in both clauses—is clear in any case: Do not be free in taking and stingy in giving!

■ **6** The next verse[47] also breathes Jewish devotional almsgiving and the practice of donation to the poor: those who have acquired something in the right way (through the work of their hands) should give to the poor because this serves to atone for their sins. The correct text, in my opinion, reads:[48] ἐὰν ἔχῃς διὰ τῶν

ἔστιν ("because of the double-minded, who dispute in their heart whether these things are so or not").

36   *Epit.* 10 is also referred to prayer, but there the obscure πότερον ἔσται ἢ οὔ is omitted.

37   Cf. Jas 1:6 and the section on διψυχία in *Hermas Man.* 9.1: μηδὲν ὅλως διψυχήσῃς αἰτήσασθαί τι παρὰ τοῦ θεοῦ ("Be not at all double-minded about asking anything from God"). Further: μὴ γίνου δίψυχος ἐν προσευχῇ σου· μακάριος γὰρ ὁ μὴ διαστάσας ("Be not double-minded in your prayer; for blessed is the one who does not doubt"), Ps.-Ignatius *Ad Heronem* 7.1 (Funk and Diekamp, *Patres apostolici,* 2.230); "It is just as impossible that someone who is of divided heart should enter the holy place. Anyone who is doubtful in prayer becomes dark, and the angels are not in accord with him [or her]. Therefore at all times have undivided hearts in the Lord," *Apoc. Elijah* 24.5–12 (cf. Wolfgang Schrage, *Die Elia Apokalypse* [JSHRZ 5.3; Gütersloh: Mohn, 1980] 238). Schaff (*Church Manual,* 175) also thought in connection with this passage of the commandment that forbids hesitancy in prayer.

38   Harnack (*Lehre,* 15; "Prolegomena," 54 n. 9) refers the statement to the final judgment by God.

39   The quotation from an unknown source in *1 Clem.* 23.3–4 and *2 Clem.* 11.2–7 warns against διψυχία, which no longer expects the coming of the *Kyrios.*

40   There is a similar suggestion by Kleist, *Didache,* 156

n. 31. Audet (*Didachè,* 330) translates: "You shall not cease to ask about what will happen to you or not," and interprets: "This is the situation of the judge who, in the presence of the parties, begins to weigh the consequences that his judgment will have for himself."

41   "But can πότερον ἔσται ἢ οὔ be interpreted in this way?" (Knopf, *Lehre,* 17).

42   The topic of charity was already discussed in *Did.* 1.5–6; the doublet occurs because of the composition: 1.5–6 is a passage by the Didachist (although the question whether the Didachist used given materials, and if so which ones, can remain open), while 4.5–8 is part of the tractate.

43   Verse 5/*Barn.* 19.9a.

44   Wengst, *Didache,* 72 (with *Doctrina* and *Constitutions*): τὴν χεῖρα.

45   The saying of the Lord in Acts 20:35 (cf. *1 Clem.* 2.1) makes a different point.

46   BAGD, *s.v.*; Knopf, *Lehre,* 17: closing the hands to giving. Windisch, *Barnabasbrief,* 401: holding one's hands together when giving. Cf. συνεσπακὼς τοὺς δακτύλους in Lucian *Timon* 13 (*Opera,* ed. Macleod, 1.315).

47   Verse 6/*Barn.* 19.10 (end).

48   Thus also Bihlmeyer, *Apostolischen Väter,* 3; and Wengst, *Didache,* 72.

χειρῶν σου, δώσεις λύτρωσιν ἁμαρτιῶν σου.[49] Alms cover sins and rescue from death.[50]

■ **7–8b** Verse 7 emphasizes generous giving of alms.[51] The one who gives should neither hesitate beforehand[52] nor grumble afterward.[53] Instead, those who give should recall that their alms will be returned; in particular, they should think *who* it is who will repay[54] their alms, namely, God![55] Still, this little tractate on almsgiving has another surprise in store: in v. 8[56] the obligation to give alms is expanded to the maximum possible—even to the readiness to surrender the right to own property. From one who is in need[57] one dare not turn away.[58] Instead, the pious should share everything with their "brothers and sisters"[59]—meaning fellow members of the religious community for whom this version of the tractate was written.[60] The ultimate consequence of this is that no individual continues to call anything his or her own private property: καὶ οὐκ ἐρεῖς ἴδια εἶναι. At this point the commandment of compassion and care for the neighbor has attained its sharpest and most consistent development.

Excursus: Common Possessions

The formulation recalls the Greek proverb "friends have everything in common."[61] There can scarcely be any connection with the tradition of the (supposed) community of goods among the Pythagoreans.[62] In fact it is questionable whether we should understand *Did.* 4.8 in the sense of a demand for a "community of goods," or whether it would not be better to think of this as "a disposition of property in principle for

49 Δώσεις λύτρωσιν is correct: cf. H, *Canons*: δός, ἵνα ἐργάσῃ εἰς λύτρωσιν ("Give so that you might work for redemption") is a clarification in *Constitutions* (*Barnabas*: ἐργάσῃ εἰς λύτρωσιν). Also purely a clarification is δὸς εἰς ἄφεσιν in *Epitome*. Lietzmann (*Didache*, 7) conjectures: δώσεις ⟨εἰς⟩ λύτρωσιν (homoioteleuton). Drews ("Apostellehre," 264) ventured the conjecture δὸς εἰς λύτρωσιν, and was followed by Klauser, *Doctrina*, 18; and Audet, *Didachè*, 230. It appears that δώσεις was lacking in the source of *Doctrina*. The resulting text reads: *Si habes per manus tuas redemptionem peccatorum non dubitaris dare* ("If you have through your hands the redemption of sins, do not hesitate to give"). Thus the Latin combines vv. 6 and 7. This is certainly secondary. The reading given above is indeed hard, but comprehensible. In my opinion, conjectures are not necessary. Drews ("Apostellehre," 264) produces the artificial ἐὰν ἔχῃς ("if you can"), with no comma after χειρῶν σου; the phrase διὰ τῶν χειρῶν σου is made dependent on δώσεις. The *Life of Shenoute* reads: "As long as you can, give to the poor, so that your many sins may be taken away."

50 Tob 4:10; 12:9; Sir 3:30; Dan 4:27 LXX; rabbinic examples in Str–B 2.561–62 and 4.554–55; Christian examples include 1 Pet 4:8; *2 Clem.* 16.4; Polycarp *Phil.* 10.2.

51 Verse 7/*Barn.* 19.10 (end).

52 Διστάζειν, as in *Hermas Sim.* 5.4.3. On this subject, cf. Prov 3:28; *Ps.-Phocyl.* 22 (cf. *Sib. Or.* 2.78Ψ); *Hermas Sim.* 9.24.2.

53 Γογγύζειν is used somewhat differently here than γόγγυσος in *Did.* 3.6. In the same vein: *1 Clem.* 2.7.

54 Ἀνταποδότης is a rare word, absent from secular Greek usage, and found in the Greek OT only in Jer 28:56 Symmachus; cf. BAGD, *s.v.* The word appears here and in the parallels in *Barnabas, Canons,* and

Constitutions. It is typical of the language of the tractate. *Doctrina* has (*huius mercedis bonus*) *redditor*. Lampe notes at this point John Chrysostom *Hom.* 22.2 *In Hebr.* (*PG* 63.156), and Thalassius *Centuriae* 1.63 (*PG* 91.1433B).

55 ὁ (H reads ἡ) ἀνταποδότης. In this regard, cf. Sir 12:2; Tob 4:14; *T. Zeb.* 6.6; 8.1–3; Luke 14:14; *2 Clem.* 20.4.

56 Verse 8a has no parallel in *Barnabas*; v. 8b is paralleled by *Barn.* 19.8.

57 Τὸν ἐνδεόμενον in H; the article is absent in *Canons, Epitome* (ἐνδεούμενον), *Constitutions*, and Wengst, *Didache*, 72.

58 Cf. 5.2: ἀποστρεφόμενοι τὸν ἐνδεόμενον. Sir 4:5: ἀπὸ δεομένου μὴ ἀποστρέψῃς ὀφθαλμόν ("Do not avert your eye from the needy"). Cf. also Prov 3:27.

59 *Barnabas* has τῷ πλησίον σου.

60 Audet, *Didachè*, 332–33. Audet believed he could locate this *fraternité* in the Jewish *anawim* (p. 333).

61 According to Timaeus in Diogenes Laertius *Lives* 8.10 (Hicks, 2.328), Pythagoras was the first to shape this proverb: εἶπέ τε πρῶτος, ὥς φησι Τίμαιος, κοινὰ τὰ φίλων εἶναι ("According to Timaeus, he was the first to say 'friends have all things in common'"). Cf. also Plato *Rep.* 4.424A (Burnet); 5.449C; Aristotle *Nicomachean Ethics* 9.11.1159b.31 (Bekker); 10.8.1168b.7–8; Cicero *De officiis* 1.16.51 (Atzert, 18); Philo *Abr.* 235; *Ps.-Clem. Rec.* 10.5.6 (GCS 2.327); Iamblicus *Vita Pythagorica* 30.168 (Deubner, 94).

62 Porphyry *Vita Pythagorica* 20 (des Places, 45): οὗτοι δὲ καὶ τὰς οὐσίας κοινὰς ἔθεντο κτλ. ("They made their possessions common, etc.")

63 Gerhard Schneider, *Die Apostelgeschichte* (2 vols.; HThK 5.1–2; Freiburg: Herder, 1980) 1.291. Schneider continues: "it would happen from time to time that there would be a transfer of property for

the benefit of the community"—to adopt Gerhard Schneider's phrase describing the conditions in the primitive community at Jerusalem.[63] The starting point for whatever demand we may read in the *Didache* was, in any case, the Old Testament and Jewish tradition, which emphasized responsibility for the neighbor in need. This motive has been raised in the tractate to encompass limitless benevolence—even to the point of renouncing one's right to private property.[64] There is no need to suppose an influence from the Essene tradition[65] on this tractate. Nor, obviously, was there any thought in the original pre- or non-Christian tractate of the primitive Christian community as depicted in Acts 2:44–45; 4:32–37.[66] It is difficult to say how the Didachist understood the text of the tractate. The prescriptions he gives later, in chaps. 12–13, point in any case to an almost matter-of-fact joy in giving and readiness to sacrifice within the group (now with a Christian motive), an attitude by which the individual member achieved social security.[67] Hereafter the Didachist gives no further attention to the problem of private property in his own remarks.

■ **8c** Verse 8c presents reasons, after the fact, for what has just been commanded, in the form of a *qal-waḥomer* conclusion: εἰ γὰρ ἐν τῷ ἀθανάτῳ κοινωνοί ἐστε, πόσῳ μᾶλλον ἐν τοῖς θνητοῖς.[68] Τὸ ἀθάνατον is the immortal, eternal, heavenly good, while τὸ θνητόν is the good that is mortal, earthly, and passing.[69] One day they will share in the heavenly goods! In accordance with this great gift, the lesser can also be expected: that they now already have earthly goods in common.[70]

To this point (4.1–8), we have found ourselves, so to speak, in the realm of "community life." Now (vv. 9–11), the parenesis turns to the οἶκος. The following admonitions have to do with correct behavior in the household. What we read in these verses is a kind of "household code."

■ **9** Verse 9[71] begins with the duties of the paternal head of the household toward his own children. The warning first expressed, not to withdraw ("withhold one's hand")

---

the benefit of those in need."

64 One should note that here the renunciation of property is not demanded on eschatological grounds (as it was of the disciples in the Jesus tradition).

65 1QS 1.11–12; 5.2; 6.2–3, 19–20; 7.6–10; Josephus *Bell.* 2.122; *Ant.* 18.20; Philo *Omn. prob. lib.* 77. By contrast, CD is familiar with private property (at least for one part of the community): 14.12–17. For the whole subject, see Braun, *Qumran*, 1.42–43, 143–49.

66 For the problems in Acts, cf. Ernst Haenchen, *Die Apostelgeschichte* (7th ed.; KEK 3; Göttingen: Vandenhoeck & Ruprecht, 1977) 191–93, 226–28 (ET: *The Acts of the Apostles* [Oxford: Blackwell, 1971] 192, 230–35); Hans Conzelmann, *Die Apostelgeschichte* (2d ed.; HNT 7; Göttingen: Vandenhoeck & Ruprecht, 1972) 37, 44–45 (ET: *Acts of the Apostles* [Hermeneia; Philadelphia: Fortress Press, 1987] 23–24, 36); Schneider, *Apostelgeschichte*, 1.283–88, 362–68.

67 From these passages one gets the impression that anyone who belonged to the group, i.e., the church, acquired a certain measure of social security through the solidarity of the group. Cf. the remarks of Wengst, *Didache*, 35.

68 A similar conclusion, although in a different context, is found in Rom 15:27.

69 The contrasting of θνητός and ἀθάνατος was common, of course. Cf. BAGD, *s.v.* θνητός. In the most general sense: Dio Chrysostom 37.30 (Lamar Crosby, 4.28); Josephus *Ant.* 11.56; regarding the immortal soul in contrast to the mortal body: Plutarch *Moralia* 960B (Helmbold, 12.324); *Diogn.* 6.8; this is hermetically interpreted in *Corp. Herm.* 1.15 (Nock and Festugière, 1.11). In Philo *Rer. div. her.* 265, we read of the contrast between the human νοῦς and the divine πνεῦμα. Closest to our passage is the (apocalyptic) contrast in 1 Cor 15:53–54 (θνητόν – ἀθανασία).

70 *Barnabas* has as contrast τὸ ἄφθαρτον – τὰ φθαρτά, which may be original. While *Didache* (*Barnabas*) and *Canons* agree in contrasting "mortal/immortal" (*Life of Shenoute* has a contrast between "passing things" and "eternal [goods]"), *Epitome* reads εἰ γὰρ ἐν τῷ θανάτῳ κοινωνοί ἐστε, πόσῳ μᾶλλον ἐν τοῖς θνητοῖς ("If you are partners in death, how much more should you be sharers in things mortal"); *Doctrina* (apparently) supports this: *Si enim mortalibus socii sumus . . .* ("if we are sharers in things mortal . . ."). Giet ("Enseignement," 233) suggests that ἐν τῷ θανάτῳ may be original. But Schlecht's conjecture (*Doctrina*, 110), *si enim in immortalibus* ("if in things immortal"), has much in its favor, and the expression in *Epitome* may well be an arbitrary alteration.

71 Verse 9/*Barn.* 19.5c.

109

from one's own children,[72] includes more than what it expressly says, namely, the acceptance of responsibility for them and their παιδεία ("upbringing, education"). The principal duty of παιδεία is formulated in the subsequent demand: from their youth onward, children[73] are to be brought up in the fear of God.[74] The admonition to fear God (or the people who are God's representatives) is one of the fixed elements among the instructions in the so-called household code in our context.[75] What is required of the father in the *Didache* is regarded by Polycarp (*Phil.* 4.2) as the educational duty of the mother,[76] and is formulated generally in *1 Clem.* 21.6.[77] Motifs from common Hellenistic morality will have been as influential here[78] as the Old Testament/Jewish commandment of יראת אלהים or יראת י׳ or ״יראת י׳ ("fear of God" or "fear of the Lord") in the sense found in the wisdom tradition.[79]

■ **10** The next verse[80] turns to obligations toward slaves. The master is urged not to treat his male and female slaves harshly.[81] This prohibition is grounded by: μήποτε οὐ μή[82] φοβηθήσονται τὸν ἐπ᾽ ἀμφοτέροις θεόν.[83] The master should consider that his slaves believe and hope in the same God as he; also, the master must take into

account that his slaves (if he treats them badly) will become bitter and will lose their reverence for the God in whom he and they believe.[84] The author of the text is probably thinking of household slaves and presumes that master and slave belong to the same cult; that is, the original reference was probably to Jewish or (more likely) gentile slaves who had become "God-fearers" or proselytes and thenceforth shared the religion of their owners. At the Christian level, the thought is already of the Christian οἶκος: the slaves worship the *Kyrios* Jesus as their Lord. The owners' religion, which the slaves have also accepted, will become unworthy of belief if the master treats the slaves badly.

The next clause (v. 10c) is difficult to imagine within the presumed Jewish source; if we do not want to give it a completely forced interpretation, it must presuppose some Christian ideas: οὐ γὰρ ἔρχεται (sc. ὁ θεός) κατὰ πρόσωπον καλέσαι, ἀλλ᾽ ἐφ᾽ οὓς τὸ πνεῦμα ἡτοίμασεν. This sounds like a Christian addition, and since the passage is also transmitted in *Doctrina* and *Barnabas*,[85] we must suppose that the recensions of the tractate behind *Barnabas* on the one hand, and *Doctrina* and *Didache* on the other, had already undergone Christian redaction[86]

---

72 For the meaning of the metaphor τὴν χεῖρα ἀπό τινος αἴρειν, see BAGD, *s.v.* αἴρω, and such English expressions as "withdraw from someone," "leave someone in the lurch."

73 Wengst (*Didache*, 72) has (διδάξεις) αὐτούς (with *Doctrina, Epitome*, and *Constitutions*). This can scarcely be right.

74 Cf. Ps 33:12, δεῦτε, τέκνα, ἀκούσατέ μου· φόβον κυρίου διδάξω ὑμᾶς ("Come listen to me, children; I shall teach you fear of the Lord").

75 1 Pet 2:17 (τὸν θεὸν φοβεῖσθε); *1 Clem.* 21.6; Polycarp *Phil.* 4.2; also Eph 5:21; 6:5; Col 3:22.

76 Καὶ τὰ τέκνα παιδεύειν τὴν παιδείαν τοῦ φόβου τοῦ θεοῦ ("To educate children in the fear of the Lord").

77 Τοὺς νέους παιδεύσωμεν τὴν παιδείαν τοῦ φόβου τοῦ θεοῦ ("Let us teach the young the lesson of fear of the Lord").

78 Horst R. Balz, "φοβέω κτλ.," *TDNT* 9 (1974) 193–94.

79 On this, see Joachim Wanke, "φοβέω κτλ.," *TDNT* 9 (1974) 202–3. Cf. esp., as well, the *Testaments of the Twelve Patriarchs* (Balz, "φοβέω κτλ.," *TDNT* 9 [1974] 205–6).

80 Verse 10/*Barn.* 19.7c.

81 Ἐν πικρίᾳ ἐπιτάσσειν τινί means telling someone in an angry manner to do something. See BAGD,

s.v. πικρία. *Doctrina: in ira tua non imperabis* ("you shall not give a command in your anger").

82 For μήποτε οὐ μή, cf. BDF, §370 (4); BDR, §370 (6): "So that they may not lose their fear."

83 *Doctrina* has changed the meaning slightly: *timeat utrumque dominum et te* ("Let him fear both the Lord and you").

84 Here there is a certain kinship between the *Didache*, on the one hand, and the household codes in Colossians and Ephesians, on the other. Cf. Col 4:1: (οἱ κύριοι) εἰδότες ὅτι καὶ ὑμεῖς ἔχετε κύριον ἐν οὐρανῷ ("for you know that you have a Master in heaven"); Eph 6:9 (οἱ κύριοι) εἰδότες ὅτι καὶ αὐτῶν καὶ ὑμῶν ὁ κύριός ἐστιν ἐν οὐρανοῖς καὶ προσωπολημψία οὐκ ἔστιν παρ᾽ αὐτῷ ("for you know that both of you have the same Master in heaven, and with him there is no partiality"). Of course this is not sufficient for us to suppose that there is a *literary* relationship. For the parallel in Lactantius *Inst. Epit.* 59(64).3 (CSEL 19.744), see above, Introduction, §2b.

85 *Barnabas* even reads ὅτι οὐκ ἦλθεν, which insinuates Christian ideas still more strongly. In *Epitome* the passage that would correspond to *Did.* 4.10–11 is missing.

86 See above, Introduction, §6b.

87 In this respect it is striking that in *Barnabas* and

(if only superficially).[87] Ἔρχεται can, but does not necessarily, refer to the parousia of the *Kyrios* (cf. the aorist tense in *Barnabas*); or is the reference in the *Didache* also to the first coming of Jesus? He comes, or came, in fact, not κατὰ πρόσωπον καλέσαι; that is (in context), his saving call, through which people are invited into the church,[88] is not limited by the social boundaries of this world. He calls both free and slave into his service, and so to salvation.[89] He was sent to call ἐφ᾽ οὓς τὸ πνεῦμα ἡτοίμασεν. The syntax and meaning of this clause are uncertain. One may[90] resolve it either as: ἀλλ᾽ ἔρχεται ἐπὶ τούτους, οὓς τὸ πνεῦμα ἡτοίμασεν,[91] in which case it means that the *Kyrios* comes (without regard for social station) to those whom the *Pneuma* (subject) has prepared for his coming; or one may resolve it as ἀλλὰ (ἔρχεται) καλεῖν τούτους, ἐφ᾽ οὓς τὸ πνεῦμα ἡτοίμασεν,[92] in which case θεός is to be considered the subject and πνεῦμα the object, and the clause intends to say that God comes to call those for whom God has prepared the Spirit as the eschatological saving gift.[93] In both cases predestinarian motifs underlie the text. In the first, the elect are prepared for salvation by the Spirit (*spiritus est causa salutis*), and in the second instance the

Spirit is given as eschatological gift to the elect (*spiritus est donum salutis*).[94] In any case the emphatically solemn rhetoric is intended, in context, to make clear that, compared to the salvation mediated by the Spirit, or compared to the Spirit as saving gift, all social distinctions lose their meaning. From this point of view (and on the basis of the specifically Christian and eschatological motivation) still another admonition to the slave owner follows: not to treat one's slaves with bitterness.[95]

■ **11** Verse 11[96] is addressed, then,[97] to the slaves; it holds up to them their duties with respect to their owners. The content of the admonition is conventional (in the framework of the household code tradition): slaves should be subject[98] to their[99] owners, and this is given a religious motivation: in the earthly *kyrios* the slave encounters the type of the heavenly *Kyrios*, namely, God.[100] The hendiadys ἐν αἰσχύνῃ καὶ φόβῳ ("with respect and reverence") represents another conventional motif of the household code tradition.[101]

Didache there is no change of subject: it remains θεός, so that in what follows divinity is implicitly predicated of Jesus. In *Doctrina*, *dominus* is the subject.

88 Καλεῖν here refers to the eschatological call, as often in the NT and the Apostolic Fathers: *Barn.* 5.9; 14.7; 19.7; *1 Clem.* 32.4; 57.4; 59.2; 65.2; *2 Clem.* 1.2, 8; 2.4, 7; 5.1; 9.4, 5; 10.1; *Hermas Sim.* 8.1.1; 9.14.5.

89 Κατὰ πρόσωπον here does not refer to personal presence (Acts 25:16; 2 Cor 10:1; Gal 2:11; *Barn.* 15.1; Polycarp *Phil.* 3.2), but is used in the sense of "preferential"; cf. BAGD, *s.v.* (Οὐ) κατὰ πρόσωπον corresponds to "impartial," in context: without regard for social status.

90 Cf. Knopf, *Lehre*, 19.

91 It is thus interpreted, e.g., by Bauer (BAGD, *s.v.* ἑτοιμάζειν); Harnack, *Lehre*, 16; Jacquier, *Doctrine*, 116; Kleist, *Didache*, 18; Audet, *Didachè*, 338–39; Wengst, *Didache*, 75.

92 This is the interpretation of Rordorf and Tuilier, *Doctrine*, 163. *Doctrina*: *sed in quibus spiritum invenit* (f² has added *humilem* above the line, more specifically above the word *invenit*).

93 It could also be καλεῖν τούτους, οὓς προώρισεν ("to call those whom he predestined"); cf. Rom 8:29–30.

94 Rordorf and Tuilier (*Doctrine*, 163 n. 5) impute a Qumran influence, and refer to 1QS 4.26 and *T. Benj.* 8.2.

95 The doublet of the reasoning (μήποτε οὐ μὴ φοβηθήσονται . . . and οὐ γὰρ ἔρχεται . . .) also speaks for the supposition that in v. 10c we have an accretion, from the tradition-historical standpoint, namely, a later Christian interpolation; it is, however, predidachistic, as the parallels show.

96 Verse 11/*Barn.* 19.7b.

97 Paired and reciprocal parenesis is part of the style of the household codes.

98 Cf. Col 3:22–25; Eph 6:5–8; 1 Pet 2:18–25; 1 Tim 6:1–2; Titus 2:9–10; Ignatius *Poly.* 4.3.

99 H reads: τοῖς κυρίοις ἡμῶν [sic]. Bryennios (Διδαχή, 22) emended: ὑμῶν, which is generally accepted.

100 For this idea (although without the use of the term τύπος), cf. Col 3:22–23; Eph 6:5.

101 See on v. 9 above.

4

g. Epilogue of the "Way of Life" (4.12–14)

12   You shall hate all wickedness and all that is not pleasing to the Lord.

13   You shall not abandon the commandments of the Lord but shall keep what you have received, without adding or subtracting anything.

14   In the assembly you shall confess your faults, and you shall not approach with a bad conscience to make your prayer. This is the way to life.

Analysis

In principle the listing of the commandments of the "way of life" ends with v. 11. What follows in vv. 12–14 looks back over the completed list: v. 12 summarizes the ἐντολαί (commandments) in the most general way; v. 13 warns against neglecting or changing the commandments as handed down; v. 14 orders confession before the assembled community as a purification before prayer (in common). All these injunctions have the character of an epilogue. Finally, v. 14c brings the *subscriptio*, which concludes the *expositio viae vitae*.[1]

Comment

■ **12** The warning against any kind of hypocrisy[2] can, in the overall context of the concluding parenesis, only mean that one should guard against every kind of sin;[3] the commandments listed in what has preceded must be carried out. Thus the subsequent warning (rearranged in *Barnabas*)[4] is to be understood in the same sense: (μισήσεις) πᾶν ὃ μὴ ἀρεστὸν τῷ κυρίῳ ("hate all that is not pleasing to the Lord").[5] This summarizes and emphasizes the consistent keeping of the commandments.[6]

■ **13** The verse[7] continues: οὐ μὴ ἐγκαταλίπῃς ἐντολὰς κυρίου. The ἐντολαὶ κυρίου are the commandments and admonitions quoted in what has gone before.[8] Ἐντολὰς ἐγκαταλείπειν means to neglect the (given) commandments. Contrasted to this is φυλάσσειν δὲ ἃ παρέλαβες, to keep the commandments that have been received.[9] But it is also part of φυλάσσειν to preserve the commandments received from changes and falsifications, hence μήτε προστιθεὶς μήτε ἀφαιρῶν, a rule with an extensive history that appears in a wide variety of meanings.[10] In this passage Deut 4:2 is probably the model: οὐ προσθήσετε πρὸς τὸ ῥῆμα, ὃ ἐγὼ ἐντέλλομαι ὑμῖν, καὶ οὐκ ἀφελεῖτε ἀπ᾽ αὐτοῦ· φυλάσσεσθε τὰς ἐντολὰς κυρίου τοῦ θεοῦ ὑμῶν, ὅσα ἐγὼ ἐντέλλομαι ὑμῖν σήμερον ("You must neither add anything to what I command you nor take away anything from it, but keep the

---

1   *Epit.* 11 has the material corresponding to *Did.* 4.12–14 in a different arrangement.

2   The parallel in *Barn.* 19.2–3 is in a different context.

3   The word is used analogously to LXX ὑποκριτής = חָנֵף; cf. Audet, *Didachè*, 344; Rordorf and Tuilier, *Doctrine*, 164–65 n. 2; for the LXX usage, see U. Wilckens, "ὑποκρίνομαι," *TDNT* 8 (1972) 563–64; and this commentary at *Did.* 2.6. Wilckens postulates (p. 569) for *Did.* 4.12: "But the sense of 'dissembling, hypocrisy,' is also found," which is inconsistent. I am not able to recognize any relationship to Qumran (so Rordorf and Tuilier, *Doctrine*, 164–65 n. 2). But the reference (ibid.) to *2 Enoch* 61.1 is correct (in both recensions; Gottlieb N. Bonwetsch, *Die Bücher der Geheimnisse Henochs* [TU 44.2; Leipzig: Hinrichs, 1922] 51 and 100).

4   See n. 2 above.

5   Wengst, *Didache*, 74: τῷ θεῷ οὐ ποιήσεις (for θεῷ cf. *Barnabas* and *Doctrina*; for ποιήσεις, *Doctrina* and *Apostolic Constitutions*).

6   Cf. Deut 6:17–18: φυλάσσων φυλάξῃ τὰς ἐντολὰς κυρίου τοῦ θεοῦ σου . . . καὶ ποιήσεις τὸ ἀρεστὸν καὶ τὸ καλὸν ἐναντίον κυρίου τοῦ θεοῦ ὑμῶν ("Surely you shall keep the commandments of the Lord your God . . . and you shall do what is pleasing and good before the Lord your God"). Cf. Deut 12:25, 28; 13:19; more distantly Wis 9:10–11.

7   *Barn.* 9.2 (end) and 11b. Verse 13a has been omitted in *Doctrina*.

8   Knopf, *Lehre*, 19.

9   For this manner of expression cf., remotely, 1 Tim 1:12, 14 (παραθήκη).

10   The extensive history of the formula or rule and its many meanings were given by Willem C. van Unnik, "De la Règle Μήτε προσθεῖναι μήτε ἀφελεῖν dans

commandments of the Lord your God with which I am charging you today").[11] For similar formulations cf. Deut 13:1; Jer 26:2 (33:2 LXX); Prov 30:5–6 LXX; *1 Enoch* 104.10–13; *Ep. Arist.* 310–11 (SC 89.232, 234); Josephus *Ant.* 1.17; *Ap.* 1.42; *Rev* 22:18b, 19, and so on.[12] Of course it is precisely the pious person who takes the commandments seriously, as here demanded, who will know when they are imperfectly fulfilled.

In that case (v. 14)[13] such a person should confess his or her sins (ἐξομολογήσῃ τὰ παραπτώματά σου) publicly, before the assembled community (ἐν ἐκκλησίᾳ).[14]

That very probably means that the commandments that have been listed serve as an aid to examination of conscience for *confessio* and *conversio*. Only *after* completing a confession of sins (and the repentance it involves) can and may the sinner join in the common[15] prayer (v. 14b)[16] without being accused by an "evil" conscience (i.e., without συνείδησις πονηρά).[17]

The final statement, which has the character of a *subscriptio*, αὕτη ἐστὶν ἡ ὁδὸς τῆς ζωῆς (v. 14c),[18] marks the end of the *expositio viae vitae*.[19]

---

l'histoire du Canon," *VC* 3 (1949) 1–36.

11 "The usage in Barnabas and the Didache goes directly back to Deuteronomy" (van Unnik, "Règle," 35).

12 Cf. the rich material and its history in van Unnik, "Règle." The formula is found in *Epit.* 11, and returns twice in the *Canons of the Apostles*, at *Can.* 14.3 (φυλάξεις ἃ παρέλαβες, μήτε προσθεὶς μήτε ὑφαιρῶν ["Guard what you have received, neither adding to it nor taking from it"]) and in *Can.* 30 (φυλάξαι τὰς ἐντολὰς μηδὲν ἀφαιροῦντας ἢ προστιθέντας ἐν τῷ ὀνόματι τοῦ κυρίου ἡμῶν, ᾧ ἡ δόξα εἰς τοὺς αἰῶνας, ἀμήν ["to guard the commandments, neither taking away nor adding anything, in the name of our Lord, to whom be glory forever. Amen."]). I suspect that the formula was removed from its original context by the compiler of the source for *Canons* and *Epitome* (which was quite logical as far as the material was concerned) and that it was then placed at the end of the book (*Epit.* 11 and *Can.* 14.3). The compiler of the *Canons* then repeated the formula in a different form in chap. 30.

13 *Barn.* 19.12b.

14 Ἐν ἐκκλησίᾳ is lacking in *Barnabas* and *Epitome* (the whole first sentence is missing from *Doctrina*), and probably does not come from the source (so also Knopf, *Lehre*, 19) but is an addition by the Didachist (Harnack, *Lehre*, 17). *Constitutions* also lacks ἐν

ἐκκλησίᾳ. The Constitutor apparently no longer thinks of a public confession before the assembled community. Here, in *Did.* 4.14, ἐκκλησία is the individual community, differently from the traditional passages in 9.4 and 10.5. See Knopf, *Lehre*, 27. The suggestions of Peterson ("Probleme," 150) are fantastic.

15 I consider it highly improbable that προσευχή refers to *private* prayer (so Drews, "Apostellehre," 265). Cf. Knopf, *Lehre*, 19: "Προσευχή is probably prayer in common with the community, scarcely individual prayer in one's chamber, in spite of σου." See Rordorf and Tuilier, *Doctrine,* 69 n. 1 ("without any doubt").

16 The thought here is of individual confessions *coram ecclesia* (cf. Knopf, *Lehre*, 19). But Poschmann (*Paenitentia secunda,* 90) interpreted this differently. According to him "confession in this general sense is to be understood as a common prayer for forgiveness of sins, somewhat like the later Confiteor." In 14.1 it is the Didachist who speaks.

17 Cf. Heb 10:22; *Hermas Man.* 3.4.

18 *Barnabas:* ἡ ὁδὸς τοῦ φωτός.

19 With this "*subscriptio*" the text of *Epitome* concludes. See above, Introduction, §6a.

a. Introduction (5.1a)

1a   **And the way that leads to death is this.**
     Above all, it is evil and full of accursed-
     ness . . .

The introductory expression ἡ δὲ τοῦ θανάτου ὁδός
ἐστιν αὕτη (v. 1a) corresponds exactly to the clause
introducing the *via vitae* in 1.2a.[1] It functions as a title.
As the previous section began (in 1.2) with a fundamental commandment (πρῶτον ἀγαπήσεις τὸν θεόν),
the key word πρῶτον is repeated here: πρῶτον πάντων
πονηρά ἐστι καὶ κατάρας μεστή.[2] The statement that
the way of death is πονηρά seems banal; however, the
phrase "full of accursedness" (κατάρας μεστή, also
attested in *Barn.* 20.1) is important. This appears to be
an old tradition with which this part of the tractate
began. The phrase κατάρας μεστή is found in our literature only here and in *Barn.* 20.1.[3] Κατάρα probably
means the divine "curse" that strikes the violator of the
law.[4] If the way of death is a way beset with curses, one

may in turn conceive the way of life as a "way full of
blessing" (ὁδὸς εὐλογίας μεστή).

The development of the theme follows. Understandably enough, however, the author of the tractate was not
able to present anything by way of explication of the way
of death other than a doublet of the series of prohibitions in 2.2–7—although now in the form of a vice list.

---

1   *Barn.* 20.1a deviates sharply from *Did.* 5.1: ἡ δὲ τοῦ
μέλανος ὁδός ἐστιν σκολιὰ καὶ κατάρας μεστή.
ὁδὸς γάρ ἐστιν θανάτου αἰωνίου μετὰ τιμωρίας, ἐν
ᾗ ἐστιν τὰ ἀπολλύντα τὴν ψυχὴν αὐτῶν ("But the
way of the Black One is crooked and full of cursing,
for it is the way of death eternal with punishment,
and in it are the things that destroy their soul"). Is
this (from the point of view of tradition history)
more original than the text in the *Didache*? *Doctrina*
reads *Mortis autem via est illi contraria* ("the way of
death is, however, contrary to that one").

2   Πρῶτον πάντων πονηρά ἐστι has no parallel in
Barnabas and may be only a mechanical approxima-

tion of *Did.* 1.2. *Doctrina* has *primum nequam et male-
dictis plena*. . . .

3   But cf. Ps 9:28: οὗ ἀρᾶς τὸ στόμα αὐτοῦ γέμει καὶ
πικρίας καὶ δόλου ("whose mouth is filled with bitterness and deceit"), and Ps 13:3: ὧν τὸ στόμα ἀρᾶς
καὶ πικρίας γέμει ("whose mouth is filled with
cursing and bitterness," quoted in Rom 3:14).

4   Cf., remotely, Heb 6:7–8 and the κατάρας τέκνα in
2 Pet 2:14 (although there the reference is to false
teachers).

5 b. Catalog of Vices (5.1b–2)

1b [Characteristic of it are] acts of murder, adultery, passion, fornication, theft, idolatry, magic, mixing poisons, robbery, false witness, hypocrisy, duplicity, guile, pride, malice, willful stubbornness, avarice, obscene speech, jealousy, insolence, arrogance, boastfulness, lack of fear <of God>.

2 [Characteristic of it are also] people who persecute the good, who hate truth, who love falsehood, who do not know the merit of righteousness, who do not adhere to what is good or to just judgment, who watch not for the good, but for evil, who are far from mildness and patience, who love what is futile, who are out for recompense, who do not show mercy to a poor person, who are not distressed by [the plight of] the oppressed, who do not know him who made them, [who are] child murderers, who destroy what God has formed, who turn away from the needy person, who oppress the person who is distressed, [who are] defenders of the rich [and] unjust judges of the poor—[people who are] sinners in everything that they do.

Analysis

This catalog consists of two parts. In the first part (v. 1b), twenty-three vices are listed;[1] in the second part (v. 2), we find nineteen groups of evildoers.[2] The beginning of the catalog (roughly the first half of the first part) has a different sequence in *Doctrina*. This is one of the passages in which *Doctrina* deviates rather sharply from H. The expressions ὑποκρίσεις, διπλοκαρδία, and δόλος, sequential in H, have nothing corresponding to them in *Doctrina* (and the same is true, in turn, of the *affectiones* in *Doctrina*, for which there is no correspon-

dence in H). Beginning with ὑπερηφανία, *Doctrina* again corresponds to the *Didache*, although ὕψος seems to appear twice in *Doctrina*, as *superbia* and as *altitudo*.

The vice list in *Barn.* 20.1 deviates still more sharply from *Did.* 5.1.[3] Only from *Did.* 5.2 onward are *Didache* and *Barnabas* again parallel, although with deviations. On the whole, the catalog in the *Didache* text seems more orderly than that in *Doctrina*, or certainly in *Barnabas*.[4] One may ask which has the older or oldest version.[5] The remaining differences between *Didache* and *Doctrina* are attributable either to the didachistic

1   For ἀφοβία (θεοῦ)? at the end of v. 1, see below.
2   Wengst (*Didache*, 74) conjectured οὐ φοβούμενοι τὸν θεόν at the end of 5.1, and adds that phrase to the following sequence. In this way, he obtains twenty-two vices (eleven each in plural and singular), and (because he counts his conjecture with the list of vices) twenty groups of evildoers. Cf. Wengst, *Didache*, 75 n. 48.
3   This is true of the number of vices (the catalog in *Barnabas* is shorter), the sequence, and also by virtue of the fact that the series in *Barnabas* is singular from the outset, while *Didache* and *Doctrina* begin with plural expressions and only later fall into the singular. There is no parallel in the *Didache* for παράβασις.
4   Audet, *Didachè*, 349: "5.1 is the 'way of death' in the instruction to the Gentiles." *Did.* 5.2 is supposed (cf. what was said above) to stem from another situation

from the point of view of tradition history, and to be a later addition, "an adaptation of the instruction to the poor on the original plan of the *Duae viae*" (*Didachè*, 349). *Did.* 5.2 is said to come from the same hand to which we owe the introduction to the "instruction to the poor" (ibid.).
5   We can determine that there is a certain parallelism (stronger at the beginning) between *Did.* 2.2–7 and 5.1. Is the later ordering from the hand of the redactor (who intervened to establish some order, at least at the beginning) different from the original order of the sources? Or is this order the original?

redaction or to a confusion in the tradition behind *Doctrina*. Certainty cannot be obtained.[6]

Comment

■ **1b** At the outset we can discern an arrangement of the list of vices. As it had at 2.2, *Didache* first models itself on the sequence of the Decalogue, treating violations of the fifth, sixth, and seventh commandments. The text thus begins, here also, with "acts of murder" (φόνοι; cf. οὐ φονεύσεις in 2.2),[7] and continues with a listing of sins against the sixth commandment, "adultery, passion, fornication" (μοιχεῖαι, ἐπιθυμίαι, πορνεῖαι; cf. 2.2, οὐ μοιχεύσεις . . . οὐ πορνεύσεις, although nothing corresponds to ἐπιθυμία at that point). Then follow, as in 2.2, the sins against the seventh commandment, "thefts" (κλοπαί; in 2.2, οὐ κλέψεις). At that point the sequence oriented to the Decalogue ends.

Then follow—as before—sins of false religion, beginning with "idolatry" (εἰδωλολατρίαι), then "magic" (μαγεῖαι) and "sorcery" (φαρμακίαι; there is nothing corresponding to εἰδωλολατρίαι in 2.2, but cf. 3.4; cf. also in 2.2 οὐ μαγεύσεις, οὐ φαρμακεύσεις). The following "acts of robbery" (ἁρπαγαί) could correspond to the phrase οὐκ ἐπιθυμήσεις τὰ τοῦ πλησίον in 2.3 (?).

Next follow four vices that have to do with falsity within and without (cf. 2.3–5): "false witness, hypocrisy, duplicity, guile" (ψευδομαρτυρίαι, ὑποκρίσεις, διπλοκαρδία, and δόλος). Compare ψευδομαρτυρίαι with οὐ ψευδομαρτυρήσεις in 2.3. Ὑποκρίσεις here is not "sin," as in 2.6 and 4.12, but "hypocrisies, falsifications," or "misrepresentations."[8] Compare διπλοκαρδία[9] with διγνώμων, δίγλωσσος, and διγλωσσία in 2.4. Note that with the word διπλοκαρδία the series moves to the singular. Δόλος[10] is lacking in 2.3–5, but cf., at least for the content, 2.5.

In the series "pride" (ὑπερηφανία;[11] cf. ὑπερήφανος in 2.6), "malice" (κακία; cf. κακοήθης in 2.6), and "willful stubbornness" (αὐθάδεια; cf. αὐθάδης in 3.6), at least pride and stubbornness belong together. Then follow (although no connection is evident) "avarice" (πλεονεξία; cf. οὐκ ἔσῃ πλεονέκτης in 2.6), "obscene speech" (αἰσχρολογία; αἰσχρολόγος in 3.3), and "jealousy" (ζηλοτυπία; cf. ζηλωτής in 3.2).

The next three vices, "insolence" (θρασύτης; θράσος in 3.9), "arrogance" (ὕψος; οὐχ ὑψώσεις σεαυτόν and ὑψηλά in 3.9), and "boastfulness" (ἀλαζονεία), again constitute a group. Only ἀλαζονεία has not been mentioned before.[12]

The first part of the catalog may well have ended with the summary phrase "lack of fear of God" (ἀφοβία θεοῦ; thus *Barn.* in S^c H V; cf. *deum*[13] *non timentes* in *Doctrina*) or (more probably) only ἀφοβία (*Constitutions, Barnabas* in S*). The word is lacking here in H and should probably be conjectured.[14] Θεοῦ or *deum* is a subsequent interpretation, but it correctly represents the intended meaning of ἀφοβία. All vices are summarized in a lack of φόβος toward God (cf. 4.9). As φόβος θεοῦ is the epitome of the right way, so is ἀφοβία (Θεοῦ) the epitome of the way that leads to death.[15]

■ **2** Thus the first series in the catalog comes to an end. The second series consists of a listing not of vices but of evildoers.[16] This catalog also has parallels in *Barn.* 20.2, including the sequence. There are no discernible subdi-

---

6   Agreements between the *Didache* and the vice list in Mark 7:21-22/Matt 15:19 and in *Hermas Man.* 8.3-5 do not indicate literary relationships. Koester (*Synoptische Überlieferung*, 163-70) and Rordorf and Tuilier (*Doctrine*, 167 n. 1) find striking parallels (?) to 1QS 4.9-10.

7   *Barnabas* and *Doctrina* transpose: μοιχεία (*moechationes*), φόνος (*homicidia*).

8   See above, p. 92 n. 48.

9   For the construction of this word see BDF, §120 (4); BDR, §120 (5); it occurs only here and in the parallel in *Barnabas*. Again, it is a characteristic expression of the tractate.

10 Common in vice lists: *Corp. Herm.* 13.7 (Nock and Festugière, 2.203); Mark 7:22; Rom 1:29; *1 Clem.* 35.5 (δόλους). It is also found frequently in the NT and a few times in the Apostolic Fathers.

11 From here on *Didache* and *Doctrina* are again parallel in sequence.

12 In vice lists: *1 Clem.* 35.5; *Hermas Man.* 6.2.5; 8.5. Otherwise: Jas 4:16; 1 John 2:16; frequently in *1 Clem.* 13.1; 14.1; 16.2; 21.5; 35.5; 57.2.

13 In f^2 *deum* has been added above the line.

14 With Franz Xaver Funk, *Doctrina duodecim apostolorum: Canones Apostolorum ecclesiastici ac reliquiae doctrinae de duabus viis. Expositiones veteres* (Tübingen: Laupp, 1887) 14; Bihlmeyer, *Apostolischen Väter*, 4; Rordorf and Tuilier, *Doctrine*, 166. Klauser (*Doctrina*, 20) and Audet (*Didachè*, 232) conjecture ἀφοβία θεοῦ. Harnack (*Lehre*, 18) and Lietzmann (*Didache*, 8) stand by the text transmitted in H. Cf. Niederwimmer, "Textprobleme," 123. Wengst (*Didache*, 74) conjectures οὐ φοβούμενοι τὸν θεόν. Cf. on this his remarks at *Didache*, 75 n. 50.

15 Cf. Prov. 15:16: Κρείσσων μικρὰ μερὶς μετὰ φόβου

visions. The initial phrase διῶκται ἀγαθῶν is, once again, a characteristic expression of the tractate.[17] The subsequent contrast is stated in *parallelismus membrorum*: μισοῦντες ἀλήθειαν/ἀγαπῶντες ψεῦδος.[18] The phrase οὐ γινώσκοντες μισθὸν δικαιοσύνης[19] means: they know nothing about the reward for righteous deeds, because they do not do any righteous deeds. Entirely captive to the Jewish(-Christian) milieu in its phrasing is the following οὐ κολλώμενοι ἀγαθῷ[20] οὐδὲ κρίσει δικαίᾳ.[21] *Barnabas* continues: χήρᾳ καὶ ὀρφανῷ οὐ προσέχοντες (which may be original). Ἀγρυπνοῦντες οὐκ εἰς τὸ ἀγαθόν,[22] ἀλλ᾽ εἰς τὸ πονηρόν: they care "not for what is good, but for what is evil."[23] The vices listed are contrasted to the attitude of the *anawim* (see above): they are typical of the powerful and of tyrants, hence the continuation: ὧν μακρὰν[24] πραΰτης καὶ ὑπομονή.[25] These last two phrases are a hendiadys, describing *the virtue of the anawim*.[26] The phrase μάταια ἀγαπῶντες ("who love what is futile") is inspired, perhaps uncon-

sciously, by Ps 4:3 (ἀγαπᾶτε ματαιότητα).[27] Διώκοντες ἀνταπόδομα ("who are out for recompense")[28] is (again perhaps unconsciously?) quoted from Isa 1:23. The reprimand is directed at those who are continually seeking to be rewarded for their deeds.

The next two clauses are in *parallelismus membrorum*:
οὐκ ἐλεοῦντες πτωχόν,[29]
οὐ πονοῦντες ἐπὶ καταπονουμένῳ.

The καταπονούμενος is the oppressed person.[30] Πτωχός and καταπονούμενος are parallel to one another. In addition, the play on words in πονεῖν – καταπονούμενος should be noted;[31] it presupposes a Greek original for the tractate.[32] The οὐ γινώσκοντες τὸν ποιήσαντα αὐτούς are those who forget God. Cf. ὁ θεὸς ὁ ποιήσας

κυρίου / ἢ θησαυροὶ μεγάλοι μετὰ ἀφοβίας ("Better is a little with the fear of the Lord than great treasure and trouble without it"). Cf. also ἀφοβία with πλάνη, ἀπιστία, etc., in the vice list in *Ps.-Clem. Hom.* 1.18.3 (GCS² 1.32).

16 There is no occasion here for source-critical or tradition-historical hypotheses. The transition is, in fact, as unimportant as that from plural to singular in 5.1.

17 Διώκτης Hos 6:8 Symmachus; 1 Tim 1:13. It was frequently used later by the Fathers; cf. Lampe, *s.v.* On this topic, cf. *1 Clem.* 45.4: ἐδιώχθησαν δίκαιοι, ἀλλ᾽ ὑπὸ ἀνόμων ("the righteous were persecuted, but by the lawless").

18 For the last, cf. Ps 4:3: ἵνα τί ἀγαπᾶτε ματαιότητα καὶ ζητεῖτε ψεῦδος ("How long will you love vain words and seek after lies?"); and the φιλῶν καὶ ποιῶν ψεῦδος in Rev 22:15.

19 Objective genitive; *Doctrina* has (secondarily) *mercedem veritatis*. Regarding μισθὸν δικαιοσύνης, cf. μισθὸς (τῆς) ἀδικίας, Acts 1:18; 2 Pet 2:15.

20 Κολλώμενοι τῷ ἀγαθῷ, Rom 12:9. Characteristic of the same milieu is *T. Ash.* 3.1: Ὑμεῖς οὖν, τέκνα μου, μὴ γίνεσθε κατ᾽ αὐτοὺς διπρόσωποι, ἀγαθότητος καὶ κακίας· ἀλλὰ τῇ ἀγαθότητι μόνῃ κολλήθητε ("But you, my children, do not be two-faced like them, one good and the other evil; rather, cling only to goodness").

21 Cf. John 7:24, and the contrary in Polycarp *Phil.* 6.1. Of divine judgment: 2 Thess 1:5; Rev 16:7. Of Jesus' eschatological judgment: John 5:30.

22 Ἀγρυπνεῖν is used metaphorically. For Ἀγρυπνεῖν

εἰς, cf. Eph 6:18; ἀγρυπνεῖν ἐπί, Dan 9:14 LXX; ὑπέρ, Heb 13:17.

23 *Doctrina* has preserved the metaphor: *pervigilantes non in bono sed in malo*. Barnabas: ἀγρυπνοῦντες οὐκ εἰς φόβον θεοῦ.

24 *Barnabas*: μακρὰν καὶ πόρρω.

25 *Doctrina* has *superbia proxima* instead of ὑπομονή, and nothing corresponding to the following μάταια ἀγαπῶντες.

26 Cf. *Did.* 3.7–8.

27 Cf. also Prov 12:11.

28 *Doctrina*: *remuneratores*.

29 This is a common expression in Proverbs: ἐλεῶν δὲ πτωχούς, 14:21; ἐλεᾷ πτωχόν, 14:31; ὁ ἐλεῶν πτωχόν, 19:17; 22:9; τῷ ἐλεῶντι πτωχούς, 28:8.

30 Cf. Acts 7:24; James Hope Moulton and George Milligan, *Vocabulary of the Greek Testament* (Grand Rapids: Eerdmans, 1930) 331; esp. *BGU* 4.1188.17 (from the time of Augustus): καταπονούμενος ὑπὸ τῶν τελωνῶν. BAGD (*s.v.*) refers to UPZ 110.87–88: δ[ι] τοὺς ἐν τῇ πόλει καὶ διὰ νυκτὸ[ς] καὶ ἡμέρας ἐν | ταῖς λειτουργίαις καταπονουμένου <<νενου>>ς.

31 Walter Bauer reproduces the play on words (Walter Bauer, *Griechisch-deutsches Wörterbuch zu den Schriften des Neuen Testaments und der frühchristlichen Literatur* [ed. Kurt and Barbara Aland; 6th ed.; Berlin: de Gruyter, 1988]); BAGD, *s.v.*, has "toil for [the one who is] downtrodden."

32 In *Barnabas* this is followed by εὐχερεῖς ἐν καταλαλιᾷ, which is lacking in *Didache* and *Doctrina*.

σε in 1.2.[33] Compare φονεῖς τέκνων[34] with οὐδὲ γεννηθὲν ἀποκτενεῖς in *Did.* 2.2. Φθορεῖς πλάσματος ("who destroy what God has formed") is rendered correctly, with interpretation, in *Doctrina* as *avortuantes* (*sic*, for *abortantes*).[35] The verbal echo between φονεῖς and φθορεῖς again suggests a Greek original for the tractate. What follows is again *parallelismus membrorum*:

ἀποστρεφόμενοι τὸν ἐνδεόμενον,[36]

κατωπονοῦντες τὸν θλιβόμενον,

and materially it is a repetition of the attitude previously deplored: οὐκ ἐλεοῦντες πτωχόν κτλ. (see above).

πλουσίων παράκλητοι,[37]

πενήτων ἄνομοι κριταί

is also *parallelismus membrorum*. Παράκλητος is someone who intervenes on behalf of another.[38] Its use here is ironic: they ought to act as advocates for the poor and needy, but no; they turn out instead to be advocates for the rich! The whole thing recalls the style of prophetic cursing. The superabundance of sins is summarized in the word πανθαμάρτητος.[39]

---

33 On this matter, cf. also Wis 15:11: ὅτι ἠγνόησεν τὸν πλάσαντα αὐτόν ("because they failed to know the one who formed them"); and Hos 5:4: τὸν δὲ κύριον οὐκ ἐπέγνωσαν ("they do not know the Lord").

34 Wis 12:5: τέκνων τε φονὰς ἀνελεήμονας ("their merciless slaughter of children").

35 Schlecht, *Doctrina*, 62. For the betacism, cf. Leo Wohleb, *Die lateinische Übersetzung der Didache kritisch und sprachlich untersucht* (SGKA 7.1; Paderborn: Schöningh, 1913; repr., New York: Johnson, 1967) 8.

36 *Doctrina*: *avertentes se a bonis operibus* ("turning yourself away from good works")—perhaps to avoid a doublet with *non miserantes pauperum . . .* etc.?

37 *Doctrina* has *advocationes iustorum devitantes*. There is nothing corresponding to the second line.

38 Cf. BAGD, *s.v.*

39 This term is found only here, *Barn.* 20.2, and *Apostolic Constitutions*. It is thus practically speaking a hapax legomenon. The expression is again characteristic of the language of the tractate. It is omitted in *Doctrina*.

5   **c. Final Admonition (5.2 [end])**

2 (end)   **Children, from all this [or: from all these men]
may you [pl.] be preserved.**

The long list of evils and evildoers is followed by this summary expression, at the same time a warning and wish: ῥυσθείητε, τέκνα, ἀπὸ τούτων[1] ἁπάντων. The final sentence is lacking in *Barnabas*. The address, τέκνα,[2] again recalls the sapiential character of 3.1–6. It is of no consequence whether ἀπὸ τούτων ἁπάντων refers to the evildoers just named (masculine), or to the vices previously listed (neuter).

---

1   Ῥύεσθαι ἀπό τινος is a genitive of separation: BDF, §180.1; BDR, §180.1 and (1).

2   *Doctrina* has the singular, *Abstine te fili*. . . . Audet (*Didachè*, 232) conjectures (unnecessarily) ῥυσθείητι, τέκνον. *Constitutions* also has the plural.

6

1   **See to it that no one leads you astray from this way of the teaching, since [the person who would do so] teaches apart from God.**

2   **If you can bear the entire yoke of the Lord, you will be perfect, but if you cannot, do what you can.**

3   **As for food, bear what you can, but be very much on your guard against food offered to idols, for [to eat it] is worship of dead gods.**

Comment

■ **1** The Two Ways tractate concluded appropriately (in the recension available to the Didachist) with a brief parenetical epilogue, now attested by 5.2 (end) and also by 6.1: Ὅρα, μή[1] τίς σε πλανήσῃ ἀπὸ ταύτης τῆς ὁδοῦ[2] τῆς διδαχῆς, ἐπεὶ παρεκτὸς θεοῦ σε διδάσκει. The Didachist dropped the rest of the epilogue from the source[3] and added, instead, an appendix (6.2–3) covering questions that he found important in the context of baptismal instruction.[4]

Excursus: An Original Parenetic Epilogue

The literary situation is therefore as follows: The Two Ways tractate, in the recension available to the Didachist, concluded with a parenetic epilogue comparable to the epilogue that we now find at the end of *Doctrina*.[5] It begins, basically, with the final phrase in *Doctr.* 5.2 and continues in *Doctr.* 6.1 and 6.4–5:

(5.2 [end])   *Abstine te fili ab istis omnibus*

(6.1)   *et vide ne quis te ab hac doctrina avocet,*
           et si minus extra disciplinam doceberis.

(6.4)   *Haec in consulendo si cottidie feceris,*
           prope eris vivo deo;
           quod si non feceris,
           longe eris a veritate.

(6.5)   *Haec omnia tibi in animo pone*
           et non deceperis[6] de spe tua,
           sed per haec sancta certamina
           pervenies ad coronam.

("My child, keep yourself from all these and see to it that no one leads you astray from this teaching or that you receive teaching without discipline. If you act with this in mind every day, you will be near the living God. If you don't do so, you will be far from the truth. Put all these things in your mind and you will not be deprived of your hope. But through these holy contests you will win a crown.") The beginning is still present in the *Didache* (in what is probably a more original version):

(5.2 end)   Ῥυσθείητε, τέκνα, ἀπὸ τούτων ἁπάντων.

(6.1)   Ὅρα, μή τίς σε πλανήσῃ ἀπὸ ταύτης τῆς
           ὁδοῦ τῆς διδαχῆς,
           ἐπεὶ παρεκτὸς θεοῦ σε διδάσκει.[7]

The Didachist suppressed the rest of the epilogue. I call this the *epilogus primus*; with it[8] the Two Ways tractate, in the recension available to *Doctrina* and *Didache*,[9] originally came to an end.[10] Its language and way of thinking are Jewish or Jewish-Christian.[11] The Didachist could not use this entire epilogue in

---

1   Ὅρα μή κτλ. with the aorist subjunctive: BDF, §364.3; BDR, §364.3.

2   Πλανᾶν ἀπὸ τῆς ὁδοῦ ("stray from the path") is good OT language; cf. Deut 11:28; Wis 5:6. See also the similar expressions in Isa 53:6 (*1 Clem.* 16.6) and 2 Pet 2:15.

3   Audet (*Didachè*, 352) differs. According to him the original *Duae viae* tractate probably concluded with 6.1.

4   Harnack's suggestions (*Apostellehre*, 30) that the Jewish source may have contained instructions about food regulations and similar matters at this point (and similar suggestions by Seeberg [*Wege*, 39–40], namely, a passage about food regulations) are revealed by the text of *Doctrina* to be without foundation.

5   In my opinion this epilogue goes back to recension C[1], which was available to *Didache* and *Doctrina*. I infer a different eschatological epilogue for recension B (from which come *Barn.* 21.2–4 and *Can.* 14).

6   *Deceperis* in f; *deciperis* in f[1]; *decipieris* conjectured by Lietzmann, *Didache*, 9.

7   Cf. also *Fides patr.* 3: ὅρα ἄνθρωπε, μή τίς σε ἀποστήσει (cf. the *v.l.* in *PG* 28.1639C) ἐκ τῆς πίστεως ταύτης, ἐπεὶ παρεκτὸς θεοῦ εἴης ("See then, man, that no one remove you from this faith, since then you would be separated from God").

8   More precisely: with the text, which we can no longer reconstruct in detail, that stands as the *source* behind *Did.* 5.2 (end) + 6.1, and *Doctr.* 5.2 (end) + 6.1, 4–5.

9   The same must be true, however, of the source that was the ultimate basis for *Fides patrum*.

10   In saying this I have obviously decided already that the source had no apocalyptic conclusion com-

the context of his book[12] and therefore restricted his quotation of it to 5.2 (end) as the conclusion of the exposition of the "Way of Death." From the rest of the epilogue he selected only the motif of warning (ὅρα μή τίς κτλ. in 6.1), and omitted the rest. In place of the text that followed, the Didachist inserted in 6.2–3 an appendix to the two-ways section of his book (therefore 6.2–3 is redactional).[13] At the same time, *Doctrina* has its own history (independent of the *Didache*). What we now read as its conclusion:

(6.6) *Per dominum Iesum Christum regnantem*
  et dominantem
  cum deo patre et spiritu sancto
  in saecula saeculorum. Amen.

("Through the Lord Jesus Christ, who reigns and rules with God the Father and the Holy Spirit forever and ever. Amen.") represents a later addition (*epilogus secundus*), which must certainly have been added to the text of *Doctrina* in the course of its history within the Latin tradition.[14]

■ **2** The redactor would therefore have concluded the quotation from his source at *Did.* 6.1. What he now added in 6.2–3 has the character of interpretation and expansion. The very first section, in 6.2, is the *crux interpretum*: εἰ μὲν γὰρ δύνασαι βαστάσαι ὅλον τὸν ζυγὸν τοῦ κυρίου, τέλειος ἔσῃ· εἰ δ᾽ οὐ δύνασαι, ὃ δύνῃ, τοῦτο ποίει. It is true that the expressions themselves are immediately intelligible: Ζυγὸν βαστάζειν is to be taken metaphorically, and here has the special meaning "to bear, endure, and keep a divine command; to be in a

position to execute it" (hence δύνασθαι βαστάσαι).[15] There is a parallel (although only a formal one) in Acts 15:10, where the text reads: ἐπιθεῖναι ζυγὸν ἐπὶ τὸν τράχηλον τῶν μαθητῶν ὃν οὔτε οἱ πατέρες ἡμῶν οὔτε ἡμεῖς ἰσχύσαμεν βαστάσαι ("by placing on the neck of the disciples a yoke that neither our ancestors nor we have been able to bear"). Here ζυγός is the divine command or instruction, as we occasionally find in Jewish usage. Thus, for example, Wisdom calls people to accept her yoke (Sir 51:26; Matt 11:29–30); the rabbis speak of the "yoke of the Torah," or the "yoke of the commandments," and so on, as well as of a "yoke" in the absolute sense, by which they mean the yoke of God. A characteristic expression is "to take up the yoke of the kingdom of heaven."[16] But (as Büchsel has pointed out),[17] ζυγὸν βαστάζειν does not correspond to the rabbinic קבל עול מלכות השמים (which would be ζυγὸν δέχεσθαι). Ζυγὸν βαστάζειν does not mean "take the yoke upon oneself," but "bear or endure the yoke."[18] Thus it is clear that in this passage it is a question of whether the individual Christian is in a position to bear the divine ordinances in their entirety (ὅλον τὸν ζυγόν). If so, such a one will be τέλειος, that is, one who fulfills the divine commands to the full;[19] if not, it is conceded that the person should concentrate on the part of the commandments that he or she is able to fulfill (ὃ δύνῃ, τοῦτο ποίει).

11 For the *certamina* in *Doctr.* 6.5, cf. 1QS 4.17–18; for *corona*, 1QS 4.7 and Braun, *Qumran*, 2.186–87. The echoes are very remote, and one would omit them altogether if there were not a tradition-historical connection between 1QS 3.13–4.26 and the Two Ways tractate.

12 The Didachist did not end the book at this point. It was his intention to add some additional parts concerning the order of worship and the rules of the community. Nevertheless, he probably took some inspiration from the conclusion of his source in adding an eschatological prospect to his text in chap. 16 (q.v.). But the material in chap. 16 does not come from the tractate.

13 So also Drews, "Apostellehre," 267; Knopf, *Lehre*, 20; 6.2–3 could scarcely be the work of an interpolator, as Audet thinks (*Didachè*, 107–8, 352–53).

14 For this formula, cf. Schlecht, *Doctrina*, 66; Giet, *L'Énigme*, 98 n. 16.

15 For δύνασθαι βαστάσαι, cf. Epictetus *Dissertationes* 3.15.9 (Schenkl, 279): ἄνθρωπε, σκέψαι πρῶτον τί ἐστι τὸ πρᾶγμα, εἶτα καὶ τὴν σαυτοῦ φύσιν ("Man,

parable to *Didache* 16. On this, see below at 16.1–8.

consider first what the business is, and then your own natural ability, what you can bear"). Cf. also ὅσον δύνασαι in *Barn.* 19.8; more remotely, οὐ δύνασθε βαστάζειν ἄρτι in John 16:12.

16 On this whole subject, see Str–B 1.608–10; Karl Georg Kuhn, "מלכות השמים in Rabbinic Literature," *TDNT* 1 (1964) 572–74; Friedrich Büchsel, "βαστάζω," *TDNT* 1 (1964) 596 n. 5; Karl Rengstorf, "ζυγός in the N.T.," *TDNT* 2 (1964) 898–901.

17 Büchsel, "βαστάζω," *TDNT* 1 (1964) 596 n. 5.

18 Cf. τὸν ζυγὸν τοῦ λόγου (sc. Χριστοῦ) βαστάζειν in Justin *Dial.* 53.1 (Goodspeed, 152). The paradoxical formulation ὁ ζυγὸς τοῦ χάριτος ("the yoke of grace," *1 Clem.* 16.17) intends to say that this yoke does not lay a burden on someone, but on the contrary it is grace. Identical in subject (although the word is given a more negative qualification) is *Barn.* 2.6: ὁ καινὸς νόμος τοῦ κυρίου ἡμῶν Ἰησοῦ Χριστοῦ, ἄνευ ζυγοῦ ἀνάγκης ὤν ("The new law of our Lord Jesus Christ, being without the yoke of necessity").

19 Τέλειος ἔσῃ ("you will be perfect") of course reminds us of καὶ ἔσῃ τέλειος in *Did.* 1.4 (q.v.). In

With these reflections we have already sketched the general framework that defines this section. It remains unclear, for the moment, what exactly is meant by the expression ὅλος ὁ ζυγός ("the entire yoke") and what its content may be.[20] Various answers have been given by scholars over the years. It has been proposed that ὅλος ὁ ζυγός refers especially to the rigoristic requirements of an encratitic morality, including sexual asceticism in particular.[21] In that case, the τέλειος would be the ascetic who renounces marriage, although this is not demanded of everyone. Average Christians are simply asked to do what they can; that is, they need not renounce marriage (like the τέλειος) if they are not able to do it.[22] In favor of this interpretation of the passage is that in the early period certain rigorists (heretics, to be sure) sometimes combined baptism and the renunciation of marriage.[23] In addition, one could call on the context in support of this interpretation of the passage: in 6.2–3 the Didachist would be discussing two special ethical questions, namely, in 6.2 whether baptism implies renunciation of marriage (which he would deny), and in 6.3 the question of asceticism with regard to food.

Alfred Stuiber[24] has presented a different idea.[25] According to him, 6.2–3 concerns a "Jewish supplement to the Jewish teaching about the two ways."[26] The *Sitz im Leben* would be the diaspora synagogue and its propaganda. "Because the Law was given only to Israel, it is only the people of Israel who are obligated to observe it. For the God-fearing Gentiles the moral law is sufficient. But it is still highly welcome when these Gentiles also observe the ritual laws insofar as that is possible, because that can prepare for complete conversion."[27] Stuiber must then suppose that *Doctrina* never had this addition, or that it was eliminated by the Christian redactor of *Doctrina*; to explain the fact that the Jewish supplement (6.2–3) was allowed to remain in the Christian *Didache* he must then suggest "carelessness on the part of the Christian compiler,"[28] although this seems rather a last-ditch solution.

The correct interpretation is probably to be found by following the suggestion of Rordorf and Tuilier,[29] according to whom ὅλος ὁ ζυγὸς τοῦ κυρίου now[30] means the law of Christ, as the Didachist had revealed at the beginning in the *sectio christiana sive evangelica*. The phrase τέλειος ἔσῃ, in any case, reveals the pen of the

---

both cases it is the didachistic redactor who is speaking. This will be discussed more fully below.

20 *Constitutions* no longer understood this section, or did not accept its thesis, and thus omitted it.

21 Harnack, *Lehre*, 19–21; idem, "Prolegomena," 43: probably the primary thought is of total sexual abstinence. Knopf, *Lehre*, 21: "The ideal is to live a life of total celibacy: anyone who can do that is a τέλειος."

22 Knopf (*Lehre*, 21) gives precision to this idea: "With ὃ δύνη we are to think of temporary and restricted asceticism, renunciation of marital intercourse during particular times (cf. 1 Cor 7:5)."

23 Niederwimmer, *Askese*, 176–86.

24 Stuiber, "Ganze Joch," 323–29. Schaff (*Church Manual*, 182) had already decreed that what is intended is "the ceremonial law."

25 Stuiber's arguments against the first interpretation ("Ganze Joch," 325–26), however, are very questionable. He then suggests (pp. 326–27) a "*Jewish-Christian*" interpretation according to which what is at stake is the yoke of the Torah (and, in fact, the particular issue of circumcision); but he then rejects this interpretation as well (p. 327). The "Jewish-Christian" interpretation (to use Stuiber's terminology) has recently reappeared in the work of Wengst (*Didache*, 95–96 n. 52). He considers it possible that the statement was originally Jewish in its intent, but

it now stands in a Jewish-*Christian* document and must therefore be interpreted differently. "The expression refers to the Old Testament law, even under Christian auspices, and the verse then regards it as not necessary, but still desirable that gentile Christians should also observe this law" (p. 96). Audet (*Didachè*, 353–54) had already said something similar (of the interpolator), and Wengst refers to this.

26 Stuiber, "Ganze Joch," 327.

27 Stuiber, "Ganze Joch," 328.

28 Stuiber, "Ganze Joch," 328.

29 Rordorf and Tuilier, *Doctrine*, 32–33.

30 Rordorf and Tuilier consider Stuiber's derivation possible. "Still, it remains equally necessary to be precise about the sense in which this instruction is repeated in the *Didache*" (*Doctrine*, 32; cf. also n. 4). That *Did.* 6.2 refers back to 1.3–6 was something already suggested by Seeberg, *Wege*, 39. He also proposed that here a Christian had given a new meaning to an existing Jewish text (pp. 39–40).

31 Rordorf and Tuilier, *Doctrine*, 32–33.

32 Rordorf and Tuilier (*Doctrine*, 33) refer to Ps.-Cyprian *De centes.* 14 (Reitzenstein, p. 79, ll. 132–35), where this passage may be quoted. See above, Introduction, §2b. I would like to set aside the question whether that sermon means the same thing as this *Didache* passage. Rordorf and Tuilier

Didachist (cf. 1.4).[31] Thus the Didachist now (after concluding the Two Ways teaching) recalls once again, and in a special way, the commandments of the Lord he quoted in 1.3b–2.1. They are for him the "yoke of the Lord" (for which he takes up a traditional Jewish way of speaking), and so the "new law of Christ," even when the term is not spoken. He has no illusions about the radical nature of the Lord's commandments; those who are not able to fulfill these commandments completely should at least do what they can.[32] If this interpretation is correct, it seems consistent to me to attribute 6.2 (as well as the next verse, 6.3) to the body of the didachistic redaction.

■ **3** The Didachist now treats a special problem for catechumens in this context: περὶ δὲ τῆς βρώσεως, concerning commandments about food. Cf. *Barn.* 10.10: ἔχετε τελείως καὶ περὶ τῆς βρώσεως ("be perfect also about food") and, although restricted to εἰδωλόθυτα, 1 Cor 8:4. This refers obviously to the commandments and prohibitions regarding food in the Old Testament and Jewish tradition.[33] The Didachist requires that they be kept to the extent that it is possible for each individual— ὃ δύνασαι βάστασον (the formula echoes what has gone

before).[34] Thus while the compulsory nature of these prescriptions has been relaxed, there is no fundamental abrogation of the food laws here. While the author considers the relaxation of food laws (except for εἰδωλόθυ-τα) permissible in individual cases (the degree of relaxation apparently to be measured by the individual's judgment), he remains strict with regard to εἰδωλόθυτα: the eating of meat offered to idols is absolutely forbidden,[35] and this is because the eating of sacrificed meat is nothing less than worship of the dead gods, the idols.[36] The phrase λίαν πρόσεχε[37] paints a picture of anxious avoidance of idol worship. The attitude toward the eating of the ἱερόθυτον ("sacred meat," as the Gentiles call it) corresponds more or less to that in Acts 15:20 par.[38] and Rev 2:14, 20.[39]

Let us now look back at *Did.* 6.2–3. What is the function of this section within the work as a whole? If my description is correct, 6.2 has an interpretive character. The Didachist directs the attention of the reader (or hearer) *back*, beyond the advice in the previous passages, to the eschatologically conditioned beginning in which logia from the Jesus tradition were quoted (1.3b–2.1). Indeed, he makes clear to the reader (or hearer) once

also refer (*Doctrina*, 33 n. 4) to the *Liber graduum*. (For my part, I would like to see the graded ethics of the *Liber graduum* clearly distinguished from the view evident in *Did.* 6.2.)

33 According to Harnack (*Lehre*, 21) this is not about the OT and Jewish food laws, but specifically about the eating of flesh. Knopf, *Lehre*, 21: "Refusal of certain things (Acts 15:20, 28), as well as strict fasting on bread and water, but only for a time (*Hermas Sim.* 5)." This is improbable.

34 From the continuation it is evident that this refers to all food laws except for the prohibition of εἰδω-λόθυτα. On this point the Didachist's judgment is more rigorous.

35 The question is thus not "sharing in the sacrificial meal for idols," which is forbidden to Christians in any case, "but eating the flesh of the sacrificial animals" (Knopf, *Lehre*, 21).

36 The idea that foreign gods are nothing matches the judgment of the OT and Jewish tradition, which was taken over by the church as a matter of course. Cf. 1 Cor 8:4; 10:20; *2 Clem.* 3.1: ὅτι ἡμεῖς οἱ ζῶντες τοῖς νεκροῖς θεοῖς οὐ θύομεν καὶ οὐ προσκυνοῦμεν αὐτοῖς ("For we who are living do not sacrifice to dead gods nor do we worship them"); *Diogn.* 2.4–5; *Sib. Or.* 8.393–94 (Jewish or Christian?) δαίμοσι ποι-ήσουσι νεκροῖς, ὡς οὐρανίοισιν,/θρεσκείαν ἄθεον καὶ ὀλέθριον ἐκτελέοντες ("They will do [these

things] for dead demons, as if they were heavenly beings, performing a godless and destructive worship"). Rabbinic texts may be found in Str–B 3.53–60, 377–78.

37 Προσέχειν ἀπό both here in 6.3 and afterward in 12.5 is the work of the Didachist.

38 There is, however, no special reference to the "apostolic decree" (Kleist differs, *Didache*, 5, as does Audet, *Didachè*, 354–57). The other prohibitions are lacking. See Rordorf and Tuilier, *Doctrine*, 33–34.

39 Is the Didachist's position the same as Paul's? Andreas Lindemann (*Paulus im ältesten Christentum* [BHTh 58; Tübingen: Mohr, 1979] 175) writes that while nothing is said about care for the conscience of one's neighbor, "the fundamental attitude is the same as in Paul: the demons are 'nothing,' therefore 'dead'; but for that very reason there can be no question for Christians of owing them any kind of homage" (p. 175). Giet (*L'Énigme*, 191) differs; according to him the *Didache* is stricter than Paul. This question can scarcely be answered at all, because Paul and the *Didache* are on quite different levels of tradition. Later examples of prohibition of eating meat sacrificed to idols can be found in Aristides *Apol.* 15.5 (Goodspeed, 20); Justin *Dial.* 34.8 (Goodspeed, 130); *Ps.-Clem. Hom.* 8.4.2 (GCS² 1.118); 8.1 (120); 8.19.1 (129).

again what high demands the *Kyrios* had raised, demands whose fulfillment is the work of the τέλειος (and him or her alone). The Christian who is not among the τέλειοι should not be dismayed by the high demands stated in 1.3b–2.1, but should fulfill them to the degree that is possible for him or her.

So much for 6.2. In contrast, 6.3 touches a special question that was scarcely mentioned in the tractate but is now added because it was apparently important to the communities for whom the Didachist wrote. This is the question of the attitude one should take toward the Old Testament and Jewish food laws, or to the eating of meat sacrificed to pagan idols. The Didachist's answer is again nuanced: The eating of meat sacrificed to idols is absolutely forbidden; as for the other food laws, individuals may observe them to the extent possible for each one.

Of these two additions, 6.2 is of special importance. Taken together with 1.3b–2.1 it allows us to see how the didachistic redactor has more strongly Christianized the text of the Jewish source (which had received only a superficial Christian veneer before this). Only by means of 1.3b–2.1 was the traditional moral teaching given an eschatological qualification, and 6.2 serves as an interpretation that emphasizes the importance of the *sectio* for understanding the whole. To put it another way: the tractate on the Two Ways that is here quoted is meant, in the intention of the Didachist, to be read in the light of 1.3b–2.1 and 6.2.

Beginning with *Did.* 7.1 we enter a completely different realm. The Didachist had planned to follow his quotation of the Two Ways teaching with a section on the rites commonly used in his communities. The moral catechism is thus succeeded by an "agenda." In it the Didachist apparently makes use of liturgical traditions and probably had a fixed, written set of instructions as his source. To the old tradition (i.e., the source) he adds passages from his own pen.

The old "agenda" the Didachist copied contained two ritual actions, baptism (βάπτισμα) and Eucharist (εὐχαριστία); cf. 1 Corinthians 10–11. (We cannot say whether the communities of the *Didache* were acquainted with other ritual actions.) The exposition in the text first regulates the ritual for baptism, with citation of the ἱερὸς λόγος or "sacred formula" (*Did.* 7.1b). In connection with the directions for baptizing, we encounter the key word "fasting" (i.e., the text speaks of baptismal fasting before the action of baptism in 7.4). This word occasions a short excursus on the question of fasting and, in that connection, on prayer (8.1–3). Thereafter the discussion returns to a depiction of the cultic actions, and then turns to the Eucharist (9.1–10.7). In this section, first the benedictions spoken at the beginning of the

meal are cited (9.1–4), then follows (9.5) a rubric concerning admission to the meal celebration (which I believe to be an addition by the Didachist). Next, 10.1–6 relates the prayers of thanksgiving to be spoken *post coenam* (after the meal). In my opinion 10.7 is another rubrical observation from the pen of the Didachist.

Therefore the whole is constructed as follows:
1. On baptism (7.1–4)
1a. Addition (or excursus): On fasting and prayer (8.1–3)
  a. How to fast (8.1)
  b. How to pray (8.2–3)
2. On the Eucharist (9.1–10.7)
  a. Prayers for the full meal, benedictions over wine and bread (9.1–4; rubric in 9.5)
  b. Prayers of thanksgiving and preface, benedictions after the full meal (10.1–6; rubric in 10.7).

1. On Baptism (7.1–4)

7

1   As for baptism, baptize in this way: Having said all this beforehand, baptize in the name of the Father and of the Son and of the Holy Spirit, in running water.
2   If you [sg. through vv. 2–4] do not have running water, however, baptize in another kind of water; if you cannot [do so] in cold [water], then [do so] in warm [water].
3   But if you have neither, pour water on the head thrice in the name of Father and Son and Holy Spirit.
4   Before the baptism, let the person baptizing and the person being baptized—and others who are able—fast; tell the one being baptized to fast one or two [days] before.

Analysis
Even if the basis of chap. 7 comes from the tradition received by the Didachist, this cannot be true of 7.1b (ταῦτα πάντα προειπόντες, βαπτίσατε). This clause, which connects the liturgical tradition after the fact with the Two Ways tractate, must be the work of the redactor. In my opinion the concession in 7.2–3 is also redac-

tional, in contrast to the original and more rigorous command to baptize "with living water" (ἐν ὕδατι ζῶντι). I also consider 7.4a to be old tradition, and 7.4b redactional. On the whole the section is constructed in such a way that the rubric (7.1a) must originally have been followed by the baptismal formula with the directions about using ὕδωρ ζῶν. Verses 2–3 offer redactional interpretations on the phrase ὕδωρ ζῶν. Verse 4 is appended to deal with the question of baptismal fasting. The closest parallel to this whole section is in Justin *1 Apol.* 61.2–3 (Goodspeed, 70).

Comment

■ **1** I consider the rubrical title περὶ δὲ τοῦ βαπτίσματος, οὕτω βαπτίσατε ("As for baptism, baptize in this way," 7.1a) to be old and believe that it was part of the source.[1] The Didachist wanted to combine the text of the source with the preceding "catechism," and therefore inserted ταῦτα πάντα προειπόντες, βαπτίσατε ("Having said all this beforehand, baptize," 7.1b).[2] By means of this note from the Didachist the preceding tractate acquires its particular social setting.[3] Whereas the Didachist, by inserting 1.3b—2.1 and 6.2–3, gave a more strongly Christian character to the source, he now explicitly defines its function, namely, within the church's life and especially its missionary activity. Thus the Two Ways tractate takes its place in the context of baptismal catechesis, and specifically as instruction before baptism.[4] We can no longer say with certainty whether the Didachist thinks that the text of chaps. 1–6 should be recited verbatim before baptism (i.e., within the context of the ritual action),[5] or whether he means simply that this text is the basis for the catechetical instruction that precedes the rite.[6] In any case, the teaching in chaps. 1–6 is incomplete, and we can be sure that the candidates for baptism received other additional instruction.[7]

Verse 1c quotes the sacred formula of baptism, framed in rubrical expressions:

(βαπτίσατε)	(Baptize)
εἰς τὸ ὄνομα τοῦ πατρὸς	in the name of the Father
καὶ τοῦ υἱοῦ	and of the Son
καὶ τοῦ ἁγίου πνεύματος	and of the Holy Spirit
(ἐν ὕδατι ζῶντι).	(in living water).

Thus the cultic action is fixed in two respects, with regard to the baptismal formula, which is to be spoken during the baptism, and with regard to the "elements" to be used in the ritual action.

The three-part[8] formula is identical with that in Matt 28:19:

Matthew: βαπτίζοντες[9] αὐτοὺς εἰς τὸ ὄνομα
Didache: βαπτίσατε εἰς τὸ ὄνομα

---

1. Analogous is περὶ δὲ τῆς εὐχαριστίας, οὕτω εὐχαριστήσατε (*Did.* 9.1). In this I am proceeding on the assumption that this was a Christian (even though Jewish-Christian) source.

2. Audet (*Didachè*, 58–62, 358) unnecessarily considers this phrase a subsequent gloss. To the contrary: Nautin, "Composition," 206–7; Rordorf, "Two Ways," 154–55; Wengst, *Didache*, 16 n. 54. Rordorf ("Baptism," 213) calls ταῦτα πάντα προειπόντες redactional, as I do. But for him 7.1 belongs with 6.3, which he assigns to the liturgical source (p. 211). Cf. also Rordorf and Tuilier, *Doctrine*, 170 n. 3.

3. One may recall at this point that Athanasius also (*Epistula Festalis* 39, § 11; Preuschen, *Analecta*, 2.45) counted the *Didache* among the writings that are suitable reading for candidates for baptism.

4. It has occasionally been pointed out in this connection that the prebaptismal instruction offered by the Two Ways tractate reveals no dogmatic themes: cf. Harnack, *Lehre*, 22; Vööbus, *Liturgical Traditions*, 19–20. But it is wrong to conclude from this that there was no dogmatic instruction at all in the *Didache* communities. In Bigg and MacLean, *Doctrine*, 19, one may read the sober judgment: "It is going too far to suggest that the *only* preparatory teaching for baptism was that given in chs. i–vi;

wherever the Three Names were used there must have been some definite instruction as to their meaning." According to John Lawson (*A Theological and Historical Introduction to the Apostolic Fathers* [New York: Macmillan, 1961] 79) it is possible that ταῦτα πάντα does not refer to chaps. 1–6 but to oral teaching. This suggestion is quite improbable.

5. Harnack, *Apostellehre*, 2; Funk, *Patres apostolici*, xv; Greiff, *Pascharituale*, 121–26.

6. Knopf, *Lehre*, 21.

7. See n. 4 above.

8. In *Did.* 9.5 we find the short formula εἰς ὄνομα κυρίου; cf. Acts 2:38; 8:16; 10:48; 19:5; *Hermas Vis.* 3.7.3. Rordorf ("Baptism," 217) believes, in accordance with the dominant teaching, that the one-part formula from *Did.* 9.5 is the oldest baptismal formula, and that the three-part formula in 7.1, 3 originated later. Does this dominant teaching really describe the historical situation? Also questionable are Rordorf's additional reflections on the history of the baptismal formula ("Baptism," 217–18); cf. also nn. 11 and 12 below.

9. Variant reading βαπτίσαντες (B D).

10. Schaff, *Church Manual*, 184.

11. Koester, *Synoptische Überlieferung*, 191: the formula does not come from Matthew's Gospel but "from the praxis of the community." For Koester (follow-

Matthew: τοῦ πατρὸς καὶ τοῦ υἱοῦ καὶ τοῦ ἁγίου πνεύματος.

Didache: τοῦ πατρὸς καὶ τοῦ υἱοῦ καὶ τοῦ ἁγίου πνεύματος.

The agreement of the formulae is not explained by the *Didache*'s quoting Matthew's Gospel[10] but—naturally—by their common dependence on the liturgy. Matt 28:19 and *Did.* 7.1 (and 7.3) represent the oldest attestations of the three-part formula.[11] Cf. Justin *1 Apol.* 61.3 (Goodspeed, 70): ἐπ᾽ ὀνόματος γὰρ τοῦ πατρὸς τῶν ὅλων καὶ δεσπότου θεοῦ καὶ τοῦ σωτῆρος ἡμῶν Ἰησοῦ Χριστοῦ καὶ πνεύματος ἁγίου τὸ ἐν τῷ ὕδατι τότε λουτρὸν ποιοῦνται ("they then perform the bath in the water, in the name of the Father of the universe and of our Savior Jesus Christ and of the Holy Spirit"); and further at 61.10 and 13 (Goodspeed, 71).[12]

The "element" with which baptism is to be performed is explicitly called ὕδωρ ζῶν (βαπτίσατε . . . ἐν ὕδατι ζῶντι), a Semitism for מים חיים, "living water," that is, flowing, fresh spring water. This direction indicates a Jewish-Christian interest. The Levitical rite in Lev 14:5–9, 50–53 demands, among other things, the use of "living water" for purification from leprosy[13]—that is, fresh spring water (as distinct from standing water in a cistern). Note also the bath for purification of the זב (one with a discharge) in Lev 15:13.[14] In addition, the water for purification in Numbers 19 is to be prepared

from "living water" (Num 19:17). Compare also, from the early Jewish period, the sprinkling with water for purification in 1QS 3.9, and the ritual bath in flowing water in *Sib. Or.* 4.165: ἐν ποταμοῖς λούσασθε ὅλον δέμας ἀενάοισιν ("wash the whole body in perennial rivers"). In the mishnaic tradition (see below) "living water," that is, pure, flowing spring water, has the highest rank within the classification of kinds of water (*m. Mik.* 1.8). In *Did.* 7.1 it is, of course, not a question of Jewish ritual practices[15] but of baptism; nevertheless, in the demand that ὕδωρ ζῶν (i.e., the best and most effective kind of water) be used for baptism we sense the influence of Jewish traditionalism.[16] We may even suspect that at an earlier stage of Jewish-Christian praxis that peeks through here flowing water was required, without exception, for the performance of baptism, because only this kind of water was supposed to have the necessary power of lustration.[17]

■ **2–3** This (suggested) view of things was no longer adopted by the author of the subsequent text, namely, the redactor. On the contrary, if there is a lack of ὕδωρ ζῶν, that is, fresh spring or river water, it is permissible to baptize with other kinds of water (v. 2).[18] Various kinds of water are mentioned, in descending order of acceptability: (ὕδωρ) ψυχρόν, which probably means water taken or diverted from a spring or river but still

ing well-known models), however, the analogous formula in Matt 28:19 is apparently secondary. Thus for him the *Didache* passage is the oldest attestation (p. 192). Vööbus (*Liturgical Traditions*, 36–39) has still a third interpretation, that the trinitarian formula arose only around the middle of the 2d century. It was subsequently introduced not only into Matthew's Gospel but also into *Didache* 7. The one-part baptismal formula in *Did.* 9.5 is the original. But there is no real reason to suppose that there is a gloss in 7.1, 3. Moreover, in my opinion, 9.5 is redactional. See below.

12   In *Dial.* 39.2 (Goodspeed, 135), it appears that Justin is alluding to the one-part formula. Rordorf ("Baptism," 217–18) assigns the two formulae to the Jewish-Christian (one-part) and gentile Christian (three-part) missions. But no argument for that can be derived from the *Didache* at any rate. Instead, the *Didache* seems to use the two formulae promiscuously.

13   The complicated Levitical rite is prescribed in Lev 14:4–9. Lev 14:50–53 deals with leprosy in houses.

Cf. Karl Elliger, *Leviticus* (HAT 4; Tübingen: Mohr [Siebeck], 1966) 186–91. For this question and the whole section, cf. also Leonhard Goppelt, "ὕδωρ," *TDNT* 8 (1972) 320, 332.

14   LXX B A has only ὕδατι. On the whole subject, see Elliger, *Leviticus*, 198.

15   Peterson ("Probleme," 159 n. 48) claims, "It is possible that in the *Didache* directions regarding (probably Jewish-Christian) baths have been mixed with directions for baptism." This is entirely speculative.

16   We owe the correct understanding of this passage to Klauser, "Taufet," 177–83; and Vööbus, *Liturgical Traditions*, 22–23. Both Klauser (p. 178) and Vööbus (p. 23) also assume that baptism *in aqua viva* was the practice of Christians from the beginning.

17   For Vööbus (*Liturgical Traditions*, 25) the text reflects the course of a development that abandoned an originally strict praxis.

18   According to Audet (*Didachè*, 357–67), vv. 2–4 are the work of an interpolator. In my opinion the redactor speaks in vv. 2–3. So also, previously, for Rordorf ("Baptism," 213–15) vv. 2–3 are redaction-

possessing its original, "cool" temperature.[19] If that is not available baptism may be performed ἐν (ὕδατι) θερμῷ. This does not mean water that has been "warmed" (perhaps out of concern for the sick),[20] but probably standing water in cisterns or the like, that is, water that no longer has its fresh temperature.[21] Finally, in case neither is available (one might add, in sufficient quantity), ἔκχεον εἰς τὴν κεφαλὴν τρὶς ὕδωρ κτλ. (v. 3).[22]

The water is to be poured[23] three times over the head of the one to be baptized,[24] apparently in reference to the three-part formula that — not accidentally — is again[25] repeated here. Cf. Tertullian *Adversus Praxean* 26.9 (CChrSL 2.1198): *Nam nec semel sed ter ad singula nomina in personas singulas tinguimur* ("We baptize not all

at once but three times, for each of the names of each of the persons [of the Trinity]").[26]

Excursus: Types of Water

The whole of *Did.* 7.2 is apparently concerned with the evaluation of types of water in descending order from best (ὕδωρ ζῶν) to less and less good (ψυχρόν, θερμόν). Cf. the classification of kinds of water in six classes (although in ascending order) in the rabbinic tradition (*m. Mik.* 1.1–8);[27] the *Didache* is not, of course, concerned with Jewish rites of lustration but with the sacrament of baptism. In addition, the classifications do not always agree in detail. The Jewish tradition is still influential, but in principle it has already been ruptured. The point in *Did.* 7.2–3 is that one should use the most appropriate water available for baptism. Still, the effect of baptism is unques-

al, as is v. 4b. In this respect the shift to the singular is not the decisive argument (the change of number is not compelling in itself); what is key to the decision is the concession made toward a formerly strict praxis. In addition, it may be said that the singular can scarcely be addressed to the leaders of the communities, because the Didachist appears not yet acquainted with the monepiscopate. See below. Schöllgen ("Church Order," 48, 66) suspects that 7.2, 3, 4b was a piece of tradition.

19 Vööbus, *Liturgical Traditions*, 24.

20 That was the earlier opinion: Bryennios, Διδαχή, 29 n. 4; Harnack, *Lehre*, 23; Funk, *Patres apostolici*, 1.18; Drews, "Apostellehre," 268; Knopf, *Lehre*, 22. Peterson ("Probleme," 160–61) suggested a sectarian praxis. To the contrary, and correctly: Vööbus, *Liturgical Traditions*, 24.

21 Vööbus, *Liturgical Traditions*, 24. For the meaning of cold water in Jewish baptizing groups, Vööbus (p. 24 and nn. 50 and 51) refers to Bannus in Josephus *Vita* 11: ψυχρῷ δὲ ὕδατι τὴν ἡμέραν καὶ τὴν νύκτα πολλάκις λουόμενον πρὸς ἁγνείαν ("frequently washing himself with cold water day and night for the sake of purity"), and the Elkesites in Hippolytus *Ref.* 9.16.1 (GCS 3.254): καὶ βαπτίζεσθαι ἐν ψυχρῷ τεσσαρακοντάκις ἐπὶ ἡμέρας ἑπτά ("and baptizing in cold water forty times in seven days").

22 The baptism spoken of here has nothing to do with the baptism of the *clinici*.

23 Ἐκχεῖν for pouring water is found only here in our literature.

24 For the pouring of the water over the baptizand, cf. the sarcophagus of Santa Maria Antiqua in Rome, 3d century (Frederik van der Meer and Christine Mohrmann, *Atlas of the Early Christian World* [London: Nelson, 1966] plate 45); the wall paintings in the catacombs of Saints Peter and Marcellinus,

4th century (plate 396); the lid of a grave from ca. 400 (plate 397). Cf. also the illustrations in Pillinger, "Taufe," after p. 160. Pillinger ("Taufe," 152–60) has attempted to show that the *Didache* presumes a "kind of baptisterium" (p. 157).

25 Minus the article.

26 Cf. also Hippolytus *Apost. Trad.* 21 (SC 11.84–96). [Ed. On this passage in general see also Nathan Mitchell, "Baptism in the Didache," in Jefford, *Context*, 226–55.]

27 1.1: "There are six grades among pools of water, one more excellent than another. The water in ponds. . . ." 1.6: "More excellent is the water of a rain-pond before the rain-stream has stopped." 1.7: "More excellent is a pool of water containing forty *seahs*. . . . More excellent is a well whose own water is little in quantity and which is increased by a greater part of drawn water." 1.8: "More excellent are smitten waters which render clean such time as they are flowing water. More excellent than they are living waters" (Herbert Danby, *The Mishnah* [Oxford: Clarendon, 1933] 732–33). See Str–B 1.108–9. Particular kinds of water are suited or not suited to particular lustrations (cf. Str–B 1.108–9).

28 The suggestion of Drews ("Apostellehre," 268) that the author is not so much concerned with the pouring of the water as with the baptismal formula itself is misleading; it anachronistically separates what the text takes for granted as belonging together. The tendency is quite different. Rigorous demands regarding the water for baptism are being liberalized. In my opinion reflections like this speak in favor of the supposition that vv. 2–3 are redactional. The redactor is still influenced by the milieu of Jewish-Christian traditions, but is judiciously stepping outside them when these traditions appear

tioned even if the water is less suitable and even if baptism consists solely of pouring water on the head.[28] This presumes that baptism normally takes place outdoors;[29] in addition, the discussion can best be located in a region that notoriously suffers from water shortages (which makes Egypt most unlikely).[30]

We should note in passing that the whole question also plays a certain part in the *Ps.-Clementine* tradition.[31] There is still an influence from Jewish-Christian tradition perceptible in Hippolytus *Apost. Trad.* 21 (Sahidic) (SC 11.80): *Sit aqua fluens in fonte* (κολυμβήθρα) *vel fluens de alto. Fiat autem hoc modo, nisi sit aliqua necessitas* (ἀνάγκη). *Si autem necessitas* (ἀνάγκη) *est permanens et urgens, utere* (χρῆσθαι) *aquam quam invenis* ("Let there be flowing water in the font, but flowing from above. Let it be done in this fashion, unless there be some other need. If, however, there is some continuing and pressing need, use whatever water you find"). The mentality is somewhat the same here as in the *Didache*.[32] Understandably the gentile Christianity of a later period no longer experienced this problem. Tertullian *De bapt.* 4.3 (CChrSL 1.280): *ideoque nulla*

distinctio est, mari quis an stagno, flumine an fonte, lacu an alveo diluantur ("Therefore there is no difference whether one uses for lustration ocean water or standing water, a river or a fountain, a lake or a spring").[33]

■ **4** The next verse adds a rule about fasting, which is to precede baptism as support and preparation.[34] In my view v. 4a again comes from the liturgy that served as source for the Didachist.[35] Προνηστεύειν ("fast beforehand") is a rare word,[36] found only here in early Christian literature.[37] Those who are to fast include (1) the one who baptizes, (2) the one to be baptized, and (3) εἴ τινες ἄλλοι δύνανται ("others if they are able"). "The baptizer and baptizand *must* fast, and others *may*" (Knopf, *Lehre*, 22). For the fasting of the one to be baptized, cf. Justin *1 Apol.* 61.2 (Goodspeed, 70): εὔχεσθαί τε καὶ αἰτεῖν νηστεύοντες παρὰ τοῦ θεοῦ τῶν προημαρτημένων ἄφεσιν διδάσκονται ("They are taught to pray and ask from God forgiveness for their previous sins, while they fast"). Hippolytus *Apost. Trad.* 20

---

29 — Thus probably also Justin *1 Apol.* 61.3 (Goodspeed, 70): ἔπειτα ἄγονται ὑφ᾽ ἡμῶν ἔνθα ὕδωρ ἐστί ("then they are brought by us to where there is water"). Pillinger ("Taufe") differs.

30 Knopf, *Lehre*, 22. See above, Introduction § 7b.

31 The term ζῶν ὕδωρ is found in the (reconstructed) *Kerygmata Petrou: Contestatio* 1.2 (GCS² 1.3); cf. *Ps.-Clem. Hom.* 11.26.2 (167) and 26.4 (ibid.), although there in the framework of a gnosticizing baptismal doctrine. The baptismal water is called ζῶν ὕδωρ "not only because it is flowing river or spring water, but because 'living water' is what imparts ζῆν [life]" (Georg Strecker, *Das Judenchristentum in den Pseudoklementinen* [2d ed.; TU 70; Berlin: Akademie-Verlag, 1981] 202; for the baptismal doctrine of the *Kerygmata* in general, pp. 196–209). Lacking the term "living water," and without the gnosticizing point, but still shaped by the Jewish tradition of the special lustrative power of flowing spring or river water, or seawater, is a series of passages from the later strata of the *Pseudo-Clementine* novel, as Strecker pointed out (*Judenchristentum*, 202 n. 2): *Hom.* 11.35.1 (171: ἀγαγών με εἰς τὰς ἐν τῇ θαλάσσῃ πλησίον οὔσας πηγάς, ὡς εἰς ἀέναον ἐβάπτισεν ὕδωρ, "leading me to the fountains that are near the sea, he baptized me in the ever flowing water"); cf. *Rec.* 6.15.2 (GCS 2.196); *Hom.* 11.36.2 (GCS² 1.172); *Hom.* 9.19.4 (GCS² 1.139): ἀενάῳ ποταμῷ ἢ πηγῇ ἐπεί γε κἂν θαλάσσῃ ἀπολουσάμενοι); cf. *Rec.* 4.32.2 (GCS 2.162). The *Pseudo-*

to him inappropriate; in doing so, he is orienting himself to the Great Church.

Clementine tradition is, in any case, more traditionalist (in relation to the Jewish-Christian tradition) than the *Didache* in restricting baptism to the kinds of water listed.

32 Other examples from the early period are found in Klauser, "Taufet," 179. Klauser believed he could show that the Latin term *fons* for the baptismal font echoed the old custom (pp. 180–81).

33 According to Klauser ("Taufet," 180) this passage in Tertullian is polemical in its intention (against the demand for *aqua viva*).

34 For the motifs associated with Christian baptism (nothing needed to be said about these in the text), cf. Dölger, *Taufritual*, 80–86; Knopf, *Lehre*, 22; Vööbus, *Liturgical Traditions*, 20.

35 Cf. Rordorf, "Baptism," 215.

36 LSJ and BAGD, *s.v.*, indicate only Herodotus 2.40 (Hude) and Hippocrates *De nat. mul.* 95, προνηστεύσασαν ἐπὶ δύο ἡμέρας ("they fast beforehand for two days," Littré, 7.412; cf. *De morb. mul.* 1.78; Littré, 8.178).

37 Lampe, *s.v.*, notes, besides *Didache*, Ammonius of Alexandria, *Fragmenta in Acta apostolorum* 13.2 (*PG* 85.1541A). Wengst (*Didache*) has νηστευσάτω in this passage like *Constitutions*.

(Sahidic) (SC 11.78): *Ieiunent* (νηστεύειν) *qui accipient baptismum, in parasceve* (παρασκευή) *sabbati* (σάββατον) ("Those who are to be baptized fast on the day of preparation for the Sabbath"). Tertullian *De bapt.* 20.1 (CChrSL 1.294): *Ingressuros baptismum orationibus crebris, ieiuniis et geniculationibus et pervigiliis orare oportet* ("It is fitting for those who will undergo baptism to pray with frequent prayers, fasts, genuflections and vigils"). Fasting by the baptizer and others before baptism is found (implicitly) in *Ps.-Clem. Hom.* 13.12.1 (GCS² 1.199); cf. (explicitly) *Rec.* 7.37.1 (GCS 2.214). Justin, however, already attests community participation in the fast in the continuation of the passage quoted above: ἡμῶν συνευχομένων καὶ συννηστευόντων αὐτοῖς ("while we pray and fast along with them").[38] This practice of joining in the fast with others appears to have declined very early.[39] It is striking that even v. 4b speaks only of the fasting of the one to be baptized. Here again (as in vv. 2–3) the command appears in the singular; in my opinion, v. 4b is also part of the redaction.[40] At the time of this redaction, only the person to be baptized still fasted. In addition, the redactor, perhaps in a polemic against other usages, fixes the length of the fast: πρὸ μιᾶς (sc. ἡμέρας), that is, the one to be baptized fasts for one whole day before baptism.[41] In summary, in chap. 7 the Didachist took over a more rigorous Jewish-Christian source, liberalized it by adding to it, and adjusted or adapted it to his own situation.

---

38 For the whole, see Johannes Behm, "νῆστις," *TDNT* 4 (1967) 933–35; Johannes Schümmer, *Altchristliche Fastenpraxis*, 164–78.

39 Vööbus, *Liturgical Traditions*, 21. Dölger (*Taufritual*, 87) connects the order in *Did.* 7.4 with the one-day or two-day Easter fast of the entire community. This can scarcely be correct.

40 Rordorf, "Baptism," 215. Κελεύεις [or κελεύσεις, Bryennios's conjecture, Διδαχη, 29, and elsewhere] δὲ νηστεῦσαι . . . can scarcely be addressed to the leader of the community (cf. the cautious suggestions of Rordorf, ibid.).

41 For this expression, cf. *Hermas Sim.* 6.5.3: τί πρὸ μιᾶς ἔπραξεν ("what he had done one day before").

A baptismal fast πρὸ μιᾶς is prescribed in *Ps.-Clem. Hom.* 13.11.4 (GCS² 1.199). On this subject (fasting on the day before baptism), cf. also *Hom.* 13.9.3 (198); *Rec.* 7.34.3 (GCS 2.213); *Hom.* 13.10.7 (198); *Rec.* 7.35.7 (214); *Hom.* 13.12.1 (199); *Rec.* 7.37.1 (214). Still, the *Pseudo-Clementines* are also familiar with prebaptismal fasting over more than one day: *Hom.* 3.73.1 (83), a fast of three months before baptism; *Hom.* 11.35.1 (171); *Rec.* 3.67.1–5 (141). The differences in length are probably to be explained by more or less strict forms of fasting: Schümmer, *Altchristliche Fastenpraxis*, 167–68.

1a. Addition: On Fasting and Prayer

The key word "fasting" (*Did.* 7.4) suggested the introduction of a number of further directions regarding fasting in general (thus these regulations no longer concern baptismal fasting in particular). Associated with these is a section on prayer—in accordance with the traditional combination of fasting and prayer.[1] This was the origin of chap. 8, which has the character of an excursus within the section on community rituals. It is clear that 8.1–3 is an addition. That need not mean, of course, that this section was only introduced after the fact. In my opinion it is rather the case that the Didachist is again writing on the basis of the tradition available to him. Only the clause ὡς ἐκέλευσεν ὁ κύριος ἐν τῷ εὐαγγελίῳ αὐτοῦ (in 8.2) is attributable to the redactor.

8

a. How to Fast (8.1)

1 Let your fasts not [take place] with [those of] the wicked. They fast on Monday and Thursday; you, though, should fast on Wednesday and Friday.

Comment

■ **1** The introductory phrase αἱ δὲ νηστεῖαι ὑμῶν ("your fasts") makes immediately clear that Christians fast regularly (we might say: as a matter of course). These are freely chosen days of fasting imposed by individual Christians on themselves. (Nothing is said about the motives for such fasting.) Thus this section is not intended to introduce the custom of fasting but simply to fix the commonly accepted custom in a certain way and with more precision. In particular (as will appear immediately) this specification has to do with the *time* for fasting. The whole passage presupposes the customary fasting of pious Jews, to which the customs of those addressed by this text are primarily and generally oriented. It is, however, the intention of the text to make a distinction in the choice of times in order to document the difference between Christian fasting and that of pious Jews. Christian fasting is to be distinguished from that of the ὑποκριταί.[2] Probably here as well as elsewhere,[3] ὑποκριτής is a designation for "deviants," or "the wicked," those who have turned away from true religion. Thus in this passage it is probably a general reference to

---

1   Cf. Ezra 8:23; Neh 1:4; 9:1–2; Pss 35:13; 69:11–13; 109:24–26; Jer 14:12; Dan 9:3; Joel 1:14; 2:12; Jdt 4:9–12; 1 Macc 3:47–54; 2 Macc 13:12; Tob 12:8; Matt 6:5–13 and 6:16–18 par.; Luke 2:37; 18:10–14; Acts 13:2–3; 14:23.

2   This obviously recalls Matt 6:16–18: "The author of the Didache seems to refer his readers to the hypocrites about whom the Gospel of Mt. speaks; in speaking of fasting, he has in mind the words of Mt. which prescribe not to fast like the hypocrites" (Massaux, *Influence*, 3.155). This can scarcely be the case. Koester (*Synoptische Überlieferung*, 202) writes: "The content of the

rule for fasting is . . . quite different in Matthew and the *Didache*." The word ὑποκριταί does refer to Matthew, "at least to the legal saying reproduced in Matt 6:16–18, which may, of course, have been known to the *Didache* from independent tradition" (p. 203). In my opinion there *may* be a recollection of the Jesus tradition behind this verse, but there *need not* be.

3   Cf. above, at *Did.* 2.6 and 4.12. Wilckens, "ὑποκρίνομαι," *TDNT* 8 (1972) 569: "ὑπόκρισις is apostasy from God and from orthodoxy."

the pious of Israel; it is improbable that it means the Pharisees in particular.[4] In the blanket condemnation[5] (ὑποκριταί) we find the expression of the contrast between two groups. The concern is not with individuals but with the overall phenomenon of a group whose piety is being rejected. The hypocrisy of the others need not be proved; it is already established, for both the writer and the addressees. The ὑποκριταί fast δευτέρᾳ (sc. ἡμέρᾳ) σαββάτων, that is, on Monday, and πέμπτῃ (sc. ἡμέρᾳ), that is, on Thursday. To distinguish themselves from those others the Christians should fast on different days, namely, τετράδα (sc. ἡμέραν), that is, on Wednesday, and παρασκευήν,[6] that is, on the eve of the Sabbath, which is Friday.[7] The weekdays are designated according to the customary Jewish reckoning.[8] This passage provides the oldest attestation of Christian fasting on those two days of the week.

The sharp polemic against the ὑποκριταί, and the necessity of distinguishing oneself from the fasting customs of the pious Jews by the choice of other fast days, presumes (on the one hand) an ongoing, close contact between the communities reflected here and their Jewish environment. On the other hand, the text requires us to suppose that these communities are in the process of separating themselves from the religious communion of Israel, or else they have already done so.

Excursus: Jewish Fasting Practice

The text of the *Didache* alludes to the fasting customs of pious and enlightened Jews that established individual, private days of fasting in addition to those that were obligatory for all. Here it is necessary again to differentiate between occasional and regular private fasting; the latter (not only, but frequently) took place two days a week (cf. Luke 18:12), and Monday and Thursday were commonly chosen for this.[9] The most zealous private fasters included the Haberim, but they had no generally obligatory rule for fasting on Mondays and Thursdays. On this whole subject, see Str–B 2.241–44; 4.77–114; Johannes Behm, "νῆστις," *TDNT* 4 (1967) 929–31.

The rules for Jewish-Christian liturgical praxis copied by the Didachist probably refer also to freely chosen private fasting, not to obligatory fasting by the entire community.[10] The choice of fast days[11] is based on a deliberate deviation from the Jewish fast days.[12] We cannot say for certain why the choice fell

---

4   Thus Bryennios, Διδαχή, 30 n. 1; Schaff, *Church Manual*, 187. The key text in Matt 6:16, ὅταν δὲ νηστεύητε, μὴ γίνεσθε ὡς οἱ ὑποκριταὶ σκυθρωποί κτλ., has no reference to a class or group (although in Matthew it is not the time, as in the *Didache*, but the type of fasting that is criticized; see n. 2 above). In the *Didache*, ὑποκριταί can mean the Jews in general, the Pharisees in particular, or (still more generally) the pious of Israel. I consider this last the most probable interpretation. Interesting also is Rordorf, "Didachè," 23 n. 30: "probably . . . Christians who are tempted to imitate Jewish practices." This possibility was already considered by Schümmer, *Altchristliche Fastenpraxis*, 84.

5   Wilckens, "ὑποκρίνομαι," 569. Wilckens also points to the usage in the Pastorals (1 Tim 4:2); *Hermas Sim.* 8.6.5; 9.18.3; 19.2–3; and in his n. 57 to the contrary passage in *Gen. Rab.* 48.6, on Gen 18:1: "Whenever *channufa* occurs in Scripture, it refers to heresy" (*Midrash Rabbah I, Genesis I*, trans. Freedman, 407).

6   For the accusatives τετράδα and παρασκευήν, cf. BDF, §161.3.

7   This passage may be quoted in *Lib. grad.* 7.20 (Kmosko, 183). See above.

8   Str–B 1.1052; Eduard Lohse, "σάββατον κτλ.,"

TDNT 7 (1971) 6–7. Cf. *Const.* 5.14: δευτέρᾳ σαββάτων . . . τῇ τρίτῃ τοῦ σαββάτου . . . τῇ δὲ τετράδι . . . (14.1) . . . καὶ τῇ πέμπτῃ . . . (14.6) . . . παρασκευῆς οὔσης (14.10). . . .

9   Cf. Schümmer, *Altchristliche Fastenpraxis*, 84–99; on the Pharisees' fasting: Epiphanius *Pan.* 16.1.5 (GCS 1.211). For the choice of days: Str–B 2.243 n. 2.

10 This was different at a later time; cf. as early as *Didasc.* (Syriac) 21 (CSCO 407.208; 408.192). We cannot discuss here Tertullian *De ieiun.* (CChrSL 2.1257ff.) and the questions associated with it (e.g., the intensification of fasting among the Montanists).

11 For this whole question, cf. also Cremer, *Fastenansage*, 10–21.

12 It is important that also in the *Didasc.* (Syriac) 21 the fast days are deliberately distinguished from the corresponding usage in Jewish communities: "However, [fast] not according to the custom of the former people, but according to the new covenant which I have set up to [*sic*] you" (CSCO 408.191). I do not believe that the *Didascalia* here depends on the *Didache*. (See above.)

13 Hans Lietzmann considered this interpretation accurate (*A History of the Early Church* [4 vols. in 2; trans. Bertram Lee Woolf; 3d ed.; London:

on Wednesday and Friday. Later these two days were associated with events in the Lord's passion, with Friday (understandably enough) being connected with the day of the Lord's death, and Wednesday (for example) with the day of his arrest (thus *Didasc.* [Syriac] 21 [CSCO 407.208; 408.191–92]).[13] But nothing of this nature can be suggested for the *Didache*.[14] The association with the days of the passion was alto-gether a subsequent invention. Knopf attempted to show[15] that Tuesday or Wednesday and Friday were the only possible alternatives to the Jewish fast days, but why, in that case, the choice fell on Wednesday is something we cannot say.[16]

Lutterworth, 1953] 1.69). Schümmer (*Altchristliche Fastenpraxis*, 97–98) thought of the events of the passion in general.

14 Audet, *Didachè*, 368–69; Josef Blinzler, "Qumran-Kalender und Passionschronologie," *ZNW* 49 (1958) 243–44.

15 Knopf, *Lehre*, 23.

16 Blinzler (*ZNW* 49 [1958] 245) inquired whether the choice of Wednesday was influenced by the calendar of the Qumran Essenes. Annie Jaubert ("Jésus et le calendrier de Qumrân," *NTS* 7 [1960/61] 27–28) favors the influence of the old priestly calendar for the question of the choice of Wednesday and Friday. All this is highly improbable.

b. How to Pray (8.2–3)

2 And do not pray as the wicked [do]; pray
instead this way, as the Lord directed in his
gospel:
Our Father who are in heaven,
May your name be acclaimed as holy,
May your kingdom come,
May your will come to pass on earth as it does
in heaven.
Give us today our daily bread,
And cancel for us our debt,
As we cancel [debts] for those who are indebt-
ed to us,
And do not bring us into temptation,
But preserve us from evil [or, from the evil
one].
For power and glory are yours forever.
3 Pray this way thrice daily.

Analysis

The directions for fasting are followed by others on prayer (*Did.* 8.2–3). Just as Christians should be distinguished from pious Jews by fasting on different days, so also their prayer customs should differ. Christians should (regularly, as we will learn) use a different prayer from that of the "hypocrites" (ὑποκριταί). It seems reasonable to think that this allusion to the prayer of the ὑποκριταί refers concretely to the *Shemoneh Esreh*, the *Tefillah* as such.[1] It is by no means necessary (although of course it is possible) to suppose the individual Jewish Christians within the region of this liturgy's tradition still regularly prayed the *Tefillah*.[2] In any case this is forbidden by the liturgical and catechetical instructions here. The Lord's prayer is to take the place of the Jewish *Tefillah*. But the instruction in *Did.* 8.2 has nothing to do with the introduction of the cursing of the *minim*[3] in the twelfth benediction of the *Tefillah*.[4]

Comment

■ **2** The Didachist may have (clumsily) inserted the passage ὡς ἐκέλευσεν ὁ κύριος (= Jesus)[5] ἐν τῷ εὐαγγελίῳ αὐτοῦ ("as the Lord directed in his gospel") into the

1 For the *Tefillah* see Str–B 1.406–7; 2.696–702 (times of prayer); 4.208–10; Ismar Elbogen, *Der jüdische Gottesdienst in seiner geschichtlichen Entwicklung* (1913; repr. Hildesheim: Olms, 1962) 27–41 (ET: *Jewish Liturgy: A Comprehensive History* [Philadelphia: Jewish Publication Society; New York: Jewish Theological Seminary of America, 1993] 24–37); Karl Georg Kuhn, *Achtzehngebet und Vaterunser und der Reim* (WUNT 1; Tübingen: Mohr, 1950) 10–26.

2 This is suggested as a possibility by Drews, "Apostellehre," 269; more definitely by Knopf, *Lehre*, 23.

3 For the *Birkat Ha-Minim*, see Str–B 4.218–19; Elbogen, *Jüdische Gottesdienst*, 36–41, 252–53 (ET: *Jewish Liturgy*, 45–46, 200–201), with the otherwise widespread but questionable opinion that the twelfth benediction was deliberately aimed at (Jewish) Christians; see Johann Maier, *Jüdische Auseinandersetzung mit dem Christentum in der Antike* (EdF 177; Darmstadt: Wissenschaftliche Buchgesellschaft, 1982) 136–41, with bibliography.

4 It is uncertain whether the *Birkat Ha-Minim* refers at all to Jewish Christians (among others); it is questionable whether the benediction was meant to make public the identity of the heretics (as has often been asserted); and it is equally problematic whether the benediction played any role at all in the separation of church and synagogue. Cf. now the skepticism of Maier, *Jüdische Auseinandersetzung*, 137–41; and previously Günter Stemberger, "Die sogenannte 'Synode von Jabne' und das frühe Christentum," *Kairos* 19 (1977) 16–21. See Peter Schäfer, "Die sogenannte Synode von Jabne: Zur Trennung von Juden und Christen im ersten/zweiten Jhdt. n Chr.," now collected in his *Studien zur Geschichte und Theologie des rabbinischen Judentums* (AGJU 15; Leiden: Brill, 1978) 45–55 ("in any case not exclusively against Jewish Christians or [later] Christians," p. 51); in the same place he denies that the benediction served to separate church and synagogue.

5 Likewise, title 4.1 (bis) (?); 6.2; 9.5 (bis); 10.5; 11.2 (bis); 11.4, 8; 12.1; 14.1; 15.1, 4; 16.1, 7, 8. To the contrary: 4.12, 13; 14.3 (bis) (?).

Table 9

Matt 6:9–13	Did. 8.2	Luke 11:2–4
Πάτερ ἡμῶν ὁ ἐν τοῖς οὐρανοῖς	Πάτερ ἡμῶν ὁ ἐν τῷ οὐρανῷ	Πάτερ,
ἁγιασθήτω τὸ ὄνομά σου,	ἁγιασθήτω τὸ ὄνομά σου,	ἁγιασθήτω τὸ ὄνομά σου,
ἐλθέτω ἡ βασιλεία σου,	ἐλθέτω ἡ βασιλεία σου,	ἐλθέτω ἡ βασιλεία σου,
γενηθήτω τὸ θέλημά σου	γενηθήτω* τὸ θέλημά σου	
ὡς ἐν οὐρανῷ καὶ ἐπὶ γῆς·	ὡς ἐν οὐρανῷ καὶ ἐπὶ γῆς·	
τὸν ἄρτον ἡμῶν τὸν ἐπιούσιον	τὸν ἄρτον ἡμῶν τὸν ἐπιούσιον	τὸν ἄρτον ἡμῶν τὸν ἐπιούσιον
δὸς ἡμῖν σήμερον·	δὸς ἡμῖν σήμερον,	δίδου ἡμῖν τὸ καθ᾽ ἡμέραν·
καὶ ἄφες ἡμῖν τὰ ὀφειλήματα ἡμῶν,	καὶ ἄφες ἡμῖν τὴν ὀφειλὴν ἡμῶν,	καὶ ἄφες ἡμῖν τὰς ἁμαρτίας ἡμῶν,
ὡς καὶ ἡμεῖς ἀφήκαμεν τοῖς	ὡς καὶ ἡμεῖς ἀφίεμεν τοῖς	καὶ γὰρ αὐτοὶ ἀφίομεν παντὶ
ὀφειλέταις ἡμῶν·	ὀφειλέταις ἡμῶν·	ὀφείλοντι ἡμῖν·
καὶ μὴ εἰσενέγκης ἡμᾶς	καὶ μὴ εἰσενέγκης ἡμᾶς	καὶ μὴ εἰσενέγκης ἡμᾶς
εἰς πειρασμόν,	εἰς πειρασμόν,	εἰς πειρασμόν.
ἀλλὰ ῥῦσαι ἡμᾶς ἀπὸ τοῦ πονηροῦ.	ἀλλὰ ῥῦσαι ἡμᾶς ἀπὸ τοῦ πονηροῦ·	
	ὅτι σοῦ ἐστιν ἡ δύναμις καὶ ἡ δόξα	
	εἰς τοὺς αἰῶνας.	

*H has (mistakenly) γεννηθήτω, which has been emended since Bryennios.

source. The prayer to be spoken thus appears as a direct order from the *Kyrios*, a mandate that the Lord commanded "in his gospel." By εὐαγγέλιον, the Didachist means either the living voice of the gospel or a written gospel.[6] It is difficult to decide. In any case the gospel of the *Kyrios* is seen by this author as an obligatory instruction. The word ἐκέλευσεν is characteristic. The Lord establishes an order and a commandment in the gospel that regulates what Christians are to do.[7] This is true in general (and will appear again and again; cf. *Did.* 11.3 and 15.3–4). In the concrete case the instruction of the Lord is particularly concerned with the prayer to be used by Christians.[8] For the Didachist the *Kyrios* in his gospel had, among other things, given specific directions regarding prayer.

The prayer that follows, the Lord's Prayer, would have been found already in the liturgy that served the Didachist as source, but it is utterly impossible to decide whether the Didachist modified the given wording (perhaps according to the liturgical tradition familiar to him, or according to the wording of a gospel text before him). It is clear only that the text of the prayer as we now have it agrees strongly with the one handed on by Matthew,

---

6 Knopf, *Lehre*, 23: *Evangelium* is "naturally not *one* particular, individual gospel, but, according to common usage, the proclamation of and about the Lord." The author must already have Matthew 6 in mind for the entire passage, however, and he alludes to it in writing ἐκέλευσεν ὁ κύριος ("the Lord directed"); Lake ("Didache," 28) claims, "the writer seems clearly familiar with a definite statement of Christ's teaching, though hardly a written one, cf. αὐτοῦ after ἐν τῷ εὐαγγελίῳ." Ἐκέλευσεν is also said to indicate oral tradition (p. 30); Massaux (*Influence*, 3.145, and passim) thinks it alludes to the Gospel of Matthew; Koester (*Synoptische Überliefe-*

rung, 10) thinks that "*evangelium*" in *Did.* 8.2 means the *viva vox*, "although an interpretation in terms of a written gospel is not entirely impossible" (p. 203). Cf. p. 209: "In retrospect we may say that . . . the word εὐαγγέλιον in *Did.* 8.2 does, in fact, appear to refer to oral preaching." Cf. also p. 240. For the whole subject, see n. 10 below, and Introduction, §7a(2).

7 For the gospel as *regula vitae christianae* see above, Introduction, § 7a(2).

8 Οὕτω probably does not fix the wording (any more than does οὕτως in Matt 6:9); instead, it characterizes the prayer that follows as a paradigm; so G. J.

with some characteristic deviations from the latter.[9] It is hard to suppose that the *Didache* quotes directly from the text of Matthew's Gospel.[10] The agreements would rest on a common liturgical tradition.

Excursus: The Text of the Lord's Prayer

We will trace the differences between the *Didache* and the Matthean text.[11] The singular ἐν τῷ οὐρανῷ ("in heaven") in place of the plural in Matthew is essentially meaningless.[12] In the "fifth petition" we find τὴν ὀφειλήν ("debt") against Matthew's τὰ ὀφειλή-ματα ("debts").[13] The *Didache*'s ἀφίεμεν ("we forgive") is interesting. Cf.:
1. Matt 6:12 ἀφήκαμεν ℵ* B Z f¹ pc vg^st sy^p. h; Gregory of Nyssa^pt.
2. Matt 6:12 ἀφίομεν D (L) W Δ Θ 565 pc sy^c? co? (thus also Luke 11:4)

3. Matt 6:12 ἀφίεμεν ℵ¹ f¹³ 𝔐 sy^c? co? Cl.
In this scheme (2) and (3) are only dialectal variants. Is the present tense original, and is the *Didache* version older than the Matthean at this point?[14] Or does the aorist ἀφήκαμεν reflect an Aramaic perfect—and if so, in what sense?[15]

It is important that the *Didache* contains a formulated doxology at the end of the prayer. Clearly, the form of the Our Father handed on by Q did not yet have such a doxology; it is lacking in the Lukan text and also in the original text of Matthew. Adolf Schlatter and Joachim Jeremias have instructed us, however,[16] that the Our Father was one of the prayers "with the 'seal,' i.e., with a freely formulated conclusion." This means that, from the beginning, the one who prayed such prayers formulated a conclusion to the last petition ex tempore. It is in the nature of things that over time "a fixed form of the doxology"[17]

Bahr, "The Use of the Lord's Prayer in the Primitive Church," *JBL* 84 (1965) 154. Nevertheless, the agreements between Matthew and the *Didache* show that the paradigm of the Lord's Prayer was already more or less fixed in this sphere of tradition.

9   Cf. Ernst Lohmeyer, *Das Vaterunser* (5th ed.; Göttingen: Vandenhoeck & Ruprecht, 1962) 7 (ET: *The Lord's Prayer* [New York: Harper & Row, 1965] 15–16). Cf. also the synopsis in table 9. Schöllgen, "Church Order," 66: *Did.* 8.2 is tradition.

10   Thus Funk, *Patres apostolici,* 1.19; Hemmer, *Doctrine,* xcv; Schaff, *Church Manual,* 188; Massaux, *Influence,* 3.154–55. To the contrary: Koester, *Synoptische Überlieferung,* 203–9; Audet, *Didachè,* 171–73; Lohmeyer, *Vaterunser,* 7 (ET: *Lord's Prayer,* 16); Giet, *L'Énigme,* 200; Rordorf and Tuilier, *Doctrine,* 86. Against Koester, most recently J. B. Bauer, "Aspekte des Kanonproblems," *Meqor Hajjim: Festschrift für Georg Molin zum 75 Geburtstag* (Graz: Akademische Druck-und Verlagsanstalt, 1983) 30–31. The arguments presented by Koester, says Bauer, are not conclusive. The *Didache*'s ἀφίεμεν was also found in the Koine text of Matthew's Gospel and in the version in the *Apostolic Constitutions*; the latter also has ἐν τοῖς οὐρανοῖς and ὀφειλήματα (the last again, in my opinion, not persuasive, because it is reasonable to suppose that the Constitutor used his text of Matthew to make corrections). Bauer asserts: "However the problem now stands, whether the Didachist knew the Gospel of Matthew or not, that he records the Matthean form can also be understood in this way: He knew not only this longer version but also the shorter text of the Our Father as it is found in Luke, and he wished, so to speak, to inculcate the longer version as canonical" (p. 31; with reference to J. B. Bligh). This can scarcely be

the case. Wengst (*Didache*, 26–27) has now also asserted that this passage is a citation from Matthew's Gospel. The liturgy or a written source are not genuine alternatives (p. 26), and the deviations from the traditional text of Matthew "do not weigh heavily" (p. 27).

11   These differences are noted in table 9 by the use of underlining in the text of the *Didache*.

12   Koester (*Synoptische Überlieferung,* 206) suggested that the singular in the *Didache* might even be original. Gerhard Schneider, "Das Vaterunser des Matthäus," in *À Cause de l'Évangile: Études sur les Synoptiques et les Actes offertes au P. Jacques Dupont, O.S.B., à l'occasion de son 70e anniversaire* (LD 123; Paris: Cerf, Publications de Saint-André, 1985) 63 n. 23: the singular is secondary. The *Apostolic Constitutions* has the plural ἐν τοῖς οὐρανοῖς (probably corrected according to the familiar text of Matthew).

13   Koester (*Synoptische Überlieferung,* 206) considered whether the didachistic or Matthean form is the older. Schneider ("Vaterunser," 63 n. 23) thinks this is probably a secondary accommodation. The *Apostolic Constitutions* again accommodated to Matthew with τὰ ὀφειλήματα.

14   Cf. the suggestions in Koester, *Synoptische Überlieferung,* 206–7. Differently Joachim Jeremias, *Theology,* 196 n. 2: ἀφίομεν or ἀφίεμεν are softenings ("so far as there is no question of Lucan influence").

15   Jeremias, *Theology,* 201: "ἀφήκαμεν goes back to the Aramaic šebaqnan, which is meant as a *perfectum coincidentiae* and is therefore to be translated: 'as *herewith* we forgive our debtors.'"

16   Adolf Schlatter, *Der Evangelist Matthäus* (6th ed.; Stuttgart: Calwer, 1963) 217; Jeremias, *Theology,* 203. Cf. also Joachim Jeremias, "Abba," in idem, *Abba,* 170–71 (ET: *The Prayers of Jesus* [SBT 2.6;

was adopted. Such a fixed form for the doxology appears for the first time here in the *Didache*; it later emerges (although expanded; see below) in the "majority text" of Matt 6:13 (end) (L W Θ 0233 f[13] 𝔐 f q bo[pt]).[18] We do not know when and where these doxologies emerged. The passage in 1 Chr 29:11–12 that is often adduced as the model for them is too far removed in its wording. Rabbinic traditions also offer only analogies. Cf. the doxology: "praised be the name of his glorious kingdom forever and ever." This is how the priest and people respond to the great confession of sins in the temple cult (Str–B 1.423). The same benediction was spoken after the beginning of the Shema (Str–B, ibid.); compare also the *Alenu* prayer, whose conclusion is introduced by "for thine is the kingdom" (Str–B, ibid.). The object of the benediction is always the kingdom, as is the beginning of the doxology to the Matthean Our Father as later attested by the "majority text." Here we should note that it is precisely this kingdom benediction, with which the later doxology of the Lord's Prayer in Matt 6:13 in the majority text begins, that is lacking in the *Didache*. The *Didache* doxology is accordingly

not in three parts (kingdom, power, glory), but only two (power and glory). In addition we note that the mention of the kingdom is also lacking in the Sahidic version of the doxology to the Lord's Prayer (Matt 6:13 [end]), and the same is true of one manuscript of the Fayyumic. Thus the two-part textual form of the doxology in the *Didache* agrees with the Coptic witnesses just listed (with the sole exception of the "Amen," which is lacking in the *Didache*):[19]

Sahidic:[20]
ϫⲉ ⲧⲱⲕ ⲧⲉ ⲧϭⲟⲙ
ⲙⲛ̄ ⲡⲉⲟⲟⲩ
ϣⲁ ⲛ̄ⲓⲉⲛⲉϩ[21]
ϩⲁⲙⲏⲛ.

Didache:
ὅτι σοῦ ἐστιν ἡ δύναμις
καὶ ἡ δόξα
εἰς τοὺς αἰῶνας.

This should be compared with the text of a fragment in the Fayyumic(?) dialect: ϫⲉ ⲧⲱⲕ ⲧⲉ ⲧϭⲁⲙ ⲙⲛ̄ ⲡⲉⲁⲩ ϣⲁⲉⲛⲉϩ ϩⲁⲙⲏⲛ.[22] Characteristic of all these examples is the absence of the first member, ἡ βασιλεία καί ("the kingdom and").[23] The agreement of the *Didache* with this form of the text is remarkable. Nevertheless, it would be difficult to draw conclusions from this regarding the origins of the *Didache*.[24]

London: SCM, 1967] 106–7). The quotation is from *Theology*, 203.

17 Jeremias, *Theology*, 203.

18 For the variants in 2148 pc g[1] k sy[c.p] sa, see the information in Nestle-Aland. In particular, for the absence of the kingdom benediction in sa (and fay), and in the forms in k and sy[c], see immediately below.

19 It is true that the kingdom benediction is also lacking in k, but the text of k shows only a one-part form overall. See n. 23 below.

20 Text from George Horner, *The Coptic Version of the New Testament in the Southern Dialect Otherwise Called Sahidic and Thebaic* (7 vols.; Oxford: Clarendon, 1911–24; repr. Osnabrück: Zeller, 1969) 1.46. Identical in its text is the version of ms. sa 9 (New York, Pierpont Morgan Library, M 569), not yet appearing in Horner's edition. Cf. Franz-Jürgen Schmitz and Gerd Mink, eds., *Liste der koptischen Handschriften des Neuen Testaments, I: Die sahidischen Handschriften der Evangelien, 1. Teil* (ANTF 8; Berlin and New York: de Gruyter, 1986) 19–24. The text of this passage was very kindly provided for me by Franz-Jürgen Schmitz of the Institut für neutestamentliche Textforschung.

21 Some mss. read ⲡⲁⲙⲁϩⲧⲉ instead of ⲡⲉⲟⲟⲩ; f[1] (cf. Horner, *Coptic Version,* 47) reads ⲉⲛⲉϩ ⲛ̄ⲉⲛⲉϩ instead of ⲛ̄ⲓⲉⲛⲉϩ (cf. also the text of 2148 pc k).

22 Text from J. David, "Fragments de l'Évangile selon Saint Matthieu en dialecte moyen-égyptien," *RB,* n.s. 7 (1910) 80–92. The text consists of three fragments of Matthew's Gospel, the first of which (originally

edited by M. Maspero) contains Matt 5:46–6:18 with lacunae. David locates the fragments "in the central Egyptian dialect that has customarily been called Fayyumic" (p. 80). The text in question is on p. 84 of the article. The Middle Egyptian version of Codex Scheide (ed. Hans-Martin Schenke [TU 127; Berlin: Akademie-Verlag, 1981] 64) has no doxology with the Lord's Prayer. The Bohairic version is split. Parts of it evidence the (three-part) doxology, and others have the text of the Lord's Prayer without a doxology. Cf. George Horner, *The Coptic Version of the New Testament in the Northern Dialect Otherwise Called Memphitic and Bohairic* (3 vols.; Oxford: Clarendon, 1898–1905; repr. Osnabrück: Zeller, 1969) 1.38–39.

23 In Codex Bobbiensis (k), not only is the corresponding term to ἡ βασιλεία καί lacking, but also that for καὶ ἡ δόξα. The text contains only a one-part doxology. At the same time (with 2148 pc sa[ms]), the additional τῶν αἰώνων is presupposed: *quoniam est tibi virtus in saecula saeculorum* (Itala 1.31). In the Cureton Syriac the corresponding term for ἡ δύναμις καί is absent. See the other variants in Nestle-Aland.

24 Harnack (*Lehre*, 26; and "Prolegomena," 168–70) originally saw this agreement with the Sahidic tradition as an indication of the *Didache*'s origins in Upper Egypt. Should we consider the possibility of a subsequent adaptation of the *Didache* text to the Sahidic version, so that we would have to conjecture the original *Didache* text? Still, the three-part text is also attested in the *Apostololic Constitutions*. But the

More important than the (purely accidental?) agreement of our *Didache* doxology with the Coptic textual witnesses just mentioned is another matter. The specific form of the doxology in *Did.* 8.2 is found again in the doxology of the meal prayers in 10.5, and with only slight variation also in 9.4. In general, the doxology of the Lord's Prayer and those of the meal celebration in chaps. 9–10 belong together, as the following synopsis illustrates:

(a) ὅτι σοῦ ἐστιν ἡ δύναμις καὶ ἡ δόξα εἰς τοὺς αἰῶνας (8.2)

(b) σοὶ ἡ δόξα εἰς τοὺς αἰῶνας (9.2)

(b) σοὶ ἡ δόξα εἰς τοὺς αἰῶνας (9.3)

(a) ὅτι σοῦ ἐστιν ἡ δόξα καὶ ἡ δύναμις διὰ Ἰησοῦ Χριστοῦ εἰς τοὺς αἰῶνας (9.4)

(b) σοὶ ἡ δόξα εἰς τοὺς αἰῶνας (10.2)

(b) σοὶ ἡ δόξα εἰς τοὺς αἰῶνας (10.4)

(a) ὅτι σοῦ ἐστιν ἡ δύναμις καὶ ἡ δόξα εἰς τοὺς αἰῶνας (10.5).

The constancy of the formula forces us to view the doxology of the Lord's Prayer that appears in the *Didache* alongside those of the meal celebration. The one-part short formula (b) is contrasted with the long formula (a), which has two parts.[25] In each of these formulae the mention of the βασιλεία is lacking. In conclusion, the *Didache* tradition is acquainted with a doxology existing in a short and a long form, both of which have found their way into the meal prayers and the Lord's Prayer. We cannot exclude the possibility that their original *Sitz im Leben* was in the meal prayers and that they were transferred from there to the Lord's Prayer.

The presentation of the Lord's Prayer is followed in v. 3 by a rubrical note: the readers or hearers are called upon to speak this prayer three times a day.[26] This corresponds to the Jewish custom of having a fixed time for prayer "three times each day" (Dan 6:9, 11, 12 LXX: τρὶς τῆς ἡμέρας).[27] The provision in the *Didache* (or that of the liturgist) maintains the Jewish τρὶς τῆς ἡμέρας but requires the replacement of the Jewish prayer with something different: namely, the Lord's Prayer just cited. In this way also the Christians show themselves different from the ὑποκριταί. This passage in *Did.* 8.3 is of immense importance for the history of Christian worship. It may be noted that the hours for the threefold daily prayer are not yet fixed.[28]

In summary, the whole section *Did.* 8.1–3 reveals a Jewish-Christian community in the process of setting itself apart in polemical fashion from its surrounding Jewish environment. This distinction is brought into action in this passage by means of the rejection of specific ritual customs of Judaism and their replacement by ritual customs proper to Christians.

Apostololic Constitutions would have been accommodated here to the text of Matthew, which was familiar to its author, and the *two-part* form of the doxology (to be discussed immediately below), which has its parallels in the doxologies of the meal prayers, speaks against a conjecture in the *Didache* text. See below.

25 For the one-part formula cf. Rom 11:36b; for the two-part formula see the similar expressions in 1 Pet 4:11; Rev 1:6.

26 Of course, this refers to *private* prayer: Harnack, *Lehre*, 27; Klauser, *Doctrina*, 22; Mattioli, *Didache*, 95ff.; denied by Clerici, *Einsammlung*, 95; and Wrege, *Bergpredigt*, 103: "public, liturgical praxis of the communities." Our passage may be quoted in *Lib. grad.* 7.20 (Kmosko, 186).

27 For the usage in the tannaitic period, see Str–B 2.697–702.

28 Funk differs (*Patres apostolici*, 1.20) and thinks

already of the hours of "*terce, sext,* and *none.*" Tertullian *De orat.* 25 (CChrSL 1.272–73) attests prayer at the third, sixth, and ninth hours (with biblical and trinitarian reasoning), but distinguishes these hours of prayer from the *legitimis orationibus, quae sine ulla admonitione debentur ingressu lucis et noctis* ("the legitimate prayers, which, without any command, ought to be offered at first light and at dusk," 25.5 [272–73]). The hours of *terce, sext,* and *none* are also found in Tertullian *De ieiun.* 10.3 (CChrSL 2.1267). Clement of Alexandria *Strom.* 7.7, 40.3 (GCS[2] 3.30) mentions the third, sixth, and ninth hours as times for prayer, "but the Gnostic prays throughout life" (ἀλλ᾽ οὖν γε ὁ γνωστικὸς παρὰ ὅλον εὔχεται τὸν βίον). See Origen *De orat.* 12.1 (GCS 2.325); Cyprian *De Dominica Oratione* 34 (CSEL 3.1.292).

2. On the Eucharist (9.1–10.7)

General

With the transition to 9.1 we approach a high point in the *Didache*. The next chapters, 9 and 10, offer an archaic liturgical formulary without peer in the early period of Christian literature. In *Didache* 9–10 we have the oldest formula for the Christian eucharistic liturgy. These chapters have engaged researchers most intensively from the very beginning. As we might well expect, they also present us with a long series of difficult problems of interpretation.

1. *Didache* 9.1–10.7 is a long, circumscribed section[1] consisting of prayers (before the meal: 9.2b, 3b, 4; after the full meal: 10.2–5), liturgical acclamations (10.6), and rubrical instructions (9.1, 2a, 3a, 5; 10.1, 7). There is no general depiction of the celebration, only an account of specific prayers. The ancient formulary appears to have been augmented by glosses from the hand of the redactor (9.5 and 10.7).[2] Each gloss is found at the end of a section. Thus what we have before us is:

a. the ancient, even archaic text of the source (liturgy): 9.1–4 and 10.1–6;

b. the redactional additions of the Didachist: 9.5 and 10.7. We will discuss the problems of the *myron* prayer below.

It has often been observed that the prayers before and after the meal are in some sense parallel.[3] These parallels can be illustrated as follows:

(9.1) Περὶ δὲ τῆς εὐχαριστίας, (10.1) Μετὰ δὲ τὸ ἐμπλησθῆναι
οὕτως εὐχαριστήσατε· οὕτως εὐχαριστήσατε
—

(9.2) πρῶτον περὶ τοῦ ποτηρίου·
Εὐχαριστοῦμέν σοι, (10.2) Εὐχαριστοῦμέν σοι,
πάτερ ἡμῶν, πάτερ ἅγιε,
ὑπὲρ τῆς ἁγίας ἀμπέλου ὑπὲρ τοῦ ἁγίου ὀνόματός
σου
Δαυὶδ τοῦ παιδός σου, οὗ κατεσκήνωσας
ἐν ταῖς καρδίαις ἡμῶν,
καὶ ὑπὲρ τῆς γνώσεως
καὶ πίστεως καὶ ἀθανα-
σίας,
ἧς ἐγνώρισας ἡμῖν ἧς ἐγνώρισας ἡμῖν

διὰ Ἰησοῦ τοῦ παιδός σου· διὰ Ἰησοῦ τοῦ παιδός σου·
σοὶ ἡ δόξα εἰς τοὺς αἰῶνας. σοὶ ἡ δόξα εἰς τοὺς
αἰῶνας.

(9.3) περὶ δὲ τοῦ *ἄρτου·
Εὐχαριστοῦμέν σοι, (10.3) σύ,
πάτερ ἡμῶν, δέσποτα παντοκράτορ,
ὑπὲρ τῆς ζωῆς καὶ γνώσεως ἔκτισας τὰ πάντα ἕνεκεν
ἧς ἐγνώρισας ἡμῖν τοῦ ὀνόματός σου,
τροφήν τε καὶ ποτὸν
ἔδωκας τοῖς ἀνθρώποις
εἰς ἀπόλαυσιν,
ἵνα σοι εὐχαριστήσωσιν,
ἡμῖν δὲ ἐχαρίσω
πνευματικὴν τροφὴν καὶ
ποτὸν καὶ ζωὴν αἰώνιον
διὰ Ἰησοῦ τοῦ παιδός σου· διὰ ⟨Ἰησοῦ⟩ τοῦ παιδός
σου.
(10.4) περὶ πάντων εὐχαριστοῦμέν
σοι, ὅτι δυνατὸς εἶ·
σοὶ ἡ δόξα εἰς τοὺς αἰῶνας. σοὶ ἡ δόξα εἰς τοὺς
αἰῶνας.

(9.4) ὥσπερ ἦν τοῦτο ⟨...⟩ (10.5) μνήσθητι, κύριε,
διεσκορπισμένον
ἐπάνω τῶν ὀρέων τῆς ἐκκλησίας σου τοῦ
καὶ συναχθὲν ἐγένετο ἕν, ῥύσασθαι αὐτὴν
ἀπὸ παντὸς πονηροῦ
καὶ τελειῶσαι αὐτὴν
ἐν τῇ ἀγάπῃ σου,
οὕτω συναχθήτω σου καὶ σύναξον αὐτὴν
ἡ ἐκκλησία
ἀπὸ τῶν περάτων τῆς γῆς ἀπὸ τῶν τεσσάρων ἀνέμων
⟨...⟩
εἰς τὴν σὴν βασιλείαν· εἰς τὴν σὴν βασιλείαν,
ἣν ἡτοίμασας αὐτῇ·
ὅτι σοῦ ἐστιν ἡ δόξα ὅτι σοῦ ἐστιν ἡ δύναμις
καὶ ἡ δύναμις καὶ ἡ δόξα
διὰ Ἰησοῦ Χριστοῦ —
εἰς τοὺς αἰῶνας. εἰς τοὺς αἰῶνας.
(10.6) ἐλθέτω χάρις
καὶ παρελθέτω
ὁ κόσμος οὗτος.
Ὡσαννὰ τῷ θεῷ Δαυίδ.
εἴ τις ἅγιός ἐστιν,
ἐρχέσθω·
εἴ τις οὐκ ἔστι, μετα-

---

1 According to Pillinger ("Taufe," 156–57; cf., previously, Kraft, *Didache*, 63–64 and 167–68), chaps. 9–10 belong with what immediately precedes them. These two chapters constitute "an integral part of the baptismal liturgy" (p. 156). This can scarcely be the case. Cf. Rordorf and Tuilier, *Doctrine*, 42.

2 Audet (*Didachè*, 375), on the contrary, attributes 9.1, 2a, 3a, 5; 10.1, 7 to the author. For Schöllgen

("Church Order," 66) 9.2–4 and 10.2–6 are tradition.

3 Cf. now the German synopsis in Clerici, *Einsammlung*, 5–6.

$$\nu o\epsilon i\tau\omega\cdot$$
$$\mu\alpha\rho\alpha\nu\alpha\vartheta\acute{\alpha}\cdot\ \acute{\alpha}\mu\acute{\eta}\nu.$$

(9.5)   (10.7)

*H reads $\kappa\lambda\acute{\alpha}\sigma\mu\alpha\tau o\varsigma$. For the emendation to $\acute{\alpha}\rho\tau o\upsilon$, see the commentary on 9.3.

2. Very early it was noticed[4] that, in a whole series of passages, the meal prayers in the *Didache* have Jewish prayers as their models.[5] (See the details in the commentary below.) We must suppose that the ties of the community tradition expressed in these prayers to the Judaism of their environment were still very strong.[6] This is true, in any case, for the liturgy and the communities behind it. We may say, with a grain of salt, that the table prayers in the *Didache* rest to a great extent on Jewish models, although those had been strongly Christianized.[7] The literary findings reflect the social situation of the Jewish-Christian group from whose ranks these prayers originally issued.[8] To what, however, do the prayers really refer?

3. After the introductory liturgical formula $\pi\epsilon\rho\grave{\iota}\ \delta\grave{\epsilon}$ $\tau\tilde{\eta}\varsigma\ \epsilon\grave{\upsilon}\chi\alpha\rho\iota\sigma\tau\acute{\iota}\alpha\varsigma$ ("As for the thanksgiving"), the reader of a later era expects to find directions for the sacrament of the Eucharist, and that expectation is heightened by the context. Chap. 7 described baptism, and chaps. 9–10 are to deal with the Lord's Supper. But what emerges in chaps. 9–10 is surprising in a number of ways. The sequence of elements appears to be reversed. The liturgical directions begin with the prayer of blessing over the wine (9.2), and only then follows the blessing of the bread (9.3–4).[9] Still more striking is that the words of institution are absent; it is also questionable whether the prayers of blessing contain any reference at all to the kerygma of the passion.[10] In addition, the expression in 10.1 ($\mu\epsilon\tau\grave{\alpha}\ \delta\grave{\epsilon}\ \tau\grave{o}\ \grave{\epsilon}\mu\pi\lambda\eta\sigma\vartheta\tilde{\eta}\nu\alpha\iota$) implies a full meal. Under these circumstances the question arises whether chaps. 9–10 really deal with the sacrament of the Lord's Supper. This has been one of the crucial problems in *Didache* research from the outset.

---

4 Cf., e.g., Klein, "Gebete," 133–46.

5 Vokes was unwilling to accept the influence of Jewish liturgy (in line with his fiction theory); instead, he attempted to have recourse to NT expressions as models, and to assert that the prayers in the *Didache* bore only a distant resemblance to Jewish prayers. Cf. Vokes, *Riddle*, 179–82, 185–86, 193, 203. In fact, there is only one problem in this regard: possible relationships to the Gospel of John. For this, see below.

6 Betz ("Eucharist," 245, 253) assigns the prayers, in their original form, to Aramaic-speaking communities. This is unnecessary. Their home is rather a Hellenistic Jewish Christianity.

7 Betz ("Eucharist," 256) finds wisdom traditions determinative for the prayers. This is questionable. It is certainly wrong, however, to conclude from this, as he does, that the prayers cannot be "a product of Hellenistic thought" ("Eucharist," 258). Rordorf ("Didachè," 7) remarks correctly that the prayers constitute "the hinge" between the Jewish tradition of prayer and the eucharistic anaphora prayers of a later time.

8 A separate problem is whether Johannine texts or motifs have influenced *Didache* 9–10. On this, see above, p. 47 n. 35, and p. 48 n. 40. In modern research, Erwin R. Goodenough ("John a Primitive Gospel," *JBL* 64 [1945] 173–75) has tried to find in *Didache* 9–10 (besides dependence on Jewish liturgy) reminiscences of the narrative of the miraculous multiplication of loaves in John 6 (interpreted eucharistically by Goodenough). Moule ("Note,"

240–43) also advocated the dependence of *Did.* 9.4 on John 6. Finally, Lucien Cerfaux ("La multiplication des pains dans la liturgie de la Didachè," *Bib* 40 [1959] 943–58), in agreement with Goodenough and Moule, has posited references in the table prayers to John 6 and 11:52. But the situation may be as follows: (1) The relationships between the table prayers and John 6 and 11:52 are superficial and accidental; literary and tradition-historical relationships are excluded; (2) in some places (see above, p. 48 n. 40]) there are distant parallels to individual motifs in the Gospel of John, esp. chap. 17 and 11:52, although contextual differences are determinative in each case; the common features may be adequately explained by common dependence on a third entity, namely, the language of the Christian liturgy. Betz ("Eucharist," 255–56) considers the possibility not of literary but of tradition-historical kinship, esp. with John 6, 15, and 17; cf. the list on p. 255.

9 1 Cor 10:16–17 is not a parallel. Klauck, *Herrenmahl,* 262: "the cup-bread sequence does not indicate a different liturgical praxis, . . . but rests on a reversal by Paul (as in v. 21)."

10 This is asserted by Sandvik, *Kommen des Herrn,* 59–60; "life" in *Did.* 9.3; 10.2–3 is said to refer to the resurrection and "servant" to Jesus' suffering. There would thus, in fact, be an anamnesis of Jesus' passion, "but here the accent is on his resurrection, not on his death" (p. 60).

11 Harnack, *Lehre,* 28–36; idem, "Prolegomena," 58–60. Harnack thought that the Eucharist was cele-

4. What kind of meal is this, then?

a. Among those who considered it to be eucharistic are Harnack,[11] Völker,[12] Greiff,[13] Middleton,[14] Creed,[15] Richardson,[16] Bosio,[17] Glover,[18] and Kraft.[19] There is an especially interesting variant in the work of Hans Lietzmann.[20] In his interpretation this is "an agape introduced by a eucharistic celebration."[21] *Did.* 9.1–5 describes the eucharistic celebration, and this was followed by an *agape,* which was a complete meal (between chaps. 9 and 10). The *agape* meal was then in turn followed by the prayers of thanksgiving in 10.1–6; the text in 10.6 (part of the eucharistic liturgy) is misplaced.[22] This description played a particular role within the framework of Lietzmann's conception of the twofold origins of the Eucharist.

b. Among those who considered this meal an *agape* were F. Kattenbusch,[23] Connolly,[24] Vokes,[25] Dix,[26] Adam,[27] and Gero.[28]

c. Drews had his own solution to the problem: the meal prayers in chaps. 9–10 are said to refer to "a Lord's Supper celebrated in the form of a unified, complete community meal," while chap. 14 describes the official Sunday Eucharist of the local community, led by a bishop.[29] Knopf's judgment was similar. He wrote of the prayers in chaps. 9–10, "What we have here is a celebration in a smaller group where there is still a genuine meal (10.1), whereas [chap.] 14 refers to the celebration of the whole community, on Sunday, without a meal: the Mass with the consumption of the sacrament alone, as in Justin *1 Apol.* 67."[30]

d. The opinion that the prayers in chaps. 9–10 are *agape* prayers followed by the Eucharist in 10.6 has been widely adopted.[31] The most important arguments for this idea are found first in the work of Zahn[32] and later

---

brated as part of the *agape* (*Lehre,* 28), as "a genuine meal" (*Apostellehre,* 3). Cf. also "Prolegomena," 60: "This complete obscuring of the death of Christ and the forgiveness of sins is characteristic of the postapostolic or, better, the non-Pauline origin of the prayers."

12 Karl Völker, *Mysterium und Agape: Die gemeinsamen Mahlzeiten in der Alten Kirche* (Gotha: Klotz, 1927) 105–7, 126–28, and passim.

13 *Paschariuale,* 109–11, and passim.

14 "Eucharistic Prayers," 259–61.

15 "Didache," 374, 386–87.

16 "Teaching of the Twelve Apostles," 165–66: "a period when the Lord's Supper was still a real supper, and when the joyful and expectant note of the Messianic Banquet had not yet been obscured by the more solemn emphasis on the Lord's Passion" (p. 166).

17 *Padri apostolici,* 1.21.

18 "Quotations," 26–27.

19 Kraft (*Didache,* 168) thinks of an "annual Baptism-Eucharist-service" as the *Sitz im Leben* for chaps. 9–10.

20 *Mass,* 188–94, at 189-90.

21 Lietzmann, *Mass,* 190.

22 Lietzmann, *Mass,* 192–93.

23 "Messe, I: Dogmengeschichtlich," *RE*³, 12.671.

24 Richard H. Connolly, "Agape and Eucharist in the Didache," *DRev* 55 (1937) 477–89.

25 *Riddle,* 197–207.

26 *The Shape of the Liturgy* (repr. of 2d ed.; London: Black, 1970; New York: Seabury, 1982) 90.

27 "Herkunft," 32–33 (combined with certain remarks on the *myron* prayer: see below).

28 Gero, "Ointment Prayer," 82; for his remarks in this connection regarding the *myron* prayer, see below.

29 "Untersuchungen," 74–79, esp. 78–79 (quotation on p. 79).

30 Knopf, *Lehre,* 24. Cf. Klein, "Gebete," 144–45: the meal in chap. 9 is a festive Sabbath meal held in the evening, at the beginning of the Sabbath (perhaps also a baptismal meal occasioned by the baptisms performed on Friday evening). On the Sabbath the community celebrates a festive, full-course meal, and on the Lord's day (chap. 14) the Eucharist.

31 For the sequence of the two celebrations the following variants have been proposed:
  · Originally, the full meal could have been inserted in the sacramental celebration (cf. "after dining," μετὰ τὸ δειπνῆσαι in 1 Cor 11:25), so that the sequence would have been: eucharistic bread, full meal, eucharistic wine.
  · At an early date the full meal was transferred to the beginning of the celebration (as it appears in the *Didache*), so that the sequence "*agape*"–Eucharist resulted. Cf. also *Ep. apost.* 15, Ethiopic (*NTApoc,* 1.257–58).
  · The reverse sequence (Eucharist–*agape*) is attested in the *Didache,* according to Lietzmann.
  · Finally, there is also early evidence of the separation of Eucharist and *agape.*

32 *Kanon,* 3.293–98. The prayers in chap. 9 are *agape* prayers. "The prayers in *Doctr.* 10 constitute the

in that of Arthur Darby Nock,[33] August Arnold,[34] Martin Dibelius,[35] and others. *Agape* prayers (or table prayers for the community meal) followed by the Lord's Supper are also suggested by, among others, Bultmann[36] and Jeremias,[37] and with caution by Stuiber,[38] Vielhauer,[39] and (again cautiously) now Rordorf and Tuilier as well.[40]

e. Audet produced a remarkable variant on this model.[41]

f. Vööbus completed a thorough investigation[42] in which he again spoke in favor of interpreting this as a eucharistic celebration. Chaps. 9–10 are eucharistic prayers, and the fact that the meal is a full-course dinner need not disturb us because Eucharist and *agape* had not yet been separated. Finally, Johannes Betz, adopting and correcting an idea of Peterson,[43] advocated the idea that

the table prayers in the *Didache* were originally eucharistic prayers, but the redactor of the document has made them *agape* prayers.[44]

g. Most recently Wengst has defended the idea that chaps. 9–10 depict nothing but a full-course meal.[45] It bears the name $\varepsilon\dot{v}\chi\alpha\rho\iota\sigma\tau\dot{\iota}\alpha$, but it has nothing to do with the Christian Lord's Supper. The celebration spoken of in chaps. 9–10 is purely a meal for the satisfaction of hunger, and nothing else.[46]

5. It seems to me that if we are to reach a conclusion in this matter we must begin with *Did.* 10.6, a text that must be placed before the sacramental Communion.[47] This means that the Eucharist in our sense, that is, the sacramental Lord's Supper, must begin *after* chap. 10. It is characteristic that Lietzmann, who defended a differ-

---

transition from the *agape* to the sacrament proper" (p. 296).

33 "Liturgical Notes," 390–91.

34 *Der Ursprung des christlichen Abendmahls im Lichte der neuesten liturgiegeschichtlichen Forschung* (2d ed.; FThSt 45; Freiburg im Breisgau: Herder, 1939) 26–31.

35 "Mahl-Gebete," 126–27: "the special *sacred action*, whatever its makeup, *did not occur between 9 and 10, but after 10.6*. Between 9 and 10 is only the meal proper" (p. 126). He then says (p. 127) that the sacred action following 10.6 is the Eucharist.

36 *Theology of the New Testament* (trans. Kendrick Grobel; 2 vols.; New York: Scribner's, 1951–55) 1.151: "It does appear to be true that the words of 10:6 are to be understood as a transition to the sacramental Eucharist, the liturgy of which does not need to be set down because it was familiar to all. But then it is clear that two celebrations of entirely different kind have been secondarily combined. Therefore, the celebration implied in Did. 9 and 10 existed at first by itself, and it must have been from it that the Lord's Supper took over the title 'Eucharist' ('Thanksgiving'), which is a very strange term for the sacrament of the Lord's Supper."

37 *Eucharistic Words*, 117–18, 134.

38 "Eulogia," 914; cf. also 919.

39 *Geschichte*, 38–39.

40 Rordorf and Tuilier, *Doctrine*, 40–41. Cf. also Rordorf, "Didachè," 15–16; Moll, *Opfer*, 106–15.

41 Audet, *Didachè*, 372–77. At 405–7 he distinguishes between the "breaking of the bread" (which, however, is not to be understood as an *agape*) and the Eucharist itself (which follows chap. 10). The whole celebration is a vigil. It is introduced by the breaking of bread. *Did.* 10.6 is the transitional formula: the baptized move to another room for the Eucha-

rist proper, the "great 'eucharist.'"

42 *Liturgical Traditions*, 63–74.

43 Peterson, "Probleme," 168–71. Behind the prayers in chaps. 9–10 of the Bryennios text are remnants of ancient eucharistic prayers of the Egyptian church, or a church prayer (in chap. 10). For the Novatianist (?) redactor of the document responsible for the the Bryennios version, these prayers have been devalued and (in chap. 10) abbreviated to table prayers for ascetic circles.

44 So Betz, "Eucharist," 251–53. Betz counts *Did.* 9.2–4; (9.5); 10.2, 3b–5 among the ancient parts. The blessing of the cup (9.2) has been shifted by the redactor; 10.3a is a later addition by the redactor, and 10.1 is also redactional. Klauck (*Herrenmahl*, 263) uses the same explanation as Betz and sees the table prayers as reflecting the influence of the Hellenistic synagogue, as does Dibelius (see below).

45 Wengst, *Didache*, 43–56. Bread and wine are sufficient for the satisfaction of hunger. "From the fact that this eucharist had the character of a full meal we may by no means conclude that the meal consisted of anything more than, or different from, bread and wine. Bread was *the* food for satisfaction of hunger" (p. 45).

46 Of course, in that case, *Did.* 10.6 creates difficulties. Wengst admits (*Didache*, 46) that "originally" (as he says) this was "a fragment of a Lord's Supper liturgy." But the text in its present context has lost that function. In that case, however, how did this liturgical text come to be placed at the end of the prayer of thanksgiving? This "may be because of its eschatological orientation" (p. 47).

47 Vööbus's attempt (*Liturgical Traditions*, 70–74) to show that *Did.* 10.6 is redactional (p. 73), and in fact "a general admonition and warning to the readers of the manual reminding them of the demand for

ent position, raised objections to the placement of 10.6.[48] If we allow the text to stand as it has been handed down we have scarcely any other choice but to suppose that 10.6 is the invitation to the Lord's Supper, which follows immediately thereafter. In that case, however, the meal envisioned in *Did.* 10.1 cannot be a Eucharist in the sacramental sense, but only a community meal. This is indicated also by ἐμπλησθῆναι, if we do not attempt to interpret it artificially against its context.[49] In that case the difficulty otherwise produced by the "reversed" sequence of wine and bread in 9.2–4 disappears. If we are to suppose that the sacramental meal follows after *Did.* 10.6 it seems plausible (with Rordorf)[50] to understand the prayer of thanksgiving in 10.2–6 as also a kind of "preface" preceding the sacrament to follow; the text itself, in its individual phrases, favors this interpretation.

Thus we find the following progression of the liturgy: community meal ("*agape*"?) as meal for satisfaction of hunger, introduced in each part (9.2–4) by short blessings of wine and bread (in which the formularies point to Jewish blessings of wine and bread as models); after the full meal (10.1) follows the prayer of thanksgiving (modeled on the Jewish prayer after meals, but strongly Christianized), which at the same time introduces the celebration of the Lord's Supper (10.2–5); this prayer in turn is followed by the invitation (10.6) and then (or

after the free prayers of the prophets: 10.7) the Lord's Supper itself.

Two major objections may be raised against this interpretation. First, the rubric in *Did.* 9.1 speaks expressly of εὐχαριστία. If we are to maintain the position just enunciated we must suppose that εὐχαριστία here does not have the ordinary, sacramental sense, but describes the nonsacramental community meal. This would be a singular but early usage of the word, not yet restricted to the sacrament. Correspondingly, εὐχαριστεῖν in 9.1 and 10.1 would mean the speaking of the prayers of blessing that are to be offered at the community celebration.[51] These propositions would be in harmony with the archaic character of the liturgy given here.

A second difficulty results from the absence of the words of institution. If, understandably enough, one is not satisfied with Bultmann's solution (the liturgy of the Lord's Supper "[did] not need to be set down because it [was] familiar to all"),[52] one might be tempted to suppose that there is a deliberate suppression of the words of institution, in order not to profane them.[53] This supposition is awkward, however, because there is no evidence at this early period for the so-called arcane discipline.[54] Thus there remains an unresolved problem at this point.

---

purity as a requirement of preparedness" (p. 74), is not persuasive.

48 See p. 141 above.

49 Ἐμπλησθῆναι can be understood metaphorically; cf. Rom 15:24 and the linguistic parallels for that verse in BAGD. Thus Karl Völker (*Mysterium und Agape: Die gemeinsamen Mahlzeiten in der Alten Kirche* [Gotha: Klotz, 1927] 107) thought of a spiritual satisfaction in *Did.* 10.1. But even Zahn (*Kanon*, 3.293) wrote, "Here, however, it is a matter of eating bread and drinking wine, and hence ἐμπλησθῆναι is to be understood as the satisfaction of hunger and thirst." Cf. also the analogous μετὰ τὸ δειπνῆσαι in 1 Cor 11:25, and the replacement of the didachistic ἐμπλησθῆναι by μετὰ δὲ τὴν μετάληψιν in *Const.* 7.26.1 (because there, in *Constitutions*, the author is thinking not of a full meal but of the sacrament).

50 "Didachè," 18. Cf., however, Arthur Darby Nock, "Liturgical Notes," *JTS* 30 (1929) 391; and Stuiber, "Eulogia," 912: "The participants in the meal are invited to the prayer after the meal in a special address concluding, simultaneously, the eating,

drinking, and table conversation. This invitation and the prayer after the meal that follows provided the formal basis for the later Christian eucharistic prayer."

51 I believe that the redactor's usage was already different, i.e., more advanced. The term εὐχαριστία in 9.5 (redactional) could already include the Lord's Supper. Something analogous is then true of εὐχαριστεῖν in 10.7 and 14.1.

52 *Theology of the New Testament*, 1.151.

53 This is suggested by Rordorf and Tuilier, *Doctrine*, 40 n. 2. One should compare Jeremias, *Eucharistic Words*, 132–37.

54 "To this time there is not a single secure proof of the existence of a Christian 'arcane discipline' in the first two centuries," Otto Perler, "Arkandisziplin," *RAC* 1 (1950) 671.

a. Prayers for the Full Meal (9.1–5)

1	As for thanksgiving, give thanks this way.
2	First, with regard to the cup:

"We thank you, our Father,
For the holy vine of David your servant,
   which you made known to us
     through Jesus your servant.
To you be glory forever."

3 And with regard to the *Bread:
"We thank you, our Father,
For the life and knowledge
   which you made known to us
     through Jesus your servant.
To you be glory forever.

4 As this < . . . > lay scattered upon the
   mountains
and became one when it had been gathered,
So may your church be gathered into your
   kingdom from the ends of the earth.
For glory and power are yours,
   through Jesus Christ, forever."

5 Let no one eat or drink of your thanksgiving
[meal] save those who have been baptized in
the name of the Lord, since the Lord has said
concerning this,
"Do not give what is holy to the dogs."

Comment

■ **1** *Didache* 9.1 is an introductory rubric. Περὶ δὲ τῆς εὐ-χαριστίας corresponds formally to περὶ δὲ τοῦ βαπτίσματος in 7.1; cf. also 11.3 (where, however, it is an imitation by the redactor). Εὐχαριστία in 9.1 is (in the sense indicated in the analysis above) a term for the blessing to be spoken and, at the same time, it is probably also the designation for the community meal to follow, whose character is determined by such benediction(s). Here in 9.1, however, εὐχαριστία does not yet refer to the sacramental Eucharist of the Lord's

Supper. The following οὕτως εὐχαριστήσατε is to be understood in the same sense: the following is the manner[1] in which you are to pray the benedictions.[2]

■ **2** This verse gives the first of the two benedictions that are to be spoken. This is the blessing over the cup. That the cup is mentioned first[3] is probably connected with the fact that at a Jewish meal with guests the first cup was given before the meal, and each person spoke a blessing over it.[4] The action presumed by the liturgy is not described, but it can be guessed: the one presiding at the meal[5] takes the cup filled with wine (in ancient

---

1   Οὕτως does not fix the wording, but offers a paradigm. See above at *Did.* 8.2.

2   We cannot go into the complicated history of the word εὐχαριστεῖν here, but this much can be said: if the Jewish-Christian community meal described here was combined with the sacramental Lord's Supper it is understandable that the designation of the community meal (namely, εὐχαριστία, after the εὐχαριστεῖν = ברך that made it what it was) was transferred over time to the Lord's Supper (or its elements). Hermann Patsch ("Abendmahlsterminologie außerhalb der Einsetzungsberichte: Erwägungen zur Traditionsgeschichte der Abendmahlsworte," *ZNW* 62 [1971] 218) advocated the position that εὐχαριστεῖν with object, in our literature, has no eucharistic (i.e., sacramental) reference, whereas absolute εὐχαριστεῖν (without an object) does

indeed have eucharistic (sacramental) significance. The usage in *Did.* 9.2–3 (where Patsch thinks of the sacrament) would be an exception. Thus even within his proposal the usage of the *Didache* is seen as inconsistent; this makes the entire proposal questionable. Εὐχαριστεῖν and εὐλογεῖν are used unsystematically in the NT (as has often been observed: cf. Hans Conzelmann, "χαίρω κτλ.," *TDNT* 9 [1974] 411). Both translate ברך. But the choice of εὐχαριστεῖν for ברך is not entirely accurate. In our texts, εὐχαριστεῖν always means "thank," not "praise" (in spite of what Audet says, *Didachè*, 377–78). At most one may suppose that the meaning "to praise" is echoed because of the underlying ברך.

3   Audet (*Didachè*, 405) concludes from the late position of the bread (and from 9.3) that the primary accent lies on that element, and thus explains the meal as the "breaking of bread."

custom, a mixture of wine and water), lifts it a little above the surface of the table, and speaks the following blessing or a similar text:

1. Εὐχαριστοῦμέν σοι, πάτερ ἡμῶν,
2. ὑπὲρ τῆς ἁγίας ἀμπέλου Δαυὶδ τοῦ παιδός σου,
   ἧς ἐγνώρισας ἡμῖν διὰ Ἰησοῦ τοῦ παιδός σου·
3. σοὶ ἡ δόξα εἰς τοὺς αἰῶνας.

Part (1) expresses the blessing addressed to God; (2) formulates, in two succinct clauses, the object over which the praise and thanksgiving are spoken; (3) concludes the brief formula with a doxology. This doxology may be the response of those gathered at the table.[6] The whole formulation is connected, here and in 9.3, with Jewish meal prayers. Indeed, 9.2 is based on the most common Jewish blessing over cup or wine: "Blessed art thou, Lord our God, Ruler of the universe, who creates the fruit of the vine."[7] The differences between the model and this prayer should be noted; they vary in importance.[8] In place of ברוך אתה ("Blessed be you") we find εὐχαρι-

στοῦμέν σοι ("We give you thanks"), but this is only a formal difference without "theological" significance. In place of the address "Lord our God, Ruler of the universe," we read "our Father" (πάτερ ἡμῶν).[9] This predication certainly expresses the self-concept of the group, who understand themselves as the table company of children who receive the goods of time and eternity from the hand of the heavenly Father.[10] An important change from the background prayers is the statement about the object for which thanks are given. The phrase ἁγία ἄμπελος ("holy vine") takes up the Jewish expression פרי הגפן ("fruit of the vine") and thus clearly shows its dependence on traditional Jewish wine blessings. The "fruit of the vine" has been replaced, however, by the expression "holy vine of David."[11] The obscure phrase

---

4 Str-B 4.616. There is occasionally a reminiscence of the kiddush (on this, with corrections of false ideas: Jeremias, *Eucharistic Words*, 26–29). Kiddush is "a *blessing* pronounced at the beginning of each Sabbath or feast day," by the head of the household (Jeremias, *Eucharistic Words*, 26). Kiddush is spoken over a cup of wine; a blessing of the wine then follows. Among those who proposed that the sequence in *Did.* 9.2 especially reflects that of the kiddush (more precisely of the blessing of wine connected with the kiddush) were Klein, "Gebete," 134–35; Middleton, "Eucharistic Prayers," 261–62; Vööbus, *Liturgical Traditions*, 163. The attempt to create a special connection to the kiddush is, in my opinion, unnecessary. In that case, one would have to posit that the meal celebration in the *Didache* liturgy originally took place on every Sabbath eve, and in fact Klein did propose that ("Gebete," 144).

5 The Jewish blessing of wine before the meal is spoken by each individual, and not (as is the blessing of bread) by one (namely, the head of the household) in the name of all.

6 This was suggested by Dibelius, "Mahl-Gebete," 119.

7 Cf. *m. Ber.* 6.1 (ed. Holtzmann, 72–73).

8 Dibelius attempted to show that the basis is not the older Jewish blessing of wine, but a spiritualizing form created in the Hellenistic synagogue ("Mahl-Gebete," 119; now in A. F. Verheule, ed., *Religionsgeschichtliche Studien: Aufsätze zur religionsgeschichte des hellenistischen Zeitalters* [NovTSup 50; Leiden: Brill, 1979] 231–85). (See also his analogous suggestions for the following prayers.) See ear-

lier Lietzmann, *Mass*, 189–90, with reference to the well-known analysis of Wilhelm Bousset on the source of the prayers in *Const.* 7.33–38 ("Eine jüdische Gebetssammlung im siebenten Buch der Apostolischen Konstitutionen," *Nachrichtungen der Göttingen Wissenschaftlicher Gesellschaft, Philosophisch-Historischer Klasse* [1915] 435–89). Vööbus (*Liturgical Traditions*, 160–62) expressed some reservations about this. There is cautious agreement with Dibelius in Wengst, *Didache*, 53 n. 177, and passim.

9 In general, for the predication of "father" to God in contemporary Judaism, see the overviews in Str–B 1.392–96, 410; Gottlob Schrenk, "πατήρ κτλ.," *TDNT* 5 (1967) 978–82; H.-W. Kuhn, "ἀββά," *EDNT* 1 (1990) 1–2; Otto Michel, "πατήρ," *EDNT* 3 (1993) 53–57; Jeremias, *Abba*, 19–22 (ET: *Prayers*, 15–18). For the predication אבינו, "our father" (combined with מלכנו, "our king"), in the Jewish literature of the early common era (1st to late 2d century), cf. esp. Jeremias, *Abba*, 28–33 (ET: *Prayers*, 24–29).

10 There can scarcely be a direct influence of the "Abba, Father" of the post-Easter experience of the Spirit (Rom 8:15; Gal 4:6).

11 I am not convinced that the term ἁγία ἄμπελος is reminiscent of the Jewish kiddush (thus Klein, "Gebete," 134–35; Vööbus, *Liturgical Traditions*, 163).

ἁγία ἄμπελος Δαυίδ[12] is symbolic language.[13] It probably alludes to the whole matter of salvation[14] (since ὑπὲρ τῆς ἁγίας ἀμπέλου parallels ὑπὲρ τῆς ζωῆς καὶ γνώσεως in the second benediction in 9.3).[15] Thus ἁγία ἄμπελος is probably a metaphor for salvation itself.[16]

The more precise definition (ἀμπέλου) Δαυὶδ τοῦ παιδός σου, which is puzzling at first, acquires its meaning in what follows: ἧς ἐγνώρισας[17] ἡμῖν διὰ Ἰησοῦ τοῦ παιδός σου. That is, God has shown, has revealed,[18] the holy vine (eschatological salvation) through Jesus,[19] God's servant. I understand this to mean that in the presence of the cup and the wine, which are earthly gifts, the thoughts of the community are directed farther, to the *heavenly* good, which God has given to God's own and which can be understood through the metaphor of the "holy vine." The concepts are thus transparent: the subject of revelation is God, and its object is the "holy vine," that is, salvation, and more specifically eschatological salvation, which was once promised but has now been given. "We thank you for the holy vine that you promised to David, your servant, and that you have now revealed through Jesus, your

---

12 To Harnack (*Lehre*, 29), the whole expression was puzzling. Peterson ("Probleme," 170) has declared the whole benediction incomprehensible. The Bryennios text is said to be secondary; in fact, "it appears that [in it] an attempt has been made to transform the eucharistic prayer into a table prayer." See above, Introduction, §3a.

13 In my opinion the formula in *Did.* 9.2 does not create a reference to the blood of Christ (thus Klein, "Gebete," 135; Greiff, *Pascharituale*, 70–72). Differently Clement of Alexandria *Quis dives salv.* 29.4 (GCS² 3.179): οὗτος (ὁ) τὸν οἶνον, τὸ αἷμα τῆς ἀμπέλου τῆς Δαβίδ, ἐκχέας ἡμῶν ἐπὶ τὰς τετρω- μένας ψυχάς ("This is the one who pours the wine, the blood of the vine of David, onto our wounded souls"). One may ask whether Clement is quoting the *Didache* (while changing its meaning)—for the contrary opinion, see above, Introduction, §2a—or whether this symbolism is familiar to him, also, apart from the *Didache*. The other instances favor the latter position. Origen *Hom.* 6.2 *in Iudic.* (Lommatzsch, 11.258): *antequam verae vitis, quae adscendit de radice David, sanguine inebriemur* ("Before we drink of the blood of the true vine, which rose from the root of David"). *P. Dêr Balizeh*, IIv., lines 6ff. (Roberts and Capelle, *Euchologium*, 26; cf. van Haelst, "Nouvelle reconstitution," 449): ὁ οἶνος ο[ὗτος] ὁ ἐξελθὼν ἐκ τῆ[ς ἁγίας ἀ]μπέλου Δ[αυεὶδ] καὶ τὸ ὕδωρ ἐξ ἀμ[νοῦ ἀμώ]μου ("This is the wine which has come from the holy vine of David and the water from the blameless lamb"). Here the liturgical expression "David's vine" is combined by means of Christian interpretation (John 15:1–8) with John 19:34.

14 Dibelius, "Mahl-Gebete," 120. The considerations he raises in this connection can be allowed to rest. Cf. also Wengst, *Didache*, 49.

15 Thus the meaning of the symbol is different from that in the OT, where Israel is frequently represented by the metaphor of the vine: Hos 10:1; Jer 2:21; Ps 80:8–13; cf. 2 Esd 5:23 (of Judah: Ezek 15:1–8; 17:6; 19:10–14). When Wisdom appears as a vine in Sir 24:17 we are already approaching the use of the image that lies behind John 15:1–6. But *Did.* 9.2 has nothing to do with these interpretations. This is not a derivation of the common OT metaphor in which the vine stands for Israel or Judah, so that we should understand the holy vine to be the church as the new, eschatological people of God (this is the interpretation of Gibbins, "Liturgical Section," 375–76, 383; J. Vernon Bartlet, *Church-Life and Church-Order during the First Four Centuries with Special Reference to the Early Eastern Church-Orders* [ed. Cecil J. Cadoux; Oxford: Blackwell, 1943] 20; Vööbus, *Liturgical Traditions*, 126; Rordorf and Tuilier, *Doctrine*, 45; Sandvik [*Kommen des Herrn*, 61–62] sees it as an image of the church as temple). Nor is it the interpretation appearing in Sir 24:17; John 15:1–8, which sees the vine as representing the one who brings salvation. It is obviously not a reference to the Messiah either, in spite of *2 Bar.* 36–40 (the rule of the Messiah); *Cave of the Treasure* 51.4 (Carl Bezold, *Die Schatzhöhle* = "*Mēᶜārath gazzē*" = [*The Cave of treasures/La caverne des trésors*]: *eine Sammlung biblischer Geschichten aus dem sechsten Jahrhundert jemals Ephraem Syrus zugeschrieben* [2 vols. in 8; Leipzig, 1883–88; repr. Amsterdam: Philo, 1981]). This interpretation of *Did.* 9.2 fails by the very fact that a distinction is drawn in 9.2 between ἄμπελος and παῖς (Vööbus, *Liturgical Traditions*, 125). The work of Rainer Borig, *Der wahre Weinstock* (Munich: Kosel, 1967), is not helpful for our specific question.

16 Betz ("Eucharist," 264–67) sees a whole group of intentions: "the expected Davidic messiah and wisdom" (p. 266), but ultimately the table community as well (p. 267).

17 Ἧς ἐγνώρισας is an attraction; the same is found also in 9.3 and 10.2. Cf. BAGD, *s.v.* γνωρίζω. For the attraction of the relative, see BDF, §294; BDR, §294.

18 This is, of course, the meaning of γνωρίζειν here. Cf. also 9.3; 10.2. This word is found in the *Didache* only in the fixed expressions of the meal prayers: ἧς

servant!"[20] It is uncertain whether, in this connection, one is meant to think of concrete promises to David in the Old Testament; the expression may have been formulated without any concrete scriptural reference in mind.[21] The designation of Jesus as παῖς σου (sc. ϑεοῦ) is certainly not a Christian imitation of a Jewish model, which would only have spoken of David as the "servant of God."[22] Instead, διὰ Ἰησοῦ τοῦ παιδός σου, which reappears verbatim in 9.3; 10.2, 3, is an old liturgical expression.[23] We know that παῖς is seldom predicated of Jesus. It appears primarily (although not exclusively) in liturgical material.[24] Reference to Jesus as "servant of God" has an archaic flavor.[25] We could imagine that this was deliberate in view of the occasional inclination of liturgical language to speak in solemn, ancient expressions that border on foreignness. More probably, however, the basis lies in tradition history: the whole predidachistic liturgy stemmed from the early Jewish Christianity of Palestine. The idea of Jesus as παῖς (ϑεοῦ) would then be a sign of the antiquity of the tradition found here.[26] Accordingly, παῖς (ϑεοῦ) here and in 9.3; 10.2–3 does not (yet) mean "child of God" but rather "servant of God." Παῖς σου = עבדך. In the context of our table prayers, then, it is difficult to posit any allusion to the servant of God in Deutero-Isaiah. One cannot say with greater certainty what special associations were combined in this exalted title for Jesus within our tradition. Only the office of the παῖς ϑεοῦ as eschatological mediator of salvation and as revealer (γνωρίζειν), his relationship to David, and the schema of promise and

---

ἐγνώρισας ἡμῖν διὰ Ἰησοῦ . . . (9.2, 3; 10.2). It is characteristic of the language of these table prayers.

19 The simple Ἰησοῦ is striking (Harnack, *Lehre*, 29–30). Thus also in 9.3; 10.2; contrast διὰ Ἰησοῦ Χριστοῦ in 9.4 (where, however, παῖς is lacking).

20 Cf. Dibelius, "Mahl-Gebete," 120, who recalls the expression in Isa 55:3 (wrongly cited by Dibelius as 55:33): Τὰ ὅσια Δαυὶδ τὰ πιστά.

21 Cf. Dibelius, "Mahl-Gebete," 120. Precisely if the (otherwise obscure) expression "vine of David" (ἄμπελος Δαυίδ) acquires its meaning only by means of the continuation (ἧς ἐγνώρισας κτλ.), it is not very likely that this expression can be explained as something pre-Christian, namely, Hellenistic Jewish, that was then added to the relative clause by Christian editors, as Dibelius would have it. Instead, the text is more readily understood within the Christian schema of "promise fulfilled," as is the paralleling of David with Jesus.

22 The expression Δαυὶδ ὁ παῖς σου (cf. Luke 1:69; Acts 4:25) corresponds to דוד עבדך; cf. the *Shemoneh Esreh* (Babylonian recension) 15 v.l. (Willy Staerk, *Altjüdische liturgische Gebete ausgewählt und mit Einleitungen* [KIT 58; Bonn: Marcus and Weger, 1910] 18); *Habhinenu* prayer, recensions a and b (Staerk, *Gebete*, 20); Musaph prayer for Rosh Hashanah 1 (Staerk, *Gebete*, 23). See Joachim Jeremias, "παῖς ϑεοῦ," *TDNT* 5 (1967) 681 n. 184.

23 There is a similar association of David and Jesus as παῖς (ϑεοῦ) in Acts 4:25–30; in v. 25 David (cf. Luke 1:69), and in vv. 27 and 30 Jesus (although Jesus is ἅγιος παῖς). Still, we should note that in Acts 4:27, 30 (and earlier in 3:13, 26) παῖς = υἱός. Ulrich Wilckens (*Die Missionsreden der Apostelgeschichte* [3d ed.; WMANT 5; Neukirchen-Vluyn: Neukirchener-Verlag, 1974] 164) concludes "with some assurance to a pre-Lukan tradition of proof of prophecy, . . .

in which the title υἱός from Ps 2:7 and the title παῖς from Isa 42:1 were fused."

24 Cf. Acts 3:13, 26; 4:27 (ἅγιος παῖς), 30 (same); then in *Barn.* 6.1; 9.2; *1 Clem.* 59.2, 3, 4; *Mart. Polyc.* 14.1, 3; 20.2. Somewhat distant: Matt 12:18 (following Isa 42:1). For later material, see Harnack, "Bezeichnung," 224–38.

25 "The solemn, archaic-sounding expression παῖς ϑεοῦ" (Knopf, *Lehre*, 26).

26 Harnack was the first to observe that the *pais* predication is ancient in its origins ("Bezeichnung," 212–14); this has often been repeated. The genealogy of the predication is disputed: the question is whether there was a distinctive *pais* Christology, and in particular whether there is reference to the "ʿebed YHWH" songs. From the (already boundless) literature, let me mention only some examples: Jeremias, *Abba*, 191–216 (ET: *TDNT* 5 [1967] 700–716); Oscar Cullmann, *The Christology of the New Testament* (rev. ed.; trans. Shirley C. Guthrie and Charles A. M. Hall; Philadelphia: Westminster, 1963) 51–82; Morna D. Hooker, *Jesus and the Servant* (London: SPCK, 1959); M. Rese, "Überprüfung einiger Thesen von Joachim Jeremias zum Thema des Gottesknechtes im Judenthum," *ZThK* 60 (1963) 21–41; Wilckens, *Missionsreden,* 163–68; Ferdinand Hahn, *Christologische Hoheitstitel* (5th ed.; Göttingen: Vandenhoeck & Ruprecht, 1995) 54–66, 386–87 (ET of 1st ed.: *Titles of Jesus in Christology: Their History in Early Christianity* [trans. Harold Knight and George Ogg; New York: World, 1969] 54–67]; Jan-Adolf Bühner, "ἀγαϑός," *EDNT* 3 (1993) 5–6. For further literature, see *ThWNT* 10.2 (1974) s.v. παῖς κτλ.; Joachim Jeremias, "παῖς κτλ.," *TDNT* 5 (1967) 636–37.

fulfillment (in 10.3, then, probably in relation to the Lord's Supper) are clearly evident.[27]

Then follows the doxological conclusion σοὶ ἡ δόξα εἰς τοὺς αἰῶνας (v. 2c), which we can best think of as a response by those present at the meal.[28]

■ **3** Verse 3 gives the second benediction, the blessing of bread, introduced by the rubric περὶ δὲ τοῦ κλάσματος. This suggests that we should understand κλάσμα to mean the bread broken at the meal celebration.[29] In that case, the plural περὶ δὲ τῶν κλασμάτων would seem more appropriate. The problem appears again in 9.4, where H gives us τοῦτο κλάσμα, and the parallels from later liturgies have ἄρτος in the analogous location.[30] Peterson has pointed out that κλάσμα is a technical term in the eucharistic language of Egypt; it refers to the particle of the host.[31] The expression would then have entered the text of the *Didache* at a secondary stage. According to Vööbus also, κλάσμα is secondary.[32] The original text may have had ἄρτου.[33] This emendation is

probably correct. The secondary κλάσμα instead of ἄρτος could also be an indication of the Egyptian character of the H tradition.

The wording of the prescribed prayer is parallel in construction to the blessing of wine (see above):

1. Εὐχαριστοῦμέν σοι, πάτερ ἡμῶν,
2. ὑπὲρ τῆς ζωῆς καὶ γνώσεως,
    ἧς ἐγνώρισας ἡμῖν διὰ Ἰησοῦ τοῦ παιδός σου·
3. σοὶ ἡ δόξα εἰς τοὺς αἰῶνας.[34]

As *Did.* 9.2 was based on the traditional Jewish blessing over the cup, so here the Jewish blessing of bread lies behind the formulation. "Blessed art thou, Lord our God, Ruler of the universe, who brings forth bread from the earth."[35] For part (1), see above. Part (2) names the schema in accordance with the divine gift, namely, "life" (ζωή) and "knowledge" (γνῶσις).[36] While this is stated by means of a metaphor in the blessing of the wine ("the holy vine of David"), here at the blessing of the bread it is predicated directly. Ζωὴ καὶ γνῶσις sounds almost like

---

27 For the association of the παῖς title with revelation, see nn. 34 and 39 below. See Harnack, "Bezeichnung," 234–35. The predication παῖς (ϑεοῦ) is thus characteristic of the table prayers in the *Didache*. For the redactor this predication probably had, on the whole, the value of a venerable liturgical relic. It is characteristic of him that when he is formulating his own text, namely, in 9.5, he immediately turns to a different predication: κύριος.

28 Differently Audet (*Didachè*, 401–2), who conjectures ἀμήν, and understands that to be the response of the gathered community.

29 Bryennios, Διδαχή, 35 n. 4: "Κλάσμα ὁ ἐν τῇ εὐχαριστίᾳ κλώμενος ἄρτος." See BAGD, *s.v.*; Schaff, *Church Manual*, 192.

30 Serapion *Euchologion* 13.13 (Funk, *Didascalia*, 2.174); *P. Dêr Balizeh* IIv., lines 3–4 (Roberts and Capelle, *Euchologium* 26; and van Haelst, "Nouvelle reconstitution," 449); (Ps.-)Athanasius *De virg.* 13 (von der Goltz, TU, n.s. 14.1a [1906] 47.4–5). *Const.* 7.15.3 reflects the *Didache*'s source as follows: ὥσπερ ἦν τοῦτο διεσκορπισμένον καὶ συναχθὲν ἐγένετο εἰς ἄρτος ("As this was scattered and brought together as one bread").

31 Erik Peterson, "Μερίς: Hostienpartikel und Opferanteil," in idem, *Frühkirche*, 99–100. Κλάσμα cannot mean "the broken bread" but only "the fragment." Here, however, it cannot be translated that way. "Hence I see no other possibility of overcoming the difficulty than to suppose that the word κλάσμα in chap. 9 of the *Didache* has entered the text under the influence of the Egyptian liturgy" (p. 100).

32 Charles Bigg ("Notes on the *Didache*," *JTS* 6 [1905] 413) had already pointed to the connection with the Egyptian liturgy (and claimed the use of this term as evidence for the late origin of the *Didache*, p. 414).

32 *Liturgical Traditions*, 89, 146–48; idem, "Background," 83.

33 On this whole subject, cf. Niederwimmer, "Textprobleme," 124–25; now also Wengst, *Didache*, 78, 97–98. The thesis that κλάσμα comes from the eucharistic language of Egypt would still not provide evidence of the originally eucharistic character of the prayer (as Peterson wishes to say: "Probleme," 168–69). Cf. also Wengst, *Didache*, 98.

34 Cf. (Ps.-)Athanasius *De virg.* 13 (von der Goltz, 47.3–4):
    1. εὐχαριστοῦμέν σοι πάτερ ἡμῶν
    2. ὑπὲρ τῆς ἁγίας ἀναστάσεώς σου·
        διὰ γὰρ Ἰησοῦ τοῦ παιδός σου ἐγνώρισας ἡμῖν αὐτήν . . .

35 Cf. *m. Ber.* 6.1 (ed. Holtzmann, 72–73).

36 According to Peterson ("Probleme," 178) the original Egyptian liturgy mentioned ἀνάστασις as an element of salvation (as does *De virg.* 13), and this would have been replaced by ζωή in the Bryennios text; in addition, γνῶσις would have been inserted. See the doubts about this proposal expressed in Vööbus, *Liturgical Traditions*, 86–87.

37 Remotely comparable is *Diogn.* 12.2–3, where Gen 2:9 is interpreted.

38 Ζωή in *Did.* 1.1, 2, and 4.14 comes from different traditions, but in the mind of the Didachist there is no difference between ζωή in 9.3 and 10.3.

a hendiadys.[37] Ζωή is the "life eternal" (ζωὴ αἰώνιος) for which 10.3 also gives thanks.[38] Cf. "immortality" (ἀθανασία) in 10.2. This is the true, genuine, real life, the life that alone deserves the name, in contrast to the earthly alienation characterized by death. Γνῶσις should be understood in an analogous sense. It is the gift for which 10.2 also gives thanks, and is related to the γνῶσις κυρίου in 11.2 (redaction). Knowledge here does not mean the intellectual apprehension of objects, but the revealed knowledge of God, the insight into the hidden meaning of life and the universe that is bestowed by revelation, the uncovering of what would otherwise be radically alien and hidden from the human being. The opposite of this was the ignorance and obscurity of earthly life.[39] When, moreover, the key word γνῶσις is absent in the concomitant passage of the *Apostolic Constitutions*, it is difficult to draw from that fact the conclusion that καὶ γνώσεως was originally absent from the text of the *Didache* as well, and that it was only added in the course of the text's later development.[40] It has a solid place in *Did.* 10.2, and it is also original in 9.3. Dibelius's hypothesis[41] that this was a prayer originally stemming from Hellenistic Jewish circles that had

already prayed in a spiritual sense for the heavenly manna is without any support.[42]

Ἧς ἐγνώρισας ἡμῖν διὰ Ἰησοῦ τοῦ παιδός σου (v. 3b) corresponds, word for word, to the phrase in the blessing of the cup (9.2). Again we may suppose that σοὶ ἡ δόξα εἰς τοὺς αἰῶνας (v. 3c) was spoken as a response by the participants at the meal.[43]

■ **4** Unlike the blessing of the wine, the blessing of bread is followed by another prayer that, with restrained pathos, establishes an important relationship between the unity of the bread and the eschatological gathering of the church. The symbolism that emerges here reappears (with appropriate variations) in many later liturgical prayers.[44] Let me only mention (Ps.-)Athanasius *De virg.* 13 (von der Goltz, 47.4–9); Serapion *Euchologium* 13.13; (Funk, *Didascalia*, 2.174, 18–22); *P. Dêr Balizeh* fol. IIv., lines 3–11;[45] plus, of course — though not an independent witness — *Const.* 7.25.3;[46] cf. table 10.[47] Still, one need not suppose that in any of these cases (apart from *Constitutions*, of course) there is a direct literary dependence on the *Didache*. What we find here, apparently, is

39 Thus the text here is not speaking of knowledge of Scripture (as in *Barn.* 1.5, etc.; *Hermas Vis.* 2.2); the concept is also free from polemic (cf., in contrast, Ignatius *Eph.* 17.2): this would also be out of place in a liturgical formula. But the tradition in which the *Didache* operates is utterly free from any hint of danger from Gnosticism. By contrast, *1 Clem.* 59.2 and *Mart. Pol.* 14.1 offer significant material parallels to the concept of γνῶσις in the *Didache*, because here the office of the *pais* is the communication of knowledge: *1 Clem.* 59.2, διὰ τοῦ ἠγαπημένου παιδὸς αὐτοῦ Ἰησοῦ Χριστοῦ, δι᾽ οὗ ἐκάλεσεν ἡμᾶς ἀπὸ σκότους εἰς φῶς, ἀπὸ ἀγνωσίας εἰς ἐπίγνωσιν δόξης ὀνόματος αὐτοῦ ("through his beloved servant, Jesus Christ, through whom he has called us from darkness into light, from ignorance into the glorious knowledge of his name"); *Mart. Pol.* 14.1, Κύριε ὁ θεὸς ὁ παντοκράτωρ, ὁ τοῦ ἀγαπητοῦ καὶ εὐλογητοῦ παιδός σου Ἰησοῦ Χριστοῦ πατήρ, δι᾽ οὗ τὴν περὶ σοῦ ἐπίγνωσιν εἰλήφαμεν ("Lord, God almighty, Father of your beloved and blessed servant, Jesus Christ, through whom we have received knowledge of you"). These passages are also important because both belong to the liturgy: the passage from the *Martyrdom of Polycarp* is probably from the anaphora prayer of the community at Smyrna. Cf. Harnack, "Bezeichnung," 221.

40 Cf. the suggestions of Peterson, "Probleme," 178. Wengst (*Didache*, 78) deleted καὶ γνώσεως.

41 "Mahl-Gebete," 120–21.

42 Cf.: "We will first suppose, hypothetically. . . . It may thus be supposed . . . " ("Mahl-Gebete," p. 120). Betz ("Eucharist," 260–61) differs: behind *Did.* 9.3, he thinks, was Gen 2:9; the ancient eucharistic prayers (and Betz considers the prayers in chaps. 9–10 to be such prayers) understood the eucharistic gifts as the gifts of paradise.

43 Audet (*Didachè*, 402) conjectures ἀμήν as the response.

44 Moreover, there is a variant of the same idea in *Did.* 10.5.

45 Roberts and Capelle, *Euchologium*, 26; van Haelst, "Nouvelle reconstitution," 449.

46 For these parallels, see Clerici, *Einsammlung*, 104–8.

47 See the further parallels in Clerici, *Einsammlung*, 108–12. Cf. esp. Cyprian *Ep.* 63.13 (CSEL 3.2.712): *quo et ipso sacramento populus noster ostenditur adunatus, ut quemadmodum grana multa in unum collecta et conmolita et conmixta panem unum faciunt, sic in Christo qui est panis caelestis unum sciamus esse corpus, cui coniunctus sit noster numerus et adunatus* ("And under this same sacred image our people are represented as having been made one, for just as numerous grains are gathered, ground, and mixed all

Table 10

Did. 9.4	(Ps.-)Athanasius *De virg.* 13	Serapion *Euchologium* 13.13	*P. Dêr Balizeh,* IIv. ll. 3–11[1]
ὥσπερ ἦν	καὶ καθὼς	καὶ ὥσπερ	*[Καὶ ὃν τρό]πον*
τοῦτο	ὁ ἄρτος οὗτος	ὁ ἄρτος οὗτος	*ο[ὗ]τος ὁ ἄρ]τος*
διεσκορπισμένον[2]	ἐσκορπισμένος[3] ὑπάρχει	ἐσκορπισμένος ἦν	*ἐσκορπισμένος ἦν*
ἐπάνω τῶν ὀρέων	ὁ ἐπάνω	ἐπάνω τῶν ὀρέων	*[ἐ]πάνω [τῶν ὀρέων]*
—	ταύτης τῆς τραπέζης		*καὶ βο[υ]νῶν καὶ ἀρουρῶν*
καὶ συναχθὲν	καὶ συναχθεὶς	καὶ συναχθεὶς	*κα[ὶ συμμ]γεὶς*
ἐγένετο ἕν,	ἐγένετο ἕν,	ἐγένετο εἰς ἕν,	*ε[γέν]ετο ἓν σῶμα, . . .*
—	—	—	*(lines 6–9)[4]*
οὕτω συναχθήτω	οὕτως ἐπισυναχθήτω	οὕτω καὶ τὴν ἁγίαν	*οὕτ[ως,] ἐπ[ισύνα]ξον*
σου ἡ ἐκκλησία	σου ἡ ἐκκλησία	σου ἐκκλησίαν σύναξον	*τὴ[ν] καθολικὴν [ἐκ]κλη]σίαν*
—	—	—	*τοῦ Ἰ(ησο)ῦ Χ(ριστο)ῦ].[5]*
ἀπὸ τῶν περάτων	ἀπὸ τῶν περάτων	ἐκ παντὸς ἔθνους[6]	—
τῆς γῆς	τῆς γῆς	. . .	
εἰς τὴν σὴν βασιλείαν·	εἰς τὴν βασιλείαν	καὶ ποίησον μίαν	
—	σου,	ζῶσαν καθολικὴν ἐκκλησίαν.[7]	
ὅτι σοῦ ἐστιν ἡ δόξα	ὅτι σοῦ ἐστιν ἡ δύναμις		
καὶ ἡ δύναμις	καὶ ἡ δόξα		
διὰ Ἰησοῦ Χριστοῦ	—		
εἰς τοὺς αἰῶνας.	εἰς τοὺς αἰῶνας τ. αἰώνων,		
—	ἀμήν.		

[1] I am citing the text of van Haelst, but not in the lines of the papyrus; the lines are adjusted to this synopsis.

[2] My emendation; see below.

[3] *V.l.* διεσκορπισμένος (cf. von der Goltz, 47.4–9).

[4] Lines 6–9: . . . οσω [. . . καθ]ὼς ὁ οἶνος ο[ὗτος]/ὁ ἐξελθὼν ἐκ τῆ[ς ἁγίας ἀ]μπέλου Δ[αυεὶδ] καὶ τὸ ὕδωρ ἐξ ἀμ[νοῦ ἀμώ]μου καὶ σύμ[μικτα] .ειο ἐγένετο ἓν [μυ]στήριον.

[5] The words of institution follow.

[6] Added: καὶ πάσης χώρας καὶ πάσης πόλεως καὶ κώμης καὶ οἴκου.

[7] In 13.14 there follow the words of institution over the cup.

an especially ancient piece of liturgy. Our passage presents the oldest example in a liturgical formula.[48]

Excursus: The Text of the Prayer

There may have been an occasion for improvement of the *Didache* text at three different points. (1) Κλάσμα may not be original (see above). The original may have been ἄρτος, but in that case the whole syntax would have to be changed.[49] It seems simpler to me to delete κλάσμα in 9.4 as a later (Egyptian) addition; then the conjectural <τό>[50] would also be superfluous. The *Apostolic Constitutions* has preserved the original text: ὥσπερ ἦν τοῦτο διεσκορπισμένον.[51] The suggested conjectures by Jean Magne are highly imaginative.[52] (2) Διὰ Ἰησοῦ Χριστοῦ could be a later

together to make one loaf of bread, so in Christ, who is the bread of heaven, we know there is but one body and that every one of us has been fused together and made one with it"; trans. G. W. Clarke, *The Lettters of St. Cyprian of Carthage,* vol. 3: *Letters 55–66* [New York and Mahwah, N.J.: Newman, 1986] 105); and 69.5 (CSEL 3.2.754): *nam quando Dominus corpus suum panem vocat de multorum granorum adunatione congestum, populum nostrum quem portabat indicat adunatum* ("For when the Lord calls bread His own body—and bread is a conglomerate of many individual grains, made into one – he signifies that we, the people whom He bore, are unit-ed into one"; trans. G. W. Clarke, *The Lettters of St. Cyprian of Carthage,* vol. 4: *Letters 67–82* [New York and Mahwah, N.J.: Newman, 1989] 56). (The comparison is then continued with regard to the wine.) J. Gribomont has investigated the motif of *ecclesiam adunare* in the Roman canon ("Ecclesiam adunare: Un echo de l'eucharistie africaine et de la Didachè," *RThAM* 27 [1960] 20–28). Interesting in the present context is the suggestion that the expression can be traced to the influence of the "African" liturgy (p. 26). Gribomont posits the influence of the *Didache* on the African liturgy (p. 27: hardly likely), but he himself raises the objection that there could be expansion (so Audet).[53] It is absent from the parallels in Ps.-Athanasius and in *Did.* 10.5. The text seems to be established, however, by the δι᾽ αὐτοῦ in *Const.* 7.25.4. (3) In the doxology we should perhaps establish the sequence: ὅτι σοῦ ἐστιν ἡ δύναμις καὶ ἡ δόξα . . . εἰς τοὺς αἰῶνας; cf. *Did.* 10.5 and the parallel text in Ps.-Athanasius *De virg.* 13.

The Old Testament root and foundation of the passage is found in the prophetic hope for the gathering of the people of Israel in the day of salvation.[54] Cf. Isa 11:12: καὶ συνάξει τοὺς ἀπολομένους Ἰσραὴλ καὶ τοὺς διεσπαρμένους Ἰούδα συνάξει ἐκ τῶν τεσσάρων πτερύγων τῆς γῆς ("And he will gather the lost of Israel and the scattered ones of Judah he will gather from the four corners of the earth"); Jer 39:37 LXX: ἰδοὺ ἐγὼ συνάγω αὐτοὺς ἐκ πάσης τῆς γῆς, οὗ διέσπειρα αὐτοὺς . . . καὶ ἐπιστρέψω αὐτοὺς εἰς τὸν τόπον τοῦτον ("Behold I gather them from all the earth where I scattered them . . . and I shall return them to this place"); Ezek 11:17: καὶ συνάξω αὐτοὺς ἐκ τῶν χωρῶν, οὗ διέσπειρα αὐτοὺς ἐν αὐταῖς, καὶ δώσω αὐτοῖς τὴν γῆν τοῦ Ἰσραήλ ("and I shall gather them from the lands where I scattered them, and I shall give them the land of Israel"); Zech 2:10 LXX: ἐκ τῶν τεσσάρων ἀνέμων τοῦ οὐρανοῦ συνάξω ὑμᾶς, λέγει κύριος ("From the four winds of the heaven I shall gather you, says the Lord").[55] This hope entered into the prayer language of Judaism; see *Shemoneh*

Esreh (Palestinian recension) 10: "Raise a banner for the gathering of our exiles; praised art thou, YHWH, who gathers the scattered of your people Israel!"[56] Cf. the Babylonian recension: "Raise a banner to gather all our exiles from the four ends of the earth into our land; praised art thou, YHWH, who gathers the scattered of your people Israel."[57] Cf. the Musaph prayer for Rosh Hashanah 4;[58] and, finally, a blessing with the schema *ahaba rabba*: "bring us together in peace from the four corners of the earth, and bring us in upright ways into our land."[59]

Israel's hope for the reunion of those who have been separated has entered, mutatis mutandis, into the primitive Christian hope for the final assembly of the elect. Cf. Mark 13:27: "And then he will send his angels and gather the [his] elect from the four winds, from the end of the earth to the end of heaven" (καὶ τότε ἀποστελεῖ τοὺς ἀγγέλους καὶ ἐπισυνάξει τοὺς ἐκλεκτοὺς [αὐτοῦ] ἐκ τῶν τεσσάρων ἀνέμων ἀπ᾽ ἄκρου γῆς ἕως ἄκρου οὐρανοῦ; cf. Matt 24:31). For this theme, cf. also John 11:52.[60] It is obvious why this hope found expression in the church's liturgies. Of course the adoption of the Jewish motif within the Christian liturgy required certain adaptations: What this community implores is no longer the gathering of Israel and the triumphant reunion of the whole people, but the gathering of the church ἀπὸ περάτων

---

common dependence on a "paleo-Christian liturgy" (ibid.). Cf. also the doubts regarding the acceptance of a relationship to the *Didache* in Clerici, *Einsammlung*, 135–42.

48 Clerici has discussed the changes experienced by this motif at a later time. We will not pursue the matter here. Cf. the interpretation of the later history in Clerici, *Einsammlung*, 104–12.

49 Cf. the suggestions of Vööbus, *Liturgical Traditions*, 88–89, 146–48 (following Peterson); and see above, n. 31.

50 Usually included since Gebhardt.

51 Niederwimmer, "Textprobleme," 124–25; now also Wengst, *Didache*, 80.

52 "Klasma, sperma, poimnion: Le voeu pour le rassemblement de Didachè IX, 4," in P. Lévy and E. Wolff, eds., *Mélanges d'histoire des religions offerts à Henri-Charles Puech* (Paris: Presses universitaires de France, 1974) 206–7. According to Magne, σπέρμα previously stood where κλάσμα is now, and still earlier (in harmony with OT models) it was ποίμνιον. In addition, Magne (p. 208) makes the *Didache* a product of Gnosticism.

53 Audet, *Didachè*, 234.

54 For the prehistory of the symbolism in *Did.* 9.4 (10.5), see Riesenfeld, "Brot von den Bergen," 145–47; Clerici, *Einsammlung*, 67–92.

55 Cf. also Deut 30:1–5; Isa 27:13; 43:5–7; 56:8; Jer 23:8; 31:8, 10; Ezek 28:25; 34:11–16; 37:21; 39:27; Mic 4:12; Pss 106:47; 147:2; Neh 1:8–9; 1 Chr 16:35; Sir 36:11; 51:12(f); 2 Macc 1:27; 2:7, 18; Tob 13:5; *Ps. Sol.* 8.28; 11.2ff.; 17.26, 44. This motif plays a special part later in the *Testaments of the 12 Patriarchs* (cf. Clerici, *Einsammlung*, 76–77): *T. Jud.* 23.5; *T. Iss.* 6.2–4; *T. Dan* 5.8–9; *T. Naph.* 4. The leading of Israel home is occasionally combined with the salvation of the "nations": *T. Ash.* 7.2–3; *T. Benj.* 9.2 (but do these statements belong to a subsequent layer?). For the linguistic parallels with the *Didache*, cf. also *T. Naph.* 6.7: "We were all scattered to the ends of the earth" (διεσπάρημεν οὖν οἱ πάντες ἕως εἰς τὰ πέρατα); and *T. Ash.* 7.2: "You will be scattered to the four corners of the earth" (ὑμεῖς διασκορπισθήσεσθε εἰς τὰς τέσσαρας γωνίας τῆς γῆς). See Clerici, *Einsammlung*, 76.

56 Holtzmann, *Berakot*, 16.

57 Holtzmann, *Berakot*, 20.

58 Staerk, *Gebete*, 24.

59 Staerk, *Gebete*, 6; German translation in Str–B 1.398.

60 Later: *Mart. Pol.* 22.3: ἵνα κἀμὲ συναγάγῃ ὁ κύριος Ἰησοῦς Χριστὸς μετὰ τῶν ἐκλεκτῶν αὐτοῦ εἰς τὴν οὐράνιον βασιλείαν αὐτοῦ—the final wish of the author ("May the Lord Jesus gather me as well with his elect into his heavenly kingdom"). In contrast, it

τῆς γῆς and its being brought home into the βασιλεία (sc. τοῦ θεοῦ).[61] In the liturgy of the *Didache* the hope for eschatological reunion of the separated is related to the meal celebration.[62] As the bread eaten at the common meal συναχθὲν ἐγένετο ἕν, so will the church be—on that day. It should be obvious on the face of it that the symbolism of *Did.* 9.4a should not be examined with logical stringency: the phrases about what was (previously) "scattered on the hillsides,"[63] and is (now) gathered into one,[64] do not strictly describe some particular techniques in farming and bread production,[65] but are simply intended to point to and beyond the one common element (with respect to bread and church): *one* bread from the διεσκορπισμένον "on the surrounding hills"; *one* church from many who are now dispersed throughout the world.[66]

The prayer almost constitutes an "interpretive saying." As the bread has come into being through the gathering of grains once scattered on the surrounding hills,[67] so may God gather the diaspora of the church[68] from the ends of the earth[69] into God's reign. The βασιλεία is understood in an eschatological sense as the realm of the end time, in which all dispersion will be at an end. God's reign is determinative for the church.

The community gathered for the meal responds[70] to this prayer by saying: ὅτι σοῦ ἐστιν ἡ δόξα καὶ ἡ δύναμις διὰ Ἰησοῦ Χριστοῦ εἰς τοὺς αἰῶνας.[71]

■ **5** At this point the Didachist[72] has inserted a rubrical comment. Only those baptized (in the name of the Lord)[73] may take part; only they may eat and drink "of your thanksgiving [meal]." It is not clear whether here

---

seems to me that the ἑνότης motif in John 17:11, 20–23 belongs in a different context.

61 God's *basileia*: in *Did.* 8.2 (in the quotation of the Lord's Prayer) and in 10.5, the material parallel to 9.4. It seems questionable to me whether the *Didache* text thinks directly of the metaphor of "harvest" for the "judgment of the world" in connection with the gathering of the scattered (Riesenfeld, "Brot von den Bergen," 146–47).

62 Cf. earlier 1 Cor 10:17, although there with regard to the Eucharist; Ignatius *Eph.* 20.2. As the parallels show, the motif had its later *Sitz im Leben* primarily in the anaphora of the Eucharist. The same motif reappears in *Did.* 10.5, a prayer that looks back in gratitude to the "*agape*" but at the same time looks forward to the sacrament.

63 Ἐπάνω τῶν ὀρέων remains uninterpreted thus far. Riesenfeld ("Brot von den Bergen," 149–50) suggested a connection with Isa 40:4, and recalls 1 Bar. 5.5–8 and *Ps. Sol.* 11.2–4. This is highly questionable.

64 Η reads καὶ συναχθὲν ἐγένετο ἕν. Wengst (*Didache* 80) decided (with *Constitutions*) for εἷς ἄρτος instead of ἕν.

65 For information on the ritual gathering of wheat for the eucharistic bread, see Adam, "Herkunft," 57–61, who sees in it evidence of the "east Syrian roots of the *Didache*" (p. 57).

66 The interpretation presented here avoids making claims with regard to Johannine reminiscences. There is sometimes a different tendency in recent research, e.g.: Goodenough, "John a Primitive Gospel," *JBL* 64 [1945] 174–75, who sees in this passage (besides dependence on Jewish liturgy) reminiscences from the Fourth Gospel (chap. 6); also Moule, "Note," 240–43. Moule finds the received interpretation problematic (instead of κλάσμα, one

would tend to expect ἄρτος, and instead of διεσκορπισμένον rather διεσπαρμένον; συνάγειν must remain odd in the traditional interpretation, and why ἐπάνω τῶν ὀρέων? pp. 240–41). These difficulties are largely eliminated if (with Moule, "Note," 242) one refers *Did.* 9.4 to "the gathering of the κλάσματα after the feeding of the multitude" (sc. according to John 6). Even the ἐπάνω τῶν ὀρέων would be explained, namely, as an echo of John 6:3 (εἰς τὸ ὄρος). To the contrary, and correctly, Riesenfeld, "Brot von den Bergen," 143–45. Lucien Cerfaux has contradicted Riesenfeld's presentation and again established connections to John 6 and 11:52, although not necessarily literary connections ("La multiplication des pains dans la liturgie de la Didachè," *Bib* 40 [1959] 943–58). Against the presentations by Goodenough, Moule, and Cerfaux: Clerici, *Einsammlung*, 92–102; Vööbus, *Liturgical Traditions*, 137–57; idem, "Regarding the Background of the Liturgical Traditions in the Didache: The Question of Literary Relation between Didache IX,4 and the Fourth Gospel," *VC* 23 (1969) 81–87. I also regard the derivation from the Fourth Gospel as out of place. Cf. also Rordorf and Tuilier, *Doctrine*, 46 n. 3. Possible relationships to John 11:52 can be adequately explained by their dependence on a common liturgical tradition. On the work of Magne, see above, p. 151 n. 52.

67 For the uncontracted genitive plural ὀρέων, see BDF, §48; BDR, §48.

68 On this see Kurt Niederwimmer, "Kirche als Diaspora," *EvTh* 41 (1981) 294. "The ἐκκλησία, here and in 10.5, is the whole community (differently from 4.14)." See also Knopf, *Lehre*, 27; and previously Harnack, *Lehre*, 31.

69 For τὰ πέρατα τῆς γῆς, cf. *T. Naph.* 6.7; Matt

εὐχαριστία means the entire meal celebration or the foods themselves. It is also uncertain whether εὐχαριστία at this point refers simply to the nonsacramental meal of the community (which has been the subject thus far),[74] or whether (and recall that we are looking at a redactional text) the term already includes the sacramental Lord's Supper that will follow at 10.6. I consider the latter more probable.

Here again (cf. *Did.* 1.6), the Didachist has the tendency to give authority to his remarks by adding a supportive quotation (v. 5b): καὶ γὰρ περὶ τούτου εἴρηκεν[75] ὁ κύριος introduces a quotation from the Jesus tradition. The subsequent quotation, μὴ δῶτε τὸ ἅγιον τοῖς κυσί, is found word for word in Matt 7:6; however, it is not certain that the Didachist is quoting Matthew's Gospel.[76] In the *Didache* we should consider the possibility of oral tradition, or a quotation from an unknown apocryphal gospel. The Didachist interprets the logion[77] as an authoritative confirmation of the prohibition he has just expressed. If Jesus forbade giving what is holy to the dogs, he thus forbade (*also at any rate*)[78] the giving of the sacred food to the unbaptized.[79] Hence τὸ ἅγιον = the sacred food (possibly we should expand this to mean that οἱ ἅγιοι = the baptized), and οἱ κύνες = the unbaptized.[80] The concept τὸ ἅγιον can certainly refer to the food of the Christian community meal;[81] it is more prob-

---

12:42/Luke 11:31; *1 Clem.* 36.4 (= Ps 2:8); Ignatius *Rom.* 6.1; *Hermas Sim.* 8.3.2.

70 Dibelius, "Mahl-Gebete," 121–22.

71 The response may originally have been: ὅτι σοῦ ἐστιν ἡ δύναμις καὶ ἡ δόξα εἰς τοὺς αἰῶνας. See above. Audet conjectures ἀμήν (*Didachè*, 401).

72 Betz ("Eucharist," 249) differs: this is "old tradition, not first composed by the redactor of the *Didache* but taken over."

73 For the formulation οἱ βαπτισθέντες εἰς ὄνομα κυρίου, cf. the baptismal formula in *Did.* 7.1, 3, and above, pp. 126–27 nn. 8, 11, and 12.

74 Stuiber, "Eulogia," 915: "If this is a liturgical agenda, εὐχαριστία would refer to the foods over which the one εὐχαριστία is spoken as table prayer."

75 Cf. *Did.* 1.6: ἀλλὰ καὶ περὶ τούτου δὲ εἴρηται; and 16.7: ἀλλ' ὡς ἐρρέθη, both of which are redactional.

76 Obviously, Massaux (*Influence*, 3.156) thinks here of a quotation from Matthew, as does Hagner, *Use*, 280. To the contrary: Koester, *Synoptische Überlieferung*, 198–200, 240. Wengst (*Didache*, 28) is inclined once again to think of Matthew. The logion is also found in *Gos. Thom.* (Coptic) 93: "Do not give what is holy to the dogs, because they will throw it on the dung heap" (cf. Leipoldt, 49). Cf. also Basilides in Epiphanius *Pan.* 24.5.2 (GCS 1.262).

77 For the aporetic question (as I see it) about the meaning of the *mashal* in Matthew's Gospel, cf. Erich Klostermann, *Das Matthäusevangelium* (4th ed.; HNT 4; Tübingen: Mohr [Siebeck], 1971) 66–67; Otto Michel, "κύων," *TDNT* 3 (1967) 1101–3; Sigfred Pedersen, "κύων," *EDNT* 2 (1991) 332; Ulrich Luz, *Matthew 1–7: A Commentary* (trans. Wilhelm C. Linss; Minneapolis: Augsburg, 1989) 418: "The logion is a riddle. Neither (a) its origin nor (b) its original meaning nor (c) its meaning in the Matthean context can be completely made clear."

78 Καὶ γὰρ περὶ τούτου. Strictly speaking, the redactor does not say that the Jesus saying refers *only* to this case. We can understand him to mean, "The word of the Lord, which you know, forbidding us to give what is holy to the dogs, can *also* be interpreted to mean that it is forbidden to give the eucharist to the unbaptized." Gregory Dix differs: Christ's prohibition applies not only to the sacramental Eucharist, but also to the community meal (*The Shape of the Liturgy* [2d ed.; repr., London: Black, 1970; New York: Seabury, 1982] 92–93).

79 Otto Michel ("κύων," *TDNT* 3 [1967] 1103) sees a material relationship between the Jesus saying and its interpretation in the *Didache*: "The cultic form of the saying of Jesus suggests that it be applied also to the Church's worship."

80 Rev 22:15 is somewhat different, and different again is the polemic against false teachers in Phil 3:2; 2 Pet 2:22; Ignatius *Eph.* 7.1. Who are the κύνες in Matt 7:6? The unworthy hearers of the proclamation? Or the Gentiles? Or the false brethren? Or the apostates?

81 Cf. Richard H. Connolly, "Agape and Eucharist in the Didache," *DR* 55 (1937) 488; Rordorf and Tuilier, *Doctrine*, 39 n. 1. Indeed, we should note the regulation for the catechumens at the *agape*: Hippolytus *Apost. Trad.* 26–27 (SC 11.102–5); cf. *Die Canones Hippolyti* 33.2.172 (ed. Achelis [TU 6.4; Leipzig: Hinrichs, 1891] 106–7); more remotely comparable is *Ps.-Clem. Rec.* 2.70.5–6; 71.1–3 (GCS 2.92–93) and—with regard to monastic community meals—Ps.-Athanasius *De virg.* 13 (ed. von der Goltz [TU, n.s. 14.2a; Leipzig: Hinrichs, 1906] 47–48): "If

able, however, that we should assume that the Didachist is not thinking simply of the community meal that has been the subject before this. Instead he includes the sacramental celebration of the Lord's Supper, and his prohibition applies in a special sense to that celebration.[82]

a woman catechumen is found at the table, do not let her pray with the believers, neither sit down to eat your bread with her . . . for are you not holy to the Lord God, and is not your food and drink sanctified?" (ἐὰν δὲ εὑρεθῇ κατηχουμένη ἐν τῇ τραπέζῃ, μὴ συνευχέσθω μετὰ τῶν πιστῶν, οὐδὲ μὴ καθίσῃς φαγεῖν τὸν ἄρτον σου μετ᾽ αὐτῆς . . . οὐ γὰρ ἅγια εἶ κυρίῳ τῷ θεῷ, καὶ τὸ βρῶμά σου καὶ τὸ πόμα σου ἡγιασμένον ἐστί). For the exclusion of the novices from the ritual meal at Qumran, see 1QS 6.16–17, 20–21.

82   Possibly serving as a bridge to the redactor's interpretation is the circumstance that, in Jewish tradition, τὸ ἅγιον is sometimes used for "sacrificial meat." Cf. Klostermann, *Matthäusevangelium*, 1102–3; Luz, *Matthew 1–7*, 418.

10

b. Prayer of Thanksgiving (Eucharist) (10.1–7)

1   When you have had your fill, give thanks this
     way:
2   "We thank you, holy Father,
       For your holy name,
          which you made dwell in our hearts,
       And for the knowledge and faith and immor-
          tality,
          which you made known to us
          through Jesus your servant.
       To you be glory forever.
3   You, almighty Lord, created all things for the
          sake of your name,
          and you gave food and drink to human
             beings for enjoyment,
          so that they would thank you;
       But you graced us with spiritual food and
          drink and eternal life
          through <Jesus> your servant.
4   *For all things, we thank you, Lord, because
          you are powerful.
       To you be glory forever.
5   Be mindful, Lord, of your church,
          to preserve it from all evil
          and to perfect it in your love.
       And < . . . > gather it from the four winds,
          into the kingdom which you have prepared
             for it.
       For power and glory are yours forever.
6   May grace come, and may this world pass by.
       Hosanna to the God of David!
       If anyone is holy, let him come.
       If anyone is not, let him repent.
       Maranatha! Amen."
7   Allow the prophets, however, to give thanks as
       much as they like.

Comment

■ **1** With 10.1 the Didachist returns to the quotation of
his source. Verse 1 is a rubrical commentary on the liturgical agenda. The meal took place between chaps. 9 and
10. The phrase μετὰ δὲ τὸ ἐμπλησθῆναι suggests that
the preceding meal was a full meal for satisfaction of
hunger (cf. John 6:12: ὡς δὲ ἐνεπλήσθησαν).[1]

In *Did.* 10.2–5 the liturgy hands on the prescribed
prayer of thanksgiving after the meal. It functions, at the
same time, as the transition to the sacramental liturgy
that follows. The prayer consists of three benedictions

(the first in v. 2, the second in vv. 3–4, and the third in
v. 5), each introduced by an address (πάτερ ἅγιε in v. 2,
δέσποτα παντοκράτορ in v. 3, κύριε in v. 5), and concluded by a doxology (σοὶ ἡ δόξα εἰς τοὺς αἰῶνας in vv.
2 and 4; ὅτι σοῦ ἐστιν ἡ δύναμις καὶ ἡ δόξα εἰς τοὺς
αἰῶνας in v. 5).

The model for this long prayer is (as has long been
acknowledged) the Jewish prayer after meals, the *Birkat
Ha-Mazon.*[2] This is introduced by the "invitational blessing," after which the one who is to recite the benediction
takes the cup of blessing, lifts it slightly from the table,

---

1   Cf. also Luke 6:25; Acts 14:17, and μετὰ τὸ δειπνῆ-
     σαι in 1 Cor 11:25. On the whole subject, see above,
     p. 143 n. 49. Klein ("Gebete," 142) refers to Deut
     8:10; cf. Audet, *Didachè,* 431. The passage plays a
     role as a scriptural basis for the Jewish table prayer
     (cf. Holtzmann, *Berakot,* 79; Str–B 4.632), and the
     blessings that follow are, in part, constructed on the
     model of Jewish table prayer.

2   For the *Birkat Ha-Mazon,* see Holtzmann, *Berakot,*
     78–79; Str–B 4.631–32; Klein, "Gebete," 140–41;
     and particularly Finkelstein, "Birkat Ha-Mazon,"
     211–62; cf. also Middleton, "Eucharistic Prayers,"
     263–67; Hruby, "Birkat Ha-Mazon," 205–22.

and recites the text of the prayer after meals.[3] We may presuppose corresponding actions (with the exception of the invitational benediction?) for the ritual now before us. The text of the Jewish table prayer was expanded in the course of time, so that it would be difficult to attempt to re-create its original wording.[4] The witness of Gamaliel II is important for establishing the extreme age of the original three benedictions (*m. Ber.* 6.8a).[5] The fourth benediction is a later accretion (and yet it is old!).[6] Still, the parts of the Jewish and Christian prayers do not correspond. The first part of the *Didache* prayer (v. 2) is constructed more according to the model in 9.2 and 9.3;[7] only the second part (vv. 3–4) recalls, in its content, the first Jewish benediction (and yet v. 4 is a direct reflection of a passage in the second benediction); finally, the third part of the *Didache* prayer (v. 5) is reminiscent of the third Jewish benediction. Of course the motifs of the Jewish "model" have been fundamentally reinterpreted.[8] Even from a formal point of view, however, we may observe crucial differences.

■ **2** The first benediction is constructed according to the same scheme as the prayers in 9.2 and 9.3, with element (2) doubled:

1. Εὐχαριστοῦμέν σοι, πάτερ ἅγιε,
2. ὑπὲρ τοῦ ἁγίου ὀνόματός σου,
   οὗ[9] κατεσκήνωσας ἐν ταῖς καρδίαις ἡμῶν,
   καὶ ὑπὲρ τῆς γνώσεως καὶ πίστεως καὶ ἀθανασίας,
   ἧς ἐγνώρισας ἡμῖν διὰ Ἰησοῦ τοῦ παιδός σου·
3. σοὶ ἡ δόξα εἰς τοὺς αἰῶνας.

The community praises God[10] who has made the divine ὄνομα ("name") to dwell in it—namely (as we are probably meant to understand), through and since baptism.[11] Ὄνομα (more precisely: τὸ ἅγιον ὄνομά σου)[12] is God's epiphany, God in person.[13] Κατασκηνοῦν (for שכן)[14] plays on God's "dwelling," God's presence; in this way[15] God makes a dwelling for the divine name—secretly and invisibly, but really and effectively—in our innermost being, ἐν ταῖς καρδίαις ἡμῶν,[16] that is, in the heart and center of a person.[17] The continuation, καὶ ὑπὲρ τῆς γνώσεως . . . , is parallel to ὑπὲρ τοῦ ἁγίου ὀνόματος . . . and continues the listing of the goods of salvation. We should probably understand this to mean that through this very indwelling of God (God's holy name, as the OT-flavored text says) we are given salvation, knowledge, faith, and immortality. While the goods

---

3   See the details in Str–B 4.627–34; Jeremias, *Eucharistic Words*, 110.

4   This is attempted by Finkelstein, "Birkat Ha-Mazon," 223–35; Hruby, "Birkat Ha-Mazon," 207–16.

5   Holtzmann, *Berakot*, 77–79.

6   The wording of the first three benedictions was, however, also expanded and changed over time. On this see Finkelstein, "Birkat Ha-Mazon," 261–62; Hruby, "Birkat Ha-Mazon," 205–22.

7   Still, as a rule the first benediction in *Didache* 10 is paralleled with the second benediction of the Jewish prayer after meals. See Finkelstein, "Birkat Ha-Mazon," 216. Dibelius also ("Mahl-Gebete," 122–23) paralleled *Did.* 10.2 with the *Birkat Ha-Arez,* but then suggested (in line with his hypothesis) that the text should be understood "as a Hellenistic development of the Hebrew prayer after meals" (p. 122), or as "a prayer after meals used in Greek Judaism" (p. 123), and that this was then Christianized in the *Didache.* But these ideas are, altogether, quite arbitrary.

8   These differences are analyzed esp. by Finkelstein, "Birkat Ha-Mazon," 213–19, although I cannot agree with him at every point.

9   Attraction: cf. BDF, §294; BDR, §294.

10   Πάτερ ἅγιε as in John 17:11. The expression is found in the NT and the Apostolic Fathers only there and in *Did.* 10.2. See the further connections between *Did.* 10.2, 5 and John 17 described by Clerici (*Einsammlung*, 97), who correctly emphasizes that "despite these common themes . . . no literary dependence [can be] established." Instead, we should think of a common liturgical tradition (ibid.). Wengst (*Didache,* 81 n. 77) writes: "Both passages [Wengst is thinking of πάτερ ἅγιε in John 17:11 and *Did.* 10.2] make it likely that the address 'holy Father' is derived from liturgical language." Cf. also *Odes Sol.* 31.5 (Charlesworth, 115–16); "*Pater sancte,*" *Acts of Peter* (against Simon) 27 (Lipsius-Bonnet, 1.74).

11   Wilhelm Michaelis, "κατασκηνόω," *TDNT* 7 (1971) 389; Rordorf, "Didachè," 19; unrestrictedly: Knopf, *Lehre,* 28.

12   For τὸ ἅγιον ὄνομα ("the holy name"), cf. ἅγιον καὶ φοβερὸν τὸ ὄνομα αὐτοῦ ("his holy and awesome name"), Ps 110:9; τὸ ὄνομα τὸ ἅγιον, Lev 18:21; (+ μου) 22:2; καὶ ἅγιον τὸ ὄνομα αὐτοῦ, Luke 1:49; τὸ μεγαλοπρεπὲς καὶ ἅγιον ὄνομα αὐτοῦ ("his magnificent and holy name"), *1 Clem.* 64.

13   Similarly Drews, "Apostellehre," 270; Knopf, *Lehre,* 28; Audet, *Didachè,* 431. Ὄνομα here stands for what the Greeks would call οὐσία.

14   Cf. Michaelis, "κατασκηνόω," *TDNT* 7 (1971) 387.

15   Κατασκηνοῦν is not intransitive, but transitive, or rather causative: cf. Ps 22:2; Jer 7:12; Ezek 43:7.

156

of salvation in 9.3 were ζωή ("life") and γνῶσις ("knowledge"), now γνῶσις ("knowledge"), πίστις ("faith"),[18] and ἀθανασία ("immortality") are named.[19] The goods of salvation that God bestows are mediated and revealed through Jesus, the "servant."[20] The next expressions, ἧς ἐγνώρισας κτλ., and σοὶ ἡ δόξα εἰς τοὺς αἰῶνας, correspond directly to the conclusions of the prayers in 9.2 and 3.[21] The stylistic relationship of the three prayers in 9.2; 9.3; and 10.2 is quite clear.

■ **3–4** The second benediction then follows the motifs of the Jewish prayer after meals (see above),[22] beginning with the *Birkat Hassan.* As reconstructed by Finkelstein,[23] the oldest version of this benediction in the prayer was: "Blessed art thou, O Lord, our God, king of the universe, who feedest the whole world with goodness, with grace, and with mercy."[24] It is uncertain to what extent the Jewish model for the *Didache* prayer had already been expanded beyond the reconstructed original form.[25] The prayer in the *Didache* is constructed as follows:

1. σύ, δέσποτα παντοκράτορ,
2. ἔκτισας τὰ πάντα ἔνεκεν τοῦ ὀνόματός σου, τροφήν τε καὶ ποτὸν ἔδωκας τοῖς ἀνθρώποις εἰς ἀπόλαυσιν, ἵνα σοι εὐχαριστήσωσιν, ἡμῖν δὲ ἐχαρίσω πνευματικὴν τροφὴν καὶ ποτὸν καὶ ζωὴν αἰώνιον διὰ Ἰησοῦ[26] τοῦ παιδός σου.
3. περὶ[27] πάντων εὐχαριστοῦμέν σοι, ὅτι δυνατὸς εἶ· σοὶ[28] ἡ δόξα εἰς τοὺς αἰῶνας.

The prayer first calls upon God, the δεσπότης παντοκράτωρ ("almighty Lord") who created all things. The address δέσποτα[29] is made more explicit by the addition

---

16 H has mistakenly written ὑμῶν; this was emended by Bryennios, Διδαχή, 37 and n. 4.

17 For this expression and its earlier history, cf. Jer 7:12: (εἰς τὸν τόπον . . .) οὗ κατεσκήνωσα τὸ ὄνομά μου ἐκεῖ ἔμπροσθεν ("the place where I caused my name to dwell previously"); Ezek 43:7: ἐν οἷς κατασκηνώσει τὸ ὄνομά μου ("among whom he will cause my name to dwell"); 2 Esd 11:9: κατασκηνῶσαι τὸ ὄνομά μου ("to cause my name to dwell"); *Ps. Sol.* 7.6: ἐν τῷ κατασκηνοῦν τὸ ὄνομά σου ἐν μέσῳ ἡμῶν ἐλεηθησόμεθα ("in causing your name to dwell among us we will be shown mercy"). Our text speaks of God's dwelling in our hearts, which is revealed through baptism. For the indwelling of God, Christ, and the Spirit, cf. Rom 8:9; 1 Cor 14:25; Jas 4:5; *Barn.* 16.9; Ignatius *Eph.* 15.3. For Christians as God's temple: 1 Cor 3:16; 6:19; 2 Cor 6:16, and Ignatius *Eph.* 15.3.

18 In the *Didache* also at 16.2, 5.

19 Ἀθανασία appears only here in the *Didache*; we find τὸ ἀθάνατον in 4.8. For ἀθανασία, cf. Ignatius *Eph.* 20.2 (in a eucharistic context); ζωὴ ἐν ἀθανασίᾳ ("life in immortality") as one of the δῶρα τοῦ θεοῦ ("gifts of God"): *1 Clem.* 35.2 (with πίστις). In *Acts of John* 109 (18) (22.1, p. 208.6 in Bonnet), Christ is called upon in the eucharistic prayer: "Root of immortality and font of incorruption" (ῥίζα τῆς ἀθανασίας καὶ ἡ πηγὴ τῆς ἀφθαρσίας).

20 Wengst (*Didache*, 80, following the Georgian), has deleted ἡμῖν after ἐγνώρισας. But cf. the parallels in 9.2 and 3.

21 Audet again conjectures ἀμήν as a response (*Didachè*, 401).

22 Dibelius, "Mahl-Gebete," 123, referred to *m. Ber.* 6.8b ("Whoever drinks water for his/her thirst speaks praise: 'through the word all things came to be'" [Holtzmann, *Berakot*, 81]) and unnecessarily regarded this reference as more important than that to the *Birkat Hassan.*

23 Finkelstein, "Birkat Ha-Mazon," 227.

24 The translation follows that in Jeremias, *Eucharistic Words*, 110.

25 The clause later added (?—Hruby differs, "Birkat Ha-Mazon," 208), "blessed art thou, Lord, who nourishes all things," corresponds to the doxology in the *Didache* prayer: σοὶ ἡ δόξα κτλ. The phrase "for the sake of [God's] great name," lacking in the reconstructed oldest form, appears to be attested already by the *Didache*. See below.

26 On this, see below, n. 37.

27 On this, see below, n. 46.

28 On this, see below, n. 41.

29 Addressing God as δεσπότης is something inherited from Hellenistic Jewish tradition. In the NT see Luke 2:29; Acts 4:24; Rev 6:10; with reference to Jesus: 2 Pet 2:1; cf. Jude 4, and indirectly perhaps 2 Tim 2:21. Δεσπότης occurs only here in the *Didache*. As predicated of God in the Apostolic Fathers: *Barn.* 1.7; 4.3; *Hermas Vis.* 2.2.4–5; *Sim.* 1.9; and frequently in *1 Clement.* Especially characteristic of the present context is ὁ δεσπότης τῶν ἀπάντων, *1 Clem.* 8.2; δημιουργὸς καὶ δεσπότης τῶν ἀπάντων, 20.11; cf. 33.2; ὁ δεσπότης ὑπάρχει τῶν ἀπάντων,

of παντοκράτωρ;[30] as creator, God is at the same time the universal ruler over all creatures.[31] God is not only the one who created all things "for the sake of the divine name,"[32] however, but at the same time the creator is the one who graciously holds the world in being. The world here means especially human beings, who receive food and drink from God's hand[33] precisely in order to give thanks to God.[34]

To this point the prayer does not follow the Jewish model word for word, but its motifs are certainly the same. With ἡμῖν δὲ ἐχαρίσω κτλ. ("you graced us, etc.") it deliberately steps beyond its Jewish model.[35] God gives earthly food and drink to all people, but to us, namely, the Christians, God gives πνευματικὴν τροφὴν καὶ ποτόν[36] ("spiritual food and drink"; πνευματική is

emphasized), and thereby ζωὴν αἰώνιον ("eternal life"). This gift, in fact, occurs διὰ Ἰησοῦ τοῦ παιδός σου.[37] Πνευματικὴ τροφή or (πνευματικὸν) ποτόν is not a "spiritualizing" expression,[38] but can be understood as a look ahead to the sacramental Lord's Supper, for which this prayer is a transitional preparation. The expression describes the bread and wine of the Lord's Supper as sacramental food. Compare the possibly pre-Pauline expressions πνευματικὸν βρῶμα and πνευματικὸν πόμα in 1 Cor 10:3–4. In this, the sacramental food, all earthly food is perfected, elevated to the spiritual plane, and transformed. It conveys more than earthly life: it provides ζωὴ αἰώνιος.[39]

■ **4** The benediction concludes with a phrase that (in comparison to the others) is somewhat expanded: περὶ

52.1; σὺ γάρ, δέσποτα, ἐπουράνιε βασιλεῦ τῶν αἰώνων, 61.2; cf. also *Diogn.* 3.2 and ὁ γὰρ δεσπότης καὶ δημιουργὸς τῶν ὅλων θεός in *Diogn.* 8.7.

30   2 Cor 6:18; frequent in Revelation (1:8; 4:8, etc.); *1 Clem.* Title; 2.3; 32.4; 56.6 (from Job 5:17); 60.4; 62.2; *Hermas Vis.* 3.3.5; Polycarp, *Phil.* Title; *Diogn.* 7.2; then in the creeds: cf. Heinrich Denzinger, *Enchiridion symbolorum: definitionum et declarationum de rebus fidei et morum* (Barcelona: Herder, 1963) 1–19. It occurs only here in the *Didache*.

31   Cf. 3 Macc 2:2: Κύριε, κύριε, βασιλεῦ τῶν οὐρανῶν καὶ δέσποτα πάσης κτίσεως, ἅγιε ἐν ἁγίοις, μόναρχε, παντοκράτωρ ("Lord, Lord, King of the heavens and Ruler of all creation, Holy one among the holy ones, Monarch, Almighty"); *Diogn.* 7.2: ὁ παντοκράτωρ καὶ παντοκτίστης καὶ ἀόρατος θεός ("The all-ruling and all-creating and unseen God"); cf. also *Const.* 7.38.1.

32   The expression "for the sake of the divine name" recalls the Jewish model; cf. n. 25 above. It is true that this phrase is lacking in the reconstructed oldest form of the Jewish prayer.

33   For εἰς ἀπόλαυσιν, cf. (ὁ θεὸς ὁ παρέχων) ἡμῖν πάντα πλουσίως εἰς ἀπόλαυσιν ("God who richly provides us with everything for our enjoyment"), 1 Tim 6:17; πρὸς ἀπόλαυσιν, *1 Clem.* 20.10; BAGD, *s.v.*

34   Wengst (*Didache*, 80) (following the Coptic and *Constitutions*) has eliminated ἵνα σοι εὐχαριστήσωσιν. But at this point *Constitutions* diverges altogether from its source, and the omission in the Coptic may be accidental.

35   Dibelius ("Mahl-Gebete," 123) differs. He supposes that the expression ἡμῖν δὲ ἐχαρίσω πνευματικὴν τροφὴν καὶ ποτόν "and possibly also καὶ ζωὴν αἰώνιον" comes from the spiritualizing Hellenistic

Jewish model that he posits. The first part that is again Christian would then be the final phrase (p. 124). All this is said without any proof.

36   For τροφὴ καὶ ποτόν, BAGD, *s.v.* ποτόν, refers to Josephus *Ant.* 7.159, and Longus 2.7.4 (Schönberger, 74): καὶ οὔτε τροφῆς ἐμεμνήμην οὔτε ποτὸν προσεφερόμην ("I neither remembered food nor approached drink").

37   Note the sequence "food–drink" in contrast to *Did.* 9.2–3, but in harmony with 9.5. The prayer has regard for the eucharistic elements. For the contrast between "earthly" and "spiritual/sacramental," cf. Ignatius *Rom.* 7.3 (φθορά/ἄφθαρτος); Justin *1 Apol.* 66.2 (Goodspeed, 74–75); Irenaeus *Adv. haer.* 4.18.5 (SC 100.610–13). For the final phrase H has only διὰ τοῦ παιδός σου, but Ἰησοῦ should be added, following the Coptic (cf. also the Georgian). Thus Schmidt, "Koptische Didache-Fragment," 85, 97. Cf. the expressions in *Did.* 9.2, 3; 10.2.

38   Thus Dibelius, "Mahl-Gebete," 124; cf. n. 35 above. In a different sense (namely, a *Christian* spiritualizing of the Jewish model): Finkelstein, "Birkat Ha-Mazon," 214.

39   "*Did.* 10.3–4 extols the eucharistic gift as the fulfilment of the gifts of creation which confer temporal life" (Leonhard Goppelt, "πίνω κτλ.," *TDNT* 6 [1968] 147).

40   For ὅτι δυνατὸς εἶ, cf. Ps 88:9; Peterson ("Probleme," 171) refers to Karl Preisendanz, *Papyri Graecae Magicae: Die griechischen Zauberpapyri* (2 vols.; Leipzig and Berlin: Teubner, 1928) 2.101 (13.275–76).

41   H's σύ should be emended: the Coptic has the equivalent of σοί. Harnack (*Lehre*, 33) conjectured σύ· σοὶ, which is possible but unnecessary. See Niederwimmer, "Textprobleme," 126.

πάντων εὐχαριστοῦμέν σοι, ὅτι δυνατὸς εἶ:[40] σοὶ[41] ἡ δόξα εἰς τοὺς αἰῶνας ("For all things, we thank you, Lord, because you are powerful").[42] Verse 4a could be regarded as a later addition,[43] if it were not for the fact that there is evidence of a parallel in the Jewish prayer after meals (not in the first benediction, but in the second): "And we praise you for all. . . ."[44] The reminiscence of the Jewish model[45] suggests the reading attested by the Coptic version: περὶ πάντων (rather than the πρὸ πάντων in H).[46] Cf. also *Mart. Pol.* 14.3: διὰ τοῦ-το καὶ περὶ πάντων σὲ αἰνῶ, σὲ εὐλογῶ, σὲ δοξάζω ("Therefore for all things I praise you, bless you, and glorify you"); and *Const.* 7.38.1: Εὐχαριστοῦμέν σοι περὶ πάντων, δέσποτα παντοκράτωρ ("We give you thanks for all things, almighty master"); and 7.38.4: περὶ πάντων σοι διὰ Χριστοῦ εὐχαριστοῦμεν ("for all things we give thanks to you through Christ").[47]

■ **5** The third benediction in the *Didache* prayer is distantly reminiscent of the third benediction in the Jewish prayer after meals. The original version reconstructed by Finkelstein[48] is said to have been: "Have mercy, O Lord, our God, on Israel thy people, and on Jerusalem, thy city, and upon Zion, the dwelling place of thy glory, and upon thy altar and thy temple. Blessed art thou, O Lord, thou who buildest Jerusalem."[49] Among the later expansions (?) is the call for relief from all distress. With regard to the *Didache* prayer, finally, we should also recall an addition to the third benediction of the *Birkat Ha-Mazon* that is prayed on the Passover eve, in which the motif of remembrance has a role to play.[50] It is true that the things that recall the Jewish prayer have been Christianized in *Did.* 10.5. The *Didache* does not pray for Israel or Jerusalem, but for the church of God; the *memento* motif and the plea for redemption are adapted accordingly.[51] The prayer is constructed as follows:

1. μνήσθητι, κύριε,
2. τῆς ἐκκλησίας σου
    τοῦ ῥύσασθαι αὐτὴν ἀπὸ παντὸς πονηροῦ
    καὶ τελειῶσαι αὐτὴν ἐν τῇ ἀγάπῃ σου,
    καὶ σύναξον αὐτὴν ἀπὸ τῶν τεσσάρων ἀνέμων
    < . . . >[52]
    εἰς τὴν σὴν βασιλείαν, ἣν ἡτοίμασας αὐτῇ·
3. ὅτι σοῦ ἐστιν ἡ δύναμις καὶ ἡ δόξα
    εἰς τοὺς αἰῶνας.

The introductory μνήσθητι, κύριε, may recall the insertion, cited above, in the third benediction of the

---

42 After αἰῶνας the Coptic adds ⳉⲁⲙⲏⲛ (and follows it with a *signum dispositionis*). Dibelius ("Mahl-Gebete," 122) and Koester (*Synoptische Überlieferung*, 194) regard this as the original text. Audet also adopts it (*Didachè*, 401). In that case "amen" would be the response of the congregation. It is problematic, however; see Niederwimmer, "Textprobleme," 126.

43 Or is it out of order? Drews ("Apostellehre," 270–71) suggested, following von der Goltz, that rearrangements need to be made in vv. 3 and 4. Knopf's opinion (*Lehre*, 28) is similar. This suggestion is unnecessary. According to Lietzmann (*Mass*, 191–92) v. 4a is in the wrong place, "but we can no longer determine the original—which may not even have been in these prayers" (p. 236).

44 Cf. the text in its various versions: Finkelstein, "Birkat Ha-Mazon," 228, 247–48. According to Finkelstein (p. 229), this was a later insertion.

45 Observed already by Klein, "Gebete," 143 (although Klein read πρὸ πάντων . . .).

46 For περί: Dibelius, "Mahl-Gebete," 124; Klauser, *Doctrina*, 24; Wengst, *Didache*, 80. The old editions read πρό, with H, but so does Audet, *Didachè*, 236. Rordorf and Tuilier (*Doctrine* 180) read πρό, but note (p. 181 n. 3) that the Coptic probably has the correct reading. On this question, see Niederwimmer, "Textprobleme," 125–26.

47 Peterson, "Probleme," 171 and n. 86. Peterson (p. 171) calls attention also to the similar introductory formula ὑπὲρ πάντων. See the examples there.

48 Cf. the various versions and the analysis in Finkelstein, "Birkat Ha-Mazon," 230–33, 253–58. The original text, as suggested by Finkelstein, is on pp. 230 and 233. So also Hruby, "Birkat Ha-Mazon," 215.

49 The translation follows Jeremias, *Eucharistic Words*, 110.

50 Following Jeremias's translation (*Eucharistic Words*, 252): "Our God, and God of our fathers, may there arise, and come, and come unto, be seen accepted, heard, recollected and remembered, the remembrance of us and the recollection of us, and the remembrance of our fathers, and the *remembrance of the Messiah, son of David, thy servant*, . . . and the remembrance of Jerusalem thy holy city, and the remembrance of all thy people, the house of Israel. May their remembrance come before thee, for rescue, goodness." According to Jeremias (*Eucharistic Words*, 252), this addition "may go back in essence to the time of Jesus."

51 Dibelius, "Mahl-Gebete," 124–25: the original prayer concluded at 10.4, and 10.5 was a later addition, "a special prayer for the church" (p. 125). The doublet σύναξον αὐτὴν κτλ. (cf. 9.4) is said to show

Birkat Ha-Mazon, but somewhat also the *Shemoneh Esreh* (Palestinian) 7: "Look upon our suffering . . . and save us for your name's sake."[53] But the *memento* motif as such goes back much farther. The Lord is called upon in many ways to remember the covenant, Israel, and the Messiah, and to take action to save those who are God's own.[54] The *memento* of the *Didache* is also within this tradition, but the motif has been translated into a Christian context, as the continuation shows.[55] In any case, the precondition for the prayer in the *Didache* is faith that God has entered into a covenant with the church and that promises are involved. When the community cries out to God μνήσθητι, κύριε, it prays for the fulfillment of the promises: "here we have . . . the primeval form of all the commemorations in the later liturgies."[56]

This is now made more concrete in three petitions (τοῦ ῥύσασθαι αὐτήν . . . τελειῶσαι αὐτήν . . . σύναξον αὐτήν . . .).[57] The first petition, (τοῦ) ῥύσασθαι αὐτήν (sc. τὴν ἐκκλησίαν) ἀπὸ παντὸς πονηροῦ[58] ("to preserve it from all evil"), could possibly be related to a similar expression in the third benediction of the Jewish prayer after meals.[59] One may also compare the expression quoted above from the *Tefillah*. But here the object of the prayer is the ἐκκλησία. The second petition, (τοῦ) τελειῶσαι αὐτήν (sc. τὴν ἐκκλησίαν) ἐν τῇ ἀγάπῃ σου ("to perfect it in your love"), refers to the eschatological perfection of the church.[60] Τελειοῦν here means "to complete," "to bring to perfection."[61] The perfection of the church is thought of either in a moral sense (in which case it is divine love[62] by and through which the church reaches perfection, by being made holy),[63] or—and this is more probable—in an eschatological sense (in which case we should understand ἐν τῇ ἀγάπῃ σου as the love of God that perfects the church in unity).[64] The unity of the church in the end time is, in any case, the matter of the third and last petition: καὶ σύναξον αὐτήν . . . ("gather it, etc."). We have already seen this motif in *Did.* 9.4. Compare:

---

that this is an addition. It is true that there is a possibility of "Jewish influence" in μνήσθητι κτλ., but "in the content, we can no longer make a distinction between the Jewish foundation and the Christian superstructure" (ibid.).

52   I regard τὴν ἁγιασθεῖσαν (H) as a later gloss. See below.

53   Holtzmann, *Berakot*, 15.

54   Closest in language is Ps 73:2: μνήσθητι τῆς συναγωγῆς σου, ἧς ἐκτήσω ἀπ᾽ ἀρχῆς ("remember your congregation, which you acquired long ago"). For more on this, see Otto Michel, "μιμνήσκομαι," *TDNT* 4 (1967) 675-76; G. Schmidt, "Μνήσθητι: Eine liturgiegeschichtliche Skizze," in *Viva vox Evangelii: Eine Festschrift für Landesbischof D. Hans Meiser zum 70. Geburtstag am 16. Februar 1951* (Munich: Lutherische Kirchenamt in Hannover, 1951) 259-64; Clerici, *Einsammlung*, 48-64; Vööbus, *Liturgical Traditions*, 166–69.

55   For the reforming undergone by the tradition, see Clerici, *Einsammlung*, 57, 60-63; and Vööbus, *Liturgical Traditions*, 168.

56   Lietzmann, *Mass*, 192. Lietzmann's remark (n. 2) that this topos did not appear in the OT and Jewish tradition has since been refuted.

57   The object of each petition is the church. In *Did.* 4.14 (didachistic redaction? see above, p. 113 n. 14) the reference is to the individual congregation, while in the prayers in 9.4 and 10.5 it is the entire community; similarly, in 11.11 it seems that ἐκκλησία means the whole church.

58   For ῥύσασθαί τινα ἀπό τινος (thus also in 8.2), cf.

BDF, §180.1; BDR, §180 (1); and the examples in BAGD, *s.v.* Of course, this is not a quotation from Matt 6:13 (Massaux, *Influence*, 3.162). John 17:15 has τηρεῖν αὐτοὺς ἐκ τοῦ πονηροῦ ("to protect them from the evil one"), but there is no literary relationship.

59   "Deliver us, deliver us, YHWH, our God, with great haste from all our difficulties" (from the German translation by Holtzmann, *Berakot*, 79). According to Finkelstein's and Hruby's analyses (see above), this passage is one of the later additions.

60   Vööbus (*Liturgical Traditions*, 126 n. 84) refers to Papyrus Egerton 5 (Harold I. Bell and Thomas C. Skeat, eds., *Fragments of an Unknown Gospel* [London: British Museum, 1935] 58): εἰρήνευσον, οἰκονόμησον, τελίωσον τ[ὸν] λαὸ[ν] ὃν ἐκτίσω, τὸν λαὸν τὸν [π]εριούσιον ("Pacify, govern and perfect the people whom you have created, the special people"). The text is from the 4th–5th centuries (p. 56).

61   Gerhard Delling, "τέλος κτλ.," *TDNT* 8 (1972) 84.

62   In any case ἀγάπη σου is subjective genitive, not objective (as Clerici wanted to see it: *Einsammlung*, 96).

63   Cf. *1 Clem.* 49.5: ἐν τῇ ἀγάπῃ ἐτελειώθησαν πάντες οἱ ἐκλεκτοὶ τοῦ θεοῦ ("All the elect of God have been perfected in love"). Cf. also 50.3: οἱ ἐν ἀγάπῃ τελειωθέντες. See Vööbus, *Liturgical Traditions*, 127–29.

64   Cf. John 17:23. John 17 in part recalls the motifs of the *Didache* prayers, not because the *Didache* is dependent on John but because motifs from the

Did. 9.4
οὕτω συναχθήτω
σου ἡ ἐκκλησία
ἀπὸ τῶν περάτων
τῆς γῆς
εἰς τὴν σὴν βασιλείαν

Did. 10.5
καὶ σύναξον
αὐτὴν
ἀπὸ τῶν τεσσάρων
ἀνέμων
εἰς τὴν σὴν βασιλείαν

We should by no means conclude from this doublet that 10.5 is a later addition.[65] For the synaxis ἀπὸ τῶν τεσσάρων ἀνέμων ("from the four winds"), cf. especially Zech 2:10 LXX; Mark 13:27 par.[66] The appositional phrase that follows in H (τὴν ἁγιασθεῖσαν, "once it is sanctified") is textually suspect.[67] It is lacking in the Coptic and in the *Apostolic Constitutions*. In my opinion it represents a later gloss.[68]

The gathering of the church is an eschatological event, when the church will enter into God's *basileia* of the end time. The idea is that the reign of God is the future of the church. The church is seen as the people of God on pilgrimage, and the goal of their journey is the reign of God.[69] The reign of God has been prepared for the church.[70]

Then follows the doxology, ὅτι σοῦ ἐστιν ἡ δύναμις καὶ ἡ δόξα εἰς τοὺς αἰῶνας ("for power and glory are yours forever"), which concludes the prayer,[71] presumably to be understood as the response of the congregation.

■ 6 The eucharistic prayer has come to an end. We immediately expect the note that we now find in v. 7 (about the free prayer of the prophets). But before that comes v. 6, which, from both a literary and a material point of view, is one of the most difficult *cruces interpretum* in the *Didache*.

Excursus: The Difficulties of 10.6

First of all it is clear that in 10.6 we are faced with a different type of discourse than in the preceding verses. In that regard there is an obvious caesura between vv. 5 and 6. What follows in v. 6 is no longer part of the prayer of thanksgiving; its genre is that of ritual acclamation.[72] The verse consists of a series of short sentences, apparently quite loosely connected. This observation also corresponds to the tradition-historical findings: while the preceding prayers make use of models drawn from the Jewish meal prayers, the same is not true of v. 6. Old Testament and Jewish traditions continue to play a role here, but the text that follows is no longer derived from concrete Jewish meal prayers, as were the prayers that preceded it.[73] The *Sitz im Leben* of v. 6 is the ἀγαλλίασις of the primitive Christian meal celebration. These are jubilant cries anticipating the vanishing of this world and the coming of the new, combined with invitation and warning associated with the eucharistic Communion.

With these eschatologically oriented, almost ecstatic cries, the meal comes to an end—as has been supposed. This opinion can, however, stand unassailably only for 10.6a. The expressions in 10.6b (the formula of invitation and warning) apparently do not belong at the end of the Communion but rather at the beginning. Thus v. 6 is an important indication that now, and only now, is the communion of the Lord's Supper beginning—that is, that the preceding meal was an *agape* or a celebration similar to an *agape*.

In addition, Lietzmann was probably right in thinking that the whole passage should be read as a dialogue:

Liturgist: Ἐλθέτω Χάρις καὶ παρελθέτω ὁ κόσμος οὗτος.
Congregation: Ὡσαννὰ τῷ υἱῷ[74] Δαβίδ.

---

liturgy have entered into John 17. Cf. above, p. 140 n. 8.

65 Thus Dibelius, "Mahl-Gebete," 125. Cf. n. 51 above.

66 See above, commentary on 9.4.

67 Vööbus, *Liturgical Traditions*, 93. Nevertheless, I cannot share Vööbus's concerns and suggestions regarding the *basileia* clause here and in 9.4 (ibid., p. 90).

68 Niederwimmer, "Textprobleme," 119. Cf. now also Wengst, *Didache*, 82.

69 Massaux (*Influence*, 3.163) sees the expression ἣν ἡτοίμασας αὐτῇ as representing literary dependence on Matt 25:34.

70 Vööbus (*Liturgical Traditions*, 13) interprets this quite differently: he suspects an older predecessor form in which the unity of the church was not yet conceived eschatologically and was not connected with the coming of God's reign.

71 The Coptic has again added ⲀⲘⲎⲚ, which Dibelius ("Mahl-Gebete," 122) and Audet (*Didachè*, 236) regard as original. The Coptic again has a *signum dispositionis* after ⲀⲘⲎⲚ.

72 In the NT we might compare Eph 5:14b.

73 Finkelstein ("Birkat Ha-Mazon," 216–17, 234) differs. He sees in *Did.* 10.6 a reflection of the prayers beginning with הרחמן that follow the fourth benediction in the Jewish prayer after meals (cf. the translation in Str–B 4.632). This is quite unlikely.

74 This is the reading adopted by Lietzmann (*Mass*, 193). In the edited text (*Mass*, 188) he reads θεῷ, with Δαβίδ in both places. H has the abbreviated proper name δαδ.

Liturgist: Εἴ τις ἅγιός ἐστιν, ἐρχέσθω· εἴ τις οὐκ ἔστιν, μετανοείτω. Μαραναθά.
Congregation: Ἀμήν.[75]
This means, however, that we have here, in εἴ τις ἅγιός ἐστιν . . . , the invitation to Communion, and in the next part a warning against unworthy participation in it.

With this transition to the sacramental Communion the celebration reaches its climax in the ritual acclamations.

Verse 6a, first of all, abruptly directs attention to the parousia. The community now gathered for the meal is the advance guard of eternity and—standing as it does immediately before the sacramental union—desires nothing more deeply than the final disappearance of this world and the arrival of the one that is to come.[76] The

χάρις[77] whose coming is implored is eschatological salvation.[78] The sentence ἐλθέτω χάρις καὶ παρελθέτω ὁ κόσμος οὗτος ("may grace come, and may this world pass by")[79] is formulated as a petition. The community cries out for redemption,[80] that is, for the passing away of the present and the coming of the future world.[81] The following cry, "Hosanna!" is the oldest example of the use of "hosanna" in Christian ritual.[82] Ὡσαννά (= הוֹשַׁעְנָא for הוֹשִׁיעָה נָּא)[83] is the acclamation found in Ps 118:25 (MT) that had retained a place in the Jewish liturgy for special feast days.[84] Originally a plea for help, it had in the course of time become an expression of praise.[85] It is apparently to be understood in the same way here. With a solemn "hosanna" the community rejoices in God,[86]

---

75 Lietzmann, *Mass*, 193. It is true that Lietzmann regards the dialogue "as a supplement to the main formulary."

76 For early Christian prayer for the parousia, or in turn for the delay of the eschaton, cf. the information in Harnack, *Lehre*, 34–35.

77 Χάρις (H) is to be preferred to ὁ κύριος, which is presumed by the Coptic version; Dibelius ("Mahl-Gebete," 125) differs. Franz J. Dölger (*Sol Salutis: Gebet und Gesang im christlichen Altertum. Mit besonderer Rücksicht auf die Ostung in Gebet und Liturgie* [LWQF 16/17; Münster: Aschendorff, 1972] 207–8) explains that χάρις is a designation for Jesus (see below n. 78), and this was still evident to the copyist: "he deliberately substitutes the commonly understood formula for the secret name *charis*" (p. 208).

78 The reference is said to be to "sacramental grace and hence the sum of Messianic salvation" (Hans Conzelmann, "χαίρω κτλ.," *TDNT* 9 [1974] 400). That *charis* is here synonymous with *logos* = Jesus (suggested by Dölger, *Sol Salutis*, 206–8; Lietzmann, *Mass*, 193 n. 2; Kleist, *Didache* 9.161 n. 66) is something I join Conzelmann (*TDNT* 9.400) in regarding as less probable. The commentary on this passage may be found in 1 Pet 1:13: ἐλπίσατε ἐπὶ τὴν φερομένην ὑμῖν χάριν ἐν ἀποκαλύψει Ἰησοῦ Χριστοῦ ("Hope in the grace brought to you by the revelation of Jesus Christ"). Klauck (*Herrenmahl*, 360) thinks, as did Conzelmann, of the union of the sacramental and eschatological coming of *charis*.

79 For παρέρχεσθαι in this sense, cf. Mark 13:30 par., 13:31 par.; 2 Cor 5:17; 2 Pet 3:10; less directly *1 Clem.* 27.5. Ἀπῆλθαν: Rev 21:1. Ὁ κόσμος οὗτος (the central apocalyptic concept) appears only here in the *Didache*.

80 See Rom 8:23.

81 After ⲚⲀⲢⲈ ⲠⲈⲒⲔⲞⲤⲘⲞⲤ ⲤⲒⲚⲒ ("Let this cosmos pass away"), Coptic again has ⲀⲘⲎⲚ (and *signum dispositionis*). This "amen" is accepted by Dibelius, "Mahl-Gebete," 122; Audet, *Didachè*, 236.

82 For "hosanna" in the *Didache* see Sandvik, *Kommen des Herrn*, 37–40.

83 Eduard Lohse, "ὡσαννά," *TDNT* 9 (1974) 682 n. 6 and 683 n. 14.

84 Str-B 1.845–47; Lohse, "ὡσαννά," 682; Sandvik, *Kommen des Herrn*, 37.

85 Lohse, "ὡσαννά," 682; Sandvik, *Kommen des Herrn*, 37.

86 The wording is uncertain:
(1) ὡσαννὰ τῷ θεῷ Δαυίδ (H)
(2) ὡσαννὰ τῷ οἴκῳ Δαυίδ (Coptic; Audet, *Didachè*, 62–67, 236, 420; Mattioli, *Didache*, 147)
(3) ὡσαννὰ τῷ υἱῷ Δαυίδ (*Constitutions*; Bryennios, Διδαχή, 38).
Reading (3) is probably a simple assimilation to Matt 21:9, 15. Reading (2) gives less meaning, in context, than reading (1). (Audet assesses the situation differently; on pp. 62–67 he gives an extensive argument for his decision.) It is understandable how the other readings may have been built up on the basis of (1). (For the reading θεῷ, see now also Wengst, *Didache*, 82; cf. ibid., p. 83 n. 88.) Dibelius ("Mahl-Gebete," 126 n. 10) suggested as the original text ὡσαννὰ τῷ θεῷ οἴκου Δαυίδ (?). For the whole subject see Niederwimmer, "Textprobleme," 126–27. The "hosanna" acclamation in the *Didache* does not come from Matthew's Gospel but from liturgical tradition: Koester, *Synoptische Überlieferung*, 198; Lohse, "ὡσαννά," 684.

87 Differently Knopf, *Lehre*, 29: "Here Christ is the God of David."

88 "The community experiences the meal as an anticipation of the parousia," writes Sandvik, *Kommen des*

who sends the Messiah, the son of David.[87] Future and present eschatology are intertwined.[88]

In contrast, v. 6b is not a jubilant cry, but an invitation and a warning. Εἴ τις ἅγιός ἐστιν, ἐρχέσθω ("if anyone is holy, let him come") concerns the conditions for admission to the Lord's Supper.[89] The formula appears to be ancient liturgical material, and to underlie 1 Cor 16:22 in a similar form:

1 Cor 16:22	*Did.* 10.6
	εἴ τις ἅγιός ἐστιν, ἐρχέσθω·
εἴ τις οὐ φιλεῖ τὸν κύριον ἤτω ἀνάθεμα. μαραναθά.	εἴ τις οὐκ ἔστιν, μετανοείτω· μαραναθά.[90]

The phraseology of the *Didache* is reminiscent of the acclamation in the later liturgies: τὰ ἅγια τοῖς ἁγίοις ("holy things for holy people") and especially John Chrysostom *Homily* 17.5 *in Hebr.* (*PG* 63.133): Ὅταν γὰρ εἴπῃ, Τὰ ἅγια τοῖς ἁγίοις, τοῦτο λέγει· Εἴ τις οὐκ ἔστιν ἅγιος, μὴ προσίτω ("For when he says, 'Holy things for holy people,' he means, 'If someone is not holy, let him not approach'").[91] Here, as there, the cry

has the tone of a warning. One who is holy, and only such a one, may approach. One who is not should do penance. In the *Didache*, ἅγιος describes either, in simple terms, the baptized person (in which case μετανοείτω represents baptism)—this would make the content of this passage identical with *Did.* 9.5—or else (and this is more probable) this text appeals to those already baptized to come as ἅγιοι to the Lord's Supper; this is not something that the status of *baptizatus* implies without further qualification.[92] Thus I am unable to perceive any contradiction between 9.5 and 10.6.[93]

The subsequent μαραναθά ("Come, Lord")[94] should probably be understood in terms of the immediate context. That is, it does not refer directly back to v. 6a (ἐλθέτω χάρις κτλ.), but continues and deepens the warning expressed in v. 6b (μετανοείτω). Thus we cannot arrive at an understanding of the expression in this passage directly by interpreting the Aramaic expression[95] (although it is probable that it implies an imperative sense in the present context as well);[96] instead, the

---

Herrn, 40. Sandvik takes the same view in interpreting "maranatha." I have some reservations about this; see below.

89 I must say that this opinion is not undisputed. Cf. Harnack, *Lehre*, 36; Jacquier, Διδαχή, 130; Schaff, *Church Manual*, 61, 197; Knopf, *Lehre*, 29; Greiff, *Pascharituale*, 50. In that case one might consider it a call to join the church. (Greiff, if I have understood him correctly, seems to be thinking of an eschatological entry.) Against the interpretation stated above it is objected that the early church had no eucharistic procession. But ἐρχέσθω can be understood in a broader sense. Audet's opinion (*Didachè*, 413) is arbitrary: "ἐρχέσθω is not necessarily the equivalent of προσερχέσθω." The one who is "holy" is said to be the one who is baptized, the call to repentance is a call to baptism for those who are not yet baptized, and the whole is a "rite of 'passage' between the 'breaking of bread' and the great 'eucharist'" (p. 415). The baptized are now invited to the great eucharist, the Eucharist proper, and in the meantime they must move from one room to another. According to Audet there is a contradiction between *Did.* 10.6 and 9.5: 10.6 (the ancient liturgy) presupposes that even those who are not baptized participate in the breaking of bread, while 9.5 (the author) forbids it (*Didachè*, 415).

90 Bornkamm, "Anathema," 164–76; Vielhauer, *Geschichte*, 38. Frequently Lucian *Alexander* 38 (Macleod, 2.348) is referred to as a parallel: Εἴ τις ἄθεος ἢ Χριστιανὸς ἢ Ἐπικούρειος ἥκει κατάσκοπος τῶν ὀργίων, φευγέτω ("If any atheist or Christian or Epicurean comes as a spy of our rites, let him flee").

91 Peterson, "Probleme," 172–73. For Peterson these observations support his thesis that in *Did.* 10.6 we find "only fragments of Mass texts and not, for example, rudimentary witnesses to a liturgy from apostolic times" (p. 172). Peterson also asks (in light of his hypothesis regarding the location of the Bryennios text) "whether the formula μετανοείτω in the Bryennios text . . . does not, perhaps, presume a developed technical language in ascetic circles" (p. 173).

92 Cf. 1 Cor 11:27–29; Rordorf and Tuilier, *Doctrine* 69 n. 2.

93 Audet, *Didachè*, 415; Bornkamm, "Anathema," 171–72.

94 Written as a single word in H.

95 Cf. the methodological notes of Peterson, Εἷς θεός, 131. That I am, nevertheless, inclined to understand "maranatha" in *Did.* 10.6 differently from Peterson is a separate matter.

96 As is well known, analysis and interpretation of the

meaning is ultimately determined by the immediate context.[97] That context (v. 6b) has the character of a call to repentance. Accordingly, $\mu\alpha\rho\alpha\nu\alpha\vartheta\acute{\alpha}$ probably calls for the Lord's coming and at the same time recalls that the eschatological advent of the *Mar/Kyrios* will be the advent of the judge. Thus (similarly to 1 Cor 16:22) this cry has a minatory character. It points to the eschatological judgment of the *Kyrios*, who will bring his law into effect, and hence calls sinners to repentance: $\mu\epsilon\tau\alpha$-$\nuο\epsilon\acute{\iota}\tau\omega$–$\mu\alpha\rho\alpha\nu\alpha\vartheta\acute{\alpha}$![98] The "amen" that follows is the response of the congregation.

■ **7** I consider v. 7 to be an added rubrical remark by the Didachist, applying to a problem that apparently was important to the communities for which he wrote. We are to understand that the preceding prayers are to be used as a paradigm for the meal celebration. As liturgists—not in the intention of the liturgy itself, but probably in the mind of the Didachist—one would ordinarily think of the *episkopoi* of 15.1 (q.v.). In the communities

of the *Didache*, however, the freewheeling charism of the prophets is still active, and, as I shall show, the Didachist makes an effort to show as much concern for these prophets as for the local officials.[99] While the prayers in chaps. 9–10 offer a more or less obligatory text as paradigm for the meal prayers of the local officials,[100] the prophets were able to formulate their prayers freely:[101] *Τοῖς δὲ προφήταις ἐπιτρέπετε εὐχαριστεῖν, ὅσα θέλουσιν*. This clause can be understood to mean either that the prophets have the right to add their own, freely formulated prayers *after* those preceding, or (and this is more probable) that the prophets (as liturgists) simply have the right to formulate the meal prayers ad libitum and are not limited by the given paradigms. In any case 10.7 reflects a situation that was typical for the Didachist, in which the community is still acquainted with the work of the prophets but is more and more often led by local, resident officials (the *episkopoi*); cf. 15.1–2. The appearance, without explanation, of the key

verb as (present) perfect or imperative are both possible in terms of the language itself. Joseph A. Fitzmyer wishes to trace the expression to "an imperative with the elision of the reduced vowel and initial *aleph* because of the preceding long *a*" ("New Testament *Kyrios* and *Maranatha* and Their Aramaic Background," in idem, *To Advance the Gospel: New Testament Studies* [New York: Crossroad, 1981] 228). For "maranatha" in general, cf. Hans Georg Kuhn, "$\mu\alpha\rho\alpha\nu\alpha\vartheta\acute{\alpha}$," *TDNT* 4 (1967) 471–72; Gerhard Schneider, "$\mu\alpha\rho\alpha\nu\alpha\vartheta\acute{\alpha}$," *EDNT* 2 (1991) 385; Hans Peter Rüger, "Aramäisch im Neuen Testament," *TRE* 3 (1978) 607; Peterson, *Εἷς θεός*, 130–31; Bornkamm, "Anathema," 164–76; Charles F. D. Moule, "A Reconsideration of the Context of *Maranatha*," *NTS* 6 (1959/60) 307–10; Siegfried Schulz, "Maranatha and Kyrios Jesus," *ZNW* 53 (1962) 125–44; William F. Albright and Christopher S. Mann, "Two Texts in I Corinthians," *NTS* 16 (1969/70) 271–76; Sandvik, *Kommen des Herrn*, 13–18; Matthew Black, "The Maranatha Invocation and Jude 14, 15 (1 Enoch 1:9)," in Barnabas Lindars and Stephen S. Smalley, eds., *Christ and Spirit in the New Testament: In Honour of C. F. D. Moule* (Cambridge: Cambridge University Press, 1973) 189–96; Fitzmyer, "New Testament *Kyrios*," 218–35; Klauck, *Herrenmahl*, 358–63.

97 After recording the prayer that the Lord come (ⲚⲀⲢⲈϤⲒ ⲆⲒⲬⲈⲚⲠ̄Ⲭ̄Ⲥ̄), the Coptic also offers what amounts to an interpretive gloss, ⲠⲬ̄[Ⲥ] ⲀϤⲒ ("the Lord has come"). This interpretation, equivalent to the Greek ὁ κύριος ἦλθεν (likewise the Georgian)

has no claim to originality. Lietzmann (*Mass*, 193) wished to find a double meaning: Our Lord, come! (namely, for the parousia), and: Our Lord has come! (namely, now, in the sacrament); so also Betz, "Eucharist," 271–72; Sandvik, *Kommen des Herrn*, 17, either: "Lord, come to your parousia, and come now, while we are gathered for the meal," or "Lord, as you are already here at our meal, come to your parousia."

98 Peterson (*Εἷς θεός*, 130–31) has gone too far in supposing, wrongly, that the words "maranatha, amen" are used here in an apotropaic-exorcistic sense. Cf. Moule, "Reconsideration." Correctly against Peterson: Kuhn, "$\mu\alpha\rho\alpha\nu\alpha\vartheta\acute{\alpha}$," *TDNT* 4 (1967) 471 n. 47; Bornkamm, "Anathema," 170. I see the connections as follows: the maranatha formula had its origins primarily in an invocation of Christ, calling for his parousia. Its original *Sitz im Leben* was the Eucharist. In 1 Cor 16:22 and *Did.* 10.6b the formula appears to be present especially to sharpen the call for repentance. Cf. Bornkamm, "Anathema," 170.

99 See below, commentary on 15.1.

100 Richard P. C. Hanson has shown that in the 2d century, and until the middle of the 3d, if not even longer, the bishops exercised freedom in formulating the anaphora (as long as they maintained the conventions prescribed) ("The Liberty of the Bishop to Improvise Prayer in the Eucharist," *VC* 15 [1961] 173–76).

101 For ἐπιτρέπειν τινί with the infinitive, cf. BAGD, *s.v.*

164

word προφῆται ("prophets") reveals 10.7 as an addition by the hand of the Didachist.

Excursus: The Addition in the Coptic Version

The Coptic text has a famous insertion at this point:[102] "But (δέ) because of the word of the oil of anointing (? [ст]ноγϥι: see immediately below) give thanks, saying: 'We thank you, Father, for the oil of anointing (? ステ]ноγ]ϥι) that you have made known through Jesus your Son (ϣнрı; the Coptic has the same word also in 10.3 end; but at this point, as in 10.3, the Coptic word was certainly intended to reflect παῖς). Thine is (the) glory forever. Amen (ἀμήν).'"[103] Schmidt ("Koptische Didache-Fragment," 85 and 94) rendered ステноγϥι as μύρον, and translated ϣнрı as παῖς. Thus he arrived at the following reconstruction: περὶ δὲ τοῦ λόγου τοῦ μύρου οὕτως εὐχαριστήσατε λέγοντες· Εὐχαριστοῦμέν σοι, πάτερ, ὑπὲρ τοῦ μύρου οὗ ἐγνώρισας ἡμῖν διὰ Ἰησοῦ τοῦ παιδός σου· σοὶ ἡ δόξα εἰς τοὺς αἰῶνας· ἀμήν ("Concerning the word of the *myron*, give thanks in the following way, saying, 'We give you thanks, Father, for the *myron* which you have made known to us through Jesus your child. To you be the glory forever. Amen").[104]

Amazingly enough there is a quite analogous prayer at the same position in *Const.* 7.27.1–2. A synopsis of the two prayers looks this way:

Coptic	Constitutions
περὶ δὲ τοῦ λόγου τοῦ μύρου (?)	Περὶ δὲ τοῦ μύρου
οὕτως εὐχαριστήσατε λέγοντες·	οὕτως εὐχαριστήσατε·
—	—
Εὐχαριστοῦμέν σοι, πάτερ,	Εὐχαριστοῦμέν σοι, θεὲ δημιουργὲ τῶν ὅλων,
ὑπὲρ τοῦ μύρου (?)	καὶ ὑπὲρ τῆς εὐωδίας τοῦ μύρου[105]
—	καὶ ὑπὲρ τοῦ ἀθανάτου αἰῶνος
οὗ ἐγνώρισας ἡμῖν	οὗ ἐγνώρισας ἡμῖν
διὰ Ἰησοῦ τοῦ παιδός σου, σοὶ ἡ δόξα	διὰ Ἰησοῦ τοῦ παιδός σου, ὅτι σοῦ ἐστιν ἡ δόξα
—	καὶ ἡ δύναμις
εἰς τοὺς αἰῶνας· ἀμήν.	εἰς τοὺς αἰῶνας· ἀμήν.

It is immediately apparent that the *Apostolic Constitutions* on the whole, although not necessary in every detail, contains the later form of the *myron* prayer.[106] The church order of Hippolytus also has, immediately after the eucharistic prayers, a prayer of blessing for the presentation of the oil (Hippolytus *Trad. Apost.* 5 [SC 11.54]); cf. also the *Oratio pro oleis*

---

102 Col. 1, ll. 15 (end)–20 (beginning). The text is most readily found in Lefort, *Pères apostoliques*, CSCO 135.32 (on this, see Gero, "Ointment Prayer," 68 n. 4). For the whole of what follows, cf. Niederwimmer, "Textprobleme," 119–21.

103 From the German translation by Schmidt, "Koptische Didache-Fragment," 85, 87 (with a single alteration). The notes in parentheses (except for δέ and ἀμήν) are mine.

104 Nevertheless, Schmidt supposed that the text of the Greek source deviated in part: "Koptische Didache-Fragment," 95. For the question of the linguistic placement of the text, see above, Introduction, §4a. I do not venture to decide whether, in *Or.* 9271, we have a copy of a Coptic source or an attempt at a translation from the Greek. See above, p. 25.

105 Cf. 7.44.2: σὺ καὶ νῦν τοῦτο τὸ μύρον δὸς ἐνεργὲς γενέσθαι ἐπὶ τῷ βαπτιζομένῳ, ὥστε βεβαίαν καὶ πάγιον ἐν αὐτῷ τὴν εὐωδίαν μεῖναι τοῦ Χριστοῦ σου, καὶ συναποθανόντα αὐτὸν συναναστῆναι καὶ συζῆσαι αὐτῷ ("Grant now that the *myron* be visible on the baptizand, so that the sweet aroma of Christ might remain firm and settled in him, and so that, having died with him he might arise and live with him"). The ὑπὲρ τῆς εὐωδίας τοῦ μύρου in *Const.* 7.27 may be original (in contrast to the Coptic). So also Wengst, *Didache*, 82.

106 Bihlmeyer (*Apostolischen Väter*, 20) reconstructed the original wording of the prayer (which he considered the genuine text of the *Didache*) as follows: περὶ δὲ τοῦ μύρου οὕτως εὐχαριστήσατε· Εὐχαριστοῦμέν σοι, πάτερ ἡμῶν (or ἅγιε), ὑπὲρ τοῦ μύρου, οὗ ἐγνώρισας ἡμῖν διὰ Ἰησοῦ τοῦ παιδός σου· σοὶ ἡ δόξα εἰς τοὺς αἰῶνας· (ἀμήν). Peterson differs ("Probleme," 157): Περὶ δὲ τοῦ μύρου οὕτως εὐχαριστήσατε. Εὐχαριστοῦμέν σοι πάτερ ὑπὲρ τῆς εὐωδίας τοῦ μύρου καὶ ὑπὲρ τοῦ ἀθανάτου αἰῶνος, οὗ ἐγνώρισας ἡμῖν διὰ Ἰησοῦ τοῦ παιδός, ὅτι σοῦ ἐστιν ἡ δόξα καὶ ἡ δύναμις εἰς τοὺς αἰῶνας ἀμήν. Wengst (*Didache*, 82) reconstructs the text as follows: περὶ δὲ τοῦ μύρου οὕτως εὐχαριστήσατε· εὐχαριστοῦμέν σοι, πάτερ, ὑπὲρ τῆς εὐωδίας τοῦ μύρου, οὗ ἐγνώρισας ἡμῖν διὰ Ἰησοῦ τοῦ παιδός σου· σοὶ ἡ δόξα εἰς τοὺς αἰῶνας· ἀμήν. Wengst considers this text the original ("at least . . . possibly," *Didache*, 59).

et aquis oblatis after Communion in the *Euchologion* of Serapion 17 (Funk, *Didascalia*, 2.179–80).

It is not clear whether the *myron* prayer in *Did.* 10.7 (Coptic) is a prayer of blessing over the oil of the sick (for the oil of the sick, cf. Mark 6:13; Jas 5:14–15),[107] or whether it is a blessing of the oil used at baptism.[108] For example, Bihlmeyer[109] thought primarily of the oil used for anointing the sick,[110] while Peterson[111] referred it to the "oil for the postbaptismal anointing."[112] The *myron* prayer undoubtedly gives (at first glance) the impression of antiquity, and for that reason the passage is occasionally regarded as a genuine element of the *Didache* text[113] that was then suppressed by H (or its source) for one reason or another.[114] *Const.* 7.27 can then be adduced to demonstrate that at the time of the compiler of the *Apostolic Constitutions*, the *Didache* still had a *myron* prayer at this point. Of course, the argumentation can be reversed. Hippolytus's church order and the *Euchologion* of Serapion indicate the tendency to add a prayer over the oil of anointing to the eucharistic formula. Such a prayer could also have been interpolated into the *Didache* text (at a later date) and have

traveled from there into *Const.* 7.27.[115] The *myron* prayer in the *Didache* would thus be a subsequent interpolation[116] in line with later liturgical usage. Vööbus[117] has pointed to the striking λέγοντες (eliminated by the *Apostolic Constitutions*), which does not correspond to the linguistic usage of the *Didache* rubrics.[118] Another indication is even more important. While the prayers of the *Didache* give thanks for the gifts of salvation, that is, for spiritual food and drink, the *myron* prayer in the Coptic gives thanks for the *myron* itself.[119] Observations like these suggest that the *myron* prayer represents nothing but an imitation of the table prayers.[120] In addition, the compiler of *Constitutions* attempted (by introducing the phrase καὶ ὑπὲρ τοῦ ἀθανάτου αἰῶνος) to accommodate the text more fully to the table prayers.[121]

This picture would change if Stephen Gero's suppositions were correct.[122] His starting point is the key word ⲥⲧⲓⲛⲟⲩϥⲓ, which shapes this whole section.[123] Schmidt (inspired by the parallel in *Const.* 7.27.1–2) interpreted ⲥⲧⲓⲛⲟⲩϥⲓ as the rendering of *myron*,[124] and that has remained the dominant interpretation. The first doubts were raised by Lefort,[125] according

107 Serapion *Euchologion* 17 is a prayer over the oil for the sick. Its relationship to the prayer over the oil in Hippolytus *Apost. Trad.* 5 is uncertain. According to the Latin version, this was the oil for the sick.

108 For the topic of anointing the sick and the anointing with oil before and after baptism, as well as baptism with oil, cf. Dölger, *Taufritual*, 137ff. (on the prebaptismal anointing); Heinrich Schlier, "ἀλείφω," *TDNT* 1 (1964) 229–32; Vööbus, *Liturgical Tradition*, 43–44.

109 *Apostolischen Väter*, xx.

110 As does Wengst, *Didache*, 58.

111 "Probleme," 162.

112 Vööbus (*Liturgical Traditions*, 45–50) treats the connection between εὐωδία – μύρον and baptism. *Const.* 7.22.2–3 suggests that baptism is in view. Here a distinction is made between the ἔλαιον ἅγιον of the prebaptismal anointing and the μύρον of the postbaptismal anointing. Schlier ("ἀλείφω," *TDNT* 1 [1964] 231 n. 8) suggested that in *Did.* 10.7 (Coptic) there might be "evidence . . . of the confluence of water baptism with baptism in oil, as in Act. Thom." That is off the mark.

113 Bihlmeyer, *Apostolischen Väter*, xx; Peterson, "Probleme," 156–68; Kraft, *Didache*, 169; considered as a possibility by Wengst, *Didache*, 59, 82 (text).

114 Peterson ("Probleme," 158–68, at 162) has expressed an imaginative idea about this: that the use of oil at baptism was suppressed, both in chap. 7 and in chap. 10, for dogmatic reasons. He suggests that in the Bryennios text it "may have something to do with a Novatianist recension of the *Didache*."

115 From this it would then follow that the Constitutor already had an interpolated *Didache* text before him. See above, Introduction, §5.

116 Schmidt, "Koptische Didache-Fragment," 95; Klauser, *Doctrina*, 25; Audet, *Didachè*, 67–70; Rordorf and Tuilier, *Doctrine* 48; Niederwimmer, "Textprobleme," 119–21; in detail, Vööbus, *Liturgical Traditions*, 54–56.

117 *Liturgical Traditions*, 56.

118 Previously Schmidt ("Koptische Didache-Fragment," 95) had drawn attention to this, and also pointed to the problematic περὶ δὲ τοῦ λόγου τοῦ μύρου. Both are signs of interpolation. "Therefore it is my opinion that this prayer was inserted by someone later, when the *Didache* began to be used in the liturgies of the Egyptian church" (ibid.). Cf. also Audet, *Didachè*, 69.

119 Vööbus, *Liturgical Traditions*, 56–57.

120 Peterson's argument ("Probleme," 158) that "the μύρον prayer [is] closely aligned stylistically with the prayers in chapters 9 and 10" would thus be superfluous; the characteristic variants show that we are simply dealing with an imitation. See Audet, *Didachè*, 69; Vööbus, *Liturgical Traditions*, 57.

121 Vööbus, *Liturgical Traditions*, 57.

122 Gero, "Ointment Prayer," 67–70.

123 "It is obvious that the exegesis of this passage depends entirely on the interpretation one gives to the word *stinoufi*" (Gero, "Ointment Prayer," 68).

124 Schmidt, "Koptische Didache-Fragment," 85: μύρον, oil of anointing. More cautiously Horner, "New Papyrus Fragment," 227: "the holy chrism, the

to whom one should expect ϭⲟϣⲛ, not ⲥⲧⲓⲛⲟⲩϥⲓ, as the word corresponding to μύρον.[126] Lefort translated ⲥⲧⲓⲛⲟⲩϥⲓ, as in the past, with "perfume."[127] For Gero this meaning makes clear that the Coptic blessing prayer cannot be a *myron* prayer, and any questionable reference to the sacrament of baptism is also excluded. But in that case what does ⲥⲧⲓⲛⲟⲩϥⲓ mean? Gero's thesis is that "the text is a *prayer over incense burned at the solemn communal meal* described in *Didache* 9 and 10."[128] Gero is compelled to combine this theory with a series of further hypotheses. Ultimately what results for him is the following picture: the meal depicted in chaps. 9–10 is an archaic community meal at which a prayer of blessing was spoken over incense, which was then burned.[129] The *Didache* prayer is thus a blessing of incense and a genuine element of the *Didache*. The Egyptian redactor of the *Apostolic Constitutions* took the text in a different direction. He no longer understood this archaism[130] and arbitrarily reinterpreted the text. Now, for the first time, the incense was replaced by the baptismal *myron*.[131] Gero suspects a similar lack of understanding of the archaic usage behind the archetype of H and the Georgian that ultimately led to the passage being eliminated entirely.[132]

Unfortunately this stimulating hypothesis is hampered by certain difficulties. To begin with, it is clear that ⲥⲧⲓⲛⲟⲩϥⲓ is certainly regarded as a saving gift revealed by God to God's own people "through Jesus." This important statement would scarcely be applicable to incense. In addition, Gero ignores the observations of Schmidt, Audet, and Vööbus about the imitative language indicating the secondary character of the Coptic prayer.[133] Finally, Gero (like all the advocates of the hypothesis of genuineness) has difficulty in explaining the omission of this passage in H (and the Georgian).

The result is that, in spite of Gero's ingenious presentation, it is still preferable to hold to the judgment that the Coptic prayer of blessing is secondary, and that it was probably a prayer over the oil of anointing. The linguistic difficulty of the use of the word ⲥⲧⲓⲛⲟⲩϥⲓ for μύρον must still be taken into account.[134] The development would therefore have been as follows. (1) In the original *Didache* the entire passage was not present. (2) At a relatively early time (ca. 200 c.e. or earlier?)[135] the text of the *Didache* experienced an interpolation at this point, the interpolation of a *myron* prayer imitating the archaic language of the preceding prayers in the *Didache*. (3) The compiler of the *Apostolic Constitutions* had the interpolated text before him; he incorporated this passage, but not without changing some details, as was his custom. (4) The noninterpolated text continued its independent existence and constituted the basis for the archetype of H and the Georgian.

---

aroma or sweet-smelling μύρον" (with reference to *Const.* 7.27).

125 *Pères apostoliques*, CSCO 136.26 n. 13. In line with Lefort's reservations, Adam ("Herkunft," 31–35) developed a hypothesis of his own, based on the idea of a Syriac source, and supposing Syriac ܒܣܡ or ܒܣܡܐ as the basis for ⲥⲧⲓⲛⲟⲩϥⲓ (with the meaning "refreshment," here specifically the *agape* celebration). According to this, the word simply refers to the preceding *agape* meal, and the prayer transmitted by the Coptic is nothing but the "concluding prayer, expressing thanks for the whole celebration in the simplest words" (p. 33). See the critique of this position in Vööbus, *Liturgical Traditions*, 44–45; and Gero, "Ointment Prayer," 72 n. 29.

126 Gero ("Ointment Prayer," 69 n. 10) referred correctly to Luke 23:56 (Sahidic)—although there μύρον is represented by ⲥⲧⲟⲓ, as noted already by Lefort, *Pères apostoliques*, CSCO 136.26 n. 13—and Ezek 27:17 (Bohairic), where ⲥⲧⲓⲛⲟⲩϥⲓ represents μύρον. Walter E. Crum (*Coptic Dictionary* [Oxford: Clarendon, 1962] 363A) includes both these examples (as well as a reference to the *Didache* passage), although placing them under the rubric "fragrant substance, incense"; and Gero writes: "But Lefort is clearly correct in saying that a Coptic translator normally would not have chosen *stinoufi* to render *myron*" (ibid.).

127 *Pères apostoliques*, CSCO 136.26 l. 6. Gero, "Ointment Prayer," 69 n. 12: "*Stinoufi* can be analyzed as *sti*, 'smell,' plus *noufi*, 'good.'" Thus the direct Greek equivalent would be εὐωδία.

128 Gero, "Ointment Prayer," 70.

129 Gero, "Ointment Prayer," 82–84.

130 An interpretation in terms of the eucharistic incensing is excluded because that custom is post-Constantinian. For a full discussion see Gero, "Ointment Prayer," 74–80.

131 Gero, "Ointment Prayer," 81, 84.

132 Gero, "Ointment Prayer," 84.

133 See above, pp. 165–66.

134 This difficulty may possibly be resolved by noting that in the Greek text the interpolation in fact alternated μύρον with εὐωδία (as we now read in the text of the *Apostolic Constitutions*). Cf. Schmidt, "Koptische Didache-Fragment," 95: "I suspect that the Greek *Vorlage*, like the *Apostolic Constitutions*, read ὑπὲρ τῆς εὐωδίας τοῦ μύρου, because the Coptic has the same word for εὐωδία and μύρον." Cf. also the text in Wengst, *Didache*, 82.

135 On this, see Vööbus, *Liturgical Traditions*, 58.

At 11.1 the mode of discourse changes again. The quotation from the liturgy (expanded at the end by the redactor in *Did.* 10.7) is finished. What now follows is a series of canonical instructions concerned with the relationship of the local communities to the itinerant charismatics and other traveling sisters and brothers, with questions having to do with confession, the choice of local officials, and finally problems of church discipline: these make up chaps. 11–15. It appears that we are now looking at the part of the *Didache* that can be called a "church order" in the narrower sense of the term.

Did. 11.1–2 represents the transition to this section. With πάντα τὰ προειρημένα (v. 1), the redactor refers to the preceding chapters of the work, and with the phrase ὃς ἂν οὖν ἐλθὼν διδάξῃ ὑμᾶς . . . he is already introducing the material that follows.

The whole section (chaps. 11–15) seems to be organized as follows:
1. Transition (11.1–2)
2. On the reception of itinerant apostles and prophets (11.3–12)
3. First appendix: On the reception of other traveling brothers and sisters (12.1–5)
4. Second appendix: On the duty to house prophets who desire to remain in the community, and duties toward teachers (13.1–7)
5. On confession and reconciliation (14.1–3)
6. On the election of bishops and deacons (15.1–2)
7. On church discipline (15.3–4)

The structure of this section becomes apparent when we clarify its tradition-historical and literary origins.[1] The Didachist (I believe) again makes use of a written source, which he then expands and brings up to date by means of additions from his own pen. In fact, what he has before him is an ancient text that deals with situations within the Christian community that have significantly (although not entirely) changed at the time when the Didachist is writing. That is, the literary layers reflect different situations: The ancient tradition available to the Didachist speaks of itinerant charismatics, apostles, and prophets who visit resident Christians for brief periods of time. Thus there is a contrast between the itinerant apostles and prophets on the one hand and the resident groups on the other. The situations presupposed by the predidachistic source could have held true for particular regions within early Christianity in the border regions of Syria and Palestine, and may have endured throughout the final decades of the first century. But between the time of this old tradition and the time of the Didachist things have changed within the region supplying the traditions for the *Didache*. There is nothing said any longer about itinerant apostles; the group of charismatics is now composed of prophets and teachers, whereby the prophets are still to be regarded as itinerants who now, at least in part, desire to become resident. As a result the Didachist sees a need to give advice applicable to this situation. *Did.* 11.1–2 shows that something analogous is true of the teachers. A further specific assignment falling to the Didachist is the division of responsibility between the two sets of leaders: the charismatics on the one hand and the office-holders within the community (the *episkopoi* and *diakonoi*) who, unlike the charismatics, have served from the beginning as local, resident officials within the community.

This description involves a specific assessment of the literary strata in this chapter.[2] I do not think it is necessary to posit two redactional levels.[3] It is sufficient to dis-

---

1. On this, see Niederwimmer, "Itinerant Radicalism," 323–27. [Ed. See now also Stephen J. Patterson, "The Legacy of Radical Itinerancy in Early Christianity," in Jefford, *Context*, 313–29.]

2. Audet assigns *Did.* 11.1–2 to D¹; D² begins with 11.3 and includes the instructions that the apostolic author subsequently added to his work (Audet, *Didachè*, 110–15, 436). For the analysis by Schille, "Recht," 84–103, cf. the critique in Niederwimmer, "Itinerant Radicalism," 323–24 n. 8. In my opinion, the approximating result of the analysis of chaps. 11–14 in Giet, *L'Énigme*, 219–24, 234–37, is artificially complicated.

3. Giet proposes two redactions: chap. 15 is said to be a "later addition" (*L'Énigme*, 243), and chap. 16 may also go back to a postdidachistic redaction (p. 256). Rordorf and Tuilier, *Doctrine*, 49, 63, 93–94, and passim: chaps. 14–15 are probably postdidachistic, as is chap. 16. On this, see above, p. 43 n. 13.

tinguish between the predidachistic tradition and the didachistic redaction (a single redaction to which, I must admit, one must attribute a relatively great amount of the material in these chapters). Each of these two layers corresponds to a particular social situation.[4] In my opinion, ancient predidachistic tradition is found only in 11.4–12; the rest is to be attributed to redaction[5]—that is, in this part of the book the Didachist does not appear merely as a compiler and redactor but offers rather long expositions from his own pen. That he formulates on his own much more extensively than in other parts of the

book is connected with the changed social conditions. The Didachist attempts (in these matters as well) to remain faithful to his tradition, but at the same time he feels called upon to accommodate that tradition to the present time and therefore to give instructions applicable to the new social situation.

---

4   De Halleux ("Ministers," 300–302) goes much farther. He not only rejects (correctly) the idea of a second redaction, but wishes to see chaps. 11–15 altogether as a literary unit (which is probably wrong). It is true that in his polemic against the contemporary model of Harnack (a polemic that is correct in principle) he mistakenly overlooks the development undergone by the charismatic groups in the traditional region of the *Didache*. In addition he attempts to show that the apostles, prophets, and teachers in the *Didache* were always one and the same group—the prophets. (This last point was already made by Kretschmar, "Askese," 141: "The summary, all-inclusive name for these charismatics is 'prophet' [11.4ff.; 13.3]".) Even Wengst (*Didache*, 23), who does not collapse the three groups of charismatics into one, attempts to see chaps. 11–15 as a literary unit and has, for that reason, rejected my description (p. 23 n. 83). Wengst's skepticism is

countered, however, by the argument that I consider strong: that in 11.4–12 the focus is on the itinerant apostles and itinerant prophets, while in the later passages nothing more is said about the apostles; instead, the text speaks only of prophets and teachers (cf. esp. 15.1–2). The inclusion of the traditional section 11.4–12 is explained (apart from the conservative attitude of the compiler) by the fact that this piece of tradition refers to the prophets who, even at the time the *Didache* was written, continued to play a role in the community.

5   Niederwimmer, "Itinerant Radicalism," 325–26. Kraft (*Didache*, 62) has correctly seen that 11.3–12 is the heart of the tradition. When he proceeds to assign the rest of chaps. 11–15 to various layers of tradition (pp. 62–63), I consider this excessive analysis. For the question whether 11.11 may be partly or entirely redactional, see below.

11

1 **Accordingly, receive anyone who comes and teaches you all that has been said above.**

2 **If the teacher himself turns away and teaches another doctrine so that he destroys [the correct teaching], do not listen to him, but [if he teaches] so that justice and knowledge of the Lord increase, receive him as the Lord.**

Comment

■ **1** This text is redactional. The Didachist creates a bridge between the liturgical agenda quoted before this and the next piece of tradition available to him, which speaks of itinerant apostles. Hence the phrase ὃς ἂν οὖν ἐλθών κτλ. (v. 1). Ταῦτα πάντα τὰ προειρημένα ("all that has been said above") appears to refer to chaps. 1–10,[1] that is, the whole of the preceding text. The author intends the hearers to take his writing as a standard by which to judge teachers who are unfamiliar to them. Δέξασθε αὐτόν ("receive [anyone]") anticipates δεχθήτω ὡς κύριος ("receive him as the Lord"), which the Didachist found in his *Vorlage* (cf. v. 4). Δέχεσθαι here means, in concrete terms, "receiving" an arriving teacher into the house.[2] The key word δέχεσθαι returns more than once in what follows, at 11.2, 4; 12.1. The situation is thus one in which the communities are being visited by traveling teachers. Hospitality requires that they be received politely, and the fraternal/sororal unity of Christians with one another further motivates the command. Yet there are betrayers at work. How can the genuine teacher be distinguished from the false? The Didachist's answer is, Test the teachers who come to you, to discover whether their teaching agrees with what has just been presented to you.

■ **2** The instruction δέξασθε αὐτόν corresponds to the warning that follows. The latter applies to cases in which the διδάσκων does not correspond to the διδαχή as given. I expand στραφείς with ἀπὸ ταύτης τῆς διδαχῆς: this refers to someone who has "turned away" from the correct teaching. Such a one teaches a different doctrine, ἄλλην διδαχήν.[3] To εἰς τὸ καταλῦσαι ("to destruction") one must mentally add τὴν διδαχήν,[4] but one could also include δικαιοσύνην or γνῶσιν, as the continuation shows.[5] The positive side is then again considered, somewhat awkwardly: εἰς δὲ τὸ προσθεῖναι δικαιοσύνην καὶ γνῶσιν κυρίου ("so that justice and knowledge of the Lord increase," v. 2b). This expression

---

1 Ταῦτα πάντα τὰ προειρημένα recalls ταῦτα πάντα προειπόντες in *Did.* 7.1—both of them redactional. Πάντα is missing from the Coptic—by mistake?

2 Mark 6:11 par.; Matt 10:40–41; Luke 10:8, 10. Cf. 2 Cor 7:15; Col 4:10. On the acceptance of a bishop in a strange community, see Ignatius *Rom.* 9.3. On the reception of sisters and brothers, see Ignatius *Phld.* 11.1.

3 Audet (*Didachè*, 70–71, 110–11, 236) adopted the plural ἄλλας διδαχάς from the Coptic title of the book, in line with his theory. This can scarcely be correct.

4 Harnack, *Lehre*, 37; materially identical is Funk, *Patres apostolici*, 1.25–26: τὰ προειρημένα or τὴν διδαχὴν προειρημένην. For καταλύειν in the sense of "do away with, abolish, annul," cf. BAGD, *s.v.*

5 For the whole, cf. 2 John 10: εἴ τις ἔρχεται πρὸς ὑμᾶς καὶ ταύτην τὴν διδαχὴν οὐ φέρει, μὴ λαμβάνετε αὐτὸν εἰς οἰκίαν καὶ χαίρειν αὐτῷ μὴ λέγετε ("do not receive into the house or welcome anyone who comes to you and does not bring this teaching"). The parallel is not accidental; the *causa* of 2 John is quite analogous to the *Didache* in its concern for the question of the attitude of local Christians toward itinerant teachers. In addition see Ignatius *Eph.* 9.1: ἔγνων δὲ παροδεύσαντάς τινας ἐκεῖθεν, ἔχοντας κακὴν διδαχήν· οὓς οὐκ εἰάσατε σπεῖραι εἰς ὑμᾶς, βύσαντες τὰ ὦτα ("I have learnt, however, that some from elsewhere have stayed with you, who have evil doctrine; but you did not suffer them to sow it among you, and stopped your ears"). Here it is already the episcopal officer who, by the power of the office, warns a community (not his own) against itinerant false teachers.

is clumsy[6] but the reader understands that προσθεῖναι is the positive contrast to καταλύειν.[7] We thus find an opposition established between the teacher who "dissolves" righteousness and knowledge and the teacher who "increases" both.[8] Δικαιοσύνη[9] and γνῶσις[10] constitute a characteristic hendiadys ("justice and knowledge"), and κυρίου is associated with both. The *Kyrios* is probably Jesus here.[11] Both "righteousness" and "knowledge" are, for the Didachist, the descriptive terms for the "essence" of the new faith. This new faith brings with it specific knowledge (namely, of the Lord), and that in turn creates the new righteousness that is characteristic of the new society. Hence, for a teacher who increases righteousness and knowledge, the command is to "receive him as the Lord" (δέξασθε αὐτὸν ὡς κύριον).

In using this formulation, the Didachist is dependent on the segment of tradition to be discussed just below (see *Did.* 11.4), but in a broader sense he is relying on the primitive Christian principle according to which the *Kyrios* himself appears in his messengers.[12] The messenger is to be received like the one who sent him or her; hence the true teacher is to be received as if the *Kyrios* himself had entered the house. In fact it is literally true that, when such a true messenger enters the house, it is the Lord himself who enters!

---

6   Before this clause we should imagine something like ἐὰν δὲ διδάσκη. . . . See Harnack, *Lehre,* 37; Knopf, *Lehre,* 30.

7   Προστιθέναι is already found in the assurance formula in *Did.* 4.13, where it is used negatively; here it is positive.

8   That is, such a one brings new righteousness and knowledge in addition to what is (already) present in the community.

9   Μισθὸς δικαιοσύνης in *Did.* 5.2 clearly comes from a different tradition-historical context.

10   For knowledge as one of the goods of salvation in the predidachistic liturgical agenda see *Did.* 9.3 and 10.2.

11   For the predication of "*Kyrios,*" see above, p. 134 n. 5.

12   The closest material parallel is Matt 10:40–41; cf. also John 13:20; Ignatius *Eph.* 6.1.

2. On the Reception of Itinerant Apostles and Prophets (11.3–12)

General

The next section, *Did.* 11.3–12, is a complete unit in itself. Verses 4–6 speak of the apostles, while vv. 7–12 focus on the prophets. I consider the introductory expression in 11.3 redactional. In detail, the pericope can be subdivided as follows:[1]

    a. Introduction (11.3)
    b. On itinerant apostles (11.4–6)
      (1) The dignity of the apostle (11.4)
      (2) The criteria for distinguishing true apostles from false (11.5–6)
    c. On itinerant prophets (11.7–12)
      (1) The dignity of the prophet (11.7)
      (2) The decisive criterion for distinguishing genuine prophets from pseudo-prophets (11.8)
      (3) Three specific cases (11.9–12)

[1]Cf. Niederwimmer, "Itinerant Radicalism," 326–27 n. 16.

11

a. Introduction (11.3)

3   In the matter of apostles and prophets, act this way, according to the ordinance of the gospel.

Comment

■ **3** In my opinion *Did.* 11.3 comes from the pen of the Didachist.[1] For the superscription with περί cf. 7.1; 9.1. These superscriptions are drawn from existing tradition. I therefore believe that the Didachist has formulated such a superscription by analogy in 11.3. Περὶ δὲ τῶν ἀποστόλων καὶ προφητῶν thus looks forward to what is to come, that is, the piece of tradition that the Didachist is about to quote. It does, in fact, speak of "apostles and prophets" (and only these).[2] In the Didachist's interpretation, the exposition to follow agrees with the "ordi-nance of the gospel." Therefore he introduces it with κατὰ τὸ δόγμα τοῦ εὐαγγελίου οὕτω ποιήσατε. The reference to the "gospel" (singular) is characteristic of the redactor; see 8.2; 15.3, 4. What is meant is either the *viva vox evangelii* or a written gospel whose text the Didachist can presume to be extant among his readers and hearers.[3] It can be called δόγμα τοῦ εὐαγγελίου

---

1   Here, according to Audet (*Didachè*, 110–15, 436), D² begins. Audet (pp. 110–11) sees in *Did.* 11.1–2 the conclusion of the original *Didache* (D¹), and adopts the reading of the Coptic, ἄλλας διδαχάς (see above).

2   De Halleux's explanation ("Ministers," 306–7) is very forced. He tries to understand the καί as explicative (because of the absence of τῶν before

προφητῶν), and thus arrives at the idea that in the *Didache* apostles and prophets represent a *single* group: "the prophets of the apostolic genre." Cf. also at 13.2 below.

3   Examples: Massaux, *Influence*, 3.163–64: *Did.* 11.3–9 is composed of recollections from the Gospel of Matthew; Koester, *Synoptische Überlieferung*, 10–11: *Did.* 15.3 already refers to a written gospel, but

because in it the *Kyrios* presents his binding instructions;[4] cf. ὡς ἐκέλευσεν ὁ κύριος ἐν τῷ εὐαγγελίῳ αὐτοῦ ("as the Lord commanded in his gospel," 8.2). There seems to be no problem in thinking of the *Kyrios* as lawgiver, and because, in the understanding of the Didachist, the gospel contains the decrees of the *Kyrios*, it is easy enough to speak of a δόγμα τοῦ εὐαγγελίου.[5]

whether this is the case already here in 11.3 remains uncertain; Klauser, *Doctrina,* 25: the text appears to be reminiscent of Matt 7:15–20; 10:5–42; Audet (*Didachè,* 442) thinks of the gospel that was written and circulated between D[1] and D[2]; for Vielhauer (*Geschichte,* 254), the expression δόγμα τοῦ εὐαγγελίου refers "probably to oral preaching"; Wengst (*Didache,* 27–28) suspects references to the Gospel of Matthew here as well, and in particular the Matthean missionary discourse. For the question of the Didachist's knowledge of an apocryphal gospel, see above, p. 51.

4   Cf. τρία οὖν δόγματά ἐστιν κυρίου ("there are,

then, three teachings of the Lord") in *Barn.* 1.6; further in 9.7, and βεβαιωθῆναι ἐν τοῖς δόγμασιν τοῦ κυρίου καὶ τῶν ἀποστόλων ("to be confirmed in the teachings of the Lord and of the apostles") in Ignatius *Magn.* 13.1; cf. Acts 16:4. Δόγμα in this passage means "instruction, prescript, decree" (sc. of the gospel).

5   As the reference to the δόγμα τοῦ εὐαγγελίου corresponds to the phrase ὡς ἐκέλευσεν ὁ κύριος in *Did.* 8.2, so οὕτω ποιήσατε corresponds to οὕτω προσεύχεσθε in 8.2.

11   b. On Itinerant Apostles (11.4–6)

4   **Let every apostle who comes to you be received as the Lord.**

5   **He shall stay <only> one day, or, if need be, another [day] too. If he stays three days, he is a false prophet.**

6   **When the apostle leaves, let him receive nothing but [enough] bread [to see him through] until he finds lodging. If he asks for money, he is a false prophet.**

Analysis

Only now does the quotation from an ancient, predidachistic tradition begin. In terms of genre the piece of tradition (vv. 4–12) is one of the "community rules for dealing with itinerant charismatics":[1] cf. Matt 10:40–42.[2] The subject here is an archaic institution, preceded by the group of Jesus' disciples, and spreading thereafter within certain regions of the post-Easter church, although under much altered conditions.[3] *Did.* 11.4–12 is evidence for the existence of this institution of itinerant charismatics in the last years of the first century C.E. It should probably be located in the border region between Palestine and Syria.

Comment

■ **4** Πᾶς δὲ[4] ἀπόστολος ἐρχόμενος πρὸς ὑμᾶς ("Every apostle who comes to you") initially means the first and most venerable group of Christians, who expected a hospitable welcome from local believers.[5] The representatives of this group bore the honorable title ἀπόστολος,

which here is evidently not yet restricted to the Twelve.[6] The group of itinerant apostles is open, and their number is indeterminate.[7] It seems certain that ἔρχεσθαι πρὸς ὑμᾶς referred to a repeated occurrence. The arriving apostles are (as the continuation will show) homeless messengers without property, existing on the contributions of the Christian sisters and brothers with fixed residences. As messengers of the *Kyrios* they are entitled to a hospitable welcome and support, and this is to be given them. The instruction says: δεχθήτω ὡς κύριος (v. 4b),[8]

---

1   Gerd Theißen ("Legitimation und Lebensunterhalt: Ein Beitrag zur Soziologie urchristlicher Missionare," *NTS* 21 [1974/75] 201). Theißen includes Matt 10:40–42 and *Didache* 11 in this genre.

2   For comparable material see the contrasting genre of rules for traveling messengers (Mark 6:6b–13; Matt 10:5–26; Luke 9:1–6; 10:1–12). Cf. also 1 Cor 9:14.

3   Cf. only Kretschmar, "Askese," 129–35, and Niederwimmer, "Itinerant Radicalism," 321–22 (with reference to the relevant investigations of Gerd Theißen).

4   Pierre Nautin ("Notes critiques sur la Didachè," *VC* 13 [1959] 118) considers δέ a mistake and deletes it, as does Wengst, *Didache*, 82. Δέ is absent in the Coptic and Ethiopic.

5   For the general subject of hospitality in antiquity, cf. Otto Hiltbrunner, Denys Gorce, and Hans Wehr, "Gastfreundschaft," *RAC* 8 (1972) 1061–1123; Michaela Puzicha, *Christus peregrinus: Die Fremdenaufnahme (Mt. 25,35) als Werk der privaten Wohltätigkeit im Urteil der Alten Kirche* (Münsterische

Beiträge zur Theologie 47; Münster: Aschendorff, 1980) 8–11. Still, one should consider that the hospitality required and expected of Christians, which is the subject of the next section, was superseded by eschatological motivation.

6   For Audet (correctly) it is here not the Twelve who are spoken of but (questionably) the apostles mentioned in the title of the *Didache* as he deduces it (*Didachè*, 446).

7   There are no fundamental statements here about the office of apostle—of course! For the addressees of the text those kinds of assessments are a matter of course and need not be communicated to them. The theme of the tradition is not theological reflection on the office of apostles but the concrete, particular question about how they are to be hospitably received in a given locality.

8   Massaux (*Influence*, 3.164) suspects an echo of Matt 10:40. For the relationship to the Synoptic tradition, cf. Koester, *Synoptische Überlieferung*, 209–10. The phrase is absent in Coptic and Ethiopic but is probably original (against Wengst, *Didache*, 82).

that is, in the persons of his messengers the Lord himself is a guest in the house.[9]

■ **5** Now come some regulations regarding the length of an apostle's stay and the provisions to be given to such an apostle for continuing the journey (vv. 5–6). These regulations also serve as a criterion for distinguishing true from false apostles. The remarks are addressed (as is the whole of the traditional section) to locally resident Christians. Among other things, they have need of distinguishing marks that will enable them to protect themselves against deceivers. When a previously unknown Christian appears with a claim to be an apostle, how is the truth of the claim to be measured? The first criterion applies to the length of stay: οὐ μενεῖ δὲ ‹εἰ μὴ› ἡμέραν μίαν ("he shall stay ‹only› one day," v. 5a).[10] The strikingly rigorous rule shows that (1) radical homelessness is one of the factors in the existence of apostles in the *Didache*, and (2) they did not appear as ongoing or even temporarily resident functionaries in these communities. Instead, their life is itinerancy. Their office is proclamation, preaching to the whole world. The horizon of their activity (even though this is not expressly stated in the text) is its eschatological motivation. They seek, as we might say, provisional lodging for only one day at a time, in order to move on.[11] Still, there was also the rule ἐὰν δὲ ᾖ χρεία,[12] καὶ τὴν ἄλλην [sc. ἡμέραν] ("if need be, another [day] too")—to which we may add μενεῖ (v. 5b). That is, there may be a case of necessity in which the apostle is absolutely unable to travel farther on the following day (for whatever reason).[13] In such cases an additional day is allowed. There is, however, an immediate further restriction: τρεῖς δὲ ἐὰν μείνῃ, ψευδοπροφήτης ἐστίν ("If he stays three days, he is a false prophet," v. 5c).[14] It should really say ψευδοαπόστολος rather than ψευδοπροφήτης, but the one supplying the tradition is apparently unfamiliar with the word *pseudoapostolos*[15] and therefore chooses instead—out of sheer desperation—a word familiar[16] from Old Testament and Jewish language, but probably already from Christian usage as well, "false prophet."[17]

■ **6** There is a further admonition concerning the guest's provisions when travelling onward on the following morning (or after two days): ἐξερχόμενος δὲ ὁ ἀπόστολος μηδὲν λαμβανέτω εἰ μὴ ἄρτον, ἕως οὗ αὐλισθῇ ("let him receive nothing but bread until he finds lodging"). The Christians resident in the place who have offered hospitality to the itinerant apostle are required to provide the bare necessities for the continuation of the journey. At the same time the special character of apostolic itinerancy emerges once again here; it is a life based on a willing abandonment of everything beyond what is really and absolutely necessary. The appropriate concern is always limited to the next day's needs. Therefore the apostle, when continuing the journey, is to be provided with food for (only) the next day[18]—not more. In the evening the apostle will find welcome in another Christian house. Moreover, the host's provision for the apostle is limited to the products of nature: ἐὰν δὲ ἀργύριον αἰτῇ,[19] ψευδοπροφήτης (rather than ψευδοαπόστολος) ἐστί ("if he asks for money, he is a false prophet," v. 6b). This recalls the prohibitions of Jesus against taking wallet or money on missionary activity:

---

9   See above, on *Did.* 11.2.

10   Additional εἰ μή: Harnack, *Lehre,* 39, taking it from the editions. This correction is attested by the Ethiopic.

11   A lengthy residence by itinerant apostles is out of the question. As we will see immediately below, the case is different with the itinerant *prophets.*

12   More common is χρείαν ἔχειν; see BAGD, *s.v.* For ἐὰν ᾖ χρεία, Bauer notes the parallel in Diodorus Siculus *Bibl. Hist.* 1.19.5 (Oldfather, 1.62).

13   Knopf (*Lehre,* 30–31) writes correctly: "we should probably think of difficult circumstances that delay the departure rather than the pastoral needs of the community."

14   The Ethiopic has modified this. According to that version an apostle may remain up to three days.

15   This is attested for the first time in 2 Cor 11:13 and is probably an ad hoc construction by Paul. The word is then again absent from the writings of the Apostolic Fathers and reappears for the first time in Hegesippus (Eusebius *Hist. eccl.* 4.22.6); Justin *Dial.* 35.3 (Goodspeed, 130); Tertullian *De praescr.* 4.4 (CChrSL 1.190); *Ps.-Clem. Hom.* 16.21.4 (GCS² 1.228); *Const.* 6.9.6. Highly instructive is Rev 2:2.

16   The concept is used frequently in the rest of the *Didache*. In the Apostolic Fathers, it is also found in *Hermas Man.* 11.2.4, 7 (bis).

17   No consequences may be drawn from the use of the term ψευδοπροφήτης regarding the equation of ἀπόστολος and προφήτης. Correctly: Rordorf and Tuilier, *Doctrine,* 52.

18   Cf., however, Mark 6:8: μὴ ἄρτον and Luke 9:3: μήτε ἄρτον.

19   Wengst, *Didache,* 84: λαμβάνῃ (following the Coptic).

μὴ εἰς τὴν ζώνην χαλκόν ("no money in their belts," Mark 6:8); μήτε ἀργύριον ("nor money," Luke 9:3); μὴ κτήσησθε χρυσὸν μηδὲ ἄργυρον μηδὲ χαλκὸν εἰς τὰς ζώνας ὑμῶν ("Take no gold, or silver, or copper in your belts," Matt 10:9);[20] μὴ βαστάζετε βαλλάντιον ("Carry no purse," Luke 10:4). They appear as those who are radically poor for God's sake, who have ceased to try to make their lives secure on the basis of property, but instead have surrendered themselves completely to God's care, which nourishes them from day to day through the gifts of their friends. In all this they simultaneously appear as the ambassadors of a new world to come.

---

20   According to Massaux (*Influence,* 3.164–65), the
      Didache is also dependent on Matthew here.

7 **Do not test any prophet who speaks in the Spirit, and do not judge him, for all sins will be forgiven, but this sin will not be forgiven.**

8 **Not everyone who speaks in the Spirit is a prophet but only the one whose behavior is the Lord's. So the false prophet and the prophet will be recognized by their behavior.**

9 **No prophet who orders a meal in the Spirit eats of it himself; if he does, he is a false prophet.**

10 **If any prophet teaching the truth does not do what he teaches, he is a false prophet.**

11 **No prophet, who is reliable and true, who acts for the earthly mystery of the church but does not teach [others] to do what he himself does, shall be judged by you, for his judgment is with God. The ancient prophets acted in the same way.**

12 **You shall not listen to anyone who says in the Spirit, "Give me money, or something," but if he is asking that something be given for others who are in need, let no one judge him.**

Analysis

After the apostles, the prophets are now named as the second group of charismatics. That they also (initially, and here in *Did.* 11.7–12) are thought of as *peregrinantes* is intimated by the context; this is in turn confirmed by 13.1–7, where the text speaks of prophets who wish to settle in the communities.[1]

Comment

■ **7** The section begins with a warning: καὶ πάντα προφήτην λαλοῦντα ἐν πνεύματι οὐ πειράσετε οὐδὲ διακρινεῖτε ("Do not test any prophet who speaks in the Spirit"). To prophets belongs λαλεῖν ἐν πνεύματι.[2] A prophet is πνευματικός· ἐν πνεύματι and speaks πνευματικά. Prophets are found to be πνευματικός and give instructions to their fellow Christians. The reader of the macrocontext is also aware of the rule in *Did.* 10.7 (formulated by the Didachist) according to which prophets are expressly granted the right to give thanks however they wish. That text, however, is a redaction within the predidachistic tradition. To return to the source: πειράζειν here means to "put someone to the test,"[3] and διακρίνειν in this location means "make a judgment" on someone,[4] apparently after the completion of the testing.[5] Both are forbidden; the prophet who speaks in the Spirit is not to be put to the test.[6] This is so because to put those who speak in the Spirit to the test means testing the Spirit working within them, and that would be a sin against the Holy Spirit: πᾶσα γὰρ ἁμαρτία ἀφεθήσεται, αὕτη δὲ ἡ ἁμαρτία οὐκ ἀφεθήσεται. Neither of these statements is quoted as a dominical saying (at

---

1 One should note that no limitation is placed on the length of a prophet's stay as there was for the apostles in *Did.* 11.5.

2 Cf. ἐν πνεύματι θεοῦ λαλεῖν, 1 Cor 12:3. In 14:2 the text speaks of λαλῶν γλώσσῃ· πνεύματι δὲ λαλεῖ μυστήρια. Cf. also *Hermas Man.* 11.5, 8, and 9: καὶ πλησθεὶς ὁ ἄνθρωπος ἐκεῖνος τῷ πνεύματι τῷ ἁγίῳ λαλεῖ εἰς τὸ πλῆθος καθὼς ὁ κύριος βούλεται ("and that man, filled with the Holy Spirit, speaks to the multitude as the Lord wishes").

3 BAGD, *s.v.*

4 BAGD, *s.v.*

5 Knopf differs (*Lehre*, 31), agreeing with Drews

("Apostellehre," 273): "We cannot say how πειράζειν and διακρίνειν are to be distinguished, but the former may refer to the behavior of the prophet and the latter to the prophet's speech."

6 The community is not to arrogate to itself the right to criticize.

7 Massaux (*Influence*, 3.165) differs; cf. also Hagner, *Use*, 280. Massaux posits dependence on Matt 12:31. Cf., to the contrary, Koester, *Synoptische Überlieferung*, 215–17.

8 For the topic of the discernment of spirits or the distinction between real and false prophecy, cf. Matt 7:15–20; 1 Thess 5:20–22; 1 Cor 12:3, 10;

least not overtly). At the same time, there is a tradition-historical relationship between this passage and the logion in Mark 3:28–29 (Matt 12:31) and Matt 12:32/ Luke 12:10 (Q). Our version of the logion can scarcely be traced to Mark/Matthew or to Q (or Matthew/Luke); it probably represents a separate form of the tradition.[7] The reference to the Son of man (Q) is absent, as is any relationship to Jesus' miracles (Mark). Here in the *Didache* the logion is connected with the early Christian prophets.

■ **8** Now of course this does not mean that all those who appear as prophets are genuinely what they seem.[8] The genuine prophets can be distinguished by the τρόποι κυρίου, as the text says, using an extremely characteristic expression.[9] Τρόποι describes the prophets' way of life;[10] by it the genuine prophets can be recognized:[11] ἀπὸ τῶν καρπῶν αὐτῶν ἐπιγνώσεσθε αὐτούς ("you will know them by their fruits," Matt 7:16; cf. v. 20);[12] *Hermas Man.* 11.7: ἀπὸ τῆς ζωῆς δοκίμαζε τὸν ἄνθρωπον τὸν ἔχοντα τὸ πνεῦμα τὸ θεῖον ("Test the man who has the divine Spirit by his life"); cf. *Man.* 11.16: δοκίμαζε οὖν ἀπὸ τῶν ἔργων καὶ τῆς ζωῆς τὸν ἄνθρωπον τὸν λέγοντα ἑαυτὸν πνευματοφόρον εἶναι ("Test, then, from his life and

deeds, the man who says that he is inspired"). Indeed, here it is especially the τρόποι κυρίου by which the true prophets will be known. "*Kyrios*" means Jesus. Thus the true prophet is in continuity with the lifestyle and praxis of Jesus—the earthly Jesus![13] This reference to the way of life of the earthly Jesus does not appear here by accident—if there is really a social and tradition-historical connection between the discipleship movement of Jesus (in which the ἀκολουθοῦντες oriented themselves to Jesus' way of life) and the itinerant prophets of the *Didache* tradition.

■ **9** Next comes the discussion of particular cases. The one first mentioned is not entirely clear: καὶ πᾶς προφήτης ὁρίζων[14] τράπεζαν ἐν πνεύματι[15] οὐ φάγεται ἀπ᾽ αὐτῆς.... Ὁρίζειν τράπεζαν seems to mean "order a meal."[16] The prophet who has arrived as a guest gives an order that a meal (for the needy of the community?) should be prepared.[17] A prophet who takes part in the meal is a false prophet (v. 9b).[18]

■ **10–11** Then follows[19] a second characteristic for distinguishing true from false prophets. The one who teaches the truth (ἡ ἀλήθεια), but does not do it, is a false prophet.[20] Now (v. 11)[21] the text addresses a special case,

---

9 *Did.* 11.1–2 is *not* valid with regard to prophets. Schöllgen ("Church Order," 54) interprets thus: v. 7 is said to formulate the "prohibition against putting prophets to the test while they speak in the Spirit," so that spiritual speech cannot be put to the test. The distinction, on the contrary, emerges of itself out of their way of life (vv. 8–12).

10 Cf. BAGD, *s.v.*; and the "*laudatio*" in SIG 2.783.10–11: αἰεὶ καὶ καθ᾽ ἡμέραν ἐπινοῶν τῇ πόλει πλεῖόν τι παρέχεσθαι, τὴν μὲν ἐπείκειαν τῶν τρόπων γεγεννημένος ("always thinking how to provide something more for the city, being most proper in manner"); and *Ep. Arist.* 144 (SC 89.172): πρὸς ἁγνὴν ἐπίσκεψιν καὶ τρόπων ἐξαρτισμὸν δικαιοσύνης ἕνεκεν σεμνῶς πάντα ἀνατέτακται ("All [these ordinances] were ordained in a solemn fashion with a view toward chaste behavior and the fashioning of behavior on account of righteousness").

11 Wengst (*Didache*, 84) reads, with the Coptic: γνώσεσθε τὸν προφήτην εἰ ἀληθινός ἐστιν ("recognize whether the prophet is true").

12 Cf. Giorgio Otranto, "Matteo 7,15–16a e gli ψευδοπροφῆται nell' esegesi patristica," *VetChr* 6 (1969) 33–45.

13 Massaux (*Influence*, 3.165–66) understands *Did.* 11.8

14:37; 1 John 4:1–3; *Hermas Man.* 11.

as a recollection of Matt 7:15–21.

14 H has the mistaken ὁ ῥίζων (which may already have been in its *Vorlage*). It was emended by Bryennios, Διδαχή, 43.

15 Wengst (*Didache*, 84) deletes ἐν πνεύματι (with the Coptic).

16 BAGD, *s.v.*

17 Audet (*Didachè*, 450) thinks that this is probably the meal celebration in chaps. 9–10. That is questionable. Cf. Knopf, *Lehre*, 31.

18 *Hermas Man.* 11.12 lists the faults of the false prophets, including καὶ εὐθὺς ἰταμός ἐστι καὶ ἀναιδὴς καὶ πολύλαλος καὶ ἐν τρυφαῖς πολλαῖς ἀναστρεφόμενος καὶ ἐν ἑτέραις πολλαῖς ἀπάταις ("He is instantly impudent and shameless and talkative and lives in great luxury and in many other deceits").

19 Wengst, *Didache*, 84: καὶ πᾶς . . . ; H: πᾶς δέ. . . .

20 Ignatius *Eph.* 15.1: καλὸν τὸ διδάσκειν, ἐὰν ὁ λέγων ποιῇ ("Teaching is good if the teacher does what he says"). Cf. also *Ps.-Clem. Ep. ad virg.* 1.11.8 (Hugo Duensing, "Briefe," 176).

21 Wengst (*Didache*, 84) again deletes δέ.

one that we again can no longer fully understand. To begin with, whatever it concerns applies only to the προφήτης δεδοκιμασμένος,[22] ἀληθινός, that is, the "true and tested" prophets.[23] Then the crucial clause reads: (προφήτης) ποιῶν εἰς μυστήριον κοσμικὸν ἐκκλησίας, μὴ διδάσκων δὲ ποιεῖν, ὅσα αὐτὸς ποιεῖ. This text constitutes a classic *crux interpretum* in the *Didache*. Its formulation is probably cryptic by design,[24] although the original audience certainly understood what it was about. In contrast it appears that even the Coptic and Ethiopic translators no longer understood the text.[25]

Excursus: The Crux of 11.11

The Coptic version (in the German translation by Carl Schmidt)[26] reads: "who teaches and attests a worldly (κοσμικός) tradition (παράδοσις) in the church (ἐκκλησία)." The question is whether there ever was a Greek form of the text corresponding to this or whether the Coptic form does not represent, instead, an ad hoc alteration by the translator, who no longer understood the Greek text before him. Something analogous may be said of the Ethiopic version, which reads at this point (in the English translation by George Horner):[27] "who acts in the assembly of men and acts unlawfully." Attempts to work with the Coptic[28] or Ethiopic text as a basis do not take us any farther. It is the text of H that must be explained. It is obscure, but at least it has integrity.[29]

(1) Some interpreters[30] have attempted to arrive at an understanding of this passage by recourse to the expression following in v. 11c, ὡσαύτως γὰρ ἐποίησαν καὶ οἱ ἀρχαῖοι προφῆται, with reference to the familiar symbolic actions of the Old Testament prophets.[31] They then attribute something similar or analogous to the Christian prophets of the *Didache* as well. In that case one could understand the text to say that the *Didache* prophets sometimes clarify or illustrate their prophetic witness through symbolic actions.[32] This opinion can be given concrete shape by reference to the analogy, implicit in the concept of μυστήριον κοσμικόν, between the heavenly and earthly realms. The text could then be understood to mean that the Christian prophets (following their OT models), by means of certain actions, present heavenly mysteries in an earthly manner[33]—most probably the union between Christ and the church.[34] In the first place, however, it is clear that in fact only the *Old Testament* prophets could be meant by ἀρχαῖοι προφῆται (and not, e.g., the prophets of the earliest Christian period).[35]

(2) Moreover, the text (as Harnack first rightly realized, in principle, despite his false interpretation of

---

22 For δεδοκιμασμένος, cf. 1 Thess 2:4; 2 Cor 8:22; 1 Tim 3:10; *1 Clem.* 42.4; 44.2; 47.4.

23 In fact, δεδοκιμασμένος, ἀληθινός could be a clarifying addition by the Didachist; cf. προφήτης ἀληθινός in 13.1, and the ἐπίσκοποι καὶ διάκονοι . . . ἀληθεῖς καὶ δεδοκιμασμένοι in 15.1. Or does the whole of v. 11 come from the Didachist? Verse 12 would follow very well after v. 10.

24 Cf. Knopf, *Lehre*, 32.

25 The Georgian version (apart from two meaningless alterations) contains the H text.

26 "Koptische Didache-Fragment," 89.30–32.

27 *The Statutes of the Apostles or Canones ecclesiastici* (London: Williams & Norgate, 1904) 193, ll. 22–23. Cf. Duensing in Adam, "Herkunft," 36.

28 Adam ("Herkunft," 29) returns to the Coptic text and suggests—in line with his fundamental thesis—a Syriac *Vorlage*. He posits that the Syriac would have had ܐܡܪ, reflected in the Greek version by ποιεῖν and in the Coptic by ⲡⲁⲣⲁⲇⲟⲥⲓⲥ (p. 30). Otherwise, in the interpretation of the substance, Adam arrives at a conclusion that, in my opinion, is correct.

29 Drews, "Apostellehre," 274; Audet, *Didachè*, 451. Differently Bigg and MacLean (*Doctrine*, 36), who suggest a corrupted text.

30 I restrict myself to the only two attempts at interpretation that are worth consideration (as Drews,

31 "Apostellehre," 274, observes correctly as well). For the symbolic actions of the OT prophets cf. (1 Sam 15:27–28); 1 Kgs 11:29–40; 2 Kgs 13:14–19; Hos 1:2–11; Isa 20:2–6; Jer 19:1, 10–13; Ezek 4:1–3, etc. In the NT see Acts 21:10–11. For the early Christian interpretation of these kinds of OT prophetic actions (together with other motifs, e.g., in Num 21:8–9), reference is occasionally made, in connection with this passage in the *Didache*, to *Barn.* 12.6–7; Justin *Dial.* 94.2 (Goodspeed, 209); Irenaeus *Adv. haer.* 4.20.12 (SC 100.668–75).

32 This was first suggested by Bryennios (Διδαχή, 44 n. 16) and is also proposed, with caution, by Schaff (*Church Manual*, 203), who also suggested Hicks's interpretation as the most likely possibility after this one (giving a review of Hicks's work). Cf. also Zahn, *Kanon*, 3.301: "He (i.e., the prophet) sometimes accompanies his prophetic speech, as did the 'ancient prophets,' with symbolic actions, which under some circumstances may appear unedifying."

33 Taylor, *Teaching*, 81–92, 150–51. Somewhat differently A. Broek-Utne ("Eine schwierige Stelle in einer alten Gemeindeordnung [Did. 11,11]," *ZKG* 54 [1935] 576–81): the reference is to eschatological mysteries known only to the prophet, who alone is permitted "to accomplish deeds that would not be recommended for others" (p. 580).

the term ἀρχαῖοι προφῆται)[36] can be understood still more concretely if one thinks not of a symbolic action, but of the whole of the prophet's way of life, namely, a *matrimonium spirituale*, a spiritual marriage in which the prophet lives with his companion.[37] This marriage (as the key phrase μυστήριον κοσμικὸν ἐκκλησίας would suggest) is ecclesiologically motivated; that is, it represents the union of the *Kyrios* with his bride, the church.[38] The advantage of this interpretation is that it achieves a focused meaning for an otherwise baffling text; the disadvantage is that it requires us to locate the beginnings of the institution of spiritual marriage relatively early. It may be, however, that the community at Corinth was already acquainted with spiritual marriage in Paul's time (cf. 1 Cor 7:36–38).[39]

If these suggestions are correct, the passage should be interpreted as follows: it may happen that the prophet will not arrive alone but accompanied by a Christian woman with whom he lives in a spiritual marriage. This may have been somewhat alienating for many Christians (and in fact it is only permitted for genuine prophets). In such a case the local Christians should recall that this spiritual marriage has (as we would now say) the charac-

ter of a "real symbol." In it the heavenly syzygy between Christ and the church is made visible through an earthly illustration; it is present in the ascetic union of the two Christians. What the prophet does is thus done as an earthly reflection of the heavenly mystery of the church (namely, its syzygy with the *Kyrios*).[40] Spiritual marriages are here (in the *Didache*) explicitly approved—although with certain provisos—and they are defended against the objections that may have been expressed by individual fellow Christians,[41] on the condition that the prophet in question does not say that his way of life is not the one and only way that is obligatory for all Christians (i.e., διδάσκων δὲ ποιεῖν, ὅσα αὐτὸς ποιεῖ).[42] If the prophet lives in his spiritual marriage without trying to impose that way of life on others, then: οὐ κριθήσεται ἐφ᾽ ὑμῶν· μετὰ θεοῦ γὰρ ἔχει τὴν κρίσιν ("he shall not be judged by you, for his judgment is with God," v. 11b). Finally, the text introduces one last argument to make the institution of spiritual marriage more comprehensible. The prophets who live in this way thus correspond typologically only to the Old Testament prophets who behaved in the same way (as is said *totum pro parte* in v. 11c). We therefore have a double typology before us. On the one

---

34 Harris, *Teaching*, 71–72: "*Revera ita fere verba obscura explicanda sunt*" ("Indeed the obscure words should be so explained" Funk, *Patres apostolici*, 1.29).

35 Against Harnack, *Lehre*, 46–47. For this expression, cf. Josephus *Ant.* 12.413; and Luke 9:8, 19: προφήτης τις τῶν ἀρχαίων ἀνέστη ("one of the ancient prophets had arisen").

36 Harnack, *Lehre*, 44–47; idem, "Prolegomena," 121.

37 This is the interpretation of (among others) Drews, "Apostellehre," 276; Knopf, *Lehre*, 32–33; Günther Bornkamm, "μυστήριον κτλ.," *TDNT* 4 (1967) 824–25 ("probably"); Hans von Campenhausen, *Kirchliches Amt und geistliche Vollmacht* (2d ed.; BHTh 14; Tübingen: Mohr, 1963) 78 n. 10 (ET of 1st ed.: *Ecclesiastical Authority and Spiritual Power in the Church of the First Three Centuries* [London: Black, 1969] 73 n. 119); Mattioli, *Didache*, 150 n. 75 (perhaps); Adam, "Herkunft," 43; Kretschmar, "Askese," 137 and n. 18; Wengst, *Didache*, 85 n. 100, and 98. Of course, one should take leave of Harnack's false interpretation of ἀρχαῖοι προφῆται (which Wengst also adopted, with some caution). The necessary reflection on this was already presented by Drews, "Apostellehre," 276.

38 The basic passages for the concept of the syzygy are Gen 1:27 and 2:24. This concept could serve as a foundation both for marriage (as in Eph 5:22–24)

and for renunciation of marriage by individuals, as well as for spiritual marriage. On the whole subject, see Niederwimmer, *Askese*, passim.

39 For the discussion of this, see Niederwimmer, *Askese*, 116–20.

40 The alternative proposed by Drews is false: "Then it is not a matter of illustrating the relationship between Christ and the community; rather, one should live according to that relationship."

41 By contrast, when the *Ps.-Clementine Epistula ad virgines* speak against living with the παρθένοι, they are polemicizing against an institution that has already become depraved; cf. 1.10.1 (Duensing, "Briefe," 175) and the whole second letter (Duensing, "Briefe," 180–88). These letters probably originated in the 3d century (Altaner and Stuiber, *Patrologie*, 47; cautiously also Duensing, "Briefe," 168). Adam ("Herkunft," 48) pleads, to the contrary, for a period "about 170." Their origin in eastern Syria appears to me to be certain. As regards the *Didache*, however, that is not an argument for locating the *Didache* in eastern Syria, contrary to what Adam says.

42 The point of the Coptic version is different: see above. Adam ("Herkunft," 43) suggested: "The Syriac version to be detected behind the Coptic

hand, spiritual marriage corresponds to its heavenly model, namely, the union of the *Kyrios* with his bride, the church; on the other hand, however, the prophet living in a spiritual marriage repeats, in typological fashion, the model (understood in a salvation-historical sense) of the Old Testament prophets. One can see that in this (isolated) passage some of the "theological" convictions of the *Didache* tradition, or of the Didachist, peek through, and yet it is characteristic of the unique quality of this book (and its sources) that the didactic implications are not expounded nor given full scope but remain merely as hints, and that they appear unsystematically, in a way that seems almost accidental, as if evoked by particular situations.

■ **12** Finally, the concluding verse of the section discusses one last case. The admonition corresponds to v. 6b. A prophet is disclosed as a false prophet if, when (supposedly) speaking ἐν πνεύματι, he demands money or something of value (ἕτερά τινα).[43] In that case, one

should not listen to him (cf. 11.2). It is a different matter if the prophet makes such demands on behalf of the needy (ὑστεροῦντες).[44] In that case: μηδεὶς αὐτὸν κρινέτω ("let no one judge him"; cf. οὐ κριθήσεται ἐφ᾽ ὑμῶν in v. 11).

This ends the quotation from the predidachistic tradition.[45] The ordering of the instructions remains to be considered. Each time, the dignity of the charismatics is first emphasized (11.4, 7); only then follow the criteria by whose aid one can distinguish false prophets from genuine apostles or prophets. That means that, for those who handed on this tradition, the first matter of concern was apology for the charismatics; only secondly was there interest in a polemic against the false prophets.

---

fragment appears to be a description of previous circumstances." That can scarcely be true.

43 Cf. *Hermas Man.* 11.12b.

44 Wengst (*Didache* 44) has ἄλλον (with the Ethiopic) instead of ἄλλων ὑστερούντων (H).

45 We should recall that in 11.11 it is possible that either a part or the whole is a redactional text.

3. First Appendix: On the Reception of Other Traveling Christians (12.1–5)

In the next part the Didachist's text begins. He turns first to the problem of the reception of noncharismatic Christians. His source seems not to have offered anything of the sort, although this question requires an answer within the overall context and may even have been of special importance for the ecclesiastical situation of his own time.

The structure of the section is as follows:
a. Reception and testing of new arrivals (12.1)
b. Travelers passing through (12.2)
c. Persons newly arrived who desire to remain (12.3–5).

12

a. Reception and Testing of New Arrivals (12.1)

1   **Let everyone who comes in the name of the Lord be received, and then, when you have taken stock of him, you will know—for you will have insight—what is right and false.**

■ **1** Here, as the larger context shows, and in contrast to the charismatics (apostles and prophets) who were the subject just previously, πᾶς δὲ ὁ ἐρχόμενος (v. 1a) can only refer to noncharismatic Christians. Ἐρχόμενος πρὸς ὑμᾶς[1] ἐν ὀνόματι κυρίου ("who comes in the name of the Lord") means that a stranger arrives in a place and asks to be received, asserting Christian identity.[2] The phrase is "Bible language"—cf. Ps 117:26, quoted in Mark 11:9 (Matt 21:9; Luke 19:38); John 12:13; and Matt 23:39/Luke 13:35 (Q).[3] This expression is meant to make clear that the guest is under the special protection of the Lord. The admonition to receive the traveler (δεχθήτω) is founded not only on the conventional rules regarding guests but also and especially on the fact that a Christian is asking to be received by fellow Christians.[4]

Before any kind of testing, the new arrival is to be received unquestioningly as a guest.[5] Only then is it proper to examine the guest.

Ἔπειτα δέ (v. 1b) follows the sequence indicated above. The rule of hospitality is preserved, for the new arrival has received shelter and food; now (and only now) can the testing of the guest begin. Δοκιμάσαντες αὐτόν ("when you have taken stock of him")[6] is formulated in very general terms.[7] Γνώσεσθε (sc. δεξιὰν καὶ ἀριστεράν)[8] here means that on the basis of a successful testing the local Christians will be able to make a judgment about the new arrival. Γινώσκειν δεξιὰν καὶ ἀριστεράν is again a biblicism: cf. Jonah 4:11. "Knowing right hand from left" (literally "judging left and right") means discerning what is right and what is false, in this

---

1   Πρὸς ὑμᾶς is lacking in H (probably through oversight, because the Georgian version has it). The phrase is attested by Coptic, Ethiopic, and the *Apostolic Constitutions*. See Niederwimmer, "Textprobleme," 127. Differently Rordorf and Tuilier, *Doctrine,* 188 and 188–89 n. 3; Wengst, *Didache,* 84.

2   *Kyrios* = Jesus. Ἐν ὀνόματι κυρίου = ὡς χριστιανός. Such a one comes and speaks the name of Jesus, i.e., declares that he or she is a Christian.

3   Cf. also the similar expression in 1 Sam 17:45. It is applied christologically in John 5:43.

4   One can scarcely split hairs over the fact that it no

longer explicitly says "receive him or her as the Lord" (11.2; cf. 11.4).

5   "Apparently this rule is inspired by fear of sinning against those who bear the name of the Lord. It is better to support someone who is unworthy than to turn away a worthy person" (Drews, "Apostellehre," 277).

6   This αὐτόν can refer to the following γνώσεσθε.

7   1 John 4:1; *1 Clem.* 42.4 are only distant parallels. *Hermas Man.* 11.7 speaks of the *dokimasis* of the prophets.

8   The object of γνώσεσθε is probably δεξιὰν καὶ

case distinguishing genuine Christians from impostors who only want to exploit and misuse Christian hospitality. The testing that is called for here presumes that there have been bad experiences connected with Christian hospitality. It is to be noted that the testing and decision are still the right of individual Christians; this is not a prerogative of local officials. No criteria for the testing are mentioned. It is a matter for the insight of individuals: σύνεσιν γὰρ ἕξετε. Σύνεσις ("insight") is apparently given special associations through the preceding γνώσεσθε ("you will know").[9]

ἀριστεράν, so that the phrase σύνεσιν γὰρ ἕξετε is to be read as a parenthesis; this was suggested already by Bryennios (in a letter to Harnack). Harnack adopted it (*Lehre*, 48) with reservations. Cf. also Knopf, *Lehre*, 33; and Audet, *Didachè*, 238. It is true that the text is uncertain at this point: Coptic, Ethiopic, and the *Apostolic Constitutions* have, or witness to, ἔχετε, which may be original (adopted by Audet, *Didachè*, 454; and Wengst, *Didache*, 84). H

reads ἔξεται, which has been emended, since Bryennios (Διδαχή, 45), to ἕξετε.

9 For σύνεσιν ἔχειν, cf. *Hermas Sim.* 9.22.2, 3. Σύνεσις is a special favorite of Hermas, "but with no broad distribution" (Hans Conzelmann, "συνίημι," *TDNT* 7 [1971] 896 n. 74).

12 b. Travelers Passing Through (12.2)

2 If the person who comes is just passing through, help him as much as you can, but he shall not stay with you more than two or three days—if that is necessary.

■ **2** Now some individual cases are discussed. In the first (v. 2) the new arrival is only traveling through. Παρόδιος (occurring only here in our literature) really means "beside the road, located on the road."[1] In this passage the word is used as a substantive and has the unique meaning "the one traveling through."[2] The injunction to "help him" (Βοηθεῖτε αὐτῷ ὅσον δύνασθε) calls for generous care of the guest, who is to be provided with everything that can be offered for the stay and for the continuing journey. This generous hospitality to their counterparts is one of the most striking characteristics of the adherents of the new faith.[3] It is also true here that hospitality is not to be misused; hence the stipulation "not to stay" (οὐ μενεῖ δὲ πρὸς ὑμᾶς εἰ μὴ δύο ἢ τρεῖς ἡμέρας). The reader naturally recalls the similar expressions in 11.5 (although they had a different sense there). In fact, the παρόδιος is to be permitted to remain more than one day, "if need be," ἐὰν ᾖ ἀνάγκη (cf. ἐὰν δὲ ᾖ χρεία in 11.5).[4]

---

1 Especially applied to walls, doors, and windows; cf. the information in LSJ, *s.v.;* and Edwin Mayser, *Grammatik der griechischen Papyri aus der Ptolemäerzeit* (2d ed.; 2 vols.; Berlin: de Gruyter, 1936) 1.3.102. Gregory of Nyssa interprets (*In Cant. cant. hom. II, PG* 44.793A) the parable of the fourfold field and paraphrases παρὰ τὴν ὁδόν with κἂν παρόδιός τε καὶ πεπατημένη. See the other patristic uses of παρόδιος in Lampe, *s.v.*

2 BAGD, *s.v.* It should be εἰ μὲν παροδίτης (or παροδεύων) ἐστὶν ὁ ἐρχόμενος, and perhaps we should conjecture it that way. For παροδίτης, see LSJ, *s.v.,* esp. *Sib. Or.* 14.33; for παροδεύων in this sense see Ignatius *Eph.* 9.1 and *Rom.* 9.3.

3 For the theme of early Christian hospitality (φιλοξενία), cf. Luke 14:12–14; Rom 12:13; 1 Pet 4:9; 1 Tim 3:2; 5:10; Titus 1:8; Heb 13:1; *1 Clem.* 1.2; *Hermas Man.* 8.10; *Sim.* 8.10.3; 9.27.2; Justin *1 Apol.* 67.6 (Goodspeed, 76); Aristides *Apol.* 15.7 (Goodspeed, 21); Dionysus of Corinth, in Eusebius *Hist. eccl.* 4.23.10; Otto Stählin, "ξένος," *TDNT* 5 (1967) 20–25; Ceslas Spicq, *Notes de Lexicographie Néo-Testamentaire* (2 vols. and Sup; OBO 22.1–3; Fribourg: Éditions Universitaires; Göttingen: Vandenhoeck & Ruprecht; Paris: Gabalda, 1978–82) 2.932–35 (ET: *Theological Lexicon of the New Testament* [trans. and ed. James D. Ernest; 3 vols.; Peabody, Mass.: Hendrickson, 1994] 3.454–57); Denys Gorce, "Gastfreundschaft: C. Christlich," *RAC* 8 (1972) 1103–7.

4 The Didachist has formulated his instructions in the style of the *Vorlage.* Still (apart from the difference in content regarding the length of time), the primary difference to be noted is between the apostles, who are obligated to constant *peregrinatio,* and the fellow Christians, who are (from time to time) on journeys.

**c. Persons Newly Arrived Who Desire
to Remain (12.3–5)**

3   If he wants to settle in with you, though, and
        he is a craftsman, let him work and eat.
4   If he has no craft, take care in your insight that
        no Christian live with you in idleness.
5   If he is unwilling to do what that way calls for,
        he is using Christ to make a living. Be on your
        guard against people like this.

■ **3** The next case is εἰ δὲ θέλει πρὸς ὑμᾶς καθῆσθαι.[1] Thus a situation is proposed in which the new arrival intends to settle in one place. In such an instance, what claim does he have to community support? Three possibilities are discussed. The first is that the new arrival has learned a trade or craft and can exercise it: τεχνίτης ὤν.[2] In that case the community is not obligated to offer assistance or shelter: Ἐργαζέσθω καὶ φαγέτω, that is, such persons should earn their daily bread through their own efforts.[3]

■ **4** A second possibility is that the new arrival does not have a craft or trade to practice (οὐκ ἔχει τέχνην),[4] and hence cannot live from it. Such a case is referred to the σύνεσις ("insight") of the community.[5] Concretely this would mean that the community shall see to it[6] that the new arrival will find work. The community, however, must take care in all cases to prevent any Christian among them from living in idleness.[7] Ἀργός (from ἀ-εργός) refers here not to the unemployed but to the idle and lazy. Χριστιανός[8]—originally probably a description by outsiders,[9] and still apparently avoided by Paul—is here, in the text of the Didachist, already a common and unproblematic self-designation.[10] Χριστιανός is a title of honor, and the name of Christian is not to be dishonored by those who bear it.[11] That would happen, however, if the community were to tolerate an idle beggar in its midst, someone living as a parasite at others' expense.

■ **5** The series of casuistic assertions concludes with a third possibility, εἰ δ᾽ οὐ θέλει οὕτω ποιεῖν, that is, the situation that occurs when someone is unwilling to live by the labor of his or her hands. In such a case the person in question calls dishonor upon the name of Christian and is not a χριστιανός, but (as the play on words has it) a χριστέμπορος. The community must guard itself against such persons.[12]

---

1   Cf. the casuistry: εἰ μὲν παρόδιός ἐστιν . . . (v. 2), εἰ δὲ θέλει . . . καθῆσθαι (v. 3), εἰ δὲ οὐκ ἔχει τέχνην . . . (v. 4), εἰ δ᾽ οὐ θέλει οὕτω ποιεῖν . . . (v. 5).

2   Cf. Acts 19:24, 38; Rev 18:22; *Diogn.* 2.3.

3   Obviously that does not exclude the possibility that the brothers and sisters will offer assistance in the exercise of his or her craft locally, as, e.g., in finding a place of work. Cf. Acts 18:3.

4   Τέχνην ἔχειν is a common expression: cf. BAGD, *s.v. Hermas Sim.* 9.9.2: ταύτην τὴν τέχνην οὐκ ἔχω. . . .

5   Cf. above at *Did.* 12.1: σύνεσιν γὰρ ἔξετε.

6   Προνοεῖν πῶς means "take care, that . . . "—cf. BAGD, *s.v.*

7   Cf. 2 Thess 3:10–12; *Didasc.* (Syriac) 13 (CSCO 407.153–54/408.139–41); *Ps.-Clement Ep. ad virg.* 1.11.1–2 (Duensing, 175–76).

8   Erik Peterson, "Christianus," in idem, *Frühkirche*, 64–87; Hans Conzelmann, *Acts of the Apostles* (Hermeneia; Philadelphia: Fortress, 1987) 88–89; Walter Grundmann, "χρίω," *TDNT* 9 (1974) 536–37, 576; Gerhard Schneider, "Χριστιανός,"

EDNT 3 (1993) 477–78. Wengst (*Didache*, 86) reads μενεῖ rather than ζήσεται χριστιανός, in dependence on the Ethiopic.

9   Acts 11:26; cf. Acts 26:28; later: 1 Pet 4:16 (the name "Christian" as an accusation—μὴ αἰσχυνέσθω, δοξαζέτω δὲ τὸν θεὸν ἐν τῷ ὀνόματι τούτῳ ["do not consider it a disgrace, but glorify God because you bear the name"]); *Mart. Pol.* 12.2. Among Gentiles: Tacitus *Annales* 15.44.2 (Koestermann, 356; for the variants *chrestiani* and *christiani* cf. the text-critical notes on the passage); Suetonius *Nero* 16.2 (Ihm, 231); Pliny *Ep.* 10.96 (Mynors, 388–89); 97 (340); Lucian *Alex.* 25 (Macleod, 2.343); 38 (2.348); *De morte Peregr.* 11–13 (3.191–92); 16 (3.193).

10   As in Ignatius *Eph.* 11.2; 14.2 (*v.l.*); *Magn.* 4; *Rom.* 3.2; *Pol.* 7.3; *Mart. Pol.* 10.1; 12.1. Ignatius also constructs the adjective in *Trall.* 6.1 and the substantive χριστιανισμός in *Magn.* 10.1, 3; *Rom.* 3.3; *Phld.* 6.1. Cf. *Mart. Pol.* 10.1.

11   Peterson ("Christianus," in idem, *Frühkirche*, 87) has expressed reservations about the genuineness of the

Excursus: Using Christ to Make a Living

The word χριστέμπορος[13] is not attested before *Did.* 12.5 and may represent a neologism by the Didachist. Ὁ ἔμπορος is, in the broad sense, someone who travels, and then specifically (and this is at the basis of the didachistic construction of the word) a merchant, more properly a wholesale merchant who undertakes business journeys to distant places, in contrast to the κάπηλος, the small, local merchant.[14] A χριστέμπορος is apparently someone who "deals in" Christ, that is, who misuses Christian faith and the name of Christ for personal enrichment.[15] On this subject cf., for example, 1 Tim 6:5; *2 Clem.* 20.4. For the term χριστέμπορος, cf. the Syriac version of the *Ps.-Clementine Ep. ad virg.* 1.10.4 in the German translation by Duensing, 175.35–36: (regarding the itinerant teachers, who) "do business, with the aid of winning words, with the name of Christ"; 1.11.4: "doing business in the name of Christ" (Duensing, 176.10);[16] 1.13.5: "workers who regard fear of God and righteousness as a source of profit" (179.34–35).[17] The Greek text, lost at this point, could have offered

χριστέμπορος.[18] The word χριστέμπορος then occurs again in Hippolytus *Fragm. in Ruth* (GCS 1.2.120); Ps.-Ignatius *Trall.* 6.2 (Funk and Diekamp, *Patres apostolici*, 2.98), οὐ Χριστιανοὶ ἀλλὰ χριστέμποροι ("not Christians but sellers of Christ"); *Magn.* 9.5 (126), οἱ χριστέμποροι, τὸν λόγον καπηλεύοντες καὶ τὸν Ἰησοῦν πωλοῦντες ("the Christ-sellers, who merchandise the word and sell Jesus"); Athanasius *Fragmenta in Matthaeum* (PG 27.1381A); Basil *Ep.* 240.3 (PG 32.897A); Gregory Nazianzus *Or.* 21.31 (PG 35.1117C): Καθαίρει μέν γε τὸ ἱερὸν τῶν θεοκαπήλων, καὶ χριστεμπόρων ("he cleanses the temple of merchants of God, sellers of Christ"); *Or.* 40.11 (PG 36.372C): μηδὲ γενώμεθα Χριστοκάπηλοι[19] καὶ Χριστέμποροι ("Let us not become merchants of Christ and Christ-sellers"); Chrysostom *Hom. 6.1 in 1 Thess.* (PG 62.430); Antiochus monachus Hom. 37 (PG 89.1548A); Alexander of Alexandria *Ep. Alex.* (in Theodoret *Historia ecclesiastica* 1.4.3; GCS 19.9) has χριστεμπορία (a printing error in the text).

word Χριστιανός in the original *Didache* text. This can scarcely be correct.

12 For προσέχειν, cf. *Did.* 6.3, which is also from the pen of the Didachist.

13 Cf. the examples in Lampe, *s.v.*; William Telfer, "The *Didache* and the Apostolic Synod of Antioch," *JTS* 40 (1939) 265 n. 1; and Adam, "Herkunft," 38–39.

14 Later, then, the term χριστοκάπηλος does emerge; see below (cf. καπηλεύειν τὸν λόγον τοῦ θεοῦ, 2 Cor 2:17, where Paul adopts and varies a common polemical expression directed against pseudophilosophy; see the examples in Hans Windisch, "καπηλεύω," *TDNT* 3 [1967] 604–5). Ludwig Mitteis and Ulrich Wilckens (*Grundzüge und Chrestomathie der Papyruskunde* [1.1; Leipzig: Teubner, 1912; repr. Hildesheim: Olms, 1963] 268) refer to the frequent compounds with ἔμπορος (e.g., σιτέμποροι). In my opinion this common usage constitutes the precondition for the clever and ironic construction χριστέμπορος. From a different perspective, constructions like χριστόγονος, χριστομάχος, and other similar words are parallels.

15 The construction χριστέμπορος is probably chosen with a view to the brothers and sisters who appear to be *on journey*, but who then prove to be pseudo-Christians. According to Adam ("Herkunft," 38), this is an "understandable contrast to χριστοφόρος" (?). Adam asserts in this connection (p. 38) that this is based on a specifically Syrian usage that frequently described the Christian as a "merchant" (in the sense of Matt 13:44).

16 Adam ("Herkunft," 39) prefers the translation: "but they sell evil things in the name of Christ."

17 The Coptic fragment (Lefort, *Pères apostoliques*, CSCO 135.35–43 and 136.29–37) unfortunately has no text for this passage.

18 Adam, "Herkunft," 39. That the *Didache* must be directed to "the same kinds of communities that can be deduced from the *Epistolae ad virgines*" (ibid.) by no means follows from this.

19 Χριστοκάπηλος is also found in Isidore of Pelusium *Ep.* 1.90 (PG 78.245A).

4. Second Appendix: On the Duty to Support Prophets Who Desire to Remain in the Community, and Duties toward Teachers (13.1–7)

While at the time of the Didachist there was no longer any need to expect itinerant *apostles*, the itinerant *prophet* continued to be a familiar figure in the community. Alongside them there now appeared διδάσκαλοι (about whom the ancient tradition in *Did.* 11.4–12 had not had anything to say).

The problem treated in *Did.* 13.1–7 is a new one, characteristic of the time of the Didachist: the prophet arrives with the intention of settling down in the local community.[1] The local community must be instructed about how to behave in such situations. The dominant theme of the whole is the prophet; teachers are spoken of only in passing.

The structure is as follows:[2]

a. Fundamental principles (13.1–2)

b. Directions for the distribution (13.3–7).[3]

[1] Differently Audet, *Didachè,* 455–56. He sees no new relationship here and does not acknowledge the picture of the increasingly resident character of the "itinerant hierarchy."

[2] Niederwimmer, "Itinerant Radicalism," 327 n. 17.

[3] For Audet's thesis on the origins of *Did.* 13.3 and 13.5–7, as well as the originality of v. 4, see below.

13

a. Fundamental Principles (13.1)

1   Every true prophet who wants to settle in with you deserves his food. 2/ In the same way, a true teacher, too, deserves his food, just as a worker does.

Comment

■ **1** The Didachist first states the fundamental principle in reference to the prophets; afterward, in vv. 3–7, he gives the principle more concrete detail. If one of the prophets (who, we are to understand, was previously homeless) desires to settle in the local community (καθῆσθαι as in 12.3), that should be permitted.[1] (The precondition that this must be a *genuine* prophet is made clear, in passing, by the use of προπήτης ἀληθινός.) The problem is not the prophet's settling down but the question of a livelihood. The basic rule for this is that he

must "deserve his food": ἄξιός ἐστι τῆς τροφῆς αὐτοῦ. This is quoted as a valid legal principle. In its full form (as its repetition in v. 2 will show) it reads: ἄξιος ὁ ἐργάτης τῆς τροφῆς αὐτοῦ. Cf. Matt 10:10b/Luke 10:7b (Q?): ἄξιος γὰρ ὁ ἐργάτης τῆς τροφῆς (Luke: τοῦ μισθοῦ) αὐτοῦ. See further 1 Tim 5:18b (τοῦ μισθοῦ), where the logion appears as a scriptural (?) quotation.[2] It is difficult to decide whether the principle is regarded by the

[1] The prophet apparently has this right; in contrast, it would be unthinkable for the itinerant apostles in the *Didache* (cf. 11.5).

[2] For this logion cf. Erich Klostermann, *Das Matthäusevangelium* (4th ed.; HNT 4; Tübingen: Mohr, 1971) 87; Martin Dibelius and Hans

Didachist as a saying of the Lord,[3] or simply as a binding legal principle from tradition. He is probably, however, construing it as a command from the Lord (as the continuation in vv. 5 and 7—κατὰ τὴν ἐντολήν—suggests).[4] In the nature of things the Didachist intends thereby to give statutory effect to the principle that locally resident Christians are obligated to provide a livelihood for the prophets who desire to settle among them. The office of prophet itself is adequate reason for this obligation of support. It gives a legal claim to τροφή. Thus here the principle of ἐργαζέσθω καὶ φαγέτω ("let him work and eat," Did. 12.3) does not apply. Instead, the prophets need not live from the work of their hands; the community must provide for their daily needs.

■ 2 The verse provides an analogous rule for teachers—as before, this applies only to the genuine teacher, διδάσκαλος ἀληθινός (or, as the text says, the community is to guard itself against the ψευδοδιδάσκαλος: Did. 11.1–2). It is true for the teachers (as for the prophets) that they are "worthy of their food," that is, that the community is obliged to provide for their livelihood.[5]

Excursus: The "Teacher"

The Didache speaks of the διδάσκαλος only here, in 11.1–2, and in 15.1–2. The word refers neither to the (itinerant) apostles nor to the prophets,[6] but to a

---

Conzelmann, The Pastoral Epistles (Hermeneia; Philadelphia: Fortress, 1972) 78–79; I. Howard Marshall, The Gospel of Luke (New International Greek Testament Commentary; Grand Rapids: Eerdmans, 1978) 412–27, esp. 420–21; Francis Wright Beare, The Gospel According to Matthew (San Francisco: Harper & Row, 1981) 243; Gottfried Holtz, Die Pastoralbriefe (4th ed.; ThHK 13; Leipzig: Evangelische Verlagsanstalt, 1986) 126–27; Joseph A. Fitzmyer, S.J., The Gospel According to Luke (X–XXIV) (AB 28A; Garden City, N.Y.: Doubleday, 1985) 841–50, esp. 848; and esp. A. E. Harvey, "'The Workman Is Worthy of His Hire': Fortunes of a Proverb in the Early Church," NovT 24 [1982] 209–21. The logion raises a number of open questions: Is the form with τροφή (Matthew) or that with μισθός (Luke and 1 Timothy) earlier? Is the γραφή in 1 Tim 5:18b a supposed quotation from the OT, from an apocryphal work, or perhaps even a quotation from Luke's Gospel? Or does the reference to γραφή apply merely to v. 18a? These questions need not be answered here. In the nature of things what we have here is a general legal principle that appeals, in the fashion of ḥokmah, to wisdom and the assent of reason (sit venia verbo: an immediately obvious fundamental principle of "natural law"). We may leave aside the question whether it stems originally from the Jesus tradition or was adopted by it. Harvey ("Workman," 211 n. 9) refers to μισθὸν μοχθήσαντι δίδου ("give a wage to the one who has toiled") in Ps.-Phocyl. 19 (cf. Sib. Or. 2.74 ψ), and πονοῦντα δ᾽ ἄξιον/μισθὸν φέρεσθαι ("one who toils is worthy to receive pay") in Ps.(?)-Euripides Rhesus 161–62. The Christian maxim is universally valid and therefore applicable to a variety of cases. In the Jesus tradition it refers to the disciples; for Paul (who appears only to allude to it

in 1 Cor 9:14) it refers, correspondingly, to the post-Easter missionaries; in Did. 13.1 it applies to the prophets; and in 1 Tim 5:18b it refers to the presbyters. Common to all these cases is that a general principle is given special application to a different set of significant persons in a religious community. Cf. also the quotation in Ps.-Clem. Hom. 3.71.3 (GCS² 1.82): τοῦ μισθοῦ.

3 The question remains open whether this is oral or written tradition and, if it is written, whether (in this case) it comes from the Gospel of Matthew or perhaps from an apocryphal writing. Harnack (Lehre, 50) concluded: "Here again the author draws on a saying of the Lord in Matthew's version." Similarly Massaux, Influence, 3.166; Hagner, Use, 280; cf. Wengst's reflections, Didache, 28–29. He writes that a quotation from the Gospel of Matthew is (in spite of the possibilities considered by Koester, Synoptische Überlieferung, 212–13) "by far the most probable" (Wengst, Didache, 28 n. 102).

4 Nonetheless, the explicit command in vv. 3–7 to give ἀπαρχή to the prophets who take the place of the high priest in the OT (v. 3) is best understood as a Christian command, namely, a command from the Lord, and especially as a consequence of the logion quoted by the Didachist in Did. 13.1 and 2.

5 Did. 13.2 repeats the binding commandment again, this time in more detail: the Didachist shows that the full text (as known to him) was: ἄξιός ἐστιν ὁ ἐργάτης τῆς τροφῆς αὐτοῦ. This form of the text agrees almost word for word with Matt 10:10b. The Didachist's form is made awkward by the insertion of ὥσπερ ὁ ἐργάτης. It is explained by the unbalanced combination of two statements: ἐστὶν ἄξιος τῆς τροφῆς αὐτοῦ and the complete quotation of the formula.

6 De Halleux ("Ministers," 311) differs, identifying

189

charismatic office different from both of them.[7] The διδάσκαλος was still absent from the old tradition in 11.4–12, but is mentioned here quite deliberately. Taken in context, 13.2 strongly suggests[8] (and this is confirmed by 11.1–2) that the charismatic teachers had also begun their work as itinerants. It is also true of the teachers in the *Didache* (as of its prophets) that at the time of the Didachist it sometimes (or even fre-

quently) occurred that they wished to become resident in one place. Hereafter 15.1–2 (q.v.) will treat the relationship between the charismatic teachers and the "local clergy." Nothing is said about the function of the διδάσκαλοι, nor did anything need to be said as far as the readers of this document were concerned, because they were all familiar with the person and work of the διδάσκαλος.[9]

the teacher with the prophet. The reference would be to the prophet *as* teacher. And because, ultimately, prophet and apostle are also identified (cf. "Ministers," 307), all these words, in principle, refer only to a *single* group. See above, p. 173 n. 2.

7   On the teachers in the *Didache,* see Stempel, "Lehrer," 209–17. In my opinion, however, Stempel has overestimated the role and function of the teacher in the *Didache.* See the general information now in Zimmermann, *Lehrer,* passim; on the *Didache* esp. pp. 141–43.

8   It is true that *Did.* 13.2 lacks a specific reference to θέλων καθῆσθαι. The Didachist could also include the teachers (having already spoken once of the community's obligation to provide sustenance) without necessarily implying that they, like the prophets, originally belonged among the *peregrinantes.* But 11.1–2 alone already compels us to con-

clude that the teachers in the *Didache* must also have begun as itinerant charismatics.

9   Zimmermann (*Lehrer,* 142) thinks with reference to the teachers that "because they must have been resident in larger numbers than the prophets they may well have been the middle term between the triadic charismatic offices and the *episkopoi/diakonoi* (15.1). The whole *Didache* can certainly be regarded as the product of such a διδάσκαλος." I cannot see that "the content of this office had surely undergone an essential change with increasing distance from Judaism" (p. 143; cf. also p. 218). Zimmermann's remarks must be read within the context of his thesis about the existence of an early Jewish-Christian Pharisaic teaching office (cf. pp. 218–19).

13

b. Directions for the Distribution (13.3–7)

3 So when you [sg.] take any firstfruits of what is produced by the winepress and the threshing floor, by cows and by sheep, you [sg.] shall give the firstfruits to the prophets, for they are your [pl.] high priests.

<4 If, however, you [pl. throughout v. 4] have no prophet, give [them] to the poor.>

5 If you [sg. throughout vv. 5–7] prepare dough, take the firstfruits and give them according to the commandment.

6 Likewise, when you open a jar of wine or oil, take the firstfruits and give them to the prophets.

7 Take the firstfruits of money and clothing and whatever [else] you own as you think best and give them according to the commandment.

Comment

■ **3** The text just preceding had spoken of the $\tau\rho o\varphi\acute{\eta}$ due to the charismatics. Now vv. 3–7[1] give a more precise indication of what is meant by $\tau\rho o\varphi\acute{\eta}$ (whereby it is striking that now the text speaks explicitly and solely of prophets as the recipients of these benefits). First mentioned are the $\grave{\alpha}\pi\alpha\rho\chi\grave{\eta}$ $\gamma\epsilon\nu\nu\eta\mu\acute{\alpha}\tau\omega\nu$ $\lambda\eta\nu o\hat{\upsilon}$ $\kappa\alpha\grave{\iota}$ $\acute{\alpha}\lambda\omega\nu o\varsigma$, $\beta o\hat{\omega}\nu$ $\tau\epsilon$ $\kappa\alpha\grave{\iota}$ $\pi\rho o\beta\acute{\alpha}\tau\omega\nu$. The term $\gamma\acute{\epsilon}\nu\nu\eta\mu\alpha$ ("firstfruits"), strictly speaking, applies only to the last two expressions.[2] In fact H reads $\gamma\epsilon\nu\eta\mu\acute{\alpha}\tau\omega\nu$, but this (in contrast to *Constitutions* $\gamma\epsilon\nu\nu\eta\mu\acute{\alpha}\tau\omega\nu$) is probably a simplification.[3] $\Gamma\epsilon\nu(\nu)\acute{\eta}\mu\alpha\tau\alpha$ $\lambda\eta\nu o\hat{\upsilon}$ means the product of the winepress—therefore the wine—while $\gamma\epsilon\nu(\nu)\acute{\eta}\mu\alpha\tau\alpha$ $\acute{\alpha}\lambda\omega\nu o\varsigma$ is the product of the threshing floor, the grain. The whole expression is biblical; cf. Num 18:30

(although there it is $\gamma\acute{\epsilon}\nu\eta\mu\alpha$).[4] $Bo\hat{\omega}\nu$ $\tau\epsilon$ $\kappa\alpha\grave{\iota}$ $\pi\rho o\beta\acute{\alpha}\tau\omega\nu$ ("cows and sheep") is constructed by analogy to the preceding pair.[5] Thus the prophets are entitled to bread, wine, and meat from cattle and sheep; in fact they are entitled to the $\grave{\alpha}\pi\alpha\rho\chi\acute{\eta}$, the firstfruits, the gifts that were originally dedicated to God and then belonged to the temple, that is, to the priests. With the term $\grave{\alpha}\pi\alpha\rho\chi\acute{\eta}$[6] (awkwardly used twice), the Didachist deliberately adopts a term from Old Testament cultic language.[7] He decrees that the cultic demand of Scripture (the OT) that the $\grave{\alpha}\pi\alpha\rho\chi\acute{\eta}$ be surrendered as an offering is now translated into an obligation toward the Christian prophets active in the community. *To them* is due the

---

1 Possibly quoted in *Lib. grad.* 13.2 (Kmosko, 307): see above, pp. 12–13. For the question whether *Did.* 13.3 is quoted in *Didascalia apostolorum*, see above, p. 15. According to Audet (*Didachè*, 106–10, 238–40, 453, 457–58) *Did.* 13.3, 5–7 is an interpolation (while 13.4 is to be regarded, in addition, as a later gloss: p. 458).

2 $\Gamma\acute{\epsilon}\nu\nu\eta\mu\alpha$ is "*that which is produced* or *born* (of living creatures), *child, offspring*" (BAGD, *s.v.*). Bauer remarks (ibid.) that the use of the term here is "justifiable because the last two nouns refer to animals."

3 Bryennios ($\Delta\iota\delta\alpha\chi\acute{\eta}$, 47) conjectured $\gamma\epsilon\nu\nu\eta\mu\acute{\alpha}\tau\omega\nu$, as do the later editions throughout. Differently Rordorf and Tuilier, *Doctrine*, 190: $\gamma\epsilon\nu\eta\mu\acute{\alpha}\tau\omega\nu$. Is this possibly correct?

4 $\H{O}\tau\alpha\nu$ $\grave{\alpha}\varphi\alpha\iota\rho\hat{\eta}\tau\epsilon$ $\tau\grave{\eta}\nu$ $\grave{\alpha}\pi\alpha\rho\chi\grave{\eta}\nu$ $\grave{\alpha}\pi'$ $\alpha\grave{\upsilon}\tauo\hat{\upsilon}$, $\kappa\alpha\grave{\iota}$ $\lambda o\gamma\iota\sigma\vartheta\acute{\eta}\sigma\epsilon\tau\alpha\iota$ $\tauo\hat{\iota}\varsigma$ $\Lambda\epsilon\upsilon\acute{\iota}\tau\alpha\iota\varsigma$ $\acute{\omega}\varsigma$ $\gamma\acute{\epsilon}\nu\eta\mu\alpha$ $\grave{\alpha}\pi\grave{o}$ $\acute{\alpha}\lambda\omega\nu o\varsigma$ $\kappa\alpha\grave{\iota}$ $\acute{\omega}\varsigma$ $\gamma\acute{\epsilon}\nu\eta\mu\alpha$ $\grave{\alpha}\pi\grave{o}$ $\lambda\eta\nu o\hat{\upsilon}$ ("When you have set apart the best of it, then the rest shall be reckoned to the Levites as produce of the threshing floor, and as produce of the winepress").

5 But cf. Deut 12:6, 17; and similarly 2 Esdr 20:37.

6 The repetition of the word $\grave{\alpha}\pi\alpha\rho\chi\acute{\eta}$ is striking. The repetition paints the solemn, cultic action.

7 For $\grave{\alpha}\pi\alpha\rho\chi\acute{\eta}$ in the LXX, see Gerhard Delling, "$\grave{\alpha}\pi\alpha\rho\chi\acute{\eta}$," *TDNT* 1 (1964) 484–85; Alexander Sand, "$\grave{\alpha}\pi\alpha\rho\chi\acute{\eta}$," *EDNT* 1 (1990) 116–17. Verses 3–7 are held together by the key word $\grave{\alpha}\pi\alpha\rho\chi\acute{\eta}$ (vv. 3 bis, 5, 6, 7). The constantly recurring expression $\tau\grave{\eta}\nu$ $\grave{\alpha}\pi\alpha\rho\chi\grave{\eta}\nu$ $\lambda\alpha\beta\acute{\omega}\nu$, $\delta\acute{o}\varsigma$ ($\delta\acute{\omega}\sigma\epsilon\iota\varsigma$) describes the solemn action of cultic offering, originally the sacrifice belonging to God alone. The $\grave{\alpha}\pi\alpha\rho\chi\acute{\eta}$ is "taken," and then given to the prophets (representing the OT priests, or [as the Didachist sees it] the high priests).

ἀπαρχή of what God gives to humanity, and this is because they, the prophets, take the place in the Christian community that belonged to the high priests in Israel. Indeed the prophets *are* "your" high priests (*Did.* 13.3b).[8] Therefore, the cultic offering that the Old Testament community owed to its high priests now belongs to them.[9] We may ask whether the terminology (according to which the prophets appear as ἀρχιερεῖς) allows us to conclude that the prophets led worship in the *Didache* communities.[10] *Did.* 10.7 seems to presume that at the time of the *Didache* the local officials led worship, but the prophets had the right to charismatic prayer; 15.1–2 shows both groups in leadership functions (see below).

Excursus: The Didachist and Judaism

This passage at 13.3 is important for understanding the position of the Didachist with respect to Judaism. The Old Testament cultic law is transferred, rather freely, to the new, ecclesiastical situation and is altered accordingly. In order to underscore the status of the prophets and to insure that the community recognizes its obligation to care for them, the Didachist parallels[11] the Christian prophets of his own time with the ἀρχιερεῖς of the old covenant, thus making the prophets (metaphorically) the "high priests" of Christians.[12] This is a striking formulation, and it has no direct parallels in early Christian literature.[13]

■ **4** Then in v. 4 the text is interrupted by a parenthetical remark, ἐὰν δὲ μὴ ἔχητε προφήτην, δότε [sc. τὴν ἀπαρχήν] τοῖς πτωχοῖς.[14] This statement is probably (as Audet has suggested)[15] a later, but still very old, gloss.[16] This is the expression of a time when even the prophets have become a rarity. In such cases the community should give its offerings to the poor.

■ **5** Verse 5 is connected to the discussion in v. 3 and continues it. The guiding word of vv. 3–5 remains ἀπαρχή, the gifts that are due the prophets. Σιτίαν

---

8   There is a characteristic alteration in *Const.* 7.29.1: πᾶσαν ἀπαρχὴν γεννημάτων ληνοῦ, ἅλωνος βοῶν τε καὶ προβάτων δώσεις τοῖς ἱερεῦσιν. Now it refers to the Christian priests. Cf. 2.26.3, where the Constitutor (dependent on the *Didascalia apostolorum*; cf. n. 12 below) parallels the high priests with the bishops, the priests with the presbyters, and the Levites with the deacons.

9   This is expressed only as a general idea. For the OT prescriptions regarding priests' incomes cf. Deut 18:3–4; Num 18:8–32; Ezek 44:30; Neh 10:32–39; 2 Chr 31:4–10. The OT is aware of prescriptions for *priests'* income, but there are no specific regulations for the income of the *high* priest. The error in the *Didache* casts a revealing light on the Didachist. For the real income of the high priest at the time of Jesus, see Joachim Jeremias, *Jerusalem in the Time of Jesus* (Philadelphia: Fortress, 1969) 150–51. The episode in 2 Kgs 4:42 (a gift of firstfruits to an OT prophet) was apparently less suitable for the Didachist's argument.

10   Thus Rordorf and Tuilier, *Doctrine,* 52–53; differently de Halleux, "Ministers," 312.

11   The system of thought that lies behind this is obviously that of typological exegesis, even if this is not expressed and perhaps is not even brought to the level of consciousness (cf. earlier, at *Did.* 11.11). We should also take note of the elements that are brought to bear to make up the Didachist's demonstration: (a) the ἐντολὴ (κυρίου), which was quoted in vv. 1–2; and (b) the typological interpretation of the OT. The *mandata Domini* and the OT (unreflec-

tively interpreted in Christian fashion) are the instances to which the redactor appeals.

12   Compare the contrary position of Tertullian *De bapt.* 17.1 (CChrSL 1.291): *summus sacerdos, si qui est, episcopus . . .* ("the high priest, if anyone, is the bishop") and *Didasc.* (Syriac) 9 (CSCO 401.103; 402.100); and (Latin) 25.20–21 (TU 75.41). For the question whether the *Didascalia* is quoting the *Didache* at this point, see above, p. 15.

13   Harnack, *Lehre,* 52.

14   Wengst, *Didachè,* 86: τῷ πτωχῷ (with *Constitutions* and the Ethiopic).

15   Audet, *Didachè,* 458. He considers *Did.* 13.3, 5–7 an interpolation (106–10, 238–41, 453, 457–58), so that according to him the gloss is to be regarded as a gloss within an interpolation. But the positing of an interpolation in chap. 13 is questionable. Cf. Niederwimmer, "Itinerant Radicalism," 326. Against the supposition that there is a gloss in v. 4, see Wengst, *Didache,* 40 n. 136.

16   Cf. Niederwimmer, "Textprobleme," 121. That the text in *Const.* 7.29.2 seems to be presupposed does not speak against this. One must presume that this is a relatively ancient gloss in the *Didache* text.

17   Ἡ σιτία is rare. Hesychius (ed. Schmidt, 3.35) has δαπάνημα, βρῶμα, σιτηρέσιον, but appears to confuse τὰ σιτία and σιτεία: cf. the notes ad loc. In the *Apophthegmata patrum* (PG 65.192A), σιτία may be dough, i.e., bread dough (καὶ λαβὼν σιτίαν εἰς τὸ ἀρτοκοπεῖον, ἐποίησεν ἄρτους, "Taking dough into the bakery, he made loaves of bread"); in 196B

ποιεῖν is a *crux interpretum* for linguistic reasons. This phrase may mean "prepare dough."[17] When that has been done,[18] the rule is: τὴν ἀπαρχὴν λαβὼν δὸς κατὰ τὴν ἐντολήν. The phrase κατὰ τὴν ἐντολήν is characteristic of the style of the Didachist (cf. 1.5 and the repetition in 13.7). In the present passage (and in 13.7) it appears that the reference is to a commandment of the Lord,[19] most probably the admonition ἄξιός ἐστι (ὁ ἐργάτης) τῆς τροφῆς αὐτοῦ just cited (vv. 1–2).[20] The effort to give as concrete a determination as possible to the sacred offerings to be made for the prophets also affects the following verses (vv. 6–7).

■ **6–7** The next verse concerns the offering of wine and oil.[21] Both are preserved in earthen containers or jars (κεράμιον). Finally, v. 7 speaks of money. The following

ἱματισμός (in spite of Knopf's protest)[22] has its usual meaning here: "clothing." Καὶ παντὸς κτήματος ("whatever else") makes clear that the preceding list is only a set of examples, and in principle every kind of property is subject to the obligation to make offerings of the ἀπαρχή. The succession of the three final phrases is noteworthy. Λαβὼν τὴν ἀπαρχήν ("take the firstfruits") again recalls the cultic nature of the gifts; ὡς ἄν σοι δόξη ("as you think best") liberates the givers from any kind of niggling legalism and appeals to the generosity of individuals; δὸς κατὰ τὴν ἐντολήν finally makes clear again, in conclusion, that the offering here demanded rests on a binding "commandment" of the *Kyrios*.[23]

(Ἀπῆλθον οὖν εἰς τὸ ἀρτοκοπεῖον ποιῆσαι δύο σιτίας, "They·therefore went off to the bakery to make two loaves of bread") and C (ἐποίησα ἐξ σιτίας . . . ἐποίησα τὰς δύο σιτίας, "I made six loaves . . . I made the two loaves") the word could simply mean bread. Bonifaz Miller (*Weisung der Väter* [Freiburg im Breisgau: Lambertus, 1965]) translates the first example as "grain" (p. 105), but understands σιτίας in the other three passages as "bread" (109). I do not want to exclude the possibility that the striking σιτίαν in the *Didache* passage is the work of the copyist, while the original text may have read ἐὰν σιτία (from σιτίον) ποιῆς. (The Ethiopic reads "bread," while the *Apostolic Constitutions* paraphrases: ἄρτοι θερμοί.)

18 According to Drews ("Apostellehre," 278) and Knopf (*Lehre,* 35) one should add, by inference: and when the dough has been baked into bread. But see n. 17 above.

19 According to Drews ("Apostellehre," 278) a quotation from "an unknown gospel source." See idem, "Untersuchungen," 63–67, where he postulates a source of dominical commandments. Cf. above at *Did.* 1.3–7.

20 Another possibility is that ἐντολή refers to the OT commands. This is less probable; the use of the singular is also against it.

21 The Ethiopic has the addition καὶ μέλιτος. The

text of the *Apostolic Constitutions* has still more interpolations.

22 Knopf refers to "the piece of cloth, either purchased or woven by oneself, that is to be cut correctly" (*Lehre* 35).

23 Georg Schöllgen, "Die Didache—ein frühes Zeugnis für Landgemeinden?" *ZNW* 76 (1985) 141: "It is not very likely that . . . all the required ἀπαρχαί are demanded of every member of the community; in that case, the *Didache* would have anticipated a twofold offering from the produce of the grain harvest: first at threshing (v. 3) and then again when bread is baked (v. 5); there is then a similar double offering of grapes and wine (vv. 3 and 6). Hence it is more likely that, as regards the individual ἀπαρχαί, there were different possibilities for fulfilling one's obligation to support the prophets." (For Schöllgen's protest against the interpretation of v. 3, or vv. 3–7, as indicating *rural* conditions, see above, p. 54.)

5. On Confession and Reconciliation (14.1–3)

1   Assembling on every Sunday of the Lord, break bread and give thanks, confessing your faults beforehand, so that your sacrifice may be pure.

2   Let no one engaged in a dispute with his comrade join you until they have been reconciled, lest your sacrifice be profaned.

3   This is [the meaning] of what was said by the Lord: "'to offer me a pure sacrifice in every place and time, because I am a great king,' says the Lord, 'and my name is held in wonder among the nations.'"

Analysis

The text is redactional. Its subject is not really the Sunday worship service[1] but the particular issue of confession, or reconciliation, as precondition for the purity required for the carrying out of the sacrifice that is brought before God in the meal celebration. To that extent chap. 14 is not a doublet of chaps. 9–10.[2] In the whole section comprising chaps. 11–15, the Didachist has in view the local community to which he is giving instructions for good order and church discipline. Thus he now arrives at a discussion of the questions of internal community life, and so deals with dissension, reconciliation, confession, and the purity of sacrifices. The presumption that chap. 14 belongs to a later, *second* redaction[3] does not seem compelling.[4]

Comment

■ **1** The whole clause κατὰ κυριακήν . . . εὐχαριστήσατε (v. 1a) simply constitutes the introduction to the central statement, which will follow only in v. 1b. The Didachist wants to speak about confession and the purity of sacrifices, and for that purpose he places the reader in the time of the Sunday worship service. The description of

---

1   Thus, e.g., Harnack, *Lehre*, 53; Drews, "Apostellehre," 279; Knopf, *Lehre*, 35. For Drews and Knopf chaps. 9–10 are about a private meal celebration, and only at chap. 14 does the text begin to speak about the official Sunday Eucharist of the community. Cf. above, p. 141. They then have difficulties with the context and must emphasize that in the section on the Sunday celebration the author restricts himself to the discussion of a *single* point (namely, the question of the forgiveness of sins). For Klauser, Audet, and Vööbus, see n. 2 below.

2   Differently (and characteristically) Klauser, *Doctrina*, 28: "*Cur hoc loco denuo de eucharistia sermo fiat, non bene perspicitur. Forsitan hoc capitulum paulo postea additum est*" ("Why there should be discussion of the Eucharist at this place is not clear. Perhaps the chapter was added somewhat after"). Audet has an easier time of it here because he ascribes the chapter to D²: "The author returns to the subject, not because he is a bad writer, or because he had, oddly enough, forgotten something, or because he is compiling his materials at random, or because someone else had created a subsequent interpolation of 14:1–3, but simply because experience has demonstrated, in the meantime, the inadequacy of the instructions in 9–10" (*Didachè*, 460). Vööbus (*Liturgical Traditions*, 78) has still another explanation: The author (in

light of the mention of the prophets) makes a digression *ad vocem* "prophets" in chaps. 11–13 and returns, in chap. 14, to the subject of the Eucharist; (for Vööbus the prayers in chap. 9 are eucharistic prayers: see above, p. 142); but this time it is not the Eucharist as such that is the topic, "but the subject of the confession of sins and its significance in relation to the cultic life. If so, then this chapter is not a repetition at all" (ibid.).

3   Rordorf and Tuilier, *Doctrine*, 49, 63, 93. Rordorf ("Didachè," 23) raised the question whether the (second) redactor of the *Didache* did not return to the subject of Sunday because his community was inclined to σαββατίζειν (?). So also Rordorf and Tuilier, *Doctrine*, 65. See below, p. 195 n. 9.

4   One must admit that *Did.* 15.1–2 represents an interruption. *Did.* 14.1–3 is only continued and concluded by 15.3–4. See below. That does not compel us to see 15.1–2 as a later insertion. It is simply a digression. At 15.3 the author again takes up the thread he had dropped.

5   Audet, *Didachè*, 72–73, 240, 460.

6   *Const.* 7.30.1 has paraphrased: τὴν ἀναστάσιμον τοῦ κυρίου ἡμέραν, τὴν κυριακὴν φαμεν ("the day of the resurrection of the Lord, we say the 'Lord's day'"), thus showing that it found both κυριακήν and κυρίου in the source. It is possible that a

the time, κατὰ κυριακὴν δὲ κυρίου ("the Sunday of the Lord"), is striking and obviously pleonastic. We expect καθ᾽ ἡμέραν δὲ κυρίου (as Audet has conjectured),[5] but it is proper to maintain the pleonastic text provided by H.[6] For the omission of ἡμέρα, cf. Jer 52:12: ἐν . . . δεκάτῃ τοῦ μηνός, and the expression ἀγοραῖοι ἄγονται in Acts 19:38.[7] Thus it is also possible, in early Christian language, for κυριακή to stand alone (in place of κυριακὴ ἡμέρα, Rev 1:10), as in Gos. Pet. 9.35 (SC 201.56): Τῇ δὲ νυκτὶ ᾗ ἐπέφωσκεν ἡ κυριακή; and 13.50 (62): Ὄρθρου δὲ τῆς κυριακῆς ("in the night in which the Lord's day dawned"); cf. Ignatius Magn. 9.1: μηκέτι σαββατίζοντες, ἀλλὰ κατὰ κυριακὴν ζῶντες ("no longer celebrate the Sabbath, but live for the Lord's day"). Κυριακή here, as in this Didache passage, is

already a familiar term for the day of the week that is consecrated by the resurrection of the Lord.[8] The community is accustomed to gather on that day. This is the custom that our passage presumes: συναχθέντες.[9] The Didachist orders that a Eucharist be celebrated on every Lord's day when the community comes together: κλάσατε ἄρτον καὶ εὐχαριστήσατε. There is something of a parallel to the whole in Acts 20:7: Ἐν δὲ τῇ μιᾷ τῶν σαββάτων συνηγμένων ἡμῶν κλάσαι ἄρτον ("On the first day of the week when we met to break bread"); cf. also Ignatius Eph. 20.2: συνέρχεσθε . . . ἕνα ἄρτον κλῶντες ("join in the common meeting . . . breaking one bread"). What, more precisely, does the double expression (κλάσατε ἄρτον and εὐχαριστήσατε) mean in this passage? Does κλάσατε ἄρτον[10] refer to the breaking of

---

Semitism underlies this pleonasm: Τὰ σάββατα κυρίου (Lev 23:38; cf. Exod 20:10) would have been replaced by Christians with ἡ κυριακὴ κυρίου (Taylor, Teaching, 61). Cf. nn. 3 and 9.

7   BAGD, s.v. ἀγοραῖος.

8   For the resurrection on the first day of the week see esp. John 20:1, 19; for the celebration on the Lord's day as the day of resurrection cf. (in addition to the passages mentioned hereafter) John 20:26; 1 Cor 16:2; Barn. 15.9; Justin 1 Apol. 67.3 (Goodspeed, 75); 67.7 (76); Dial. 24.1 (117); 41.4 (138); 138.1 (260). The stato die in Pliny Ep. 10.96.7 (Mynors, 339) would also refer to Sunday. Cf. b. ʿAbod Zar. 6b (Eduard Lohse, "σάββατον," TDNT 7 [1971] 29 n. 227); Werner Foerster, "κυριακός," TDNT 3 (1967) 1095–96; Lohse, "σάββατον," 28–35. C. W. Dugmore has raised some problems about the received interpretation of this passage in the Didache ("Lord's Day and Easter," in Neotestamentica et Patristica: Eine Freundesgabe, Herrn Professor Dr. Oscar Cullmann zu seinem 60. Geburtstag überreicht [NovTSup 6; Leiden: Brill, 1962] 275–77). He suggests the day of Easter for κυριακή: "If we take κυριακή in its later meaning of 'Sunday,' we get 'on the Sunday of the Lord.' Since every Sunday is the Lord's Day, the Sunday of the Lord can only mean the Sunday on which he rose from the dead, i.e. Easter Sunday, but the phrase is infelicitous" (p. 276). Dugmore also (p. 277) understands the paraphrase in Const. 7.30.1 (see n. 6 above) as referring to the day of Easter. All this is highly questionable.

9   The Didachist is not aware of a Sabbath celebration in the community. For the Sabbath observance of later, heretical, and especially gnostic-influenced Jewish Christianity, cf. Lohse, "σάββατον," 32–34. This Didache passage is interpreted differently by Rordorf and Tuilier (Doctrine, 65; cf. earlier

Rordorf, "Didachè," 23): The specific reference to Sunday could be an indirect polemic against σαββατίζειν. Rordorf and Tuilier even consider this very probable (with references to Gal 4:8–11; Col 2:16–17; Ignatius Magn. 9.1–2), and they wish to explain the pleonasm κατὰ κυριακὴν τοῦ κυρίου from that standpoint. The formulation would be intended to exclude the Sabbath as the day for celebration.

10 Breaking of bread, as in the Jewish ritual, at the beginning of the meal (see above, commentary on 9.3): Mark 8:6 par.; 8:19; Matt 14:19; Luke 24:30; Acts 20:11; 27:35 (cf. κατακλᾶν in Mark 6:41 par.); at Jesus' final meal: Mark 15:22 par.; 1 Cor 11:24; as post-Easter, probably eucharistic meal: 1 Cor 10:16; Acts 2:46; 20:7; cf. Ps.-Clem. Hom. 14.1.4 (GCS² 1.204): τὸν ἄρτον ἐπ᾽ εὐχαριστίᾳ κλάσας καὶ ἐπιθεὶς ἅλας ("having broken the bread for thanksgiving and having put salt on it"). For the whole, cf. κλάσις τοῦ ἄρτου ("breaking of the bread"), Luke 24:35; Acts 2:42. The literature is legion; for an overview, see, e.g., Johannes Behm, "θύω," TDNT 3 (1967) 726–43; Jeremias, Eucharistic Words, passim; Emmanuel von Severus, "Brotbrechen," RAC 2 (1954) 620–26; Gerhard Delling, "Abendmahl II. Urchristliches Mahl-Verständnis," TRE 1 (1977) 56–57; Joachim Wanke, "κλάω," EDNT 2 (1991) 295–96; Klauck, Herrenmahl, 259–64, and passim. Literature in Wanke, "κλάω," 295; and ThWNT 10/2.1138–43.

195

bread as meal for satisfaction of hunger, and εὐχαριστή-σατε to the sacramental Eucharist proper?[11] Or are the two expressions a hendiadys, together describing the meal celebration culminating in the Eucharist? The latter is probably more likely. In any case, with εὐχαριστήσατε the author is thinking of the benedictions given in chaps. 9–10, and perhaps also of the free εὐχαριστεῖν of the prophets (10.7). The redactor would already have included here in 14.1 (as in 10.7) the eucharistic prayers in the narrower sense.

As I have said, however, the whole previous clause, which speaks of the Sunday celebration, serves simply to establish a precondition for the central statement of the text, which is now stated. *Before* the breaking of bread and thanksgiving, the members of the congregation are to acknowledge their sins, to "confess," in order that the sacrifice to be carried out during the meal will be ritually pure (v. 1b). That is the point at which the Didachist is aiming in v. 1. The Two Ways tractate had already called

for a public confession of sins (see above at 4.14; ἐν ἐκκλησίᾳ may be an addition by the Didachist). This subject is now resumed.[12] Προεξομολογεῖσθαι[13] appears only here in our literature,[14] and describes a confession of sins *before* the beginning of the Eucharist.[15] Παραπτώματα ("faults") is used as in 4.3, 14. The confession of sins purifies those participating in the Eucharist and constitutes the precondition for the purity of the sacrifice presented at the meal: ὅπως καθαρὰ ἡ θυσία ὑμῶν[16] ᾖ. Here καθαρά means "ritually pure." *Const.* 7.30.2 interprets this with a paraphrase, ὅπως ἄμεμπτος ᾖ ἡ θυσία ὑμῶν καὶ εὐανάφορος θεῷ ("and so let your sacrifice be blameless and acceptable to God").[17] What is meant by θυσία, the sacrifice to be presented at the meal?[18] It seems tempting to understand θυσία to refer to the sacred action of the eucharistic celebration,[19] or more precisely to associate it with the eucharistic elements (as, e.g., Justin does in *Dial.* 41.3 [Goodspeed, 138]).[20] In that case *Did.* 14.1–3[21] would

---

11   Cf. Audet (*Didachè*, 460–61), who refers κλάσατε ἄρτον to the breaking of bread and εὐχαριστήσατε to the Eucharist proper. Cf. his interpretation of chaps. 9–10 above, p. 142.

12   The Didachist formulates in a manner reminiscent of *Did.* 4.14; cf. there (ἐν ἐκκλησίᾳ) ἐξομολογήσῃ τὰ παραπτώματά σου with 14.1: προεξομολογησάμενοι τὰ παραπτώματα ὑμῶν.

13   H reads προσεξομολογησάμενοι, as do Rordorf and Tuilier, *Doctrine*, 68, 192 (earlier Rordorf, "Rémission des péchés," 286 n. 4; and idem, "Didachè," 25 n. 37). Nonetheless, the emendation in Harnack, *Lehre*, 54, going back to von Gebhardt, which most of the editions have accepted, should be maintained as correct. Cf. προειπόντες, *Did.* 7.1, and προνηστευσάτω, 7.4. The *Apostolic Constitutions* has καὶ ἐξομολογούμενοι (although in a different sense).

14   Lampe, *s.v.*, refers otherwise only to Joannes Jejunator (?), *Sermo de poenitentia*, PG 88.1929B. He does not have προσεξομολογεῖσθαι.

15   Poschmann, *Paenitentia secunda*, 89. I consider it improbable that the two *Didache* quotations (4.14 and 14.1) refer to 1 Cor 11:28, as Poschmann supposes (ibid.). A further question is whether the author is thinking of individual confessions in the presence of the congregation (or before the bishop or another fellow Christian), or simply of a common confession by the whole congregation. (Poschmann supposes the latter, p. 90; Rordorf, "Rémission des péchés," 286, agrees; as does Moll, *Opfer*, 110.) On this subject, see above p. 113 n. 16.

In addition Poschmann considers it important that in the *Didache* nothing is said about an absolution (*Paenitentia secunda*, 92).

16   H has a mistake, ἡμῶν, which was emended by Bryennios, Διδαχή, 49. Cf. also *Constitutions*.

17   For the pure sacrifice of the eschatological community cf. 1 Pet 2:5; Heb 13:10; Jas 1:27, etc.

18   "During the first three centuries the Eucharist was understood in a threefold way as sacrifice. The sacrifice presented to God is, first of all, the prayers, second, the bread and wine, . . . third, the sacred action at the altar itself as analogue to the sacrifice of the death of Christ" (Lietzmann, *Mass*, 68).

19   E.g., Harnack, "Prolegomena," 139; Knopf, *Lehre*, 36: "θυσία: the Eucharist as sacrifice"; Lietzmann, *Mass*, 193; Drews, "Apostellehre," 279: θυσία refers to the Lord's Supper, not merely the prayers, as sacrifice. The proof of this is said to be the Malachi quotation that follows; see Koester, *Synoptische Überlieferung*, 214–15.

20   Περὶ δὲ τῶν ἐν παντὶ τόπῳ ὑφ᾽ ἡμῶν τῶν ἐθνῶν προσφερομένων αὐτῷ θυσιῶν, τοῦτ᾽ ἔστι τοῦ ἄρτου τῆς εὐχαριστίας καὶ τοῦ ποτηρίου ὁμοίως τῆς εὐχαριστίας, προλέγει [sc. the prophet Malachi, 1:10–11] τότε ("concerning the sacrifices offered to him by us, the nations, in every place, that is, the bread of the Eucharist and, likewise, the cup of the Eucharist"). Justin, however, is also acquainted with the other idea according to which the eucharistic prayers are a sacrifice to God: *Dial.* 117.1 (Goodspeed, 234).

represent the oldest explicit instance of the understanding of the Lord's Supper as a sacrifice.[22] This interpretation, however, is uncertain. The context permits still another possibility: that $\vartheta v\sigma\iota\alpha$ refers in a special sense to $\epsilon\dot{v}\chi\alpha\rho\iota\sigma\tau\dot{\eta}\sigma\alpha\tau\epsilon$. The sacrifice that is spoken of so often here would then be the eucharistic prayer offered by the congregation.[23] It is stained if guilty persons speak it, but it is pure if their guilt is removed. But is this alternative a justifiable interpretation of the *Didache* text? No matter how unsatisfying it may appear to a later, more reflective consciousness, one cannot exclude the possibility that these alternatives are utterly foreign to the state of mind reflected in the text (and other, similar texts); that is, the tradition that comes to light here associates the sacred meal with the idea of sacrifice in the most general way, without making detailed specifications about what precisely is to be understood by "sacrifice" in this instance.[24] That seems to be the most appropriate understanding of the *Didache* text. In any

case, it is true that participation in the $\vartheta v\sigma\iota\alpha$ demands moral purity as ritual purity—and the prior purification by *exhomologesis* is intended in that sense.

■ **2** The demand for purity is made concrete by means of an additional rule. The sacrifice is pure if it comes from those who are reconciled—by which we should apparently understand the ranks of the holy community of the end time, in which there is no longer any trace of enmity (v. 2).[25] With $\pi\tilde{\alpha}\varsigma\ \delta\dot{\epsilon}\ \ddot{\epsilon}\chi\omega\nu\ \kappa\tau\lambda$. the Didachist again resumes the style of the rules in 11.4–6. Ἀμφιβολία really means "hemmed in on both sides, attacked," and then "ambiguity, doubt, confusion";[26] but these meanings of the word yield no sense in this passage. Here it must mean something like "quarrel."[27] Τὴν ἀμφιβολίαν ἔχειν μετά τινος then means: "to be in a state of enmity with someone."[28] Whether ἑταῖρος here means "the neighbor" in the broader sense or more narrowly the members of the same religious group,[29] fellow Christians in

---

21 The term $\vartheta v\sigma\iota\alpha$ is used three times (the third in the quotation from Malachi).

22 *1 Clem.* 44.4 may be considered older, but the meaning of the phrase δῶρα τῆς ἐπισκοπῆς there is uncertain. Otherwise one must obviously distinguish between the explicit examples and the idea itself; the latter can be older than the former. Thus, e.g., it seems to me that 1 Cor 10:16–22 implicitly presupposes the idea of the Eucharist as sacrifice.

23 Thus, e.g., Harris (*Teaching*, 106), with reference to the quotation in Ps.-Cyprian *De aleat.* 4 (CSEL 3.3.96): *ne inquinetur et inpediatur oratio vestra* ("lest your prayer be troubled and impeded"); Johannes Behm, "$\vartheta\dot{v}\omega$," *TDNT* 3 (1967) 189–90 (cautiously). Wengst thinks that $\vartheta v\sigma\iota\alpha$ probably means first of all the prayers spoken by the congregation and second, in a broader sense, "the congregation itself as those who celebrate" (*Didache*, 55).

24 It seems to me that the statements of Audet (*Didachè*, 462–63) tend in the same direction, as do especially those of Vööbus, *Liturgical Traditions*, 107: "According to all the canons of typology, this [the reference of the word $\vartheta v\sigma\iota\alpha$ to the Eucharist] is the answer which must be given. However, for the sake of circumspection, the question should be raised whether the same notion also covered prayer, thanksgiving, hymns, in one word, all the acts of worship. There are reasons for thinking that the line between these acts and the εὐχαριστία as 'sacrifice' par excellence was not yet sharply drawn." Vööbus adds (pp. 107–8) that $\vartheta v\sigma\iota\alpha$ here does not yet have the usual meaning of propitiation for sins.

Cf. also Frank, "Maleachi 1,10ff.," 72: "It is impossible on the basis of the text to attempt to define the precise referent of 'sacrifice,' whether the congregation's prayer of thanksgiving or the breaking of bread. All that is permitted us is the conclusion that the whole action of the congregation on Sunday is understood as a sacrifice before God." According to Moll (*Opfer*, 110) $\vartheta v\sigma\iota\alpha$ refers to "the whole action"; 115: "the sacrificial *gifts* in particular," or rather "the . . . eucharistic prayer of thanksgiving spoken over the bread, which remains symbolically attached to the sacrificial gifts."

25 Rordorf, "Rémission des péchés," 289: "The penitential stance thus has not only a vertical dimension, the sincere confession of sins before God, the holy one, but also a horizontal dimension, namely, reconciliation among brothers and sisters." For the quotation of the present passage in Ps.-Cyprian *De aleat.* 4, see above, Introduction §2b.

26 Cf. LSJ, *s.v.*: "state of being attacked on both sides"; "ambiguity," "doubt," "uncertainty of mind."

27 BAGD, *s.v.* Lampe refers (*s.v.*) to Leontius of Naples *Vita Johann. Eleemos.*, ed. Gelzer, pp. 12-13: ὥστε μηδένα ἔχειν πρὸς τὸν πλησίον αὐτοὺς μάχην ἢ ἀμφιβολίαν ("so that no one my hold toward his neighbor a dispute or quarrel").

28 "Τὴν before ἀμφιβολίαν is unusual. Von Gebhardt suggested τινά" (Knopf, *Lehre*, 36). Audet, *Didachè*, 463: a Semitism (with reference to Moulton, *Grammar*, 2.430).

29 Cf. Dittenberger, ed., *Orientis Graeci Inscriptiones Selectae*, 2.573.1.

this case,[30] is not clear. The only thing that is obvious is the rule that Christians may not participate in worship (probably more precisely the eucharistic meal) until they have reconciled with their foes. The verb for "to be reconciled," διαλλάσσεσθαι as in Matt 5:24, like the didachistic rule as a whole, recalls the dominical saying in Matt 5:23–24. First go and be reconciled to your brother or sister, and then come and offer your gift (in Matthew 5, of course, this would be the sacrifice in the temple at Jerusalem; in *Didache* 14 it is the sacrifice brought by the church).[31] Anyone taking part in the sacrifice without being reconciled would desecrate the community's sacrifice. Κοινοῦσθαι ("to be profaned") is a common expression in cultic language.[32] It is the opposite of καθαρά (v. 1). While in v. 1 the point was to call people to confess before offering the sacrifice, in v. 2 it is to call them to reconciliation.

■ **3** Strikingly enough, however, the Didachist supports his demand not by appealing to the Lord's words in Matt 5:23–24, but by means of an Old Testament quotation, namely, Mal 1:11, 14, which calls for a θυσία καθαρά ("pure sacrifice"). The introductory formula (αὕτη γάρ ἐστιν ἡ ῥηθεῖσα ὑπὸ κυρίου) makes it obvious that what follows is a quotation.[33] *Kyrios* here probably does not refer to Jesus.[34] The text of the Septuagint (?) is quoted freely.[35] In the second part (Mal 1:14) the quotation is more exact than in the first (1:11).[36] The text of Mal 1:10–14 has otherwise played a significant role in the early church's scriptural citations.[37] For the most part it serves as a standard argument for the purpose of distin-

---

30 Koester (*Synoptische Überlieferung*, 215 n. 1) rightly criticizes what Knopf says (*Lehre*, 36) about the "narrowing" of the rule "limiting it to the community" that thus takes place.

31 The Didachist does not designate his advice as a word of the Lord, but it is possible that he is thinking of the logion: thus with assurance Harnack, *Lehre*, 55; Drews, "Apostellehre," 279. According to Massaux (*Influence*, 3.156–57), we should consider literary dependence on Matthew. According to Koester (*Synoptische Überlieferung*, 214) the author draws "on the treasure of freely circulating community rules." Koester constructs thus: Mark 11:25 rests on the same tradition but has already Christianized the logion. The Didachist "Christianized" the logion "in an entirely different way than in Mark 11:25" (ibid.).

32 Friedrich Hauck, "κοινωνικός κτλ.," *TDNT* 3 (1967) 809; Franz Georg Untergassmair, "κοινός," *EDNT* 2 (1991) 302–3.

33 Cf. ἀλλὰ καὶ περὶ τούτου δὲ εἴρηται in *Did*. 1.6 and καὶ γὰρ περὶ τούτου εἴρηκεν ὁ κύριος in *Did*. 9.5 (both redactional). These introductory formulae are characteristic for the Didachist.

34 Differently Funk, *Patres apostolici*, 33: *Kyrios* = Jesus: "*Jesu Christo dictum Veteris Testamenti attribuitur*." Likewise Wengst, *Didache*, 31.

35 Mal 1:11b LXX   *Did*. 14.3b
    . . . καὶ ἐν παντὶ τόπῳ   ἐν παντὶ τόπῳ
    –   καὶ χρόνῳ
    θυμίαμα προσάγεται   προσφέρειν
    τῷ ὀνόματί μου   μοι
    καὶ θυσία καθαρά . . .   θυσίαν καθαράν·

    Mal 1:14b LXX   *Did*. 14.3c
    διότι βασιλεὺς   ὅτι βασιλεὺς
    μέγας ἐγώ εἰμι,   μέγας εἰμί,

    λέγει κύριος   λέγει κύριος,
    παντοκράτωρ,   –
    καὶ τὸ ὄνομά μου   καὶ τὸ ὄνομά μου
    ἐπιφανὲς   θαυμαστὸν
    ἐν τοῖς ἔθνεσιν.   ἐν τοῖς ἔθνεσιν.

The combination of Mal 1:11b and 14b is unusual. It is probably explained by the fact that the Didachist does not intend to polemicize (against Judaism); hence vv. 12–13 are omitted from the quotation, as Frank ("Maleachi 1,10ff.," 71) correctly pointed out. Cf. Audet, *Didachè*, 464; Moll (*Opfer*, 112) speaks of a "selection process" that he traces to the Didachist. There is a similar combination of vv. 11 and 14 in Clement of Alexandria *Strom*. 5.14.136.2–3, but one need not suggest influence from the *Didache* (against the note in GCS³ 2.418). Muilenburg (*Literary Relations*, 91–92, 95) suggested that *Did*. 14.3 is a quotation from the *Hebrew* text. Indeed the θαυμαστόν in the *Didache* text (Mal 1:14b), against ἐπιφανές (LXX, as well as Clement of Alexandria in the passage cited), is striking. According to Muilenburg it better reflects the Hebrew נורא than does the LXX word (which is a misunderstanding of the Hebrew text). But θαυμαστόν would not be a good translation either: cf., in contrast, ἐπίφοβον in Aquila, Symmachus, and Theodotion (Muilenburg, *Literary Relations*, 92). Against positing a translation from the Hebrew is Vokes, *Riddle*, 91; he suggested that θαυμαστόν is a reminiscence of Ps 8:2 (there is a typographical error in his text at this point) or Deut 28:58. A different problem arises from the added καὶ χρόνῳ in *Did*. 14.3b. It recalls the version of Targum Jonathan: "and on every occasion when you do My will" (in R. P. Gordon, "Targumic Parallels to Acts XIII 18 and Didache XIV 3," *NovT* 16 [1974] 287). Gordon says of the text of the *Didache*, "Here the

guishing the new Christian ritual observance from that of the old covenant. That contrast, however, is not emphasized here in *Did.* 14.3 (at least not overtly). In the context of the *Didache*, the quotation from Malachi is simply intended to verify the demand for a pure sacrifice.[38] The quotation is linked to the remarks in 14.1–2 by means of the key phrase ϑυσία καϑαρά. The author was probably already thinking of the ϑυσία καϑαρά in the Malachi text when formulating *Did.* 14.1.

In retrospect we find a more or less cogent train of thought here. While in chaps. 11–13 the Didachist had, in a sense, looked outward (toward the arriving guests of the community), in chaps. 14–15 he looks inward (at the relationships within the community itself). In doing so he touches on two groups of questions: on the one hand the moral status of the community, and on the other hand problems that arise with regard to the leadership of the community (the subject of chap. 15). In the first instance he decrees that the community may only offer its eucharistic sacrifice in a pure state when (1) the members have been purified of sin by a previous confession, and (2) all quarrels have been cleansed away by a prior reconciliation. Only in this way can the sacrificing community be clean; only in this way can it offer the pure, eschatological sacrifice prophesied by Malachi.[39]

At this point the train of thought is interrupted. The real continuation of the topic here introduced is to be found in *Did.* 15.3. Inserted between these two parts is a section on problems of community leadership, probably inspired by the association of "presiding at the Eucharist with the Eucharist itself."[40]

---

readings of MT (and LXX) and Targum Jonathan are combined in ἐν παντὶ τόπῳ καὶ χρόνῳ" (p. 288). Of the two possibilities suggested by Audet, *Didachè*, 463–64 (a reminiscence of an old, lost form of the text, or an accommodation of the text to the church's sacrifice), Gordon, while writing "although there is indeed an ancient text," nevertheless considers the latter more likely, namely, "that both the Targum and *Didache* have adapted Mal i 11 to suit their own particular doctrinal needs" (p. 288).

36 For ϑαυμαστόν, which is still remarkable, see n. 35 above. One may ask whether it is possible to conclude from the free quotation of the OT that the Didachist may also have quoted the Gospel text before him (if he had one) with the same freedom.

37 Justin *Dial.* 28.5 (Goodspeed, 122); 41.2 (138); 116.3 (234); 117.1 (234) and 4 (235); Irenaeus *Adv. haer.* 4.17.5–6 (SC 100.592–95); Tertullian *Adv. Marc.* 3.22.6 (CChrSL 1.539); 4.1.8 (1.546); *Adv. Iud.* 5.4, 7 (2.1351, 1352); Clement of Alexandria *Strom.* 5.14, 136.2–3 (GCS³ 2.418), etc. Cf. Frank, "Maleachi 1,10ff.," 70–72. The *Didache* quotation appears to be "the earliest Christian application of the saying in Malachi" (p. 71).

38 "The prophetic promise has now been fulfilled" (Frank, "Maleachi 1,10ff.," 72).

39 The method of scriptural interpretation this time is not especially typological; rather it follows the general principle of prophecy and eschatological fulfillment.

40 Funk (*Patres apostolici*, 33) emphasized χειροτονή-σατε <u>οὖν</u> ἑαυτοῖς ἐπισκόπους καὶ διακόνους (*Did.* 15.1), from which follows that the *episkopoi* and *diakonoi* administer the eucharistic liturgy. Similarly Drews, "Apostellehre," 280; Knopf, *Lehre*, 37; Audet, *Didachè*, 464–65. This is probably correct. J. Mühlsteiger ("Verfassungsrecht der Frühkirche," *ZKTh* 99 [1977] 272) remarks: "The Sunday synaxis . . . appears to have been perceptibly disrupted by the irregular availability of prophets and teachers; this called for a remedy. The directive in *Did.* 15.1 about the selection of bishops and deacons thus appears as a practical consequence of the necessity of a regular eucharistic celebration on Sunday."

15

1   Select, then, for yourselves bishops and dea-
     cons worthy of the Lord, mild-tempered men
     who are not greedy, who are honest and
     proven, for they too perform the services of
     prophets and teachers for you.
2   So do not disregard them, for they are the per-
     sons who are honored <by God> among you,
     together with the prophets and the teachers.

Analysis

This text is another that in my opinion need not be
attributed to a second redaction;[1] it comes from the pen
of the Didachist. The section is evoked by the contrasting situations of itinerant or resident charismatics on the
one hand and the "local clergy" on the other. The local
communities have begun (probably long since) to choose
officials from their own ranks, so that the itinerant
charismatics, or those who are now settling down, col-
lide with the group of officeholders representing the
local community. The *Didache* is concerned to achieve a
resolution between these two groups.[2]

Comment

■ **1a–b** First of all the Didachist calls on the community
to choose their own officers or representatives from
among themselves (v. 1a). That call can scarcely be
understood to mean that he is thereby introducing a new
custom; rather he is expressing an opinion (also intended to establish a rule) regarding already existing usages.
We must in all probability understand the text to mean
that the choice of officers is the business of the whole
community.[3] The injunction to choose officers is, at any
rate, addressed to the entire (individual) congregation.

The procedure for making the choice is not prescribed.
Χειροτονεῖν here means "choose" or "elect," not
"appoint."[4] Those who are chosen bear the titles
ἐπίσκοποι καὶ διάκονοι; this is most probably to be
understood to mean that a number of ἐπίσκοποι and/or
διάκονοι are to work in each community.[5] Therefore, in
the region from which the tradition of the *Didache*
comes, (1) there is not yet a monepiscopate. (2) The
community officers do not include the group called
πρεσβύτεροι.[6] The phrase in the *Didache* that mentions
bishops and deacons recalls Phil 1:1 (σὺν ἐπισκόποις
καὶ διακόνοις),[7] and given that this parallel is not accidental we would have to recognize the retarded nature
of the development of canon law in the *Didache*'s milieu
(Philippians would have to be about a half century earlier than the redactional level of the *Didache*). The
absence of presbyters apparently indicates that the development of the "local clergy" perceptible in the *Didache*'s
milieu was not specifically Jewish-Christian in its influences.[8] Further, (3) the ἐπίσκοποι καὶ διάκονοι are not
itinerant charismatics but ecclesiastical officials "on the
local scene." (4) One becomes a bishop or deacon not by
being called to follow the *Kyrios* in the same pointed

---

1   Rordorf and Tuilier, *Doctrine*, 49, 63, 93. There are
     also some propositions regarding the posterior
     character of chap. 15 in Kraft, *Didache*, 64, 174
     ("This is one of the most recently composed
     sections of the *Didache*"); and Giet, *L'Énigme*,
     240–44.
2   Niederwimmer, "Itinerant Radicalism," 333–38.
     One should note that the observations regarding
     the canonical-legal developments in the region of
     the *Didache*'s tradition do not permit any generaliz-
     ing conclusions. Cf. also the restrictions in
     Schöllgen, "Church Order," 69–70. Schöllgen
     emphasizes as well (pp. 62, 69) that the Didachist
     does not introduce any new offices. But were there
     really no conflicts at all between the two groups (p.
     70)?
3   Giselbert Deussen emphasizes the differences
     between this and *1 Clement* ("Weisen der Bischofs-

     wahl im 1. Clemensbrief und in der Didache," *ThGl*
     62 [1972] 132).
4   Χειροτονεῖν, "elect" or "choose": 2 Cor 8:19;
     Ignatius *Phld.* 10.1; *Smyrn.* 11.2; *Pol.* 7.2; "appoint":
     Acts 14:23; Titus 1:9 *v.l.* (cf. also the *subscriptiones* to
     2 Timothy and Titus); BAGD, *s.v.*; Eduard Lohse,
     "χείρ κτλ.," *TDNT* 9 (1974) 433–34; Horst Balz,
     "χειροτονέω," *EDNT* 3 (1993) 464–65.
5   Kleist (*Didache*, 164 n. 91) suggests another possi-
     bility: "the plural 'bishops' was perhaps meant to
     mean 'a bishop and his presbyters'" (?).
6   In the *Apostolic Constitutions* the presbyters are
     promptly added (7.31.1).
7   *1 Clem.* 42.4–5 and 1 Tim 3:1–10 must be excluded
     as parallels.
8   Cf. Rordorf and Tuilier, *Doctrine*, 77.
9   The *Apostolic Constitutions* has expanded these.
10   For the literary genre of the text, cf. 1 Tim 3:1–10;

sense that still marks *Did.* 11.4–12, but by being elected by a local congregation. Finally, (5) the function of bishops and deacons is therefore not ordered to the whole church, but to the needs and tasks in the individual congregation by whom they were elected.

Here follow some very concise[9] directions regarding the qualifications required of candidates for the office of ἐπίσκοπος or διάκονος (v. 1b).[10] The most general qualification is that they be "worthy of the Lord," ἄξιοι τοῦ κυρίου (sc. Ἰησοῦ).[11] Other, special attributes follow: ἄνδρες πραεῖς ("mild-tempered men"),[12] ἀφιλάργυροι ("not greedy," they have to handle the community's funds);[13] ἀληθεῖς ("honest"), δεδοκιμασμένοι ("proved," i.e., not neophytes—only tried and tested Christians may be chosen as officers of the community).[14]

■ **1c–2** Finally, vv. 1c and 2 regulate the relationships between the prophets and teachers on the one hand and the local officials on the other (a relationship that appar-

ently was not always without friction). The Didachist's language is carefully chosen here. Λειτουργεῖν λειτουργίαν is paronomasia;[15] the meaning of the expression in context, unfortunately, is not completely clear.[16] In any case, it refers to the sacred office that prophets and teachers as well as the "local clergy" perform for the community.[17] The point of the statement in v. 1c is clear: both groups should be able to function alongside and in cooperation with each other. It is generally conceded that the prophets and teachers exercise a sacred office in the community; the congregation must recognize that

---

5:17–25; Titus 1:5–9; 1 Pet 5:1–5; Polycarp *Phil.* 5.2; 6.1. Similar admonitions, much expanded, are found in the *Didascalia apostolorum*; cf. *Didasc.* (Syriac) 3 (CSCO 401.27–30/402.27–30); 4 (401.52–58/402.43–49); 7–8 (401.75–102/402.67–98); 11–12 (407.127–48/408.119–34); 16 (407.172–76/408.155–60). Harnack pointed out that in the *Didache* the required qualifications are the same for ἐπίσκοποι and διάκονοι without distinction (*Lehre*, 57); cf. also Audet, *Didachè*, 465.

11   Cf. Ignatius *Eph.* 2.1, ὁ θεοῦ ἄξιος καὶ ὑμῶν; *Rom.* 10.2, ἄξιοι θεοῦ καὶ ὑμῶν ("worthy of God and of you"); *Eph.* 4.1, τὸ γὰρ ἀξιονόμαστον ὑμῶν πρεσβυτέριον, τοῦ θεοῦ ἄξιον ("for your justly famous presbytery, worthy of God"); compare, in a broader sense, *Eph.* 15.1; *Magn.* 12.

12   For this, cf., e.g., 1 Tim 3:3 (the bishop); the admonition in 1 Pet 5:3 (the presbyters); Polycarp *Phil.* 5.2, εὔσπλαγχνοι (the deacons); 6.1 εὔσπλαγχνοι, εἰς πάντας ἐλεήμονες ("compassionate and merciful to all," of the presbyters).

13   1 Tim 3:3 (the bishop); Polycarp *Phil.* 5.2 (the deacon); cf. similar statements in Titus 1:7 (the bishop); 1 Pet 5:2 (the presbyters).

14   For ἀληθεῖς, δεδοκιμασμένοι, cf. δεδοκιμασμένος, ἀληθινός in *Did.* 11.11 (the prophets); ἀληθινός in 13.1 (the prophets); ἀληθινός in 13.2 (the teachers). If 11.11 comes from the Didachist, these may be characteristic expressions from his pen.

15   On this see, BDF, §488, 1a; BDR, §488, 1a.

16   For this word group see Hermann Strathmann and Rudolf Meyer, "λειτουργέω," *TDNT* 4 (1967)

215–31; *ThWNT* 10/2.1162–63 (literature); Ceslas Spicq, *Notes de Lexicographie Néo-Testamentaire* (2 vols. and Sup; OBO 22.1–3; Fribourg: Éditions Universitaires; Göttingen: Vandenhoeck & Ruprecht; Paris: Gabalda, 1978–82) 1.475–81 (ET: *Theological Lexicon of the New Testament* [trans. and ed. James D. Ernest; 3 vols.; Peabody, Mass.: Hendrickson, 1994] 2.378–84); Horst Balz, "λειτουργία," *EDNT* 2 (1991) 347–49; Emil Joseph Lengeling, "Liturgie," *Handbuch theologischer Grundbegriffe* 2 (1973) 75–97. In this passage the concept is already intended as a designation for Christian worship, and it refers especially to the activity of the prophets and teachers and that of the local officers. This language is clearly distinct from that in the NT (apart from Acts 13:2, where a later usage is visible). Compare from the early period *1 Clem.* 44.2–6. For the development of usage in this regard (for which the example in *Did.* 15.1 is very important), cf. Strathmann, "λειτουργέω," *TDNT* 4 (1967) 228–29; Lengeling, "Liturgie," 76; Balz, "λειτουργία," *EDNT* 2 (1991) 349.

17   Contrasted here are on the one hand the προφῆται καὶ διδάσκαλοι and on the other the ἐπίσκοποι καὶ διάκονοι. Nothing is said about the apostles in the first group because at the time of the Didachist there appear to have been no more apostles. Differently de Halleux, "Ministers," 313; he also concludes here, from the absence of the article before διδάσκαλοι in the phrase προφῆται καὶ διδάσκαλοι, that they are one and the same group (see above at *Did.* 13.2).

the local officials *also* (καὶ αὐτοί is emphatic) perform this kind of sacred service for the community.[18]

■ **2** The Didachist's remarks apparently serve to protect the elected local officials from disparagement: μὴ οὖν ὑπερίδητε αὐτούς ("do not disregard them," i.e., the bishops and deacons: v. 2a).[19] Ὑπεροράω means to overlook someone, that is, to disparage or have a low opinion of them.[20] Rather they have the same rank as the prophets and teachers; both groups together (αὐτοὶ . . . μετὰ τῶν προφητῶν καὶ διδασκάλων) make up the list of those who are τετιμημένοι ὑμῶν (v. 2b). To τετιμη-μένοι[21] we should probably add τοῦ θεοῦ,[22] and the whole expression would then mean: "those among you who are honored by God, those among you to whom God has assigned a special τιμή, a special rank." This

designation, please note, applies to *both* groups; it is obvious as regards the itinerant charismatics, but it is also true of the local officials, who are equally entitled to this honorable title. The last statements (vv. 1c and 2) probably indicate that the local officials, together with the prophets and teachers (or, to the extent that the last two groups are absent, they alone) lead the worship service that formerly was in the hands of the prophets and teachers alone.[23] It remains striking, in all this, that nothing is yet said about an obligation to support the "local clergy." For the time being that is reserved to the other group (cf. 13.1–3, 5–7).[24]

---

18 I believe it is wrong to assume (as in Harnack's view of the history) that the *episkopoi* and *diakonoi* originally had purely administrative functions and only later assumed the teaching office of the charismatics. See Niederwimmer, "Itinerant Radicalism," 337 n. 56.

19 Rordorf and Tuilier (*Doctrine*, 194 n. 1) refer to *Apoc. Pet.* (NHC 7.3), p. 79, lines 23–31 (James M. Robinson, ed., *The Nag Hammadi Library in English* [3d ed.; San Francisco: HarperCollins, 1990] 376). The bishops and deacons are rejected there (in a gnostic context), however, for entirely different reasons.

20 As in *Barn.* 3.3 (a free quotation of Isa 58:7). See BAGD, *s.v.*

21 Comparable, but somewhat distant, are Clement of Alexandria *Strom.* 6.13, 107.2 (GCS³ 2.485); *Hypotyposes* in Eusebius *Hist. eccl.* 2.1.3 (προτετιμημένοι); Hippolytus *De Antichr.* 2 (GCS 1.2.4).

22 Ὑμῶν is a partitive genitive; both these suggestions are already in Harnack, *Lehre*, 58.

23 *Did.* 15.1–2 excludes the Montanism hypothesis: Creed, "Didache," 384.

24 The relationships in chaps. 11–14 and 15 are described quite differently by Gottfried Schille ("Das Recht der Propheten und Apostel — gemeinderechtliche Beobachtungen zu Didache Kapitel 11–13," in Paul Wätzel and Gottfried Schille, eds.; *Theologische Versuche* [Berlin: Evangelische Verlags-Anstalt, 1966] 102–3, and passim). For a critique see Niederwimmer, "Itinerant Radicalism," 338 n. 60.

15

3   Correct one another not in anger but in peace,
as you have [received] it in the gospel; and let
no one speak to anyone who wrongs another—let him not hear [a word] from you—until
he has repented.

4   Perform your prayers and your almsgiving and
all that you undertake as you have [received]
it in the gospel of our Lord.

Analysis

After the digression in *Did.* 15.1–2 the Didachist returns
to the theme introduced in 14.1–3. Thus 15.3–4 would
more logically follow 14.3.[1] In my opinion 15.3–4 is
again redactional, which means that it comes from the
pen of the Didachist.[2] Characteristic of him is the
double reference to the "gospel." The presupposition
for the entire passage to follow is the image of the community as an eschatological brother- and sisterhood in
which mutual peace reigns, and in which each member
is responsible for the others. The community itself exer-
cises the right of discipline, and the most extreme
means at its disposal is excommunication. An appeal
to institutions outside the community is still unthinkable.[3]

Comment

■ **3** The section begins with the commandment of mutual fraternal/sororal correction: ἐλέγχετε ἀλλήλους.[4]
One brother or sister engages in dialogue with another,
confronts him or her with the fault committed, and calls
him or her to repentance (cf. Matt 18:15 par.).[5] But this
correction should not be done in wrath; rather it should
be (as we would now say) "nonaggressive" and should
not destroy the brotherly or sisterly harmony between
the one doing the correcting and the one who is corrected: μὴ ἐν ὀργῇ ἀλλ᾽ ἐν εἰρήνῃ ("not in anger but in
peace").[6] The admonition to meet one another not in an
aggressive manner but with a harmonious attitude is
something that can be read in the "gospel" (ὡς ἔχετε ἐν

1   Thus Knopf (*Lehre*, 38), who in particular would
prefer to attach it to *Did.* 14.2: "If the case in 14.2
occurs, and those concerned cannot be reconciled
with one another, the other members of the community should intervene and gently put them right."
Similarly at an earlier period Drews, "Apostellehre,"
280–81. For the explanation of the interpolation in
15.1–2 see above, p. 194 n. 4.

2   Not from a second redaction: see above.

3   For the quotation in Ps.-Cyprian *De aleat.* 4, see
above, Introduction, §2b.

4   Ἐλέγχειν occurs twice in the tractate: at *Did.* 2.7
and 4.3. The history of this theme's origin explains
why it recurs more than once within the book.

5   This is the duty of the one who presides over the
community in 1 Tim 5:20; 2 Tim 4:2; Titus 1:9, 13;
2:15. One should not see the contrast (here the *cor-
rectio* is the concern of all, while there it is the duty
of the officeholders) as an alternative. Poschmann
(*Paenitentia secunda*, 95–96) sees this correctly. On
the *Didache* passage he comments, "Correction and
punishment of the sinner appears, in principle, to
be the duty of all the faithful. But it is apparent
from the nature of the thing, and it is also not difficult to discern from the form of admonition itself,
that ultimately this 'judging' will be done by one in
authority among the brothers and sisters." "In addi-

tion, the association of the bishops and deacons
with the function of correction is also expressed . . .
by the transitional particle δέ. Concretely we are
thus to picture the situation here also in such a way
. . . that the case requiring discipline has been discussed in the assembled community, but in the first
instance the church leaders, as the authoritative
representatives of the community, were the agents
of judicial functions" (p. 96).

6   Εἰρήνη is here the equivalent of "peace, harmony."
See BAGD, *s.v.* Cf. *1 Clem.* 63.2: ἐκκόψητε τὴν
ἀθέμιτον τοῦ ζήλους ὑμῶν ὀργὴν κατὰ τὴν ἔντευ-
ξιν, ἣν ἐποιησάμεθα περὶ εἰρήνης καὶ ὁμονοίας
("Root out the wicked passion of your jealousy
according the entreaty for peace and concord which
we have made in this letter"). Rordorf ("Rémission
des péchés," 295 n. 3) refers among other passages
to 1QS 5.24–25: "each should reproach his fellow in
truth, in meekness and in compassionate love for
the man. No-one should speak to his brother in
anger or muttering" (trans. of Florentino García
Martínez, *The Dead Sea Scrolls Translated* [2d ed.;
Leiden: Brill; Grand Rapids: Eerdmans, 1996] 9). A
more distant comparison is with *T. Gad* 6.3: καὶ ἐὰν
ἁμάρτῃ εἴς σε, εἰπὲ αὐτῷ ἐν εἰρήνῃ ("and if someone sins against you, speak to him in peace").

τῷ εὐαγγελίῳ).[7] This appears to mean a written gospel book,[8] but it is not clear which one. The admonition here expressed, which the author finds in his gospel book, is reminiscent of Matt 5:22[9] or 18:15–17. But the question is whether he really had Matthew's Gospel at hand[10] and not some other gospel unknown to us.[11]

The next rule (*Did.* 15.3b) seems to apply to the cases of those who persist in sin despite brotherly or sisterly correction.[12] Cf. the casuistry in Matt 18:15–17. Sin is described as an ἀστοχεῖν κατὰ τοῦ ἑτέρου. Ἀστοχεῖν means "to miss the goal, to fall away."[13] In this passage it is used in a specific sense: ἀστοχεῖν κατά τινος must mean "to fall short, to sin *against* someone."[14] Πᾶς ἀστοχῶν κατὰ τοῦ ἑτέρου[15] thus refers to someone who errs by sinning against someone else. What must happen

in such a case? Μηδεὶς λαλείτω μηδὲ παρ᾽ ὑμῶν ἀκουέτω means "no one should speak with him or her, nor should he or she hear (anything) from you,"[16] which is practically the equivalent of excommunication,[17] although only until the moment of repentance (ἕως οὗ μετανοήσῃ).

■ **4** The verse sounds like an epilogue. The author has just expressed his opinion on the topic of church discipline and other questions touching Christian life now occur to him: εὐχαί, ἐλεημοσύναι καὶ πᾶσαι αἱ πράξεις ("prayers, almsgiving, and all that you undertake"). For the Lord's Prayer, which is to be prayed three times a day, see above at *Did.* 8.2–3. It is possible that nothing is said about fasting because the author remembers what had already been said in 8.1.[18]

---

7   Cf. *Did.* 8.2; 11.3.

8   Examples of this interpretation: the passage "seems to indicate the existence of a written gospel" (Kleist, *Didache*, 165 n. 97); Vielhauer, *Geschichte*, 253–54: in *Did.* 8.2 the "gospel" means the gospel *viva vox*, but, in contrast, *Did.* 15.3 seems "to point to a written document" (p. 254). *Did.* 15.4 could refer to the *viva vox*, but 15.3 speaks against that. At the same time, even here (namely, in *Did.* 15.3–4, in comparison with *2 Clem.* 8.5) the concept of "gospel" is "still understood in terms of content, not in a literary sense" (ibid.). Koester, *Synoptische Überlieferung*, 10–11: *Did.* 15.3 and 4 appear to refer already to a written gospel. For Koester's opinion on 8.2 and 11.3, see above, p. 51. For *Did.* 15.3–4, see also Koester, 240. Rordorf and Tuilier (*Doctrine*, 88) suggest for *Did.* 15.3–4 (and *only* for these verses) a reference to a written gospel, "and this note confirms once again that this chapter is probably a later addition." Cf. also 194 n. 4. For the whole question see above, Introduction, §7a. Is this a reference to an apocryphal gospel of the Q type? (Cf. Rordorf, "Rémission des péchés," 293.) Audet (*Didachè*, 182 and frequently elsewhere) suggested a gospel related to Matthew.

9   Matt 5:22 forbids wrath in general, however, and does not refer to fraternal or sororal correction.

10 Examples of this interpretation: Funk (*Patres apostolici*, 35) suggested an allusion to Matt 18:15–17; cf. Drews, "Apostellehre," 282; Massaux (*Influence*, 3.167) considered that passage and possibly Matt 5:22 as well; Koester, *Synoptische Überlieferung*, 210–11: only Matt 18:15 is possible, but a more stringent proof of knowledge of Matthew's Gospel cannot be produced; Rordorf and Tuilier, *Doctrine*, 194 n. 4: possibly comparable to Matt 18:15–20;

Wengst, *Didache*, 25–26: the passage presupposes the Gospel of Matthew.

11 In addition one gets the impression that the author simply refers to the gospel but does not quote it. According to Koester (*Synoptische Überlieferung*, 240) that is generally true of the *Didache* as a whole.

12 Drews, "Apostellehre," 282; Knopf, *Lehre*, 38.

13 In our literature it is otherwise applied to falling away from faith (and similar instances): 1 Tim 1:6; 6:21; 2 Tim 2:18; *2 Clem.* 17.7. Cf. BAGD, *s.v.*

14 BAGD, *s.v.*; Lampe, *s.v.*: "hence *err*, i.e., act unjustly."

15 Harris (*Teaching*, 9) emended to ἑταίρου (cf. *Did.* 14.2). This was also considered by Audet (*Didachè*, 483), but in the edition, at p. 240, he has ἑτέρου.

16 This phrase is a crux. Knopf (*Lehre*, 38) calls it a "tautology and a difficult construction." The shift in the subject causes difficulty; in μηδεὶς λαλείτω, the community is the subject, while in μηδὲ . . . ἀκουέτω, the subject seems to be the ἀστοχῶν(!). Something like καὶ μηδεὶς ἀκουέτω αὐτοῦ would be simpler. Or is this a corruption of the text, as Harnack (*Lehre*, 59) had already suggested? Pierre Nautin ("Notes critiques sur la Didachè," *VC* 13 [1959] 119–20) suggested an expansion: μηδεὶς . . . παρ᾽ ὑμῶν ἀκουέτω (περὶ αὐτοῦ). This may be correct.

17 This was denied by Harnack, *Lehre*, 60. Drews, "Apostellehre," 282: "[the sinner] is to be excluded both from the Lord's Supper and from contact with the community." Poschmann, *Paenitentia secunda*, 95: "It should be noted that all are obligated to refuse contact with the unrepentant sinner, even though he or she has only sinned against a single individual." For Poschmann's further suggestions regarding the subject of church discipline see above at n. 5.

Almsgiving is ultimately part of (Jewish-) Christian religious devotion; cf. above, at *Did.* 1.5–6. The phrase πᾶσαι αἱ πράξεις includes everything that could otherwise be listed specifically as part of Christian behavior. The Didachist does not intend to go into detail; he is content with a sweeping reference to "the gospel." The formula in v. 3 is repeated and expanded: ὡς ἔχετε ἐν τῷ εὐαγγελίῳ τοῦ κυρίου ἡμῶν.[19] It seems improbable that the Didachist was thinking specifically of Matthew 6 at this point.[20]

---

18 Massaux (*Influence*, 3.157 n. 32) differs: "The 'acts' (πράξεις) may very possibly represent the third element of good works, namely fasting."
19 See above at v. 3.
20 Massaux, *Influence*, 3.157; also Wengst, *Didache*, 26.

General Comment

With *Did.* 16.1 begins the concluding section of the book, which contains an eschatological text. More precisely one must distinguish between a parenetic section (16.1–2) and an apocalyptic section (16.3–8). The latter breaks off sharply at 16.8. The whole seems to be organized as follows:

1. Eschatological parenesis (16.1–2)
2. The apocalypse (16.3–8)[1]
    a. The appearance of false prophets and the collapse of the Christian community (16.3–4a)
    b. The appearance of the Antichrist (16.4b–d)
    c. The great apostasy and the preservation of the faithful (16.5)
    d. The revelation of the three signs of the truth (16.6–7)
    e. The arrival of the *Kyrios* (16.8) . . .

The conclusion of the apocalypse is unfortunately lost in H and can no longer be reconstructed in detail from *Constitutions* or the Georgian version; it is probable, however, that the apocalypse in the *Didache* ended originally with a short reference to the final judgment of the world.[2]

The eschatological conclusion of the *Didache* has been repeatedly associated with the Two Ways tractate. Chap. 16 (or parts of chap. 16, or the source of the chapter) is then regarded as the original conclusion of the Two Ways tractate. The Didachist then would have copied the tractate in chaps. 1–6 of the *Didache* and returned to his source in chap. 16, which constituted the conclusion of the tractate.[3] The principal argument in favor of this hypothesis making chap. 16 (or its prior forms) part of the tractate may be the observation that the tractate, in the form available to *Barnabas* (and similarly the *Canons of the Apostles* as well), very probably had an eschatological conclusion, which is demonstrable in the form found in *Doctr.* 6.4–5. (The text of the epilogue, however, is different.) Something similar has been proposed regarding the source of the *Didache*. Chap. 16 is said therefore to come from the eschatological final section of the Two Ways tractate, or more precisely from the version of the tractate that was available to the Didachist as a source. The principal argument against this is the observation that while *Did.* 1.1–6.1 has parallels (some of them very close) in the *Doctrina apostolorum* (setting aside the *sectio evangelica*), the same is no longer true for *Didache* 16.

---

1   The defining elements are as follows: ἐν γὰρ ταῖς ἐσχάταις ἡμέραις (v. 3a) opens this section; αὐξανούσης γὰρ τῆς ἀνομίας (v. 4a) is part of the previous section. The remaining organization is indicated by the numerative (καὶ) τότε in vv. 4b, 5, 6 (including the scriptural proof in v. 7), 8. Cf. Philip Vielhauer and Georg Strecker, "Apocalyptic in Early Christianity," in *NTApoc*, 2.589–91. Consider also the similar beginnings:
v. 4b: καὶ τότε φανήσεται
v. 5a: τότε ἥξει
v. 6a: καὶ τότε φανήσεται
v. 8: τότε ὄψεται.

2   Section (e) thus probably dealt, originally, with "the coming of the *Kyrios* to judge the world." Aono (*Entwicklung*, 169–74) has insisted that *Didache* 16 is lacking the idea of judgment. He finds it absent as early as 16.2b as well as in what follows. Aono can only maintain this judgment, however, by having the apocalypse in the *Didache* (despite *Constitutions* and the Georgian) end with 16.8. He considers it "more probable that the author deliberately ended chapter 16 just as the other manuscripts [*sic*] read" (p. 171). To this it should be said that, as certainly as anything can be, 16.8 (if only for paleographical reasons: see below) is *not* the end of the original *Didache*. Rather, in the original, judgment would

indeed have been mentioned in what followed, as the paraphrases in the *Apostolic Constitutions* and the Georgian still show.

3   This hypothesis seems to have appeared first in the work of P. Savi (cf. Ehrhard, *Altchristliche Litteratur*, 51 and n. 1, 55). Ehrhard himself also accepted this idea (p. 51). It later found a number of adherents, e.g., Hemmer, *Doctrine*, xciv (probably); cf. earlier at xxix; Creed, "Didache" 379; Drews, "Untersuchungen," 68–73 (for the source redacted by the Didachist); Knopf, *Lehre*, 2: "In the original of this proselyte catechism, which was available to the author of the *Didache*, the greater part of chap. 16, the apocalyptic final scene (16.3–7) was very probably present. Possibly 16.2 was also part of the Jewish document because there is again a clear parallel to this passage in *Barn.* (4.9–10)." In more recent times see esp. Koester, *Synoptische Überlieferung*, 160: "*Did.* 16: a little apocalypse that was probably combined with the 'ways' even before its inclusion in the *Didache*." Cf. also pp. 173, 190. Koester therefore speaks of the "apocalypse of the ways" (p. 173). In addition see Kamlah, *Paränese*, 214. Against the combining of chaps. 1–6 with chap. 16 are Rordorf and Tuilier, *Doctrine*, 81–83; Vielhauer, *Geschichte*, 731–35; Aono, *Entwicklung*, 164–65, 256–57.

Table 11

Did. 16.1–2	Luke 12:35	Matt 24:42	Matt 25:13	Mark 13:35 (cf. 33)
(1a) γρηγορεῖτε ὑπὲρ τῆς ζωῆς ὑμῶν·		γρηγορεῖτε οὖν,	Γρηγορεῖτε οὖν,	γρηγορεῖτε οὖν·
(1b) οἱ λύχνοι ὑμῶν μὴ σβεσθήτωσαν, καὶ αἱ ὀσφύες ὑμῶν μὴ ἐκλυέσθωσαν,[1]	Ἔστωσαν ὑμῶν αἱ ὀσφύες περιεζωσμέναι καὶ οἱ λύχνοι καιόμενοι.			
	Matt 24:44/Luke 12:40 (Q)			
(1c) ἀλλὰ γίνεσθε ἕτοιμοι·	(. . .) καὶ ὑμεῖς γίνεσθε ἕτοιμοι,			
οὐ γὰρ οἴδατε τὴν ὥραν, ἐν ᾗ	ὅτι ᾗ οὐ δοκεῖτε ὥρᾳ (Luke: ᾗ ὥρᾳ οὐ δοκεῖτε)	ὅτι οὐκ οἴδατε ποίᾳ ἡμέρᾳ	ὅτι οὐκ οἴδατε τὴν ἡμέραν	οὐκ οἴδατε γὰρ πότε
ὁ κύριος ἡμῶν	ὁ υἱὸς τοῦ ἀνθρώπου	ὁ κύριος ὑμῶν	οὐδὲ τὴν ὥραν.	ὁ κύριος τῆς οἰκίας
ἔρχεται.[2]	ἔρχεται.	ἔρχεται.		ἔρχεται . . .
(2a) πυκνῶς δὲ συναχθήσεσθε ζητοῦντες τὰ ἀνήκοντα ταῖς ψυχαῖς ὑμῶν·				
	Barn. 4.9			
(2b) οὐ γὰρ ὠφελήσει ὑμᾶς ὁ πᾶς χρόνος — τῆς πίστεως ὑμῶν, ἐὰν μὴ ἐν τῷ ἐσχάτῳ καιρῷ — τελειωθῆτε.	. . . οὐδὲν γὰρ ὠφελήσει ἡμᾶς ὁ πᾶς χρόνος τῆς ζωῆς καὶ τῆς πίστεως ἡμῶν, ἐὰν μὴ νῦν ἐν τῷ ἀνόμῳ καιρῷ καὶ τοῖς μέλλουσιν σκανδάλοις, ὡς πρέπει υἱοῖς θεοῦ, ἀντιστῶμεν.			

[1] Cf. Eph 6:14; 1 Pet 1:13.
[2] Cf. *2 Clem.* 12.1.

This can only be explained if either *Didache* or *Doctrina* has better preserved the original conclusion of the source; in light of *Did.* 6.1 I prefer the latter option. The simplest and least forced explanation may well be that the Didachist found in his source (the Two Ways tractate) a short eschatological epilogue (note: short and not apocalyptic in its content), somewhat in the form in which it now appears in *Doctr.* 6.1 and 6.4–5 (*Barnabas* 21/*Canons* 14 rest on another, perhaps older version). The Didachist, when he came to this point, omitted the epilogue he found in his source (except for 6.1), for understandable compositional reasons. Now, at the end of his whole document, he inserts in its place an eschatological conclusion; in its content, however, it is not derived from the Two Ways tractate.[4]

But where does the material in chap. 16 come from? The answers given to this question are sometimes combined with the hypothesis just discussed, according to which chap. 16 belonged to the Two Ways tractate (in one or another version); sometimes they are independent of that hypothesis. Cf. also tables 11–15 (derived from Koester, *Synoptische Überlieferungen*, 175–90).

1. According to the traditional view, chap. 16 is dependent on Matthew, and specifically Matthew 24:[5] cf. Harnack,[6] Funk,[7] Robinson,[8] Vokes,[9] Johnson,[10] Massaux,[11] Richardson,[12] Stommel,[13] Hagner,[14] and others.[15] Beyond this, other literary models enter into consideration. Thus the Gospel of Luke could be quoted (e.g., Connolly,[16] Richardson[17]); Pauline letters could have been used (e.g., Johnson,[18] Stommel[19]); there could be dependence on *Barnabas* (thus, e.g., Harnack,[20] Robinson,[21] Connolly,[22] Vokes,[23] Muilenburg,[24] Richardson[25]). There is no disputing that *Did.* 16.7 quotes the Old Testament, namely, Zech 14:5. Is chap. 16 therefore a compilation of various literary texts?[26] "It will be clearly seen that the *Didache*'s Apocalypse is founded on that in Matt. XXIV, enriched from various New Testament sources, from *Barnabas,* and from the Old Testament."[27] Massaux's opinion is more

---

4   See above, p. 38 n. 62, and the commentary below on *Did.* 16.1. From among the other presentations let me mention those of Drews and Bammel. Drews ("Untersuchungen," 69–70) suggested (to list only the most important points) various recensions of the basic document with different conclusions. One (already shortened) form can still be discerned behind *Barnabas* 21/*Canons* 14; another, still further shortened, is in *Doctrina*. In contrast, *Didache* 16 is probably closest to the original form because Drews suspected "that originally a longer apocalypse constituted the conclusion of D" (p. 70). Bammel ("Schema," 253–62) differs. He investigates the eschatological epilogues of related documents and comes to the conclusion that these epilogues were subject to extensive changes (p. 257). Hence one may not regard *Didache* 16 in its present form as simply the original conclusion of the Two Ways tractate in the source. In addition there were two types of eschatological epilogues: "The one looks toward the blessed end, the other points to the judgment, and only in that connection to the μισθός" (p. 258). Bammel assigns *Didache* 16 to this second type. Chap. 16 is not, however, a unit; vv. 1–2 are an eschatological parenesis while vv. 3–8 are the "depiction of the cosmic eschatology" (p. 259). In v. 2b the characteristic epilogue type appears, and it leads in vv. 3–8 to a digression (p. 259). The resumption of the thread dropped in v. 3 has been lost from H. The original conclusion should be sought in a formula close to the Georgian text (p. 260). But what we now read in vv. 3–8 is a subsequent "apocalyptic inflation" (p. 261).

5   Cf. *Did.* 16.1a/Matt 24:42
     Did. 16.1c/Matt 24:42 and 44
     Did. 16.3/Matt 24:11–12 and 7:15
     Did. 16.4a/Matt 24:12 and 10
     Did. 16.4b/Matt 24:24
     Did. 16.4d/Matt 24:21
     Did. 16.5b/Matt 24:10
     Did. 16.5c/Matt 24:13 (10:22b)
     Did. 16.6a/Matt 24:30a

Did. 16.6b/Matt 24:31
[*Did.* 16.7/Matt 25:31]
Did. 16.8/Matt 24:30b; 26:64.

6   Harnack, *Lehre*, 60.

7   Funk, *Patres apostolici*, 35: "*Summa capitis ex Evangelio secundum Matthaeum 24 hausta est*" ("The bulk of the chapter is drawn from Matthew 24").

8   Robinson, *Didache*, 68.

9   Vokes, *Riddle*, 111.

10 Johnson, "Motive," 118–19.

11 Massaux, *Influence*, 3.167–73.

12 Richardson, "Teaching," 165.

13 Stommel, "Σημεῖον," 27–42; and A. J. B. Higgins, "The Sign of the Son of Man (Matt XXIV,30)," *NTS* 9 (1962/63) 380–82.

14 Hagner, *Use*, 280.

15 There is an original variation on this in Butler, "Relations," 276–83. Aono (*Entwicklung*, 186, 188) posits indirect dependence on Matthew.

16 Connolly, "Streeter on the Didache," 374–75.

17 Richardson, "Teaching," 165.

18 Johnson, "Motive," 119: "The Antichrist is introduced into Matthew's scheme in language that suggests 2 Thessalonians 2:9."

19 Stommel, "Σημεῖον," 27–33, 32: 2 Thessalonians and Galatians.

20 Harnack, *Lehre*, 60; idem, "Prolegomena," 287–88; idem, *Apostellehre*, 12–13.

21 Robinson, *Didache*, 66–68.

22 "Barnabas and the Didache," 166–67; idem, "Streeter on the Didache," 376.

23 Vokes, *Riddle,* 111.

24 Muilenburg, *Literary Relations*, 159–60.

25 Richardson, "Teaching, "163, 165.

26 Cf., e.g., the judgment of Muilenburg, *Literary Relations*, 163: "a cento of N. T. writings and Barnabas."

27 Vokes, *Riddle*, 111. The apocalypse in the *Didache* "is an artificial catena of New Testament and other passages" (p. 143). The idea of the Montanist origins of the *Didache*, which Vokes originally connected with this, can be left entirely out of the discussion here.

Table 12

Did. 16.3	Matt 24:11–12	Mark 7:15
(3a) ἐν γὰρ ταῖς ἐσχάταις ἡμέραις πληθυνθήσονται οἱ ψευδοπροφῆται[1] καὶ οἱ φθορεῖς,	καὶ πολλοὶ ψευδοπροφῆται ἐγερθήσονται	Προσέχετε ἀπὸ τῶν ψευδοπροφητῶν,
(3b) καὶ στραφήσονται τὰ πρόβατα εἰς λύκους,[2] καὶ ἡ ἀγάπη στραφήσεται εἰς μῖσος·[3]	καὶ πλανήσουσιν πολλούς· καὶ διὰ τὸ πληθυνθῆναι τὴν ἀνομίαν ψυγήσεται ἡ ἀγάπη τῶν πολλῶν.	οἵτινες ἔρχονται πρὸς ὑμᾶς ἐν ἐνδύμασιν προβάτων, ἔσωθεν δέ εἰσιν λύκοι ἅρπαγες.

For the whole, cf. Justin 1 *Apol.* 16.13 (Goodspeed, 37) and *Dial.* 35.3 (130).
[1] Cf. Mark 13:5–6 par., 12–13 par.; 1 Tim 4:1–5; 2 Pet 3:3; *Apoc. Pet.* 1–2 (Akhmimic fragment, fol. 10r; Adolf von Harnack, *Bruchstücke der Evangelien und der Apokalypse des Petrus* [2d ed.; TU 9.2; Leipzig: Hinrichs, 1893] 16), etc.
[2] Cf. Matt 10:16/Luke 10:3 (Q).
[3] Cf. *2 Bar.* 48.35.

cautious:[28] *Didache* 16 depends on Matthew, and what the Didachist wrote in chap. 16 "seems to comment" on the Matthean text.[29] One could still ask whether, beyond that, there was influence from Luke;[30] in addition the chapter incorporates thematic (not literary) apocalyptic motifs that are attested in Paul and Revelation.[31]

2. Glover suggested another solution to the problem, positing here (as in other echoes of the Synoptic tradition) a literary influence from some form of the Q tradition.[32]

3. Still another possibility was suggested by the attempt of Drews to clarify the outstanding questions.[33] At first he adopted the traditional opinion according to which chap. 16 depends on Matthew,[34] but that did not suffice for him. He attempted to explain the specifically literary relationships as follows: For him, the source of *Didache* 16 was part of the Two Ways tractate (see above). The author of the source had used a Jewish basic document, in fact the same one that is the basis of Mark 13.[35] The Didachist in turn, while using the Gospel of Matthew, had reworked the Jewish source, Christianized it, "but also quite freely elevated it to match his own point of view."[36] Following a similar direction, Koester subjected this chapter to a penetrating analysis.[37] He reconstructed a complicated tradition history. The Synoptic material in *Didache* 16 is said to be made up of three different strands of tradition: (a) 16.1, 6, and 7 come from generally available apocalyptic material; (b) 16.4b,[38] 5, and 8 are from a Jewish source, which also

---

28 Massaux, *Influence*, 3.167–73 (analysis); 3.173 (summary conclusion).
29 *Influence*, 3.173.
30 *Influence*, 3.173.
31 *Influence*, 3.173.
32 Glover, "Quotations," 21–23. Cf. his concluding suggestions on pp. 28–29.
33 Drews, "Untersuchungen," 70–73.
34 Drews, "Untersuchungen," 71.
35 Drews, "Untersuchungen," 72. This is, however, quite inadequately demonstrated.
36 Drews, "Untersuchungen," 72.
37 Koester, *Synoptische Überlieferung*, 173–90.

38 Would this be v. 4b–d in our numbering?
39 Koester, *Synoptische Überlieferung*, 189. Thus Matthew 24 was not used (against Drews).
40 Koester, *Synoptische Überlieferung*, 190.
41 Koester, *Synoptische Überlieferung*, 190.
42 Kloppenborg, "Matthaean Tradition," 54–67.
43 His most important observations are that *Did.* 16.7 quotes not Matthew but the LXX ("Matthaean Tradition," 59; on this cf. the earlier work of Koester, *Synoptische Überlieferung*, 187); *Did.* 16.6 "corresponds to Matt 24:30–31 *only* at those points at which Matthew turned from Mark to his special source" (p. 65). On the other hand, Kloppenborg's

Table 13

Did. 16.4	Matt 24:12		
(4a) αὐξανούσης γὰρ	καὶ διὰ τὸ πληθυνθῆναι		
τῆς ἀνομίας	τὴν ἀνομίαν . . .		
	Matt 24:10		
	καὶ τότε		
	σκανδαλισθήσονται πολλοὶ		
μισήσουσιν ἀλλήλους	καὶ ἀλλήλους παραδώσουσιν		
καὶ διώξουσι	—		
καὶ παραδώσουσι,[1]	καὶ μισήσουσιν ἀλλήλους . . .		
	Matt 24:24	**Mark 13:22**	
(4b) καὶ τότε φανήσεται	ἐγερθήσονται γὰρ	ἐγερθήσονται γὰρ	
ὁ κοσμοπλάνης[2]	ψευδόχριστοι	ψευδόχριστοι	
ὡς υἱὸς θεοῦ	καὶ ψευδοπροφῆται	καὶ ψευδοπροφῆται	
καὶ ποιήσει	καὶ δώσουσιν	καὶ δώσουσιν	
σημεῖα καὶ τέρατα,[3]	σημεῖα μεγάλα καὶ τέρατα	σημεῖα καὶ τέρατα . . .	
(4c) καὶ ἡ γῆ παραδοθήσεται			
εἰς χεῖρας αὐτοῦ,			
	Matt 24:21	**Mark 13:19**	**Dan 12:1 (Theodotion)**
(4d) καὶ ποιήσει	ἔσται γὰρ τότε	ἔσονται γὰρ	καὶ ἔσται
	—	αἱ ἡμέραι ἐκεῖναι	—
ἀθέμιτα,[4]	θλῖψις μεγάλη	θλῖψις	καιρὸς θλίψεως,
ἃ οὐδέποτε γέγονεν	οἵα οὐ γέγονεν	οἵα οὐ γέγονεν τοιαύτη	οἵα οὐ γέγονεν
ἐξ αἰῶνος.	ἀπ᾽ ἀρχῆς κόσμου . . .	ἀπ᾽ ἀρχῆς κτίσεως . . .	ἀφ᾽ οὗ γεγένηται
			ἔθνος . . .

[1] 4 Ezra 6:24; *2 Bar.* 70.3.
[2] 2 John 7; 2 Thess 2:3–4, 8-9; Justin *Dial.* 110.2 (Goodspeed, 226); *Sib. Or.* 3.68; *Apoc. Pet.* 2 (Ethiopic; *NTApoc,* 2.669); Hippolytus *De Antichr.* 6.2 (GCS 1.2, p. 8).
[3] 2 Thess 2:9; Rev 13:13; 19:20; *Apoc. Pet.* (see above); and elsewhere.
[4] Justin, *Dial.* 110.2 (Goodspeed, 226).

served as a source for Mark 13; (c) 16.3, 4a, and 5 go back to "another piece of apocalyptic tradition" that would also have been used in Matt 24:10–12.[39] Still, the whole would probably have been available to the Didachist in a Christian recension.[40] "We have here a parallel process to the origins of the Christian apocalypse in the Synoptics."[41]

4. Most recently John S. Kloppenborg has minutely analyzed *Did.* 16.6–8 (and given a cursory analysis of 16.3–5).[42] His conclusion is that *Didache* 16 is dependent neither on Matthew nor on Mark 13 (or the source for Mark 13),[43] but on a tradition on which the corresponding special material in Matthew also depends. "*Did* 16.3–8 agree with Matthew only when Matthew is using

argumentation on pp. 62–63 (as far as it concerns the conclusion of v. 8) is problematic. If *Did.* 16.8 were dependent on Matthew, according to Kloppenborg one should expect the concluding phrase to be μετὰ δυνάμεως καὶ δόξης πολλῆς; the absence of this final phrase is said to show, however, that the *Didache* is also not dependent on Mark 13. But in saying this Kloppenborg overlooks the

fact that the conclusion of the *Didache* has been lost; moreover, the Georgian presumes precisely the phrase that Kloppenborg finds missing here. In contrast, it really is striking that "Did 16.8 *agrees with Mt 24:30 at those points where Matthew disagrees with Mark*" (p. 63; Kloppenborg apparently means ἐπί vs. ἐπάνω and τοῦ οὐρανοῦ).

211

Table 14

Did. 16.5–6

	Matt 24:10	*Apoc. Pet.* 1 (Ethiopic; *NTApoc*, 2.668)	Mark 13:27	1 Thess 4:16	1 Cor 15:52
(5a) τότε ἥξει ἡ κτίσις τῶν ἀνθρώπων εἰς τὴν πύρωσιν τῆς δοκιμασίας,					
(5b) καί σκανδαλισθήσονται πολλοὶ καὶ ἀπολοῦνται,	καὶ τότε σκανδαλισθήσονται πολλοὶ καὶ ἀλλήλους παραδώσουσιν . . .				

Matt 24:13 (10:22b; Mark 13:13b)

| (5c) οἱ δὲ ὑπομείναντες
ἐν τῇ πίστει αὐτῶν
σωθήσονται[1]
ὑπ᾽ αὐτοῦ τοῦ
καταθέματος. | ὁ δὲ ὑπομείνας
εἰς τέλος
οὗτος σωθήσεται. | | | | |

Matt 24:30a — *Apoc. Pet.* 1 (Ethiopic; *NTApoc*, 2.668)

| (6a) καὶ τότε φανήσεται
τὰ σημεῖα
τῆς ἀληθείας·[2]
πρῶτον σημεῖον
ἐκπετάσεως ἐν οὐρανῷ, | καὶ τότε φανήσεται
τὸ σημεῖον
τοῦ υἱοῦ τοῦ ἀνθρώπου
—
ἐν οὐρανῷ . . . | so shall I come . . .
—
with my cross
going before my face. . . .[3] | | | |

Matt 24:31 — Mark 13:27 — 1 Thess 4:16 — 1 Cor 15:52

| (6b) εἶτα σημεῖον
φωνῆς σάλπιγγος,
καὶ τὸ τρίτον
ἀνάστασις νεκρῶν· . . . | καὶ ἀποστελεῖ τοὺς
ἀγγέλους αὐτοῦ
μετὰ σάλπιγγος μεγάλης[4]
. . . | | καὶ τότε ἀποστελεῖ τοὺς
ἀγγέλους καὶ . . . | —
καὶ ἐν σάλπιγγι θεοῦ,
καταβήσεται ἀπ᾽
οὐρανοῦ . . . | —
ἐν τῇ ἐσχάτῃ σάλπιγγι·
σαλπίσει γάρ . . . |

[1] Dan 12:12 (Theodotion); 4 Ezra 6:25, etc.
[2] For the three signs, cf. *Sib. Or.* 2.188.
[3] Further parallels in the commentary at 15.6.
[4] א etc.; σάλπιγγος φωνῆς μεγάλης· B etc.; σάλπιγγος καὶ φωνῆς μεγάλης D etc.

his special source. Agreements with Mark are registered only when Mark was quoting common and widely known apocalyptic sayings (e.g., Dan 7:13; 12:12)."[44] It follows that *Did.* 16.3–8 most probably rests on a "free-floating apocalyptic tradition"[45] that was also known to Matthew (as special material). Matthew and the *Didache* used this tradition independently of one another.[46] Matthew incorporated it in his Markan source while the *Didache* placed it (probably with redactional alterations)[47] at the end of the book.

44 Kloppenborg, "Matthaean Tradition," 66. Cf. his table at this point.
45 Kloppenborg, "Matthaean Tradition," 67.
46 Kloppenborg, "Matthaean Tradition," 67; cf. earlier, at p. 65.
47 Kloppenborg, "Matthaean Tradition," 65.

Table 15

Did. 16:7–8	Matt 25:31		Zech 14:5b
(7) οὐ πάντων δέ,			
ἀλλ᾽ ὡς ἐρρέθη·	...		... καὶ
Ἥξει ὁ κύριος	...		ἥξει κύριος ὁ θεός μου
καὶ πάντες οἱ ἅγιοι	καὶ πάντες οἱ ἄγγελοι		καὶ πάντες οἱ ἅγιοι
μετ᾽ αὐτοῦ.	μετ᾽ αὐτοῦ ...		μετ᾽ αὐτοῦ.

	Matt 26:30b	Mark 13:26	Luke 21:27	Dan 7:13
(8) τότε ὄψεται	καὶ ὄψονται	καὶ τότε ὄψονται	καὶ τότε ὄψονται	...
ὁ κόσμος	—	—	—	
τὸν κύριον	τὸν υἱὸν τοῦ ἀνθρώπου	τὸν υἱὸν τοῦ ἀνθρώπου	τὸν υἱὸν τοῦ ἀνθρώπου	ἐπὶ
ἐρχόμενον ἐπάνω	ἐρχόμενον ἐπὶ	ἐρχόμενον ἐν	ἐρχόμενον ἐν	τῶν νεφελῶν
τῶν νεφελῶν	τῶν νεφελῶν	νεφέλαις	νεφέλῃ	τοῦ οὐρανοῦ
τοῦ οὐρανοῦ ...[1]	τοῦ οὐρανοῦ	—	—	ὡς υἱὸς ἀνθρώπου
(with power and	μετὰ δυνάμεως	μετὰ δυνάμεως	μετὰ δυνάμεως	ἤρχετο ...
great glory ...	καὶ δόξης πολλῆς·	πολλῆς καὶ δόξης.	καὶ δόξης πολλῆς.	(μετὰ ... ἐρχόμενος
Georgian)				... Theodotion)

	Matt 26:64	Mark 14:62	Luke 22:69
	... ἀπ᾽ ἄρτι ὄψεσθε	... καὶ ὄψεσθε	ἀπὸ τοῦ νῦν δὲ ἔσται
	τὸν υἱὸν τοῦ ἀνθρώπου	τὸν υἱὸν τοῦ ἀνθρώπου	ὁ υἱὸς τοῦ ἀνθρώπου
	καθήμενον ἐκ δεξιῶν	ἐκ δεξιῶν καθήμενον	καθήμενος ἐκ δεξιῶν
	τῆς δυνάμεως	τῆς δυνάμεως	τῆς δυνάμεως τοῦ θεοῦ.
	καὶ ἐρχόμενον ἐπὶ	καὶ ἐρχόμενον μετὰ	
	τῶν νεφελῶν	τῶν νεφελῶν	
	τοῦ οὐρανοῦ.	τοῦ οὐρανοῦ.	

[1] Cf. 4 Ezra 13:3; Rev 1:7; Justin, *1 Apol.* 51.9 (Goodspeed 62); *Dial.* 14.8 (107).

16

1   Keep vigil over your life. Let your lamps not go
     out and let your loins not be weak but be
     ready, for you do not know the hour at which
     our Lord is coming.

2   You shall assemble frequently, seeking what
     pertains to your souls, for the whole time of
     your belief will be of no profit to you unless
     you are perfected at the final hour.

Comment

■ **1** One must admit that the introductory call to "keep vigil," γρηγορεῖτε κτλ. (v. 1a), appears without warning. We would at least expect γρηγορεῖτε <u>οὖν</u>. . . . This does not mean that vv. 1–2 are quoted from a source. In my opinion the Didachist is formulating for himself here (as also in v. 2), making use of traditional parenetic material and particularly such material as is associated with the Christian anticipation of the end. Γρηγορεῖν[1] (in a transferred sense) is sometimes, as here, a characteristic expression in eschatologically motivated parenesis, especially in the imperative; cf. Mark 13:35 par.; Matt 25:13; 1 Cor 16:13.[2] Γρηγορεῖτε ὑπὲρ τῆς ζωῆς ὑμῶν is, however, an unusual combination.[3] It seems to mean "watch over one's life"[4] in the sense of disciplining one's body and life against the temptations of the Evil One. The Didachist does mean this, as he shows by quoting immediately from the Jesus tradition, which serves him, so to speak, as a commentary on the imperative

γρηγορεῖτε and therefore is associated with it at this point:

οἱ λύχνοι ὑμῶν μὴ σβεσθήτωσαν,
καὶ αἱ ὀσφύες ὑμῶν μὴ ἐκλυέσθωσαν (v. 1b)
("Let your lamps not be quenched
and your loins not be weak")

This is an admonitory, rousing aphorism in *parallelismus membrorum*.[5] Cf. Luke 12:35; but the differences between this and the Lukan text are too great to indicate literary dependence[6]—to say nothing of the fact that at least the metaphor of the ὀσφύες ("loins," connecting with the biblical tradition in Exod 12:11; Jer 1:17, and frequently elsewhere) is in broad Christian usage (Eph 6:14; 1 Pet 1:13). The Didachist does not make it obvious that the logion is a saying of the Lord, but he probably understood it to be one (as did his readers); he quotes the saying in the form of oral tradition (or as a quotation from a special sayings source?)[7] in which it was available to him.[8] The λύχνοι are the common oil lamps with two

1   Albrecht Oepke, "ἐξεγείρω κτλ.," *TDNT* 2 (1964) 338–39; Johannes M. Nützel, "γρηγορέω," *EDNT* 1 (1990) 264–65.

2   Γρηγορεῖν in an eschatological sense (other than the imperative usage) is found in 1 Thess 5:6; Rev 3:2–3; 16.15. For the whole subject, cf. Methodius *Symposium* 5.3.114 (GCS 55): Διὸ προσῆκεν ἄσβεστον ἐν τῇ καρδίᾳ τῆς πίστεως ἐξάψαντας τὸν λύχνον, καὶ τὴν ὀσφῦν ἀναζωσαμένους τῇ σωφροσύνῃ, ἐγρηγορέναι καὶ προσδοκᾶν ἀεὶ τὸν κύριον ("therefore it is fitting to enkindle in the heart the unquenchable fire of faith, and having girt the loins with prudence, to ever await and expect the Lord").

3   Harnack (*Lehre*, 60), also emphasizing the unusual character of the expression, still refers to Heb 13:17, where it is said of the ἡγούμενοι· ἀγρυπνοῦσιν ὑπὲρ τῶν ψυχῶν ὑμῶν ("for they are keeping watch over your souls").

4   Cf. BAGD, *s.v.* The expression could be an allusion to the Two Ways tractate and thus a further association with the beginning of the *Didache*. It is not pos-

sible to derive from this (as does Drews, "Untersuchungen," 68) an original connection between chaps. 1–6 and 16. At most this could be a deliberate allusion by the Didachist.

5   Schaff, *Church Manual*, 96.

6   In comparison to the Lukan text the positions of λύχνοι and ὀσφύες are reversed. (Cf. also the passage from Methodius in n. 2 above.) Instead of λύχνοι . . . μὴ σβεσθήτωσαν, Luke has the positive καιόμενοι; instead of ὀσφύες . . . ἐκλυέσθωσαν, Luke reads περιεζωσμέναι. Against dependence on Luke are Koester, *Synoptische Überlieferung*, 175–76; and Aono, *Entwicklung*, 178.

7   Cf. Glover, "Quotations," 22.

8   There is a truncated version of the logion (to be understood as gnostic) in *Gos. Thom.* (Coptic) 21b (trans. of Helmut Koester and Thomas O. Lambdin, in James M. Robinson, ed., *The Nag Hammadi Library in English* [3d ed.; San Francisco: HarperCollins, 1990] 129): "be on your guard against the world. Arm yourselves with great strength lest the robbers find a way to come to you."

apertures, one for the wick and another for filling the lamp with oil. For the metaphor $\mu\grave{\eta}$ $\sigma\beta\varepsilon\sigma\vartheta\acute{\eta}\tau\omega\sigma\alpha\nu$[9] it is probably correct to recall that the lamps burned all night long (originally for apotropaic reasons).[10] Not letting the lamps go out means always to be on the alert. $A\acute{\iota}$ $\acute{o}\sigma\phi\acute{\upsilon}\varepsilon\varsigma$ $\acute{\upsilon}\mu\hat{\omega}\nu$ $\mu\grave{\eta}$ $\acute{\varepsilon}\kappa\lambda\upsilon\acute{\varepsilon}\sigma\vartheta\omega\sigma\alpha\nu$ is less clear than the analogous biblical expressions in Exod 12:11; Jer 1:17, and elsewhere in the Jewish Scriptures, and then in Luke 12:35; Eph 6:14; 1 Pet 1:13. The biblical phrase means "to belt the garment which is worn ungirdled in the house or in times of relaxation, with a view to greater mobility for work, for travel, for battle, etc."[11] By contrast, the didachistic expression means "do not let your loins be flabby"[12]—but it probably implies the same imagery as that in Luke 12:35.

The two-line metaphor ($\lambda\acute{\upsilon}\chi\nu\sigma\iota$ – $\acute{o}\sigma\phi\acute{\upsilon}\varepsilon\varsigma$) was an interpretation of the introductory $\gamma\rho\eta\gamma\sigma\rho\varepsilon\hat{\iota}\tau\varepsilon$. Now in v. 1c the interpretation of the metaphor itself follows: $\grave{\alpha}\lambda\lambda\grave{\alpha}$ $\gamma\acute{\iota}\nu\varepsilon\sigma\vartheta\varepsilon$ $\acute{\varepsilon}\tau\sigma\iota\mu\sigma\iota\cdot$ $\sigma\grave{\upsilon}$ $\gamma\grave{\alpha}\rho$ $\sigma\acute{\iota}\delta\alpha\tau\varepsilon$ $\tau\grave{\eta}\nu$ $\acute{\omega}\rho\alpha\nu$, $\acute{\varepsilon}\nu$ $\hat{\eta}$ $\acute{o}$ $\kappa\acute{\upsilon}\rho\iota\sigma\varsigma$ $\acute{\eta}\mu\hat{\omega}\nu$ $\acute{\varepsilon}\rho\chi\varepsilon\tau\alpha\iota$ ("but be ready, for you know not the hour in which our Lord comes"). A similar saying is handed down both in Q (Matt 24:44/Luke 12:40) and in Mark 13:(33 and) 35; cf. Matt 24:42 and 25:13. In *Did.* 16.1 there is another, independent[13] tradition.[14] The didachistic version (probably taken again from oral tradition—or from a sayings collection?) is closer to the Q version.[15]

■ **2** Verse 2a is one of what we might call the "special materials pieces" in the final chapter. In this admonition to frequent attendance (or attendance in large numbers?) at community worship we hear the voice of a generation in which there is already the danger that first love will grow cold: the Didachist is speaking. Compare this with Heb 10:25 and *Barn.* 19.10, where similar admonitions are placed in an eschatological context. Apart from that, such warnings are traditional.[16] Understandably enough they are especially frequent in the "postapostolic" period.[17] $\Pi\upsilon\kappa\nu\hat{\omega}\varsigma$ $\sigma\upsilon\nu\alpha\chi\vartheta\acute{\eta}\sigma\varepsilon\sigma\vartheta\varepsilon$[18] ("assemble frequently") urges frequent gatherings of the community (should we understand this to mean that they should take place during the week and not only on the Lord's day?), or else that the assemblies should be large.[19] Ignatius *Eph.* 13.1 sounds very similar: $\sigma\pi\sigma\upsilon$-$\delta\acute{\alpha}\zeta\varepsilon\tau\varepsilon$ $\sigma\grave{\upsilon}\nu$ $\pi\upsilon\kappa\nu\acute{o}\tau\varepsilon\rho\sigma\nu$ $\sigma\upsilon\nu\acute{\varepsilon}\rho\chi\varepsilon\sigma\vartheta\alpha\iota$ $\varepsilon\acute{\iota}\varsigma$ $\varepsilon\grave{\upsilon}\chi\alpha\rho\iota\sigma\tau\acute{\iota}$-$\alpha\nu$ $\vartheta\varepsilon\sigma\hat{\upsilon}$ $\kappa\alpha\grave{\iota}$ $\varepsilon\acute{\iota}\varsigma$ $\delta\acute{o}\xi\alpha\nu$. $\acute{o}\tau\alpha\nu$ $\gamma\grave{\alpha}\rho$ $\pi\upsilon\kappa\nu\hat{\omega}\varsigma$ $\acute{\varepsilon}\pi\grave{\iota}$ $\tau\grave{o}$ $\alpha\grave{\upsilon}\tau\grave{o}$ $\gamma\acute{\iota}\nu\varepsilon\sigma\vartheta\varepsilon$ . . . ("Hasten then to come together more frequently for thanksgiving and praise of God. For when you come together frequently . . ."). The gathering is for the good of souls: $\tau\grave{\alpha}$ $\grave{\alpha}\nu\acute{\eta}\kappa\sigma\nu\tau\alpha$ $\tau\alpha\hat{\iota}\varsigma$ $\psi\upsilon\chi\alpha\hat{\iota}\varsigma$ means "what your souls need."[20] The reference to the usefulness of coming together is traditional: compare *Barn.* 4.10: $\grave{\alpha}\lambda\lambda'$ $\acute{\varepsilon}\pi\grave{\iota}$ $\tau\grave{o}$ $\alpha\grave{\upsilon}\tau\grave{o}$ $\sigma\upsilon\nu\varepsilon\rho\chi\acute{o}\mu\varepsilon\nu\sigma\iota$ $\sigma\upsilon\nu\zeta\eta\tau\varepsilon\hat{\iota}\tau\varepsilon$ $\pi\varepsilon\rho\grave{\iota}$ $\tau\sigma\hat{\upsilon}$ $\kappa\sigma\iota\nu\hat{\eta}$ $\sigma\upsilon\mu\phi\acute{\varepsilon}\rho\sigma\nu\tau\sigma\varsigma$ ("But when you come together seek for the common good"), and the contrary warning

The metaphor of "girding one's loins" (Leipoldt, "Shenute," p. 51) or "arming oneself" (Koester and Lambdin) is also found in *Gos. Thom.* 103.

9   Matt 25:8: $\delta\acute{o}\tau\varepsilon$ $\acute{\eta}\mu\hat{\iota}\nu$ $\acute{\varepsilon}\kappa$ $\tau\sigma\hat{\upsilon}$ $\acute{\varepsilon}\lambda\alpha\acute{\iota}\sigma\upsilon$ $\acute{\upsilon}\mu\hat{\omega}\nu$, $\acute{o}\tau\iota$ $\alpha\acute{\iota}$ $\lambda\alpha\mu\pi\acute{\alpha}\delta\varepsilon\varsigma$ $\acute{\eta}\mu\hat{\omega}\nu$ $\sigma\beta\acute{\varepsilon}\nu\nu\upsilon\nu\tau\alpha\iota$ ("Give us some of your oil, for our lamps are going out").

10   H. P. Rüger in *BHH* 2.1047. Cf. also *Rul. Ben.* 22.4 (CSEL 75², 84): *Candela iugiter in eadem cella ardeat usque mane* ("let the candle therefore in the cell burn until dawn").

11   Heinrich Seesemann, "$\acute{o}\sigma\phi\acute{\upsilon}\varsigma$," *TDNT* 5 (1967) 496.

12   Cf. BAGD, *s.v.* $\acute{\varepsilon}\kappa\lambda\acute{\upsilon}\omega$.

13   See the discussion of the relationship between *Did.* 16.1 and the Synoptic tradition in Koester, *Synoptische Überlieferung*, 176–77, with the conclusion at p. 189. Koester attributes the material in v. 1 to the whole body of common apocalyptic motifs. I would prefer to think of v. 1b as a dominical saying, and I do not consider it impossible even at v. 1c (in spite of $\acute{o}$ $\kappa\acute{\upsilon}\rho\iota\sigma\varsigma$ $\acute{\eta}\mu\hat{\omega}\nu$) that the Didachist is consciously quoting a word of the Lord from the memories contained in his oral tradition (changing it, however, by the addition of $\acute{o}$ $\kappa\acute{\upsilon}\rho\iota\sigma\varsigma$ $\acute{\eta}\mu\hat{\omega}\nu$).

14   Rev 3:3 and *2 Clem.* 12.1 offer only remote parallels.

15   Only in replacing "Son of man" with *Kyrios* does the *Didache* version more closely recall Mark and its parallels. This replacement could, however, be the work of the Didachist, for whom *Kyrios* is *the* title of exaltation for Jesus.

16   From early Judaism, cf. *m. 'Abot* 2.4b (Marti and Beer, 43): "Hillel said: Do not separate yourself from the congregation." See further in Str–B 3.743.

17   *1 Clem.* 46.2; *2 Clem.* 17.3; *Barn.* 4.10; 10.11; *Hermas Vis.* 3.6.2; *Sim.* 8.9.1; 9.26.3; Ignatius *Eph.* 13.1; 20.2; *Pol.* 4.2. Later: Ps.-Clement *Ep. Clem.* 9.2 (GCS² 1.12); *Hom.* 3.69.2 (GCS² 1.81–82).

18   $\Sigma\upsilon\nu\acute{\alpha}\gamma\varepsilon\sigma\vartheta\alpha\iota$ is reflexive, as in 14.1. Does this betray the hand of the Didachist? It is used differently in the text of the liturgical section at 9.4.

19   Funk, *Patres apostolici*, 35: either "*crebri congregamini*" or "*crebro convenite*" ("come together frequently"). The latter interpretation is said to be more probable. So also Drews, "Apostellehre," 282. To the contrary: Knopf, *Lehre*, 38; Wengst, *Didache*, 89.

20   BAGD, *s.v.* $\grave{\alpha}\nu\acute{\eta}\kappa\omega$. Wengst (*Didache*, 89 n. 128)

against the consequences of not gathering together in *Hermas Sim.* 9.26.3: μονάζοντες ἀπολλύουσι τὰς ἑαυτῶν ψυχάς ("Those who are in isolation destroy their souls"). Such admonitions already express a kind of pastoral concern. Beyond this the present passage introduces a further motivation, apparently thought to be primary: οὐ γὰρ ὠφελήσει ὑμᾶς ὁ πᾶς χρόνος τῆς πίστεως ὑμῶν, ἐὰν μὴ ἐν τῷ ἐσχάτῳ καιρῷ τελειωθῆτε ("for the whole time of your belief will be of no profit to you unless you are perfected at the final hour," v. 2b). This verse has a parallel in *Barn.* 4.9, but it can scarcely be a quotation from *Barnabas*.[21] The *Didache* has the shorter and probably older form of the aphorism:

Didache	Barnabas
οὐ γὰρ ὠφελήσει	οὐδὲν γὰρ ὠφελήσει
ὑμᾶς	ἡμᾶς
ὁ πᾶς χρόνος	ὁ πᾶς χρόνος τῆς ζωῆς
τῆς πίστεως ὑμῶν,	καὶ τῆς πίστεως ἡμῶν,
ἐὰν μὴ	ἐὰν μὴ νῦν
ἐν τῷ ἐσχάτῳ καιρῷ	ἐν τῷ ἀνόμῳ καιρῷ
—	καὶ τοῖς μέλλουσιν σκανδάλοις,
—	ὡς πρέπει υἱοῖς θεοῦ,
τελειωθῆτε.	ἀντιστῶμεν.

The additions in *Barnabas* appear secondary, and the

νῦν (on which Harnack placed so much emphasis)[22] proves nothing about the originality of that version. Ἀντιστῶμεν ("let us resist," instead of τελειωθῆτε) results in *Barnabas* from the reference to the ἄνομος καιρός ("lawless time"). The τελειωθῆτε in the *Didache* version is not connected by any thought process to *Did.* 1.4 or 6.2. The aphorism known to the Didachist (from oral tradition?) speaks of the usefulness of accepting the Christian faith.[23] This benefit, acquired over a lifetime, will be lost if the faithful should fail at the last hour. Thus ἐν τῷ ἐσχάτῳ καιρῷ ("at the final hour") the whole period of believing is once again at risk, and it is especially vital that one should not fail at that moment, in extremis.[24] The ἔσχατος καιρός is the point in time when the apocalyptic catastrophes will begin,[25] the moment at which the end of the universe and the judgment of the world come near.[26] To stand firm in faith at that hour means "being found perfect." It is only in this firmness in face of the coming trial that faith is perfected.

With ἔσχατος καιρός ("final hour") the Didachist himself has introduced the central concept for the concluding apocalypse.

---

interprets ψυχή simply as a substitute for the relative pronoun (as in *Did.* 2.7).

21 Quotation from *Barnabas* is posited by Harnack, Robinson, Connolly, Vokes, Muilenburg, and Richardson. On this, see above, p. 209 nn. 20–25. Funk (*Abhandlungen,* 117–24) gives the opposite explanation: *Barnabas* is dependent on the *Didache.* According to Drews ("Apostellehre," 282) this sentence was already in the Two Ways tractate, on which both *Barnabas* and the *Didache* depend. This was previously suggested by Ehrhard, *Altchristliche Litteratur,* 51; and after him by Creed, "Didache," 379; and Kraft, *Didache,* 15 (as a possibility).

22 Cf. note 21 above and p. 209 n. 20.

23 The reference is to eternal life as the outcome of faith.

24 Cf. 2 John 8 (although there with a view to the threat posed by false teachers).

25 Ἐν τῷ ἐσχάτῳ καιρῷ (v. 2) is taken up and interpreted by ἐν γὰρ ταῖς ἐσχάταις ἡμέραις hereafter, in v. 3. See Bammel, "Schema," 259.

26 Ἐν καιρῷ ἐσχάτῳ, 1 Pet 1:5; ἔσχατοι καιροί, Ignatius *Eph.* 11.1; ἐν ἐσχάτοις καιροῖς, *T. Iss.* 6.1.

16

a. The Appearance of False Prophets and the Collapse of the Christian Community (16.3–4a)

2. The Apocalypse

3   For in the final days false prophets and corrupters will be multiplied, and the sheep will turn into wolves, and love will turn into hate.

4a   As lawlessness increases, they will hate and persecute and betray one another.

■ **3** Ἐν γὰρ ταῖς ἐσχάταις ἡμέραις takes up the key phrase ἐν τῷ ἐσχάτῳ καιρῷ in the previous verse.[1] I believe there is a seam between vv. 2 and 3.[2] Beginning with v. 3 the Didachist quotes a small but well-organized Christian apocalypse that, at least in v. 7, he expands with a scriptural reference from his own pen, as we will see. The apocalypse begins with the temporal note "in the final days." The ἔσχαται ἡμέραι[3] are the "last days of humanity," before the end arrives. They begin (as the readers should know) with a sudden increase in the numbers of false prophets and seducers of the communities. For the notion of "being multiplied," πληθυνθήσονται, cf. Matt 24:12 (διὰ τὸ πληθυνθῆναι τὴν ἀνομίαν, "and because of the increase of lawlessness").[4] "False prophet" was a key phrase in the piece of tradition in *Did.* 11.4–12 (vv. 5, 6, 8, 9, 10)—although there without any apocalyptic reference. Φθορεῖς ("corrupters," sc. πλάσματος θεοῦ) was used quite differently in the Two Ways tractate (cf. *Did.* 5.2) than here,

where it refers to the false teachers.[5] The appearance of false teachers is a feature of the last days;[6] cf. especially Matt 24:11 and 7:15.[7] Associated with the appearance of the false teachers is the apostasy of Christian communities: στραφήσονται τὰ πρόβατα εἰς λύκους, καὶ ἡ ἀγάπη στραφήσεται εἰς μῖσος ("the sheep will turn into wolves and love will turn into hate," v. 3b).[8] The apocalypticist makes use of the familiar contrasting pair of sheep and wolves[9] and gives the metaphor a special meaning in this context: the reference to sheep that are transformed into wolves can, but need not, mean the false teachers.[10] More probable is another interpretation: "former believers will become enemies."[11] The continuation seems to describe the same process in different

---

1   Bammel, "Schema," 259.

2   This was emphasized especially by Bammel, "Schema"; however, he combines this observation with hypotheses I cannot share (cf. above, p. 209 n. 4]).

3   Singular: John 6:39–40, 44, 54; 7:37; 11:24; 12:48; *Hermas Vis.* 2.2.5. Plural: Acts 2:17; 2 Tim 3:1; Heb 1:2; Jas 5:3; 2 Pet 3:3; *Barn.* 4.9; 12.9; 16.5; *2 Clem.* 14.2; *Hermas Sim.* 9.12.3. In a different sense: *Hermas Vis.* 3.12.2.

4   Matt 24:11: the appearance of false prophets.

5   Cf. *Const.* 6.13.3, where ψευδόχριστοι, ψευδοπροφῆται, ψευδαπόστολοι, πλάνοι καὶ φθορεῖς are listed.

6   Mark 13:5–6 par., 21–22 par.; 1 Tim 4:1–3; 2 Pet 3:3–4; *Apoc. Pet.* 1–2 (Akhmimic fragment, fol. 10r.; Adolf von Harnack, *Bruchstücke der Evangelien und der Apokalypse des Petrus* [2d ed.; TU 9.2; Leipzig: Hinrichs, 1893] 16]; *Sib. Or.* 2.165–66; 3.68–74; *As. Mos.* 7.3–10; *Apoc. Elijah* 1.13–14, etc.

7   *Did.* 16.3 need not for this reason rest on Matt 24:11: Koester (*Synoptische Überlieferung*, 189) counts

v. 3 among the elements from an apocalyptic tradition behind both the *Didache* and Matt 24:10–12; similarly Kloppenborg, "Matthaean Tradition," 66.

8   Στραφήσονται – στραφήσεται is paronomasia. See BDF, §488.1; BDR, §488.1. Wengst (*Didache*, 88) eliminates στραφήσεται (with the *Apostolic Constitutions*).

9   Matt 7:15 is the closest parallel. The metaphor is also found in Matt 10:16 (Luke 10:3); John 10:12; Acts 20:29.

10   On false teachers see Günther Bornkamm, "λύκος," *TDNT* 4 (1967) 311.

11   Koester, *Synoptische Überlieferung*, 179. Koester (in view of the question of possible dependence of this passage on Matt 7:15) observes correctly that "the same image is used very frequently, and always with a difference. Therefore, common use of the same metaphor, while giving a different meaning to the image, says nothing about literary dependence" (ibid.). By contrast, there are direct quotations (of differing quality) in *2 Clem.* 5.2–4; Justin *1 Apol.* 16.13 (Goodspeed, 37); *Dial.* 35.3 (130).

words. The love that had been at work in the communities[12] is suddenly transformed into hatred[13]—a characteristic moment within the perversions of the last days.[14] The parallel in Matt 24:12, ψυγήσεται ἡ ἀγάπη τῶν πολλῶν ("the love of many will grow cold"), has a somewhat different meaning.[15]

■ **4a** Verse 4a gives a reason for the events in the communities: the increase of lawlessness (αὐξανούσης γὰρ τῆς ἀνομίας; cf. Matt 24:12).[16] It also paints a picture of the consequences, mutual hatred (μισήσουσιν ἀλλήλους καὶ διώξουσι καὶ παραδώσουσι; cf. Matt 24:10).[17]

Brothers and sisters become enemies[18] and the consequence, in the situation in which Christians are placed within society (namely, that of constant insecurity that can at any moment turn into persecution), is that one sister or brother persecutes and betrays another. Παραδώσουσι means that apostate Christians are denouncing their former fellow believers to the authorities.

---

12 This is, of course, considered as the eschatological salvation that is evident in the communities in a special way.

13 Μῖσος is in the vice list in *Hermas Sim.* 9.15.3.

14 Remotely comparable is *2 Bar.* 48.35.

15 Is there, however, a common source (so Koester, *Synoptische Überlieferung*, 189; Kloppenborg, "Matthaean Tradition," 66–67)? Has the *Didache* preserved the more original version (suggested by

Koester, *Synoptische Überlieferung*, 178–79)?

16 Καὶ διὰ τὸ πληθυνθῆναι τὴν ἀνομίαν. . . .

17 Καὶ ἀλλήλους παραδώσουσιν καὶ μισήσουσιν ἀλλήλους. Dependence on Matthew is not compelling; again there may be mutual dependence on a common tradition. See Koester, *Synoptische Überlieferung*, 189; analogously: Kloppenborg, "Matthaean Tradition," 66–67.

18 Cf. *4 Ezra* 6:24; *2 Bar.* 70.3.

16

b. The Appearance of the Antichrist (16.4b–d)

4b–d And at that time the one who leads the world astray will appear as a "son of God" and will work signs and wonders, and the earth will be given into his hands, and he will do godless things which have never been done since the beginning of time.

Comment

■ **4b–d** This new phase in the apocalyptic drama is introduced by καὶ τότε ("at that time"). The text presupposes the epiphany of the Antichrist,[1] who will blind people with signs and wonders (v. 4b; cf. Mark 13:22/Matt 24:24).[2] The Antichrist here bears the name κοσμοπλα-νής,[3] that is, the one who "leads the world astray," deceives it, betrays it: the great betrayer of the world.[4] His betrayal consists in his appearance in the form of a son of God: φανήσεται . . . ὡς υἱὸς θεοῦ.[5] The diabolical, deceptive masquerade of God's adversary is one of the typical events of the end time.[6] The next motif also stems from that field: the Antichrist deceives and seduces people by the signs and wonders he performs.[7] Closest to this *Didache* passage is *Apoc. Pet.* 2 (Ethiopic):

"that this is the deceiver who must come into the world and do signs and wonders in order to deceive."[8] The world deceiver becomes the world ruler: καὶ ἡ γῆ παραδοθήσεται εἰς χεῖρας αὐτοῦ (v. 4c).[9] That is, the whole inhabited world[10] is subjected to his seduction and will be handed over to him as a demonic *imperator mundi*.[11] In v. 4d, finally, the demonic world ruler commits wicked deeds, ἀθέμιτα,[12] such as have not occurred since the beginning of the world: ἃ οὐδέποτε γέγονεν ἐξ αἰῶνος. Behind the whole expression may be a recollection of Dan 12:1, but we should note that θλῖψις (as in the Synoptic apocalypse in Mark

1 Wilhelm Bousset, *The Antichrist Legend: A Chapter in Christian and Jewish Folklore* (London: Hutchinson, 1896); ET of *Der Antichrist in der Überlieferung des Judentums, des neuen Testaments und der alten Kirche* (Göttingen: Vandenhoeck & Ruprecht, 1895); Ernst Lohmeyer, "Antichrist," *RAC* 1 (1950) 450–57; Rudolf Schnackenburg, *The Johannine Letters: A Commentary* (trans. Reginald and Ilse Fuller; New York: Crossroad, 1992) 135–44; Josef Ernst, "ἀντί-χριστος," *EDNT* 1 (1990) 111.

2 For the relationship to the Synoptic tradition, see below.

3 H reads κοσμοπλανής, which the *Apostolic Constitutions* improves to κοσμοπλάνος: so also Bryennios, Διδαχή, 54; Harnack, *Lehre*, 62; Knopf, *Lehre*, 39; Wengst, *Didache*, 88. *Constitutions* also has (in 7.32.4) κατακρῖναι τὸν κοσμοπλάνον διάβολον. The κοσμοπλανής in the traditional text is a hapax legomenon. Commentary is provided, e.g., by 2 John 7: ὁ πλάνος καὶ ὁ ἀντίχριστος. Cf. 2 Thess 2:3–4, 8–9; Justin *Dial.* 110 (Goodspeed, 226); *Sib. Or.* 3.68; and esp. *Apoc. Pet.* 2 (Ethiopic) (*NTApoc*, 2.626). The Antichrist as πλάνος is found in Hippolytus *De Antichr.* 6 (GCS 1.2, p. 8).

4 Cf. Rev 12:9 (of the devil): ὁ πλανῶν τὴν οἰ-κουμένην ὅλην ("the one who makes the whole world go astray").

5 Υἱὸς θεοῦ appears only here in the *Didache*. Absolute υἱός (= Jesus) occurs in the liturgical section at *Did.* 7.1, 3.

6 The devil who alters his appearance is found in *Adam and Eve* 9; 2 Cor 11:14; *T. Job* 6.4; in apocalyptic contexts in *Apoc. Elijah* 3.16–18; Hippolytus *De Antichr.* 6 (GCS 1.2, p. 8): κατὰ πάντα γὰρ ἐξο-μοιοῦσθαι βούλεται ὁ πλάνος τῷ υἱῷ τοῦ θεοῦ ("the deceiver desires to be likened in every way to the Son of God," lines 1–2).

7 Cf. 2 Thess 2:9; Rev 13:13; 19:20; Beliar: *Sib. Or.* 2.167–68; 3.66–67. The Synoptic apocalypse predicts the appearance of false christs and false prophets who lead astray by means of signs and wonders: Mark 13:22/Matt 24:24. See below.

8 Translation: Hugo Duensing in *NTApoc*, 2.626.

9 There is no parallel to this sentence in the Synoptic tradition. For the subject cf. Rev 13:7b: καὶ ἐδόθη αὐτῷ ἐξουσία ἐπὶ πᾶσαν φυλὴν καὶ λαὸν καὶ γλῶσσαν καὶ ἔθνος ("And power was given to him over every tribe and people and tongue and nation").

10 Γῆ is used in this sense, as in Luke 21:35 and elsewhere. BAGD, *s.v.*

11 For παραδιδόναι τινὰ εἰς χεῖράς τινος (a biblical expression), cf. BAGD, *s.v.* παραδίδωμι.

12 Ἀθέμιτα (the substantive occurs only here in our

13:19/Matt 24:21) is replaced in the *Didache* by ἀθέμιτα.[13] It is uncertain whether our apocalypticist refers to persecution of Christians when he writes ἀθέμιτα,[14] but the continuation suggests that this is the case.[15]

literature) is from ἀθέμιτος (properly ἀθέμιστος). BAGD, *s.v.,* refers to Xenophon *Mem.* 1.1.9 (Marchant, II): τοὺς τὰ τοιαῦτα παρὰ τῶν θεῶν πυνθανομένους ἀθέμιτα ποιεῖν ἡγεῖτο ("to put such questions to the gods seemed to his mind profane"). For the subject as in the *Didache,* cf. perhaps Justin *Dial.* 110.2 (Goodspeed, 226), where it is said of the ἄνθρωπος τῆς ἀποστασίας· ὁ καὶ εἰς τὸν ὕψιστον ἔξαλλα λαλῶν, ἐπὶ τῆς γῆς ἄνομα τολμήσῃ εἰς ἡμᾶς τοὺς χριστιανούς ("The man of rebellion: he who speaks outrages against the Most High and on earth dares iniquities against us Christians").

13 Cf. also *As. Mos.* 8.1.

14 Differently Knopf, *Lehre,* 39: "horrors, wicked deeds, the worst of which is probably the divine worship that the Antichrist demands for himself."

15 Literary dependence of this passage (16.4b–d) on Matthew cannot be proved, nor can dependence on Mark. Verse 4b has no special relationship to Matthew; if there was a special connection to the Synoptic tradition it would have to consist in a relationship to some postulated pre-Markan apocalypse. *Did.* 16.4b is, however, closer to the text of *Apoc. Pet.* 2 (Ethiopic) than to the Synoptic parallels. Verse 4c is "special material" throughout. Verse 4d reflects generally available apocalyptic material, perhaps with a particular reminiscence of Dan 12:1. There is no special connection to Matt 24:21 or Mark 13:19. Koester (*Synoptische Überlieferung,* 181–82) analyzed the section and came to a negative conclusion. In this context (p. 189) he assigns it to the material that "stems from one and the same Jewish apocalypse" that would have been available as a model for *Didache* 16 and Mark 13.

16

c. The Great Apostasy and the Preservation of the Faithful (16.5)

5   **Then human creation will pass into the testing fire and many will be scandalized and perish, but those who persevere in their belief will be saved by the curse itself.**

Comment

■ **5** A new section is once again signaled by τότε. In this case the beginning has no parallel in the language of the Synoptic tradition.[1] Upon humanity, or more precisely over the human "creation" (ἡ κτίσις τῶν ἀνθρώπων, which is a singular expression),[2] will fall[3] the time of great testing (the metaphor is ἡ πύρωσις τῆς δοκιμα-σίας).[4] The continuation (v. 5b) shows that in fact it is not the whole human creation that is in view, but only the Christians. Thus it is probably the threat of persecution that is being presented here. Not all will withstand the test: καὶ σκανδαλισθήσονται πολλοὶ καὶ ἀπολοῦνται. As in the parallel in Matt 24:10,[5] the text speaks of "the great eschatological σκανδαλισμός"[6] that is descending on humanity, that is, on the Christians. Σκανδαλίζεσθαι here means to go astray from Christian faith and fall away. The consequence is ἀπολοῦνται—in the eschatological sense of "destruction." Contrasted with the apostates are the host of

those who remain faithful, who withstand the test (v. 5c; cf. Matt 10:22b; 24:13; Mark 13:13b).[7] The promise of an eschatological remnant that will be saved is a feature of apocalyptic tradition.[8] Οἱ ὑπομείναντες ἐν τῇ πίστει αὐτῶν[9] probably does not mean "to endure in faith" but "to withstand the test by means of their faith."[10] The ὑπομείναντες will receive salvation, but this is not formulated in an absolute sense; instead it is described more precisely in an additional clause: (σωθήσονται) ὑπ᾽ αὐτοῦ τοῦ καταθέματος. This expression is a *crux interpretum*.[11]

Excursus: ΚΑΤΑΘΕΜΑ

Κατάθεμα is a word that is rather rarely attested. In Rev 22:3 it probably describes (as a synonym for ἀνάθεμα)[12] the accursed, the "object that is

---

1   Drews ("Untersuchungen," 71–72) saw a parallel to Mark 13:19 (κτίσις) and concluded to a common source.

2   But compare πᾶσα ἡ κτίσις (sc. τῶν ἀνθρώπων) in Mark 16:15; *Hermas Man.* 7.5; and Col 1:23: πᾶσα κτίσις ἡ ὑπὸ τὸν οὐρανόν.

3   For the typical ἥξει in such texts, cf. *T. Lev.* 18.6; Matt 23:36; 24:14, 50 par.; (Luke 19:43); 2 Pet 3:10; (Rev 2:25; 3:3[bis]; 18.8); *1 Clem.* 23.5(bis); *2 Clem.* 12.2. Cf. also *Did.* 16.7 (Zech 14:5).

4   For this style of expression, cf. 1 Pet 4:12. See Friedrich Lang, "πύρωσις," *TDNT* 6 (1968) 951.

5   Καὶ τότε σκανδαλισθήσονται πολλοὶ καὶ ἀλλήλους παραδώσουσιν. . . . There can scarcely be literary dependence on Matthew here. Koester (*Synoptische Überlieferung*, 183–84, 189) explains the parallelism by common dependence on a "traditional piece of Jewish apocalyptic" (p. 184) that is quoted in Matt 24:10–12 as well as in parts of the *Didache* apocalypse.

6   Otto Stählin, "σκάνδαλον," *TDNT* 7 (1971) 346.

7   Ὁ δὲ ὑπομείνας εἰς τέλος οὗτος σωθήσεται. The closeness of this text to the Synoptic parallels is quite clear, but the *Didache* has the plural οἱ ὑπομείναντες rather than the singular; instead of εἰς τέλος, *Didache* reads ἐν τῇ πίστει αὐτῶν. Finally, *Didache* does not have the simple σωθή-

σονται (in place of σωθήσεται); instead, this is more closely defined by the (awkward) addition of ὑπὸ αὐτοῦ τοῦ καταθέματος. Koester (*Synoptische Überlieferung*, 189) assigns the *Didache* text to "the same Jewish apocalypse" that, he is convinced, was also used for Mark 13.

8   Cf. the macarism of the ἐμμένων in Dan 12:12 (μακάριος ὁ ὑπομένων in Theodotion), and the motif of the eschatological remnant in *1 Enoch* 90.30; 4 Ezra 7:28; 9:7–8; 12:34; 13:24, 26; *2 Bar.* 29.4; *Sib. Or.* 5.384–85: εἰρήνην δ᾽ ἕξει λαὸς σοφός, ὅσπερ ἐλείφθη, πειραθεὶς κακότητος, ἵν᾽ ὕστερον εὐφρανθείη ("A wise people, which has been taken, will have peace; having experienced wickedness so that it might later find joy"). [Ed. See also Aaron Milavec, "The Saving Efficacy of the Burning Process in *Didache* 16.5," in Jefford, *Context*, 131–55.]

9   Remotely parallel is οἱ δὲ ὑπομένοντες ἐν πεποιθήσει in *1 Clem.* 45.8.

10   Cf. BAGD, *s.v.* ὑπομένω.

11   Bryennios (Διδαχή, 54 n. 8) originally suggested among other things the conjecture ἐπ᾽ αὐτοῦ τοῦ κάτω θέματος ("on the region below," i.e., the earth). For his later remarks, see n. 14 below.

12   Zech 14:11 is quoted (although there the word is ἀνάθεμα).

cursed."[13] Later examples are found in *Acts of Philip* 28 (Lipsius and Bonnet, 2.2, p. 15); *Ps.-Clement Contestatio* 4.3 (GCS² 1.4); T. B. Mitford, ed., *The Inscriptions of Kourion* (Philadelphia: American Philosophical Society, 1971), line 23 (on a magical tablet from Kourion, late 3d century); Ps.-Justin *Quaestiones et responsiones* 121 (Otto, 3.2³, 198).[14] Lampe, *s.v.*, refers to two other passages: *Acta conciliorum oecumenicorum, collectio sabbatica* 5.32 (Schwartz, 3.88.19): ἀνάθεμα καὶ κατάθεμα; and *Acta Maximi Confessoris* 2.31 (*PG* 90.168D): ἔστω ἀνάθεμα καὶ κατάθεμα. Cf. καταθεματίζειν in Matt 26:74.[15]

How should the *Didache* passage be explained? Of the numerous attempts at interpretation only two deserve serious consideration:[16] (1) Audet read κατάθεμα as meaning "grave, death,"[17] and conjectured ἀπό instead of the ὑπό of the manuscript tradition.[18] Thus believers will be saved "from the grave."

(2) If we retain the traditional text we are pushed toward an interpretation of κατάθεμα as Christ, who was cursed by the enemies of the faith. The meaning would then be that those who remain faithful will be saved by the very one who was cursed by the enemies. This interpretation has been suggested frequently, with greater or lesser assurance; I refer, as examples, only to Harnack,[19] Richardson,[20] Aono,[21] Rordorf and Tuilier,[22] and Wengst.[23] We cannot go into the details here.[24] The second interpretation is preferable.

---

13   Johannes Behm, "ἀνάθεμα," *TDNT* 1 (1964) 354–56. [Ed. See now Nancy Pardee, "The Curse That Saves (*Didache* 16.5)," in Jefford, *Context*, 156–76.]

14   Theodoret of Cyrus? Cf. Altaner and Stuiber, *Patrologie*, 340. This text attempts to distinguish between κατάθεμα and ἀνάθεμα: κατάθεμα δέ ἐστι τὸ συνθέσθαι τοῖς ἀναθεματίζουσιν. Bryennios, who had the honor of being the first to refer to this passage, later cited it (in a letter to Harnack; cf. idem, *Lehre*, 63) as a possible interpretation of the *Didache* passage, among others. See the justified reservations about Ps.-Justin's distinction in Johannes Behm, "ἀναθεματίζω," *TDNT* 1 (1964) 355–56 n. 2.

15   There are later examples of καταθεματίζειν in Behm, "ἀναθεματίζω," *TDNT* 1 (1964) 355–56 n. 2.

16   Cf. Rordorf and Tuilier, *Doctrine*, 197–98 n. 6.

There is a long list of interpretations (as produced even in the early days of research) in Schaff, *Church Manual*, 215–16.

17   Audet, *Didachè*, 472–73.

18   Audet, *Didachè*, 242.

19   Harnack, *Lehre*, 62–63.

20   Richardson, "Teaching," 179 n. 78.

21   Aono, *Entwicklung*, 172.

22   Rordorf and Tuilier, *Doctrine*, 197–98 n. 6.

23   Wengst, *Didache*, 99 n. 137.

24   In this context reference has rightly been made to Justin *Dial.* 47.4 (Goodspeed, 145–46) on the one hand, and to Pliny *Ep.* 10.96.5 (Mynors, 338) and *Mart. Pol.* 9.3 on the other.

16   **d. The Revelation of the Three Signs of Truth (16.6–7)**

6   **And then the signs of truth will appear: first, the sign of extension in heaven; next, the signal of the trumpet call; and third, resurrection of the dead—**

7   **not of all, however, but, as it has been said, "The Lord will come and all the holy ones with him."**

■ **6** Καὶ τότε φανήσεται ("then will appear")[1] indicates the beginning of the next eschatological section. There will appear τὰ σημεῖα τῆς ἀληθείας ("the signs of truth")—in fact, three of them, as appears from what follows.[2] For the formulation in v. 6a cf. Matt 24:30a.[3] Σημεῖα τῆς ἀληθείας (for σημεῖα ἀληθινά)[4] apparently designates the following apocalyptic "signs" in contrast to the demonic signs and wonders of the *kosmoplanes* in v. 4b.[5]

The *first* sign is an ἐκπέτασις ἐν οὐρανῷ. What does the expression mean? The noun ἐκπέτασις signifies expansion, spread, extension.[6] (1) Some scholars consider this to refer to the opening of the heavens[7] as precondition for the following descent of the *Kyrios* and his holy ones.[8] (2) A reference to the cross is, however, more

probable.[9] Stommel[10] and Butler[11] recall especially the *signum extensionis ligni* ("sign of the extension of the wood") in the Latin *Didascalia* (49.8; *TU* 75.80).[12] Analogously one should add ξύλου after σημεῖον ἐκπετάσεως.[13] The sign referred to would thus be as follows: the cross of the *Kyrios* appears in the heavens as precursor of his parousia.[14] This cross (as we perhaps must suppose) was previously taken up with him into heaven;[15] now the cross reappears and announces his

---

1   Cf. v. 4b.

2   For signs that are three in number cf. the σήματα τρισσά in *Sib. Or.* 2.188–95.

3   Καὶ τότε φανήσεται τὸ σημεῖον τοῦ υἱοῦ τοῦ ἀνθρώπου ἐν οὐρανῷ ("And then the sign of the Son of man will appear in heaven"). The differences should also be noted, however: Matthew knows only *one* sign, and it is the sign of the "Son of man"—a title that is completely lacking in the *Didache*. If one supposes dependence on Matthew, *Didache* must have interpreted the Matthew passage ("sign of the Son of man"). But literary dependence is quite uncertain. Koester, *Synoptische Überlieferung*, 189: v. 6 stems from generally available apocalyptic material; Kloppenborg ("Matthaean Tradition," 66) regards "a reference to a sign appearing in heaven prior to the Parousia" as part of the apocalyptic tradition available to the *Didache* and Matthew.

4   This is an example of a "Hebrew genitive"; see Alfred Stuiber, "Drei σημεῖα," *JAC* 24 (1981) 43.

5   Karl Rengstorf, "σημεῖον κτλ.," *TDNT* 7 (1971) 261; Stuiber, "Drei σημεῖα," 43–44. Differently Harnack, *Lehre*, 63: "in contrast to the κατάθεμα, v. 5." So also Knopf, *Lehre*, 39. This is improbable.

6   The dictionaries refer to Plutarch *Moralia* 564C (de Lacy and Einarson, 7.276), in contrast to συστολή. Lampe lists only the present passage.

7   Cf. Rev 6:14.

8   Harnack, *Lehre*, 64; Drews, "Apostellehre," 283; Audet, *Didachè*, 473; Giet, *L'Énigme*, 254 n. 41. Rengstorf ("σημεῖον," 261) objects: "But if so ἐν οὐρανῷ would not fit very well." Likewise Butler, "Relations," 276. This is not compelling. But certainly ἐκπέτασις τοῦ οὐρανοῦ would be clearer.

9   Suggested by Schaff, *Church Manual*, 217; Koester, *Synoptische Überlieferung*, 190; cf. Kraft, *Didache*, 176. This was also proposed by Aono, *Entwicklung*, 173.

10   "Σημεῖον ἐκπετάσεως," 25–26. Rordorf and Tuilier (*Doctrine*, 198–99 n. 1) express cautious agreement.

11   "Relations," 279–80.

12   Cf. above, Introduction, §2c. In my opinion this is a content parallel, but scarcely an indication of literary dependence.

13   Stommel, "Σημεῖον," 26.

14   Thus this is not a reference to the appearance of the crucified one hanging on the cross (as suggested by Knopf, *Lehre*, 40; Knopf, however, also proposed the interpretation given above as [1]: cf. Johnson, "Motive," 119; Richardson, "Teaching," 179 n. 80 [possibly]), but simply the epiphany of the cross, because the appearance of the *Kyrios* is first spoken of in 16.8. See Stommel, "Σημεῖον," 29–30.

15   *Gos. Pet.* 10.39 (SC 201.58) attests the idea of the ascension of the cross.

(the *Kyrios*'s) immediate appearance.[16] There are parallels for this in later apocalyptic literature.[17] Cf. *Apoc. Pet.* 1 (Ethiopic): "so shall I *come on the clouds of heaven with a great host in my glory*; with my cross going before my face will I come in my glory."[18] Similarly, in *Ep. apost.* 16 (27) (Coptic): "with the wings of the clouds carrying me in splendour and the sign of the cross before me, will I come down to the earth."[19] In *Apoc. Elijah* 32.4–5 (the Messiah comes) "while the sign of the cross goes before him [and] the whole world will see it."[20] (3) A third interpretation has most recently been presented by Stuiber.[21] He proceeds on the assumption that the "sign of the Son of man" in Matt 24:30 refers to the standards of the Son of man in the heavens.[22] The πρῶτον σημεῖον ἐκπετάσεως ἐν οὐρανῷ in *Did.* 16.6 is to be understood analogously: Ἐκπετάσεως is "genitive of quality" or a "Hebrew genitive"; the expression stands for σημεῖον ἐκπετασθὲν ἐν οὐρανῷ and means "the banners spread out in the heavens";[23] these are probably to be thought

of concretely as cloth banners.[24] This is a possible interpretation but it is by no means fully persuasive. In light of the broad basis for the tradition of the *crux eschatologica* (see above), I prefer interpretation (2).

The *second* sign is the σημεῖον φωνῆς σάλπιγγος ("signal of the trumpet call," v. 6b), again an element of apocalyptic tradition.[25] This is "the eschatological signal which sounds forth at the end of the age."[26]

The sound of the trumpet is followed by the resurrection of the dead; in the *Didache* apocalypse this is the *third* of the "signs of truth." At the same time, the Didachist (in my opinion)[27] adds a defining commentary to the key phrase ἀνάστασις νεκρῶν: the ἀνάστασις νεκρῶν is not (yet) the general resurrection of the dead, but (first of all) the resurrection of the "saints."[28]

■ **7** The Didachist's specifying οὐ πάντων δέ ("not of all") is supported by an Old Testament quotation introduced by ἀλλ᾽ ὡς ἐρρέθη. What follows is the second explicit quotation from the Old Testament in the

---

16 What is meant by the "sign of the Son of man" in

16 What is meant by the "sign of the Son of man" in Matt 24:30? Stommel, "Σημεῖον," 27–42; and A. J. B. Higgins, "The Sign of the Son of Man (Matt. XXIV.30)," *NTS* 9 (1962/63) 380–82: this means the cross; the *Didache* is dependent on the passage in Matthew and interprets it. Similarly Butler, "Relations," 277–80: the *Didache* is dependent on Matt 24:30–31, more precisely on what Butler calls "the M(g) stream of synoptic tradition," 277; the *Didache* interprets the Matthean tradition, although Butler does not say expressly whether its interpretation is correct. For the church fathers' interpretation of the Matthean sign in terms of the cross, cf. Stommel, "Σημεῖον," 30 n. 42. But in my opinion it remains highly questionable whether the "sign of the Son of man" really means the cross. Cf. Rengstorf, "σημεῖον," 236: the formulation is not absolutely clear. "From the context one may gather only that it [sc. the sign] is something which is clearly terrifying" (235). For Glasson and Schweizer see below.

17 Entirely different is the extension of the hands (symbolizing the horizontal beam of the cross) in the gnostic *Od. Sol.* 27.1–3; cf. 42.1–2.

18 Translation by C. Detlef G. Müller in *NTApoc*, 2.625–26 (partly italics in original).

19 Similarly Ethiopic (but lacking, e.g., the key word "sign"); translation by C. Detlef G. Müller in *NTApoc*, 1.258.

20 From the translation by Wolfgang Schrage, *Die Elia Apokalypse* (JSHRZ 5.3; Gütersloh: Mohn, 1980) 251. Cf. also Ὦ ξύλον ὦ μακαριστόν, ἐφ᾽ οὗ θεὸς ἐξε-

τανύσθη, οὐχ ἕξει σε χθών, ἀλλ᾽ οὐρανὸν οἶκον ἐσόψει ("O most blessed wood, on which God was stretched out, earth will not hold you, but you will see a heavenly home," *Sib. Or.* 6.26–27); τὸ γὰρ σημεῖον τοῦ σταυροῦ ἀπὸ ἀνατολῶν ἕως δυσμῶν ἀνατελεῖ ὑπὲρ τὴν λαμπρότητα τοῦ ἡλίου καὶ μηνύσει τοῦ κριτοῦ τὴν ἔλευσιν ("The sign of the cross will rise from east to west, brighter than the sun, and it will portend the coming of the judge," Ps.-Hippolytus *De consumatione mundi* 36 [GCS 1.2, pp. 303–4]); further references in Wolfgang Schrage, *Die Elia Apokalypse* (JSHRZ 5.3; Gütersloh: Mohn, 1980) 251 n. d; Stommel, "Σημεῖον," 30–31 n. 42. On the art-historical aspects, see Josef Engemann, "Auf die Parusie Christi hinweisende Darstellungen in der frühchristlichen Kunst," JAC 19 (1976) 142–45.

21 "Drei σημεῖα," 42–44.

22 Following T. F. Glasson, "The Ensign of the Son of Man (Matt. XXIV.30)," *JTS*, n.s. 15 (1964) 299–300; cf. also Eduard Schweizer, *Das Evangelium nach Matthäus* (3d ed.; NTD 2; Göttingen: Vandenhoeck & Ruprecht, 1981) 298 (ET: *The Good News According to Matthew* [Atlanta: John Knox, 1975] 456): "the standard of the Messiah."

23 "Drei σημεῖα," 43.

24 "Drei σημεῖα," 43–44.

25 OT background: Isa 27:13; Joel 2:1; Zeph 1:16. In apocalyptic literature: 4 Ezra 6:23; *Sib. Or.* 8.239. In the NT: Matt 24:31; 1 Thess 4:16; 1 Cor 15:52. It occurs frequently in Revelation 8–11.

26 Gerhard Friedrich, "σάλπιγξ," *TDNT* 7 (1967) 87.

Didache,[29] this time from Zech 14:5: καὶ ἥξει κύριος ὁ θεός μου καὶ πάντες οἱ ἅγιοι μετ᾽ αὐτοῦ ("Then the Lord my God will come and all the holy ones with him"). The quoted version follows the LXX, with a slight change at the beginning (ἥξει ὁ κύριος instead of ἥξει κύριος ὁ θεός μου).[30] The same quotation is also found in Matt 15:31a, but the *Didache* passage does not come from Matthew; it is taken directly from Zechariah.[31] Πάντες οἱ ἅγιοι ("all the holy ones") in the text of Zechariah are probably the ἄγγελοι (as Matt 25:31a correctly interprets it). The *Didache* interprets the ἅγιοι instead as the dead Christians who are now reawakened to life.[32]

It is unnecessary to posit dependence on the Pauline passages; likewise, the relationships to Matt 24:31 are not literary. Basic to all these passages is the same widespread motif from Jewish-Christian apocalyptic. Cf. Koester, *Synoptische Überlieferung*, 189; Kloppenborg, "Matthaean Tradition," 66.

27 Verse 7 is a gloss by the Didachist. Verse 8 follows well after v. 6. Cf. also the similar citation formulae in 1.6 and 14.3.

28 Knopf (*Lehre*, 40) suggests that this could mean the resurrection for the thousand-year reign of God.

29 See above at *Did.* 14.3 (Mal 1:11, 14).

30 Wengst, *Didache*, 31: *Kyrios* (as the context shows) refers to Jesus.

31 In fact the Matthean text is farther from the text of Zechariah than is the *Didache*. See Koester, *Synoptische Überlieferung*, 187. Kloppenborg ("Matthaean Tradition," 59) also notes that *Did.* 16.7 is not dependent on Matt 25:31, but is closer to the LXX text than is Matthew. Kloppenborg ("Matthaean Tradition," 66), however, assigns the quotation from Zechariah in both cases to a common apocalyptic tradition in which Matthew and the *Didache* participate. This last is scarcely an accurate observation.

32 Harnack, *Lehre*, 64. Ἅγιοι = the Christians as early as *Did.* 4.2 (in the Didachist's interpretation). The case is different at 10.6.

e. The Arrival of the *Kyrios* (16.8)

8   **Then the world will see the Lord coming upon the clouds of heaven . . .**

■ **8** So follows (τότε) the epiphany of the *Kyrios* (= Jesus) before the entire world: ὄψεται ὁ κόσμος τὸν κύριον ἐρχόμενον ἐπάνω τῶν νεφελῶν τοῦ οὐρανοῦ ("The world will see the Lord coming upon the clouds of heaven"). The description recalls the Synoptic apocalypse in Mark 13:26/Matt 24:30b/Luke 21:27.[1] The foundational passage is Dan 7:13 LXX: καὶ ἰδοὺ ἐπὶ τῶν νεφελῶν τοῦ οὐρανοῦ ὡς υἱὸς ἀνθρώπου ἤρχετο. Cf. Theodotion: καὶ ἰδοὺ μετὰ τῶν νεφελῶν τοῦ οὐρανοῦ ὡς υἱὸς ἀνθρώπου ἐρχόμενος. The text of the *Didache*, in the sequence of its elements,[2] is closer to Mark 13:26 par. than to the text in Daniel. Again striking is the replacement of the title "Son of man" by *Kyrios*. The text is especially close to Matt 24:30b: ἐρχόμενον ἐπί or ἐπάνω τῶν νεφελῶν (in contrast to ἐν νεφέλαις in Mark 13:26 and ἐν νεφέλῃ in Luke 21:27), and τοῦ οὐρανοῦ (Matthew and *Didache* against the omission in Mark and Luke).[3] This would speak more for a dependence on Matthew rather than Mark or a source that sometimes approximates Mark 13—if there is any dependence at all. Literary dependence on Matthew, however, cannot be demonstrated with assurance even in this passage. The *Didache* quotes common apocalyptic material (from Daniel), and agrees with Matthew (against Mark) precisely at those points where both agree with Daniel.[4]

thus signaled his conviction that the conclusion of the *Didache* was missing,[5] which also means that the conclusion of the *Didache* apocalypse has been lost. I have already said that the structure of the whole document speaks in favor of this conclusion. The reader expects a depiction of the judgment of the world, and such a description must originally have concluded the text of the *Didache*.

The *Apostolic Constitutions* and the Georgian version (each in its own way) provide confirmation for this supposition. *Const.* 7.32 concludes: (4) (ἐπάνω τῶν νεφελῶν) μετ᾽ ἀγγέλων δυνάμεως αὐτοῦ ἐπὶ θρόνου βασιλείας, κατακρῖναι τὸν κοσμοπλάνον διάβολον καὶ ἀποδοῦναι ἑκάστῳ κατὰ τὴν πρᾶξιν αὐτοῦ. (5) Τότε ἀπελεύσονται οἱ μὲν πονηροὶ εἰς αἰώνιον κόλασιν, οἱ δὲ δίκαιοι πορεύσονται εἰς ζωὴν αἰώνιον, κληρονομοῦντες ἐκεῖνα, ἃ ὀφθαλμὸς οὐκ εἶδεν καὶ οὖς οὐκ ἤκουσεν καὶ ἐπὶ καρδίαν ἀνθρώπου οὐκ ἀνέβη, ἃ ἡτοίμασεν ὁ θεὸς τοῖς ἀγαπῶσιν αὐτόν, καὶ χαρήσονται ἐν τῇ βασιλείᾳ τοῦ θεοῦ τῇ ἐν Χριστῷ Ἰησοῦ ("above the clouds with his powerful angels on the royal throne, to judge the devil who leads the world astray and to requite to each according to their actions. Then the wicked will proceed to eternal punishment, but the just will proceed to eternal life, inheriting those things that eye has not seen nor has ear heard nor have they entered into the human heart, things that God has prepared for those who love him, and they will rejoice in the kingdom of God which is in Christ Jesus"). This text

Excursus: The Lost Conclusion

The words ἐπάνω τῶν νεφελῶν τοῦ οὐρανοῦ complete the text in H. The scribe placed a period after τοῦ οὐρανοῦ, leaving the rest of the line blank, and the rest of the page as well. Apparently the copyist

---

1   The same motif is also in 4 Ezra 13:3; Rev 1:7. The quotation from Justin *1 Apol.* 51.9 (Goodspeed, 62) may, as usual, be a free recollection of the Gospels. Kloppenborg ("Matthaean Tradition," 63) differs. Justin *Dial.* 14.8 (Goodspeed, 107) probably rests on Dan 7:13.

2   Subject – ἐρχόμενος – νεφέλαι. Contrast Daniel: νεφέλαι – subject – ἤρχετο (i.e., ἐρχόμενος). See Koester, *Synoptische Überlieferung*, 187.

3   But cf. Mark 14:62b: μετὰ τῶν νεφελῶν τοῦ οὐρανοῦ.

4   *Did.* 16.8: ἐπάνω τῶν νεφελῶν τοῦ οὐρανοῦ; Matt 24:30b: ἐπὶ τῶν νεφελῶν τοῦ οὐρανοῦ; Dan 7:13

LXX: ἐπὶ τῶν νεφελῶν τοῦ οὐρανοῦ; Dan 7:13 Theodotion: μετὰ τῶν νεφελῶν τοῦ οὐρανοῦ against Mark 13:26: ἐν νεφέλαις (Luke 21:27: ἐν νεφέλῃ). According to Koester (*Synoptische Überlieferung*, 188–89) v. 8 stems from the apocalyptic source that was also used for Mark 13. According to Kloppenborg ("Matthaean Tradition," 66), "an adaptation of Dan 7:13 (using either ἐπί or ἐπάνω τῶν νεφελῶν)" was part of the common tradition of the *Didache* apocalypse and Matthew.

5   Cf. Audet, *Didachè*, 73–74; and above, Introduction, §3a; Niederwimmer, "Textprobleme," 127–29.

is (if at all) a very loose reproduction of the *Didache*. The epilogue of the *Apostolic Constitutions* is extremely wordy in contrast to the brisk presentation in the apocalypse of the *Didache*. The Georgian concludes: "(coming with the clouds) with power and great glory, in order to repay every human being according to his [or her] works in his holy righteousness, before the whole human race and before the angels. Amen."[6] The *Didache might* have concluded in some similar fashion. In any case it appears that there was a Greek source for the Georgian and that it was still complete. I shall not be bold enough to attempt to reconstitute the lost conclusion of the *Didache* by conjecture.[7]

---

6   Peradse, "Lehre," 116.
7   Wengst (*Didache* 90) reconstructed: . . . ἀποδοῦναι ἑκάστῳ κατὰ τὴν πρᾶξιν αὐτοῦ.

It is not easy to locate the *Didache* within the whole sweep of the history of early Christianity. Still, one can form a more or less complete picture of this document, and from that alone it is possible to give a rather accurate estimate of the place occupied by the *Didache*.

The author of our document is an unknown but apparently influential Christian author who writes a kind of "rule book" for the communities within his area of influence some time around the turn of the century, or perhaps we could more accurately say at the beginning of the second century. The author's desire is that the communities he addresses should govern their life, worship, and church order according to this book. It seems probable that we should think of communities in Syria or in the border regions between Syria and Palestine. (Antioch seems to be eliminated by the canonical situation presumed in the *Didache*.) The didachistic communities are still strongly influenced by Jewish Christianity, but they are already clearly distinct from the synagogue. The relationship between "church" and "Israel" is not a theme of the book, but the manner in which Scripture is occasionally interpreted in the redactional parts of the document shows the direction in which that relationship is tending. The canonical situation of our author's communities is somewhat retrograde in comparison to other Christian communities of the same period. (The monepiscopate has not yet been established.) The institution of itinerant charismatics is still familiar to the communities of the *Didache*, but the apostolate is already a thing of the past, and the itinerant prophets are in the process of settling down in the communities. The author (apparently an authority) intervenes in the canonical situation to establish order, but in a very conservative and irenic spirit. He seeks an accommodation between the itinerant charismatics and the "local clergy." The author takes a similarly conservative stance in other questions of order such as those concerning baptism and the Eucharist. His characteristic manner of procedure is the same throughout: he quotes existing, sometimes archaic rules and seeks both to preserve what has been inherited and at the same time to accommodate that heritage to his own time.

The author, as I have said, is an authority for his communities. It is, however, striking that he himself never claims apostolic, episcopal, or charismatic authority. Still, we will scarcely go wrong in imagining that he himself is a respected and influential bishop. His own personality is placed in the background. His book tells us little or nothing of his "theology," if he had one at all. It is written without any theoretical claims and is entirely focused on the praxis and order of community life. Individual theological motifs are evident, but only in passing and without systematic reflection. A reconstruction of the "theology of the *Didache*" would therefore be a foolish enterprise. All we can say is that attention should be paid to the author's fundamentally conservative stance. It is no accident that over long stretches he presents not his own material but texts from his tradition (whether from written or oral sources). What he says rests on tradition. What he adds from his own pen (only hesitantly at the beginning—it is not until chap. 12 and afterward that he emerges as an independent author) reveals him as the protector, preserver, and interpreter of his traditions. This circumstance shapes the literary form of his work.

This situation in turn explains another phenomenon, namely, the constant recourse to the Old Testament γραφή, or to the "gospel" of the *Kyrios*. These references, as we have seen, are restricted to the didachistic level—that is, to the work of the author. Unfortunately we cannot determine with absolute certainty what, precisely, is to be understood by "the gospel," whether this is oral tradition or already something written. Still, it is clear that "the gospel" to which the author refers is entirely within the so-called Synoptic tradition, more precisely the sayings tradition. Equally obvious is the value and function assigned to "the gospel" within the *Didache*. For the Didachist the gospel is the decisive norm, the rule, the measuring rod of behavior, the sum total of the teachings the church has received from its *Kyrios*. The gospel, we might say, is for him the "eschatological law" (in Pauline terms the "law of faith," or the "law of the Spirit"). It is characteristic that he inserts quotations from the Jesus tradition in an attempt to elevate the teachings of the introductory Two Ways tractate (stemming from an originally Jewish source) to the level of Jesus' eschatological preaching. The eschatological character of the gospel is clearly evident to the Didachist. He is thus equally aware of the conflicts that may be associated with Jesus' eschatological demands.

This book has had an interesting history. On the one hand its heritage was adopted by the later church orders for which the *Didache* furnished the model, so to speak. On the other hand certain tendencies in this rule book led to later monastic writings; this was another occurrence that, in retrospect, bestowed on this work a special place of honor in the whole line of development. A correct understanding of the *Didache* demands that we not view it entirely in the light of later, similar documents. It must be read with a view to distinguishing the ancestral pieces of tradition, some of them very ancient, from the interventions and additions of the Didachist. Here such a differentiation (where possible, still more than has otherwise been done) is of fundamental importance for understanding the work as a whole.

Bibliography
Indices

See also Kenneth J. Harder and Clayton N. Jefford, "A Bibliography of Literature on the *Didache*," in Jefford, *Context*, 368–82.

1. Editions and Commentaries

Audet, Jean-Paul
La Didachè: Instructions des apôtres (EtB; Paris: Gabalda, 1958).

Bigg, Charles, and Arthur J. MacLean
The Doctrine of the Twelve Apostles (Translations of Christian Literature Series 1, Greek texts; London, New York, and Toronto: SPCK, 1922).

Bihlmeyer, Karl
Die apostolischen Väter: Neubearbeitung der Funkschen Ausgabe, unveränderter Nachdruck der mit einem Nachtrag von W. Schneemelcher versehenen 2. Auflage, vol. 1: *Didache, Barnabas, Klemens I und II, Ignatius, Polycarp, Papias, Quadratus, Diognetbrief* (3d ed.; Sammlung ausgewählter kirchen- und dogmengeschichtlicher Quellenschriften, 2d ser., vol. 1; Tübingen: Mohr, 1970).

Bosio, Guido
I Padri apostolici, vol. 1: *Dottrina degli Apostoli – San Clemente Romano – Lettera di Barnaba: Introduzione – Traduzione – Note* (CPS.G 7; Turin: Società Editrici Internazionale, 1940; 2d ed. 1958).

Bryennios, Philotheos
Διδαχὴ τῶν δώδεκα ἀποστόλων ἐκ τοῦ ἱεροσολυμιτικοῦ χειρογράφου νῦν πρῶτον ἐκδιδομένη μετὰ προλεγομένων καὶ σημειώσεων ἐν οἷς καὶ τῆς Συνόψεως τῆς Π. Δ., τῆς ὑπὸ Ἰωάνν. τοῦ Χρυσοστόμου, σύγκρισις καὶ μέρος ἀνέκδοτον ἀπὸ τοῦ αὐτοῦ χειρογράφου (Constantinople: Voutyra, 1883); ET (of the text only): *Teaching of the Twelve Apostles. Recently Discovered and Published by Philotheos Bryennios, Metropolitan of Nicomedia* (ed. and trans. Roswell D. Hitchcock and Francis Brown; New York: Scribner, 1884).

Drews, Paul
"Apostellehre (Didache)," in Edgar Hennecke, ed., *Handbuch zu den neutestamentlichen Apokryphen* (Tübingen: Mohr, 1904) 25–83.

Funk, Francis Xaver
Doctrina duodecim apostolorum: Canones Apostolorum ecclesiastici ac reliquiae doctrinae de duabus viis. Expositiones veteres (Tübingen: Laupp, 1887).

Idem
Patres apostolici (2d ed.; 2 vols.; Tübingen: Laupp, 1901).

Funk, Franz Xaver, and Franz Diekamp
Patres apostolici, vol. 2 (3d ed.; Tübingen: Laupp, 1913).

Giet, Stanislas
L'Énigme de la Didachè (PFLUS 149; Paris: Ophrys, 1970).

Grenfell, Bernard P., and Arthur S. Hunt
The Oxyrhynchus Papyri, vol. 15 (London: Egypt Exploration Fund, 1922) no. 1782.

Harnack, Adolf von
Die Apostellehre und die jüdischen beiden Wege (2d ed.; Leipzig: Hinrichs, 1896).

Idem
"Die Bezeichnung Jesu als 'Knecht Gottes' und ihre Geschichte in der alten Kirche," SPAW.PH (1926) 212–38.

Idem
Lehre der zwölf Apostel nebst Untersuchungen zur ältesten Geschichte der Kirchenverfassung und des Kirchenrechts (TU 2.1, 2; Leipzig: Hinrichs, 1884; repr. Berlin: Akademie-Verlag, 1991).

Harris, James Rendel
The Teaching of the Apostles (Διδαχὴ τῶν ἀποστόλων) (London: Clay; Baltimore: Johns Hopkins University Press, 1887).

Hemmer, Hippolyte M., Gabriel Oger, and A. Laurent
Doctrine des apôtres: Épitre de Barnabé (Textes et documents 5, Les Pères apostoliques 1–2; Paris: Picard, 1907, 2d ed. 1926).

Horner, George W.
"A New Papyrus Fragment of the *Didaché* in Coptic," *JTS* 25 (1924) 225–31.

Idem
The Statutes of the Apostles or Canones ecclesiastici: Edited with Translation and Collation from Ethiopic and Arabic MSS; also a Translation of the Saidic and Collation of the Bohairic Versions; and Saidic Fragments (London: Williams & Norgate, 1904).

Jacquier, Eugène
Διδαχὴ τῶν δώδεκα ἀποστόλων: *La Doctrine des douze Apôtres et ses Enseignements* (Lyons: Vitte; Paris: Lethielleux, 1891).

Klauser, Theodor
Doctrina duodecim apostolorum, Barnabae epistula (Flor Patr 1; Bonn: Hanstein, 1940).

Kleist, James A.
The Didache, The Epistle of Barnabas, The Epistles and the Martyrdom of St. Polycarp, the Fragments of Papias, The Epistle to Diognetus (ACW 6; Westminster, Md.: Newman, 1948).

Knopf, Rudolf
Die Lehre der zwölf Apostel: Die zwei Clemensbriefe (HNT.E; Die apostolischen Väter 1; Tübingen: Mohr [Siebeck], 1920).

Kraft, Robert A.
Barnabas and the Didache (The Apostolic Fathers, A New Translation and Commentary 3; New York: Nelson, 1965).

Lawson, John
  A Theological and Historical Introduction to the Apostolic Fathers (New York: Macmillan, 1961).
Lefort, L. Theophile
  Athanasius. Lettres festales et pastorales en Copte (2 vols.; CSCO 150–151; Louvain: Durbecq, 1955).
Idem
  Les Pères apostoliques en Copte (2 vols.; CSCO 135–136; Scriptores Coptici 17–18; Louvain: Durbecq, 1952).
Lietzmann, Hans
  Die Didache (Kleine Texte für Vorlesungen und Übungen 6; Bonn: Marcus and Weber, 1903).
Lilje, Hanns
  Die Lehre der zwölf Apostel: Eine Kirchenordnung des ersten christlichen Jahrhunderts (Hamburg: Furche, 1956).
Mattioli, Umberto
  La Didache dottrina dei dodici apostoli: Introduzione, traduzione e note (Rome: Edizione Paoline, 1969; 3d ed., 1980).
Niederwimmer, Kurt
  "Der Didachist und seine Quellen," in Jefford, *Context*, 15–36.
Peradse, G.
  "Die 'Lehre der zwölf Apostel' in der georgischen Überlieferung," *ZNW* 31 (1932) 111–16.
Quacquarelli, Antonio
  I Padri Apostolici (CTP 5; 4th ed.; Rome: Città Nuova Editrice, 1981).
Richardson, Cyril Charles
  "The Teaching of the Twelve Apostles, Commonly Called the Didache," in idem, *The Early Christian Fathers* (LCC 1; Philadelphia: Westminster, 1953; repr. New York: Macmillan, 1970) 161–79.
Rordorf, Willy, and André Tuilier
  La Doctrine des douze apôtres (Didachè): Introduction, Texte, Traduction, Notes, Appendice et Index (SC 248; Paris: Cerf, 1978).
Sabatier, Paul
  Διδαχὴ τῶν ιβ′ ἀποστόλων: *La Didaché ou l'Enseignement des douze Apôtres* (2d ed.; Paris: Fischbacher, 1885).
Schaff, Philip
  The Oldest Church Manual, Called the Teaching of the Twelve Apostles (2d ed.; New York: Funk & Wagnalls, 1886).
Schmidt, Carl
  "Das koptische Didache-Fragment des British Museum," *ZNW* 24 (1925) 81–99.
Taylor, Charles
  The Teaching of the Twelve Apostles with Illustrations from the Talmud (Cambridge and London: Deighton Bell, 1886).
Wengst, Klaus
  Didache (Apostellehre), Barnabasbrief, Zweiter Klemensbrief, Schrift an Diognet: Eingeleitet, herausgegeben, übertragen und erläutert (SUC 2; Munich: Kösel, 1984).

Wünsche, August
  Lehre der zwölf Apostel nach der Ausgabe des Metropoliten Philotheos Bryennios mit Beifügung des Urtextes, nebst Einleitung und Noten ins Deutsche übertragen (Leipzig: Schulze, 1884).

2. Editions of Writings Related to the *Didache*

(*Epistle of Barnabas, Doctrina apostolorum, Canons of the Apostles, Epitome, Apostolic Constitutions, Syntagma, Fides patrum, Life of Shenoute, Sentences* of Isaac of Syria, *Fragmenta Anastasiana*)

Amélineau, Émile
  Mémoires publiés par les membres de la Mission archéologique française au Caire, 1885–1886, vol. 4: *Monuments pour servir à l'histoire de l'Égypte chrétienne aux IVe, V^e, VIe et VIIe siècles* (Paris: Leroux, 1888), chap. 6: "Vie de Schnoudi," 289–478 (Arabic and French).
(Pseudo-)Athanasius
  Syntagma Doctrinae. PG 28, 836–45.
Bartlet, James Vernon
  "Fragments of the Didascalia Apostolorum in Greek," *JTS* 18 (1917) 301–9.
Batiffol, Pierre
  "Canones Nicaeni pseudepigraphi," *Revue archéologique* 3d ser. 6 (1885) 133–41.
Idem
  "Le Syntagma Doctrinae dit de Saint Athanase," in Pierre Batiffol, ed., *Studia Patristica* (Études d'ancienne littérature chrétienne; 2 vols.; Paris: Leroux, 1890) 2.119–60.
Benigni, H.
  "Didachê coptica: 'Duarum viarum' recensio coptica monastica, Shenudii homiliis attributa, per arabicam versionem superstes," *Bessarione* 3 (1898) 311–29.
Besson, M.
  "Un recueil des sentences attribué à Isaac le Syrien," *OrChr* 1 (1901) 46–60, 288–98.
Fides CCCXVIII patrum (PG 28, 1637–44).
"Fragmenta Anastasiana," in Funk, *Didascalia*, 2.52–71.
Funk, Franz Xaver, ed.
  Didascalia et Constitutiones apostolorum (2 vols.; Paderborn: Schöningh, 1905–6; repr. Turin: Bottega d'Erasmo, 1962).
Iselin, Ludwig E.
  Eine bisher unbekannte Version des ersten Teiles der "Apostellehre," gefunden und besprochen von L. E. Iselin, übersetzt von A. Heusler (TU 13.1b; Leipzig: Hinrichs, 1895).
Revillout, Eugene
  Le concile de Nicée d'après les textes coptes et les diverses collections canoniques (2 vols.; Paris: Maisonneuve, 1881–98).

Roberts, Colin H., and Bernard Capelle, eds.
  An Early Euchologium: The Dêr-Balizeh Papyrus Enlarged and Reedited (Bibliothèque du Muséon 23; Louvain: Bureau du Muséon, 1949).

Schermann, Theodor
  Die allgemeine Kirchenordnung, frühchristliche Liturgien und kirchliche Überlieferung, vol. 1: *Die allgemeine Kirchenordnung des zweiten Jahrhunderts* (SGKA Sup 3.1; Paderborn: Schöningh, 1914; repr. New York: Johnson, 1968).

Idem
  Eine Elfapostelmoral oder die X-Rezension der "beiden Wege" (VKHSM 2.2; Munich: Lentner, 1903).

Schlecht, Joseph
  Doctrina XII Apostolorum: Die Apostellehre in der Liturgie der katholischen Kirche (Freiburg im Breisgau: Herder, 1901).

3. Jewish Literature

Beer, Georg, Oscar Holtzmann, Samuel Krauss, et al., eds.
  Die Mischna: Text, Übersetzung und ausführliche Erklärung (Giessen: Töpelmann, 1912; Berlin and New York: de Gruyter, 1970–).

Bietenhard, Hans, ed. and trans.
  Der tannaitische Midrasch Sifre Deuteronomium (Judaica et Christiana 3; Bern: Peter Lang, 1984).

Bonwetsch, Gottlieb Nathanael, ed.
  Die Bücher der Geheimnisse Henochs: Das sogenannte slavische Henochbuch (TU 44.2; Leipzig: Hinrichs, 1922).

Charlesworth, James H., ed.
  The Old Testament Pseudepigrapha (2 vols.; Garden City, N.Y.: Doubleday, 1983–85).

Cohn, Leopold, and Wendland, Paul, eds.
  Philo, *Opera* (7 vols.; Berlin: G. Reimer, 1896–1930).

Danby, Herbert
  The Mishnah (Oxford: Clarendon, 1933).

Diehl, Ernst, and Douglas Young, eds.
  "Pseudo-Phocylides," in *Theognis, Ps.-Pythagoras, Ps.-Phocylides, Chares, Anonymi Aulodia, Fragmentum Teliambicum* (2d ed.; Leipzig: Teubner, 1971) 95–112.

Freedman, Harry, and Maurice Simon, eds.
  Midrash Rabbah: Translated into English with Notes, Glossary and Indices (10 vols.; London: Soncino, 1939, repr. 1969).

Geffcken, Johannes, ed.
  Die Oracula Sibyllina (GCS 8; Leipzig: Hinrichs, 1902).

Goldschmidt, Lazarus, ed.
  Der babylonische Talmud (12 vols.; Berlin: Jüdischer Verlag, 1930–36).

Holtzmann, Oskar
  Der Tosephtatraktat Berakot: Text, Übersetzung und Erklärung (BZAW 23; Gießen: Töpelmann, 1912).

Jonge, Marinus de, ed.
  The Testaments of the Twelve Patriarchs: A Critical Edition of the Greek Text (PVTG 1, 2; Leiden: Brill, 1978).

Kautzsch, Emil, et al., eds.
  Die Apokryphen und Pseudepigraphen des Alten Testaments, vol. 1: *Die Apokryphen des Alten Testaments*, vol. 2: *Die Pseudepigraphen des Alten Testaments* (Tübingen, 1900; repr. Hildesheim: Olms, 1962).

Kümmel, Werner Georg, et al., eds.
  Jüdische Schriften aus hellenistisch-römischer Zeit (Gütersloh: Gerd Mohn, 1973–).

Lauterbach, Jacob Z., ed.
  Mekilta de-Rabbi Ishmael (3 vols.; Philadelphia: Jewish Publication Society of America, 1933–35, repr. 1949).

Lohse, Eduard, ed.
  Die Texte aus Qumran (4th ed. Darmstadt: Wissenschaftliche Buchgesellschaft, 1986).

Marcus, Ralph, ed.
  Philo, *Opera*, Sup vol. 2: *Questions and Answers on Exodus* (LCL; London: Heinemann, and Cambridge: Harvard University Press, 1953, repr. 1970).

Michel, Otto, and Otto Bauernfeind, eds.
  Flavius Josephus, *De Bello Judaico*, vol. 1 (Bad Homburg: Gentner, 1960); vols. 2, 3 (Munich: Kösel, 1963–69).

Niese, Benedikt, ed.
  Flavius Josephus, *Opera* (7 vols.; vol. 6 ed. with Justus A. Destinon; 2d ed. Berlin: Weidmann, 1955).

Pelletier, André, ed.
  Lettre d'Aristée à Philocrate (SC 89; Paris: Cerf, 1962).

Rießler, Paul, ed.
  Altjüdisches Schrifttum außerhalb der Bibel (Augsburg: Filer, 1928).

Sammter, Ascher, et al., eds.
  Mischnajot. Die sechs Ordnungen der Mischna: Hebräischer Text mit Punktation, deutscher Übersetzung und Erklärung (3d ed.; 6 vols.; Basel: Goldschmidt, 1968).

Staerk, Willy, ed.
  Altjüdische liturgische Gebete ausgewählt und mit Einleitungen (KlT 58; Bonn: Marcus and Weger, 1910).

Strack, Hermann L., and Paul Billerbeck
  Kommentar zum Neuen Testament aus Talmud und Midrasch, vol. 1 (8th ed.; Munich: Beck, 1982); vol. 2 (8th ed.; Munich: Beck, 1983); vol. 3 (7th ed.; Munich: Beck, 1979); vol. 4.1–2 (7th ed.; Munich: Beck, 1978); vols. 5, 6 (ed. Joachim Jeremias and K. Adolph; 5th ed.; Munich: Beck, 1979).

van der Horst, Pieter W., *The Sentences of Pseudo-Phocylides with Introduction and Commentary* (SVTP 4; Leiden: Brill, 1978).

4. Other Christian Literature

Acts of the Martyrs
Herbert Musurillo, ed., *The Acts of the Christian Martyrs* (Oxford: Clarendon, 1972; repr. 1979).

Apologists
Edgar J. Goodspeed, ed., *Die ältesten Apologeten: Texte mit kurzen Einleitungen*(Göttingen: Vandenhoeck & Ruprecht, 1914; repr. 1984).

Athanasius
L.-Theophile Lefort, trans. and ed., *Lettres festales et pastorales en Copte* (CSCO 150–51; Louvain: Durbecq, 1955).

(Ps.-)Athanasius, *De virginitate*
Eduard von der Goltz, ed., *Ps.-Athanasius, De virginitate: λόγος σωτηρίας πρὸς τὴν παρϑένον (de virginitate): Eine echte Schrift des Athanasius* (TU, n.s. 14.2a; Leipzig: Hinrichs, 1905).

(Ps.-)Clement of Rome, *Epistula ad virgines*
Hugo Duensing, "Die dem Klemens von Rom zugeschriebenen Briefe über die Jungfräulichkeit," *ZKG* 63 (1950/51) 166–88.

(Ps.-)Cyprian, *De centesima, de sexagesima, de tricesima*
Richard Reitzenstein, "Ps.-Cyprian, *De centesima, de sexagesima, de tricesima*: Eine frühchristliche Schrift von den dreierlei Früchten des Lebens," *ZNW* 15 (1914) 60–90.

Dêr-Balizeh Liturgical Fragment
J. van Haelst, "Une nouvelle reconstitution du Papyrus liturgique de Dêr-Balizeh," *EThL* 45 (1969) 444–55.

Didascalia Apostolorum (Latin)
Erik Tidner, ed., *Didascalia Apostolorum, Canonum Ecclesiasticorum, Traditionis Apostolicae versiones latinae* (TU 75; Berlin: Akademie-Verlag, 1963).

Didascalia Apostolorum (Syriac)
Arthur Vööbus, ed., *The Didascalia Apostolorum in Syriac* (Louvain: Secrétariat du Corpus SCO, 1979) 1, chaps. 1–10, edited text (Scriptores Syri 175; CSCO 401; Louvain: Secrétariat du Corpus SCO, 1979), and English translation (Scriptores Syri 176; CSCO 402; Louvain: Secrétariat du Corpus SCO, 1979) 2, chaps. 11–26, edited text (Scriptores Syri 179; CSCO 407; Louvain: Secrétariat du Corpus SCO, 1979), and English translation (Scriptores Syri 180; CSCO 408; Louvain: Secrétariat du Corpus SCO, 1979).

Epistle of Titus
Donatien de Bruyne, ed., "*Epistula Titi, discipuli Pauli, de dispositione sanctimonii*," *RBén* 37 (1925) 47–72.

Liber graduum
Mihaly Kmosko, ed., *Liber graduum* (Patrologia Syriaca 1.3; Paris: Didot, 1926).

Origen
Opera Omnia, vol. 11: *In Libros Josuae Judicum et I Samuelis Homiliae* (ed. C. H. E. Lommatzsch; Berlin: Haude and Spener, 1841).

Rule of Benedict
Adalbert de Vogüé, *La Règle de Saint Benoît* IV (SC 184; Paris: Cerf, 1971).

Sayings traditions
Alfred Resch, *Agrapha* (2d ed.; Leipzig: Hinrichs, 1906; repr. Darmstadt: Wissenschaftliche Buchgesellschaft, 1967).

5. Gnostic Literature

Charlesworth, James H.
The Odes of Solomon: The Syriac Texts (SBLTT 13. Pseudepigrapha Series 7; Missoula: Scholars Press, 1977).

Fitzmyer, Joseph A.
"The Oxyrhynchus *Logoi* of Jesus and the Coptic Gospel according to Thomas," *TS* 20 (1959) 505–60.

Grenfell, Bernard P., and Arthur S. Hunt, eds.
"Evang. Thom. gr.," *The Oxyrhynchus Papyri* X (London: Egypt Exploration Fund, 1914) no. 1224.

Leipoldt, Johannes, ed.
Das Evangelium nach Thomas koptisch und deutsch (TU 101; Berlin: Akademie-Verlag, 1967).

Nock, Arthur D., and André-Jean Festugière, eds.
Corpus Hermeticum I, II (2d ed.; CUFr; Paris: Société d'Édition "Les belles lettres," 1960), III, IV (Paris: Société d'Édition "Les belles lettres," 1954).

Robinson, James M.
The Nag Hammadi Library in English (3d ed.; San Francisco: HarperCollins, 1990).

6. Greco-Roman Literature

Arcadius
Edmund Henry Barker, ed., *Περὶ τόνων* (Leipzig: Fleischer, 1820).

Aristotle
Immanuel Bekker and Olof Gigon, eds., *Opera*, vol. 2 (2d ed.; Berlin: de Gruyter, 1960); text reprinted from Georg Reimer edition of 1831.

Cicero
Karl Atzert, ed., *M. Tulli Ciceronis scripta quae manserunt omnia* (4, fasc. 48. BiTeu; Leipzig: Teubner, 1963).

Cleanthes
Hans Friedrich August von Arnim, ed., *Stoicorum Veterum Fragmenta* (Leipzig: Teubner, 1905, repr. 1921).

Diodorus of Sicily
Charles Henry Oldfather, ed., *Diodorus of Sicily* I (LCL; London: Heinemann; Cambridge: Harvard University Press, vol. 1, 1933, repr. 1960; vol. 3, 1939, repr. 1961).

Diphilos
Theodor Kock, ed., *Comicorum Atticorum Fragmenta* (3 vols.; Leipzig: Teubner, 1888) 2.541–80.

Epictetus
Henricus Schenkl, ed., *Epicteti Dissertationes ab Arriano digestae* (2d ed.; BiTeu; Stuttgart: Teubner, 1916, repr. 1965).

Etymologicon
Thomas Gaisford, ed., *Etymologicon Magnum* (Oxford: E. Typographeo academico, 1848).

Euripides

Gilbert Murray, ed., *Fabulae* (SCBO; vol. 1, Oxford: Clarendon, 1902, repr. 1958; vol. 2, 3d ed.; Oxford: Clarendon, 1913, repr. 1957; vol. 3, 2d ed.; Oxford: Clarendon, 1913, repr. 1957).

Euripides, *Scholia*

Wilhelm Dindorf, ed., *Scholia Graeca in Euripidis Tragoedias ex codicibus aucta et emendata,* vol. 2 (Oxford: E typographeo academico, 1863).

Herodian

August Lentz, ed., *Herodiani Technici Reliquiae* (2 vols.; Leipzig: Teubner, 1867).

Herodotus

Karl Hude, ed., *Herodoti Historiae* (3d ed.; 2 vols.; SCBO; Oxford: Clarendon, 1927; repr. 1: 1960; 2: 1958).

Hesiod

Alois Rzach, ed., *Hesiodi Carmina* (3d ed.; BiTeu; Stuttgart: Teubner, 1913, repr. 1967).

Hesychius

Johannes Alberti, Moritz Schmidt, and Rudolf Menge, eds., *Hesychii Alexandrini Lexicon* (5 vols.; Jena: Sumptibus Frederici Maukii, 1861; repr. Amsterdam: Hakkert, 1965).

Hippocrates

Émile Littré, ed., *Oeuvres complètes,* vols. 7, 8 (Amsterdam: Hakkert, 1962; repr. of the ed. of 1851 [vol. 7] and 1853 [vol. 8]).

Hyperides

Frederic G. Kenyon, ed., *Hyperidis Orationes et Fragmenta* (SCBO; Oxford: Clarendon, 1961).

Lucian

M. D. Macleod, ed., *Opera* (3 vols.; SCBO; Oxford: Clarendon, 1972–80).

Physiognomists

Richard Foerster, ed., *Scriptores Physiognomonici Graeci et Latini* (2 vols.; BiTeu; Leipzig: Teubner, 1893).

Plato

John Burnett, ed., *Platonis Opera* (5 vols.; SCBO; Oxford: Clarendon, 1900–1907, repr. 1957–62).

Pliny

Roger A. B. Mynors, ed., *C. Plini Caecili Secundi Epistularum libri decem* (SCBO; Oxford: Clarendon, 1963).

Plutarch

Harold F. Cherniss and W. C. Helmbold, eds., *Moralia,* vol. 12 (LCL; London: Heinemann; Cambridge: Harvard University Press, 1957).

Idem

P. H. De Lacy and B. Einarson, eds., *Moralia,* vol. 7 (LCL; London: Heinemann; Cambridge: Harvard University Press, 1959).

Idem

Claes Lindskog and Konrat Ziegler, eds., *Plutarchi Vitae parallelae,* vols. 1, 2 (3d ed.; BiTeu; Leipzig: Teubner, 1964).

Pollux

Erich Bethe, ed., *Onomasticon,* vol. 2 (Lexicographia Graeci 9; Leipzig: Teubner, 1937).

Porphyry

Édouard des Places, ed., *Vie de Pythagore. Lettre à Marcella* (CUFr; Paris: "Les Belles Lettres," 1982).

Sextus

Henry Chadwick, *The Sentences of Sextus: A Contribution to the History of Early Christian Ethics* (Cambridge: Cambridge University Press, 1959).

Sextus Empiricus

Hermann Mutschmann and Jürgen Mau, eds., *Sexti Empirici Opera,* vol. 3 (BiTeu; Leipzig: Teubner, 1961).

Silius Italicus

Ludwig Bauer, ed., *Punica* (2 vols.; BiTeu; Leipzig: Teubner, 1890).

Simplicius

Friedrich Dübner, ed., "Commentarius in Epicteti Enchiridion," in *Theophrasti Characteres; Marci Antonini Commentarii; Epicteti Dissertationes ab Arriano literis mandatae fragmenta et Enchiridion cum commentario Simplicii; Cebetis Tabula; Maximi Tyrii Dissertationes* (Paris: Firmin-Didot, 1840).

Suetonius

Maximilian Ihm, ed., *C. Suetoni Tranquilli Opera,* vol. 1: *De vita Caesarum libri VIII* (BSGRT; Stuttgart: Teubner, 1908, repr. 1961).

Tacitus

Erich Koestermann, ed., *Annales* (BSGRT; Leipzig: Teubner, 1965).

Theognis

Ernst Diehl and Douglas Young, eds., *Theognis, Pseudo-Pythagoras, Pseudo-Phocylides, Chares, Anonymi Aulodia, Fragmentum Teliambicum* (2d ed.; BiTeu; Leipzig: Teubner, 1971).

Vergil

Frederic A. Hirtzel, *P. Vergili Maronis Opera* (SCBO; Oxford: Clarendon, 1900, repr. 1963).

Xenophon

Edgar C. Marchant, ed., *Opera Omnia,* vol. 2 (2d ed.; LCL; Cambridge: Harvard University Press; and London: Heinemann, 1921, repr. 1962).

Inscriptions

Dittenberger, Wilhelm, ed., *Orientis Graeci Inscriptiones Selectae* (2 vols.; Leipzig: Hirzel, 1903–1905; repr. Hildesheim: Olms, 1960).

Dittenberger, Wilhelm, ed.

Sylloge Inscriptionum Graecarum (3d ed.; 4 vols.; Leipzig: Hirzel, 1915; repr. Hildesheim: Olms, 1960).

Mitford, Terence B., ed.

The Inscriptions of Kourion (Memoirs of the American Philological Society 83, no. 127. Philadelphia: American Philological Society, 1971).

Weinreich, Otto, ed.

Stiftung und Kultsatzungen eines Privatheiligtums in Philadelphia in Lydien (SHAW.PH 16; Heidelberg: Winter, 1919).

Papyri

*Ägyptische Urkunden aus den königlichen Museen zu
Berlin*: *Griechische Urkunden* (Berlin: Weidmann,
1912), vol. 4, no. 13, 117.

Grenfell, Bernard P., Arthur S. Hunt, and J. G. Smyly,
eds.
The Tebtunis Papyri I (London: H. Frowde; and
New York: Oxford University Press, 1902).

Kenyon, Frederic G., and Harold Idris Bell, eds.
Greek Papyri in the British Museum, vol. 3 (London:
British Museum, 1898), no. 354.

Kenyon, Frederick, and Harold Idris Bell, eds.
Greek Papyri in the British Museum, vol. 5 (London:
British Museum, 1917).

Preisendanz, Karl
*Papyri Graecae Magicae. Die griechischen
Zauberpapyri* (2 vols.; Leipzig and Berlin: Teubner,
1928).

Preisigke, Friedrich
Sammelbuch griechischer Urkunden aus Ägypten, vol.
1 (Strasbourg: Trubner, 1915).

7. Secondary Literature

Adam, Alfred
"Erwägungen zur Herkunft der Didache," *ZKG* 68
(1957) 1–47; repr. in idem, *Sprache und Dogma:
Untersuchungen zu Grundproblemen der Kirchengeschichte* (ed. Gerhard Ruhbach; Gütersloh: Mohn,
1969) 24–70.

Idem
"Erwägungen zur Herkunft der Didache," *ZNW* 46
(1955) 266–67.

Albright, William F., and C. S. Mann
"Two Texts in I Corinthians," *NTS* 16 (1969/70)
271–76.

Alfonsi, Luigi
"Aspetti della struttura letteraria della Διδαχή," in
Studi classici in onore di Quintino Cataudella (3 vols.;
Catania: Universitè di Catania, Facoltà di lettere e
filosofia, 1972) 2.465–81.

Idem
"Proprietà, lavoro e famiglia nella Διδαχή:
Premessa alla società dei padri," *Augustinianum* 17
(1977) 101–6.

Altaner, Berthold
"Zum Problem der lateinischen Doctrina
Apostolorum," *VC* 6 (1952) 160–67; repr. as "Die
lateinische Doctrina Apostolorum und die
griechische Grundschrift der Didache," in Günter
Glockmann, ed., *Kleine Patristische Schriften* (TU
83; Berlin: Akademie-Verlag, 1967) 335–42.

Altaner, Berthold, and Alfred Stuiber
Patrologie: Leben, Schriften und Lehre der Kirchenväter
(9th ed.; Freiburg im Breisgau, Basel, and Vienna:
Herder, 1980).

Amundsen, Leiv
"Christian Papyri from the Oslo Collection," *SO* 24
(1945) 121–47.

Aono, Tashio
Die Entwicklung des paulinischen Gerichtsgedankens

bei den apostolischen Vätern (EHS.T 137; Bern,
Frankfurt, and Las Vegas: Peter Lang, 1979).

Arnold, August
*Der Ursprung des christlichen Abendmahls im Lichte
der neuesten liturgiegeschichtlichen Forschung* (2d ed.;
FThSt 45; Freiburg im Breisgau: Herder, 1939).

Audet, Jean-Paul
"Affinités littéraires et doctrinales du Manuel de
Discipline," *RB* 59 (1952) 219–38; 60 (1953) 41–82.

Idem
"A Hebrew-Aramaic List of Books of the Old
Testament in Greek Transcription," *JTS,* n.s. 1
(1950) 135–54.

Idem
"Literary Forms and Contents of a Normal
Εὐχαριστία in the First Century," *StEv* 1 (1959)
643–62.

Bahr, G. J.
"The Use of the Lord's Prayer in the Primitive
Church," *JBL* 84 (1965) 153–59.

Baltzer, Klaus
*The Covenant Formulary in Old Testament, Jewish,
and Early Christian Writings* (trans. David E. Green;
Philadelphia: Fortress, 1975); ET of *Das
Bundesformular* (WMANT 4; Neukirchen-Vluyn:
Neukirchener Verlag, 1960).

Bammel, Ernst
"Schema und Vorlage von *Didache* 16," *StPatr* 4.2
(1961) 253–62.

Bardenhewer, Otto
Geschichte der altchristlichen Literatur (2d ed.; 5 vols.;
Freiburg im Breisgau: Herder, 1913–32; repr.
Darmstadt: Wissenschaftliche Buchgesellschaft,
1962).

Barnard, Leslie W.
"The Dead Sea Scrolls, Barnabas, the *Didache* and
the Later History of the 'Two Ways,'" in idem,
Studies in the Apostolic Fathers and Their Background
(Oxford: Blackwell, 1966) 87–107.

Bartlet, J. Vernon
*Church-Life and Church-Order during the First Four
Centuries with Special Reference to the Early Eastern
Church-Orders* (ed. Cecil J. Cadoux; Oxford:
Blackwell, 1943).

Idem
"The Didache Reconsidered," *JTS* 22 (1921)
239–49.

Bartsch, Hans-Werner
"Traditionsgeschichtliches zur 'goldenen Regel'
und zum Aposteldekret," *ZNW* 75 (1984) 128–32.

Batiffol, Pierre
"L'Agape," in idem, *Études d'Histoire et de Théologie
positive* (2 vols.; Paris: Lecoffre, 1902–5) 1.279–
311.

Idem
"L'Eucharistie dans le Nouveau Testament," in
idem, *Études d'Histoire et de Théologie positive* (2
vols.; 2d ed.; Paris: Lecoffre, 1902–5) 2.1–133.

238

Bauer, Johannes Baptist
"Aspekte des Kanonproblems," in *Meqor Hajjim: Festschrift für Georg Molin zum 75 Geburtstag* (Graz: Akademische Druck- und Verlagsanstalt, 1983) 25–42.

Beck, Hans–Georg
Kirche und theologische Literatur im byzantinischen Reich (HAW 12.2.1; Munich: Beck, 1959).

Becker, Jürgen
Untersuchungen zur Entstehungsgeschichte der Testamente der zwölf Patriarchen (AGJU 8; Leiden: Brill, 1970).

Berger, Klaus
Formgeschichte des Neuen Testaments (Heidelberg: Quelle & Meyer, 1984).

Idem
Die Gesetzesauslegung Jesu, vol. 1: *Markus und Parallelen* (WMANT 40; Neukirchen-Vluyn: Neukirchener Verlag, 1972).

Idem
"Hellenistische Gattungen im Neuen Testament," *ANRW* 2.25.2 (1984) 1031–1432.

Bergman, J.
"Zum Zwei-Wege Motiv: Religionsgeschichtliche und exegetische Bemerkungen," *SEÅ* 41/42 (1976–77) 27–56.

Betz, Hans Dieter
Lukian von Samosata und das Neue Testament: Religionsgeschichtliche und paränetische Parallelen: Ein Beitrag zum Corpus Hellenisticum Novi Testamenti (TU 76; Berlin: Akademie-Verlag, 1961).

Betz, Johannes
"Der Abendmahlskelch im Judenchristentum," in Marcel Reding, ed., *Abhandlungen über Theologie und Kirche: Festschrift für Karl Adam* (Düsseldorf: Patmos, 1952) 109–37.

Idem
"The Eucharist in the *Didache*," in Draper, *Research*, 244–75; ET of "Die Eucharistie in der Didache," *ALW* 11 (1969) 10–39.

Beyschlag, Karlmann
"Zur Geschichte der Bergpredigt in der Alten Kirche," *ZThK* 74 (1977) 291–322, repr. in idem, *Evangelium als Schicksal: Fünf Studien zur Geschichte der Alten Kirche* (Munich: Claudius, 1979) 77–92.

Bigg, Charles
"Notes on the *Didache*," *JTS* 5 (1904) 579–89; 6 (1905) 411–15.

Black, Matthew
"The Maranatha Invocation and Jude 14,15 (1 Enoch 1:9)," in Barnabas Lindars and S. S. Smalley, eds., *Christ and Spirit in the New Testament: In Honour of C. F. D. Moule* (Cambridge: Cambridge University Press, 1973) 189–96.

Blinzler, Josef
"Qumran-Kalender und Passionschronologie," *ZNW* 49 (1958) 238–51.

Boehmer, Heinrich
"Hat Benedikt von Nursia die Didache gekannt?" *ZNW* 12 (1911) 287.

Borig, Rainer
Der wahre Weinstock: Untersuchungen zu Jo 15,1–10 (SANT 16; Munich: Kösel, 1967).

Bornkamm, Günther
"Der Aufbau der Bergpredigt," *NTS* 24 (1978/79) 419–32.

Idem
"Das Doppelgebot der Liebe," in Walther Eltester, ed., *Neutestamentliche Studien für Rudolf Bultmann* (2d ed.; BZNW 21; Berlin: Töpelmann, 1957) 85–93; repr. in idem, *Geschichte und Glaube* (*Gesammelte Aufsätze* 3–4) (2 vols.; BEvTh 48; Munich: Kaiser, 1968–71) 1.37–45.

Idem
"Eschatology and Ecclesiology in the Gospel of Matthew," in Günther Bornkamm, Gerhard Barth, and Heinz Joachim Held, *Tradition and Interpretation in Matthew* (trans. Percy Scott; Philadelphia: Westminster, 1963); ET of "Enderwartung und Kirche im Matthäusevangelium," in Günther Bornkamm, Gerhard Barth, and Heinz Joachim Held, *Überlieferung und Auslegung im Matthäusevangelium* (7th ed.; WMANT 1; Neukirchen-Vluyn: Neukirchener Verlag, 1975) 13–47.

Idem
"On the Understanding of Worship. B: The Anathema in the Early Christian Lord's Supper Liturgy," in idem, *Early Christian Experiences* (New York: Harper & Row, 1969) 169–79; ET of "Zum Verständnis des Gottesdienstes bei Paulus. B: Das Anathema in der urchristlichen Abendmahlsliturgie," in idem, *Das Ende des Gesetzes: Paulusstudien (Gesammelte Aufsätze 1)* (5th ed.; BEvTh 16; Munich: Kaiser, 1966) 123–32.

Bousset, Wilhelm
Der Antichrist in der Überlieferung des Judentums, des neuen Testaments und der alten Kirche (Göttingen: Vandenhoeck & Ruprecht, 1895).

Idem
"Eine jüdische Gebetssammlung im siebenten Buch der Apostolischen Konstitutionen," NGWG (1915) 435–89; repr. in Anthonie F. Verheule, ed., *Religionsgeschichtliche Studien: Aufsätze zur Religionsgeschichte des hellenistischen Zeitalters* (NovTSup 50; Leiden: Brill, 1979) 231–85.

Braun, Herbert
Qumran und das Neue Testament (2 vols.; Tübingen: Mohr [Siebeck], 1966).

Broek-Utne, A.
"Eine schwierige Stelle in einer alten Gemeindeordnung (Did. 11,11)," *ZKG* 54 (1935) 576–81.

Brox, Norbert
Der Glaube als Weg: Nach biblischen und altchristlichen Texten (Munich and Salzburg: Pustet, 1968).

Bruce, F. F.
"Eschatology in the Apostolic Fathers," in David Neiman and Margaret A. Schatkin, eds., *The Heritage of the Early Church: Essays in Honor of the*

Very Reverend Georges Vasilievich Florovsky on the Occasion of His Eightieth Birthday (OrChrA 195; Rome: Pontificium Institutum Studiorum Orientalium, 1973) 77–89.

Bruyne, Donatien de
"Un traité gnostique sur les trois récompenses," *ZNW* 15 (1914) 280–84.

Bultmann, Rudolf
Die Geschichte der synoptischen Tradition (FRLANT 29; 9th ed. Göttingen: Vandenhoeck & Ruprecht, 1979), with additional volume edited by Gerd Theißen and Philip Vielhauer (5th ed. Göttingen: Vandenhoeck & Ruprecht, 1979); ET: *The History of the Synoptic Tradition* (trans. John Marsh; New York: Harper & Row, 1963; rev. ed., 1976).

Idem
Theologie des Neuen Testaments (ed. Otto Merk; 9th ed.; UTB 630; Tübingen: Mohr, 1984); ET: *Theology of the New Testament* (trans. Kendrick Grobel; 2 vols.; New York: Scribner's, 1951–55).

Burchard, Christoph
"Das doppelte Liebesgebot in der frühen christlichen Überlieferung," in Eduard Lohse, Chr. Burchard, and B. Schaller, eds., *Der Ruf Jesu und die Antwort der Gemeinde: Exegetische Untersuchungen Joachim Jeremias zum 70. Geburtstag gewidmet* (Göttingen: Vandenhoeck & Ruprecht, 1970) 39–62.

Burkitt, Francis Crawford
"Barnabas and the Didache," *JTS* 33 (1932) 25–27.

Butler, Basil Christopher
"The Literary Relations of Didache, Ch. XVI," *JTS,* n.s. 11 (1960) 265–83.

Idem
"The 'Two Ways' in the Didache," *JTS,* n.s. 12 (1961) 27–38.

Butler, Edward Cuthbert
"The Rule of St. Benedict," *JTS* 11 (1910) 279–88; 12 (1911) 261–68.

von Campenhausen, Hans
Kirchliches Amt und geistliche Vollmacht (2d ed.; BHTh 14; Tübingen: Mohr, 1963); ET of the 1st edition: *Ecclesiastical Authority and Spiritual Power in the Church of the First Three Centuries* (London: Black, 1969).

Carrington, Philip
The Primitive Christian Catechism: A Study in the Epistles (Cambridge: Cambridge University Press, 1940).

Casel, Odo
"Altchristliche Liturgie bis auf Konstantin d. Gr.," *JLW* 5 (1925) 230–50.

Cerfaux, Lucien
"La multiplication des pains dans la liturgie de la Didachè," *Bib* 40 (1959) 943–58.

Clerici, Luigi
Einsammlung der Zerstreuten: Liturgiegeschichtliche Untersuchung zur Vor- und Nachgeschichte der Fürbitte für die Kirche in Didache 9,4 und 10,5 (LWQF 44; Münster: Aschendorff, 1966).

Cohn, Leopold
"Philo von Alexandria," *NJKA* 1 (1898) 514–40.

Colson, Jean
L'Évêque dans les communautés primitives: Tradition paulinienne et tradition johannique de l'épiscopat des origines à saint Irénée (Unam Sanctam 21; Paris: De Latour-Maubourg, 1951).

Connolly, Richard Hugh
"Agape and Eucharist in the Didache," *DRev* 55 (1937) 477–89.

Idem
"Barnabas and the Didache," *JTS* 38 (1937) 165–67.

Idem
"Canon Streeter on the Didache," *JTS* 38 (1937) 364–79.

Idem
"Didache and Diatessaron," *JTS* 34 (1933) 346–47.

Idem
"The *Didache* and Montanism," *DRev* 55 (1937) 339–47.

Idem
"The Didache in Relation to the Epistle of Barnabas," *JTS* 33 (1932) 237–53.

Idem
"New Fragments of the Didache," *JTS* 25 (1924) 151–53.

Idem
"The Use of the *Didache* in the *Didascalia,*" *JTS* 24 (1923) 147–57.

Conzelmann, Hans
Die Apostelgeschichte (2d ed.; HNT 7; Göttingen: Vandenhoeck & Ruprecht, 1972); ET: *Acts of the Apostles: A Commentary on the Acts of the Apostles* (trans. James Limburg, A. Thomas Kraabel, and Donald H. Juel; ed. Eldon Jay Epp with Christopher R. Matthews; Hermeneia; Philadelphia: Fortress, 1987).

Creed, John Martin
"The Didache," *JTS* 39 (1938) 370–87.

Cremer, Franz Gerhard
Die Fastenansage Jesu: Mk 2,20 und Parallelen in der Sicht der patristischen und scholastischen Exegese (BBB 23; Bonn: Hanstein, 1965).

Crouch, James E.
The Origin and Intention of the Colossian Haustafel (FRLANT 109; Göttingen: Vandenhoeck & Ruprecht, 1972).

Cullmann, Oscar
Die Christologie des Neuen Testaments (5th ed.; Tübingen: Mohr, 1975); ET: *The Christology of the New Testament* (rev. ed.; Philadelphia: Westminster, 1963).

Daniélou, Jean
"Le traité de centesima, sexagesima, tricesima et le Judéo-Christianisme Latin avant Tertullien," *VC* 25 (1971) 171–81.

David, J.
"Fragments de l'Évangile selon Saint Matthieu en dialecte moyen-égyptien," *RB,* n.s. 7 (1910) 80–92.

Davis, Cyprian, O.S.B.
"The *Didache* and Early Monasticism in the East and West," in Jefford, *Context*, 352–67.

Dehandschutter, Boudewijn
"The Text of the *Didache*: Some Comments on the Edition of Klaus Wengst," in Jefford, *Context*, 37–46.

Delling, Gerhard
"Abendmahl, II. Urchristliches Mahl-Verständnis," *TRE* 1 (1976) 47–58.

Deussen, G.
"Weisen der Bischofswahl im 1. Clemensbrief und in der Didache," *ThGl* 62 (1972) 125–35.

Dibelius, Martin
"Die Mahl-Gebete der Didache," *ZNW* 37 (1938) 32–41; repr. in H. Kraft and Günther Bornkamm, eds., *Botschaft und Geschichte: Gesammelte Aufsätze*, vol. 2: *Zum Urchristentum und zur hellenistischen Religionsgeschichte* (Tübingen: Mohr, 1956) 117–27.

Dibelius, Martin, and Hans Conzelmann
Die Pastoralbriefe (4th ed.; HNT 13; Tübingen: Mohr, 1966); ET: *The Pastoral Epistles* (Hermeneia; Philadelphia: Fortress, 1972).

Dibelius, Martin, and Heinrich Greeven
An die Kolosser. Epheser. An Philemon (3d ed.; HNT 12; Tübingen; Mohr [Siebeck], 1953).

Dihle, Albrecht
Die goldene Regel (Studienhefte zur Altertumswissenschaft 7; Göttingen: Vandenhoeck & Ruprecht, 1962).

Dix, Gregory
"Didache and Diatessaron," *JTS* 34 (1933) 242–50.

Idem
The Shape of the Liturgy (repr. of 2d ed.; London: Black, 1970; New York: Seabury, 1982).

Dölger, Franz Joseph
Der Exorzismus im altchristlichen Taufritual: Eine religionsgeschichtliche Studie (SGKA 3.1–2; Paderborn: Schöningh, 1909).

Idem
"Nilwasser und Taufwasser. Eine religionsgeschichtliche Auseinandersetzung zwischen einem Isisverehrer und einem Christen des vierten Jahrhunderts nach Firmicus Maternus," in idem, *Antike und Christentum: Kultur- und religionsgeschichtliche Studien* 5 (2d ed.; Münster: Aschendorff, 1976) 153–87, esp. § 5: "*Aqua ignita*: Wärmung und Weihe des Taufwassers," pp. 175–83.

Idem
Sol Salutis: Gebet und Gesang im christlichen Altertum. Mit besonderer Rücksicht auf die Ostung in Gebet und Liturgie (LWQF 16/17; Münster: Aschendoff, 1972).

Draper, Jonathan A., ed.
The Didache in Modern Research (AGJU 37; Leiden: Brill, 1996).

Idem
"Social Ambiguity and the Production of Text: Prophets, Teachers, Bishops, and Deacons and the Development of the Jesus Tradition in the Community of the *Didache*," in Jefford, *Context*, 284–312.

Idem
"Torah and Troublesome Apostles in the *Didache* Community," *NovT* 33 (1991) 347–72.

Drews, Paul
"Untersuchungen zur Didache," *ZNW* 5 (1904) 53–79.

Dugmore, Clifford William
"Lord's Day and Easter," in *Neotestamentica et Patristica: Eine Freundesgabe Herrn Professor Dr. Oscar Cullmann zu seinem 60. Geburtstag überreicht* (NovTSup 6; Leiden: Brill, 1962) 272–81.

Ehrhard, Albert
Die altchristliche Litteratur und ihre Erforschung von 1884–1900, vol. 1: *Die vornicänische Litteratur* (StrThS.S 1; Freiburg: Herder, 1900).

Elbogen, Ismar
Der jüdische Gottesdienst in seiner geschichtlichen Entwicklung (4th ed.; Hildesheim: Olms, 1962).

Elliger, Karl
Leviticus (HAT 1.4; Tübingen: Mohr, 1966).

Emonds, Hilarius
"Abt," *RAC* 1 (1950) 45–55.

Engemann, Josef
"Auf die Parusie Christi hinweisende Darstellungen in der frühchristlichen Kunst," JAC 19 (1976) 139–56.

Felmy, Karl Christian
"'Was unterscheidet diese Nacht von allen anderen Nächten?' Die Funktion des Stiftungsberichtes in der urchristlichen Eucharistiefeier nach Didache 9f. und dem Zeugnis Justins," *JLH* 27 (1983) 1–15.

Fiensy, David
"Redaction History and the Apostolic Constitutions," *JQR* 72 (1982) 293–302.

Finkelstein, Louis
"The Birkat Ha-Mazon," *JQR*, n.s. 19 (1928/29) 211–62.

Fitzmyer, Joseph A., S.J.
The Gospel According to Luke (X–XXIV) (AB 28A; Garden City, N.Y.: Doubleday, 1985).

Idem
"New Testament *Kyrios* and *Maranatha* and Their Aramaic Background," in idem, *To Advance the Gospel: New Testament Studies* (New York: Crossroad, 1981) 218–35.

Frank, K. Suso
"Maleachi 1,10ff. in der frühen Väterdeutung: Ein Beitrag zu Opferterminologie und Opferverständnis in der alten Kirche," *ThPh* 53 (1978) 70–78.

Funk, Franz Xaver
"Die Didache in der afrikanischen Kirche," *ThQ* 76 (1894) 601–4.

Idem
 "Didache und Barnabasbrief," *ThQ* 87 (1905) 161–79.

Idem
 "Die Didache, Zeit und Verhältnis zu den verwandten Schriften," in idem, *Kirchengeschichtliche Abhandlungen und Untersuchungen* (3 vols.; Paderborn: Schöningh, 1899) 2.108–41.

Idem
 "Die Doctrina apostolorum," *ThQ* 6 (1884) 381–402.

Idem
 Untitled note on the *Didache, ThQ* 74 (1892) 522.

Idem
 "Zur alten lateinischen Übersetzung der Doctrina apostolorum," *ThQ* 68 (1886) 650–55.

Idem
 "Zur Apostellehre und apostolischen Kirchenordnung," *ThQ* 69 (1887) 276–306, 355–74.

Idem
 "Zur Didache, der Frage nach der Grundschrift und ihren Rezensionen," *ThQ* 84 (1902) 73–88; revised in idem, *Kirchengeschichtliche Abhandlungen und Untersuchungen* (3 vols.; Paderborn: Schöningh, 1907) 3.218–29.

Gamber, Klaus
 Sacrificium laudis: Zur Geschichte des frühchristlichen Eucharistiegebets (SPLi 5; Regensburg: Pustet, 1973).

Gebhardt, Oscar von
 "Ein übersehenes Fragment der Διδαχή in alter lateinischer Übersetzung," an appendix to von Harnack, *Lehre,* 275–86.

Gero, Stephen
 "The So-called Ointment Prayer in the Coptic Version of the Didache: A Re-evaluation," *HTR* 70 (1977) 67–84.

Gibbins, H. J.
 "The Problem of the Liturgical Section of the Didache," *JTS* 36 (1935) 373–86.

Giet, Stanislas
 "La Didachè: Enseignement des douze Apôtres?" *Melto* 3 (1967) 223–36.

Idem
 L'Énigme de la Didachè (PFLUS 149; Paris: Ophrys, 1970).

Idem
 "L'Énigme de la Didachè," *StPatr* 10, 1 (TU 107; Berlin: Akademie-Verlag, 1970) 84–94.

Gignac, Francis T.
 A Grammar of the Greek Papyri of the Roman and Byzantine Periods (2 vols.; Testi e Documenti per lo Studio dell'Antichità 50, 1. 2; Milan: Istituto editoriale cisalpino-La goliardica, 1976–81).

Glasson, Thomas Francis
 "The Ensign of the Son of Man (Matt. XXIV,30)," *JTS,* n.s. 15 (1964) 299–300.

Glover, Richard
 "The *Didache*'s Quotations and the Synoptic Gospels," *NTS* 5 (1958/59) 12–29.

Goodenough, Erwin R.
 "John a Primitive Gospel," *JBL* 64 (1945) 145–82.

Goodspeed, Edgar J.
 "The Didache, Barnabas and the Doctrina," *ATR* 27 (1945) 228–47.

Goppelt, Leonhard
 Der erste Petrusbrief (ed. F. Hahn; 8th ed.; KEK 12.1; Göttingen: Vandenhoeck & Ruprecht, 1978); ET: *A Commentary on I Peter* (ed. F. Hahn; trans. John E. Alsup; Grand Rapids: Eerdmans, 1993).

Gordon, R. P.
 "Targumic Parallels to Acts XIII 18 and Didache XIV 3," *NovT* 16 (1974) 285–89.

Grant, Robert M.
 The Apostolic Fathers: A New Translation and Commentary, vol. 1: *An Introduction* (New York: Nelson, 1964).

Greiff, Anton
 Das älteste Paschariuale der Kirche, Did 1–10, und das Johannesevangelium (Johanneische Studien 1; Paderborn: Schöningh, 1929).

Gribomont, Jean
 "Ecclesiam adunare: Un écho de l'eucharistie africaine et de la Didachè," *RThAM* 27 (1960) 20–28.

Haelst, Joseph van
 Catalogue des Papyrus Littéraires Juifs et Chrétiens (Paris: Publications de la Sorbonne, 1976).

Haenchen, Ernst
 Die Apostelgeschichte (7th ed.; KEK 3; Göttingen: Vandenhoeck & Ruprecht, 1977); ET: *The Acts of the Apostles* (trans. Bernard Noble et al.; Philadelphia: Westminster, 1971).

Hagner, Donald A.
 The Use of the Old and New Testaments in Clement of Rome (NovTSup 34; Leiden: Brill, 1973).

Hahn, Ferdinand
 Christologische Hoheitstitel: Ihre Geschichte im frühen Christentum (4th ed.; FRLANT 83; Göttingen: Vandenhoeck & Ruprecht, 1974).

Halleux, André de
 "Ministers in the *Didache,*" in Draper, ed., *Research,* 300–320: ET of "Les Ministères dans le Didachè," *Irénikon* 53 (1980) 5–29.

Hanson, Richard P. C.
 "The Liberty of the Bishop to Improvise Prayer in the Eucharist," *VC* 15 (1961) 173–76.

Harnack, Adolf von
 "Der apokryphe Brief des Paulusschülers Titus 'De dispositione sanctimonii,'" SPAW.PH (1925) 180–213.

Idem
 "Apostellehre," *RE*[3] 1.711–30.

Idem
 Die Apostellehre und die jüdischen beiden Wege (2d ed.; Leipzig: Hinrichs, 1896).

Idem
 "Die Bezeichnung Jesu als 'Knecht Gottes' und ihre Geschichte in der alten Kirche," SPAW.PH (1926) 212–38.

Idem

    Bruchstücke der Evangelien und der Apokalypse des Petrus (2d ed.; TU 9.2; Leipzig: Hinrichs, 1893).

Idem

    Geschichte der altchristlichen Litteratur bis Eusebius, vol. 1: *Die Überlieferung und der Bestand der altchristlichen Litteratur bis Eusebius* (Bearbeitet unter Mitwirkung von Erwin Preuschen; Leipzig: Hinrichs, 1893); vol. 2: *Die Chronologie der altchristlichen Litteratur bis Eusebius*, part 1: *Die Chronologie der Litteratur bis Irenäus, nebst einleitenden Untersuchungen* (Leipzig: Hinrichs, 1897).

Idem

    Review of P. Bryennios, Διδαχή, 1883, in *ThLZ* 9 (1884) 49–55.

Harvey, Anthony Ernest

    "'The Workman Is Worthy of His Hire': Fortunes of a Proverb in the Early Church," *NovT* 24 (1982) 209–21.

Heiligenthal, Roman

    "Goldene Regel, II: Neues Testament und frühes Christentum," *TRE* 13 (1984) 573–75.

Henderson, Ian H.

    "Style-Switching in the *Didache*: Fingerprint or Argument?" in Jefford, *Context*, 177–209.

Hengel, Martin

    Judaism and Hellenism: Studies in Their Encounter in Palestine during the Early Hellenistic Period (trans. John Bowden; Philadelphia: Fortress, 1974): ET of *Judentum und Hellenismus: Studien zu ihrer Begegnung unter besonderer Berücksichtigung Palästinas bis zur Mitte des 2. Jh.s v. Chr.* (2d ed.; WUNT 10; Tübingen: Mohr [Siebeck], 1973).

Hennecke, Edgar

    "Die Grundschrift der Didache und ihre Recensionen," *ZNW* 2 (1901) 58–72.

Idem

    "Mitteilung," *ThLZ* 49 (1924) 408.

Higgins, Angus J. B.

    "The Sign of the Son of Man (Matt XXIV,30)," *NTS* 9 (1962/63) 380–82.

Hiltbrunner, Otto, Denys Gorce, and Hans Wehr

    "Gastfreundschaft," *RAC* 8 (1972) 1061–1123.

Hitchcock, Francis Ryan Montgomery

    "Did Clement of Alexandria Know the Didache?" *JTS* 24 (1923) 397–401.

Holtz, Gottfried

    Die Pastoralbriefe (4th ed.; ThHK 13; Berlin: Evangelische Verlagsanstalt, 1986).

Hooker, Morna D.

    Jesus and the Servant: The Influence of the Servant Concept of Deutero-Isaiah in the New Testament (London: SPCK, 1959).

Hruby, Kurt

    "La 'Birkat Ha-Mazon,'" in *Mélanges liturgiques offerts au R. P. dom Bernard Botte à l'occasion du cinquantième anniversaire de son ordination sacerdotale (4 juin 1972)* (Louvain: Abbaye du Mont César, 1972) 205–22.

Hunger, Herbert

    Die hochsprachliche profane Literatur der Byzantiner (2 vols.; HAW 12.5.1–2; Munich: Beck, 1978).

Hüntemann, U.

    "Ad cap. 1 Doctrinae XII apostolorum," *Antonianum* 6 (1931) 195–96.

Jaubert, Annie

    "Jésus et le calendrier de Qumrân," *NTS* 7 (1960/61) 1–30.

Jefford, Clayton N., ed.

    The Didache in Context: Essays on Its Text, History and Transmission (NovTSup 77; Leiden: Brill, 1995).

Idem

    "Did Ignatius of Antioch Know the *Didache*?" in Jefford, *Context*, 330–51.

Idem

    "Presbyters in the Community of the *Didache*," *StPatr* 21 (1989) 122–28.

Idem

    The Sayings of Jesus in the Teaching of the Twelve Apostles (VC Sup 11; Leiden: Brill, 1989).

Idem

    "Tradition and Witness in Antioch: Acts and Didache 6," in Edgar V. McKnight, ed., *Perspectives on Contemporary New Testament Questions* (Lewiston, N.Y.: Mellen, 1992); repr. in *Perspectives in Religious Studies* 19 (1992) 409–19.

Jefford, Clayton N., and Stephen J. Patterson

    "A Note on *Didache* 12.2a (Coptic)," *Second Century* 7 (1989–90) 65–75.

Jeremias, Joachim

    "Abba," in idem, *Abba: Studien zur neutestamentlichen Theologie und Zeitgeschichte* (Göttingen: Vandenhoeck & Ruprecht, 1966) 15–67; partial ET: *The Prayers of Jesus* (SBT 2.6; London: SCM, 1967) 11–65.

Idem

    Die Abendmahlsworte Jesu (4th ed.; Göttingen: Vandenhoeck & Ruprecht, 1967); ET: *The Eucharistic Words of Jesus* (trans. Norman Perrin; 3d ed.; London: SCM, 1966).

Idem

    Jerusalem zur Zeit Jesu: *Eine kulturgeschichtliche Untersuchung zur neutestamentlichen Zeitgeschichte* (3d ed.; Göttingen: Vandenhoeck & Ruprecht, 1969); ET: *Jerusalem in the Time of Jesus: An Investigation into Economic and Social Conditions during the New Testament Period* (trans. F. H. and C. H. Cave; Philadelphia: Fortress, 1969).

Idem

    Neutestamentliche Theologie (3d ed.; Gütersloh: Mohn, 1979); ET of 1st ed.: *New Testament Theology: The Proclamation of Jesus* (trans. John Bowden; New York: Scribner's, 1971).

Idem

    Unbekannte Jesusworte (4th ed.; Gütersloh: Mohn, 1965); ET: *Unknown Sayings of Jesus* (2d ed.; London: SPCK, 1964).

Johnson, Sherman E.
"A Subsidiary Motive for the Writing of the Didache," in Massey H. Shepherd and Sherman E. Johnson, eds., *Munera Studiosa: Studies presented to W. H. P. Hatch on the Occasion of his Seventieth Birthday* (Cambridge, Mass.: Episcopal Theological School, 1946) 107–22.

Jones, F. Stanley, and Paul A. Mirecki
"Considerations on the Coptic Papyrus of the *Didache* (British Library Oriental Manuscript 9271)," in Jefford, *Context*, 47–87.

Jungmann, Josef A.
Liturgie der christlichen Frühzeit bis auf Gregor den Großen (Fribourg: Herder, 1967); ET: *The Early Liturgy to the Time of Gregory the Great* (trans. Francis A. Brunner; Notre Dame, Ind.: University of Notre Dame Press, 1959).

Kahle, Paul E., Jr.
Bala'izah: Coptic Texts from Deir El-Bala'izah in Upper Egypt (2 vols.; Oxford and London: Oxford University Press, 1954).

Kamlah, Ehrhard
Die Form der katalogischen Paränese im Neuen Testament (WUNT 7; Tübingen: Mohr, 1964).

Kattenbusch, Ferdinand
"Messe, I: Dogmengeschichtlich," *RE*[3], 12.664–97.

Kertelge, Karl
"Das Doppelgebot der Liebe im Markusevangelium," in *À Cause de l'Évangile: Études sur les Synoptiques et les Actes offertes à P. Jacques Dupont, O.S.B., à l'occasion de son 70e anniversaire* (LD 123; Paris: Cerf, 1985) 303–22.

King, G. Brooks
"The 'Negative' Golden Rule," *JR* 8 (1928) 268–279; 15 (1935) 59–62.

Klauck, Hans-Josef
Herrenmahl und hellenistischer Kult: Eine religionsgeschichtliche Untersuchung zum ersten Korintherbrief (NTAbh NF 15; Münster: Aschendorff, 1982).

Klauser, Theodor
"Taufet in lebendigem Wasser! Zum religions- und kulturgeschichtlichen Verständnis von Didache 7,1–3," in Theodor Klauser and A. Rükker, eds., *Pisciculi: Studien zur Religion und Kultur des Altertums, F. J. Dölger zum 60. Geburtstage* (AuC.E. 1; Münster: Aschendorff, 1939) 157–64; repr. in Klauser, *Gesammelte Arbeiten zur Liturgiegeschichte, Kirchengeschichte und christlichen Archäologie* (ed. Ernst Dassmann; JAC.E 3; Münster: Aschendorff, 1974) 177–83.

Klein, Gottlieb
Der älteste christliche Katechismus und die jüdische Propaganda-Literatur (Berlin: Reimer, 1909).

Idem
"Die Gebete in der Didache," *ZNW* 9 (1908) 132–46.

Klevinghaus, J.
Die theologische Stellung der apostolischen Väter zur alttestamentlichen Offenbarung (BFCTh 44,1; Gütersloh: Mohn, 1948).

Kloppenborg, John S.
"Didache 16.6–8 and Special Matthaean Tradition," *ZNW* 70 (1979) 54–67.

Idem
"The Transformation of Moral Exhortation in *Didache* 1–5," in Jefford, *Context*, 88–109.

Klostermann, Erich
Das Matthäusevangelium (4th ed.; HNT 4; Tübingen: Mohr, 1971).

Kneller, C. A.
"Zum 'schwitzenden Almosen,'" *ZKTh* 26 (1902) 779–80.

Knoch, Otto
Eigenart und Bedeutung der Eschatologie im theologischen Aufriß des ersten Clemensbriefes: Eine auslegungsgeschichtliche Untersuchung (Theophaneia 17; Bonn: Hanstein, 1964).

Idem
"Die Stellung der Apostolischen Väter zu Israel und zum Judentum: Eine Übersicht," in Josef Zmijewski and Ernst Nellessen, eds., *Begegnung mit dem Wort: Festschrift für Heinrich Zimmermann* (BBB 53; Bonn: Hanstein, 1980) 347–78.

Knox, Wilfrid L.
"περικαθαίρων (Didache III, 4)," *JTS* 40 (1939) 146–49.

Koch, Hugo
"Die Didache bei Cyprian?" *ZNW* 8 (1907) 69–70.

Idem
"Die ps.-cyprianische Schrift De centesima, sexagesima, tricesima in ihrer Abhängigkeit von Cyprian," *ZNW* 31 (1932) 248–72.

Idem
"Zur Schrift *adversus aleatores*," in *Festgabe von Fachgenossen und Freunden Karl Müller zum siebzigsten Geburtstag dargebracht* (Tübingen: Mohr, 1922) 58–67.

Koester, Helmut
Synoptische Überlieferung bei den apostolischen Vätern (TU 65; Berlin: Akademie-Verlag, 1957).

Kretschmar, Georg
"Ein Beitrag zur Frage nach dem Ursprung frühchristlicher Askese," *ZThK* 61 (1964) 27–67; repr. in K. S. Frank, ed., *Askese und Mönchtum in der Alten Kirche* (WdF 409; Darmstadt: Wissenschaftliche Buchgesellschaft, 1975) 129–79, with an addendum, 179–80.

Idem
"Frühkatholizismus: Die Beurteilung theologischer Entwicklungen im späten ersten und im zweiten Jahrhundert nach Christus," in J. Brantschen and P. Selvatico, eds., *Unterwegs zur Einheit: Festschrift für H. Stirnimann* (Fribourg: Universitätsverlag; Freiburg im Breisgau and Vienna: Herder, 1980) 573–87.

Kubo, Sakae
"Jude 22–23: Two-division Form or Three?" in
Eldon J. Epp and Gordon D. Fee, eds., *New
Testament Textual Criticism, Its Significance for
Exegesis: Essays in Honour of Bruce M. Metzger* (New
York: Oxford University Press, 1981) 239–53.

Kuhn, Karl Georg
Achtzehngebet und Vaterunser und der Reim (WUNT
1; Tübingen: Mohr, 1950).

Idem
"μαραναθά," *TDNT* 4 (1967) 466–72.

Lake, Kirsopp
"The Didache," in J. V. Bartlet, K. Lake, et al., *The
New Testament in the Apostolic Fathers* (Oxford:
Clarendon, 1905) 24–36.

Lawson, John
*A Theological and Historical Introduction to the
Apostolic Fathers* (New York: Macmillan, 1961).

Layton, Bentley
"The Sources, Date and Transmission of *Didache*
1.3b–2.1," *HTR* 61 (1968) 343–83.

Leipoldt, Johannes
"Schenute von Atripe und die Entstehung des
national ägyptischen Christentums" (TU 25.1;
Leipzig: Hinrichs, 1903).

Lengeling, Emil J.
"Liturgie," *Handbuch theologischer Grundbegriffe* 2
(1963) 75–97.

Lietzmann, Hans
"Die Entstehung der christlichen Liturgie nach
den ältesten Quellen," VBW 5 (1925/26) 45–66;
repr. in idem, *Kleine Schriften* 3 (TU 74; Berlin:
Akademie-Verlag, 1962) 3–27.

Idem
Geschichte der Alten Kirche (4 vols. in 1; 4th and 5th
eds.; Berlin and New York: de Gruyter, 1975); ET:
A History of the Early Church (4 vols. in 2; trans.
Bertram Lee Woolf; 3d ed.; London: Lutterworth,
1953).

Idem
*Mass and Lord's Supper: A Study in the History of the
Liturgy* (trans. Dorothea H. G. Reeve; Leiden: Brill,
1979); ET of *Messe und Herrenmahl: Eine Studie zur
Geschichte der Liturgie* (AKG 8; Bonn: Marcus and
Weber, 1926).

Idem
"Notizen," *ZNW* 21 (1922) 236–40.

Idem
"Zum Text der georgischen Didache," *ZNW* 31
(1932) 206.

Ligier, Louis
"The Origins of the Eucharistic Prayer: From the
Last Supper to Eucharist," *StLi* 9 (1973) 161–85.

Lindemann, Andreas
Paulus im ältesten Christentum (BHTh 58;
Tübingen: Mohr [Siebeck], 1979).

Lohmeyer, Ernst
"Antichrist," *RAC* 1 (1950) 450–57.

Idem
Das Vaterunser (5th ed.; Göttingen: Vandenhoeck &
Ruprecht, 1962); ET: *The Lord's Prayer* (New York:
Harper & Row, 1965).

Lührmann, Dieter
"Neutestamentliche Haustafeln und antike
Ökonomie," *NTS* 27 (1981) 83–97.

Luz, Ulrich
Das Evangelium nach Matthäus, vol. 1: *Mt 1–7* (EKK
I/1; Zurich, Einsiedeln, and Cologne: Benziger;
Neukirchen-Vluyn: Neukirchener, 1985); ET:
Matthew 1–7: A Commentary (trans. Wilhelm C.
Linss; Minneapolis: Augsburg, 1989).

Magne, Jean
"Klasma, sperma, poimnion: Le voeu pour le
rassemblement de Didachè IX, 4," in P. Lévy and
E. Wolff, eds., *Mélanges d'histoire des religions offerts
à Henri-Charles Puech* (Paris: Presses universitaires
de France, 1974) 197–208.

Maier, Johann
*Geschichte der jüdischen Religion: Von der Zeit
Alexander des Grossen bis zur Aufklärung mit einem
Ausblick auf das 19./20. Jahrhundert* (2d ed.;
Freiburg, Basel, and Vienna: Herder, 1992).

Idem
*Jüdische Auseinandersetzung mit dem Christentum in
der Antike* (EdF 177; Darmstadt: Wissenschaftliche
Buchgesellschaft, 1982).

Manser, Anselm
"Zur Didache I,6 aus der Vita Chrodegangi," *ThR*
8 (1909) 459–60.

Massaux, Edouard
*The Influence of the Gospel of Saint Matthew on
Christian Literature before Saint Irenaeus* (3 vols.;
Louvain: Peeters; Macon, Ga.: Mercer, 1990–93);
ET of *Influence de l'Évangile de Saint Matthieu sur la
littérature chrétienne avant Saint Irénée. Réimpression
anastatique présentée par F. Neirynck. Supplément:
Bibliographie 1950–1985 par B. Dehandschutter*
(BETL 75; Louvain: Louvain University Press and
Peeters, 1986).

Idem
"Le Texte du Sermon sur la Montagne de
Matthieu utilisé par Saint Justin," *ETL* 28 (1952),
411–48; repr. in idem, *Influence*, 725–62.

Mathys, Hans-Peter
"Goldene Regel, I: Judentum," *TRE* 13 (1984)
570–73.

McDonald, James I. H.
*Kerygma and Didache: The Articulation and Structure
of the Earliest Christian Message* (SNTSMS 37;
Cambridge and New York: Cambridge University
Press, 1980).

Meer, Frederik van der, and Christine Mohrmann
Atlas of the Early Christian World (trans. Mary F.
Hedlund and H. H. Rowley; London: Nelson,
1966); ET of *Bildatlas der frühchristlichen Welt* (ed.
Heinrich Kraft; Gütersloh: Mohn, 1959).

Mees, Michael
"Die Bedeutung der Sentenzen und ihrer auxesis
für die Formung der Jesusworte nach Didaché
1,3b–2,1," *VetChr* 8 (1971) 55–76.

Michaelis, Wilhelm
"ὁδός," *TDNT* (1967) 42–114.

Middleton, Robert Dudley
"The Eucharistic Prayers of the Didache," *JTS* 36 (1935) 259–67.

Milavec, Aaron
"The Saving Efficacy of the Burning Process in *Didache* 16.5," in Jefford, *Context*, 131–55.

Mitchel, Nathan
"Baptism in the *Didache*," in Jefford, *Context*, 226–55.

Mitteis, Ludwig, and Ulrich Wilckens
Grundzüge und Chrestomathie der Papyruskunde, vol. 1.1 (Leipzig: Teubner, 1912; repr. Hildesheim: Olms, 1963).

Moll, Helmut
Die Lehre von der Eucharistie als Opfer: Eine dogmengeschichtliche Untersuchung von Neuen Testament bis Irenäus von Lyon (Theophaneia 26; Cologne and Bonn: Hanstein, 1975).

Moule, Charles Francis Digby
"A Note on *Didache* IX.4," *JTS*, n.s. 6 (1955) 240–43.

Idem
"A Reconsideration of the Context of *Maranatha*," *NTS* 6 (1959/60) 307–10.

Mühlsteiger, J.
"Verfassungsrecht der Frühkirche," *ZKTh* 99 (1977) 129–155, 257–85.

Muilenburg, James
The Literary Relations of the Epistle of Barnabas and the Teaching of the Twelve Apostles (diss. Yale; printed, Marburg, 1929).

Nauck, Wolfgang
Die Tradition und der Charakter des ersten Johannesbriefes (WUNT 3; Tübingen: Mohr, 1957).

Nautin, Pierre
"La composition de la 'Didachê' et son titre," *RHR* 78 (1959) 191–214.

Idem
"Notes critiques sur la Didachè," *VC* 13 (1959) 118–20.

Neppi Modona, A.
"Un frammento della 'Didaché' in un nuovo papiro di Ossirinco," *Bilychnis* 20 (1922) 173–86.

Neugebauer, Fritz
"Die dargebotene Wange und Jesu Gebot der Feindesliebe: Erwägungen zu Lk 6,27–36/Mt 5,38–48," *ThLZ* 110 (1985) 865–76.

Niederwimmer, Kurt
Askese und Mysterium: Über Ehe, Ehescheidung und Eheverzicht in den Anfängen des christlichen Glaubens (FRLANT 113; Göttingen: Vandenhoeck & Ruprecht, 1975).

Idem
"Doctrina apostolorum (Cod. Mellic. 597)," in H. D. Schmidt-Lauber, ed., *Theologia scientia eminens practica; F. Zerbst zum 70. Geburtstag* (Vienna, Freiburg, and Basel: Herder, 1979) 266–72.

Idem
"An Examination of the Development of Itinerant Radicalism in the Environment and Tradition of the *Didache*," in Draper, *Research*, 321–39; ET of "Zur Entwicklungsgeschichte des Wanderradikalismus im Traditionsbereich der Didache," *WS*, n.s. 11 (1977) 145–67.

Idem
"Kirche als Diaspora," *EvTh* 41 (1981) 290–300.

Idem
"Textprobleme der Didache," *WS*, n.s. 16 (1982) 114–30.

Nissen, Andreas
Gott und der Nächste im antiken Judentum: Untersuchungen zum Doppelgebot der Liebe (WUNT 15; Tübingen: Mohr, 1974).

Nock, Arthur Darby
"Liturgical Notes," *JTS* 30 (1929) 381–95.

Oesterley, William O. E.
The Jewish Background of the Christian Liturgy (Oxford: Clarendon, 1925).

Orbán, Arpad Peter
"Die Frage der ersten Zeugnisse des Christenlateins," *VC* 30 (1976) 214–38.

Otranto, Giorgio
"Matteo 7,15–16a e gli ψευδοπροφῆται nell' esegesi patristica," *VetChr* 6 (1969) 33–45.

Oulton, John Ernest Leonard
"Clement of Alexandria and the Didache," *JTS* 41 (1940) 177–79.

Papadopoulos-Kerameus, Athanasios, ed.
Ἱεροσολυμιτικὴ Βιβλιοθήκη ἤτοι κατάλογος τῶν ἐν ταῖς βιβλιοθήκαις τοῦ ἁγιωτάτου ἀποστολικοῦ τε καὶ καθολικοῦ ὀρθοδόξου πατριαρχικοῦ θρόνου τῶν Ἱεροσολύμων καὶ πάσης Παλαιστίνης ἀποκειμένων Ἑλληνικῶν κωδίκων I. (Ἐν Πετρουπόλει· ἐκ τοῦ τυπογραφείου Β. Κιρσβαουμ, 1891; repr. Brussels: Culture et civilisation, 1963).

Pardee, Nancy
"The Curse That Saves (*Didache* 16.5)," in Jefford, *Context*, 156–76.

Patsch, H.
"Abendmahlsterminologie außerhalb der Einsetzungsberichte: Erwägungen zur Traditionsgeschichte der Abendmahlsworte," *ZNW* 62 (1971) 210–31.

Patterson, Stephen J.
"*Didache* 11–13: The Legacy of Radical Itinerancy in Early Christianity," in Jefford, *Context*, 313–29.

Perler, Otto
"Arkandisziplin," *RAC* 1 (1950) 667–76.

Peterson, Erik
"Christianus," in idem, *Frühkirche*, 64–87.

Idem
Εἷς θεός: *Epigraphische, formgeschichtliche und religionsgeschichtliche Untersuchungen* (FRLANT 41; Göttingen: Vandenhoeck & Ruprecht, 1926).

Idem
Frühkirche, Judentum und Gnosis: Studien und Untersuchungen (Rome, Freiburg, and Vienna: Herder, 1959).

Idem

"Μερίς: Hostienpartikel und Opferanteil," in idem, *Frühkirche,* 97–106.

Idem

"Über einige Probleme der Didache-Überlieferung," in idem, *Frühkirche,* 146–82.

Philippidis, Leonidas J.

Die "Goldene Regel" religionsgeschichtlich untersucht (Inaugural-Dissertation Leipzig; Eisleben: Kloeppel, 1929).

Idem

Religionswissenschaftliche Forschungsberichte über die "goldene Regel" (Athens, n.p., 1933).

Piepkorn, Arthur C.

"Charisma in the New Testament and the Apostolic Fathers," *CTM* 42 (1971) 369–89.

Pillinger, Renate

"Die Taufe nach der Didache: Philologisch-archäologische Untersuchung der Kapitel 7, 9, 10 und 14," *WS,* n.s. 9 (1975) 152–62.

Piper, John

"Love your enemies": Jesus' Love Command in the Synoptic Gospels and in the Early Christian Paraenesis: A History of the Tradition and Interpretation of Its Uses (SNTSMS 38; Cambridge and New York: Cambridge University Press, 1979).

Poschmann, Bernhard

Paenitentia secunda: Die kirchliche Buße im ältesten Christentum bis Cyprian und Origenes: Eine dogmengeschichtliche Untersuchung (Theophaneia 1; Bonn: Hanstein, 1940, repr. 1964).

Powell, Douglas

"Arkandisziplin," *TRE* 4 (1981) 1–8.

Prinz, Friedrich

Frühes Mönchtum im Frankenreich: Kultur und Gesellschaft in Gallien, den Rheinlanden und Bayern am Beispiel der monastischen Entwicklung (4. bis 8. Jahrhundert) (Munich: Oldenbourg, 1965).

Puzicha, Michaela

Christus peregrinus: Die Fremdenaufnahme (Mt. 25,35) als Werk der privaten Wohltätigkeit im Urteil der Alten Kirche (Münsterische Beiträge zur Theologie 47; Münster: Aschendorff, 1980).

Quasten, Johannes

Patrology (3 vols.; 1950–60; repr. Utrecht and Antwerp: Spectrum; Westminster, Md.: Newman, 1975).

Reicke, Bo

Diakonie, Festfreude und Zelos in Verbindung mit der altchristlichen Agapenfeier (UUÅ 5; Uppsala and Wiesbaden, 1951).

Rengstorf, Karl

"σημεῖον κτλ.," *TDNT* 7 (1971) 200–269.

Rese, Martin

"Überprüfung einiger Thesen von Joachim Jeremias zum Thema des Gottesknechtes im Judenthum," *ZThK* 60 (1963) 21–41.

Richter, Klemens

"Ansätze für die Entwicklung einer Weiheliturgie in apostolischer Zeit," *ALW* 16 (1974) 32–52.

Riesenfeld, Harald

"Das Brot von den Bergen. Zu Did. 9,4," *Eranos* 54 (1956) 142–50.

Riesner, Rainer

Jesus als Lehrer: Eine Untersuchung zum Ursprung der Evangelien-Überlieferung (Tübingen: Mohr [Siebeck], 1981).

Riggs, John W.

"The Sacred Food of *Didache* 9–10 and Second-Century Ecclesiologies," in Jefford, *Context,* 256–83.

Robinson, Joseph Armitage

Barnabas, Hermas, and the Didache: Being the Donnelan Lectures Delivered before the University of Dublin in 1920 (London: SPCK; New York: Macmillan, 1920).

Idem

"The Epistle of Barnabas and the Didache" (ed. R. H. Connolly), *JTS* 35 (1934) 113–46, 225–48.

Idem

"The Problem of the Didache," *JTS* 13 (1912) 339–56.

Rordorf, Willy

"An Aspect of the Judeo-Christian Ethic: The Two Ways," in Draper, *Research,* 148–64; ET of "Un chapitre d'éthique judéo-chrétienne: les deux voies," *RechSR* 60 (1972) 109–28.

Idem

"Baptism according to the Didache," in Draper, *Research,* 212–22; ET of "Le baptême selon la *Didachè,*" in *Mélanges liturgiques offerts au R. P. Dom Bernard Botte O.S.B. de l'Abbaye du Mont César à l'occasion du cinquantième anniversaire de son ordination sacerdotale (4 Juin 1872)* (Louvain: Abbaye du Mont César, 1972) 499–509.

Idem

"Beobachtungen zur Gebrauch des Dekalogs in der vorkonstantinischen Kirche," in William C. Weinrich, ed., *The New Testament Age: Essays in Honor of Bo Reicke* (2 vols.; Macon, Ga.: Mercer, 1984) 2.431–42.

Idem

"La Didachè," in *L'Eucharistie des premiers chrétiens* (Le Point théologique 17; Paris: Beauchesne, 1976) 7–28.

Idem

"Une nouvelle édition de la Didachè? (Problèmes exégétiques, historiques et théologiques)," *StPatr* 15 (TU 128; Berlin: Akademie-Verlag, 1984) 26–30.

Idem

"Le problème de la transmission textuelle de *Didachè* 1.3b–2.1," in F. Paschke, ed., *Überlieferungsgeschichtliche Untersuchungen* (TU 125; Berlin: Akademie-Verlag, 1981) 499–513.

Idem

"La rémission des péchés selon la Didachè," *Irénikon* 46 (1973) 283–97.

Idem

"La tradition apostolique dans la Didachè," *L'Année canonique* 23 (1979) 105–14.

Saeki, P. Y.
  The Nestorian Documents and Relics in China (Tokyo: The Academy of Oriental Culture, The Tokyo Institute, 1937).

Sandvik, Bjørn
  Das Kommen des Herrn beim Abendmahl im Neuen Testament (AThANT 58; Zurich: Zwingli, 1970).

Schäfer, Peter
  "Die sogenannte Synode von Jabne: Zur Trennung von Juden und Christen im ersten/zweiten Jhdt. n. Chr.," repr. in idem, *Studien zur Geschichte und Theologie des rabbinischen Judentums* (AGJU 15; Leiden: Brill, 1978) 45–64.

Schermann, Theodor
  "Die Gebete in Didache c. 9 und 10," in A. Biglmaier et al., *Festgabe Alois Knöpfler zur Vollendung des 60. Lebensjahres* (VKHSM 3, series 1; Munich: Lentner, 1907) 225–39.

Schille, Gottfried
  "Das Recht der Propheten und Apostel—gemeinderechtliche Beobachtungen zu Didache Kapitel 11–13," in Paul Wätzel and Gottfried Schille, eds., *Theologische Versuche* (Berlin: Evangelische Verlags-Anstalt, 1966) 84–103.

Schlatter, Adolf
  Der Evangelist Matthäus (6th ed.; Stuttgart: Calwer, 1963).

Schmidt, G.
  "Μνήσϑητι: Eine liturgiegeschichtliche Skizze," in *Viva vox Evangelii: Eine Festschrift für Landesbischof D. Hans Meiser zum 70. Geburtstag am 16. Februar 1951* (Munich: 1951) 259–64.

Schmitz, Franz-Jürgen, and Gerd Mink
  Liste der koptischen Handschriften des Neuen Testaments, vol. 1: *Die sahidischen Handschriften der Evangelien* (ANTF 8; Berlin and New York: de Gruyter, 1986).

Schnackenburg, Rudolf
  The Johannine Letters: A Commentary (trans. Reginald and Ilse Fuller; New York: Crossroad, 1992); ET of *Die Johannesbriefe* (6th ed.; HThK 13.3; Freiburg, Basel, and Vienna: Herder, 1979).

Schneider, Gerhard
  Die Apostelgeschichte, vol. 1: *Einleitung, Kommentar zu Kap. 1,1–8,40* (HThK 5.1; Freiburg: Herder, 1980).

Idem
  "Das Vaterunser des Matthäus," in *À Cause de l'Évangile: Études sur les Synoptiques et les Actes offertes au P. Jacques Dupont, O.S.B., à l'occasion de son 70e anniversaire* (LD 123; Paris: Cerf, Publications de Saint-André, 1985) 57–90.

Schöllgen, Georg
  "Die Didache—ein frühes Zeugnis für Landgemeinden?" *ZNW* 76 (1985) 140–43.

Idem
  "The *Didache* as a Church Order: An Examination of the Purpose for the Composition of the *Didache* and Its Consequences for Its Interpretation," in Draper, *Research*, 43–71; ET of "Die Didache als

Kirchenordnung: Zur Frage des Abfassungszweckes und seinen Konsequenzen für die Interpretation," JAC 29 (1986) 5–26.

Schottroff, Luise
  "Gewaltverzicht und Feindesliebe in der urchristlichen Jesustradition," in Georg Strecker, ed., *Jesus Christus in Historie und Theologie: Neutestamentliche Festschrift für Hans Conzelmann zum 60. Geburtstag* (Tübingen: Mohr, 1975) 197–221.

Schrage, Wolfgang
  Die Elia Apokalypse (JSHRZ 5.3; Gütersloh: Mohn, 1980).

Idem
  Ethik des Neuen Testaments (GNT 4; Göttingen: Vandenhoeck & Ruprecht, 1982); ET: *The Ethics of the New Testament* (trans. David E. Green; Philadelphia: Fortress, 1988).

Idem
  "Zur Ethik der neutestamentlichen Haustafeln," *NTS* 21 (1975) 1–22.

Schulz, Siegfried
  "Maranatha and Kyrios Jesus," *ZNW* 53 (1962) 125–44.

Schümmer, Johannes
  Altchristliche Fastenpraxis: Mit besonderer Berücksichtigung der Schriften Tertullians (LQF 27; Münster: Aschendorff, 1933).

Schweizer, Eduard
  Das Evangelium nach Matthäus (NTD 2; 3d ed.; Göttingen: Vandenhoeck & Ruprecht, 1981); ET: *The Good News According to Matthew* (Atlanta: John Knox, 1975).

Idem
  Matthäus und seine Gemeinde (SBS 71; Stuttgart: KBW, 1974).

Seeberg, Alfred
  Die beiden Wege und das Aposteldekret (Leipzig: Deichert, 1906).

Idem
  Die Didache des Judentums und der Urchristenheit (Leipzig: Deichert, 1908).

Idem
  Der Katechismus der Urchristenheit (ThBü 26; 1903, repr. Munich: Kaiser, 1966).

Severus, Emmanuel von
  "Brotbrechen," *RAC* 2 (1954) 620–26.

Skehan, Patrick W.
  "Didache 1,6 and Sirach 12,1," *Bib* 44 (1963) 533–36.

Smith, M. A.
  "Did Justin Know the Didache?" *StPatr* 7.1 (TU 92; Berlin: Akademie-Verlag, 1966) 287–90.

Snell, Bruno
  "Das Symbol des Weges," in idem, *Die Entdeckung des Geistes: Studien zur Entstehung des europäischen Denkens bei den Griechen* (4th ed.; Göttingen: Vandenhoeck & Ruprecht, 1975) 219–30.

Speyer, Wolfgang
"Ein angebliches Zeugnis für die Doctrina apostolorum oder Pelagius bei Pseudo-Hieronymus," *VC* 21 (1967) 241–46.

Spicq, Ceslas
Notes de Lexicographie Néo-Testamentaire (2 vols. and Sup; OBO 22.1–3; Fribourg: Éditions Universitaires; Göttingen: Vandenhoeck & Ruprecht; Paris: Gabalda, 1978–82]; ET: *Theological Lexicon of the New Testament* (3 vols.; trans. and ed. James D. Ernest; Peabody, Mass.: Hendrickson, 1994).

Stählin, Otto
"Zu dem Didachezitat bei Clemens Alexandrinus," *ZNW* 14 (1913) 271–72.

Stegmüller, Friedrich
Repertorium Biblicum Medii Aevi (11 vols.; Madrid: Consejo Superior de Investigaciones Científicas, Institute Francisco Suarez, 1950–80).

Steidle, Basilius
"Dominici schola servitii. Zum Verständnis des Prologes der Regel St. Benedikts," *BenM* 28 (1952) 397–406.

Stemberger, Gunter
"Die sogenannte 'Synode von Jabne' und das frühe Christentum," *Kairos* 19 (1977) 14–21.

Stempel, H.-A.
"Der Lehrer in der 'Lehre der zwölf Apostel,'" *VC* 34 (1980) 209–17.

Stenzel, Meinrad
"Der Bibelkanon des Rufin von Aquileja," *Bib* 23 (1942) 43–61.

Stommel, Eduard
"Σημεῖον ἐκπετάσεως (Didache 16,6)," *RQ* 48 (1953) 21–42.

Strecker, Georg
"Eine Evangelienharmonie bei Justin und Pseudoklementinen?" *NTS* 24 (1978) 297–316.

Idem
Das Judenchristentum in den Pseudoklementinen (2d ed.; TU 70; Berlin: Akademie-Verlag, 1981).

Streeter, Burnett Hillman
"The Much-Belaboured *Didache*," *JTS* 37 (1936) 369–74.

Stuiber, Alfred
"Die drei σημεῖα von Didache XVI," JAC 24 (1981) 42–44.

Idem
"Eulogia," *RAC* 6 (1966) 900–929.

Idem
"'Das ganze Joch des Herrn' (Didache 6,2–3)," *StPatr* 4.2 (TU 79; Berlin: Akademie-Verlag, 1961) 323–29.

Suggs, M. Jack
"The Christian Two Ways Tradition: Its Antiquity, Form, and Function," in David E. Aune, ed., *Studies in New Testament and Early Christian Literature: Essays in Honor of Allen P. Wikgren* (NovTSup 33; Leiden: Brill, 1972) 60–74.

Talley, Thomas J.
"The Eucharistic Prayer Tradition and Develop-
ment," in Kenneth Stevenson, ed., *Liturgy Reshaped* (London: SPCK, 1982) 48–64.

Idem
"Von der Berakah zur Eucharistia: Das eucharistische Hochgebet der alten Kirche in neuerer Forschung: Ergebnisse und Fragen," *LJ* 26 (1976) 93–115.

Taylor, Charles
"Traces of a Saying of the Didache," *JTS* 8 (1907) 115–17.

Telfer, William
"The *Didache* and the Apostolic Synod of Antioch," *JTS* 40 (1939) 133–46, 258–71.

Idem
"The 'Plot' of the Didache," *JTS* 45 (1944) 141–51.

Theißen, Gerd
"Gewaltverzicht und Feindesliebe (Mt 5,38–48/Lk 6,27–38) und deren sozialgeschichtlicher Hintergrund," in idem, *Studien*, 160–97; ET: "Nonviolence and Love of Our Enemies (Matthew 5:38–48; Luke 6:27–38): The Social Background," in idem, *Social Reality*, 115–56.

Idem
"Legitimation und Lebensunterhalt: Ein Beitrag zur Soziologie urchristlicher Missionare," *NTS* 21 (1974/1975) 192–221; repr. in idem, *Studien*, 201–30.

Idem
Studien zur Soziologie des Urchristentums (2d ed.; WUNT 19; Tübingen: Mohr, 1983); ET: *Social Reality of the Early Christians: Theology, Ethics and the World of the New Testament* (Minneapolis: Fortress, 1992).

Idem
"Wanderradikalismus: Literatursoziologische Aspekte der Überlieferung von Worten Jesu im Urchristentum," *ZThK* 70 (1973) 245–71; repr. in idem, *Studien*, 79–105; ET: "The Wandering Radicals: Light Shed by the Sociology of Literature on the Early Transmission of Jesus Sayings," in idem, *Social Reality*, 33–59.

Idem
"'Wir haben alles verlassen' (Mc. X. 28). Nachfolge und soziale Entwurzelung in der jüdisch-palästinischen Gesellschaft des 1. Jahrhunderts n. Chr.," *NovT* 19 (1977) 161–96; repr. in idem, *Studien*, 106–41; ET: "'We Have Left Everything . . .' (Mark 10:28): Discipleship and Social Uprooting in the Jewish-Palestinian Society of the First Century," in idem, *Social Reality*, 60–93.

Thraede, Klaus
"Zum historischen Hintergrund der 'Haustafeln' des NT," in Ernst Dassmann and K. Suso Frank, eds., *Pietas: Festschrift für Bernhard Kötting* (JAC.E. 8; Münster: Aschendorff, 1980) 359–68.

Torrance, Thomas F.
The Doctrine of Grace in the Apostolic Fathers (Grand Rapids: Eerdmans, 1959).

Torrey, Charles C.

"Ein griechisch transkribiertes und interpretiertes hebräisch-aramäisches Verzeichnis der Bücher des Alten Testaments aus dem 1. Jahrhundert n. Chr.," translated and annotated by Otto Eißfeldt, *ThLZ* 77 (1952) 249–54.

Tuilier, André

"Didache," *TRE* 8 (1981) 731–36.

Idem

"La liturgie dans la *Didachè* et l'essénisme," *StPatr* 26 (1993) 200–210.

Idem

"Une nouvelle édition de la Didachè (Problèmes de méthode et de critique textuelle)," *StPatr* 15.1 (TU 128; Berlin: Akademie-Verlag, 1984) 31–36.

Turner, Cuthbert H.

"Adversaria patristica," *JTS* 7 (1906) 593–95.

Turner, Eric G.

The Typology of the Early Codex (Haney Foundation Series 18; Philadelphia: University of Pennsylvania Press, 1977).

Unnik, Willem C. van

"De la Règle Μήτε προσθεῖναι μήτε ἀφελεῖν dans l'histoire du Canon," *VC* 3 (1949) 1–36.

Urban, Angel

Concordantia in Didachen (Doctrina duodecim Apostolorum) (Alph-Omega A.146; Concordantia in Patres Apostolicos 2; Hildesheim, Zurich, New York: Olms-Weidmann, 1993).

Verme, M. Del

"The Didache and Judaism: The ἀπαρχή of Didache 13:3–7," *StPatr* 26 (1993) 113–20.

Vielhauer, Philipp

Geschichte der urchristlichen Literatur: Einleitung in das Neue Testament, die Apokryphen und die apostolischen Väter (Berlin and New York: de Gruyter, 1975; repr. 1981).

Vögtle, Anton

Die Tugend- und Lasterkataloge im Neuen Testament: Exegetisch, religions- und formgeschichtlich untersucht (NTA 16/4.5; Münster: Aschendorff, 1936).

Vogüé, Adalbert de

"'Ne haïr personne.' Jalons pour l'histoire d'une maxime," *RThAM* 44 (1968) 3–9.

Vokes, Frederick E.

"The *Didache* and the Canon of the New Testament," *StEv* 3.2 (TU 88; Berlin: Akademie-Verlag, 1964) 427–36.

Idem

"The *Didache* – Still Debated," *ChQ* 3 (1970) 57–62.

Idem

The Riddle of the Didache: Fact or Fiction, Heresy or Catholicism? (London: SPCK; New York: Macmillan, 1938).

Völker, Karl

Mysterium und Agape: Die gemeinsamen Mahlzeiten in der Alten Kirche (Gotha: Klotz, 1927).

Völkl, Richard

Frühchristliche Zeugnisse zu Wesen und Gestalt der christlichen Liebe (QCVL 2; Freiburg im Breisgau: Herder, 1963).

Vööbus, Arthur

Liturgical Traditions in the Didache (Proceedings of the Estonian Theological Society in Exile 16; Stockholm: Estonian Theological Society in Exile, 1968).

Idem

"Regarding the Background of the Liturgical Traditions in the Didache: The Question of Literary Relation between Didache IX,4 and the Fourth Gospel," *VC* 23 (1969) 81–87.

Idem

Studies in the History of the Gospel Text in Syriac (CSCO Subsidia 3; Louvain: Durbecq, 1951).

Wagner, Georg

"Zur Herkunft der Apostolischen Konstitutionen," in *Mélanges liturgiques offerts au R. P. Dom Bernard Botte O.S.B. de l'Abbaye du Mont César à l'occasion du cinquantième anniversaire de son ordination sacerdotale (4 Juin 1972)* (Louvain: Abbaye du Mont César, 1972) 525–37.

Walker, Joan H.

"An Argument from the Chinese for the Antiochene Origin of the *Didache*," *StPatr* 8.2 (TU 93; Berlin: Akademie-Verlag, 1966) 44–50.

Wegman, Herman A. J.

"Une Anaphore incomplète? Les Fragments sur Papyrus Strasbourg Gr. 254," in Roelof van den Broek and M. J. Vermaseren, eds., *Studies in Gnosticism and Hellenistic Religions: Presented to Gilles Quispel on the Occasion of His 65th Birthday* (EPRO 91; Leiden: Brill, 1981) 432–50.

Weidinger, Karl

Die Haustafeln. Ein Stück urchristlicher Paränese (UNT 14; Leipzig: Hinrichs, 1928).

Wengst, Klaus

Tradition und Theologie des Barnabasbrief (AKG 42; Berlin and New York: de Gruyter, 1971).

Wibbing, Siegfried

Die Tugend- und Lasterkataloge im Neuen Testament und ihre Traditionsgeschichte unter besonderer Berücksichtigung der Qumran-Texte (BZNW 25; Berlin: Töpelmann, 1959).

Wilckens, Ulrich

Die Missionsreden der Apostelgeschichte. Form- und traditionsgeschichtliche Untersuchungen (3d ed.; WMANT 5; Neukirchen-Vluyn: Neukirchener Verlag, 1974).

Windisch, Hans

Der Barnabasbrief (HNT.E; Die apostolischen Väter 3; Tübingen: Mohr, 1920).

Winter, Paul

"Ben Sira and the Teaching of 'Two Ways,'" *VT* 5 (1955) 315–18.

Wohleb, Leo

Die lateinische Übersetzung der Didache kritisch und sprachlich untersucht (SGKA 7.1; Paderborn: Schöningh, 1913; repr. New York: Johnson, 1967).

Wohlenberg, Gustav
Die Lehre der zwölf Apostel in ihrem Verhältnis zum neutestamentlichen Schrifttum: Eine Untersuchung (Erlangen: Deichert, 1888).

Woude, A. S. van der
"Malachi's Struggle for a Pure Community: Reflections on Malachi 2:10–16," in J. W. van Henten et al., eds., *Tradition and Re-interpretation in Jewish and Early Christian Literature: Essays in Honour of Jürgen C. H. Lebram* (SPB 36; Leiden: Brill, 1986) 65–71.

Wrege, Hans Theo
Die Überlieferungsgeschichte der Bergpredigt (WUNT 9; Tübingen: Mohr, 1968).

Zahn, Theodor
Forschungen zur Geschichte des neutestamentlichen Kanons und der altkirchlichen Literatur, vol. 1: *Tatians Diatessaron* (Erlangen: Deichert, 1881); vol. 2: *Der Evangeliencommentar des Theophilus von Antiochien* (Erlangen: Deichert, 1883); vol. 3: *Supplementum Clementinum* (Erlangen: Deichert, 1884), therein: "Die 'Lehre der zwölf Apostel,'" 278–319.

Idem
Geschichte des Neutestamentlichen Kanons (1 vol. in 2 parts; Erlangen and Leipzig: Deichert, 1890–92).

Zimmermann, Alfred F.
Die urchristlichen Lehrer: Studien zum Tradentenkreis der διδάσκαλοι im frühen Urchristentum (WUNT 2.12; Tübingen: Mohr, 1984).

Select Bibliography from the Second Edition

1. Editions and Commentaries

Lindemann, Andreas, and Henning Paulsen
Die Apostolischen Väter: griechisch-deutsche Parallel-ausgabe auf der Grundlage der Ausgaben von Franz Xaver Funk/Karl Bihlmeyer und Molly Whitaker (Tübingen: Mohr [Siebeck], 1992).

Lightfoot, J. B., and J. R. Harmer
The Apostolic Fathers (rev. ed. Michael W. Holmes; Grand Rapids, Mich.: Baker, 1989).

Ruiz Bueno, Daniel
Padres apostolici: Edicion Bilingue Completa (3d ed.; Biblioteca de autores cristianos 65; Madrid: Biblioteca de autores cristianos, 1985).

Schöllgen, Georg, and Wilhelm Geerlings
Didache: Zwölf-Apostel-Lehre: Traditio Apostolica: Apostolische Überlieferung (Fontes christiani 1; Freiburg and New York: Herder, 1991)

Tugwell, Simon
The Apostolic Fathers: Outstanding Christian Thinkers (London: Chapman, 1989).

2. Sources

Apocalypse of Peter
Dennis D. Buchholz, *Your Eyes Will Be Opened: A Study of the Greek (Ethiopic) Apocalypse of Peter* (SBLDS 97; Atlanta: Scholars, 1988).

Apostolic Constitutions
Marcel Metzger, ed., *Les Constitutions Apostoliques*, Vol. 1: *Livres 1 and 2* (SC 320; Paris: Cerf, 1985), Vol. 2: *Livres 3–6* (SC 329; Paris: Cerf, 1986), Vol 3: *Livres 7–8* (SC 336; Paris: Cerf, 1987).

Cairo Geniza
Klaus Berger, *Die Weisheitsschrift aus der Kairoer Geniza: Erstedition, Kommentar und Übersetzung* (Texte und Arbeiten zum neutestamentlichen Zeitalter 1; Tübingen: Francke, 1989).

Idem
Hans-Peter Rüger, ed., *Die Weisheitsschrift aus der Kairoer Geniza: Text, Übersetzung und philologischer Kommentar* (WUNT 53; Tübingen: Mohr [Siebeck], 1991).

Clement of Alexandria
Otto Stählin, Ludwig Fruchtel, Ursula Treu, eds., *Stromata Buch I–VI* (GCS 52 (15); 4th ed.; Berlin: Akademie, 1985).

Didymus the Blind
Michael Gronewald, ed., *Psalmenkommentar (Tura-Papyrus). Teil III: Kommentar zu Psalm 29–34* (Papyrologische Texte und Abhandlungen 8; Bonn: Habelt, 1969).

Idem
Michael Gronewald, ed., *Kommentar zum Ecclesiastes (Tura-Papyrus). Teil II: Kommentar zu Eccl. 3–4, 12* (Papyrologische Texte und Abhandlungen 22; Bonn: Habelt, 1977).

Eucharistic Prayers
C. Vogel, "Anaphores eucharistiques préconstanti-niennes: Formes non traditionnelles," *Aug 20* (1980) 401–10.

Hippolytus
Bernard Botte, *La tradition apostolique de Saint Hippolyte: Essai de reconstitution* (5th ed.; A. Gerhards, ed., LWQF 39; Münster: Aschendorff, 1989).

Papyri
A. Schmidt, "P. Oxy. X 1224, Fragment 2 recto, Col I: Ein neuer Vorschlag," *ZNW* 20 (1989) 276–77.

Pseudo-Clementine Homilies
Bernhard Rehm, Georg Strecker, eds., *Die Pseudoklementinen*, Vol. 1: *Homilien* (GCS 42; 3d ed.; Berlin: Akademie, 1992).

3. Secondary Literature

Black, Matthew
"The Doxology to the Lord's Prayer with a Note on Matthew 6,13b," in Philip R. Davies, B. T. White, eds., *A Tribute to G. Vermes: Essays on Jewish and Christian Literature and History* (JSOTSup 100; Sheffield: JSOT Press, 1990) 327–38.

Behl, F.
"Das Fasten an Montagen und Donnerstagen: Zur Geschichte einer pharisäischen Praxis (Lk 13,12)," *BZ* n.F. 31 (1987) 247–56.

Brock, Sebastian
"The Two Ways and the Palestinian Targum," in Philip R. Davies, B. T. White, eds., *A Tribute to G. Vermes: Essays on Jewish and Christian Literature and History* (JSOTSup 100; Sheffield: JSOT Press, 1990) 139–52.

Delobel, Jean
"The Lord's Prayer in the Textual Tradition: A Critique of Recent Theories and Their View on Marcion's Role," in J.-M. Sevrin, ed., *The New Testament in Early Christianity: La réception des écrits néotestamentaires dans le christianisme primitif* (BETL 86; Leuven: Leuven University Press/Uitgeverij Peeters, 1989) 293–309.

Draper, Jonathan
"The Jesus Tradition in the Didache," in David Wenham, ed., *Gospel Perspectives: The Jesus Tradition Outside the Gospels* (Sheffield: JSOT Press, 1985) 269–87.

Ehrman, Bart
"The New Testamnent Canon of Didymus the Blind," *VC* 37 (1983) 1–21.

Flüsser, David
"Paul's Jewish-Christian Opponents in the Didache," in Shaul Shaked, et al., eds., *Gilgul: Essays on Transformation. Revolution and Permanence in the History of Religions Dedicated to R. J. Z.*

Werblowsky (SHR 60; Leiden, New York, and Cologne: Brill, 1987) 71–90.

Hagner, Donald A.
"The Sayings of Jesus in the Apostolic Fathers and Justin Martyr," in David Wenham, ed., *Gospel Perspectives: The Jesus Tradition Outside the Gospels* (Sheffield: JSOT Press, 1985) 233–68.

Hahn, Ferdinand
"Charisma und Amt: Die Diskussion über das kirchliche Amt im Lichte der neutestamentlichen Charismenlehre," in idem, *Exegetische Beiträge zum ökumenischen Gespräch: Gesammelte Aufsätze I* (Göttingen: Vandenhoeck & Ruprecht, 1986) 201–31.

Idem
"Prophetie und Lebenswandel: Bemerkungen zu Paulus und zu zwei Texten der Apostolischen Väter," in Helmut Merklein, ed., *Neues Testament und Ethik: Für Rudolf Schnackenburg* (Freiburg, Basel, and Vienna: Herder, 1989) 527–37.

Han-Rhinow, J. A.
"Die frühchristlichen Kirchenordnungen und ihr Amtsverständnis als Beitrag zur ökumenischen Diskussion um das Lima Dokument" (Diss. Münich, 1991).

Jenks, Gregory C.
The Origins and Early Development of the Antichrist Myth (BZNW 59; Berlin and New York: de Gruyter, 1991).

Kiilunen, Jarmo
Das Doppelgebot der Liebe in synoptischer Sicht: Ein redaktionskritischer Versuch über Mk 12, 28–34 und die Parallelen (Suomalainen Tiedeakatemian toimituksia B 250; Helsinki: Suomalainen Tiedeakatemia, 1989).

Köhler, Wolf-Dietrich
Die Rezeption des Matthäusevangeliums in der Zeit vor Irenäus (WUNT 2,24; Tübingen: Mohr [Siebeck], 1987).

Kubo, H. W.
"Das Liebesgebot Jesu als Tora und als Evangelium: Zur Feindesliebe und zur christlichen und jüdischen Auslegung des Bergpredigt," in Hubert Frankemölle, Karl Kertelge, eds., *Vom Urchristentum zu Jesus: Für Joachim Gnilka* (Freiburg, Basel, and Vienna: Herder, 1989) 194–210.

Lattke, Michael
Hymnus: Materialien zu einer Geschichte der antiken Hymnologie (NTOA 19; Freiburg: Universitätsverlag; Göttingen: Vandenhoeck & Ruprecht, 1991).

Lohmann, Hans
Drohung und Verheissung: Exegetische Untersuchungen zur Eschatologie bei den apostolichen Vätern (BZNW 55; Berlin and New York: de Gruyter, 1989).

Lührmann. Dieter
"Das Bruchstück aus dem Hebräerevangelium bei

Didymos von Alexandrien," *NovT* 29 (1987) 265–79).

Milavec, Aaron
"The Pastoral Genius of the Didache: An Analytical Translation and Commentary," in Jacob Neusner, ed., *Religious Writings and Religious Systems* (Atlanta: Scholars Press, 1989) 89–125.

Neymeyr, Ulrich
Die christlichen Lehrer im zweiten Jahrhundert: ihre Lehrtätigkeit, ihr Selbstverständnis und ihre Geschichte (Supplements to Vigiliae Christianae 4; Leiden and New York: Brill, 1989).

Ricoeur, Paul
"The Golden Rule: Exegetical and Theological Perplexities," *NTS* 36 (1990) 392–97.

Riggs, John W.
"From Gracious Table to Sacramental Elements: The Tradition-History of Didache 9 and 10," *Second Century* 4 (1984) 83–101.

Rordorf, Willy
"Does the Didache Contain Jesus Tradition Independently of the Synoptic Gospels?" in Henry Wansbrough, ed., *Jesus and the Oral Gospel Tradition* (JSNTSup 64; Sheffield: JSOT, 1991) 394–423.

Schmeller, Thomas
Brechungen: Urchristliche Wandercharismatiker im Prisma soziologisch orientierter Exegese (Stuttgarter Bibelstudien 13; Stuttgart: Katholisches Bibelwerk, 1989).

Stroker, William D.
Extracanonical Sayings of Jesus (Resources for Biblical Study 18; Atlanta: Scholars Press, 1989).

Tuckett, Christopher M.
"Synoptic Tradition in the Didache," in J.-M. Sevrin, ed., *The New Testament in Early Christianity: La réception des écrits néotestamentaires dans le christianisme primitif* (BETL 86; Leuven: Leuven University Press/Uitgeverij Peeters, 1989) 197–230.

Tuilier, Andre
"La Doctrine des Apôtres de la hiérarchie dans l'église primitive," *Studia Patristica* 18,3 (1989) 229–62.

Walker, J. H.
"A Pre-Markan Dating for the Didache: Further Thoughts of a Liturgist," in F. A. Livingstone, ed., *Studia Biblica 1978.* Vol. 3: *Papers on Paul and Other New Testament Authors* (JSNTSup 3; Sheffield: JSOT Press, 1980) 403–11.

Indices

<table>
<tr><td colspan="2">

2.68–69ψ	90[25]
2.74ψ	189[2]
2.78ψ	108[2]
2.79ψ	84
2.89–90ψ	82[96]
2.145ψ	97[17]
2.165–66	217[6]
2.167–68	219[7]
2.188	212[2]
2.188–95	223[2]
2.281	90[15]
3.37	91[35], 92[49]
3.66–67	219[7]
3.68	211[2], 219[3]
3.68–74	217[6]
3.224–30	89[10]
3.225	98[34]
4.165	127
5.384–85	221[8]
6.26–27	224[20]
8.239	224[25]
8.393–94	123[36]
8.399–401	62
14.33	185[2]

Testaments of the Twelve Patriarchs

	61[15], 65[11], 95, 96[12], 151[55]

T. Ash.

1–5	40[73]
1.3	60
1.3–5	36, 60, 62[26]
1.5	60
2	37[56]
3.1	117[20]
3.1–2	106[34]
6.4	63[29]
7.2	151[55]
7.2–3	151[55]

T. Benj.

3.1	65[11]
5.1	75[56]
6.3	97[31]

8.2	98[31], 111[94]
9.2	151[55]
10.3	65[11]

T. Dan

1–6	97[21]
5.1	65[11]
5.3	65[11]
5.8–9	151[55]

T. Gad

6.3	203[6]

T. Iss.

5.1–2	65[11]
6.1	216[26]
6.2–4	151[55]
7.2	97
7.6	65[11]

T. Jos.

11.1	65[11]
17.8	101[18]

T. Jud.

14.1	95[9]
19.1	95[9]
23.5	151[55]

T. Levi

17.11	89[7], 99[45]
18.6	221[3]

T. Naph.

1.6	66[14]
3.1	91[40]
4	151[55]
6.7	151[55], 152–53[69]

T. Reub.

2.8–9	95[9]

T. Sim.

4.8	96[9]
5.2	65[11]

T. Zeb.

5.1	65[11]
6.6	108[55]
6.7	82[96]
7.2	82[96]
8.1–3	108[55]

T. Job

6.4	219[6]

c / Qumran Literature

Community Rule (1QS)

	2[11]
1.6	98[31]
1.11–12	109[65]
3	63[28]
3–4	61[17, 62]
3.9	127
3.13–4.26	121[11]
3.18–4.26	36, 36[48], 37[56], 40[73], 61, 62[26]
3.18–19	61, 63[29]
3.20–21	61
4.2–14	61[17]
4.6–8	61[17]
4.7	121[11]
4.9–10	116[6]
4.11–14	61[17]
4.17–18	121[11]
4.26	111[94]
5.2	109[65]
5.24–25	203[6]
6.2–3	109[65]
6.16–17	154[81]
6.20–21	154[81]
7.6–10	109[65]
11.11	102

Damascus Document (CD)

2.16	98[31]
14.2	91[37]
14.12–17	109[65]

Thanksgiving Hymns (1QH)

2.21	91[37]
4.14	106[34]

Habakkuk Pesher (1QpHab)

5.3	66[20]

d / Other Jewish Literature

Josephus
    Antiquities of the Jews

1.17	113
1.189	99[52]

</td></tr>
</table>

e / Rabbinic Literature

f / New Testament

12:29–31	65	6:31	66	6:3	152[66]
12:30–31	64	6:32	76[59]	6:12	155
12:31	64	6:32–33	76[59]	6:39–40	217[3]
13	211, 220[15], 221[7]	6:32–35	75[51]	6:44	217[3]
13:5–6	210[1], 217[6]	6:33	22, 73[41]	6:54	217[3]
13:12–13	210[1]	9:1–6	175[2]	7:24	117[21]
13:13b	212, 221	9:3	176[18], 177	7:37	217[3]
13:19	211, 219–20, 220[15], 221[1]	9:8	181[35]	10:8	7
		9:19	181[35]	10:12	217[9]
3:21–22	217[6]	10:1–12	175[2]	11:24	217[3]
13:22	211, 219, 219[7]	10:3	210[2], 217[9]	11:52	48[40], 140[8], 151, 152[66]
13:26	213, 226, 226[5]	10:4	177	12:13	183
13:27	151, 161, 212	10:7b	188	12:48	217[3]
		10:8	171[2]	13:20	172[12]
13:30	162[79]	10:27	64, 65	15	140[8]
13:31	162[79]	11:2–4	135	15:1–6	146[15]
13:33	208, 215	11:31	152–53[69]	15:15	48[40]
13:35	208, 214, 215	12:10	179	16:12	121[15]
		12:15	92[46]	17	48[40], 140[8], 156[10], 160–61[64]
14:62	213	12:35	208, 214, 215		
14:62b	226[3]				
15:22	195[10]	12:40	215	17:11	48[40], 152[60], 156[10]
16:15	221[2]	12:58–59	71, 81, 83		
Luke		13:35	183		
1:49	156[12]	14:11	101[18]	17:15	160[58]
1:51	92[50]	14:12–14	185[3]	17:20–23	152[60]
1:69	147[22, 23]	14:14	108[55]	17:21–22	48[40]
2:29	157[29]	16:14	99[45]	17:23	48[40], 160[64]
2:37	131[1]	18:10–14	131[1]	17:26	48[40]
6	70[12]	18:11	92[47]	18:22	70[14], 78[68]
6:20–26	81[86]	18:12	132	19:3	70[14], 78[68]
6:25	155[1]	18:14	101[18]	20:1	195[8]
6:27	22, 74[42], 75, 76[59]	18:20	89[4]	20:19	195[8]
		19:38	183	20:26	195[8]
6:27–28	69, 74	19:43	221[3]	Acts	
6:28	73[38], 75, 76[59]	21:27	213, 226, 226[4]	1:18	117[19]
				2:17	217[3]
6:29	79[78]	21:35	219[10]	2:38	126[8]
6:29a	78	22:69	213	2:41–42	57[15]
6:29b	78, 79	23:56 Sah.	167[126]	2:42	57[15]
6:29–30	70	24:30	195[10]	2:44–45	109
6:30	71, 78, 79, 79[78, 79]	24:35	195[10]	2:45	83[105]
		John		2:46	195[10]
		5:30	117[21]	3:13	147[23, 24]
		5:43	183[3]	3:26	147[23, 24]
		6	140[8], 152[66]		

6:18	117[22]
Philippians	
1:1	200
2:22	96[12]
3:2	153[80]
Colossians	
1:23	221[2]
2:16–17	195[9]
3:5	92[46]
3:8	97[28]
3:18–4:1	104[3]
3:21–4:1	104[5]
3:22	110[75]
3:22–23	111[100]
3:22–25	111[98]
4:1	110[84]
4:10	171[2]
1 Thessalonians	
2:4	180
2:5	92[46]
4:6	92[46]
4:16	212, 224[25]
5:6	214[2]
5:20–22	178[8]
5:22	97[17]
2 Thessalonians	
1:5	117[21]
2:3–4	211[2], 219[3]
2:8–9	211[2], 219[3]
2:9	209[18], 211[3], 219[7]
3:10–12	186[7]
1 Timothy	2
1:2	96[12]
1:6	204[13]
1:10	89[7], 90[25]
1:12	112[9]
1:13	117[7]
1:14	112[9]
1:18	96[12]
2:8–15	104[3]
3:1–10	200[7, 10]
3:2	185[3]
3:3	201[12, 13]
3:10	180[22]
4:1–3	217[6]

4:2	132[5]
5:10	210[1]
5:17–25	201[10]
5:18a	189
5:18b	188, 189, 189[2]
5:20	203[5]
6:1–2	104[3], 111[98]
6:5	187
6:17	158[33]
6:21	204[13]
2 Timothy	
1:2	96[12]
2:1	96[12]
2:21	157[29]
3:1	217[3]
3:2	92[50], 99[45]
4:2	203[5]
Titus	2
1:4	96[12]
1:5–9	201[10]
1:7	97[19], 99[52], 201[13]
1:9	200[4, 5]
1:13	200[5]
2:1–10	104[3]
2:9–10	111[98]
2:12	76, 77
2:15	200[5]
Philemon	
10	96[12]
Hebrews	
1:2	217[3]
6:7–8	114[4]
10:22	116[17]
10:25	215
12:25	105[10]
13:1	185[3]
13:7	105[10]
13:10	196[17]
13:17	117[22], 214[3]
James	
1:6	107[37]
1:8	106[34]
1:22	91[42]
1:27	196[17]

3:1–12	91[38]
3:9	73[38]
3:14	97[22]
3:16	97[22]
4:5	157[17]
4:6	92[50]
4:8	106[34]
4:16	116[12]
5:3	217[3]
5:12	90
5:14–15	166
1 Peter	70[12]
1:5	216[26]
1:13	162[78], 208, 214, 215
2:5	196[17]
2:11	70[14], 76
2:11–3:17	76[62]
2:17	110[75]
2:18–25	111[98]
2:18–3:7	104[13]
2:19	75[51]
4:8	108[50]
4:9	185[3]
4:11	138[25]
4:12	221[4]
4:16	186[9]
5:1–5	201[10]
5:2	201[13]
5:3	201[12]
5:5	92[50]
2 Peter	
2:1	157[29]
2:3	92[46]
2:10b	99[52]
2:14	92[46], 98[31], 114[4]
2:15	62, 117[19], 120[2]
2:22	153[80]
3:3	210[1], 217[3]
3:3–4	217[6]
3:10	162[79], 221[3]
1 John	
1:6–7	61[19]
2:1	96[12]

2:12 96[12]
2:16 116[12]
2:28 96[12]
3:7 96[12]
3:17 83[105]
3:18 91[42], 96[12]
4:1 183[7]
4:1–3 179
4:4 96[12]
5:21 96[12]

2 John
7 211[2], 219[3]
8 216[24]
10 171[5]

3 John
4 96[12]

Jude
4 157[29]
16 99[48]
22–23 92[55]
23 93[57]

Revelation 4
1:6 138[25]
1:7 213[1], 226[1]
1:8 158[30]
1:10 195
2:2 176[15]
2:14 123
2:20 123
2:25 221[3]
3:2–3 214[2]
3:3 215[14], 221[3]
4:8 158[30]
6:10 157[29]
6:14 223[7]
8–11 224[25]
9:21 89[13]
12:9 219[4]
13:7b 219[9]
13:13 211[3], 219[7]
16:7 214[2]
16:15 214[2]
18:8 221[3]
18:22 186[2]
18:23 89[13]
19:20 211[3], 219[7]

21:1 162[79]
21:8 89[13]
22:3 221
22:15 89[13], 117[18], 153[80]
22:18b 113
22:19 113

g / Christian Literature

Abelard
  De Eleemosyna Sermo
  (Cousin, 1.552) 85
Acta conciliorum oecumenicorum, collectio sabbatica
  5.32 222
Acta Maximi Confessoris
  2.31 222
Acts of John
  109 (18) 157[19]
Acts of Paul 4, 5
Acts of Paul and Thecla
  6 101[4]
Acts of Peter
  27 156[10]
Acts of Philip
  28 222
Acts of Thomas
  20 74
  145 74
Alexander of Alexandria
  (in Theodoret, *Historia ecclesiastica*) 187
Ammonius of Alexandria
  Fragmenta in Acta apostolorum
  13.2 129[37]
Antiochus monachus
  Homily 37 187

Apocalypse of Paul 5
Apocalypse of Peter 202[19], 211[3]
  1 Ethiopic 212, 224
  1–2 Achmimic 210[1], 217[6]
  2 Ethiopic 211[2], 219, 219[3], 220[15]

29 (NHC 7.3) 90[27]
Apostolic Church Order
  (See *Canons of the Apostles*)
Apostolic Constitutions
  4, 11[60], 15[94], 17, 17[109], 18, 19, 20, 21, 22, 22[34], 26[26], 27, 64[2], 68, 73[40, 41], 74[42], 77, 91[36], 93[56], 95[4], 97[23], 97[27, 28, 29], 99[47, 53], 108[49, 57], 118[39], 119[2], 122[20], 136[10, 12], 138[24], 149, 150, 161, 162[86], 167, 183, 184, 193[17, 21], 196[13, 16], 200[9], 219[3], 226, 227
2.1.5 35[40], 16, 101[11]
2.6.1 16, 91[34, 35]
2.26.3 192[8]
2.53.6 93[56]
4.3.1–2 81[84], 82[99]
5.14.1 132[8]
5.14.6 132[8]
6.9.6 176[15]
6.13.3 217[5]
7 17, 22, 29
7.1.1–2 28
7.1.2–18 29, 30[4]
7.1.2–32.4 17, 28–29
7.2.3 93[56]
7.2.4 28[5], 76[61]

61.2	158[29]
62.2	90[31], 158[30]
63.2	203[6]
64	156[12]
65.2	111[88]
2 Clement	19, 20[15]
1.2	111[88]
1.8	111[88]
2.4	111[88]
2.7	111[88]
3.1	123[36]
4.1–5	91[42]
5.1	111[88]
5.2–4	217[11]
8.5	204[8]
9.4	111[88]
9.5	111[88]
10.1	111[88]
11.2–7	107[39]
12.1	208[2], 215[14]
12.2	221[3]
13.1	99[51]
13.2	99[51]
13.3	99[51]
13.4	74, 75[51], 99[51]
14.2	217[3]
16.4	108[50]
17.3	77, 215[17]
17.7	204[13]
20.4	108[55], 187
Clement of Alexandria	4[3]
Hypotyposes (in Eusebius, *Hist. eccl.* 2.1.3)	202[21]
Paedagogos	
2.10, 89.1	7
2.10, 96.1	89[15]
3.12, 88.1	66[15]
3.12, 89.1	7, 89[7]
Protreptikos	
10.108.5	7, 89[7]
Quis dives salvetur	
29.4	8, 146[13]

Stromateis	
1.20, 100.4	7, 99[40]
2.19, 102.4	75[56]
2.20, 107.4–5	60[6]
2.23, 139.2	66[14]
3.4, 36.5	7
5.5, 31.1	8
5.5, 31.1–2	60[6]
5.14, 121.1	60[7]
5.14, 136.2–3	198[35], 199[37]
6.13, 107.2	202[21]
7.7, 40.3	138[28]
7.12, 69.4	75[56]
Commodian	11[65]
Carmen apologeticum	
699	11
Instructiones	
1.22.15	11
Corpus Hermeticum	
1.15	109[69]
9.10	106[24]
13.7	116[10]
16.2	91[42]
Cyprian	10[52]
Ep.	
63.13	9[44], 149[47]
69.5	9[44]
Didache	
1	61[14]
1.1	1, 31[16], 44, 59–63, 72, 148[38]
1.1a	59
1.1b	59
1.1–1.2b	32[22], 33[27]
1–3	35[41]
1.1–3a	42[7]
1.1–4.8	13
1.1–5.2	1
1–6	1, 3[13], 29, 31, 38[57], 43[13], 44[16], 59, 59[2], 63, 126, 207
1.1–6.1	30, 207

1.1–6.2	59–123
1.1–11.2	42
1.2	1, 6[30], 8[41], 10[56], 16, 34[36], 35, 37[54], 45, 64–67, 86, 114, 114[2], 118, 148[38]
1.2a	64, 114
1.2b	64, 66
1.2c	64, 66
1.2–3a	64–67
1.2–4.14	1, 64–113
1.3	6[30], 12, 15[98], 31[16], 72, 75, 76[66], 79[77], 87, 97[27]
1.3a	1, 32[22], 67, 86, 88
1.3–4	83[115]
1.3–6	86[135]
1.3–7	193[19]
1.3b	1, 73, 74, 75, 76[59]
1.3b–d	69, 73
1.3b–4	72
1.3b–4a	73–77
1.3b–5a	72, 79[80]
1.3b–2.1	1, 13[85], 14, 30[5], 31[12], 37, 42, 43[13], 67, 67[25], 68–72, 82[93], 87, 90[26], 123, 124, 126
1.3b–5.2	50[55]
1.3b–6	44, 45
1.3c	22, 72
1.3c–d	74, 76[59]
1.3c–4a	21, 67, 68
1.3d	15, 21, 22, 67, 68, 74, 75, 79[77]

	138, 139, 149[44], 151, 152–54, 152[61, 62], 155, 156[10], 159–61, 159[15], 160[57], 161
10.6	26, 46, 139, 141, 142, 142[41], 142[46, 47], 143, 161–64, 161[73], 163, 163[89, 95]
10.6a	26, 161, 162, 163
10.6b	161, 163, 164, 164[98]
10.7	21, 28, 46, 125, 139
11	28, 175[1], 192, 196
11–13	43[13, 14], 194[2], 199
11–14	202[24]
11–16	44[16], 139, 140, 143, 164–67, 166[112], 169, 178–79
11.1	169, 171
11.1–2	1, 46, 169, 171–72, 173[1], 179[9], 189, 190, 190[8]
11.1–15.4	169–205, 194
11.2	134[5], 149, 171–72, 176[9], 182, 183[4]
11.3	1, 46, 47[34], 49, 49[47],

	50, 51, 135, 144, 173, 173–74[3], 204[8]
11.3–9	173[3]
11.3–12	1, 50[55], 169, 170[5], 173–82
11.3–13.2	42[8]
11.3–13.7	17, 26, 26[29]
11.3–16.8	42
11.4	26, 134[5], 171, 172, 173, 175–76, 182, 183[4]
11.4B	175
11.4–6	1, 173, 175–77, 197
11.4–12	43[14], 46, 54, 170, 175, 188, 190, 201, 217
11.5	27, 176, 178[1], 185, 188[1], 217
11.5a	176
11.5b	176
11.5c	176
11.5–6	173
11.6	176–77, 217
11.6b	176, 182
11.7	27, 173, 179, 182
11.7–12	1, 173, 178–82
11.8	27, 173, 179, 179[13], 217
11.8–12	179[9]
11.9	179, 217
11.9b	179
11.9–12	173

11.10	26–27, 217
11.10–11	179–82
11.11	8[41], 26, 27, 46, 160[57], 170[5], 179, 180–82, 182[45], 201[14]
11.11b	181
11.11c	180, 181
11.12	27, 182
12	28
12–13	44[18], 54, 109
12.1	1, 26[26], 27, 134[5], 171, 183–84, 186[5]
12.1a	21, 183
12.1b	183
12.1–5	1, 169, 183–84
12.1–15.4	43[14], 44, 46
12.2	1, 183, 185, 186[1], 188
12.3	27, 186, 188, 189
12.3–5	1, 183, 186–87
12.4	27, 35, 186, 186[1]
12.5	8[41], 46, 123[37], 186, 186[1], 187
13.1	52, 180[23], 189[2], 189[4]
13.1–2	1, 32[24, 25], 188–90, 192[11], 193, 202
13.1–3	1, 104, 105, 169, 178, 188–93
13.2	27, 189[4, 5], 190, 190[8], 201[14, 17]

h / Greek and Latin Authors

2. Authors

Adam, Alfred
2, 2[6], 8[41], 9[42], 13,
13[79, 82, 83], 14[93], 15[95],
24[15], 25[21], 26[29], 36[47],
37–38[57], 42, 42[1, 3],
53[71, 77], 56[6], 86[132],
141, 141[27], 152[65],
167[125], 180[23, 28],
181[37, 41, 42]

Albright, William F.
164[96]

Altaner, Berthold
9[41, 47, 50], 10[52, 57], 11[59],
11[61, 65], 12, 12[69], 12[73],
12[74], 13[76, 84], 14[90],
15[94], 17[109], 19[5], 29[14],
36[47], 53[71, 77], 84[120],
86, 86[131, 132], 181[41],
222[14]

Amélineau, Émile
14[90], 34, 234

Amundsen, Leiv
21[22]

Aono, Tashio
2[8], 46[33], 47[34], 49[42],
53[71, 77], 72[30], 76[63],
207[2, 3], 209[15], 214[6],
222, 222[21], 223[9]

Arnold, August
142, 142[34]

Audet, Jean-Paul
2[5], 4[2], 5[8, 18], 6[27], 12,
18[116], 19[6, 9], 20, 20[10],
20[11, 13, 14, 15, 18], 21[22],
21[28], 22[32], 24[7, 9], 25[18],
25[22], 26, 26[27, 30], 26[31],
26[32], 27[32, 33, 38], 29[15],
36[47], 40[74, 75], 42, 42[4],
42[7, 11], 46[33], 48[41],
49[47], 51, 51[58], 51[63],
53[71], 56[8, 11], 61[19, 20],
66[20], 68[2], 71[22], 72,
72[32], 73[40], 74[47], 75[56],
76[62], 82[91, 95], 85,

85[126, 127], 86, 86[128],
86[129], 88[1, 3], 89[3, 7],
92[48], 93[62], 94[1], 95[6, 7],
96[11], 100[1, 2, 6], 105[9],
107[40], 108[49, 60], 111[91],
112[3], 115[4], 116[14],
120[3], 121[13], 122[25],
123[38], 126[2], 127[18],
133[14], 136[10], 139[1],
142, 142[41], 144[2, 3],
148[28], 149[43], 151,
151[52], 153[71], 155[1],
156[13], 157[21], 159[42, 46],
161[71], 162[82, 86], 163[89],
163[93], 166[116, 118, 120],
167, 169[2], 171[3], 173[1],
174[3], 175[6], 179[17],
180[29], 184[8], 188[1],
191[1], 192[15], 194[1, 2],
194[5], 196[11], 197[24, 28],
198[35], 199[35, 40], 201[10],
204[8, 15], 222, 222[17, 18],
223[8], 226[5]

Bahr, G. J.
135–36[8]

Baltzer, Klaus
63[28]

Balz, Horst R.
110[78], 200[4], 201[16]

Bammel, Ernst
209[4], 216[25], 217[1, 2]

Bardenhewer, Otto
6[26], 9[46], 105[57], 13[84],
14[90], 15[94], 17[109, 110],
17[112], 19[5], 53[77], 96[12]

Barnard, Leslie W.
4[5], 6[26], 15[95], 32[23],
34[38], 35[43], 36[47], 40[73],
46[33], 47[34], 53[71, 77],
56[9]

Bartlet, J. Vernon
14[94], 36[47], 42[5], 57[15],
146[15]

Bartsch, Hans-Werner
66[18]

Batiffol, Pierre
14[88, 89], 30, 34, 34[39]

Bauer, Johannes
Baptist
117[31], 136[10], 176[12],
191[2]

Beare, Francis W.
189[2]

Beck, Hans-Georg
17[114], 18[115, 118], 18[119],
18[121]

Behm, Johannes
130[38], 132, 195[10],
197[23], 222[13, 15]

Benigni, H.
14[90], 34[36]

Berger, Klaus
37[56], 60[6], 61[14], 62[24],
62[25], 65[11], 104[4]

Bergman, J.
59[4], 60[7]

Besson, M.
14[91], 29, 29[11, 12, 14],
29[15], 68[1], 76[61]

Betz, Johannes
140[6, 7, 8], 142, 142[44],
146[16], 149[42], 153[72],
164[97]

Beyer, Hermann W.
99[51]

Beyschlag, Karlmann,
74[45]

Bigg, Charles
70[9], 126[4], 148[31],
180[29]

Bihlmeyer, Karl
2, 2[6], 4[3], 107[48], 116[14],
165[106], 166, 166[109],
166[113]

Black, Matthew
164[96]

Bligh, J. B.
136[10]

Blinzler, Josef
133[14, 16]

Boehmer, Heinrich
14[92]

Borig, Rainer
146[15]

Bornkamm, Günther
2[8], 64[11], 163[90, 93],
164[96, 98], 181[37], 217[10]

Bosio, Guido
30[7], 46[33], 47[34], 53[77],
141, 141[17]

Bousset, Wilhelm
145[8], 219[1]

Braun, Herbert
61[19], 62[20], 109[65],
121[11]

Broek-Utne, A.
180[33]

Brox, Norbert
59[4]

Bruyne, Donatien de
10[51, 52], 11[66]

Bryennios, Philotheos
19–21, 19[4, 7], 20[16],
21, 28[1], 30[6], 32[23],
52[66], 53[71], 76[60], 83[116],
84[118], 111[99], 128[20],
130[40], 132[4], 135,
142[43], 146[12], 148[27, 29],
157[16], 162[86], 163[91],
166[114], 179[14], 180[32],
184[8], 191[3], 196[16],
219[3], 221[1], 222[14]

Büchsel, Friedrich
121[16, 17]

Budge, Ernest A. W.
25[18]

Bühner, Adolf
147[26]

Bultmann, Rudolf
142[36], 143, 143[52]

Burchard, Christoph
64[11], 65[11]

Burkitt, Francis C.
30[6]

Butler, Basil C.
36[47], 209[15], 223[8, 11],
224[16]

Gordon, R. P.
198–99[35]

Grant, Robert M.
53[77]

Greeven, Heinrich
104[4]

Greiff, Anton
42[5], 46[33], 47[35], 126[5],
141, 141[13], 146[13],
163[89]

Grenfell, Bernard P.
21, 21[21, 22, 23, 26], 74,
75

Gribomont, Jean
150[47]

Grundmann, Walter
186[8]

Haelst, Joseph van
9[43, 44], 53[76], 146[13],
148[30], 149[45], 150[1]

Haenchen, Ernst
109[66]

Hagner, Donald A.
46[32, 33], 70[10], 153[76],
178[7], 189[3], 209,
209[14]

Hahn, Ferdinand
36[50], 147[26]

Halleux, André de
44[20], 170[4], 173[2],
189–90[6], 192[10], 201[17]

Hanson, Richard P. C.
164[100]

Harnack, Adolf von
4[3], 6[28], 7[33], 9[46], 11[66],
18[116, 120], 27, 28[1, 3, 4],
28[5], 32[23, 24], 34[39],
36[47, 49], 37[57], 46[33],
52[65], 53[73], 56[4], 57[13],
68[2], 79[80], 80[83], 86[135],
93[58, 59], 96[15], 104[9],
106[25], 107[38], 111[91],
113[14], 116[14], 120[4],
122[21], 123[33], 126[4, 5],
128[20], 137[24], 138[26],

140[11], 141, 146[12],
147[19, 26], 148[27], 149[39],
152[68], 158[41], 162[76],
163[89], 170[4], 171[4],
172[6], 176[10], 181[35, 36],
181[37], 184[8], 189[3],
192[13], 194[1], 196[13, 19],
198[13], 201[10], 202[18],
202[22], 204[16, 17], 209,
209[6, 20], 210[1], 211[3],
216, 216[21], 217[6],
219[3], 222, 222[19],
223[5, 8, 32]

Harris, James Rendel
19[18], 28[1], 36[51], 52[66],
181[34], 197[23], 204[15]

Harvey, Anthony
Ernest
189[2]

Hauck, Friedrich
100[2, 3, 5], 198[32]

Heiligenthal, Roman
66[18]

Hemmer, Hippolyte M.
7[33], 8[38, 41], 9[42], 18[116],
75[53], 136[10], 207[3]

Hennecke, Edgar
35[43], 36[48], 39[69], 52[66]

Higgins, Angus J. B.
209[13], 224[16]

Hiltbrunner, Otto
175[5]

Hitchcock, Francis
Ryan Montgomery
7[37]

Hofius, O.
99[51]

Holtz, Gottfried
189[2]

Holtzmann, Oskar
151[56, 57], 155[1, 2], 156[4],
157[22], 160[53, 59]

Hooker, Morna D.
147[26]

Horner, George W.
24, 24[1, 9, 12], 25[16], 26,

26[28, 32], 27[32], 137[20, 21],
137[22], 166–67[124], 180

Horst, P. W. van der
37[52], 62[22], 89[8, 12, 13],
90[15, 17, 20, 25]

Hruby, Kurt
155[2], 156[4, 6], 157[25],
159[48], 160[59]

Hunt, Arthur S.
21, 21[21, 22, 23, 26], 74,
75

Hüntemann, Ulricus
86[135]

Iselin, Ludwig E.
14[90]

Jacquier, Eugène
7[33], 53[56], 111[91]

Jaubert, Annie
133[16]

Jefford, Clayton N.
7[30], 24[3], 25[22], 63[28],
72[25]

Jeremias, Joachim
136, 136[14, 15, 16],
137[17], 142, 142[37],
143[53], 145[4, 9], 156[3],
147[22, 26], 157[24], 159[49],
159[50], 192[9], 195[10]

Johnson Sherman E.
47[33, 34], 49[42], 53[71],
57[15], 209, 209[10, 18],
223[14]

Jones, F. Stanley
24[3]

Kahle, Paul E., Jr.
25, 25[19, 20]

Kamlah, Ehrhard
59[4], 61[14], 62[25], 63[28],
207[3]

Kattenbusch,
Ferdinand
141, 141[23]

Kertelge, Karl
65[11]

Klauck, Hans-Josef
140[9], 142[44], 162[78],
164[96], 195[10]

Klauser, Theodor
108[49], 116[14], 127[16],
129[32, 33], 138[26], 159[46],
166[116], 174[3], 194[1, 2]

Klein, Gottlieb
36[50], 140[4], 141[30],
145[4, 11], 146[13], 155[1],
155[2], 159[45]

Kleist, James A.
53[71], 57[15], 93[58],
107[40], 111[91], 123[38],
162[78], 200[5], 204[8]

Kloppenborg, John S.
46[33], 63[28], 210[42], 211,
211[43], 212[44, 45], 212[46],
212[47], 217[7], 218[15, 17],
223[3], 225[26, 31], 226[1, 4]

Klostermann, Erich
153[77], 154[82], 188[2]

Kmosko, Mihaly
13[78, 79]

Kneller, C. A.
84[120, 122], 85

Knopf, Rudolf
7[33], 53[77], 57[13], 59[4],
60[9], 66[19], 75[49], 80[82],
83[103], 90[26], 91[42, 43],
93[55, 57, 58, 59], 95[8],
97[29], 100[3], 101[14],
105[9, 18], 107[46], 111[90],
112[8], 113[14], 113[16],
121[13], 122[21], 122[22],
123[33, 35], 126[6], 128[20],
129, 129[30, 34], 133,
133[15], 134[2], 135[6],
141, 141[30], 147[25],
152[68], 156[11, 13], 159[42],
162[87], 172[6], 176[13],
178[5], 179[17], 180[24],
184[8], 193[18, 22], 194[1],
196[19], 197[98], 198[30],

199[40], 203[1], 204[12], 204[16], 207[3], 215[19], 219[3], 220[14], 223[5, 14], 225[28]

Knox, Wilfrid L.
98[37]

Koch, Hugo
9[47], 10[52]

Koester, Helmut
47[33], 49, 49[49], 50[49], 50[54], 51, 51[57, 62], 56[9], 64[7, 8, 9, 10], 66[18], 68[3], 69[6], 70[8], 71[22], 72, 72[27, 28, 29], 73[37], 74[46], 75[53], 76[59], 78[67], 79[77], 79[78, 79], 80[82], 81[89], 82[91], 83[110, 112], 83[115], 88[3], 107[41], 116[6], 126[11], 131[2], 135[6], 136[10, 12, 13, 14], 153[76], 159[42], 162[86], 173[3], 175[8], 178[7], 189[3], 196[19], 198[30], 198[31], 204[8, 11], 207[3], 208, 210, 210[37, 39], 210[40], 210[41, 43], 214[6], 215[13], 217[7, 11], 218[15, 17], 220[15], 221[5, 7], 223[3, 9], 225[26, 31], 226[2, 4]

Kraft, Robert A.
27, 45, 32[25], 36[47], 40[75], 42-43[11], 53[71], 53[73], 82[91], 139[1], 141, 141[19], 166[113], 170[5], 201[1], 216[21], 223[9]

Kretschmar, Georg
170[4], 175[3], 181[37]

Kubo, Sakae
92[55]

Kuhn, H. W.
145[9]

Kuhn, K. G.
121[16], 134[1], 164[96, 98]

Lake, Kirsopp
46[33], 135[6]

Lang, Friedrich
221[4]

Lawson, John
30[6], 126[4]

Layton, Bentley
44[16], 46[33], 48[37], 52[66], 70, 70[17], 71, 71[18, 19], 71[20, 22], 72, 74[46], 75[53], 76[59, 66], 79[77, 78], 80[83], 81[86, 87], 82[90], 83[103], 83[106, 112], 86[128, 130]

Lefort, L. Theophile
4-57, 24, 24[3, 4], 25, 25[18], 165[102], 166-67, 167[125, 126], 187[17]

Leipoldt, Johannes
14[90], 153[76], 214-15[8]

Lengeling, Emil J.
201[16]

Lietzmann, Hans
22[29], 108[49], 116[14], 120[5], 132[13], 141, 141[20, 21, 22, 31], 142, 145[8], 159[43], 160[56], 161, 161[74], 162[75, 78], 164[97], 196[18, 19]

Lindemann, Andreas
49[42], 123[39]

Lohmeyer, Ernst
136[9, 10], 219[1]

Lohse, Eduard
65[11], 132[8], 162[83, 84], 162[85], 162[86], 195[86], 195[8, 9], 200[4]

Lührmann, Dieter
xv, 104[4]

Luz, Ulrich
153[77], 154[82]

MacLean, Arthur J.
9[42, 43], 36[47], 46[33], 48[36], 52[66], 53[71], 56[9], 68[3], 70[9], 126[4], 180[29]

Magne, Jean
150, 151[52], 152[66]

Maier, Johann
134[3, 4]

Mann, Christopher S.
164[96]

Manser, Anselm
84[120]

Marshall, I. Howard
189[2]

Massaux, Edouard
47[33, 34], 48[36], 64[4], 66[17], 70, 70[10], 131[2], 135[6], 136[10], 153[76], 160[58], 161[69], 173[3], 175[8], 177[20], 178[7], 179[13], 189[3], 198[31], 204[10], 205[18, 20], 209, 209[11], 210[28, 29, 30, 31]

Mathys, Hans-Peter
66[18]

Mattioli, Umberto
42, 43[12, 15], 68[3], 138[26], 162[86], 181[37]

Mees, Michael
72[32]

Meyer, Rudolf
210[16]

Michaelis, Wilhelm
38[58], 59[4], 60, 60[6], 156[11, 14]

Michel, Otto
145[9], 153[77, 79], 160[54]

Middleton, Robert Dudley
43[16], 46[33], 48[37], 53[73], 141, 145[4], 155[2]

Mirecki, Paul A.
24[3]

Mitteis, Ludwig
187[14]

Moll, Helmut
142[40], 196[15], 197[24], 198[35]

Moule, Charles F. D.
47[33, 35], 140[8], 152[66], 164[96, 98]

Mühlsteiger, J.
199[40]

Muilenburg, James
7[32], 9[42], 15[95], 30[6, 9], 31[15], 32[17], 35[43], 36[47], 36[51], 46[31], 48[36], 52[66], 53[77], 68[3], 70, 70[11], 94[1], 100[7], 198[35], 209, 209[24, 26], 216[21]

Musurillo, Herbert
8[41]

Nauck, Wolfgang
61[19]

Nautin, Pierre
42[11], 49[47], 68[2, 3], 69[7], 126[2], 175[4], 204[16]

Neugebauer, Fritz
73[37]

Niederwimmer, Kurt
20[19, 20], 22[32], 25[22], 31, 31[14], 76[62], 91[41], 97[26], 98[38], 116[14], 122[23], 148[33], 151[51], 152[68], 158[41], 159[42], 159[46], 161[68], 162[86], 165[102], 166[116], 169[1], 169[2], 170[5], 173, 175[3], 181[38, 39], 183[1], 188[2], 192[15, 16], 200[2], 202[18], 202[24], 226[5]

Nissen, Andreas
65-66[11]

Nock, Arthur Darby
142, 142[33], 143[50]

Nützel, Johannes M.
214[1]

Oepke, Albrecht
214[1]

Orbán, A. P.
10[52]

Otranto, Giorgio
179[12]

Oulton, John Ernest Leonard
7[36]

ⲉⲓⲥⲩ︦ⲧ︦ ⲡⲉⲗⲁϥⲓⲛⲧⲏⲛⲛⲟⲩⲁⲗⲗⲁ
ⲗⲁ ⲉⲡⲧⲁ ϥⲧⲛ̄ⲧⲉⲓⲛⲏⲁⲛ
ⲛⲓⲩⲣⲁⲙⲁⲥ ⲛ̄ϫⲓ ⲛⲉⲡⲣⲟⲫⲏⲧⲏⲥ
ⲛ̄ⲧⲉⲛⲓⲟⲩⲁⲓ̄ ⲩⲡⲛⲁⲉⲉⲧⲏⲛⲉ
ⲭⲁⲓⲥ ⲓⲛⲛⲟⲩ ⲡⲛⲛⲉⲟⲩ ⲙⲁⲭⲉⲙⲁ
ⲛ̄ⲏⲓⲛⲉⲛ ⲁⲙⲧ̄ⲓ ⲉⲙⲉ ⲛⲕⲉ ⲓⲕⲉⲛ
ⲡⲉⲣⲥ ⲧⲙⲛⲥⲟⲧⲉ ⲱϣⲟⲡⲓ ⲁ ⲉⲛ
ⲧⲁ ⲁⲥ ⲛ̄ ⲁⲛ ⲭⲗⲁⲥ ⲛ̄ⲏⲧ ⲛ̄ⲉⲧⲃⲉ
ⲗⲁⲓⲛⲓ ⲉ ⲩ ⲭⲁ ⲓⲙ̄ⲡⲉⲣⲧⲉ ⲗ ⲁ ⲡⲧ̄
ⲙⲁ ⲧ̄ⲛ ⲕⲡⲓⲛⲉⲙⲁϥ ⲟⲩ ⲁⲛ ⲛⲓ ⲃⲓ
ⲛ ⲁⲉ ⲧⲛ ⲛⲛⲟⲩ ϣⲁ ⲅⲁ ⲧⲉ ⲛ̄ⲓⲙ
ⲡⲣⲉⲛ ⲡ ⲡⲣ︦ⲥ︦ ϣⲁⲡⲟⲩⲉⲣⲁ ⲧⲛ
ⲛ̄ ⲧ̄ⲛ ⲁⲉ ⲁ ϣⲕ ⲓⲙ̄ⲁ ⲓⲛⲛ
ϥⲁⲩⲱ ⲥⲟⲩⲱⲛ̄ϥ ⲟⲩⲛ ⲧⲏ
ⲧⲓ ⲙⲉⲩⲓ ⲱ︦ⲧ︦ ⲛⲛⲟⲩⲉⲓ ⲙⲉⲓ
ⲛ̄ⲁⲟⲩⲓ ⲛⲉ ⲙ ⲙ̄ⲛ ⲛⲁ ⲑⲭⲁ ⲉ ⲉ ϣⲱ
ⲡⲓ ⲛⲉⲟⲩⲉ ⲓ ⲉ ⲧ̄ⲛⲛⲟⲩ ϣⲁⲣⲁ ⲧⲛ
ⲉ ⲣⲁⲛ ⲓ ⲧⲉ ⲓ ⲱⲛ ⲧⲁ ⲉⲓⲙ̄ⲉⲗⲁ ϥ